D1262150

A Concise History of
Canada's First Nations

Second Edition

Olive Patricia Dickason with William Newbigging

OXFORD
UNIVERSITY PRESS

OXFORD

UNIVERSITY PRESS

8 Sampson Mews, Suite 204, Don Mills, Ontario M3C 0H5
www.oupcanada.com

Oxford University Press is a department of the University of Oxford.
It furthers the University's objective of excellence in research, scholarship,
and education by publishing worldwide in

Oxford New York

Auckland Cape Town Dar es Salaam Hong Kong Karachi
Kuala Lumpur Madrid Melbourne Mexico City Nairobi
New Delhi Shanghai Taipei Toronto

With offices in

Argentina Austria Brazil Chile Czech Republic France Greece
Guatemala Hungary Italy Japan Poland Portugal Singapore
South Korea Switzerland Thailand Turkey Ukraine Vietnam

Oxford is a trade mark of Oxford University Press
in the UK and in certain other countries

Published in Canada
by Oxford University Press

Copyright © Oxford University Press Canada 2010

The moral rights of the author have been asserted

Database right Oxford University Press (maker)

First Published 2010

All rights reserved. No part of this publication may be reproduced,
stored in a retrieval system, or transmitted, in any form or by any means,
without the prior permission in writing of Oxford University Press,
or as expressly permitted by law, or under terms agreed with the appropriate
reprographics rights organization. Enquiries concerning reproduction
outside the scope of the above should be sent to the Rights Department,
Oxford University Press, at the address above.

You must not circulate this book in any other binding or cover
and you must impose this same condition on any acquirer.

Previous edition copyright © 2006 Oxford University Press Canada

Library and Archives Canada Cataloguing in Publication

Dickason, Olive Patricia, 1920–
A concise history of Canada's first nations / Olive Patricia Dickason & Willian Newbigging.—2nd ed.
New version of Canada's First Nations.

Includes index.

ISBN 978-0-19-543242-8

1. Native peoples—Canada—History—Textbooks. I. Newbigging, William, 1963–
II. Dickason, Olive Patricia, 1920– . Canada's First Nations. III. Title.

E78.C2D536 2010   971.004'97   C2010-900543-0

Cover image: 'Eagle Holman—Survival vs. Desire' by Vernon Asp

This book is printed on permanent (acid-free) paper ♾ .

Printed and bound in Canada.

1 2 3 4 – 13 12 11 10

Contents

List of Maps

'I am an Indian. I am proud to know who I am and where I originated. I am proud to be a unique creation of the Great Spirit. We are part of Mother Earth. . . .

We have survived, but survival by itself is not enough. A people must also grow and flourish.'

Chief John Snow, *These Mountains Are Our Sacred Places*
(Toronto: Samuel Stevens, 1977).

Acknowledgements

I wish to thank the people at the Canadian Circumpolar Institute at the University of Alberta, and, in particular, Nancy Gibson, the director of the Institute, for providing the enthusiasm and resources to get this project going, in the first edition. Thanks also to Moira Calder, who worked closely with me throughout the first edition, and to William Newbigging for his assistance on the second edition. Special thanks to Elaine Maloney, Cindy Mason, Patti Laboucane-Benson, Malcolm King, Jeanette Buckingham, and Carl Urion, as well as to Gerdy and Jacques Aarts. We are also grateful to the anonymous reviewers who provided input to this edition and to Dr Richard Tallman, copy editor for both editions of *A Concise History* as well as for the four editions of the original work.

All who assisted me with *Canada's First Nations*, either individually or through the institutions with which they are affiliated, have contributed indirectly to this book, and I am still grateful for their input and support.

In acknowledging the help of all those named and unnamed who have contributed so much, I should still point out that the responsibility for the contents and orientation of this book is mine alone.

Olive Patricia Dickason

Without question my first acknowledgement must be to Olive Dickason, who established the text upon which I have worked and without whom this second edition of *A Concise History of Canada's First Nations* would not exist. Thanks also are due to two friends, Dr Harvey Feit, FRSC, and Professor Howard Webkamigad, my colleague in the Department of Anishinaabe-mowin at Algoma University. They gave invaluable assistance on a number of points. I am also indebted to the skilled editors at Oxford University Press, Peter Chambers and Richard Tallman, for their dedication and guidance. The anonymous reviewers took their task seriously and helped improve the manuscript. I thank them for their obvious commitment to our craft. On a more personal note I would like to thank my wife, Kathryn Kohler, my editor of the first resort, and our children, Cameron and Janet, for their patience while this work was in preparation.

William Newbigging
Algoma University

Introduction

Canada, it used to be said by non-Aboriginals with more or less conviction, is a country of much geography and little history.[1] The ethnocentricity of that position at first puzzled, and even confused, Amerindians, but it has lately begun to anger them. How could such a thing be said, much less believed, when their people have been living here for thousands of years?

History, for its part, has been described as a document-bound discipline. If something was not written, preferably in an official document, it was not historical. Thus, pre-literate societies were excluded from history and labelled prehistoric, or perhaps proto-historic. The best they could hope for was to become historic by extension, when they came into contact with literate societies. In other words, Canada's history began with the arrival of Europeans.

As if that were not restrictive enough, another limitation was added: Canada's history has been usually presented as beginning not with the first Europeans, the Norse, who arrived here about AD 1000, but with the French, who came first as fishermen and later as explorers in the sixteenth century, and stayed to settle in the seventeenth. The arbitrariness of this is evident when it is realized that the English preceded the French in exploratory voyages, at least one of which, that of John Cabot (d. 1498?), or rather, to use his Italian name, Giovanni Caboto, sailing under the English flag, dated back to 1497. Pushed into the background were the Portuguese, who were also here before the French, exploiting the rich fisheries off the North Atlantic coast, as well as the Basques (usually referred to as Spanish), who may have preceded all the other Europeans of this period in their pursuit of whales. The list of Europeans does not end there. By the turn of the fifteenth century into the sixteenth, the waters off Canada's North Atlantic coast were the scene of intense international activity, and by 1600 there may have been up to a thousand European ships a year engaged in commercial activities in Canada's northeastern coastal waters.

Such activity would not have been possible without the co-operation and participation of the first nations of the land. When it came to penetrating the interior of the continent, Amerindians and Inuit guided the way for the European 'explorers', equipped them with the clothing and transportation facilities they needed, and provided them with food. Their contributions in economic terms alone were substantial and can probably never be properly assessed.[2] In the most profound sense of the term, they are Canada's founding peoples.

Because they were oral, rather than literate, peoples (even those who did possess a form of writing had not developed it into a widely shared form of communication), reconstructing their pre-contact history in the Western sense of the term is a daunting task. Canadian historians have, in the past, found it much easier to ignore the earlier period; hence the blinkered view of Canada as a 'young' country.

Europeans found the Americas populated by a variety of peoples who, in broad terms, shared a general civilization, somewhat as the newcomers did themselves in their own homelands, in spite of a dazzling array of cultural particularities. This variety tended to obscure a world view that saw humans as part of a cosmological order depending on a balance of reciprocating forces to keep the universe functioning in harmony. This contrasts with the Judeo-Christian view of a cosmos dominated by a God in the image of man. In this perspective man is in a privileged position, as up to a certain point he can control nature for his own benefit. These ideological approaches were reflected in their respective technologies: where Europeans used metals for tools and weaponry, Amerindians used them mainly to express their sense of cosmological order.[3]

In telling the story of the meeting of these disparate civilizations, this book begins with the first appearance of humans in the Americas. Since little is positively known about those distant events, I have described various theories without attempting to nail down the 'truth'. This applies also to the development of agriculture and the rise of city-states. As British archaeologist Ian Hodder has observed, without certainty 'we do not have the right to impose our own universals on the data and to present them as truth.'[4] A challenging aspect of our very early history is that so much remains to be found out.

Chapter 1 looks at Canada's First Nations as Europeans first found them, setting the scene (at least in part) for the story of the interactions that followed, which comprises the bulk of the work.

The early contact period (Chapters 2 to 4) begins with the brief presence of the Norse but is concerned mainly with interactions of Amerindians and French and with how the two peoples set about developing working relationships. The British takeover in 1763, and the opening of the West to the fur trade and later to non-Aboriginal settlement (Chapters 5 to 7), heralded a difficult period for the Amerindians, as their traditional world became steadily less secure under advancing colonial pressures. Attempts to counter this movement with pan-Amerindian alliances (which had begun during the French regime and had been vigorously suppressed) met with failure on the battlefield. The turning point was the War of 1812 (Chapter 8), the last of the colonial wars, which ushered in a new way of life for Amerindians as British imperial power became firmly established (Chapter 9). The drive to assimilate Amerindians took on a new intensity; this period saw the beginning of the great land-cession treaties, by which the British sought to extinguish what limited land rights they recognized for Amerindians, and

Indians sought to work out as congenial arrangements as they could for accommodating themselves to the new order of things (Chapter 10). This was also the period that saw the rise of the Métis, the 'New Nation' born of Indians and Euro-Canadians, who in 1869–70 would make their first stand for their place in the British imperial order.

The rapid disappearance of the buffalo herds of the western Plains precipitated an even more desperate resistance on the part of the Métis, as well as Cree to a lesser extent (Chapters 11 and 12). This led Canada to inaugurate a campaign of legislating Aboriginal cultures out of existence (Chapters 13 and 14). The Far North, which until this point had been the purview of whalers and trappers, neither of whom directly attacked the Native way of life, suddenly attracted the attention of southerners when its placer gold was discovered. The Klondike gold rush became a Canadian legend, and the isolation that had protected traditional lifestyles was severely cracked. It was not shattered, however, until after World War II when new technology made exploitation of northern resources economically feasible (Chapter 15).

The Electronic Age also gave a new meaning to oral traditions, and Canada's original peoples—both Amerindian and Inuit, as well as Métis—began to campaign for their rights. No longer was industrial development allowed to ride roughshod over Native rights, at least not without a protest. The Mackenzie Valley Pipeline Inquiry marked a change in attitudes, and the James Bay and Northern Quebec Agreement brought a modification in procedures. An important ongoing example of this change is in Alberta where the Samson Cree Nation continues to press for revenues from their oil and gas reserves. But established ways of doing and thinking can die hard, as the 'Indian Summer' of 1990, the Wet'suwet'en decision of 1991, and the postponement of the second phase of the James Bay project at Great Whale River so dramatically illustrate. These and other developments led Ottawa to launch its first major official inquiry in co-operation with First Nations into the situation and the concerns of its Aboriginal citizens. As the five-volume report of the Royal Commission on Aboriginal Peoples made clear, what they are asking for is full and equal partnership in the Canadian federation (Chapters 16 and 17).

First Nations have become politically sophisticated in their campaigns to salvage what they can of their territories and traditional values; the term 'Aboriginal right', originally applied only to land, has now come to include self-government. Canada has been slow to acknowledge the First Nations' right to an ongoing interest in their lands and has continued to insist on extinguishment of Aboriginal right in return for specified benefits, mostly of an economic nature but also including political concessions. Both Indians and Inuit have become steadily less inclined to accept such arrangements, and in some cases (such as the Mohawk and Dene) they flatly reject them as violations of their basic rights. Events at Douglas Creek south of Caledonia, Ontario, have served to remind Canadians of the continuing problems associated with neglecting these issues. Unless the government negotiates self-determination, Amerindians could become a permanently disaffected group, as happened with the Irish in Great Britain. Anthropologist Michael Asch made that point when he observed that denying minorities the right to negotiate their concerns with those in power virtually assures resort to violence.⁵ Canada once made a reputation for itself as a peacekeeper on the international scene, a reputation it is having difficulty in maintaining, if it has not already lost it, within its own borders. The Residential Schools Settlement Agreement of 2007 may be a sign that positive change is coming, but at the present it remains only a promise.

The Problem of Interpretation

A word about Amerindian tribal classifications is necessary. Labels such as 'Cree', 'Huron', 'Beaver', 'Haida' were imposed by Europeans and do not represent how the people termed themselves, at least aboriginally. In some cases a single label, such as 'Cree', 'Abenaki', or 'Odawa', included a number of distinct groups, more or less closely related by language. These three all belong to the Algonkian language group. The term 'Algonkian' or 'Algonkin' as used in this work refers to language; 'Algonquin' or 'Algonquian' refers to a particular people living in the Eastern Woodlands who are Algonkian speakers and who on first contact were allied to the Hurons. While many of the Europeanized labels have come to be accepted by the Aboriginal peoples, some have not. For instance, the tundra-dwellers of the Arctic objected to 'Eskimo' on the grounds that it was pejorative as it had come to be popularly believed that it came from an Ojibwa term that translated as 'eaters of raw meat', despite the opinion of linguists that it actually derived from a Montagnais term meaning 'she nets a snowshoe'.⁶ The tundra-dwellers won their point, and their term for themselves, 'Inuit' ('the people', 'Inuk' in the singular), has been officially accepted. The Montagnais and Naskapi, referred to as two separate (although closely allied) people in early documentation, today consider themselves to be one, 'Innu'. However, since the terms 'Montagnais' and 'Naskapi' are solidly entrenched in the literature, these names will be retained for the sake of clarity, particularly when citing early documentation. When the context is modern-day, 'Innu' will be used.

This leads to the problem of a general name for New World peoples. Although the term 'Indian' is recognized as originating in a case of mistaken identity, it has come to be widely accepted, particularly by the Aboriginal peoples themselves. The trouble with that term, of course, is that it is also used for the people of India, who with some justification claim prior right. Francophones have solved the problem by using 'amérindien', which is specific to the Americas, or 'autochtone', which translates as Aboriginal. Anglophones have not reached such an accord; in Canada, 'Native' has come to be widely used, but it is not accepted in the United States on the grounds that anyone born in that country is a native, regardless of racial origin. In Canada, 'Aboriginal' is becoming widely used by Indians as well as non-Indians. 'Amerindian' has not received popular acceptance in English-language Canada and has even less in the United States. However, as it avoids the ambiguities of 'Indian' and 'Native', and is more specific than 'Aboriginal', it is my term of preference.

Problems of translating concepts and even words from one language to another are notorious for misleading the unwary. The word 'father' is a good example of this.

For sixteenth- and seventeenth-century Europeans, the connotations of the term included authority and control of the family. In Amerindian languages, the term implied a protector and provider, who could be influential but who lacked authority in the European sense, particularly among matrilineal societies, where mothers had the say over children. The authority figure in such societies was the maternal uncle. When the Iroquois, for instance, referred to the French king as 'father', they were not placing themselves under his authority. If that had been their intention, they would have used the term 'uncle', which they never did.[7]

Amerindian personal names can present difficulties for non-Indians. Since spellings have not, for the most part, been standardized, there is a great variety to choose from. I have mentioned some of these choices, but it was not possible—or even desirable—to try and list them all. The English versions of these names present another problem; for the most part, the best that can be hoped for is an approximation that touches on only a limited aspect of a range of possible meanings.

Place names, on the other hand, are in a separate category. In Amerindian practice, they indicate geographical or ecological characteristics, or else recall a historic event that happened on the spot. Unlike Europeans, and with one major exception, Amerindians do not name places or geographical features after persons or tribes. The exception concerns reserves, sometimes named after individuals, such as Ahtahkakoop, Poundmaker, and Mistawassis. Northern Quebec has switched to Inuktitut for its place names.

Problems of interpretation take on a totally different aspect when considering early European accounts of the Americas. For one thing, as one scholar, Ian S. MacLaren, has pointed out, words that were used in the sixteenth or eighteenth centuries might have different meanings today. For another, what appeared in print could differ markedly from what the author had written. Publishers were sometimes more concerned about sales than about accuracy.[8] Since the printed word should not be taken automatically at face value, the researcher is left with the necessity of cross-checking with whatever other sources are available. These are usually few, and sometimes non-existent.

Another area that calls for caution is that of dating. Two systems are used in this work: the standard Gregorian calendar with which we are all familiar for the historic period, which uses the abbreviations BC (before Christ) and AD (anno domini, 'year of our Lord'); and the scientific calendar based on radiocarbon dating for the prehistoric period, which refers to dates in years BP (before present). Where the Gregorian calendar uses the birth of Christ as a pivotal point, radiocarbon dating uses the year 1950.

A final reminder: the Indian Act applies only to 'status' Indians, that is, those who are registered and listed in the official band rolls. Non-status Indians and Métis are legally classed as ordinary citizens. In the interests of simplicity and readability, the distinction is usually not referred to in the text, except in some specific instances where clarity calls for it. The term 'Métis' is used in its French sense, mixture, usually applied to the crossing of human races, without specifying which ones. On the Labrador coast, people of mixed ancestry are known to the Inuit as 'Kablunangajuit' and to non-Aboriginals as 'liveyeres', 'settlers', or perhaps 'Labradorians'.

1 At the Beginning

When Europeans stumbled on the Caribbean islands in the late fifteenth century, they found Amerindians in what they considered to be their cultural infancy. Most assumed the islanders were a young people who could have been there for only a few hundred years. A few, however, recognized traces of early habitation and realized that this must have happened over long periods.[1] How long a time that was is still not known.

The traditions of the Amerindians tell us that America is their land of origin,[2] emphasizing and confirming the peoples' attachment to the land. The west coast Gitksan people maintain that the Upper Skeena River Valley, in the northwest part of the land that came to be called the Americas, is their Garden of Eden. The Salish Thompson River people, also living on the west coast, and the Ojibwa of the Great Lakes area both believe that their first ancestors were born of the earth. The traditional belief of one Anishinabe nation, the Nassauakueton Odawa, is that people were born when a sucker swam onto dry land and laid eggs in the sand.[3] The Athapaskan Beaver, whose land is in the north, hold that humans crawled through a hollow log to reach earth.[4] According to Iroquoian tradition, the mother of humanity, Aataentsic, fell through a hole in the sky and landed on a tortoise swimming in a world covered only by water. When the tortoise saw Aataentsic falling, it ordered the aquatic animals to dive to the bottom of the sea to find earth to pile on its back to cushion Aataentsic's landing.[5] From physical and linguistic evidence, we know that humans were present in the Americas at least by 17,000 BP ('before present') and perhaps by 50,000 BP or even earlier.[6]

On another plane, the Northwest Coast Tsimshian have legends in which migration is a theme.[7] Today it is widely accepted that at several periods during the late Pleistocene geological age, a land bridge connected Asia and North America and that some Amerindians crossed from the Old World to the New on foot during these times.[8] The first identifiable bridge dates back to about 75,000 years ago. The last one ended about 14,000 years ago.[9] **Beringia**, as this land bridge is called by scientists, at one point was more than 2,000 kilometres wide, more like a continent than a bridge. Once believed to have been a grassy and often boggy plain, recent studies have revealed

Time Line

75,000–15,000 BP	Ice Ages (Wisconsin glaciation), when Bering Strait land bridge was accessible for migration from Asia.		Plains and mixing with Plano (rippled flaking of spear and knife points) peoples creates Plains culture.
11,000 BP	Bifacially flaked (fluted) stone points and knives dated to 11,000 years ago have been found and identified by archaeologists at both the Asian and North American sides of Beringia. Campsites of peoples of different cultural traditions scattered throughout North and South America. Northwest Coast culture established, based on salmon fishing and sea hunting—a sedentary culture with permanent settlements due to rich land and sea resources.	7000 BP	Earliest known domestication of corn, in central Mexico.
		5300–1500 BP	Archaeological evidence suggests Chinese contact in Americas.
		4300 BP	Agriculture introduced in Northeast Woodlands: squash.
		3500–2000 BP	Olmec, the 'mother' of American civilizations, in Gulf of Mexico region.
		3000 BP	First local cultivated plant in Northeast: sunflower.
		1500 BP	Corn first cultivated in Canada, in present-day Ontario.
		1000	Tobacco cultivated in Ontario; beans soon followed. Norse landing and brief settlement on northern tip of Newfoundland.
10,600–8700 BP	Domesticated plants in Central and South America: gourds, avocados, beans, squash.		
10,000–8000 BP	Hunting of bison by means of drives and jumps begins.		
8500 BP	Domestication of dogs as pack and sled animals and for hunting.	1200s	Squash (and sunflowers) first grown domestically in Ontario, thus completing triad of the famous 'three sisters'—corn, beans, squash.
8000 BP	Migration of eastern Early Archaic peoples to western		

that it was covered with birch, heath, and shrub willow,[10] food for such animals as mammoth, mastodon, giant bison, and saiga antelope—and the predators that preyed on them. That human hunters followed the herds is a reasonable assumption. These newcomers travelled mainly from north to south, either along the coast or further inland. Some looped south of the glaciers, then headed north again as the ice retreated. Algonkian speakers who occupy so much of Canada's Subarctic forest, the **taiga**, at some point in time fanned northward from the Great Lakes, and the buffalo hunters of the northwestern Plains came from two directions, south and east. The Athapaskans (Dene), on the other hand, began to move south after living in the Far North since about 9,000 years ago, following a volcanic eruption near White River.[11] The forebears of the Inuit, the last Native peoples to settle in what is today Canada, spread eastward across the Arctic from Siberia.

There is no reason to conclude, however, that because Beringia offered a convenient pedestrian route, it was therefore the only one available or used. Nor is there any reason to believe that Beringia's inhabitants were land-bound, ignoring the rich marine life on and off its coasts. The sea also offered options. In the Pacific, the Japanese current sweeping from the Asiatic coast eastward to the Americas provided a natural aquatic highway. Certainly, sea voyages were occurring elsewhere. In some respects, deep-sea sailing is not as dangerous as coasting, and both are easier than walking.[12] Whether on foot or on water, or a combination of both, Amerindians reached the southern tip of South America by at least 11,000 BP. The High Arctic was the last region to be populated, after 5000 BP.

The person who fell to earth from the sky is a common theme in Amerindian creation stories. Sometimes the person left an impression, as on this rock near Prince Rupert, BC. *(National Museums of Canada, 70401)*

By 11,000 years ago—about the time of the last known mammoth and mastodon kills—campsites of peoples with different economic adaptations and cultural traditions were scattered throughout the two continents. In that period, and during the next 3,000 years or so, some 200 species of major animals disappeared from the Americas. We do not know what caused these extinctions, any more than we know what caused that of the dinosaurs. Perhaps big-game hunters tipped the balance as their population expanded. On the other hand, some scientists believe that mammoth kills were rare.[13]

Whatever the reason, the disappearance of the giant mammals does not seem to have changed people's hunting patterns, as such game as bison and caribou had always been important. If there was a population drop, it did not last long. People survived for the same reason then as later: by being adaptable. The way of life that developed, called Archaic by researchers, would last in some places until long after the arrival of Europeans. This way of life was based on the exploitation of a wide variety of food sources coupled with one of humanity's great strides forward in technology—the development of stone and bone tools.

The Spread of Tool-Building Technology

Stone Age technology reached its highest point of development in the Americas, in delicately crafted projectile points and, later, in the massive constructions of the Maya, Mexica, and Inca. The Inca created the largest Stone Age empire in the world,[14] the 'realm of the Four Quarters', which incorporated more than 200 ethnic groups. Working with stone required detailed and accurate observation, on the one hand, and a workable social organization, on the other. Technology, Stone Age or otherwise, is the product of an accumulated fund of knowledge (Box 1.1).

Around 11,200–10,500 BP, the making of **fluted points** displaced earlier forms of manufacture. It spread among the nations with extraordinary speed.[15] The hunters who made these tools concentrated on bison or caribou, depending on the region. Later, from about 10,000 to 8000 BP, their descendants on the western Plains, who now used the Plano point, identifiable by distinctive ripple fluting, were hunting bison by means of drives. Drives became common in Canada around 5000 BP.

At the same time, people in the Eastern Woodlands developed a style of point called Early Archaic by researchers, characterized by distinctive side notching of points for hafting. About 8000 BP, these eastern peoples migrated to the western Plains, where they came in contact with peoples who used the Plano point. Out of this interaction, the Plains cultures developed.[16]

Box 1.1   Stone Age Technology

In some ways, **Stone Age** technology was very efficient indeed. Cutting edges, for example, could be sharper than metal. The war club of the Mexica, with its serrated edges made with a row of obsidian blades inserted into a wooden base, could cut a man's head off with one blow. Even simple stone fleshing blades were quite efficient for processing game. Metal's big advantage was durability. Stone broke easily, so that early tool and weapon makers were kept busy with repairs. One of the results of all this activity was a great variety of artifacts and styles. Archaeologists have identified the tools used in making these elegant points. In some cases, they can identify the work even of individuals.

A successful Stone Age technician had to know his materials: where to find them, how to work them, how they would behave under different conditions, and what he could use them for. Many of the construction and sculpture achievements of the pre-contact Americas were once thought to be impossible with a Stone Age technology. For that reason, scientists attributed them to vanished races and even to creatures from outer space. Now, we know that they were within the capabilities of the Stone Age craftsmen.

A latter-day stone-knapper, Don E. Crabtree, when faced with the necessity for heart surgery, insisted on making the required tools from obsidian. The result was faster healing and less scarring than would have been the case with steel instruments.

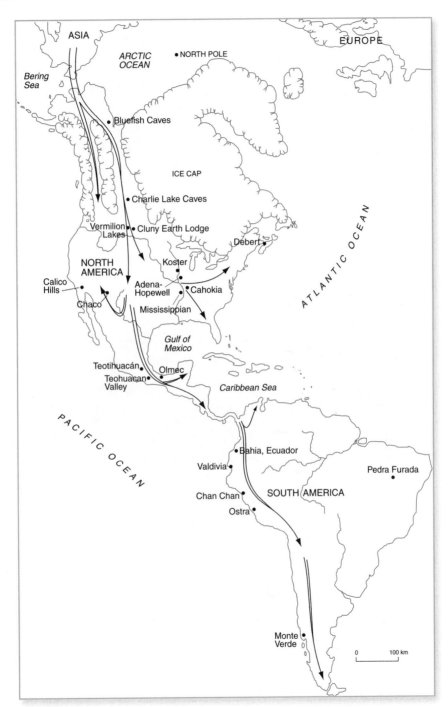

1.1 Possible land route for first human entry into the Americas, as well as some archaeological sites

Source: Alvin M. Josephy, Jr, *The Indian Heritage of America* (New York: Knopf, 1969), 36.

These finely crafted tools are from the High Plains and date to about 11,000 years ago. Shown are stone knives of various sizes and, in the left foreground, a dark projectile point made by the people of the Clovis cultural complex. Its diagnostic feature is the concave 'fluting' at the base. The dowel-like objects are casts of spear foreshafts that had been made of bone. *(David L. Arnold © National Geographic Society, Washington, DC, courtesy Anzick-Hargis Collection)*

Meanwhile, still another lifestyle had appeared on the Northwest Coast, beginning about 11,000 BP. It centred on salmon fishing and sea hunting, and also had distinctive leaf-shaped projectile points.[17] Receptivity to new ideas and willingness to experiment characterized these Stone Age craftsmen. For that reason, not all peoples everywhere—even those who followed similar ways of life—had the same type of tool kit. Not all Amerindians, for example, hafted stone points to bone or wooden bases. Similarly, tools associated with seed grinding have restricted distribution in South America but are widespread in southern and western North America. The development of grinding tools made a wider variety of seeds available for food, such as the small seeds of grasses and amaranths.[18]

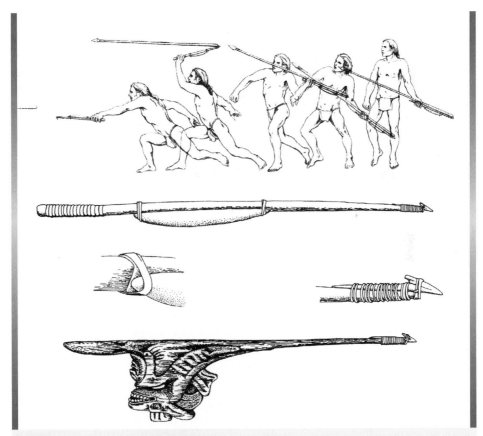

Before the more efficient bow and arrow rendered it obsolete, the spear-thrower—atlatl—was a part of the hunter's tool kit. The notched atlatl gave extra power to hurling a spear. A weight attached to the underside of the atlatl added to its effectiveness. An unusually elaborate weight, in the form of a plumed serpent holding a human head, is shown at the bottom. Carved out of yew-wood with inlaid white-shell eyes, it has been radiocarbon-dated to 17,000 years ago. It was dredged up from the Skagit River, about 50 kilometres south of the Canada–US border, in Washington state. *(University of British Columbia Museum of Anthropology Collection; sketch reproduced with permission from Knut R. Fladmark, Simon Fraser University)*

At one time, researchers thought the bow and arrow appeared in the Americas about AD 250.[19] More recent evidence suggests that Paleo-Eskimos had them much earlier.[20] The bow and arrow had more firepower and a greater range and accuracy than the atlatl (spear thrower), which they replaced. They were also easier to make.[21] Ropemaking, netting, and basketmaking appeared very early, during the late Pleistocene.[22]

How did people use these tools and artifacts? Archaeologists have concentrated on the hunting aspect, because hunting leaves recognizable debris, but what about gathering and processing? The Stone Age tool kit was as useful for cutting and preparing wood, bark, and bast, as well as for gathering and preparing foods such as roots and fruit, as it was for dressing meat and hides. However, little is known about these early tools used for collecting and grinding, because plant products were perishable and tended to disappear without a trace.

At the time of the first certainly known European contact with North America, that of the Norse about AD 1000, most of the nations of the area that would become Canada were hunters and gatherers.[23] This way of life had evolved over thousands of years and grew out of an intimate knowledge of resources and the best way of exploiting them. From this knowledge of how and where plants would grow, however, New World people were already developing a new technology for managing food resources—farming.

New World Farmers—The Three Sisters and Hundreds of Others

Agriculture seems to have developed independently, within a span of a few thousand years at the end of the last Ice Age, in several widely separated regions of the globe: the Near East, the monsoon lands of Southeast Asia, China, Mesoamerica, Peru, and the Amazon. A sudden and unexplained jump in the atmosphere's carbon dioxide (CO_2), which occurred about 15,000 years ago, might provide the explanation. This increase in CO_2 made photosynthesis—the process by which plants convert sunlight into energy—more efficient, increasing their growth rate and size. That might have triggered their domestication and the emergence of farming. Squash seeds found in a Mexican cave have been dated to 10,000 years ago.[24] Bottle gourds may have been among the first domesticated crops in the Americas. In Mexico they were being grown by 9000 BP.[25] Gourds were domesticated before corn, and so were squash and avocados. The last two date to about 8700 BP. Various beans, chili peppers,[26] and amaranth are at least as old. Probably, plant domestication began in several different places with various plants.

There are no definite answers as yet as to why humans turned from collecting to cultivating plants in certain areas but not in others that seem equally suitable. The pressures of growing populations might have caused big-game hunters to turn to farming, but there is no physical evidence of this. Moreover, the switch in lifestyle was not all that sudden or complete.[27]

Fishing, a form of collecting, seems to have played a part in these early attempts at resource management. Classic Mayan agriculturalists, for instance, were also fish farmers.

The people who hunted on the northwestern Plains, on the other hand, harvested plants, such as the prairie turnip ('white apple'), which they had to observe carefully to determine the right time to gather it for drying and pulverizing for winter use.[28] There is also some evidence that they moved plant stocks from one location to another. People in Central and South America cultivated crops that would be grown as far north as the climate permitted and that, eventually, would extend production capacity in the Old World, corn and potatoes being the best known.

The 'New' World Produced Crops for Many Climates and Conditions . . .

New World domesticated plants that made the largest contribution to world agriculture were all of undisputed American origin, developed by Amerindian farmers. Corn (maize) and potatoes are the best known, although tomatoes, peanuts, pineapples, and cacao (from which chocolate is made) are not far behind. Amerindians originally grew more than a hundred species of plants that are still routinely farmed today. Amerindians grew the most famous of all Amerindian crops, tobacco, for diplomatic, ritual, and some medical uses.

In the Northeastern Woodlands of North America, agriculture was introduced with the cultivation of squash, *c.* 4300 BP, probably via southern trade, and the first local plant, the sunflower, was not domesticated until about 3000 BP. In all, the Huron at the time of contact were growing up to 17 varieties of maize and eight types of squash in the Great Lakes area. As well, they gathered more than 30 varieties of wild fruit and at least 10 kinds of nuts, besides other varieties of wild foods.[29] Corn was the first cultivated food crop to reach what is now southern Ontario, and that not until

Huron women preparing corn, from Father François Du Creux, *Historiae Canadensis*, 1664. The woman on the right is using a mortar and pestle to crush the grain while tending a baby, who can be seen on a cradleboard. *(Library and Archives Canada)*

after AD 500. It remained the only crop for five centuries. Tobacco appeared about AD 1000, with beans following somewhat later.

Squash (with sunflowers) did not reach southern Ontario until the thirteenth century, finally completing the triad of the famous **'three sisters'** in the northernmost limits of its range. The time this took could have been that needed for the plants to be adapted to a shorter growing season. By the sixteenth century, the triad—corn, beans, and squash—was being grown throughout agricultural America. As crops, the three sisters benefited the soil when sown together: beans capture nitrogen in the air and release it into the soil; squash roots are extensive and help prevent soil erosion; and the tall corn stalks provide the other plants with some protection from hail, damaging wind, and excessive sunlight. This gave the 'three sisters' a sustainability and permanence lacking in modern agriculture.[30] As food they reinforced each other nutritionally when combined in diets.

The changeover to agriculture seems to have been a mixed blessing, however. For one thing, its higher reliance on starchy foods meant more dental problems. For another, if people relied too heavily on corn in the diet without protein supplements, it could result in a population smaller in stature than ancestral hunters/gatherers and with shorter lifespans.[31]

Whatever its benefits or drawbacks, plant domestication could not have occurred without an extensive botanical knowledge already in place, as is suggested by the vast number of plants that were used for medicinal purposes (Box 1.2). It was no accident that agriculture developed first in warm, moderately rainy latitudes, where plant diversity was greatest and ecological conditions allowed the necessary freedom for experimentation with a comparatively simple technology. Northerners were no less skilful and experimental in exploiting their resources, but the restrictions of their environment in combination with their Stone Age technology, ingenious as it was, meant that they had fewer options.

Box 1.2   Herbal Medicine

The plant world always has been the major source of medicines. (According to the Cherokee, animals brought diseases and plants provided the cures.) Recollect missionary Chrestien Le Clercq (*c.* 1641–after 1700) would report from Acadia, where he was from 1675 to 1686: 'Amerindians are all by nature physicians, apothecaries, and doctors, by virtue of the knowledge and experience they have of certain herbs, which they use successfully to cure ills that seem to us incurable.'[32] That this knowledge had roots that went deep into the past is not questioned. The process by which the Amerindians acquired their herbal lore is not clearly understood, but there is no doubt about the results. Amerindians originally used more than 500 drugs that are still used today.[33]

... But Few Animals Suitable for the Farmyard

Amerindian agriculture concentrated on plants rather than animals, in contrast to the European practice, but did not ignore animals. In the New World, however, there were few candidates for the farmyard. The Peruvians domesticated the llama and the guinea pig. Llamas were mainly beasts of burden but also provided hides, wool, and meat. Farming developed in conjunction with hunting among, for example, the Iroquoian farmers and also occurred in the boreal forest.[34]

1.2   Aboriginal population densities

Source: Carl Waldman, *Atlas of the North American Indian* (New York: Facts on File, 1985).

Dogs were widely (but not universally) present. Some peoples sacrificed dogs in rituals and ate them as ceremonial food. Others used them as work animals. In the North, they pulled sleds but were also raised for food.[35] On the Plains, they were pack animals and also hauled the products of the hunt and camp equipment by means of the travois, a V-shaped frame of tipi poles lashed together with hide. On the Northwest Coast, Amerindians had a variety of dog with a white woolly coat that provided fibres for weaving. In the northern forests, dogs were trained for hunting.

As one observer remarked, turkeys domesticated themselves, as they appreciated the food available in settlements and the detritus from agricultural activity. Amerindians also domesticated other types of fowl and birds but, on the whole, depended on hunting and fishing for their protein even as some of them became sedentary.

Even where no animals existed for possible domestication, however, the possibility of resource management existed and was exploited. New World farmers and hunters controlled game to a surprising extent. They used fire to control directly the movements of animals, such as those of the buffalo on the Plains, and to modify vegetation, which in turn influenced the animals' feeding patterns. For instance, by the sixteenth century, the farming peoples of the Northeastern Woodlands of North America had transformed their habitat into one particularly suitable for deer—the so-called 'deer parks'.[36] Non-agricultural Californians used the same technique for the same purpose: to have deer on hand when needed.

Furthermore, even though agriculture was closely associated with the development of permanent settlement, particularly as populations grew, the process of settling permanently in one location could begin without an agricultural base. What is essential for a sedentary way of living is an assured supply of food in one place, a situation not necessarily dependent on agriculture, at least in the distant period we are considering, when populations were usually small. Archaeological evidence indicates that permanent villages in the Americas date back to 15,000–13,000 BP, before the domestication of plants. In the area that would become Canada, permanent settlement began at least 9,000 years ago.[37]

Geography and Cultural Adaptations

As groups of people settled various regions across the northern half of the continent of North America they adapted to different climates and to the resources that those regions provided. These vast geographic differences help us to understand the differences in cultural adaptations made by the groups of people who settled the area that would become Canada. Ecologists divide Canada into broadly defined ecological regions called biomes, ecozones, or biotic provinces, which differ immensely based on climate, flora, fauna, and soil types. These distinct regions, however, commonly have transitional zones between them that show some characteristics of both regions. Two of Canada's ecozones cover most of what is now northern Canada. The tundra in the Far North is a region with an extremely cold climate, little vegetation, and maritime mammals such as polar bears, whales, walrus, and harp seals. Adjacent to the tundra, chiefly in northern Ontario but also, to a lesser extent, in northern Quebec and Manitoba, is the Hudson Bay Lowland. There are trees in this biotic province, mainly black spruce and tamaracks, but they tend to be smaller than members of these species growing in warmer climates. This region supports caribou herds, muskox, and Arctic hare, among many other species.

Extending from the Atlantic Ocean all along the rugged uplands of the Canadian Shield to the northern reaches of the present-day Prairie provinces, and into northern British Columbia, the Northwest Territories, and Yukon, is the boreal forest (taiga). This densely wooded area of coniferous trees includes black spruce, white spruce, white pine, red pine, and eastern cedar, as well as a few broadleaf deciduous species such as white birch. The moose, the beaver, and the black bear are the most important of the region's animals. To the south is the Great Lakes transitional ecozone. The climate of this area of the Great Lakes and the St Lawrence Valley is moderated by the huge inland seas that are the Great Lakes. As the name implies, the area includes the flora and fauna of both the boreal forest and of the Carolinian forest to the south. The Carolinian species include broadleaf deciduous trees such as maple, ash, and oak. Deer are the most important large animal of the Carolinian forest.

To the west of the Great Lakes and south of the Shield and the boreal forest lie the grasslands of the Canadian Plains. This area is called the grasslands or prairie ecozone, although the agricultural development of the nineteenth and twentieth centuries has rendered it the most dramatically transformed region in the world. The grasslands that stretched from the woodlands in the east to the Rocky Mountains in the west supported massive herds of bison. Furthest west, along the Pacific coast, lies the temperate Pacific maritime biotic province. This region is dominated by huge mountains in the east and by the cedar forests of the coastal ranges in the west. It is populated by grizzly bears, elk, and bighorn sheep on land and by salmon in the coastal waters and rivers.

The environment of each of these biomes provided resources that in turn shaped the cultural adaptations of the particular groups. In the Far North the Inuit were hunter/gatherers. They hunted seals, walruses, whales, caribou, and muskox. Ivory from walrus tusks had a great value. The Inuit gathered edible seaweed called *kuanniq*, Arctic berries, bone, and soapstone. These comparatively meagre resources provided them with all they needed to eat and to clothe themselves. The harsh climate and their relative isolation helped to shape their world view. The culture of the Inuit is rich with tales of travelling vast distances to hunt and to find food. Relationships in Inuit communities were less formal or hierarchical than in other societies as people sought ways of adapting to their sparsely populated region.

The resources of the Hudson Bay Lowland and of the tundra–boreal forest transition zone to the east supported the Cree in the Hudson Bay region, as well as Inuit farther to the north in present-day Quebec and Innu to the east in Quebec and Labrador. These people hunted for caribou and other game, and they sought berries, grasses, roots, and tubers. Like the Inuit, the relative isolation of the James Bay Cree (and the Wood Cree and Swampy Cree who populated the lands to the west of Hudson Bay) and of the Innu, and their adaptations to the region's extreme climate, kept them in small family hunting groups with more informal social relations. Cree and Innu stories, like those of the Inuit, focus on travel and hunting themes and identify the necessities of the world around them with reference to the environmental features that shaped their culture.

The Ojibwa people are a good example of a group who lived in the region of the boreal forest. The Ojibwa hunted for moose and beaver and gathered tubers, berries, and birchbark. Unlike the Inuit, Innu, and Cree, the Ojibwa were active traders in the pre-contact period. The ecological basis for trade was more easily exploited by the Ojibwa than by those groups further to the north because of the relative proximity of trading partners. The Ojibwa traded the thick beaver pelts of the region north of Lake Superior to the Odawa and Huron peoples to the south. In return they received the horticultural products of those people: corn and tobacco. Like the Cree, the Ojibwa lived in small family hunting groups and followed an annual round in search of different kinds of fish and game. Ojibwa people were patrilocal: young couples lived with the male's family, probably because their economy was dominated by hunting, a male pursuit according to the gender division of labour.

The Great Lakes transitional region was the most diverse of all of Canada's regions as it included the flora and fauna of two bordering ecozones. This meant that the two peoples who lived in the region, the Odawa and the Hurons, had made complex cultural adaptations to their environment. They fished for the whitefish of the Great Lakes; they hunted the moose and beaver of the boreal forest and the deer of the Carolinian forest. They practised horticulture, growing corn, beans, squash, and tobacco along the northern fringe of the growing zones for these crops. The Odawa manufactured mats from the rushes of the Carolinian forest and birchbark canoes and boxes from the birch trees. The Hurons made wooden clubs, mortars, and pestles from the hardwood of the Carolinian trees. Both groups gathered blueberries, nuts, birchbark, and other non-timber forest products. Most importantly, their economic diversity gave both groups the impetus to trade, and this led to a relatively high level of contact with other groups. Both the Odawa and Hurons held large feasts at specified times of the year in order to trade and to renew alliances with their neighbours. Both groups were matrilocal, as horticulture—an activity led by women—dictated living with the mother's family. Although they were similar in terms of their cultural adaptations, the Odawa and Hurons had important differences. The Odawa spoke an Algonkian language, like the Cree, Innu, and Ojibwa peoples to the north and east. The Hurons spoke an Iroquoian language, like the Eries, Neutrals, Petuns, and Five Nations to the south and east. Like other Iroquoians, the Hurons lived in longhouses and relied more heavily on horticulture than did the Odawa.

The people of the Blackfoot Confederacy of what is now southern Alberta cannot be understood without reference to the bison (buffalo), the most important resource of the grasslands. The Blackfoot, like the Plains Cree, made shelters and garments from bison hides and subsisted on bison meat, either fresh or dried as *pemmican*. The Blackfoot also gathered berries, tubers, grasses, and other products of the grasslands. They lived in larger groups as bison hunting required the participation of large communities, and as a result they had a more formal social structure. Not surprisingly, the bison played a large role in Blackfoot storytelling.

In the moderate Pacific maritime region, people such as the Haida established large, palisaded, permanent villages. They built huge canoes out of giant cedar trees and fished the coastal waters. Haida culture is best represented by their exquisite totem poles, expressions of their beliefs and their warrior ethic as they sought to defend their territory and its rich resource base from external threats.

Social Development

For a variety of reasons, including the geographic and economic determinants discussed above, social development varied throughout the Americas. Some hunting and gathering societies continued in their traditional pattern. Others picked up aspects of agricultural cultures. This could happen even when peoples associated with each other in trade or war. For example, the people who hunted buffalo on the northern Plains traded with the farming Mandans. The way of life of each was richer for their interchange, yet each retained its specific character. Similarly, there were farming peoples who retained the hunting-gathering mode even as some of their neighbours developed into city-states, and, in one or two cases, empires. And while most Amerindian societies operated on an egalitarian basis, some societies, especially those that were more sedentary and had a rich resource base, such as on the west coast, developed complex hierarchies based on kinship.

Egalitarian and Hierarchical Societies

Egalitarian societies did not separate authority from the group as a whole. In some cases, they even went to considerable lengths to ensure that such a separation did not occur. In those societies, available resources were open to all, and their leaders used influence rather than force.[38] Free sharing ensured that the superior skills of, say, a hunter benefited the group rather than just the individual hunter. The power of chiefs depended on their ability to provide for their followers. The leaders' role was to represent the common will. They did not use force, and they would have quickly lost their positions if they had tried. This lent extreme importance to eloquence, the power to persuade. A chief's authority was 'in his tongue's end; for he is powerful in so far as he is eloquent'. Failure in this regard meant loss of position.[39] Among the Mi'kmaq, a chief

Box 1.3   Individualism and Discipline

The warrior and the soldier symbolize the difference between egalitarian and state societies. In the Eastern Woodlands, the warrior—in Iroquoian terms, the bearer of the bones
of the nation, a responsibility that included the duty to fight for it—was his own man, to the
point of being able to quit a war party without losing face.[40] A soldier, however, under the
command of his superior officer, could be court-martialled or even shot for such behaviour.
In any case, he would be disgraced.

For the Amerindian, discipline was an individual matter.[41] It included the ability to go for
long periods with little or no food and to withstand torture; calm endurance of inconven-
iences, hardships, and suffering; capacity to resist fatigue; and the ability to think for oneself
in battle.[42] The Amerindian code of bravery in warfare was unlikely to call for dying while
trying to maintain an untenable position, as that of the Europeans often did.

could attract followers, but they were not subordinated to their leader's will,[43] except,
perhaps, in time of war. Even in warfare, however, among many groups the individual
was essentially his own leader (see Box 1.3). Perhaps most important of all, chiefs were
expected to set an example for their people, in particular by being generous. Instead
of gaining wealth through their positions, they could end up the poorest of the group
because of the continual demands made on their resources.[44]

Selection of leaders was based on qualification, although the sons of chiefs often
succeeded their fathers. Besides the established leader, certain individuals, because
of their particular skills and spiritual powers, could be chosen by social consensus
to organize and lead such group activities as the buffalo hunt, a raid, or a seasonal
transfer in the pursuit of food. However, the authority involved in such positions
lasted only as long as the task or project at hand. Should a rival chief appear or
factionalism result in a split, the dissident group could always break away and establish itself elsewhere. In order to avoid this factionalism, some groups, including the
Anishinabek of the Great Lakes, maintained both hereditary chiefs and chiefs chosen
by consensus.

The general lack of quarrelling or interpersonal conflict in Amerindian communities
impressed Europeans, who wondered how peaceful relations could prevail without the
threat of force in the background. Amerindians, for their part, were not impressed
when they saw Europeans being afraid of their captains, 'while they laugh at and make
sport of theirs'.[45]

Such observations indicate how easy it was for Europeans to miss the subtleties
of Amerindian social controls. Respect was exceedingly important, and within their
spheres of competence, the chiefs did have authority.[46] One European visitor reported
in the eighteenth century that some chiefs were skilful leaders, as they knew 'how to
confine their commands within the limits of their power'.[47]

In chiefdoms (in Canada, found on the Northwest Coast), on the other hand, the chiefs did have power, up to and including that of life and death in certain cases. In America, permanent settlement seems to have been necessary for the development of chiefdoms, which, in a few cases, became states. However, the old idea that hunters/gatherers were kept so busy finding food that they had no time for cultural matters is not true. Chiefdoms did develop in non-agricultural societies, such as those of the Northwest Coast, as well as in agricultural societies, such as the agricultural peoples of the Gulf of Mexico, the southern Atlantic coast, and in some regions in between.

The Northwest Coast was the only area in what is now Canada where **chiefdoms** developed (such as those of the Haida, Nuu'chah'nulth, Kwakwaka'wakw, and Tsimshian). They had clearly marked class divisions between chiefs, nobles, and commoners based on wealth and heredity. There was also grading within each class.[48] Overriding class and even tribal distinctions among the northern tribes (Tlingit, Haida, and Tsimshian) was the division of each of these groups into two parts that researchers call 'moieties',[49] in turn subdivided into clans, which recognized descent only through the female line. Farther south, the Kwakwaka'wakw, Bella Coola, and Nuu'chah'nulth, on the other hand, had no such moieties. They reckoned descent through both the female and the male lines, and practised a ritual life characterized by secret societies. These traits were less evident among the Coast Salish. In general, their chiefs also had less power. The Salish word for *chief* translates best as 'leader'.

Chiefdoms varied considerably in their social complexities and centralization of authority. What they had in common was concern with rank based on lineage, through which their redistributive economies functioned. As well, they developed sophisticated artistic traditions, each in a different sphere (the Californians in basketry, the Northwest Coasters in woodwork, the Ohioans and Mississippians in stone sculpture and shell and copperwork, the east coasters in feather work and hide painting, and the Adena-Hopewell-Mississippian [*c.* 3000 BP] in monumental earthworks).

Some of these chiefdoms, especially those that were non-agricultural, lasted until the arrival of Europeans. Those with an agricultural base could support denser populations. Where they reached comparatively large proportions, such as at **Cahokia** (in present-day Illinois), which during its peak (1050–1250, although it lasted for about 500 years) had a population estimated at 30,000 to 40,000, the distinction between chiefdom and state becomes blurred. Cahokia had the largest and densest pre-contact population north of the Rio Grande and was bigger than contemporaneous London, England.[50]

Why some societies shifted from being egalitarian groupings of mobile peoples to become hierarchical sedentary or semi-sedentary chiefdoms, and eventually to become the social complexities of city-states, still puzzles historians.[51] If there is debate as to how humans came to be in the Americas, there is impassioned argument as to how they became urbanized.

The Cultural Exchange between the 'New' World and the 'Old'

What were the factors that led to the rise of city-states? Did the great metropolises of Central and South America develop completely independently? Did other cultures influence them along the way? If so, what other cultures were involved, and when did they make contact?

Thus baldly stated, the question assumes an either/or characteristic that probably is too simple. There is no serious argument against contacts and diffusion between various New World centres. In fact, many of these have been traced (the spread of the use of tobacco, for instance, or the cultivation of corn).[52] Even so, certain questions about intercultural contacts need to be kept in mind. What was their nature, and how important were they? How did they interact with indigenous cultures already in place? The questions take on another character (and become heated) when we consider the possibility of overseas contact between the Americas and the Old World. Answers arrived at in the present state of our knowledge must be considered as tentative, a pushing back of frontiers perhaps, but not final solutions.

If there were non-Amerindian influences at work in the Americas, they most likely came by the easiest and quickest route available—the sea. Long before the present era, the people of ancient southeastern China became known as Pai-Yueh, the Navigators. We can only speculate as to where these early sailors went. However, the peanut, an American plant, has turned up at two coastal Chinese sites dating to about 5300–4800 BP,[53] and two varieties of chickens considered to be native to Asia were established in America when the Spanish arrived.[54]

Chinese records tell of a search for islands in the Eastern (Pacific) Ocean where drugs for longevity could be found, as well as 'magical beings and strange things'. One such expedition, around 2200 BP, resulted in 3,000 young men and women being sent a few years later. Their mission was to establish a trade in the drug, but they were never heard from again. The mention of magical drugs brings South America to mind, but likely we will never know for certain. In AD 458, Chinese records tell us, the monk Hwui Shan, with four companions, sailed to the east and reached the land of Fu-Sang, believed to be in present-day Mexico, where he stayed for 40 years, returning to China in 499.[55]

In 1956, archaeologists discovered ceramics at Valdivia, in southwestern Ecuador, dated to 5200–4800 BP, at that time by far the oldest-known such artifacts in the Americas. Their striking resemblance to Japanese pottery set off a wave of speculation that the Japanese introduced pottery-making to the Americas. Eventually, however, even older ceramics that had no resemblance to Valdivia ware came to light, ending that particular debate but leaving open the question of the origin of New World pottery.[56]

In northeastern North America, another fully developed type of pottery called by scientists Vinette I and resembling Old World ceramics appeared about 3000 BP.[57] It could have resulted from local experimentations following exposure to the pottery of

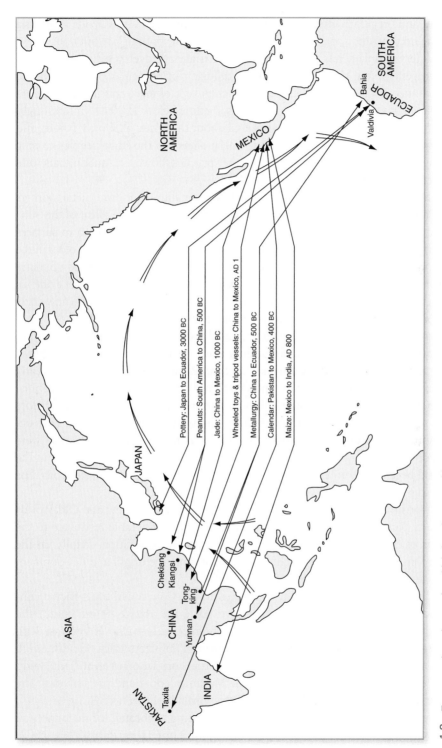

1.3   Transoceanic exchanges for which there is some evidence

Source: John Barber, 'Oriental Enigma', *Equinox* 49 (Jan.–Feb. 1990): 83–95.

the mid-Atlantic region. Otherwise, pottery might have come into Canada from Asia via Alaska and the Yukon, or from the south into the east, both before 5000 BP.[58]

The pottery problem has, if anything, fuelled the controversy over transoceanic contacts in general and their role in cultural diffusion in particular. The issue of the Japanese connection is far from dead, as a particular type of mace considered to be peculiar to Japan has surfaced in Ecuador, dated sometime before 1500 BP. (Interestingly, in the Far North, the bow and arrow appeared about this time, or shortly before, and spread rapidly southward.) Japanese and Amerindians are the only peoples to sing death songs. If there was a connection with other peoples, however, Amerindians were soon experimenting on their own.

Amerindians were the first masters of platinum metallurgy. Andean metal workers made skilful use of alloys. Peruvians manipulated sheets of gold, 'the sweat of the Sun', and silver, 'tears of the Moon', into desired forms with particular attention to surfaces and colour, a style called surface transformation.[59] Beaten metal work is even older in the Americas. The Old Copper Culture, in the Lake Superior region and to the south, dates to 6000 BP. As matters stand at the present, however, plants offer the strongest evidence of overseas connections between New and Old Worlds. Accordingly, the scene now shifts to Southeast Asia, mainly Cambodia, southern India, and the Maldive Islands.[60]

The argument here is for a trade contact, mainly with Cambodian Khmers, around AD 400–1000. Prevailing winds and currents made such commerce possible, but it could not have lasted past the thirteenth century. Plant evidence indicates an early India–America connection. Both New and Old Worlds shared bottle gourds, coconuts, and some varieties of yams. Similarly, cotton, cultivated in Mexico and in Peru before 4500 BP, seems to have Old World connections. Some argue that this could have occurred by natural processes, but botanists see this as highly unlikely.[61] People were likely involved in the hybridization, and cultivation of the domesticated plant in the New World began in northwestern South America, probably Peru.[62] Maize (corn) has added to this botanical puzzle (see Box 1.4).[63]

Not surprisingly, proponents of ancient contact between the New and Old Worlds have eagerly picked up these two cases. Since there is considerable resistance to the hypothesis of early contact before the time of European exploration, mainly on the grounds of insufficient sea-going technology at that time, the origin and development of gourds and cotton as crops are unsolved problems.

Other New World plants that have appeared in pre-Columbian trans-Pacific contexts include grain amaranth, which may have made the voyage before corn,[64] the sweet potato, peanuts, and the coconut palm. The reverse seems to be the case with an Asiatic type of rice, *Oryza latifolia*, widely grown in South America. In addition to plant evidence, the calendar of the Mexica has a partial correlation to an ancient Hindu zodiac. There are also similarities between the Mayan calendar and the alphabet. The Hindu game of pachisi and the Mexica patolli are virtually the same.[65]

Further west, we find Egypt and Phoenicia both being advocated for the honour of having reached the New World. When archaeologist **Thor Heyerdahl** (1914–2002)

Box 1.4   The Puzzle of Corn

Corn presents a puzzle in tracing the early attempts at agriculture by the peoples of the New World. By the 1500s, Amerindians were growing at least 150 varieties, adapted to a wide array of conditions.[66] However, if a wild corn once flourished, researchers have not found it. Two wild grasses related to corn—teosinte and tripsacum—still grow in the highlands of Mexico. Teosinte (the name is Mexican, meaning 'mother of corn') can be cross-bred with domesticated corn, but it needs equal hours of daylight and darkness and warm temperatures. Corn, in contrast, was being grown from Huronia in the Ontario midlands of Canada all the way through to southern Chile when Europeans arrived.

The oldest site known where corn may have been developed as a crop is in central Mexico, where tiny cobs dated to 7000 BP have been found. Stone tools for grinding corn appeared about 5,000 years ago and are still used today. The mortar and pestle also served the same purpose. Corn needed about a thousand years of selective breeding to produce the many varieties first encountered by Europeans. The main modification since has been for the cobs to become larger.

Corn cannot survive without human intervention, as it lacks the capacity to reproduce itself. It is among the most efficient crops in the world in terms of yield.[67] Its development is one of the world's great achievements in plant science.[68] To Amerindian farmers, corn has feelings and can cry.

looked for men who could recreate the ancient craft required to sail the South Atlantic, he found them at Lake Chad in North Africa and Lake Titicaca in the Andean highlands.[69] Heyerdahl has pointed out that Columbus reached the Caribbean by taking the ocean highway called the Canary Current. Carrying on a little further west, Spaniards later reached the Gulf of Mexico. It is in this region that the Olmec, the 'mother' of American civilizations, appeared suddenly in a well-settled area about 3500 BP during a time of natural disasters in and emigration from the Old World (see Box 1.5). The Olmec influenced later city-states, such as those of the Mayas.

It is not always clear, however, in which direction the influences went. For instance, glyphic writing, once assumed to be an innovation of the Olmec in the New World, was actually present centuries earlier, before 2600 BP, at Monte Albán, in the land of the Zapotecs in present-day southwestern Mexico. This was one of the only two sites of the world where writing was indisputably invented. (The other was Mesopotamia, before 5000 BP.)[70]

Heyerdahl saw no reason why early travellers, like the Spaniards at a later date, did not sail down the Pacific coast on sea-going rafts, built with balsa logs from Ecuador and equipped with sails. Heyerdahl saw the settlement of Easter Island—with its mysterious giant sculptured heads (some with carefully buried bodies), so different from the giant heads of the Olmec—as originating in the Americas.

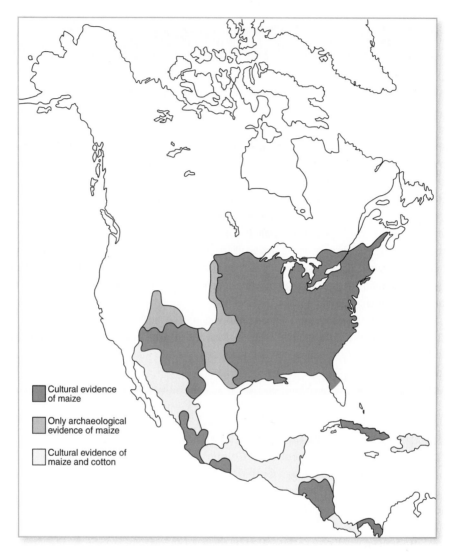

1.4   Distribution of maize and cotton in North and Central America

Source: Waldman, *Atlas of the North American Indian.*

As well, the peopling of Polynesia (including New Zealand), even if largely originating in Southeast Asia as generally accepted, would have had to come via the Americas along the only route available with the available sailing technology—the Japanese Current. The sweet potato, widespread throughout the Pacific, is an American crop. As Heyerdahl saw it, Polynesia was the last region of the world to be populated by humans, and it was by way of the Americas. Genetic studies have revealed a close relationship between South American Amerindians and Polynesians.[71]

Box 1.5 The Development of Civilizations

We do not yet understand fully how civilizations arise in the first place.[72] In the Old World, archaeologists generally believe that the process began in the Middle East, but it was not long (in archaeological terms) before civilizations developed in other locations, including the Far East. There was exchange, not only between related peoples but also with other races and cultures, and this stimulated widely varying developments. These exchanges took place over long distances involving travel by both land and water, yet they do not take away from the achievements of a particular culture.[73]

As for Old World influence on New World culture, the evidence we have is merely suggestive. The evidence accumulated so far indicates that the civilizations of the New World basically developed in the New World according to cultural adaptations that groups of people made to the various environments. If they had the benefit of cross-fertilization, which is possible and, in some cases, even probable, this would have encouraged already established processes. Some researchers deny the likelihood of any external factors powerful enough to have had an important impact. Succinctly put, civilizations were independently developed by the peoples of the western hemisphere.[74]

Whatever the outcome of these debates, one point is clear. New World prehistory was as filled with significant developments as that of the Old World. Whatever the degree of overseas influence, the civilizations that evolved in the New World were distinctively their own. Varied as the New World cultures were, they fit into a hemisphere-wide pattern, and like Europeans on the other side of the Atlantic, they shared a basic civilization. Their 'formidable originality' has led scholars to place Amerindian civilizations on a par with those of the Old World: the Han, the Gupta, and the Hellenistic Age.[75]

Important Names and Terms

Beringia	fluted points
Cahokia	Heyerdahl, Thor
chiefdoms	taiga
egalitarian societies	'three sisters'

Study Questions

1) Account for the different theories of the origins of the First Nations peoples.
2) How were the routines, assumptions, and compelling experiences of daily life shaped by adaptations to the various ecozones across Canada?

3) Discuss the ecological basis for trade that existed across the regions.
4) What explains the rise of egalitarianism among the First Nations?

Recommended Readings

Deloria, Vine, Jr. *Red Earth, White Lies: Native Americans and the Myth of Scientific Fact*. Golden, Colo.: Fulcrum, 1997.

Heyerdahl, Thor. *Early Man and the Ocean: A Search for the Beginnings of Navigation and Seaborne Civilizations*. New York: Vintage Books, 1980.

McClellan, Catharine. *Part of the Land, Part of the Water: A History of the Yukon Indians*. Vancouver: Douglas & McIntyre, 1987.

McGhee, Robert. *Canadian Arctic Prehistory*. Toronto: Van Nostrand Reinhold, 1978.

Shutler, Richard, ed. *Early Man in the New World*. Beverly Hills, Calif.: Sage, 1983.

Weatherford, Jack. *Indian Givers: How the Indians Transformed the World*. New York: Crown Publishers, 1988.

2 | First Meetings

First contacts between Europeans and New World peoples occurred over a much longer period than most people realize.[1] In what is now Canada, first meetings for which there is a reasonably acceptable record began with the Norse about 1000 BP and continued as late as 1915, when members of the Canadian Arctic Expedition met isolated bands of Inuit who were completely unknown to the Canadian government.[2] In 1918, Royal North-West Mounted Police, while on a search for an Inuk wanted for murder, were still meeting people who had never seen a non-Aboriginal.[3] In contrast, these Inuit knew of non-Aboriginals, as their ancestors had met them. In other words, first meetings with Inuit occurred, off and on, over a period of more than 900 years. The Amerindian time span for such encounters was about 400 years, with some Athapaskans of the Far Northwest being among the last to meet whites early in the twentieth century.

We can define **'first meetings'**, of course, in a number of ways. One historian has listed three basic types: collisions, relationships, and contacts, all three of which rarely occur in a pure form.[4] 'Collisions' include the transmission of disease and the slave trade. Trade, evangelization, and colonial administration characterized the second type, 'relationships'. 'Contacts' were encounters, for the most part short-lived, between Europeans and members of a non-European culture, and were usually peaceful, although they often involved ritual displays, such as flag- or cross-planting ceremonies, that could be interpreted as threats and that could lead to eventual collisions.

Contacts can be either pristine encounters—in which one or both sides had no previous knowledge of the other—or first encounters preceded by hearsay, the appearance of new trade goods through local networks, the spread of a new disease, or other evidence, such as the debris left behind by explorers. It is with these subtleties in mind that we will consider 'first contacts' here. The first recorded encounters with Europeans in the New World took place in the eastern Arctic, perhaps some of them on Baffin Island, and along the North Atlantic coast of what is now Canada. Two of the peoples most likely to have been involved, Dorset and Beothuk, have since disappeared.

Time Line

5000 BP	Head-Smashed-In Jump in southern Alberta, used for hunting of bison until 1870s, had 30 different mazeways, as many as 20,000 cairns to direct stampeding herds.		impact on subsequent inter-tribal and Indian–European relations.
4000–1000 BP	Dorset culture thrives in Far North.	1576–8	Arctic voyages of Sir Martin Frobisher, by which time Thule culture has developed into Inuit. Like other explorers, he returns to Europe with an Aboriginal, an Inuk hunter, as a 'token of possession'. The Inuk soon dies in captivity.
1000	Thule culture begins to supersede earlier Dorset in North. Norse accounts of 'Skraelings'—probably Dorset people, but may have been Beothuk.		
		1600	Inuit range extends down Labrador coast.
1497	John Cabot (Giovanni Caboto) makes landfall on east coast of Newfoundland.	1611	Subarctic Indians in James Bay meet Henry Hudson: first European contact.
1500s or earlier	Iroquoians form confederacies (Huron Confederacy, League of Five Nations) that have major	1829	Shawnadithit, a woman who was the last known Beothuk, dies.

Box 2.1   The Norse and the Skraelings

The Norse who travelled to the New World reported meeting Skraelings (from 'skrael-ingjar', meaning small, withered), who were probably Dorset.[5] The Norse thought of them possibly as folkloric creatures. They referred to them as 'trolls' and described them as 'very little people', lacking in iron, who 'use whale teeth for arrowheads and sharp stones for knives'.[6] Another description refers to them as 'small ill-favored men' with 'ugly hair on their heads. They had big eyes and were broad in the cheeks.'[7] The Norse said that the Skraelings were eager to trade the products of the hunt for weapons. That the Norse traded with the Skraelings has been inferred from the presence of European artifacts in Arctic archaeological sites, particularly burials. Even more fascinating was the discovery in Bergen, Norway, the Norwegian port for traffic with Iceland and Greenland, of a walrus figurine of Inuit workmanship. This find was made at an archaeological site dated to the thirteenth century. The written records give us no hint as to what the Skraelings thought of the Europeans.[8]

2.1   Aboriginal culture areas

Sources: Waldman, *Atlas of the North American Indian*; R. Bruce Morrison and C. Roderick Wilson, eds, *Native Peoples: The Canadian Experience* (Toronto: McClelland & Stewart, 1986).

Men of stone and bone could hold their own against the men of iron in pre-fireweapon days, and Norse settlements on northern Newfoundland and mainland Atlantic coasts did not last. There seem to have been four expeditions to Leifsbudir (Leif's booths, now thought to be the site near L'Anse aux Meadows) at the northern tip of Newfoundland, but hostilities developed between the local people and the visitors (see Box 2.1).[9] At sea, the **Little Ice Age** of *c.* 1450–1850[10] caused the ice pack to thicken, interfering with shipping, which in any event had been irregular and was decreasing due to conditions in

Europe. It eventually stopped, cutting off supplies from Norway on which the people's lifestyle (including diet) depended.[11] Eventually, the Norse abandoned their colonies.

The Inuit Meet the Kodlunas

During the time before the Europeans arrived, the ancestors of the modern Inuit were moving steadily eastward across the Arctic, displacing earlier people called **Dorset** by archaeologists (whose culture had evolved from the original Paleo-Eskimo). The **Thule**, as archaeologists have called them, reached the Atlantic coast sometime during the fifteenth century. Dorset lingered in the northern Ungava until the fifteenth century. They also held out until about the same time in Newfoundland before giving way to the Beothuk, a proto-Algonkian people who followed a way of life based on the winter caribou hunt and the summer exploitation of sea and river resources. Some pockets of Dorset may have continued until the twentieth century on Hudson Bay.[12]

Baffin Island Inuk woman and baby, taken prisoner by Martin Frobisher in 1577 during his second Arctic voyage. This depiction is by John White, who accompanied the expedition and was the first European artist to portray Inuit. *(Library and Archives Canada, ECM 64–31125)*

The Thule, like the modern Inuit but unlike the Dorset, possessed the bow and arrow, spear thrower, and sealskin-covered kayaks and umiaks. They used dogs as draft animals. They were the unchallenged masters of the tundra lands beyond the treeline, and the Amerindians seldom encroached on their domain.[13]

By the sixteenth century, however, the changing climate favoured the sea mammal-hunting activities of the Inuit, who were advancing eastward and southward down the North Atlantic coast. When they met Frobisher during his Arctic voyages in 1576–8, they were already familiar with Europeans and their ships. There was no hint about wondering if Europeans were supernatural beings, any more than there had been on the

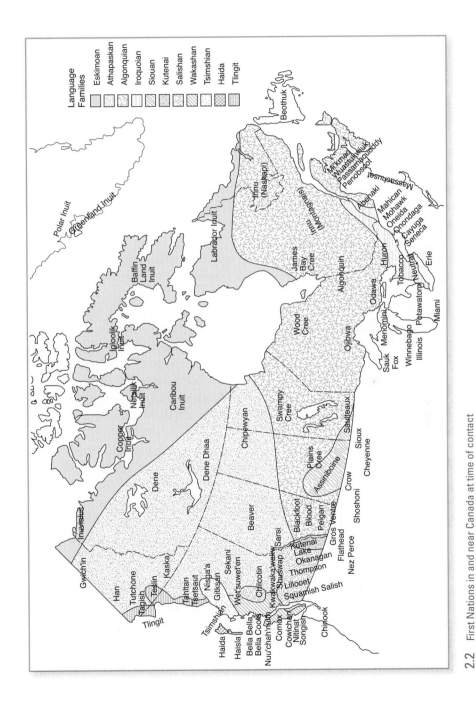

2.2   First Nations in and near Canada at time of contact

Sources: Alan D. Macmillan, *Native Peoples and Cultures of Canada* (Vancouver: Douglas & McIntyre, 1988); John Price, *Indians of Canada: Cultural Dynamics* (Scarborough, Ont.: Prentice-Hall, 1979).

North Atlantic coast when **John Cabot** (Giovanni Caboto) had made his landfall in 1497. The shock of first encounter seems to have dissipated very early in those northern regions, perhaps with the Norse, perhaps with later, unrecorded meetings. More shocks, however, would follow.

Frobisher brought back an Inuk hunter to England and displayed him as a 'token of possession', proof that the explorer had found and claimed new lands for the Queen.[14] The Inuk soon died, but others followed. The Inuit back in the Arctic, for their part, maintained an oral tradition of the time when the kodlunas (kabloonas, or Qallunaat) visited them.[15] As well, they had carefully preserved odds and ends from Frobisher's visit, such as pieces of red brick and brass rings.[16]

Kidnapping was the best possible proof that an explorer had actually reached the lands he claimed. There was also the idea that the Natives could learn the language of their captors and be used as interpreters and guides for future explorations. However, if the captives survived the trip across the Atlantic, they usually quickly succumbed in Europe to unfamiliar living conditions and diet. They were often called on to display their skill in archery, all the more because of the English pride in their reputation as the best archers in Europe. However, historians dismiss the tale that Queen Elizabeth I granted one of these Inuit visitors the unheard-of privilege of shooting some royal swans.[17]

Early English explorers referred to Inuit as 'salvages' but also as 'Indians'—in the eighteenth century, 'Esquimaux Indians' was a common term. They were reported to 'eate their meate raw' and also to 'eate grasse like bruit beasts, without table or stoole, and when their hands are imbued in blood they lick them clean with their tongues.' Although the English judged them to be 'very tractable' and 'easie to be brought to civility', they also considered Amerindians to be 'Idolaters and witches', serious charges in an age when Europeans burned witches alive at the stake and when Christians tended to consider all non-Christians to be enemies.

The English also seem to have shared with Europeans in general the belief that all New World peoples were cannibals. Later, reports became more colourful: to quote Canadian-born interpreter and trading-post clerk Nicolas Jérémie (1669–1732), 'when they kill or capture any of their enemies, they eat them raw and drink their blood. They even make infants at the breast drink it, so as to instil in them the barbarian ardour of war from their tenderest years.'[18]

The closest to sustained contact that developed between Natives of the eastern Arctic and Europeans during this period was through whaling. This began along the Labrador coast and the Strait of Belle Isle, where Inuit met with Basque whalers, and later with French. These encounters introduced Europeans to Inuit technology for deep-sea whaling, which during the seventh to the thirteenth centuries was the most advanced in the world. Combined with European deep-sea ships, that technology led to the growth of worldwide whaling.[19]

Early Inuit–European encounters followed the pattern of trading and raiding. We do not know how far this extended, but by the first half of the eighteenth century, Inuit were occasionally working with Europeans. This co-operation would reach its fullest extent during the 1800s, after operations moved to northwestern Hudson Bay and Americans became major participants.

Arctic whaling would last until the first decade of the twentieth century. The resulting reduction of whale stocks severely affected Inuit domestic offshore whaling and led to changes in hunting patterns. On the positive side, the Arctic environment, which Europeans found unattractive in the extreme, protected Inuit territory. It would be the second half of the twentieth century before there would be a serious intrusion of Canada's northernmost lands and its people.

The World Called 'New' by the Europeans Was Far from New

Europeans who wintered over in the New World to protect and maintain fishing gear and stages for drying codfish seem, on the whole, to have enjoyed a happier fate than Frobisher's captive Inuk. Soon, individuals were choosing to stay over. The first persons selected for this service were convicts, perhaps condemned criminals. Often, their function was to learn the language and way of life of the people among whom they went to live, as well as something about their land. The idea was for these 'interpreters' to report back to officials of their mother country several years later, if anyone remembered, or cared enough, to pick them up. These interpreters eventually became key factors in the Caribbean. Further north, men often entered this life willingly.

The indigenous people of the New World lived within cultural frameworks that met social and individual needs by emphasizing the group as well as the self. This was true even among those peoples, particularly in the Far North, whose groupings changed with the season and availability of food. Land, like air and water, was for the benefit of everyone, and so was communally owned. Because of Canada's extensive coastline (the longest of any nation in the world), many of the Aboriginal peoples were sea-oriented. However, the great variety in the country's geographical regions (Arctic, Subarctic, Northeastern Woodlands, Great Plains, Plateau, and Northwest Coast) resulted in many variations on fundamentally similar ways of life.[20]

Trade and Gift Diplomacy: An Important Part of Interactions

Uneven distribution of resources ensured that all of these people traded. Good relations, alliances, and the transfer of spiritual powers were important in these exchanges, rather than economic considerations. However, there could be trade with an enemy, if the parties could agree on a truce. As Jesuit Paul Le Jeune (1591–1664) observed in the St Lawrence Valley, 'Besides having some kind of Laws maintained among themselves, there is also a certain order established as regards foreign nations.' Amerindians treated any person caught breaking these rules like a thief. They sealed agreements by an exchange of gifts and hostages, which led to the formation of blood ties. Alliances were less important in the Far North, where hostilities were expressed in chance killings or raids rather than in warfare.

While Amerindians certainly appreciated the value of goods and had a good eye for quality, prestige was more important than the accumulation of wealth as such.

Amerindians measured wealth either in material goods or in immaterial rights, such as those to certain songs, dances, or rituals. Despite the emphasis on rank and material goods, the principle of sharing prevailed as far as the basic necessities of life were concerned. The kinship groups divided up the village's hunting, fishing, and gathering territories. Acquiring prestige called for generosity. Individuals traded for goods to give away on ceremonial occasions, such as the potlatch on the west coast. **Gift exchanges**—'I give to you that you may give to me'[21]—were a social and diplomatic obligation. Amerindians presented gifts when people visited each other; on special occasions, such as marriage and name-giving; or for obtaining the return of prisoners of war. Status was important in these exchanges. The higher the rank of the recipients, the greater the value of the gifts.

Gifts also sealed agreements and alliances with other peoples.[22] Amerindians did not see treaties as self-sustaining. To be kept alive, they needed to be fed every once in a while by ceremonial exchanges. Later, during the colonial wars, periodic gift distributions would be essential in maintaining the alliances that proved so useful to the colonizing powers. This was the only pay the allies received for their services as guerrillas.

Trade goods could travel long distances. For instance, obsidian, valued for tools because of its keen cutting edge and also for ceremonial purposes because of its beauty, has been found on archaeological sites far from its place of origin.[23] The copper trade was also active. Jacques Cartier's (1491–1557) men became excited when they found copper knives among Amerindians near the Saguenay, mistaking them for gold. Thus was born the legend of the Golden Kingdom of the Saguenay, which would inspire northern exploration by Europeans.[24] Most often traded were cherts and flints (silicas) for arrowheads and other tools. Various kinds of shells, depending on the region, were also much in demand for personal adornment and because of their commercial, diplomatic, and ceremonial value and use.

There is no way of knowing the extent of the trade in perishable goods.[25] We know that Amerindians traded oolichon oil (derived from candlefish), which they used as a condiment, extensively from the Pacific coast into the interior along established routes that came to be known as 'grease trails'. In eastern Canada, trade dates back at least 6,000 years.

World Views Transcended Local Cultures and Customs

Local conditions and sources of food ensured that the peoples spread across Canada led different lives within distinctive cultural frameworks. Yet they all practised severe self-discipline to stand alone against an uncertain world, along with the acquisition of as much personal power as possible.[26]

Amerindians also valued humour highly. This characteristic was one of the first to be reported of New World peoples. In the fifth century, Hwui Shan told the Chinese court, 'The People of the land [presumed to be Aleuts] are of a merry nature, and they rejoice when they have an abundance, even of articles that are of little value.'[27] They also knew how to keep their spirits up in the face of starvation. As his Montagnais hosts told Le Jeune, 'keep thy soul from being sad, otherwise thou wilt be sick; see how we do not cease to laugh, although we have little to eat.'[28]

All Amerindians observed the law of hospitality, the violation of which was considered a crime.[29] They could carry hospitality even to the point of self-impoverishment, which did not strike Europeans as a virtue.[30] They also shared the concept of the unity of the universe, although that universe was filled with powers of various types and importance. This meant that all living beings, including humans, were related—indeed, were 'people'—and had minds.[31] So did some objects that the Western world considers to be inanimate. For instance, certain stones, under certain conditions, could be alive or inhabited, and have an awareness of their surroundings.[32] In other words, things were not always as they seemed at first sight, hence the importance of the trickster.[33]

Inter-tribal hostilities were widespread in the Americas, but organized warfare was more common in the sedentary societies.[34] Amerindians did not fight to gain land. Warfare along the Northwest Coast seems to have been more widespread before and during early contact with Europeans than it later became, particularly after depopulation as a result of epidemics. In the Far North, its main purpose seems to have been to kill the enemy, but to the south the goal was to acquire slaves and possessions, especially canoes. (Those of the west coast were dugouts, the manufacture of which was slow and laborious.)[35] The Iroquois, on the other hand, used prisoners for sacrifice or adoptions, which helped them to deal with deaths in their ranks caused by the cyclical warfare. Loot was less important.[36] In the Great Lakes, wars were fought when scarcities of game animals forced rival groups to trespass into their neighbour's hunting territory. Reparations were a means of controlling killings resulting from blood feuds. Among traders such as the Huron, this developed into an elaborate system.

Indian cemetery near Skuzzy Creek, five miles below North Bend, BC, northeast of Chilliwack. The people of the region are Salishan-speaking Lower Thompson (Nlaka'pamus). *(Library and Archives Canada, PA 120111l)*

Whatever the form of their particular societies, Amerindians led full and satisfying so-cial lives within the framework of complex cosmologies. As Le Clercq saw the Mi'kmaq, they lived like 'the first kings of the earth', as in Biblical times.[37] Canada was in the northern zone of a hemisphere-wide civilization that shared many underlying assumptions, even as it divided into regional manifestations. More likely, this reflects the cultures the Amerindians brought with them. In other words, in spite of regional differences, one can speak of an American civilization in the same sense that one can speak of a European civilization.

Amerindian and European Ethos: Differences That Would Lead to Misunderstanding

The difference between the American ethos and that of the Europeans was striking. Amerindian society was, for the most part, egalitarian. Its people viewed humans as part of a transcendent universal system. Europe, on the other hand, was a society of nation-states and developing capitalism. Its people were convinced that humans were not only the centre of the universe but its controlling force.[38]

Differences were particularly evident in attitudes towards land. For Amerindians, land existed for the benefit of all. For Europeans, it was private property, individually owned. On the other hand, Amerindian cultural knowledge was a carefully guarded, individual privilege that was selectively passed on through the generations, whereas for Europeans it was generally publicly available. At the time of first contact, however, differences were not as great as they would later become.

Some Europeans could and did adapt to Amerindian life, against the wishes of colonial officials. Even so, on first arrival, the Europeans did not see any resemblances to their own way of life.[39] As late as the end of the seventeenth century, Le Clercq could repeat in all earnestness the old saying that had been around since the days of Columbus, that Amerindians had neither faith, nor king, nor law.[40] How could they, since they were not dominated by chiefs or captains with the power to command?[41]

What was clear to Europeans from the start was that Amerindians did not have the social will to unite to prevent the invasion and takeover of their lands. The ten-dency towards fragmentation had been effective for survival before contact. Later, the Europeans would use it as an instrument for their domination.

Subarctic Meetings—Different Perspectives

In 1611, more than a century after encounters had become sustained for the Inuit of the North Atlantic coast, a lone Cree presented himself to **Henry Hudson** on the shores of James Bay. On being given some tokens of friendship, he left to return with the skins of two deer and two beaver, which he offered in trade. The English obliged, and when they showed an inclination to bargain, the Cree accepted the offer but indicated he did not like it. Picking up his goods, he departed, never to be seen by the English again.

This brief encounter suggests that the Cree had a clear idea of the exchange rate he expected as well as of trading protocol, perhaps that of the north/south Native networks, which at that time operated as far north as James Bay. Hudson's Bay Company (HBC) chief factor Andrew Graham (c. 1733–1815) reported that the first Amerindians to trade with Europeans in Hudson Bay were an eastern branch of the Cree called Oupeeshepow.[42] He added that 'they relate the arrival and wintering of the unfortunate Captain Henry Hudson, as handed down to them by the tradition of their ancestors.'[43] Hudson seems to have been more eager to meet with Amerindians than the latter were to meet the English following the encounter with the lone Cree. Hudson's motives were simple: he wanted fresh meat. In this, he was disappointed, for 'though the Inhabitants set the woods on fire before him, yet they would not come to him.'[44]

The Cree, for their part, have a startlingly different remembrance of their first trade with the English. In an episode that seems to have occurred somewhat later and to have involved a group rather than just an individual, they recall that the English wanted the fur clothing they were wearing and persuaded them to trade the clothes off their backs in exchange for European garments.[45] Explorers John Davis (?1550–1605) and **Jacques Cartier** reported similar incidents, although both men reversed the perspective. As they saw it, the Amerindians were so eager for trade, they willingly parted with the clothes they were wearing, and not necessarily for European clothing.

The Cree at the mouth of the Churchill River have an oral tradition of seeing strange signs and then meeting Europeans, who invited them aboard their ship. They were not afraid to accept, because from 'the expression on the strangers' faces, they could tell they were welcome aboard.'[46] Sporadic trade did not develop into a continuing relationship at this time, however. Violence all too often marked what contact there was, although contacts were usually peaceful at first.

The 'Fish'—by Any Definition—Brought Europeans to the North Atlantic Coast, and Contact Turned into Conflict

Apart from the Inuit, mainland native North Americans who have the longest history of contact with Europeans are the Amerindians of the North Atlantic coast. This started with Cabot's visit, at a time when Christopher Columbus was between his second and third voyages and Spanish colonization of the West Indies was just beginning.

It was a contact that can best be described as casual, at least at first, although exchanges—of foods, agricultural produce, technology, and disease—occurred from the very beginning of contact in what has been called 'the Columbian Exchange' (Box 2.2). The Europeans had come not to colonize but to exploit the enormously rich fishing grounds, the whale runs up the Strait of Belle Isle between present-day Newfoundland and Labrador, and the walrus rookeries of the Madeleine Islands in the Gulf of St Lawrence. Then as now, oil was big business, and with the adoption of Inuit hunting techniques, whales became the main source of supply, along with walrus. Fish was also in demand because the European religious calendar counted 153 meatless days a year.

Exploiting sea resources, especially the cod fisheries, did not involve the type of close or sustained contact with the local population that the fur trade would later require. Until the fur trade began in earnest and European settlement got underway, the comings and goings entailed in the fisheries (a term that included whaling and walrus hunting) allowed Amerindians and Europeans to pursue their separate lifestyles without much consideration for each other. By 1600, Inuit had expanded down the Labrador coast, occasioning sporadic hostilities throughout the French regime. By the 1690s, most French settlers in Labrador were on the south shore, numbering about 40 families. The English spread along Labrador's east coast into about 30 harbours and coves, some counting only one family each.[47]

By the second half of the eighteenth century, under the British, not only was settlement expanding even more, but also white trappers were competing with Inuit for fur and game resources. Hostilities increased, with each side raiding and killing as opportunities arose. The Inuit had the advantage of a huge hinterland, inhospitable to Europeans, to which they could retreat. The situation was such that Sir Hugh Palliser, governor of Newfoundland from 1764 to 1768, issued a proclamation in 1764 urging that the 'Eskimo Indians' be treated as friends.[48] Less fortunate in this regard were the Beothuk.

The Beothuk Experience—Resistance and Genocide

We know very little about the **Beothuk**, who hunted on land and sea in what is now called Newfoundland. Not even their language is certain, although it may have been a variant of proto-Algonkian. They seem to have had an association with the Inuit. From earliest encounters, Europeans described the Beothuk as 'inhuman and wild'.

At first, however, mutual tolerance—or, perhaps, a mutual distance—operated, and visiting Basques left fishing gear and boats in whaling ports over the winter without loss or damage. In contrast to the Arctic, where whaling had provided a limited basis for co-operation between Europeans and Inuit, no common interest developed between Europeans and Beothuk. Early attempts to establish trade aborted in misunderstanding and violence.

Hostile incidents later accumulated into a feud that embittered both sides. The fishermen needed shore space for their drying racks ('flakes'). Often, they erected them on sites favoured by the Amerindians for summer fishing. Mounting irritation between Beothuk and European is only too evident in the references that have come down to us. According to France's top navigator at the time, the Beothuk had 'no more God than beasts, and are bad people.' The poet Pierre Crignon (*c.* 1464–1540) was no more complimentary: 'Between Cape Race and Cape Breton live a cruel and rude people with whom we can neither deal nor converse.'[49]

The Beothuk retreated as far as they could into the interior of the island, occasionally emerging in their cyclical rounds to attempt their traditional fishing, if the European presence did not frustrate them. Alternatively, they raided any European gear they could find.[50] Early in the seventeenth century, an English admiral reported that operations were being hampered 'because the Savages of that country . . . secretly every year come into Trinity Bay and Harbor, in the nightime, purposely to steale

Box 2.2   The Columbian Exchange

The Columbian Exchange refers to transfers, whether of goods, disease, or technology and whether intentional or unintentional, between Europe and the land the Europeans called the New World. The effects of these exchanges on the civilizations involved were profound.

Diseases*

Diseases endemic to the Americas	Bacillary and amoebic dysentery; viral influenza and pneumonia; arthritis; rickettsial (micro-organismic) fevers; viral fevers; American leishmaniasis (protozoan); American trypanosomiasis (parasitic protozoans); roundworms and other endoparasites; syphilis and pinta (both treponemal infections); and a mild form of typhus. Other illness attributed to arthritis, tuberculosis (especially spinal varieties), treponemal infections, Paget's disease (osteitis deformans), periostitis, acute osteomyelitis, and myeloma (bone cancer); dietary deficiency in maize-rich economies; anemia and dental problems.
Diseases whose existence in the Americas before 1492 is debated	Malaria, yellow fever, pulmonary tuberculosis, venereal syphilis
Diseases that were certainly introduced by Europeans, Africans, and their livestock and animals	Smallpox, measles, influenza, bubonic plague, diphtheria, typhus, cholera, scarlet fever, trachoma, whooping cough, chicken pox, tropic malaria
Diseases that were probably introduced to Europeans by Americans	Syphilis

Plants

American plants eaten by Europeans	Maize, many kinds of beans, peanuts, potato, sweet potato, sassafras, manioc (tapioca, cassava), squash, pumpkin, papaya, guava, avocado, pineapple, tomato, chili pepper, paprika, cocoa. Note: soybeans are Old World beans; some New World beans include lima, pole, curry, kidney, French, navy (haricot), snap, string, and frijole.

(continued)

American non-food plants adopted by Europeans	Tobacco, rubber, some cottons, brazilin (dye from brazilwood tree), sisal (for rope)
Old World plants imported for consumption by Europeans	Wheat, chickpeas, melons, onions, radishes, salad greens, grapevines, sugar cane, orchard fruits (e.g., olives); bananas were brought from the Canaries in 1516
Old World plants imported for commercial reasons by Europeans	Sugar, cotton, rice, indigo (for blue dye), brazilin, cochineal (red dye extracted from the female Dactylopius coccus insect), achiote (yellow dye)
Old World plants imported by Europeans for livestock	Some forage plants and clover, although most would have travelled informally, in clods of mud, folds of textiles, etc.
Old World non-edible plants imported by Europeans	Kentucky bluegrass, dandelions, daisies

Animals

Old World domesticated animals	Horses, dogs, pigs, cattle, chickens, sheep, goats, cats, donkeys**
Old World accidental imports	Old World rat

Note: This is not a complete list. Other examples of Amerindian contribution to world culture are drugs such as quinine (used in malaria prevention and cure) and cocaine and precious metals. Europeans also adopted New World technology, such as the canoe and whaling implements, whereas Amerindians embraced such things as metal knives and implements and, later, guns. In the first half of the sixteenth century, for example, the amount of silver and gold in circulation in Europe tripled. The amount that came from South America was 10 times the combined output of the rest of the world.

*There were at least 17 major epidemics between 1520 and 1600. Death toll estimates range from 30 per cent to 75 per cent. The earliest European accounts of the New World all spoke of the 'great multitudes' of people. Later, when colonization was gaining momentum, large stretches of territory were found unoccupied, as the spread of disease had preceded the European advance, and the notion of an 'empty continent' gained currency.

**The New World had some dogs and chickens. Horses had originated in the New World but became extinct.

Sources: Noble David Cook, *Born to Die: Disease and New World Conquest, 1492–1650* (Cambridge, 1998); Alfred W. Crosby, *The Columbian Exchange: Biological and Cultural Consequences of 1492* (Westport, Conn., 1972); Bruce Trigger and Wilcomb E. Washburn, *The Cambridge History of the Native Peoples of the Americas*, vol. 1 (Cambridge, 1996); Jack Weatherford, *Indian Givers: How the Indians of the Americas Transformed the World* (New York, 1988).

Sailes, Lines, Hatchets, Hookes, Knives, and such like.'[51] Few early colonizers tried to establish a working relationship.

In the hard and unforgiving landscape of Newfoundland, the Beothuk reaction to contact is easy to understand. People feared that their carefully managed resource base was being threatened by the newcomers. The technological marvels possessed by these newcomers made the threat all the more worrisome. The increased presence along the south coast of Newfoundland by the Abenaki and Mi'kmaq, and along the northwest coast by some Mi'kmaq fishing parties, served to heighten the tension. These peoples had been long-time trading partners of the Beothuk and had been welcome participants in the seal hunt. Eventually, however, they were encouraged, first by the French and then by British colonizers, to turn against the Beothuk in exchange for European weapons. The Beothuk fought back hard and, sadly, the reputation they left to history has suffered for the brave defence of their home.[52]

Once settlement began, the feuding turned into an open hunting season against the Beothuk. The situation was aggravated by the fact that after the first half of the seventeenth century, anti-colonizing English West Country fishing interests were able to influence Parliament to legislate against settlement, which was restricted if not actually placed outside of the law. Official control was sporadic, a condition that benefited the fishing industry. Newfoundland was not declared a colony until 1824. By that time, there were practically no Beothuk left. One of the last of her people, Demasduwit (Shendoreth, Waunathoake, Mary March, 1796–1819), was captured following a Beothuk raid of a salmon boat but died of tuberculosis before she could be returned to her people. The last known Beothuk, Shawnadithit, who was Demasduwit's niece, died in 1829.[53]

Amerindian Trade, Rivalry, and a Great League of Peace

Great Lakes Region

At the time of first European contact, there were at least 34 First Nations in the Great Lakes region,[54] representing cultures ranging from hunter-gatherers to agriculturalists, with variations in between. The Iroquoians and some Algonkians, such as Odawa (Ottawa) of the St Lawrence River and Great Lakes—'land of the white pine'—had adopted agriculture, in addition to hunting, and were sedentary. The Iroquoians lived in longhouses clustered in palisaded villages that had up to 1,500 inhabitants or more.[55] They moved their villages to new sites every 10 to 50 years, when local resources, such as land and firewood, became exhausted. Apart from the Algonkian-speaking Odawa, they spoke related languages.[56]

For these people, the fourteenth into the fifteenth centuries was a period of population expansion. Some villages grew; others disappeared. The 'three sisters'—corn, beans, and squash, each introduced at different times—eventually dominated the regional agricultural scene.[57] All of these factors contributed to rapid social change.[58]

Sometime during the sixteenth century, or perhaps earlier, groups of Iroquoians organized into confederacies that would have powerful impacts in regional politics.[59] The northernmost was that of the Huron,[60] an alliance of four or five nations. To the south, on the Ontario peninsula, was that of the Neutrals, about whom little is known. In the Finger Lakes region of today's central New York state was the Five Nations Confederacy.

Huronia

The Huron Confederacy was concentrated between Lake Simcoe and the southeastern corner of Georgian Bay, an area of about 2,300 square kilometres. As far north as agriculture was possible with a Stone Age technology, the Huron had about 2,800 hectares (7,000 acres) under cultivation. In **Huronia**, 'it was easier to get lost in a cornfield than in a forest.'[61] The Huron traded with the northern tribes, supplying them with corn, beans, squash, and tobacco, as well as twine for fishnets, in return for meat, hides, and furs. The beauty and bounty of the land were such that when the French first came to their country, the Huron assumed it was because France was poor by comparison.[62]

By the end of the sixteenth century, Huronia counted an estimated 30,000 people—compared to 16,000 in the Five Nations[63]—who lived in up to 25 villages. The largest, Cahiagué, belonged to the Arendarhonon (Rock) nation[64] and may have had a population of 5,000. These villages were concentrated close to each other at the centre of Huronia. Cornfields formed a surrounding belt. Because of this, all Huron could understand each other, and their language was used in the northern trade networks.

Situated at a crossroads in the North American trading networks, Huronia dominated regional trade routes. It also dominated the political scene. It had surrounded the rival Five Nations with a system of alliances that extended as far as the Susquehannocks (Andastes, Conastogas), about 800 kilometres to the south. Huronia apparently absorbed at least some of the St Lawrence Iroquoians who were dispersed during the sixteenth century, an event in which the Mohawk of the Five Nations seem to have had a hand.[65] Despite this strength, however, Huronia would rapidly disintegrate before the realignment of forces brought about by the intrusion of European trade.

People of the Longhouse

The territory of the League of Hodenosaunee (People of the Longhouse), as the **Five Nations** also called themselves, was larger than the lands of the Huron, although their population was less. The league's territory stretched from the Mohawk River in the east to the Genesee River in the west, a distance of about 180 kilometres. It was a geographic position that would come into its own after the establishment of European colonies on the east coast, as it controlled the major routes from the coast to the interior.

The Iroquois villages were much more scattered than those of Huronia. Each was surrounded by its own cornfields, and so the languages of the Five Nations[66] were more distinct from each other than those of the Huron. Although the men cleared the fields, the women did the farming. Each member nation occupied its own villages, usually two or more. Each also had its own council, as did each tribe, whose council usually met in the group's largest village. Women had the right to choose sachems (leaders selected from within certain families or clans)[67] and order their removal. Iroquois social organization included division into phratries and clans, as on the Northwest Coast.

The Great League of Peace was another name for the Iroquois Confederacy. A council of 50 chiefs representing participant tribes governed it, although not equally. Despite that fact, each tribe had one vote. The aim was to keep peace between the tribes through ceremonial words of condolence and ritual gifts of exchange.[68] They also co-ordinated

As in other First Nations, Ojibwa women played a major part in the economic life of their community. In this nineteenth-century drawing by Seth Eastman, they are shown harvesting wild rice. Amerindian care of the stands of wild rice came close to farming. *(Photo courtesy The Newberry Library, Chicago)*

external relations, which had to be by unanimous decision.[69] Centralization was not complete, however. Member tribes maintained a considerable degree of autonomy, above all in internal affairs.

Dekanawidah, 'Heavenly Messenger', said to have suffered from a speech impediment, and his disciple, Hiawatha (Hionwatha), 'One Who Combs', founded the league.[70] Its symbol was the White Tree of Peace, above which hovered an eagle, a very wise bird 'who sees afar', indicating preparedness. According to tradition, Hiawatha dedicated himself to peace when he lost his family in an inter-tribal feud. The chairman of the Great Council bore the title Thadodaho (Atotarho), after the warlike chief whom Dekanawidah and Hiawatha converted to peaceful ways.[71]

Aside from the Northwest Coast, all the other nations whose land would make up Canada hunted and gathered food, although some were also at least partly agricultural and others had felt the influence of farming cultures. The Ojibwa (Anishinabe),[72] for example, relied on an uncultivated crop, wild rice (*Zizania aquatica*). Their care of wild rice stands bordered on farming, although their dependence on wild rice was much less than that of farmers on their crops—Iroquoians grew 80 per cent of their food requirements.[73]

The Nipissings and Algonquins, both allies of the Huron, did some planting, but they were too far north for this to be an important source of food. The Montagnais also seem to have practised some slash-and-burn agriculture.[74] The Gwich'in (Kutchin, Loucheux) and related Han and Tutchone of the Yukon, like other hunting peoples, 'encouraged' the growth of medicinal plants near their encampments.[75] The Mi'kmaq and Wuastukwiuk (Maliseet) of the Atlantic coast, on the other hand, had been an agricultural people but returned to hunting and gathering. According to their traditions, they descend from a people who migrated from the south and west, and archaeologists have confirmed this.

The Bison Hunt of the Northwestern Plains

On the northwestern Plains, 'where the sky takes care of the earth and the earth takes care of the sky',[76] the population averaged less than one person per 10 square miles (26 square kilometres) when the Europeans arrived. However, there were wide fluctuations, with considerable influxes from surrounding areas during seasonal hunts. The bison hunt provided the basis for cultural patterns.[77] From about 7000 BP to 4500 BP, however, higher temperature and drought decimated the herds of giant bison by cutting down on their food supply. Afterwards, the bison were of the smaller variety with which we are familiar.

Hunters used both drives and jumps, depending on the conformation of the land. At the time of European arrival on the east coast, the use of bison jumps and drives was, if anything, increasing. The greatest number of jump sites was in the foothills of the Rocky Mountains. Pounds were more common on the Plains. In Canada, most of the drive sites are in Saskatchewan or Alberta. One of the earliest jump sites, dated to more than 5,000 years ago, was **Head-Smashed-In** in southern Alberta. It would continue to be used until the 1870s. This was an enormous site, so big that its use was an inter-tribal affair. Recent archaeology has revealed 30 mazeways along which the buffalo were driven and up to 20,000 cairns that guided the direction of the stampeding herds. Head-Smashed-In might also have been a trading centre, providing bison materials such as pemmican and hides in return for dried maize, artifacts, and possibly tobacco.[78]

These forms of hunting called for co-operation and organization within bands but also between bands and tribes. Impounding, or corralling, was the more complex method, a form of food production rather than hunting.[79]

In general, campsites were located on lookouts. Some found in Alberta include several hundred tipi rings, indicating long use. There may be more than a million such rings scattered throughout Alberta.[80] Medicine wheels, important for hunting rites, ringed the bison's northern summer range. Some were in use for at least 5,000 years.[81]

Whatever the type of communal hunting, strict regulation was involved. When several tribal nations gathered for such a hunt, camp police enforced the rules. Penalties could include the destruction of the offender's dwelling and personal belongings.[82] In contrast, when herds were small and scattered, individuals could hunt as they pleased.

Fur, Felt, and Spread of Disease

In the sixteenth century, the felt hat, which had been around for at least 200 years, became an essential fashion item in Europe. This created a strong demand for beaver fur, from which felt was made, so much so that the European beaver was trapped to near extinction. Then, in 1534, Frenchman Jacques Cartier sailed into the mouth of the river that he would name after Saint Lawrence and met men and women wearing the furs so coveted back in Europe. Cartier and others were quick to see the advantage in dealing more directly with these New World people than the fishermen had. The Amerindians, too, quickly saw the benefit for them in this trade, and set themselves up as middlemen between the Europeans and the nations further inland. Furs and the goods they were traded for would pass from hand to hand, carrying microscopic stowaways into the continent ahead of the white traders, so that European diseases, most notably smallpox, decimated groups of Amerindians long before they had direct contact with the newcomers.

Important Names and Terms

Beothuk	gift exchanges
Cabot, John	Head-Smashed-In
Cartier, Jacques	Hudson, Henry
Dorset	Huronia
'first meetings'	Little Ice Age
Five Nations	Thule

Study Questions

1) What patterns emerged from the earliest contacts between Europeans and First Nations peoples?
2) What were some of the causes of conflict between First Nations groups?
3) What were the distinctive features of the Iroquoian communities?
4) What were the distinctive features of First Nations' agriculture?

Recommended Readings

Grant, John Webster. *Moon of Wintertime: Missionaries and the Indians of Canada in Encounter since 1534.* Toronto: University of Toronto Press, 1984.

Marshall, Ingeborg Constanze Luise. *A History and Ethnography of the Beothuk.* Montreal and Kingston: McGill-Queen's University Press, 1996.

Morrison, R. Bruce, and C. Roderick Wilson, eds. *Native Peoples: The Canadian Experience,* 3rd edn. Toronto: Oxford University Press, 2004.

Paul, Daniel N. *We Were Not the Savages: A Micmac Perspective on the Collision of European and Aboriginal Civilization.* Halifax: Nimbus, 1993.

Trigger, Bruce G. *The Children of Aataentsic: A History of the Huron People to 1660,* 2 vols. Montreal and Kingston: McGill-Queen's University Press, 1976.

3

On the Eastern Edge of the Mainland

While coasting along the Gaspé during his first voyage to Canada (1534), Cartier met St Lawrence Iroquoians presumed to have come from **Stadacona** (Stadakohna), a village on the present site of Quebec City. Cartier recorded:

> They go quite naked, except for a small skin, with which they cover their privy parts, and for a few old furs which they throw over their shoulders.... They have their heads shaved all around in circles, except for a tuft on the top of the head, which they have long like a horse's tail. This they do up upon their heads and tie in a knot with leather thongs.

Although Cartier claimed that these men showed great pleasure at meeting the French, 'they had made all the young women retire into the woods, except two or three who remained, to whom we gave each a comb and a little tin bell, at which they showed great pleasure, thanking the captain by rubbing his arms and his breast with their hands.'[1] At this display of friendship, the Iroquoian leader called the other women from hiding so that they, too, could receive gifts.

This friendliness would not last, however, particularly after Cartier persuaded Chief **Donnacona** (Donnakoh-Noh, d. 1539) to let his two sons, Taignoagny (Tayagnoagny) and Domagaya, go with him to France on his return voyage. Cartier's purpose was to train them as interpreters for the fur trade, in which he was successful. However, he apparently also expected them to act in the French interest when he brought them back to Stadacona on his second voyage (1535–6), but the pair would prove to be true to their own. In Cartier's eyes, they were not only unappreciative of French hospitality; they were traitors.

Cartier was a better sailor than diplomat. The explorer had no doubt that he had 'discovered' Canada,[2] as the north shore of the Gulf of St Lawrence was called. On his first visit, he had erected crosses of possession on the Gaspé and at Stadacona.[3] Ironically, an account published later in France would describe Stadacona as a seat of royal residence.[4]

Time Line

1534	The Iroquoian village Stadacona, at present site of Quebec City, witnesses Jacques Cartier's first voyage to Canada. Two sons of Chief Donnacona accompany Cartier on his return trip to France.
1535–6	Donnacona's two sons return to Stadacona with Cartier. Cartier then kidnaps the pair plus Donnacona and other headmen and takes them back to Europe. They all die in France.
1541	Cartier's last voyage, with settlers to establish a colony. This attempted settlement lasts only two years. Hochelaga, at site of present-day Montreal, is largest Iroquoian settlement.
1603	Montagnais (Innu) meet Samuel de Champlain at Tadoussac, at the mouth of Saguenay River. Champlain joins in celebration of Montagnais victory over Iroquois. Montagnais Chief Anadabijou seals friendship pact with Champlain and French.
1608	Champlain founds Quebec on Stadacona site; all the St Lawrence Iroquoians have gone, driven away and killed in long war with Mohawks and likely, too, in battles with Mi'kmaq.
1610	Mi'kmaq Chief Membertou greets the French, who re-establish Port Royal (Annapolis Royal) in present-day Nova Scotia.
1627	Charter of La Compagnie des Cent Associés.
1629	Abenaki envoy sent to Quebec to seek closer ties with French

in trade and in their battles with Iroquois.

1629–32	The Montagnais, who were in a dispute with the French, help the English gain control of Quebec.
1635	Death of Champlain ends, for a time, the alliance between Eastern Abenaki and French.
1642	French establishment of Montreal; importance of Tadoussac as trading centre begins to wane, as does Montagnais hegemony in region.
1670s	Marriage of Pidianske, daughter of a Penobscot sagamore, to a French officer ends traditional hostility between Eastern Abenaki and Mi'kmaq: both groups now allied with French.
1671	Mi'kmaq raid fishing vessel, kill 16.
1675–6	King Philip's War in New England results in exodus of Western Abenaki to Canada.
early 1700s	Odanak (near Sorel, Que.) largest Abenaki settlement in New France.
1710	Defeat of Acadians by British.
1713	Treaty of Utrecht cedes Acadia to British, who assume France must have extinguished Aboriginal title. Mi'kmaq and Wuastukwiuk (Maliseet) caught in middle of European legal concepts but believe land is theirs—they were friends of French, not subjects.
1716	Nescambiouit, Pigwacket (Abenaki) chief, returns from being feted in France, goes to Fox to seek pan-Indian alliance.

(continued)

1720	French undercut peace negotiations between Abenaki and Iroquois.	1740	Presentation begun by French of ceremonial medals to Amerindians.
1722–4	English–Indian War, after Abenaki declare sovereignty over their ancestral lands.	1759	Robert Rogers and his Rangers attack and destroy Odanak, but it is soon re-established.
1725	Treaty of Boston signals end to English–Indian War.		

During his second voyage, Cartier sailed up the river against the wishes of the Stadaconans, who controlled upriver traffic. The Stadaconans responded by barring the Europeans from the river.[5] Cartier then kidnapped Donnacona, his two sons, and other headmen, and took them back with him to France. None of them returned to their homeland.

Cartier's third and last voyage to Canada was in 1541, when he brought settlers for a colony that Lieutenant-General Jean-François de La Rocque de Roberval (c. 1500–60) was going to establish. Roberval, however, did not arrive until the following year. By then, the Stadaconans were hostile, harassing Cartier and killing his men.[6] Cartier gave up after 10 months and returned home. Roberval did not fare any better. He was overly severe with his colonists and mistreated the Amerindians. He returned to France within the year after running out of food.[7] France's first attempt at colonizing in the New World had lasted less than two years: 1541–3.

The St Lawrence Iroquoians Cartier left behind were a farming people who, according to their location on the river, depended in varying degrees on hunting and fishing as well as on agriculture for their food supply. They all lived well, storing quantities of food, such as smoked eel, corn, beans, large cucumbers, and other fruit, for lean seasons.[8] The Stadaconans, geographically less favoured for agriculture, relied more on hunting, while the Hochelagans, on the site of today's Montreal, were more agricultural.[9]

Hochelaga was the largest of 14 villages on the north shore of the river, with about 50 longhouses and a population of 1,500. As with Stadacona, it would later be described in grandiose terms.[10] But by the early seventeenth century, not one of these villages remained, and the language spoken at Quebec during the time of Cartier was 'no longer heard in that region',[11] victims of a long war in which the Mohawk were said to have been the aggressors (see Box 3.1).[12]

Apparently, even though Europeans had been barred from the river, some of their trade goods had filtered into the interior through Amerindian networks. Soon, demand was growing faster than supplies.[13] Difficulty in obtaining items like iron axes might have been galling to the Five Nations, especially the Mohawk, who during the sixteenth century did not have direct access to European trade but who were keenly aware of neighbours who did. Resorting to warfare to obtain what they could not get

Box 3.1   The Disappearance of the Stadaconans

The period just before the arrival of the Europeans seems to have seen warfare escalate to major proportions.[14] Cartier reported that 200 Stadaconans were killed in an encounter with the Mi'kmaq two years before his second voyage.[15] The Stadaconans fished in the Gaspé during the summer, and there may have been rivalry over access to ocean resources. Trade, traditional hostilities, or European-introduced epidemics might also have been factors. Furthermore, climatic changes caused by the Little Ice Age would have been disastrous for agriculture so far north. This could have made things worse for the Stadaconans, to the point where they were no longer able to resist the attacks of the Mohawk.

However, accumulating evidence points more clearly all the time to the dynamism of Iroquoians in late pre-contact times. Profound large-scale social and cultural changes had been underway long before the arrival of the Europeans. What happened afterwards may well have been, for the most part, a continuation of these processes and developments, with European-related factors playing only a small role.[16] The St Lawrence Iroquoians probably withdrew westward, to join the Wendat (Huron Confederacy).[17]

by peaceful means, they attacked the villages controlling the St Lawrence River, particularly Stadacona. By the time **Samuel de Champlain** (*c.* 1570–1635) arrived on the scene in the early 1600s, the river was deserted except for roving Mohawk war parties, which had spread such terror that other Amerindian nations hardly dared to hunt in the area.[18]

The Innu Become Fur Trade Middlemen

In contrast to the Beothuk and Stadaconans, Algonkian-speaking Innu (the collective name for the Montagnais-Naskapi) and Mi'kmaq accommodated themselves comparatively peacefully to Europeans. It may have been the Montagnais who smoke-signalled Cartier at the mouth of the Strait of Belle Isle north of the Gulf of St Lawrence during his first voyage (1534).[19]

According to their traditions, particularly those of the Montagnais, the Iroquois had pushed the Innu into the Subarctic before the arrival of Europeans. Later, the prospect of European trade lured these hunters of the northern interior to the coast. The Naskapi of Labrador exploited maritime resources as well as caribou. The Montagnais, living in the heavily forested interior but roaming as far as Newfoundland, depended mainly on moose in winter and freshwater fish in summer.[20] When a Montagnais band agreed to let Paul Le Jeune, superior of the Jesuits of Quebec, 1632–9, winter with them in 1633–4, they warned him that 'we shall be sometimes two days, sometimes three, without eating, for lack of food; take courage, chihiné, let thy soul be strong to endure suffering and hardship.'[21]

Portage on the Moisie River, Labrador, as painted by William George Richardson Hind. *(Metropolitan Toronto Reference Library, J. Ross Robertson Collection, T–31960)*

When Champlain first met the Montagnais at Tadoussac in 1603, they were celebrating a victory over the Iroquois with their allies, the Algonquin and Maliseet. These raids and counter-raids continued until the mid-seventeenth century. In the meantime, Champlain joined in the victory celebrations at the invitation of Montagnais chief Anadabijou (*fl.* 1611) and sealed a pact of friendship with him and his people, which allowed the French to establish on Montagnais territory but which did not involve land title.[22] Anadabijou's son and heir, Miristou, later known as Mahigan Aticq Ouche ('Wolf' and 'Stag', indicating both cruelty and gentleness, d. 1628), would develop this relationship. The reason for his interest lay back in Europe: Canadian furs were in even greater demand following the Swedish capture in 1583 of Narva, the Baltic port through which Western Europe obtained furs from the Russians.

The Innu Control of the Early Fur Trade

The French were quick to take advantage of the new source for furs through alliances with the Amerindians who controlled the source of supply. They adopted Amerindian diplomatic protocol and negotiated these accords by means of gift distributions accompanied by feasting and speeches. The Montagnais, for their part, had a particular interest in cultivating the relationship, as **Tadoussac**, at the mouth of the Saguenay River on the Gulf of St Lawrence, was within their territory. Its location on the southern edge of the taiga and beyond the northern edge of agriculture, and its ease of access, had made it a favourite trading place for northern hunters and southern agriculturalists.

The Montagnais controlled the trade up the Saguenay. Therefore, they found themselves in a lucrative position as more and more European ships came to trade. Tadoussac became an outlet for interior trading networks that extended as far north as James Bay and as far west as the Great Lakes.[23] It was a position the Montagnais were to enjoy for more than half a century, until they were bypassed by the establishment of Quebec in 1608, nearly three decades after the St Lawrence had been reopened.

In its heyday, Tadoussac had 50 ships at a time in its harbour during the summer trading season. By the second decade of the seventeenth century, as many as a thousand ships a year were trading and fishing along the North Atlantic coasts and in the Gulf of St Lawrence.[24] For the northern Amerindians, it was a bonanza, as Frenchmen vied with Frenchmen and they all tried to outdo the Dutch.[25] Despite the importance of Tadoussac in the growing trade, however, the French did not establish a permanent post there until 1599.

The Europeans were not alone in benefiting from this trade. This did not mean, however, that the Amerindians instantly abandoned traditional ways of doing things or that their life was totally transformed within a generation or so. Change does not automatically alter identity. Just as Europeans benefited from Amerindian technology (toggling harpoons for whaling, moccasins for footwear, maize and potatoes as food crops), so did Amerindians from that of Europeans. In both cases, adaptations were selective and within established cultural patterns.

One item that had been popular since the early days of trading was the copper kettle. The gun, on the other hand, was not widely used by Amerindians for hunting in the Northeast until the end of the seventeenth century, although they had adopted it for warfare long before that because of the terror it induced and the imagined superiority of those who had guns. As tools of hunting, however, guns of this period were unreliable, scarce, and dependent equally on shot and powder.

That the Montagnais prospered from this early access to a wide variety of trade goods is indicated by the quantity of presents received from chiefs of different nations at the installation in 1643 of Georges Etouat (d. 1648, a Christian convert, as his given name indicates) as 'Captain' at Tadoussac. Trade had brought such prestige to the post that its holder considered himself the equal of the French governor-general at Quebec City and 'acted the Sovereign', as the Jesuits remarked sourly. The importance of the French in trade was indicated by their influence on the installation ceremonies: Etouat wore a white linen shirt, lace neckband, and scarlet cloak.[26] The name 'Etouat' was that of the position, as well as of the person holding it.

Friction between Trading Partners

There were also problems connected with the fur trade, for Amerindians as well as for traders. Sometimes this erupted into violence, and both Amerindians and Frenchmen were killed.[27] Such incidents put strains on the alliance, and Champlain's insistence on European-style punishment rather than Amerindian-style reparations when Frenchmen were the victims did nothing to ease the tensions. When the French leader arrested an Algonquin on suspicion of murder, a displeased Chief Tessouat threatened reprisals.[28] The Montagnais were so annoyed when the French established a trading monopoly and then raised prices[29] that Champlain refused to hold public baptisms for some Montagnais for fear that they would take advantage of the occasion to attack the French.[30] The Montagnais retaliated by guiding the English up the river and joining in their attack on Quebec, which resulted in its occupation by the English for three years, 1629–32.

In other cases, cultural misunderstandings led to unintended insults. One chief, who was offended with the inappropriate gift he had received from a French captain during pre-trade ceremonies at Tadoussac, told his people to come aboard the ship and help themselves to what they wanted, paying what they wished. Later, the Amerindians had second thoughts and brought extra furs to make up the value of what had been taken. Both sides agreed to forget and forgive, and 'to continue always in their old friendship'. After that, the traders were careful to ensure that they observed trading rituals properly, not the least element of which was appropriate gifts. They were not so compliant, however, when the Montagnais tried to collect tolls for rights of passage on the St Lawrence, and they quickly moved to curb such 'insolence'.[31]

Another problem area was the exchange rate. The flexibility of the French in this regard did not go down well. Once a rate had been agreed, the Amerindians expected it to be maintained. One chief, being offered a special deal for himself but excluding his people, indignantly turned it down with the words, 'I am a chief; I do not speak for myself; I speak for my people.'[32] Neither did they accept the concept of fluctuating prices according to supply and demand.

Perhaps the most serious problem of all, at least from a long-range point of view, was the overexploitation of resources that the trade encouraged. There were those, such as Jesuit historian Pierre-François de Charlevoix (1682–1761), who were appalled at the destruction. A 'handful' of French had arrived, he said, in a land abounding with wild-life. Less than a century later, it was already noticeably less so.[33] Later, David Thompson would observe that in the West 'Every intelligent Man saw the poverty that would follow the destruction of the Beaver, but there were no Chiefs to control it; all was perfect liberty and equality.'[34] Some Amerindians were reported to have joined in the slaughter, killing even the breeding stock. Such examples, however, are more a reflection on the disruptive forces associated with European contact than they are evidence of some new movement away from the time-honoured practice of careful resource management.[35]

The Trade Shifts Westward

With the establishment of Quebec, it was not long before the Montagnais found themselves replaced by the Huron as main trading partners of the French (see Chapter 4). Tadoussac, once the hub of the Canadian fur trade, lost importance as the French penetrated further and further up the St Lawrence, finally establishing Montreal in 1642.

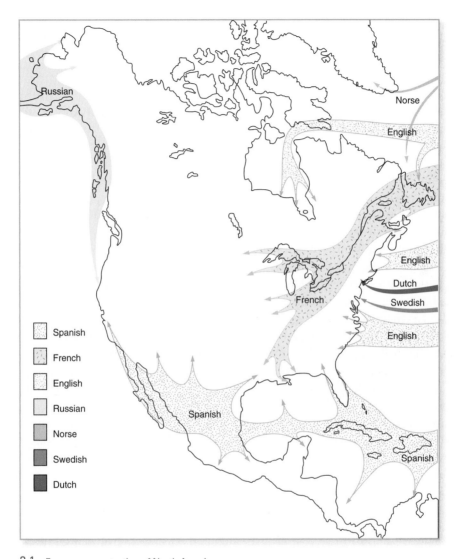

3.1   European penetration of North America

Sources: Waldman, *Atlas of the North American Indian*; Geoffrey Barroclough, ed., *The Times Atlas of World History* (Toronto: Fitzhenry & Whiteside, 1978), 161.

Despite their initially favourable trading position and the protection their Subarctic habitat afforded them, the Innu shared in the population decline that was the general Amerindian experience after the arrival of Europeans. Outside the mainstream of colonial activity, the Innu pursued their traditional way of life with little modification or interference. They shared with the Inuit the advantage of a hinterland that was both very large and very forbidding to Europeans. It would be centuries before Western technology would be capable of exploiting economically the mineral and hydroelectric potentialities of this huge area. In the meantime, the Innu controlled, at least to a certain extent, the terms of their contact.

Who 'Owns' the Land? and What Does Ownership Involve?

The coastal Mi'kmaq, like the Innu, quickly found advantage in the European presence.[36] This relationship began with the fisheries, which had first attracted European attention to the region. With their close relatives, the Maliseet, the Mi'kmaq willingly entered into the service of Europeans for a few goods or a little pay, doing 'all kinds of work, such as cleaning and butchering whales'.[37] They also hunted for marine mammals such as walrus, seals, and small whales. Before the arrival of Europeans, they had depended primarily on marine resources, including cod and bass, as well as the deep-sea swordfish, and only secondarily on those of the forests.[38]

This pattern soon reversed itself, however, as the Mi'kmaq adapted to the fur trade. Their distinctive sea-going canoes, with gunwales swelling upward at the centre, were well adapted to coastal travel as well as for crossing the Gulf of St Lawrence and going to Newfoundland. By the beginning of the seventeenth century, Mi'kmaq were sailing European shallops (keel boats pointed at both ends).[39] They also continued their pre-contact role as middlemen between the hunters of the north and the agriculturalists of the south. One of the names by which the Mi'kmaq were known, 'Taranteens', was said to mean 'traders',[40] and they treated their trading partners with courtesy.

An Amerindian custom that surprised early Europeans was that of respecting food caches and supply depots of others, even though unguarded. A group of 79 Frenchmen moved temporarily, in 1605–7, from Ile Ste Croix to Port Royal (later known as Annapolis Royal). When they returned in 1610, they found that the Amerindians had touched nothing and the paramount Mi'kmaq chief, Membertou (d. 1611), was there to greet them.[41] Trade flourished. For Europeans, the profits were great, as the Amerindians, while they did not want to be deceived, responded 'liberally to the presents that they [the French traders] make, without exacting any, since it is certain that they are well content if they get only half the value of what is received from them.'[42] Still, in trading, the Mi'kmaq were in their element, although they soon developed protective mechanisms in dealing with Europeans.[43] Some sagamores (chiefs) took a tone that the French considered haughty, making it clear, in the words of Charlevoix, 'they were honoring the Great Sagamo of the French by treating him as an equal.'[44]

Relations were not always peaceful, however. In 1671, an Amerindian raid on a fishing vessel, killing 16 men, caused so much alarm that the fishermen thereafter kept watch instead of fishing.[45] The Mi'kmaq were superb seamen. During the eighteenth century, in their war against Britain, they were taking and sailing schooners as large as 70 tons.[46] By the nineteenth century, they were operating as commercial fishermen with their own vessels.[47]

The Wuastukwiuk, also known as the Saint John River Indians, shared a similar lifestyle with the Mi'kmaq. According to Spiritan Pierre-Antoine-Simon Maillard (*c.* 1710–62), the 'Mickmakis and Mariquets, who, though different in language, have the same customs and manners . . . are of the same way of thinking and acting.' Both groups interacted successfully with Europeans in both fisheries and fur trade.

This close relationship, however, did not prevent the Wuastukwiuk and Mi'kmaq from being on hostile terms with each other as well as with branches of the Abenaki when the Europeans arrived. Their differences seem to have been smoothed over later, as they both became allies of the French, fought together during the colonial wars, and in general shared the same fate afterwards. This participation as guerrillas in the colonial wars ensured their survival in their ancestral lands. Nevertheless, they maintained a separate identity and sometimes acted separately.

English slave raids along the Atlantic coast had early aroused the hostility of the Mi'kmaq and pushed them into their alliance with the French. At the beginning, they fought for the traditional reasons of prestige and booty, as well as to help their allies, only to see their allies defeated. France's loss of Acadia in 1710 and the advent of British settlement soon put another cast on the conflict, which by that time was already a century old. At issue was a question that would permeate Amerindian–European relations: who owned the land, and what did ownership involve?

France believed that New France and Acadia were hers by right of 'discovery'.[48] As far as the French were concerned, the Amerindians did not own the land. The French merely allowed them to continue using it. The French had been making grants of land to her subjects in Acadia at least since the beginning of the seventeenth century. Earlier, trading licences had also included land rights. The charter for **La Compagnie des Cent Associés** (1627) provided for an Amerindian who became Christian to be considered in all respects French, including proprietary and inheritance rights. Any property he acquired, however, came by right of the French Crown, not by Aboriginal right.[49] Landownership had not become an issue earlier, however, in part because the French population was small. The French were also dependent on their allies, for reasons of the fur trade and war, and so took care to respect Amerindian villages and encampments.[50] Acadian colonists used areas of little interest to the Amerindians.

That this did not extend to international recognition of Amerindian sovereignty was only too clear in the **Treaty of Utrecht**, when the French ceded Acadia to the English without mentioning their Aboriginal allies. Britain, too, considered that she had gained from France clear sovereign title to the land. In fact, Britain believed the Mi'kmaq and their Aboriginal neighbours had never possessed sovereignty anyway, being mobile or semi-sedentary peoples who had not organized into states. The British did not at first consider that the principle of compensation applied in Acadia. They believed that their defeat of France meant that they did not have to compensate the local Amerindians for lands. According to British legal thinking of the day, defeated non-Christians had no rights, and settlement was a form of conquest, as English settlers brought their laws with them.[51]

The original inhabitants of the land, however, did not share France's belief it held a transferable title to the land. Far from being subjects of the French, the Mi'kmaq and Wuastukwiuk had welcomed them as friends and allies. They accepted the French king as their father, because he sent missionaries to teach them their new religion, but the idea that he had any claim on their lands, or that they owed him any more allegiance than they owed to their own chiefs, did not make sense to them. Periodically, they reminded the French that they had granted only use of their lands, which still belonged to the Mi'kmaq.[52] The Mi'kmaq also did not consider that their alliance with the French automatically implied their later subjugation to the British. As the Mi'kmaq saw it, the only right involving land that the British had gained through their conquest was the right to purchase from the Amerindians.[53]

Benefit and Cost of the English–French Rivalry

The English were well aware of the wisdom of maintaining good relations. It was not the Amerindians' importance as allies that mattered, so much as the difficulties they could cause if they were not.[54] Proclaiming George I as King of Acadia in 1762, the British asked the Amerindians for an oath of loyalty and to share their lands peacefully with the settlers they hoped would soon be coming. In return, they promised more generous annual gifts than the French had been giving, but they relied mainly on offering better trade values at 'truck houses' (trading posts run under government auspices). They also promised not to interfere with the Amerindians' religion—by that time, many of them, particularly among the Mi'kmaq, were Catholic.

The Amerindians replied that they were pleased to have religious liberty but did not see why they had to have truck houses on their lands. They thought that trade could continue as it had in the past, mostly from shipboard. As for the oath of allegiance, they had never taken one to the French King and did not see why they should do so for the British. As far as the Mi'kmaq were concerned, Acadia was their land, which they called Megumaage and which they had divided into seven districts under a system of chiefs and a paramount chief. They wanted only to continue living in their territories without fear of English encroachment.

The French held a trump card in this contest to win Amerindian loyalties: approximately a hundred missionaries who had worked in Acadia during the French regime. Canadian-born Antoine Gaulin (1674–1740) served from 1698 until 1731, retiring because of ill health. Maillard was in Acadia from 1735 until his death in 1762. The missions of Spiritan Jean-Louis Le Loutre (1709–72), from 1737 until 1755, included Acadians as well as Mi'kmaqs. The effectiveness of these missionaries stemmed at least in part from traditional Amerindian respect for shamans. France's identification of the importance of religion in Amerindian leadership and their ability to turn religious sentiments in their favour were major factors in the success of the French with their Amerindian alliances.[55] Maillard wrote that only through religion could Amerindians be rendered docile.[56]

One aspect of Christianity that resonated with some Amerindians was its rituals. Ritual was traditionally very important in Amerindian lives. In modifying the focus of ritual, the missionaries did not entirely change Amerindian taste in these matters.[57] In this, as well as in using their positions for political ends, French missionaries were so effective that in 1749 the exasperated English put a price on the head of Le Loutre.[58] In their turn, the British would adopt the French practice of using missionaries as agents of the state, particularly during the negotiations for the numbered treaties during the last part of the nineteenth century and the first part of the twentieth. Missionaries would also act as mediators in other areas, as well, until about mid-twentieth century. Meanwhile, the Mi'kmaq were far from passive in this struggle for their control.

The Mi'kmaq soon learned to play the English off against the French and, eventually, to force the French to reorganize and increase their 'gift' distributions (tools and equipment, guns, weapons, and ammunition, food, clothing). In 1751, the Mi'kmaq successfully demanded that special gift distributions to meet their needs be incorporated into the regular ones.[59] The distributions, essentially Amerindian in their ritual character, came to be combined with the European custom of awarding titles and medals. Amerindians had as much of a penchant for honours and prestige as Europeans. It would be difficult to overrate the importance both Amerindians and French attached to these ceremonies. Even the English, who had initiated the awarding of medals but who still looked on the annual gift distributions as a form of bribery, were drawn reluctantly into this form of diplomacy.[60]

Thus, although their traditional subsistence base was very quickly overexploited through the activities of the fisheries and the fur trade, the Mi'kmaq and Wuastukwiuk were able to substitute the goods and food they received from their allies to maintain their traditional lifestyle as long as the colonial wars, and consequently their own war, lasted. They were, however, severely reduced in numbers. The Mi'kmaq, who might have numbered as many as 35,000 at the time of contact, dropped to 3,000, and the Wuastukwiuk to 800. Membertou, the Mi'kmaq chief reported to have memories of Cartier, in 1610 said that in former times his people had been 'as thickly planted as the hairs upon his head', but that after the arrival of the French they had developed bad habits in respect to food and drink, which had greatly diminished their numbers.[61] 'Bad habits' do not tell the whole story, however.

Jesuit priest Pierre Biard wrote that more than half the population of Cap de la Hève died of disease in 1612, noting ominously, 'One by one the different coasts according as they have begun to traffic with us, have been more reduced by disease.' In 1617, an especially severe epidemic wreaked havoc among coastal peoples. By 1705, some French believed that it was hardly worthwhile learning about Amerindian nations, who, although once numerous, were now reduced to 'almost nothing'. It was reported that in 1,500 leagues of New France, there was only one Amerindian for every two Frenchmen.[62]

The Innu (particularly the Montagnais), Mi'kmaq, and Wuastukwiuk were the first to come into lasting relationships with the French. But the Abenaki would become the most important of the French military allies and would contribute the phrase 'French and Indians' to the colonial wars.

People of the Sunrise

The southernmost of the Atlantic coast peoples we are considering here are the Abenaki (Wabanaki), 'those living at the sunrise' (or 'dawnland people', among other variations).[63] The Abenaki are closely related to the Mi'kmaq and Wuastukwiuk as well as to other Algonkian speakers to the south.[64] Their homeland is south of the present Canada–US border, but the dislocations caused by colonial wars and European settlement meant that many Abenaki eventually found their home in Canada. Also, their alliance with the French was largely responsible for the connotations that the phrase 'French and Indians' came to assume in colonial history, especially in the United States (Box 3.2).

The first of these people known to have come into contact with Europeans, in this case the French, were the Eastern Abenaki. An account published in 1613 described between 10,000 and 14,000 souls living in 21 semi-permanent villages along 11 rivers in the region now known as Maine and New Hampshire. Bashabes (Betsabes, Bessabes, among other variations; d. 1616?) was the top man of 23 sagamores. Because of the nature of the soil and climate, and the availability of sea resources, the Eastern Abenaki farmed less intensively than Iroquoians did.

European diseases soon took their toll here as elsewhere, wiping out or drastically reducing villages from a very early date. In 1616, Father Biard reported that there were no more than 3,000 souls in the region.[65] The influx of new trade goods also caused important social and political reverberations. The availability of iron tools and weapons—metal points for spears and arrows but above all swords, cutlasses, and even muskets—inflamed long-standing rivalries.[66] The first decades of the seventeenth century saw the Abenaki, Mi'kmaq, and Wuastukwiuk all fighting each other. Cutlasses and swords were devastatingly effective, with muskets providing the *coup de grâce*.

The Abenaki did not develop an association with the French in the fisheries and fur trade as quickly as the Mi'kmaq and Wuastukwiuk did. In fact, the French at first shared the Mi'kmaq dislike of the Abenaki, calling them 'Armouchiquois', a term applied to

---

Box 3.2   The Abenaki as Guides and Warriors

The Abenaki played important roles in voyages of exploration, such as those of René Robert Cavelier de La Salle (1643–87) on the Mississippi in the 1670s and 1680s, and in military expeditions such as those of Governor-General Joseph-Antoine Le Febvre de La Barre (1622–88) in 1684 and Jacques-René de Brisay de Denonville (1637–1710) in 1687, both in the region of the Great Lakes.[67] In fact, it seems that the Abenaki were almost as active in the colonial wars of the old North West as they were in the Northeast.

Champlain's Engraved Map of 1612: two couples, one identified as Almouchiquois (Abenaki), on the right, the other as Montagnais. The French called the latter by this name because the people told the French that they were descended from a people who had migrated from a mountainous region. *(Library and Archives Canada, C–118494)*

several of the peoples in the general region. They described the Armouchiquois as being deformed, with small heads and short bodies, whose knees, when they squatted on their heels, passed their heads by more than a foot.[68] Champlain, who actually visited them, reported that, on the contrary, they had well-proportioned bodies and even found them to be of 'good disposition', but warned that they were inveterate thieves who could not be trusted. The French suspected them of cannibalism but this was far from true.[69]

Despite such attitudes, the French seemed promising to the Abenaki as trading partners and as allies, both in their traditional war against the Iroquois[70] and against the slave-raiding English. In 1613, when the English raided the French settlement of St Sauveur on the Penobscot River, the Abenaki offered to help the beleaguered survivors.[71] They followed this up in 1629 by sending an envoy to Quebec to sound out the possibilities of developing these ties. Champlain was immediately interested, because the Abenaki south of the Saco River were farmers and could possibly help provision his fledgling colony. Unable to help in the war against the Iroquois immediately, he promised to do so as soon as possible. In the meantime, he proposed a mutual assistance program involving food supplies and trade goods.[72]

The alliance proposal did not survive Champlain's death in 1635. The Abenaki quickly took advantage of their access to European goods to develop their own trading networks. The French were annoyed enough to restrict Abenaki visits to Quebec and, finally, in 1649, to warn them to stay away.[73] From this inauspicious beginning developed what became one of the most effective and long-lasting alliances in North American colonial history.

The Abenaki Fight for Their Land

In 1642, Algonquin allies of the French had brought a Sokoki (Western Abenaki) prisoner to Trois-Rivières under the impression he was an Iroquois.[74] The French moved much faster to consolidate this new relationship than they had previously done with the Eastern Abenaki. In 1651, a Jesuit missionary brought together various groups, including the Mahican (not usually included with the Abenaki, but related), to form a solid front against their traditional enemies, the Iroquois, who were being particularly annoying to the French. The Iroquois responded by intensifying their attacks.

The English taking of Acadia in 1654 and the growing intensity of the French–Iroquois War severely restricted communication between French and Abenaki. However, English settlement pressures from the south were increasing, pushing the Abenaki into the French orbit, and France's re-establishment in Acadia in 1670 led to the development of the French–Abenaki alliance. French officer Jean-Vincent d'Abbadie de Saint-Castin (1652–1707) consolidated this alliance in the 1670s when he married Pidianske (or Pidiwamiska), the daughter of Madockawando (d. 1698), **sagamore** of the Penobscots, 'people of the white rocks country', reputedly the most powerful of the Abenaki tribes.

Now the Eastern Abenaki and the Mi'kmaq were both allies of the French. The new situation did not produce unanimity within Abenaki communities, however. Splits developed between pro-French and pro-English factions, leading to a new set of internal tensions. These tensions would increase with the quickening tempo of frontier warfare.

The exodus of the Western Abenaki to Canada began as a trickle about this time.[75] It swelled into a major movement as a result of **King Philip's War**, 1675–6, the last major Aboriginal push to expel the Europeans from New England. 'King Philip' was the name the British used for Wampanoag chief Metacom (Metacomet). 'That cataclysm in New England history'[76] destroyed the Amerindian presence in southern New England (the war was fought mainly in Massachusetts and Connecticut) and helped to ignite the simultaneous Maine War between the English and the Abenaki. Clearly, the People of the Sunrise were caught in the middle of the ongoing French–English battles (see Box 3.3).

The Abenaki tried to prevent war but eventually had to take sides. They did not fight solely, or even mainly, as allies of the French but for their own lands. The English pushed them back sporadically until the final defeat of New France in 1760. The flow of refugees was particularly heavy in 1722–4 (English–Indian War) and 1744–8 (King George's War).

The Abenaki Refuse To Be Pawns in a European Game

Early in the eighteenth century, **Odanak** on the St François River near Sorel, Quebec, became the largest Abenaki settlement in New France. By the 1740s and 1750s, it was the main source for Abenaki warriors fighting in border raids. This situation resulted in one of the most famous episodes in the annals of colonial warfare, the raid of Robert Rogers and his Rangers in 1759, in which they destroyed the village.

Box 3.3   The Remaining Abenaki

Until recently, many Americans believed that the only Eastern Abenaki to survive in their traditional territories were a remnant of the Penobscot, and that Western Abenaki had all but disappeared. It has become apparent, however, that not all Abenaki withdrew into the interior or north into Canada as English settlers pre-empted their lands. Some chose to stay. But the cost was high, as they could only do so through an anonymity that amounted to a loss of public identity. Not until the 1970s did they come back into the open and begin their ongoing campaign for US federal recognition as a tribe.[77] In Canada, outside of their ancestral lands, where their French alliance drew them, most Abenaki were able to keep their public identity, and these survive as a people today.

The French soon re-established Odanak but carefully settled the new arrivals into villages situated to act as buffers against invading Iroquois and English, strengthening the defences of New France. An unplanned side effect of this policy was to promote smuggling between the French and English colonies, in which both the Abenaki and the Iroquois were active participants.[78] However, the French put aside their old objections that the Abenaki competed with them in the fur trade. Instead, they now tried to lure the Abenaki away from the English and to encourage raids against the latter.

Some of the practical needs of maintaining alliances aroused concern. Particularly contentious was the extent to which the French should adapt to Amerindian ways of doing things. The willingness of the French 'to spread themselves through the savage nations, where they adopt their manners, range the woods with them, and become as keen hunters as themselves'[79] caused concern in some circles about losing sight of *la mission civilisatrice*, particularly during the early days of the colony, when intermarriage between French and Amerindian was most frequent.[80]

The French were so successful in luring Amerindians to their side that the English began a counter-campaign. In this, they had two weapons: the promise of better deals in trade and, more important, the fact that the French had ceded Amerindian lands in the Treaty of Utrecht without even informing their Native allies. The Abenaki shared with the Mi'kmaq a stunned disbelief at the actions of their French allies. In words that would become all too familiar in later confrontations, the Amerindians asked, 'by what right did the French give away a country that did not belong to them' and which the Amerindians had no intention of quitting?[81]

The English were thus able to persuade some refugees to return. Among these were the Eastern Abenaki chiefs Mog (Heracouansit, 'One with Small Handsome Heels', *c.* 1663–1724) of Norridgewock and Atecouando ('Deer Spirit-Power', *fl.* 1701–26). Atecouando set an example, bringing his people back to Pigwacket a decade after they had left for the St François River. Some Abenaki even joined the English in fighting the Mi'kmaqs of Nova Scotia.[82]

Regretting the Treaty of Utrecht, French officials tried to make up lost ground by arguing that the English in New England were 'encroaching on [Abenaki] territory and establishing themselves contrary to the Law of Nations, in a country of which the said Indians have been from all time in possession'.[83] As for their own presence in Amerindian territories, the French pointed to their alliances to claim that they were there with the permission of the local people. With this encouragement, chiefs such as Wowurna ('Captain Joseph', *fl.* 1670–1738) of Norridgewock rejected the British claim to sovereignty over his people. Others who had gone to Canada reacted by returning to their ancestral homes and reasserting their sovereignty, even in the midst of growing English settlement. This was at least partly what the British were working for, although they never accepted Amerindian claims to sovereignty. It was certainly not, however, what the French were aiming at.

The French would have preferred to keep the Abenaki as a fighting force within their colony, where they would be easier to control. With strategic reasons in mind and also concerned with countering English manoeuvres, they tried to attract Mi'kmaq and Eastern Abenaki to settle at Ile Royale (Cape Breton; Oonumaghee to the Mi'kmaq), but with no success. Quite apart from the fact that the Amerindians did not consider the island to be good hunting territory, the Abenaki rejected the proposal that they move to serve their allies' political goals.[84] It would be 1723 before the Mi'kmaqs, harassed by the English, finally agreed to establish at Mirliguèche on Ile Royale if the French built a church for them.[85] The settlement did not last past 1750, however, when the mission moved to Sainte-Famille on Bras d'Or Lake, also on Ile Royale.

In another instance, the French tried to play on the Abenaki desire for vengeance to get them to establish on the Nicholas River, in Canada but within easy striking distance of the English. The Abenaki answer was a firm rejection. After all, the English had already hit them hard. If they were to seek revenge, it would be from their traditional villages.[86] In other words, although the French did their best to turn the Abenaki into agents for their imperial interests, the Amerindians were far from being mere pawns in their hands. So true was this that the French complained that their allies insulted them almost as much as they did the English.[87]

The French also intensified their efforts to neutralize English commercial superiority. Their most effective means for achieving this was by carefully observing the annual feasting, speech-making, and gift distribution by which they maintained their alliances. According to Philippe de Vaudreuil (*c.* 1643–1725), governor-general of New France, 1703–25, 'we treat our Indians as Allies, and not as Subjects.'[88] As with the Mi'kmaq, and allies generally, the awarding of medals and honours came to be an important element of these occasions, but reports of French ennoblement of Amerindians are apparently more legend than fact (see Box 3.4).[89]

Vaudreuil had no doubt that France's ability to maintain a presence in the Northeast was due to the Abenaki. Further, by winning the co-operation of the Abenaki, the French 'shall have completely provided for the security of Canada.'[90] What started out as a commercial venture for the French ended up as the most politically important of all their Amerindian alliances in New France.[91]

Box 3.4   The French and the Amerindians

Throughout the history of New France, the French policy towards Amerindians was consistent: treat them with every consideration, avoid violence (this was not always successful), and transform them into Frenchmen.[92] They would reach these goals through gifts, military promotions, payments for scalps, and encouraging youth to accompany Amerindians on their expeditions.[93]

The French used these four techniques throughout the period of New France, which formally ended with the 1763 Treaty of Paris. A fifth technique, tried early and later discarded, was to send 'eminent and enterprizing' Amerindians to France 'to amaze and dazzle them with the greatness and splendour of the French Court and Armie'.[94] However, Amerindians proved not to be so easily impressed, and soon they learned to take advantage of these occasions to lobby in their own interests. Once, Versailles hosted six sagamores at the same time, all of them asking for help from the French against the English.[95]

A sixth technique was ceremonial recognition, including presentation of appropriate gifts. For example, a gun or even a cannon salute for a visiting delegation and the gifts offered on such occasions were important influences on later negotiations. Most successful of all, however, were military commissions and, above all, medals. The French first proposed the presentation of medals in 1739 and implemented the policy the following year.

The French, however, were never as comfortable with their Aboriginal allies as European eyewitnesses and popular legend would have us believe. The Amerindians' concept of personal freedom made them uncertain allies at best.[96] The King of France spent a good deal of time and energy—and money—maintaining alliances with these people, whose ideas of equality and individual freedom he would not have tolerated for an instant in his own subjects.

But New France depended on its Amerindians both for trade and militarily—perhaps even for the front ranks of defence[97]—so France had to compromise some of its most cherished principles. In other words, if the French valued their alliances with the Amerindians,[98] they did so no more than they thought necessary, and for solidly practical reasons. France's Amerindian policy emerges as a blend of give and take—giving when necessary to ensure alliance in trade and war, and taking the profits of the fur trade and the benefits of military actions.

In their campaign to win the hearts and minds of the Amerindians, officials pinned their faith on the women and children. They saw the women as hard-working, and they were the ones who tended the crops.[99] French missionaries began in 1620 sending selected children to France.[100] The idea was that the children would become familiar enough with the French language and ways that they would retain them on their return to their native land and influence other Amerindians to adopt French culture. When the program did not achieve the expected results, the French discontinued it, blaming the perverseness of Amerindians.[101]

Attempts at establishing schools for Amerindian children within the colony also met with limited success. Neither day nor boarding schools worked out at first, perhaps because the French curriculum was not relevant to the Amerindian way of life.[102] Parents were also

(*continued*)

unwilling to part with their children, particularly for boarding school. French discipline was foreign to the Amerindian way, and the diet and general regimen often affected the children's health, to the point of death in some cases.[103] Slowly, the French worked out accommodations, but the situation remained far from satisfactory.

For their part, the Amerindians could not control French policy or the course of the Anglo-French conflict any more than they could that of the fur trade, but they influenced the character of all three. The view that Amerindians were 'simple savages' in an unformed state of nature waiting to be moulded by a civilizing hand was proving to be wrong.

The Abenaki Suffer in Their Allies' Defeat

In 1721, the Abenaki delivered an ultimatum to Samuel Shute, governor of Massachusetts from 1716 to 1727. In it, the Amerindians asserted their sovereignty over the territories east of the Connecticut River but said the English who were there could stay, provided no more came.[104] This was the start of the English–Indian War, a virulent three-year struggle that ended in the destruction of the Eastern Abenaki town of Norridgewock (Narantsouak) in 1724[105] and the defeat of the Pigwacket in 1725.

The war ended with the signing of the **Treaty of Boston** in 1725 and its ratification at Falmouth (Portsmouth, New Hampshire) in 1727 despite belated French attempts to prevent it. Other ratifications soon followed in Nova Scotia. However, neither treaties nor ratifications ensured peace until the final defeat of New France, a situation the English tried to deal with by calling the Amerindians rebels.[106]

Their defeat was a bitter pill for the Abenaki to swallow, particularly as they felt that their French allies had let them down. They had sought help in 1720 from Vaudreuil, but England and France were officially at peace, and the French governor was unable to respond with the wholeheartedness that the Abenaki expected.[107] The French had sent guns and ammunition, as well as Amerindian allies, but not troops, as the Abenaki had requested. Neither were the French always considerate in their treatment of their allies.[108] Under the circumstances, the Abenaki had no choice but to wind down their hostilities against the English, even though they were as convinced as ever of their rights.

The Abenaki saw the land not in the terms of absolute ownership but as the right to control its usage and products. Atecouando (fl. 1749–57) of Odanak, for example, in 1752 challenged the authority of the British to survey Abenaki lands without the Amerindians' permission, adding:

> We forbid you very expressly to kill a single beaver or to take a single stick of wood on the lands we live on. If you want wood, we will sell it to you, but you shall not have it without our permission.[109]

But the direction of events was clear. Ratifications to the 1725 peace had continued, as one group after another laid down arms despite continuing violations of their lands.

Such an act did not guarantee that the violations would stop, however, or even that the Abenakis' persons would be respected. For instance, English hunters, who were never caught, killed and robbed Nodogawerrimet, the Norridgewock sachem (d. 1765), despite the fact that he had persistently worked for peaceful coexistence.[110] Wenemouet ('Weak War Chief', d. 1730), a Penobscot chief, tried to avoid special arrangements with either of the colonizing powers and to negotiate working relationships with both. Continuing settler encroachments undermined these efforts, however, and this played into the hands of the French working to keep their alliance on a war footing.

The Pigwacket chief **Nescambiouit** ('He who is so important and so highly placed because of his merit that his greatness cannot be attained, even in thought', c. 1660–1722) was one of several Abenaki chiefs who realized that the Amerindians' only hope of curbing European expansion lay in united action. Although he had been taken to France and honoured by Louis XIV for his efforts in the French cause, in 1716 Nescambiouit went to live with the Fox, whose recent defeat had not reconciled them to French penetration into the West. The French were able to abort Nescambiouit's initiative, as well as those of his associates, but were so worried by them that they limited Abenaki travel into the *pays d'en haut* (the Great Lakes region) unless accompanied by the French.

In 1720, the Abenaki and the Iroquois exchanged wampum belts. Alarmed, the French moved quickly to stop the peace negotiations, believing that otherwise 'the colony would be lost',[111] even though they had signed a peace with the Iroquois in Montreal in 1701. A pan-Indian alliance could only have worked against French interests, as, indeed, it would have done against those of any European colonizer.

For the Abenaki, association with the French meant making the best of a bad predicament. Caught as they were in circumstances that defied their most creative efforts in war and peace, it is not surprising that they were eventually overwhelmed.

Important Names and Terms

Champlain, Samuel de	Odanak
Compagnie des Cent Associés	sagamore
Donnacona	Stadacona
Hochelaga	Tadoussac
King Philip's War	Treaty of Boston
Nescambiouit	Treaty of Utrecht

Study Questions

1) What became of the St Lawrence Iroquois?
2) What were the causes of friction between the Europeans and the Amerindians of the east coast?

3) What advantages did the French have over the English in terms of their relations with the Mi'kmaq?

4) In what ways did the French come to depend on their Amerindian allies?

Recommended Readings

Dickason, Olive Patricia. *The Myth of the Savage and the Beginnings of French Colonialism in the Americas*. Edmonton: University of Alberta Press, 1984.

Green, L.C., and Olive P. Dickason. *The Law of Nations and the New World*. Edmonton: University of Alberta Press, 1989.

Tkaczuk, Diana Claire, and Brian C. Vivian, eds. *Cultures in Conflict: Current Archaeological Perspectives*. Calgary: University of Calgary Press, 1989.

Trigger, Bruce G., ed. *Handbook of North American Indians, vol. 15: Northeast*. Washington: Smithsonian Institution, 1978.

———. *Natives and Newcomers: Canada's 'Heroic Age' Reconsidered*. Montreal and Kingston: McGill-Queen's University Press, 1985.

4 Huron, Five Nations, and Europeans

The People of the Rock Flourish with the Fur Trade

The French establishment of Quebec in 1608 as the centre for the growing fur trade quickly attracted the attention of the Huron, the leading traders in their region, which was nearly 1,300 kilometres into the interior.[1] With a sharp eye for economic advantage, Ochasteguin (*fl.* 1609) of the Huron joined an Algonquin delegation that was teaming up with the Montagnais to go and meet the French.[2] The Algonquins, with their leader Iroquet (*fl.* 1609–15), agreed. The result was the meeting with Champlain at Quebec in 1609, an event that changed the course of Canada's history.

Ochasteguin's people were the Arendarhonon, 'the People of the Rock', occupying easternmost Huronia. The third newest members of the confederacy, which they probably joined about 1590 (well after European trade goods had begun filtering into the interior), they also were the second largest in population.[3] According to Amerindian custom, Ochasteguin and members of his clan segment had the right, as the initiators, to control the new Huron trade. By 1615, all of the confederates were involved in this vast enterprise.

The largest tribe in the Huron confederacy was the Attignawantan, 'People of the Bear', a founding member. They would play host to the Jesuits and would prove to be the most open to Christianity. Another founding tribe that also was willing to accept Christianity was the Attigneenongnahac, 'Barking Dogs' or 'People of the Cord'. The Arendarhonon, on the other hand, held to their traditional beliefs despite the best efforts of the Jesuits.

Most recent arrivals were the Tahontaenrat, 'People of the Deer', who joined about 1610.[4] Like the Arendarhonons, they resisted Christianity. The possible fifth member, Ataronchronon, 'People of the Marshes', in the lower Wye Valley, probably did not have a formal role in the confederacy and may have been a subsidiary group.[5]

Time Line

1608	Samuel de Champlain establishes his habitation at Quebec.
1609	Huron leader Ochasteguin of the Arendarhonon and Algonquin leader Iroquet join forces to establish trade in meeting at Quebec with Champlain. Dutch established on Hudson River. Champlain accompanies a Huron war party in their attack on a Mohawk village, the first example of inter-tribal as opposed to inter-racial warfare.
1613	Tessouat turns Champlain around at Allumette Island in the Ottawa River.
1615	In response to 1609 invitation of Atironta, principal chief of the Arendarhonon, Champlain visits Huronia. He winters there after being wounded in battle between Huron and Iroquois that he had joined to confirm alliance.
1623	Dutch establish Fort Orange (Albany, NY).
1624	Iroquois make peace with Hurons; Algonquins to gain access to southern part of trade with French and to begin trade with Dutch.
1633	Coureur de bois Étienne Brûlé executed by Huron for dealing with their enemy, the Seneca.
1634	Jesuit missions in New France replace Recollects. Smallpox epidemics begin to decimate Algonquins and Huron.
1640s–50s	Iroquois attacks bring end to Algonquin control of Ottawa River, the route from Huronia to Quebec.

1642	Iroquois begin river blockades to disrupt trade from Huronia to Quebec.
1649	Iroquois attack and rout Huronia: two Jesuit missionaries burned at stake; Hurons burn their own villages as they flee. Some Huron take refuge on Christian Island in Georgian Bay before moving to Ancien Lorette near Quebec; others go west to Chequamegon Bay in western Lake Superior. Later, they follow their Odawa allies to Michilimackinac and then to le Détroit. Eventually, they settle in Ohio and Michigan and become known as Wyandots. Still others are captured and become Iroquois.
1668	English expedition to Hudson Bay.
1670	Hudson's Bay Company chartered, with monopoly trading rights over all lands (Rupert's Land) draining into Bay.
1670s	Ojibwa and Odawa move south into former Iroquoian territories around Lake Ontario, Lake Erie, and southern Lake Huron; Cree expand further north and west.
1671	French move into the West.
1680	League of Five Nations invades the Illinois.
1685–1713	English and French fight for dominance in the Bay, but without Amerindian allies.
1690–2	Explorer Henry Kelsey, led by his Cree family and kin, reaches northeast edge of Great Plains.

1717	Death of Thanadelthur, Chipewyan woman who had been instrumental in York Factory trade.	1754	Henley House massacre of English by Cree.
1753	Father Maillard, 'Apostle to the Micmacs', anticipates that within 50 years the Acadians would be so mixed with Mi'kmaq and Wuastukwiuk as to form 'one race'.	1772	Samuel Hearne, with Chipewyan guide Matonabbee and other Amerindians, is first European man to reach Arctic Ocean by overland route.
		1807	HBC opens schools for First Nations children at principal posts.

The intense campaign of the Jesuits to persuade all to conform to the Christian norm caused tensions, as some Huron converted and others resisted.[6] One missionary portrayed some Huron as sneering at Christianity. Wyandot leader Kondiaronk (Gaspar Soiaga, Souoias, Sastaretsi, known to the French as 'Le Rat', c. 1649–1701) would later suggest that the only reason the missionaries wanted to convert Amerindians was to have more people to collect money from. He noted that the missionaries could not prove the existence of hell. As well, Kondiaronk and his people contended with some traders who spoke of Christianity but cheated in the fur trade and stole from Aboriginal people.[7]

The Jesuits tried to ease the way to conversion by not interfering with local custom where there was no opposition to Christian values. This compromise, however, brought them into conflict with officialdom and was only partially successful. Indeed, the French state found it difficult to determine exactly what the relationship between France and the Amerindians should or could be (see Box 4.1). Motives for conversion could be more related to preferential treatment in the fur trade than to religious conviction. In 1648, when only an estimated 15 per cent of the Huron were Christian, half of those who were in the fur fleet had either converted or were preparing for it.[8] Commercial incentives were considerable. Converts were considered to be French and so entitled to the same prices for their furs as Frenchmen, much higher than those paid to non-Christians.[9]

The influx of European goods seems to have strengthened the political and economic dominance of the Huron at first. By late in the sixteenth century, these goods were penetrating inland by means of war, diplomatic exchanges, and trade.[10] The Huron prospered but kept their Stone Age technology until their dispersal because the French were reluctant to trade guns to them as long as they were not converted.[11] This mixing of religious and economic considerations meant that the first Huron to obtain a firearm was the Christian Charles Tsondatsaa.[12] In 1641, the year of Tsondatsaa's baptism, the Iroquois had 39 muskets, received in trade with the Dutch and the English. By 1643, the number had risen to 300.

Lulled by the remoteness of Huronia from both the English and themselves, the French did not consider it necessary to arm the Huron as they were doing at that time

Box 4.1   French Law and Amerindians

A thorny question that the French never fully resolved during their regime concerned whether they should treat Amerindians as allies or as subjects of the French monarch. When dealing with other European nations, particularly the English, the French consistently denied responsibility for the behaviour of their allies on the grounds that they were sovereign. When it came to dealing with Amerindians, however, officials were not always clear as to what to do. As the colony became more secure, a consensus developed favouring the enforcement of French law, the imposition of which, however, was an extremely delicate matter.

The Amerindians saw themselves as free and sovereign, and did not take kindly to being put into French prisons for breaking laws they knew nothing about and would not have accepted if they had. As an eighteenth-century Spanish visitor to Louisbourg on Ile Royale described the situation:

> These natives . . . acknowledged [the King of France] lord of the country, but without any alteration in their way of living; or submitting themselves to his laws; and so far were they from paying any tribute, that they received annually from France a quantity of apparel, gunpowder and muskets, brandy and several kinds of tools, in order to keep them quiet and attached to the French interest.[13]

In other words, the French tacitly granted the Amerindians in the colony a kind of special status. The French needed the Indians both in their struggle against the British and in the fur trade, and could not risk alienating them.[14] Particularly after the outbreak of colonial wars, the French were careful in their treatment of their Indian allies. Shortly before the end of the French regime, a contemporary observer found that:

> [The French] are assiduously caressing and courting them. Their missionaries are dispersed up and down their several cantonments, where they exercise every talent of insinuation, study their manners, nature and weaknesses, to which they flexibly accommodate themselves, and carry their points by these arts.[15]

That might be something of an overstatement, but it indicates how aware the French were of the importance of the alliances. Whenever the opportunity presented itself, however, the French imposed their laws as much as they could.

As far as the French were concerned, whether the Amerindians wanted it or not, the process of transforming them into subjects had begun the moment the French established the colony, although this transformation was not fully realized during the French regime. The importance of kinship for Amerindians, however, meant that even political and economic alliances had personal and social aspects, and kinship went beyond biology. It could also be established by means of networks of names and affiliations, such as membership in clans.

with the Abenaki, whether they were Christian or not. Nor did they properly assess the role of Huronia in keeping the Five Nations in check. The cost to the French of these misjudgements would become only too evident by mid-seventeenth century, when the Iroquois threatened the very existence of New France. The cost to the Huron would be even higher.

During the Quebec meeting of 1609, Atironta (*fl.* 1609–15), main chief of the Arendarhonons,[16] invited Champlain to visit Huronia. This pleased neither the Algonquins nor the Montagnais, both of whom traded with the French, and the Kichesipirini (Algonquins) of Allumette Island[17] in the Ottawa River took action. By a series of ruses and fostered misunderstandings, their leader, one of several chiefs named **Tessouat** (Besouat, *fl.* 1603–13),[18] was able to delay the visit until the summer of 1615.[19] A later

The French fanned the flames of rivalry among the First Nations, solidifying relations with the Huron and Algonquin through military alliances against the Iroquois. This 1632 engraving represents a 1615 attack on an Iroquois village. French infantry, to the left, are shown firing muskets in support of Huron, who are attacking with bows and arrows and fire. At this time, the French did not provide firearms to their hosts. *(Library and Archives Canada, C–005749)*

Box 4.2   Tessouat and the Kichesipirini

Huron trading sessions were 'a pleasure to watch'.[20] Delegations had to get permission to cross another's territory. Some groups tried to discourage the Hurons and others from cross-ing their territory. As the traffic between Huronia and Montreal increased, the Kichesipirini (known as Ehonkehronons to the Hurons) of Allumette Island in the Ottawa River tried to discourage the Hurons from travelling to Montreal to trade with the French. Some histor-ians have cast the Kichesipirini as middlemen, attempting to make a profit by charging tolls. In enforcing this policy, Chief Tessouat of the Kichesipirini was merely asserting what Donnacona had done a century earlier and what countless others would attempt to do later: keep the French and their dangerous technology away from potential enemies. He asserted he was keeping the French trade for the Huron but this was merely subterfuge. He also claimed he could force the French back across the sea.[21]

Tessouat also tried to prevent the French from gaining access to the Great Lakes and in 1613 he turned around Champlain and his party at Allumette Island. Tessouat could not prevent the Huron from travelling the Ottawa River, nor could he hold Champlain off perma-nently, but he did try to impede the movement of French trade goods into the Great Lakes until he could solidify his position as gatekeeper and ensure the safety and security of his people. Increasing Iroquois attacks eroded Tessouat's position in the late 1640s and early 1650s, however. In spite of their complaints against the Algonquin chief and his people, the Huron fur brigades were the first to suffer the consequences as the Iroquois reduced and eventually eliminated Tessouat's control of the river.

chief of the same name and the Algonquins of Allumette Island also instituted a system of tolls along the river that was so important to early trade and communication (Box 4.2).

When Champlain finally visited Huronia in 1615, he confirmed French desire for an alliance by joining with the Huron in an attack on an Iroquois village, probably that of the Oneida.[22] The French leader was wounded in the knee and had to be carried back to Cahiagué, where he recuperated over the winter as the guest of Atironta. The French and Huron formally concluded the alliance the following year at Quebec, with Atironta leading the Huron delegation.

In 1626, the French sent a missionary to the neighbouring Neutrals (known to the Huron as Attiwandaron, 'people who speak a slightly different language', and to the French as Neutrals because they managed to stay on peaceful terms with both Huron and Five Nations), but the Huron saw to it that he did not stay long. They viewed the move as unfavourable to their trading position.[23] On the other hand, when it suited their trading interests, they facilitated the movements of the Jesuits.[24] (This was not the first time the Huron had demonstrated their priorities when it came to trading. In 1633, they had executed coureur de bois Étienne Brûlé [c. 1592–1633] on the charge of dealing with their enemies the Seneca.[25])

The Huron alliance with the French confirmed the shift in importance of trade routes from north–south, as it had been before contact, to east–west. The immediate result of the French–Huron alliance was a blossoming of the fur trade.[26] By plugging into the network of the Huron and convincing them to emphasize furs, the French developed the trade into the main economic activity of the north. Such commerce brought prosperity to everyone involved.[27] It also attracted the attention of the Huron's Iroquois neighbours, who did not have access to the lucrative trade and who resented the Europeans' alliance with their enemy.

The Huron and Their French Allies Take the Offensive

The Huron–French alliance confirmed the hostility between the French and the Iroquois. The Montagnais, Algonquins, and Mi'kmaq, along with the Huron, had been fighting the Five Nations long before the arrival of Europeans. In trading with them, the French were stepping into a ready-made situation. This became evident in 1609, the year the Huron called on Champlain. Then, the French leader found it necessary to confirm his intentions to ally with the Algonquin and Montagnais by marching with them against the Five Nations. Champlain would later claim to have fired a shot that brought down two chiefs.[28]

The animosity between the Iroquois and the French and their allies was reconfirmed the following year, in 1610, when Champlain again joined Algonquins and Montagnais, this time in repulsing an Iroquois raiding party below Sorel.[29] With the sealing of the Huron–French alliance in 1616, the war would escalate into the most famous Amerindian–European confrontation in Canada's history. Champlain assumed that because his Indian allies were so firm in their attachment to the French, and because they so heavily outnumbered the Iroquois, it would be easy to defeat them. As the Jesuit historian Pierre-François de Charlevoix (1682–1761) explained many years later:

> He [Champlain] had not foreseen that the Iroquois, who for so long had been at odds with the Savages for a hundred leagues around them, would soon become allies with their neighbours who opposed France, and become the most powerful in this part of America.[30]

Amid Missionaries and Epidemics, the Huron Edge towards War

The Huron were eager to expand their trading operations to include the French, but neither they nor the French traders were enthusiastic about the arrival of missionaries.[31] But Champlain insisted: without missionaries, no trade. He arranged for Recollects to come to New France in 1615. That same year, the Attignawantans accepted Recollect Father Joseph Le Caron (c. 1586–1632) as the first missionary to Huronia.[32] The Jesuits would soon join the Recollects.[33] Among them was **Jean de Brébeuf** (1593–1649), who in 1626 was sent to Huronia because of his skill with languages. The Jesuits had high hopes of evangelizing the Amerindians quickly.[34] Instead, it would take Brébeuf nine years just to learn the Huron language and compile a grammar.[35]

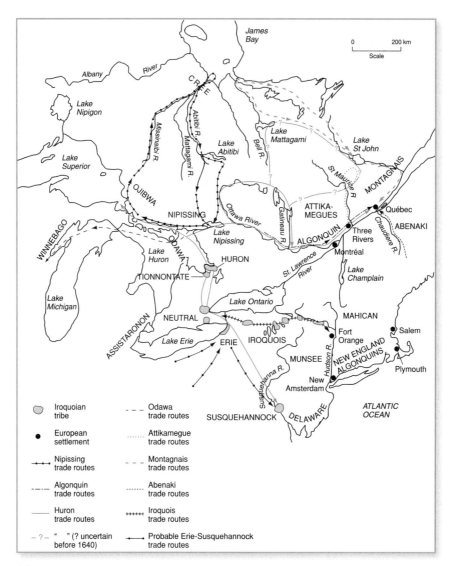

4.1 Major central and eastern trade routes, first half of 17th century

Source: Bruce G. Trigger, *Children of Aataentsic*, vol. 1 (Montreal and Kingston: McGill-Queen's University Press, 1976).

The attitude of the Jesuits was that 'if once they can be made to settle down, they are ours.'[36] Powerful trading interests, on the other hand, wanted to keep the Amerindians in the bush harvesting furs.[37] The Jesuits realized only too well that they also depended on the trade and so collaborated with it, but the tension remained unresolved.[38] Similarly, a certain tension developed over the mixing of races and the inevitability

Colonial officials and missionaries used pictures to get their message across to the Amerindians. In this drawing, from Lahontan, 1728, a missionary is demonstrating to the Huron the Christian conception of God. Despite the advantages that the French accorded to Christians, many Huron resisted these evangelical efforts. *(Library and Archives Canada, C–099231)*

of intermarriage (Box 4.3). These missionaries never completed the evangelization of Huronia, producing a few nuns among Amerindian women but not one priest among the men.[39] That is not to say, however, that the Amerindians took no interest in their black-robed visitors.

The Huron continually tested the French. In particular, they were curious about the priests' claimed powers, which they compared to those of their shamans. They were surprised, and even puzzled, when missionaries did not want to work with medicine men.[40] Puzzlement turned into hostility, especially when missionaries refused to participate and reciprocate in festivals. The Huron began to accuse them of causing the deaths of individuals who resisted them.[41]

On the lighter side, animals the French brought with them, such as dogs with floppy ears and cats, were subjects of endless interest. Indeed, cats became acceptable for gift exchanges.[42] Amerindians were intrigued with European-style doors, a grinding mill, and clocks. The sounding of the hours seemed to them to be a form of speech, indicating that the clock was alive. The Jesuits took advantage of this to tell the Huron that when it sounded four times, it was telling them to leave, thus providing themselves with free time after four o'clock.[43]

Box 4.3   The Intermarriage of Amerindians and the French

Although intermixing and intermarriage occurred independently of the formal clan arrangements of the Amerindians, they were, nevertheless, closely linked. In Canada, the mixing of
the races began long before settlement as a result of the fishing industries, particularly sea
mammal hunting (classed as 'fishing'), where Amerindian expertise was much in demand.[44]
What began informally would later become official French policy.

The seventeenth-century permanent European settlements had few women. For one
thing, Europe had barely recovered from the demographic disaster of the Black Death, and
so nations such as France did not encourage emigration on any scale. The primary purpose
of overseas expansion was resource exploitation; the settlement and growth of colonies
in new lands were of secondary importance. Thus, the first groups that came out were
largely male, sometimes selected for their particular trades skills. The official idea was
that they would intermarry with the indigenous population, producing a French population
overseas.[45] The Church approved, as long as the brides first converted to Catholicism.[46] As
Le Jeune observed, the aim was 'to make them like us'.

The climate also dictated such a course. At this time, the Western world was in the
throes of the Little Ice Age (*c.* 1320–1850). In Canada, the climate was more severe than in
Europe, even at the same latitude.[47] The problem was as fundamental as survival. Too heavy
a reliance on salted foods and lack of fresh provisions during the long winters brought
disease.[48] Amerindians had shown Cartier how to cope with the problem of scurvy during
the winter of 1535–6, but that group does not seem to have passed the knowledge on. Later
colonial attempts, such as those of Champlain, suffered severely at first. Such experiences
led to the popular view in France of Canada as 'un lieu de horreur'.[49]

In short, Europeans needed to co-operate with Amerindians to establish a viable colony. Furthermore, when it came to selecting a mate, an Amerindian or, later, a Métis had
obvious advantages. The widespread and persistent belief that Amerindians were really
white, turning brown because of certain practices, eased intermixing for the French.[50] As
well, French women sometimes married Amerindian men. Once, an Iroquois of Sault St
Louis requested a donkey to bring in family firewood, as his French wife was not used to
such work as Indian women were. He received his request.[51]

If the mixed-blood children were baptized, the French community accepted them. An
odd aside to this was the practice, particularly towards the end of the French regime, of giving illegitimate children to Amerindians. These children, as well as those the Amerindians
had taken captive from the English colonies, were raised and lived as Indians.[52] With colonization in view, officials also proposed sending French families to live among the Huron.
The Huron, seeing this as a form of exchange, thought it might be a good idea.[53] At first, they
did not see its purpose, which was to lead them into the French way of life.

We will probably never know the extent to which intermarriage occurred, because the
records are not complete. Officially, there were 120 mixed marriages during the French

regime. Unofficially, unions often occurred according to the **'custom of the country'**.[54] Maillard, 'Apostle to the Micmacs', wrote in 1753 that he expected that within 50 years the French colonists would be so mixed with the Mi'kmaq and Wuastukwiuk that it would be impossible to tell them apart.[55] Acadians seem to have been well on the way towards realizing the official goal of 'one race'. (Indeed, some have recently rediscovered this heritage and are claiming Aboriginal status.[56]) The demands of the fur trade—which was why the colony existed in the first place—encouraged this mixing.

Inevitably, such arrangements developed, not only within the fur trade but also for military alliances. This was one of the main aspects of the 'disorderliness' and 'libertinage' of the frontier that aroused the condemnation of the missionaries. In general, however, the French supported intermarriage as long as the individuals involved—including Amerindians—obeyed their rules. This, however, did not always happen.

Opposition to intermarriage first found voice in the Old Northwest, where such marriages were common. First, France restricted the right of Amerindian women to inherit their French husbands' property, a measure contrary to the charter of the Company of New France. Later, a 1735 edict required the consent of the governor or commanding officer for all mixed marriages.[57] Eventually, the goal of 'one nation' faded in the face of the emerging reality of a people who would eventually consider themselves a 'new nation'—the Métis. A new political dimension also was forming that would be far removed from the original colonial purpose of forging a New France overseas. Its consequences in the later history of Canada would be profound.

At first, of course, neither Huron nor Montagnais had any means of assessing the societies from which the French came, yet cultural influence worked both ways (Box 4.4). In any event, the evidence at hand was not enough to shake Amerindian cultural self-confidence. 'We have our way of doing things, and you have yours, as well as other nations', the Huron repeated time and again to the French.[58] If new dangers such as strange diseases were appearing in encampments, often without Europeans having ever been seen, the connection had not yet been made with these odd visitors with their ugly beards and peculiar social habits.[59]

The missionaries left during the brief English occupation of New France, from 1629 to 1632, and when France resumed control in 1633 the Recollects did not return. The **Jesuits**, however, did come back to the mission field. Hardly two years had passed after their return in 1634, however, when smallpox appeared among the Montagnais. It would soon reach the Huron. Within four years, up to two-thirds would be gone.[60] In the Amerindian view, somebody or something must be the cause. The Jesuits were the obvious suspects, particularly as they did not die of the contagion.[61] The Algonquins of Allumette Island drew the obvious conclusions and tried to scare the French away.[62] The French responded by threatening to withhold

Box 4.4   Amerindian Influence and Attitudes

For the French, everything depended on getting the mobile hunters to settle down, to start clearing the land and farming after the French model.[63] Above all, Amerindians must learn to accept centralized authority.[64] In New France and Acadia, however, the opposite was happening.[65] Indian self-confidence was such that an Iroquois once told the French 'we have learned to change Frenchmen into Hiroquois', but added diplomatically, 'let us rather say that they will become French and Hiroquois at the same time.'[66]

The French were only too well aware of this possibility. The Recollect friar Gabriel Sagard observed that the French 'become Savages simply by living with the Savages, and lose even the appearance of Christianity.'[67] He told of Étienne Brûlé making a tobacco offering at the beginning of a voyage, which was one of the most successful he had ever made[68]—this at a time when missionaries were doing their best to get hunters to settle into villages! The arrow sash, which would become a symbol of the voyageur and later of the Métis, was an adaptation of an Iroquoian burden-strap design.

Amerindian societies displayed far more strength than the French expected in their colonization of New France. Other colonizing powers had similar experiences. In the view of Charlevoix, Amerindians were 'true philosophers', as they had their priorities straight. He told of a group of Iroquois who had visited Paris in 1666, and who had seen royal residences 'and all the beauties of our great city, but who still preferred their home villages'.[69]

French officialdom was genuinely puzzled at the 'blindness' of the Amerindians to the benefits of French civilization. Some individuals showed insight, however. Paris lawyer turned historian Marc Lescarbot (c. 1570–1642) wrote, 'one cannot root out all at once customs and habitual ways of doing things from a people, whoever they are.'[70] Such perceptions, unfortunately, seldom penetrated to official levels.

trade, a serious matter for the Huron, as the French were their only source for European goods.

As if disease were not enough, drought and forest fires added to their troubles. The opportunity was obvious for the Iroquois to increase their attacks, although they, too, were suffering severely from the epidemics.[71] The Huron looked to their old allies and trading partners, the **Council of Three Fires**—the Potawatomi, Odawa, and Ojibwa—to help counter the threat from the Five Nations, but the Three Fires confederacy had little interest in mounting a large-scale attack against the Five Nations Iroquois. For one thing, the three member nations were relatively safe from the Iroquois menace. The Potawatomi were south and west of Lake Erie, the Odawa lived in villages on Manitoulin Island and at Michilimackinac, and the Ojibwa were located along the north shores of Lakes Huron and Superior. The Iroquois did not have the ability to attack at such a great distance and on so many fronts. Their one campaign against the Odawa at Michilimackinac ended in disaster and starvation for the warriors. In addition, at the first sign of an advancing Iroquois war party the threatened Ojibwa or Odawa could jump into their canoes and go for help. As long as they kept an eye on the gateways into Lake Huron, the Odawa and Ojibwa were impervious to the Iroquois threat and they had little motive to help the Huron by launching a pre-emptive strike. Meanwhile, the Five Nations Iroquois were looking to the south and east for an opportunity to join the fur trade.

For the Five Nations, the new trade posed problems. For one thing, the Iroquois had no allies with whom they could negotiate access to the French. Even when the Dutch set up at Fort Orange (Albany) in 1623, the Mahicans barred the Iroquois. The Dutch, for their part, would have liked to tap into the northern trade, but the Iroquois and Mahicans stood in the path.

The Iroquois decided to try for the Dutch trade. This meant removing the Mahican barrier. They would also have to divert their raiding activities from the St Lawrence Valley.[72] Accordingly, they made peace with the Algonquin and Huron in 1624 (which the French tried to prevent), removing the danger of enemy action from the rear and freeing themselves to attack the Mahicans, whom they finally defeated four years later. The Dutch, at first alarmed and uneasy, later accepted what had happened and opened trade relations with the Mohawk.

On their eastern front, the Iroquois established trade relations with the English. Now, they had two sources of goods. They also had shorter lines of communication, compared with the Huron, deep in the interior, who had access only to the French. The Iroquois played off the English against the Dutch, to the point where the Dutch, feeling threatened by both English and French, began to trade arms to the Iroquois. In 1636, when some Algonquins tried to cross Five Nations territory on their way to trade with the Dutch, the Mohawk killed them. The Algonquins of Allumette Island, led by Oumasasikweie (La Grenouille, 'The Frog', *fl.* 1633–6), tried to turn French–Iroquois differences to their own advantage, but their efforts backfired.[73] So ended the Mohawk–Algonquin–Huron agreement of 1624.

Meanwhile, French attempts to establish trade ties with the Iroquois failed, so Champlain moved to strengthen his colony's defences. In 1633, he requested 120 men from France.[74] He established Trois-Rivières as a buffer for Quebec in 1634 and began to fortify the St Lawrence before his death the following year. The Iroquois responded by building forts on the river from which to harass the fur brigades. Montreal, founded as a religious enterprise in 1642, quickly became a strategic outpost.

The die was cast. The French were committed to the fur-producing nations of the north for obvious commercial reasons. The Five Nations were committed to disrupting the northern trading networks for a combination of reasons, not the least of which was to keep threatened settler encroachment at bay. The war that would dominate the history of New France for a century was well on its way.

The Mohawk and Seneca Succeed in Scattering the Huron

The Iroquois (specifically, Mohawk and Seneca) began their blockades of the St Lawrence, Ottawa, and Richelieu rivers in 1642. These were successful enough that in 1644 and 1645, only one brigade in four made it to its destination.[75] In two years during the same decade, no brigades got through at all. In 1644, the French and some Mohawk negotiated a peace, each side acting independently of its allies and, in the case of the Mohawk, some of their own nation.[76] It brought the short-term benefit of the second largest flotilla, 80 canoes, getting through in 1646. The cost was the killing of a Jesuit by holdout Mohawk of the Bear clan.[77]

Two years later, in 1648, the Huron rallied, sending down 60 canoes, which picked up French reinforcements at Trois-Rivières.[78] It proved to be a hollow achievement. The brigade returned home to find three of Huronia's villages destroyed. The Iroquois changed their tactics and now were attacking settlements instead of just the convoys, taking captives for adoption to replace Iroquoian population losses from war and disease. On top of that, the French were building fortifications in Iroquois territory.[79]

The next year, 1649, when the Five Nations warriors returned in force, the Huron gave up, burned their 15 remaining villages, and dispersed. The French followed their example with their mission, sending up in smoke their dream of a new kind of Christian community in North America blending the two cultures. They also lost two of their missionaries to the fires of the stake, a common lot for captured enemies if they were not adopted.[80]

Among the Huron, the greatest death toll came from starvation the following winter. About 5,000 died on Christian Island in Georgian Bay. Of those who survived, some joined with neighbouring Tionontati (Petun, Khionontateronon) and with the Kiskakon Odawa. This group moved first to Chequamegon Bay in western Lake Superior and then to Michilimackinac, where they joined with the Kamiga Odawa. As the Five Nations threat diminished over the latter half of the seventeenth century, these people moved south to the area of Bkejwanong, the straits between Lakes Huron and Erie. There, they became known as Wyandot, a variation of their traditional name for themselves, Wendat. Several of their chiefs, among them Orontony (fl. 1739–50), entered into a trading relationship with the English.[81]

Of those who remained with the French alliance and continued to be known as Huron, about 600 returned to their ancient territories along the north shore of the St Lawrence, eventually establishing Loretteville outside of Quebec (the ancient Stadacona). Others fled to the Erie and Neutrals, only to be defeated a second time by the Iroquois. Most, however, went south to join the Iroquois. Of those we know about, the Seneca took in the Tahontaenrat (Deer) as well as some Arendarhonon (People of the Rock), although most of the latter went to the Onondaga. A few got as far as Oklahoma. In later confrontations, the French would occasionally have the odd experience of fighting Five Nations warriors who had once been their Huron allies. When the Mohawk accepted the surviving Attignawantan (Bear), however, they were taking in more than a conquered group of people.

Box 4.5   Huron Rights

In 1990, a Quebec court recognized Huron rights to vast territories in the province. Those rights were guaranteed in a safe conduct the British issued to the Huron three days before the final fall of New France in 1760.[82] The Supreme Court of Canada later upheld this decision, ruling in *R. v. Sioui* that the safe conduct was the equivalent of a treaty and was still valid. Its terms allowed Huron 'the free Exercise of their Religion, their Customs and Liberty of trading with the English'. The territory involved stretches from the St Lawrence River to James Bay and from the St Maurice River at Trois-Rivières to the Saguenay River at Tadoussac.[83]

Many of the Huron-turned-Iroquois had been previously exposed to Christian teaching. This gave the Jesuits leverage to intensify their evangelical campaign among the Five Nations. The campaign led to an out-migration from Iroquoia, mainly from Mohawk villages to settlements around Montreal, as converts sought to be near their co-religionists.[84]

In the meantime, to the west, the Wyandot of Michilimackinac gave rise to one of the most famous leaders of the Iroquois war, Kondiaronk. He would be one of the main promoters of the peace of 1701, signed at Montreal.[85]

The dispersal of Huronia occurred 34 years after Champlain's visit and the arrival of the first missionary. From being the most powerful confederacy in the region, demographically, commercially, and militarily, in a little more than a generation Huronia was scattered far and wide, its villages destroyed, its cornfields reverting back to forest (see Box 4.5). It was far more than simply a defeat of a people. A complex commercial system had been brought down, the consequences of which would reverberate in the interior of the continent, reaching as far as James Bay in the Far North.

The fall of Huronia had far-flung consequences for both Amerindians and French. Huronia had been a breadbasket not only for Amerindians but also for colonists. In New France, this led to an increase in land-clearing and in agriculture. Politically, the dispersal of Huronia signalled a development that had been underway for some time. The French started off as allies of the Amerindians. Now, the Indians were allies of the French.

The pattern of the fur trade was radically changed, also, as Montreal picked up where Huronia left off.[86] The annual brigades to Montreal, continued by the Odawa along with remnants of the Huron, diminished and eventually ceased during the 1680s. Instead, the **coureurs de bois** fanned out from Montreal into the interior: the brigades were now going the other way. Despite the difficulties of inland travel—there were 38 portages between Montreal and Grand Portage, a distance of a thousand miles—it was an opportunity that the colony seized eagerly. The Jesuits reported that 'all our young Frenchmen are planning to go on a trading expedition, to find the Nations that are scattered here and there; and they hope to come back laden with the Beaver-skins of several years' accumulation.'[87] The east–west axis, fuelled with merchandise from Europe, now prevailed.

It was as part of this movement that Pierre Esprit Radisson (*c*. 1640–1710) and his brother-in-law, Médard Chouart des Groseilliers (1618–96?), penetrated north of Lake Superior during the 1650s with the indispensable aid of Indian guides. There, they learned of the rich fur resources that the Huron so successfully had exploited. The way was being prepared for the entrance of the Hudson's Bay Company, a quasi-governmental institution that would play a major role in the Canadian fur trade for two centuries.

In the meantime, the Council of Three Fires undertook a counter-offensive. By the end of the seventeenth century, it had driven the Five Nations out of Huronia and the lands of its allies, the Tionontati and Attiwondaron. This led to the Five Nations agreeing to the Montreal peace of 1701.[88]

Huronia's Loss Is the Bay's Gain

While Europeans concentrated on the fur trade along the St Lawrence–Great Lakes systems, Amerindians were busy with their own networks, which stretched north to the Arctic and south to the Gulf of Mexico.[89] When the French finally reached Lake Mistassini in 1663, after several unsuccessful attempts, they became aware that enough trade goods were filtering through from the south to satisfy the needs of the northerners. This helps to explain why the French could not go through to the east side of James Bay by land until 1670. Amerindian networks were coping with the increased volume brought about by the European trade.[90] The people saw no reason to encourage the French to come in.[91]

Four main trade routes stretched from the St Lawrence Valley to the north.[92] After the establishment of Quebec in 1608, however, the focus of the northern trade shifted west. The result was that the two routes from Huronia to James Bay rose in importance. Huronia remained the hub of the north–south networks for 30 years, until it was destroyed in 1649. Iroquois raiding parties then went on a rampage, leaving the northern networks that had operated since distant times in disarray and cut off from access to trading goods from the south. In this realignment of forces, the Five Nations became the dominant Amerindian factor. They now controlled the main routes between the English colonies and the interior.[93] For most of the eighteenth century, the Iroquois would be the leading Amerindian players in the Northeast.

When the English sent a trading expedition to Hudson's Bay in 1668, they found that Amerindians who had once avoided contact were now eager to trade. The English organized the **Hudson's Bay Company** (HBC) and in 1670 granted it monopoly trading rights in those regions where the waters drained into the Bay. There was no question of consulting the Amerindians involved.

That same year, the Company established Fort Charles on Rupert River. The local Cree were missing the supplies they used to receive through the Amerindian networks, and Fort Charles was an instant success. This resulted in the rapid spread of HBC forts around the Bay over the next 15 years. The French countered with their own forts in the interior but found the coureurs de bois more effective.

The Amerindians now became partners in the European enterprises. Almost over-night, homeguard bands became an established feature of both English and French posts because of the shift in subsistence strategies that the fur trade brought about. Use of the total environment gave way to the specialized pursuit of fur-bearing animals. The Amerindians turned to the posts to offset the increased danger of famine caused by this switch.[94] Both French and English encouraged the presence of Amerindians around their establishments to have hunters on hand to supply them with fresh meat. Amerindians, for their part, wanted manufactured and other trade goods.

Trade Brings Changes, but Culture Remains Intact

The metal axe and cooking pot continued to be in demand as trade items.[95] The Europeans also soon assessed Amerindian preferences shrewdly enough to evolve the tomahawk, one of the first items developed by Europeans specifically for the Amerindian trade. Combining as it did the war axe with the peace pipe, it had con-notations beyond the 'practical' and fit with the Amerindian concept of the duality of nature, the dichotomy and interaction of life and death.

Brazil tobacco was also an important trade item because even in the North, where tobacco did not grow, smoking was important for rituals.[96] Amerindians also wanted shiny items such as mirrors and certain types of beads. This related to their understand-ing of the operation of the cosmos, which to them was just as practical as its material as-pect. Beads were also shaped like berries, reputed to have curative powers.[97] Europeans quickly learned to appreciate certain aspects of Amerindian technology, such as the canoe, snowshoes, toboggan, and moccasins, to mention the best-known items.

By this time, the Cree (Cristinaux, Christino, Kristinaux, Killistinaux) were already the largest single group of Canadian Amerindians. They would become even more numerous and widespread as they prospered through the fur trade. The English, ap-preciating their hunting capabilities, found the Cree to be 'of a humane Disposition'.[98] Good relations were essential to the English, and the HBC post journals made little use of the word 'savage', a term used so often in the settlements when referring to the Amerindians. The English also knew that, at any time, the French—or anyone else on the scene—might make an offer and the Amerindians might accept, destroying what the English were seeking to build. They had to secure the relationship, and they knew one way of doing so.

The First Treaties Formalized Trade Alliances

The English hoped to secure their position by entering into alliances, or 'agreements'.[99] The Amerindians were willing partners in this. After all, they, too, were negotiating for alliances, without which trade was insecure. They did not understand, however, the 'absolute propriety'—ownership—that the English believed they were acquiring.[100] The concept was completely foreign to them. Whatever the agreements were, Amerindians felt free to come to the posts, and one observer, at least, was under the impression that the HBC was paying them 'rent'—probably a reference to the ceremonial gift exchanges and other rituals that accompanied trading.[101]

Trading alliances in the North did not imply military service, because conditions in the North did not allow for wars. Amerindians and Inuit may have killed each other on sight (if they could), or even raided each other, but this never led to military campaigns. When the English and the French fought it out for dominance in the Bay, 1685–1713, Amerindian allies did not join them.

The English depended on the Amerindian **homeguards** for food when their own supplies ran out, a frequent occurrence because of the uncertainties of shipping schedules. They tried to train their own men to hunt but at first were unsuccessful.[102] Here, too, feasts and gifts kept the relationship with the homeguards functioning. Even so, relations were not always easy.

Maintenance of the posts plus the demands of the fur trade eventually depleted game in some areas. Faced with starvation, Amerindians turned to the posts for help. If such help was not given, ugly incidents could result. One occurred in 1832 at Hannah Bay, an outpost of Moose Factory, when starving Cree raided it and killed its personnel.[103] These episodes were rare, however, in the North.

The Clash and Adaptation of Cultures

Neither side was impressed with the other's food. According to Samuel Hearne (1745–92), Amerindians did not even like bread, 'for though some of them would put a bit of it into their mouths, they soon spit it out again with evident marks of dislike; so that they had no greater relish for our food than we had for theirs.'[104] Some individuals used this reaction to demonstrate their cultural superiority. Esquawino (Esqua:wee:Noa, *fl.* mid-eighteenth century), known, for obvious reasons, to the English at Moose Fort as Snuff the Blanket, would hold his clothing to his nose when he entered the fort to avoid the smell. He refused to eat food prepared in the pots there.[105]

On the other side of the picture, Hearne learned to appreciate some (though not all) Amerindian dishes.[106] He categorically dismissed the European belief that Inuit and Amerindians of the Far North were cannibals.[107] Amerindians also eventually demonstrated dietary adaptability. They became so fond of prunes and raisins that they would 'give a Beaver Skin for twelve of them to carry to their Children.' But they continued to disdain cheese, believing that it was made of 'dead Mens Fat'.[108] Huron (in common with Amerindians generally) did not like salt. In fact, they considered it to be poison (with some reason, the way Europeans were using it at the time) and refused to let their children touch it.[109]

The HBC sought at first to keep company 'servants', as they called the men who worked for them, and Amerindians apart. This, of course, turned out to be impossible.

For one thing, the Company's minimum contact policy meant restriction of its access to the interior. No European at that time could make such a trip without Amerindians acting as guides and hunters.[110] As well, the presence of women in the trading groups that arrived at the post sparked a natural interest among the servants, all of whom were male.

Women played a pivotal role in both trade and Amerindian society generally. They fished and hunted small game, prepared maple sugar and other food, and made clothing. They also collected and prepared the materials needed to repair canoes—essential to all involved in the trade, whether Aboriginal or European. John Tanner tells of an Odawa woman named Netnokwa, who led trade negotiations.[111] **Thanadelthur** (d. 1717), a remarkable Chipewyan woman, was captured by the Cree, escaped with another woman, and survived a year in the bush searching for York Factory, which she had heard about but had only a vague idea as to its location. Her companion died, and shortly afterward a party from the factory found Thanadelthur. Taken to the post, she soon became invaluable as an interpreter and in persuading her fellow tribesmen to come to the fort to trade despite the presence of their traditional enemies, the Cree.[112]

Access to areas beyond the coast depended on the navigational assistance of Amerindians. In this 1861 painting by William George Richardson Hind, an Amerindian guide draws a map on birchbark for the Labrador Peninsula expedition. *(Metropolitan Toronto Reference Library, J. Ross Robertson Collection, T–31956)*

When the HBC relaxed its rule, at least unofficially, English exploration of the interior became possible. The need for new sources of furs, and particularly the aggressive expansion of the French, made such exploration necessary to the English. The first man to undertake an extended voyage, Henry Kelsey (*c.* 1667–1724), prepared for it by living with Amerindians. During 1690–2, his Cree family guided him to the northeastern edge of the Great Plains. There, he saw the great bison herds.[113] Similarly, **Samuel Hearne** met only failure in his attempts at northern travel until he accepted the advice of his Chipewyan guide **Matonabbee** (*c.* 1737–82). Thus, Hearne became the first European man to reach the Arctic Ocean overland, in 1772.[114]

Amerindian Counter-Techniques

Even in trade, the HBC did not enjoy the control it would have liked. The Amerindians played off the English against the French, and they were quick to recognize a better deal, but they were not businessmen in the same sense as Europeans. For one thing, they were not guided to the same extent by supply and demand in setting their prices.[115] Also, they accumulated goods to satisfy social obligations and to acquire prestige rather than for personal use.

Amerindian traders were as eager as anyone to set up in business. They thought nothing of undertaking long journeys to obtain better prices.[116] Capitalizing on English–French rivalry, they would persuade hunters on their way to bayside posts to part with their best furs and then shop around for the best deal available. A disgruntled trader at Moose Fort described the entrepreneur Esquawino as 'ye grand politician of all being a free Agent travelling about, sometimes to ye French, at others to Albany & this Fort, never drinks but has always his scences about him & makes ye best of his Markett at all places.'[117] The English jailed the enterprising Captain Snuff on the charge of interfering with trade and stirring rebellion among the homeguard. Esquawino hanged himself because of loss of face.[118]

The HBC promoted contact only up to a point. The Company discouraged its men from teaching Amerindian children to read and write, fearing the Amerindians would learn English trade secrets.[119] It would be a hundred years before it would recognize the value to the trade of Amerindians (particularly those born to its own employees) and launch a training program for them. The Company opened schools in 1807 at its main posts.[120] An early problem, however, was keeping the schoolmaster at his job. The fur trade was so much more lucrative than teaching.

Amerindians and traders mixed well socially,[121] but they continued in their separate ways despite the close co-operation needed for the trade. One trader observed sadly that the only basis for friendship in the Northwest was the desire of Amerindians for European goods and the Europeans' eagerness for the Amerindians' furs.[122] One area of difficulty was reciprocity and the obligations it entailed. Ignoring accepted standards of behaviour could cause resentment and lead to trouble. In 1754, for example, the postmaster at Henley House did not provide for relatives of women who were being kept in the post. The Cree turned on the English, killed them, and looted the post.[123]

The expanding presence of the English in North America disturbed the French at Quebec deeply, and they launched two encircling movements. The first one in 1671 from the Great Lakes to the west aimed at cutting off the English at the Bay from the interior, and in 1699 to the south down the Mississippi, surrounding the Thirteen Colonies. The Iroquois became alarmed, particularly with the first move. They saw it as an attempt to cut them off from the fur resources of the North. They responded by attacking the Illinois in 1680 and stepping up their war against New France. Meanwhile, the French were doing their best to expand their own presence in the New World.

National Territories Shift as the French Push beyond the *Pays d'en Haut*

The French moved to take possession of the West formally in 1671. To mark the occasion, they assembled 14 Amerindian tribal nations at the Jesuit mission at Sault Ste Marie to witness the ceremonies of possession—the raising of a cross and a post bearing the arms of France.[124] Although the Amerindians knew of European interest in their lands, it is doubtful that they understood fully what the French were up to. They had gained a powerful new ally, one who would bring desired trade goods and who had promised to protect them from their enemies. As far as they knew, they had just concluded a good deal.

The French learned, however, that the Iroquois, whenever they came across a French metal plaque attached to a tree, tore it off and took it to the English. Thus, Jean Talon (1626–94), intendant of New France for two terms, 1665–8 and 1670–2, admitted the Iroquois probably knew that the French were claiming the West as theirs.[125] On top of that, this huge expansion was presenting the French with problems of control—their people in the **pays d'en haut** did not always behave well. Officials realized the importance of the friendship of the local Amerindians if they were to maintain a presence, and went to some trouble to keep the peace.[126]

In the 1670s, the French and the English were not the only ones expanding their territories. Ojibwa moved south from the north shore of Lake Huron into lands that had once been occupied by such Iroquoians as the Huron, Petun (Tionontati), and Neutrals, all of whom the Five Nations had dispersed during the preceding decades. The Ojibwa pushed west, eventually moving onto the Plains. They defeated the Iroquois in skirmishes throughout the last decade of the seventeenth century.[127]

The Cree also expanded their territory.[128] By 1820, they were raiding in the Mackenzie basin. To the north, the Chipewyan contained them. To the south, they followed their Assiniboine allies to take up life as buffalo hunters on the northern Plains.[129] The Cree/Assiniboine movement was partly linked to trade, at least in its later phase.[130] But the Blackfoot and their confederates, who controlled the central and southern Alberta Plains, stopped this movement.

In the Maritimes, the Mi'kmaq were not so fortunate. Advancing settlement was encroaching on them. They were in the throes of a war against the English, a confrontation that had begun early in the seventeenth century and would not end until the final defeat of France in 1760. Add to all this the century-long Iroquois War against New France (which had ended in 1701) and Canada's 'peaceful' frontier takes on the aspect of a wishful myth.

Important Names and Terms

Brébeuf, Jean de	Hudson's Bay Company
Council of Three Fires	Jesuits
coureurs de bois	Matonabbee
'custom of the country'	*pays d'en haut*
Hearne, Samuel	Tessouat
homeguards	Thanadelthur

Study Questions

1) Why did Amerindian women seek French husbands?
2) In what ways did the Jesuits compromise the Huron ability to defend themselves against the threat posed by the Five Nations?
3) Why did the Five Nations launch their attack on Huronia in 1649?
4) How did the Cree play the French against the English in the fur trade?

Recommended Readings

Bowden, Henry Warner. *American Indians and Christian Missions*. Chicago: University of Chicago Press, 1981.

Davis, Richard C., ed. *Rupert's Land: A Cultural Tapestry*. Calgary: Calgary Institute for the Humanities, 1988.

Francis, Daniel, and Toby Morantz. *Partners in Furs: A History of the Fur Trade in Eastern James Bay, 1600–1870*. Montreal and Kingston: McGill-Queen's University Press, 1983.

Houston, James. *Running West*. Toronto: McClelland & Stewart, 1989.

Jaenen, Cornelius J. *Friend and Foe: Aspects of French–Amerindian Culture Contact in the Sixteenth and Seventeenth Centuries*. Toronto: McClelland & Stewart, 1976.

Van Kirk, Sylvia. *Many Tender Ties: Women in Fur-Trade Society, 1670–1870*. Norman: University of Oklahoma Press, 1983.

5 | Some Amerindian–Colonial Wars

Unlike the British, who fought wars with Amerindians over land, and the Spanish, who saw indigenous peoples as a slave labour force for gold and silver mines, French colonizers had a purpose for establishing amicable relationships with the peoples of northeastern North America. The French needed trading partners and they quickly came to view the Mi'kmaq, the Huron, and the Odawa as allies. These alliances drew the French into war with the Five Nations Iroquois, the ancestral enemies of the Hurons and their Odawa allies. From Champlain's first excursion with a Huron war party in 1609 to the **Great Peace of Montreal** in 1701, the French fought with the Huron and the Odawa against the Five Nations Iroquois. For their part, the British waged endemic warfare against the Mi'kmaq of the east coast. Known as the Mi'kmaq War, this protracted conflict was fought over land and it lasted from about 1613 until 1761. It was a part of the Abenaki wars (see Chapter 3). All of these wars were intermittent, sometimes with pauses that lasted for years.

Equalling, or perhaps even surpassing, the Iroquois War in the intensity of emotion aroused was the Fox War (1710–38), which carried the Iroquois conflict into the Middle West after the Five Nations came to terms with the French in Montreal. The Fox War concerned territory that became part of the United States, but it involved New France almost as deeply as the Iroquois War had. The Fox War began when the Ojibwa—allies of the Odawa and therefore of the French—got into a series of disputes over encroachments into one another's ancestral hunting territories in the area between lakes Michigan and Superior. The obligations of alliance thus drew the French into a conflict that they did not want.

Iroquois War (1609–1701)

The **Iroquois War** was hard on both sides, but neither seemed able to stop.[1] The cyclical nature of the war, called the **Mourning War** by the Iroquois, was ensured by the mutually held belief that warriors killed in battle could not enter the afterlife until they had been avenged in battle. Both sides realized the futility of this belief, but it

Time Line

1609–1701	The Iroquois War, which ended with the Great Peace of Montreal.	1725	Mascarene's Treaty (Treaty No. 239) with Abenaki after fall of Norridgewock, which details how Amerindians must behave as British subjects.
1650	Mohawk and Seneca join forces to defeat and disperse Attiwandaron (Neutrals).		
1665	French sign peace treaty with League of Five Nations, except for Mohawk, whose raids on French settlements have been especially unsettling.	1734	Kiala and three other Fox leaders travel to Montreal to sue for peace: one chief pressed into galley service; Kiala sent as slave to Martinique, ends up abandoned on Guyana coast.
1675	Seneca defeat the Susquehannock.		
1687	Denonville sends dozens of captive Iroquois to France for service in galleys; 13 survivors eventually returned.	1749	Halifax established by English. Abenaki and Wuastukwiuk of Saint John River ratify Mascarene's Treaty.
1693	French and Canadiens invade Mohawk territory.	1752	Mi'kmaq chief from Shubenacadie signs peace treaty with English in Halifax.
1710–38	Fox War, involving attacks on French traders and blockading of river systems needed for French trade in Upper Midwest.	1755	Expulsion of Acadians from Nova Scotia.
1716	French besiege Fox village, killing an estimated 1,000 Amerindians.	1758	Louisbourg falls to British, who refuse to include Amerindians in terms of surrender because of earlier massacre of British prisoners at Fort William Henry in New York.
c. 1720	Tuscarora migrate north to join Iroquois, who become League of Six Nations.		
1720s	Fox war chief Kiala seeks alliance with Abenaki (and Chief Nescambiouit), Iroquois, and Chickasaw.	1782	French destroy Fort Prince of Wales on Hudson Bay; outbreak of disease leads Chipewyan to abandon area.

was difficult to eradicate. When the Algonquin war chief Pieskaret (d. 1647) killed 13 Mohawk in one engagement in 1645,[2] the Mohawk were ready to sue for peace. The French, feeling the effects in their fur trade, were only too willing to join, but they handled the negotiations clumsily. Not only did they hold meetings behind closed doors without the knowledge of allies and associates, but the peace agreement excluded their non-Christian allies as well.

The effect on the Amerindians when they learned what had happened can easily be imagined. The treaty so displeased the excluded members of the Iroquois league that it took all of the celebrated eloquence of a leading Mohawk negotiator, Kiotseaeton ('The Hook', *fl.* 1645–6), with 17 wampum belts, to persuade even some of them to go along with its terms, at least for a while.[3] Among the main holdouts were the 'nephews' of the Mohawk, the Oneida. Not surprisingly, it did not take long for hostilities to resume, more intensely than ever, although the century of warfare was interwoven with attempts at peace.

Iroquois Unity, Patched-Up Peace

In 1653, all the Iroquois joined with each other to negotiate an accord. The French accepted, even though their Amerindian allies were once more excluded. In the breathing space of a few years that followed, the Jesuits established a mission at Onondaga that would have important consequences in the future. In the meantime, the French allies received no respite. In the view of the French, the Iroquois were not interested in peace until they obtained control of the flow of beaver from the Old Northwest, deflecting it to the Dutch and then the English.[4]

Except for a period in the mid-1650s, the four decades that followed the 'patched-up peace' of 1645[5] saw the outlying areas of the colony, especially those around Montreal, become nearly impossible to farm. Sulpician missionary Dollier de Casson (1636–1701) described the 'enemy all around us . . . [they] approach like foxes, fight like lions, fly away like birds.' Iroquois warriors, he wrote, thought nothing of passing a 'whole day without moving, and hidden behind a stump' in order to dispatch a colonist.[6] 'How can we fight a war against an invisible enemy?' one Jesuit complained. He added that unless they cut down all the forests, it would be impossible to stop the raids.[7] The exasperation this type of warfare aroused in the French surfaced in a proposal that the Iroquois be exterminated.[8]

By 1646, some Huron were also doubting their alliances. The benefits of the trade were great, but they blamed the French for the recent epidemics. Some found 'that it costs them too dear, and they prefer to do without European goods rather than to expose themselves every year.'[9] Meanwhile, the Iroquois aimed to spread terror in their raids, and in this they were very effective. A Jesuit missionary, observing these same techniques among the Abenaki, said they made 'a handfull of warriors more formidable than would a body of two or three thousand European soldiers'.[10]

The Iroquois attacks fuelled the anti-French faction among the Huron. In 1648, they killed a young missionary assistant in the hope of ending the alliance and getting both French and Christianized Huron expelled from Huronia. The pro-French faction prevailed, however. The Huron gave the Jesuits a reparations payment said to have been the largest ever made by the confederacy.[11] That action, however, did not save Wendat (as the Huron referred to their confederacy) from dispersal the following year, a fate shared with their neighbours, the Tionontati (Tobacco People, Petun), specialists in growing tobacco. That was only the beginning of a series of Iroquoian victories.

In 1650, the Mohawk and Seneca joined forces to disperse the Attiwandaron (Neutrals). In keeping with their geographical position between the Huron and

Iroquois confederacies, the Attiwandaron tried to maintain relations with both sides but were more successful with the Huron. They now found themselves, in effect, swallowed whole by the Iroquois, incorporated into the league.

The Erie, who took in large numbers of Huron refugees, became the next targets. During 1654–6, the Iroquois defeated them in a series of attacks. With the Seneca defeat of the Susquehannock in 1675 after 20 years of hostilities, the Iroquois finally smashed the ring of Huron allies that had encircled them since the heyday of Huron power. Not only that, they spread their terror to tribal nations in what are today Wisconsin and Michigan, and then erupted into Illinois country.

The Guerrilla Tactics of the Mohawk

The **guerrilla warfare** waged by the Iroquois, based on surprise and speed of movement, was their preferred technique, particularly after they met with firearms. The only time the French faced an Iroquois army on an open field was in 1609, when Champlain claimed deadly results from his one shot. Whether or not that story is true, the Iroquois saw no virtue in exposing themselves to fire they could not match. For the French, the guerrilla tactics of the Iroquois were harder on nerves than on the lives of the colonists. Dollier de Casson mentioned frequent skirmishes that wounded many but killed few. The Iroquois, on the other hand, may have lost half their warriors to war and disease during the last two decades of the seventeenth century; the French lost about 200 souls.[12]

To the French—indeed, to seventeenth-century Europeans in general—guerrilla warfare was a disgraceful way of conducting a war.[13] At first, they tried to make a show of force in the European way. In 1665, they sent out the crack Carignan-Salières regiment, the pride of the French military establishment. Alexandre Prouville de Tracy, lieutenant-general of America from 1663 to 1667, soon followed. On 13 December 1665, the French signed a peace treaty at Quebec with four members of the League of Five Nations, excluding the Mohawk.[14]

Later that winter, the regiment marched towards Mohawk territory, but their Algonquin guides failed to show, and they got lost. The French army wound up near Schenectady, about three days' march from Mohawk villages. The Mohawk advised the English in Albany of the presence of the French force, and the English sent a delegation to ask what the French were doing on English territory. (Apparently, neither side knew that England and France had been at war for the past two weeks.) The French, surprised to learn that England claimed title to the region, negotiated for supplies and returned home. The expedition lost about 400 men from frostbite, exhaustion, and hunger.

Still determined to teach the Mohawk a lesson, the French returned the following September with a much larger expedition. This time, they brought Huron and Algonquin guides, with a third party bringing up the rear. Again, they did not meet any Iroquois, but they burned four Mohawk villages and destroyed food stores. The French lost 10 men in a storm.

As a result of Tracy's enterprise, the Mohawk sued for peace the following spring, in 1667. This time, the agreement held, at least for a while. The Iroquois, who at that time were involved in tribal wars from Virginia to Lac Saint Jean as well as in the West, needed time to adapt to this change in conducting international relations. The French also worked at coming to terms. In 1669, they executed three Frenchmen for killing a Seneca chief.

The destruction of their supplies apparently hit the Mohawk hard. A few years later, the Seneca presented La Salle, who was passing through their land, with 15 tanned deerskins in token of welcome. In a speech, the Seneca expressed the hope that the French would not burn their villages as they had done those of the Mohawk a few years earlier.[15] At that point, they need not have worried. The Seneca were on the leading edge of western expansion, and many of them were trading with the English. In 1670, a worried intendant Talon estimated that the Iroquois had diverted 1.2 million livres' worth of beaver. Therefore, it was important that the Seneca not be antagonized.

French Invasion in the West

The French decided that the Sault Ste Marie ceremony of 1671, when they had formally taken possession of the West, needed to be followed up. Accordingly, in 1673 Louis de Buade, Comte de Palluau et de Frontenac, governor-general of New France, 1672–82 and 1689–98, enthroned in a sedan chair, headed up the St Lawrence to found a fort at Cataracoui, now Kingston. There he met delegates from the Five Nations, who were much disturbed because the French were now in Iroquois territory. Not only were Iroquois–Odawa negotiations for a separate peace aborted, but as the French pushed westward, the Five Nations became convinced that the Europeans were outflanking them, all the more so because the Illinois had joined the French.

That same year, 1673, the Iroquois negotiated a treaty with the Odawa, promising to provide them with trade goods in return for pelts.[16] It did not last past 1700, however, when the Iroquois violated the treaty's terms by hunting in Odawa territory. In the meantime, in 1680, the league's warriors invaded Illinois country.

The French, for their part, again tried a European-style invasion of Iroquois territory, this one organized by a new governor-general, Joseph-Antoine Le Febvre de La Barre (in office 1682–5) and aimed at the Seneca (1684).[17] Illness broke out among the troops, however, forcing the army to encamp at a bay in Lake Ontario that became known as Anse de la Famine. There, the Iroquois found the French, disease-ridden and running out of food. Otreouti (Hateouati, among other variations, 'Big Mouth', *fl.* 1659–88), Onondaga orator and chief, presented the Iroquois terms. They would pay 1,000 beaver in return for damages from their raids. They were not, however, prepared to accept peace in Illinois country, nor would they guarantee protection for French traders in the region. The French had no choice but to accept, a turn of events that angered France. The government quickly recalled Le Febvre de La Barre and sent out Jacques-René de Brisay de Denonville (governor-general, 1685–9). Denonville was, after all, a professional soldier, so surely, the French believed, he could recoup this loss of honour.

In fact, Denonville's expedition against the Seneca (1687) had more casualties from disease than from fighting, but it was involved in one skirmish. Admittedly, it was an inconclusive ambush, but at least Denonville engaged the enemy. He achieved this by adopting the Iroquoian tactics of surprise, surround, give way when pressed, and speed (a quick blow and rapid withdrawal).[18] The *raid-éclair* would contribute to the reputation of Canadiens as feared forest fighters in the cycle of French–English wars that began in 1689. It had taken a century of warfare, but the French had learned, at least for North America. The English later would follow suit.

Denonville, like Tracy in 1666 against the Mohawk, destroyed Seneca villages and food stores. He also captured a group of Iroquois and sent them to France as prisoners.[19] The coup aroused a frightful row. The Jesuits were especially angry, as they saw their years of difficult missionary work among the Five Nations destroyed. Army officer Louis-Armand de Lom d'Arce de Lahontan (1666–before 1716), a caustic observer of the colonial scene, claimed that the French took prisoner friendly groups who came to settle around Fort Cataracoui. In fact, France for a long time had entertained the idea of transporting Amerindian prisoners to France, not just from New France but from the Caribbean also, and Denonville had acted under orders. In the end, though, France backed down and returned the 13 survivors.

The Seneca suffered severely from the destruction of their stores by Denonville's troops, but they soon took revenge. Their raid on Lachine on an August dawn of 1689 saw 56 of 77 habitations go up in flames, killing at least 24 residents. They had caught the French completely by surprise, and the colony was stunned.

War in Iroquois Lands

For the next few years New France was practically in a state of siege, with Montreal taking the brunt. In 1691, Iroquois burned about 30 farms at Pointe-aux-Trembles, outside of Montreal. When the habitants captured some Iroquois, they publicly burned three of them to death. The lessons of warfare worked both ways.

During the 1690s, Frontenac finally was able to move the scene of war from New France or the territories of its allies and into the lands of the Mohawk and Onondaga. The French inflicted heavy losses, and the Iroquois seriously began to consider peace.[20] Their fear that the French would surround them was becoming a reality as the latter moved down the Mississippi and founded Louisiana in 1699. The French were encircling them also with alliances with western Amerindians, particularly the Odawa and Miami, who had fought very effectively for the French against the Iroquois.[21]

The response of their English allies to the league's requests for help was not adequate, either with supplies of guns and ammunition or otherwise. For example, when the French and Canadiens invaded Mohawk lands in 1693, the forewarned English prepared for their own defence but neglected to warn the Mohawk. The latter suffered much damage and severe losses.[22]

On top of that, the English and the French signed one of their periodic peace treaties in 1697 but did not include the Five Nations in its terms. Both claimed the Iroquois as subjects. The Iroquois, of course, did not see themselves as being subject to anyone. Teganissorens (Decanasora, *fl.* last quarter, seventeenth century, and first quarter, eighteenth century), Onondaga chief and leader of the pro-French faction, dominated negotiations for 30 years.

Artful to the end, the Five Nations signed a peace with the French in Montreal in 1701 in the face of English objections. Later that same year, they cemented their alliance with the English in Albany by ceding them lands in southern Ontario. The problem was that although the Tionontati and Neutrals had occupied the area earlier, the Ojibwa defeated the Iroquois in the region during the 1690s and were now living there. The English, apparently, were unaware of this. They also did not know that the Iroquois, in a double twist, had negotiated with the French for their guarantee of hunting and fishing rights to that same region. Further, they assured the French of their neutrality in future wars but made no mention of this to the English. The Iroquois were playing both ends against the middle with great skill.[23]

In addition, the Iroquois had another ace in the hole—their access to English markets in Albany. During their hostilities against the French, they had been careful to protect their position as middlemen in the English trading system. When the French market collapsed in 1696 because of oversupply, the Iroquois offered Amerindian allies of the French safe conduct through Iroquois territories to New York markets—a brilliant move that deepened the crisis for the French in the West on both diplomatic and economic fronts. Their purpose: to win the westerners into the Iroquois–English network.[24]

The Iroquois Claim the Balance of Power, but Disease and Dissension Follow

The century of war shifted the balance of Amerindian regional power from Huronia to Iroquoia. The Five Nations emerged with expanded territory, although not as much as they claimed,[25] and despite extensive adoptions of war captives, the league suffered severe population losses. Between 1689 and 1698, it may have lost up to half of its fighting forces. Desertions to the Montreal settlements of converts contributed to this.[26] Remarkably, the Iroquois still managed to keep their confederacy intact in the face of these disasters and despite the relentless pressures of European settlement. The combination of these factors was changing Iroquois society. For one thing, **longhouses** were being abandoned in favour of single-family living units. Even so, the Iroquois identity remained strong.

Paradoxically, the Five Nations also assured the existence of New France, uniting the colonists and their allies and giving them a common purpose in the face of a common enemy. Indirectly, by knocking out Huronia and its northern trading networks, the Five Nations also facilitated the establishment of the English on Hudson Bay and forced the westward expansion of the French. These outcomes would soon lead to on-again, off-again battles between the French and the English in the North, which had a lasting impact on Amerindian groups although they were not directly involved as allies (see Box 5.1).

The seventeenth-century Ojibwa defeat of the Iroquois as depicted around 1900 in porcupine quills on birchbark by Mesquab (Jonathan Yorke), from the Rama Reserve, Lake Simcoe. Mesquab took the design from a rock painting that once stood at Quarry Point, Lake Couchiching. Working from memory, Mesquab showed two Ojibwa warriors dominating the Mohawk in the centre. According to this picture, the Ojibwa had firearms while the Iroquois did not. *(Ontario Provincial Museum [now the Royal Ontario Museum], Archaeological Report for 1904)*

Lahontan held that it had never been in the interest of New France, either economically or politically, to eliminate the Iroquois despite all the overheated rhetoric to that effect. In fact, by trying to destroy them, the French played into the hands of the English.[27] Other historians have agreed that the French failure to form a stable alliance with the Iroquois was a major factor in their 1760 defeat by the British.

There is no way of knowing the war's toll for the Five Nations. Hit by epidemics, particularly during the 1640s, they had compensated for their losses by adopting and incorporating defeated peoples. This was a technique the Iroquois used very skilfully, but which the Jesuits later would be able to use to polarize Iroquois society.[28]

The death toll eventually outran replacements, especially when the Five Nations suffered mass defections as a result of the Jesuit missionary efforts. During the 1690s, fully two-thirds of the Mohawk decamped for the two French missions around Montreal. Two factors were involved: the mass absorption of conquered peoples that had followed the dispersion of Huronia, and the work of the Jesuits.

Divisions within the Iroquois communities became bitter as missionaries made inroads. Accusing the Jesuits of working for their destruction, traditionalists began a

---

Box 5.1   The War in the Bay (1685–1782)

The struggle between the French and English in Hudson Bay, like the Mi'kmaq War (see below), was a series of disconnected raids, sometimes widely spaced in time and place, rather than a sustained conflict. These did not involve Amerindians as allies, as did the conflicts to the south. However, some posts were destroyed or were unable to meet their trade requirements.[29] The destruction of Fort Prince of Wales in 1782 and the outbreak of disease led the Chipewyan to abandon the area and move southward to Athapaskan country. Eventually, Inuit filtered into the deserted region, which later administrators would label the Keewatin District. Migrating herds of caribou provided the Inuit with a subsistence base. When they began trading with the British and Canadians at interior posts, they became known as Caribou Inuit.[30]

---

successful campaign to drive them out of Iroquoia, although they did not completely root out factionalism.[31] The Jesuits, for their part, encouraged converts to emigrate to such missionary villages as Sault St Louis (Caughnawaga, today's Kahnawake) and Prairie de la Madeleine (Kentake).[32] Within a couple of decades after the end of the conflict, the League of Five Nations became the **League of Six Nations** when the Tuscarora, fleeing from hostilities with settlers in the Carolinas, joined it. As the Iroquois laid down the gauntlet, however, their allies the Fox, one of the larger Algonkian groups of present-day Wisconsin, picked it up.

Fox War (1710–38)

The Fox (Mesquakie, as they referred to themselves; called the Outagami, or 'People of the Other Shore', by the Odawa) were trading partners with the Iroquois and so were becoming involved in the English network. They were the only Algonkians of the upper Great Lakes who opposed the French, largely because the Fox were on bad terms with the Ojibwa, an important French ally. Although the scene of their war, what has come to be called the **Fox War**, was far from the St Lawrence, in the *pays d'en haut*, it would become bitter, with the French seeking to wipe out the enemy.

When Antoine Laumet *dit* Lamothe Cadillac (1658–1730) established a fort at Detroit (called Pontchartrain) the same year that the Five Nations and the French signed their peace in Montreal, he foresaw the fort becoming the hub of the western trade. Already the French were developing trade with the Sioux. This had deeply disturbed their enemies, the Iroquois and the Fox. Cadillac must have been aware of this. Even so, he optimistically invited everyone to establish around his fort, an invitation that outraged the Wyandot, Odawa, and Ojibwa peoples who had settled in the region in the 1670s and 1680s. This outrage turned into a riot in 1706 and the French of-ficials eventually responded by removing Cadillac. In spite of the instability in the region, some Fox accepted Cadillac's invitation in 1710, but the French at the fort were suspicious and watchful. Suspicion soon turned into anger as the Fox began to attack French traders.[33]

The Fox then tried to leave the Green Bay area to join the Iroquois, but the Odawa and Ojibwa pressured the French to send forces to prevent this. The Fox responded in 1711 by blocking the Fox–Wisconsin river system, the main route from the East to the Mississippi and the Sioux. Not only did they cut the French off from access to the southwest, but they also harassed the French allies on their hunting grounds. The French, again at the urging of their Odawa and Ojibwa allies, retaliated, besieging a Fox village for 19 days and killing about a thousand men, women, and children. If the French had hoped that this would cool the situation, they were mistaken.

Finally, in 1716, the French sent out an army, possibly disguised as a trading dele-gation, the first French military expedition to penetrate so far west. Once more, the Fox fortified themselves in a village, and the French destroyed it. The Fox–Wisconsin river system was once again open for traders. Ouchala (*fl.* 1716–27), the pro-French Fox peace chief, led the peace negotiations. Among other terms, the Fox agreed to hunt to pay the costs of the war. To ensure that the Fox carried out these terms, the French took six hostages to Montreal, where two of them died of smallpox. Ouchala then delayed ratifying the agreement. By the time he did so, he was not able to prevail against the mutual recriminations concerning breaking the agreement.

In 1717 the war was rekindled, not only between the Fox and the French but also into a complex of feuds between the Fox and other tribes. As well, it raised tensions between New France and Louisiana, which felt that New France was sacrificing its trading interests.

Kiala Works for Amerindian Unity, and the French Retaliate

A new governor-general, Charles de Beauharnois de la Boische, in office from 1726 to 1747, set out to re-establish French control in the West. Two years later (1728), Paul Marin de la Malgue (1692–1753) became the French leader on the scene, which he would dominate for the next quarter-century. In the midst of the bitter campaigns that followed, the Fox, led by **Kiala** (Quiala, *fl.* 1733–4), moved to reaffirm their alliance with the Iroquois.

Kiala was the war chief who headed the anti-French faction. Seeing the need for Amerindians to unite against the European invasion, during the 1720s, besides the Iroquois, he negotiated with the Chickasaw and Abenaki, confirming old alliances and building new ones. Nescambiouit, the Abenaki chief, was involved in these discus-sions (see Chapter 3). This greatly upset the French, who saw an attempt to encircle them, cutting them off from their allies and separating New France from Louisiana. Consequently, the French went on the offensive.

In 1730, the Fox, harassed on all sides, sent two redstone axes to the Seneca, asking to come and live with them. In spite of French attempts to prevent it, the Seneca agreed, and the Fox began their migration. Cornered in 1730 by the pursuing French under Nicolas-Antoine Coulon de Villiers (1683–1733),[34] they held out for 23 days before attempting a sortie. By now, only a few hundred survived of the 1,300 Fox of a year earlier.[35] The French with their allies set about tracking down the remnants. Some groups fled west of the Mississippi. Villiers, one of his sons, and a son-in-law died in the fighting, setting off yet another punitive French expedition in 1734. This time, however, the French allies decided that matters had gone far enough. They refused to go along with the campaign, which, as a result, came to nothing.

In the meantime, in 1733, the remaining Fox had sued for peace. The following year, Kiala and three other Fox leaders surrendered in Montreal. The French sent one of the chiefs to France for service in the galleys. They sent Kiala as a slave to Martinique but instead abandoned him on the Guyana coast. The Huron of Lorette adopted his wife. The French scattered other Fox prisoners among the missions. Thus ended Kiala's dream of uniting Amerindians from the Atlantic to the Ohio Valley.

Some French allies went to Montreal to plead for their former enemies. They were having second thoughts: what was happening to the Fox could happen to them. During this period, the Sauk reconsidered their position and became such firm allies of the Fox that the two peoples ever since have been referred to together. In the final campaigns of the French, more of their allies sided with the Fox and the Sauk. As Beauharnois expressed it, 'The Savages as a rule greatly fear the French, but they do not love them.'[36]

Peace was finally achieved in 1738. The French confirmed it five years later, when Marin de la Malgue, who had stayed with the Fox in the West, led another delegation to Montreal. The Fox were no longer the enemy. From a nation that had once counted at least a thousand warriors, they could now muster barely 250. Some Fox later joined the French and fought with them against the English, including the 1755 attack that annihilated the British army led by General Edward Braddock (1695–1755) and in the Battle of the Plains of Abraham in 1759.

What can we learn from these two conflicts? For one thing, the French were more effective against the Fox than they had been for most of the war against the Iroquois—because they had adapted to forest fighting techniques. Their system of Amerindian alliances was much less stable in the *pays d'en haut* than it was eastward to the Atlantic coast. In this case, it was the English who had made the necessary adaptations to develop and hold Amerindian alliances. On the Atlantic coast, the French had had a head start and were able to forge firm alliances before the English realized the importance of this form of diplomacy. In the Great Lakes area, however, the English offered stiff competition. Amerindians, on the other hand, were beginning to realize the importance of allying with each other instead of with the invading Europeans. Although pan-Indianism barely got a hesitant start, it was enough to give the French a severe fright.

The Mi'kmaq Defend Their Land (1713–61)

As the final round of the North American colonial wars got underway, the Mi'kmaq pitched into the fray on land and sea, asserting their right to make war or peace as they willed and reaffirming their sovereignty over their land, **Megumaage**. Between 1713 and 1760, they captured well over a hundred vessels, cruising in their captured ships before abandoning them, and forcing their prisoners to serve as crew. They had no use for ships of that size, just as they had no use for artillery. This activity peaked in 1722, the year the English–Indian War broke out. Revivals of lesser proportions in the 1750s followed the establishment of Halifax in 1749 and the expulsion in 1755 of the Acadians, many of whom had blood ties with Amerindians.[37]

The turning point came in 1725, when the Abenaki sued for peace following the destruction of Norridgewock. The British took advantage of the situation to negotiate not only for peace (the Treaty of Boston) but also for a second agreement, Treaty No. 239 (also called **Mascarene's Treaty** after its main British negotiator), detailing how they expected Amerindians to behave as British subjects.[38]

The peace treaty was a blow to the French. Immediately, they claimed that the English–Indian War had not concerned them. However, an apparently unfounded report that a Canadian-born missionary, Antoine Gaulin (1674–1740), was encouraging his Mi'kmaq to sign so annoyed the French that Ile Royale's governor had to come to the missionary's defence.[39]

The treaties called for countermeasures, especially as the allies were complaining that the all-important gift distributions often did not have enough goods to go around. The French steadily increased the budget for this purpose. By 1756, it had reached 37,000 livres, not including 'extraordinary expenses' entailed when employing Amerindians.[40] The Amerindians would no longer accept promises of gifts to come. They would lead their allies only when they had goods in hand. What started as a matter of protocol to cement alliances and trade agreements ended as a means of subsistence for Amerindians and a form of protection for the French.

Even as the French spurred their allies to fight against the English, they did pause from time to time at the '*férocité inutile*' of some of their attacks. Sometimes, they even tried to curb them. In 1739, the governor of Ile Royale, seeking to calm the Amerindians' fears, asked them to keep the peace for the sake of the French King and themselves. The Amerindians, on the other hand, worried that the French and English would unite to destroy them. They observed that if they had listened less to the French, they would be having less trouble with the English, who were taking their lands and destroying their fishing. They promised to be quiet for the present but warned that they would protect themselves against those who tried to destroy them.[41] A decade later, they would have reason to make good on their threat.

The Mi'kmaq Declare War

When the British founded Halifax in 1749 in a district the Mi'kmaq called Segepenegatig, they once more failed to consult the Amerindians. Asking 'Where can we go, if we are

---

Box 5.2   War at Sea and on Land

Several characteristics distinguish the **Mi'kmaq War**. First, it was fought largely at sea. In addition, that part of it fought on land was the only case in Canada where Amerindians fought on their own lands for their own lands. In this aspect, the war in its later phases came to resemble the frontier wars in the US. Despite the fact that the Mi'kmaq and Wuastukwiuk have had one of the longest contacts with Europeans, and despite the protracted hostilities, they still are living on their ancestral lands, although only on a tiny fraction of what was once theirs.

---

to be deprived of our lands?' the Mi'kmaq adopted a European custom and formally declared war (see Box 5.2).[42] To the English, the Mi'kmaq simply were rebels.[43]

Mi'kmaq raids were effective enough for the governor to request more arms for the colonists, as 'at present above ten thousand people are awed by two hundred savages.' As the raids intensified, he issued a proclamation commanding the settlers 'to Annoy, distress, take or destroy the Savages commonly called Mic-macks, wherever they are found'.[44]

During this period, both French and English paid bounties for scalps at escalating rates, no questions asked.[45] In the midst of all this, for a brief period, the British officially encouraged marriages to Amerindian women.[46] They also gave in to the inevitable and began to be more generous in their gift distributions. This influenced the Wuastukwiuk and Abenaki of the Saint John River, in 1749, to ratify Mascarene's Treaty. The French tried to answer this by sending René, a chief from Naltigonish, to act as a counter-agent, but without success.[47]

Despite their efforts, in 1752 the French received ominous news: a ranking chief from Shubenacadie had signed a peace treaty in Halifax.[48] This treaty was a major breakthrough, not only in its effect on the course of the Mi'kmaq War but also in the terms of the treaty itself. It guaranteed hunting and fishing rights for the Amerindians and regular gift distributions. These gifts, later, would be transformed into annuity payments for surrendered lands.

The Mi'kmaq, Wuastukwiuk, and Abenaki See Their Allies Lose Ground

Further south, the fall of Fort William Henry (at Lake George, New York) in 1757—and the murder of English prisoners by French allies that followed—raised settler hysteria against Amerindians to such a pitch that when Louisbourg fell in 1758, the victorious British refused to include Amerindians in the terms of surrender. The Amerindians correctly saw this as not boding well for them, and when the British formally took over the fortress, not one Amerindian was present.

If the Amerindian factor had simply faded at Louisbourg, however, this was not true for Acadia generally. The British now had to make sure that the peace agreement included all chiefs and their people, if a general peace were to be achieved. It took the final defeat of the French in 1760 to accomplish this. A year later, they signed the peace. The Mi'kmaq, Wuastukwiuk, and Abenaki of Acadia finally acknowledged British sovereignty. In return, they were assured that they would have the full protection of British laws just as any other subject 'as long as the sun and the moon shall endure'.[49]

In this long struggle, Mi'kmaq, Wuastukwiuk, and Abenaki had shown themselves astute in turning imperial rivalries to their own advantage. After all, when it came to self-interest, there was not much to choose between Amerindians and the colonial powers. The difference lay in the fact that both France and Britain were building empires, whereas Amerindians, after a brief initial period when some tried to use European alliances to expand their own territory, soon found themselves struggling to survive. Their ability to keep the colonial powers off balance became their most formidable weapon. In this, Louisbourg's role was vital.

For the French, whatever their original intentions for building the fortress, Louisbourg's greatest military usefulness turned out to be as a headquarters for the maintenance of Amerindian alliances and the encouragement of their guerrilla warfare. For the Mi'kmaq and Wuastukwiuk, it represented a reprieve from European economic and cultural domination, because as guerrillas they were able to dictate to a surprising extent their terms as allies, particularly with the French.

The spectre of French return to Canada continued to haunt the British until the defeat of Napoleon at Waterloo in 1815. An episode in 1762 did much to keep this fear alive, when the French invested St John's, Newfoundland, for a couple of months. Hearing this news, the Mi'kmaq became edgy, giving settlers a severe fright. Reports that French from the islands of St Pierre and Miquelon off the south coast of Newfoundland were secretly supplying the Mi'kmaq also fuelled these fears, but those rumours were never substantiated. It seems that the Mi'kmaq had gone to the islands, which remained under French control, looking for priests and supplies. The French were under orders to discourage such visits, on the ground that they would only annoy the British and would serve no purpose;[50] but they seem to have helped the Mi'kmaq anyway.

Thrown back on their own resources when traditional territories had long since been overhunted, and with gift distributions cut off, the Mi'kmaq were now desperately searching for a means of subsistence. Groups went to southern Newfoundland, alarming settlers and authorities alike. In spite of official attempts to dislodge them, however, they had come to stay.[51] This once assertive, far-ranging people on sea and land now had to take what they could get, and that was not very much. In fact, the process was in reverse. Settlers were now streaming into the homelands the Mi'kmaq had fought so hard to protect.

Important Names and Terms

Fox War
Great Peace of Montreal
guerrilla warfare
Iroquois War
Kiala
League of Six Nations

longhouse
Mascarene's Treaty
Megumaage
Mi'kmaq War
Mourning War

Study Questions

1) Why did the French fight inter-tribal rather than inter-racial wars?
2) Define the term 'Mourning War'.
3) What were the causes of the Fox War?
4) What were the war aims of the French and British in the Mi'kmaq War? Study Questions

Recommended Readings

Brandão, José Antonió. *Your Fyre Shall Burn No More: Iroquois Policy toward New France and Its Native Allies to 1701*. Lincoln: University of Nebraska Press, 1997.

Coates, Kenneth S., and William R. Morrison, eds. *For Purposes of Dominion*. Toronto: Captus University Publications, 1989.

Dickason, Olive Patricia. 'Louisbourg and the Indians: A Study in Imperial Race Relations, 1713–1760', *History and Archaeology* 6 (1976): 1–206.

Edmunds, David, and Joseph L. Peyser. *The Fox Wars: The Mesquakie Challenge to New France*. Norman: University of Oklahoma Press, 1993.

Hunt, George T. *The Wars of the Iroquois*. Madison: University of Wisconsin Press, 1967.

Jennings, Francis. *The Ambiguous Iroquois Empire*. New York: Norton, 1984.

Kenyon, W.A., and J.R. Turnbull. *The Battle for the Bay 1686*. Toronto: Macmillan, 1971.

MacLeod, D. Peter. *The Canadian Iroquois and the Seven Years War*. Toronto: Dundurn Press, 1996.

Richter, Daniel K. *The Ordeal of the Longhouse: The Peoples of the Iroquois League in the Era of European Colonization*. Chapel Hill: University of North Carolina Press, 1992.

6 | The World Shifts

Defeated by Peace

The defeat of France in the New World was a disaster for many Amerindians, from the east coast to the Great Lakes and even westward. Besides depriving them of their bargaining position between two rival powers, it also cut them off with brutal suddenness from their 'presents'. To make matters worse, although the defeat of the French at Montreal in 1760 guaranteed Amerindians (particularly Britain's allies) protection for the lands they inhabited, the colonies did not enforce the agreement.[1]

British Commander-in-Chief Jeffrey Amherst (1717–97) lost no time introducing economies after the fall of Montreal. Among the first items to be cut were the gift distributions. After all, now that the French were gone, the British did not need their Amerindian allies. In Amerindian eyes, however, the annual gift-giving ceremonies not only symbolized the renewal of English–Amerindian alliances, they also were the agreed-on price by which the Amerindians allowed the English to use their lands.

To complicate matters, Amerindians had come to depend on such items as guns and ammunition. **Sir William Johnson** (Warraghiyagey, 'He Who Does Much Business'), northern superintendent for Amerindian affairs from 1755 to 1774, strongly advised Amherst against the cutback,[2] but Amherst did not listen. In coastal regions, the continuing activities of French trading ships further complicated the situation.[3] The general situation was such, however, that gift-giving remained a practical necessity and continued until 1858.

Britain had led her Amerindian allies to believe that once they drove the French out, encroaching settlers also would go and the Amerindians would get better trade deals. Instead, however, more settlers than ever moved into their territories,[4] and British traders raised their prices, claiming that they had sold unprofitably low during the war.

During hostilities, the British co-operated with Amerindian leaders in limiting the liquor trade to preserve them as allies. With peace, they lost interest in protecting the Amerindians from the traffic that was so harmful to them yet highly profitable

Time Line

1760	Fall of Montreal to British. British Commander-in-Chief Jeffrey Amherst ends 'gift' distributions to Amerindians.	1765	Pontiac signs separate agreement but does not give up Amerindian lands.
1760s–70s	Pan-Indian alliance, the Federation of Seven Fires, forms to resist loss of lands to settlers, but does not survive colonial distrust and US War of Independence.	1766	Ratification of agreements at Fort Ontario, at which Pontiac dominates.
		1769	Pontiac murdered by Illinois tribesman.
1762	Amerindian alliance, led by Pontiac, Odawa war chief, lays siege to Fort Detroit for five months.	1774	Quebec Act brings Ohio Valley and Great Lakes region under Quebec jurisdiction; Americans object that their legitimate expansion is being thwarted.
1763	Treaty of Paris effectively ends French presence in North America. Proclamation of 1763 at least partially acknowledges Amerindian territorial rights. Nine British forts, including Fort Michilimackinac, fall to Amerindians in May–June. Neolin, 'The Delaware Prophet', calls to drive Europeans back into the sea. Amherst proposes giving smallpox-infested blankets to the Odawa and Ojibwa.	1775	American invasion of eastern Canada repulsed for two weeks by Iroquois.
		1776–83	Amerindians caught up on both sides of US War of Independence.
		1783	Peace of Paris to end conflict between Britain and Thirteen Colonies completely ignores Amerindians.
1764	Peace conference at Fort Niagara formed by Sir William Johnson: 2,000 Amerindians from 19 tribes respond, but Pontiac does not go.	1784	Loyalist Iroquois granted Six Nations Reserve (Haldimand Grant) on Grand River in Upper Canada after cession of 3 million acres on Niagara Peninsula.
		late 1700s– early 1800s	Millions of acres in present-day southern and central Ontario ceded by Ojibwa and Odawa.

to the settlers.[5] Traders swarmed into Amerindian territory, where all too often they behaved badly. The Amerindians were powerless to control them, and colonial governments did not bother to do so.[6] Even though, in the words of Peter Wraxall, New York's secretary for Indian Affairs, 1750–9, trade was 'the chief Cement which binds us together', it had its perils both for Amerindians and for whites. Nonetheless, trade was the 'first Principle of our whole System of Indian politics'.[7]

The Amerindians, on whichever side they found themselves, saw the struggle between the French and English as the concern of the combatants, involving them only as fighting allies. They did not know that their lands were at stake. As more than one chief remarked, no one had conquered the Amerindians. This land was their land, and they had allowed the Europeans to come and settle on it under certain conditions, such as the gift distributions. Ojibwa chief Minweweh (Minavavana, c. 1710–70), 'The one of the silver tongue' also known as 'Le Grand Sauteur', who fought alongside the French, voiced a general sentiment when he told the British:

> Although you have conquered the French, you have not conquered us. We are not your slaves. These lakes, these woods and mountains were left us by our ancestors. They are our inheritance, and we will part with them to none.[8]

The British, uneasily aware of Amerindian fears about losing their lands, eventually moved to reassure them by at least partially acknowledging their territorial rights in the **Proclamation of 1763**, which today is embedded in the Canadian Charter of Rights and Freedoms (Constitution Act, 1982, section 25[a]).

Before this, however, discontent spread and rumours flew. Why were the British denying Amerindians the guns and ammunition they needed for the hunt, if not to wipe them out? Why were settlers being allowed to take over Amerindian lands? Even worse were the techniques that the newcomers were using to 'purchase' Amerindian lands and the extent of the lands involved. In 1756, Johnson warned about the effects of such practices. As the Amerindians observed to George Croghan (d. 1782), a successful trader who for 15 years was Johnson's right-hand man, 'in either case they would lose their Lands, & the consideration they got was soon spent, altho' the Lands remained', but in the hands of the non-Aboriginals.[9]

An Amerindian resistance loomed alarmingly close. At councils, tribal nations met to share their grievances. Out of this coalesced the **Federation of Seven Fires** (also called the Seven Nations of Canada), an alliance network linking French mission Amerindians.[10] The central fire was maintained at Kahnawake, where the members gathered every three years. The confederacy did not survive the dislocations of the US War of Independence or colonial distrust of anything that smacked of pan-Indianism, a movement first proposed by Pontiac aimed at uniting all Amerindians against the British.[11]

Colonial officials knew the causes of Native unrest.[12] A British plan to control the traders by restricting trade to the posts and to eliminate rum failed. Amerindian resentment reached the boiling point. Johnson, in alarm, called a general peace conference at Detroit in 1761. Just before it opened, he received a letter from Amherst forbidding gift-giving. Johnson considered the decision so unwise he ignored it for the moment. The truth was not long in coming out, however, as other expected distributions did not take place. By the spring of 1762, Amerindians were short of goods, particularly of ammunition.

Pontiac

Out of this troubled situation emerged Pontiac (Ponteack, Pontiague, Obwandiyag, 1712/1725–69), an Odawa war chief. We do not know much about him, and we have

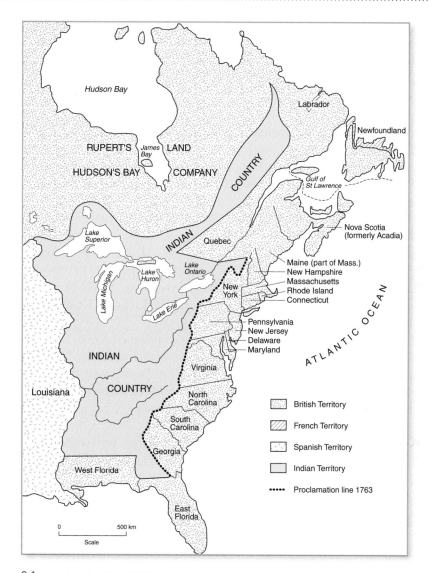

6.1 Proclamation line of 1763

Source: Waldman, *Atlas of the North American Indian*.

only a vague idea of what he looked like.[13] His personality gave rise to contradictory reports. To some, he was imperious of manner, 'proud, vindictive, warlike, and very easily offended'.[14] However, Major Robert Rogers (1731–95), who went to Detroit in the fall of 1760 with 200 of his famous Rangers, and who had reason to be grateful to Pontiac for having prevented his warriors from attacking the British contingent, found him to be a man of 'great strength of judgment and a thirst after knowledge'.[15] Pontiac seems to have supported a movement among the Amerindians that claimed a spiritual vision had called for a return to the ways of their ancestors. Like Nescambiouit of the Abenaki and Kiala of the Fox before him, Pontiac saw the need for united action against the Europeans. Also like Kiala, he was unable to achieve it on a large enough scale to change the course of events.

According to Major Rogers, Pontiac was prepared not only to accept British settlement but even to encourage it. He expected, however, to be treated with respect and honour.[16] Although he had fought on the side of the French, when Montreal fell Pontiac quickly moved to establish good relations with the British, on the strength of the latter's promises of better treatment in trade. When that did not happen, he again turned to the French, this time those who had remained in the Old Northwest, but they refused to co-operate with their former ally.

During the summer of 1762, a war belt and hatchet circulated through the Old Northwest. Resentment had been building for well over a year, encouraged by the French residents still in the area. That fall, the Seneca struck the first blow by killing two traders. A month later, two British soldiers were killed in the Ohio Valley. Pontiac, after a series of wins against the English, tried to take Fort Detroit by a ruse, but his plan was betrayed. Pontiac then laid a siege—an unusual action for Amerindians—that lasted five months.[17]

Pontiac appears to have supported a movement among the Amerindians that claimed a spiritual vision had called for the return to the ways of their ancestors. This was an early manifestation of **nativistic movements** by which Amerindians sought to cope with the invasion of their lands and missionary pressures against their way of life. Neolin ('One That Is Four', fl. 1760s), one of two known as 'The Delaware Prophet', urged his people to abstain completely from contact with whites: 'I warn you, that if you allow the English among you, you are dead, maladies, smallpox, and their poison will destroy you totally.'[18]

Minweweh and Madjeckewiss (Machiquawish, among other variations, c. 1735–c. 1805) had better luck with a similar ruse against Fort Michilimackinac, at the Straits of Mackinac connecting lakes Huron and Michigan. There, warriors organized a lacrosse game that allowed them to gain entrance to the fort and overwhelm its garrison. Between 16 May and 20 June 1763, nine British forts fell. The only posts in the war zone still in British hands were those at Detroit (Pontiac's men had given up by the end of October), Niagara, and Fort Pitt.

An expeditionary force under Colonel Henry Bouquet (1719–65), a Swiss-born officer who had learned something from Indian tactics, rescued Fort Pitt. Bouquet taught his troops to move while firing, to form a circle when pressed, and to use the bayonet, a weapon that Amerindians did not generally adopt. Despite the British success in this hard-fought engagement, by the end of the summer the Amerindians were in control of most of the Old Northwest. The system of garrisoned forts had not proven effective, and the result would be the most formidable Amerindian uprising that the British would face during the eighteenth century.

Neolin's call to drive the Europeans back into the sea seemed to be on its way to success. In his exhortations, he used a diagram painted on deerskin to show how non-Aboriginals were blocking Indians from the enjoyment of their lands.[19] As his influence rose, so did that of Pontiac despite his failure at Detroit. Prominent as he was, however, Pontiac does not seem to have been the originator of the revolt, which was more in the nature of a spontaneous combustion.[20]

Amherst's immediate reaction was to underestimate both its scope and importance. He did not have much regard for Amerindians and at first did not believe they were capable of such feats. When, finally, he was convinced, he urged the British to use every method against them, even distributing smallpox-infected blankets and the use of drugs. Those who were wise in the ways of Amerindians counselled patience, as the fire would burn itself out. The Amerindians had no use for the forts they were taking. They were after the supplies.

Indeed, the winter of 1763–4 passed without serious incident, as the Amerindians dispersed to their hunting grounds equipped with pillaged goods. When they began to run short, especially of ammunition, some voluntarily brought back prisoners in a gesture for peace. Others returned to their British alliance. The British, however, had revenge on their minds and sent out retaliatory expeditions, but they soon learned that revenge was not a realistic policy. Not only were Amerindians hard to find, even when they were located, all the British could do was either kill them or deprive them of their horses and possessions, neither of which served the purpose. Amerindian losses during the resistance were probably low. In contrast, the settlers counted about 2,000 killed or captured and tremendous property damage. Despite the toll, however, European settlement was not seriously deterred, and the fur trade had been affected hardly at all.

Johnson tried to resolve the situation by convoking a peace conference at Fort Niagara in 1764. About 2,000 Amerindians from 19 tribes answered his call, but Pontiac was not among them. Johnson's technique was to divide and conquer, dealing with each tribe separately. Among other items, he asked them to return all prisoners immediately, compensate traders for their losses, and break off relations with enemies of the British. Amerindians would submit future grievances to the commandant at Detroit. An important item was a schedule of values for trade goods.

The following year, 1765, Pontiac signed a separate agreement, in which he stipulated that France's surrender of its forts to the English did not mean that the English could automatically take over the Indians' land, as the French had been only tenants of the Amerindians. He agreed that the British could reoccupy their forts, but hunting grounds must remain undisturbed.

When the final ratification of the agreements took place in 1766, Pontiac was a dominant figure. Johnson let him speak on behalf of all, however, which did not sit well with the other chiefs. From then on, Pontiac's influence rapidly diminished. Three years later, an Illinois tribesman, said to have been bribed by an English trader, murdered him. Contrary to expectations, apart from some isolated killings, Pontiac's death did not ignite general inter-tribal warfare.[21] Still, the quiet that settled over the frontier was not a peaceful one for either the Amerindians or the frontiersmen.

The Mohawk: Forced to Choose between the British and the Americans

Amerindians had held the balance of power between two imperial rivals when France was present. Now, they found themselves jockeying for position between an imperial power, Great Britain, and her restive Thirteen Colonies, which would soon gain their independence as the United States of America. Under the earlier arrangement, both Britain and France had something to gain from Amerindian alliances. In the new situation, only Britain at first found it useful to court such arrangements. In this regard, she had stepped into France's shoes, not always a comfortable fit.

The **Quebec Act of 1774** brought the Ohio Valley and Great Lakes region under the jurisdiction of Quebec. This meant that the headquarters of the fur trade transferred from Albany to Montreal. (This shift in colonial administration superseded the arrangement contained in the Proclamation of 1763. Later, the argument would be made that it also abrogated the Proclamation's measures in respect to Indian lands, but this argument was not sustained. For further discussion of the Royal Proclamation, see below and Chapter 16.)

The British assured the Amerindians that they were protecting their territory against the illegal encroachments of settlers. The Thirteen Colonies saw things differently: they felt that they were being deliberately thwarted in a legitimate expansion. For them, the Quebec Act was provocation enough to launch their War of Independence. In 1775, Massachusetts entered into negotiations with the Mi'kmaq and Penobscots. The following year, a group of Mi'kmaq signed a treaty at Watertown, agreeing to send men to the American army. Most of the people opposed this treaty, however, and the Mi'kmaq quickly disavowed it. Using the American precedent as an excuse, General Thomas Gage, commander-in-chief of the British forces from 1763 to 1775, ordered Guy Carleton, governor of Quebec, 1766–77, to use Amerindians on the frontier. Instead, Carleton delayed. For one thing, the fur trade was booming, and Britain was building trading posts in the West.[22]

In eastern Canada, the story was different. Americans invaded in 1775, bringing the Iroquois of Kahnawake into the conflict. The Amerindians fought off two assaults but became convinced that the British were sacrificing them to save their own troops and went home. Even so, they had delayed the American invasion by nearly two weeks.

Amerindians, particularly the Iroquois, were by now deep in the conflict despite efforts to maintain the neutrality they had decided on at the beginning of the century. This split the League of Six Nations. The Mohawk, guided by the influential Mary Brant (Konwatsi?tsiaié'nni, c. 1736–96) and her younger brother, the war chief Joseph (Thayendanegea, 1743–1807), were pro-British.[23] (Joseph had made a trip to England in 1775, during which he had been lionized by British society.) So were the Cayuga. The Mohawk's 'little brothers', the Oneida, and the Tuscarora favoured the Americans.[24] The Seneca and Onondaga were divided. Lines were fluid, as inner dissensions increased. External relations also suffered, and attempts to form a united Amerindian front got nowhere. As the Iroquois phrased it, the White Tree of Peace had been uprooted.[25] On top of that, Amerindians had to face once more the unpleasant fact that siding with the losing side in a European-style war meant loss of lands.

The peace that Great Britain and the United States signed in Paris in 1783 completely ignored the Amerindians. It made no provisions for their lands in the transfer of territory to the Americans. In particular, the cession of the Ohio Valley aroused a violent reaction on the part of British allies. Americans, on the other hand, flatly rejected proposals for the establishment of a separate indigenous state. The Iroquois observed bitterly that they had not been defeated in the war, but they certainly were by the peace.

Posts and Proclamations

The British, in an effort to please their allies, did not evacuate the western posts as provided for in the treaty, a stance that led to prolonged wrangling with the Americans.[26] For Amerindians dislodged by the war, the posts became a refuge, as 2,000 fled to them during the winter of 1784.[27] For the 5,000 or so Iroquois refugees who congregated between the Genesee River and Niagara, the British negotiated with the Mississauga, as they called the Ojibwa on the north shore of Lake Ontario, and purchased land along the Grand River in Upper Canada (Ontario). (Although the original grant of 1784 has been much reduced since, the Six Nations are still there.)

American pressure eventually forced the British to abandon the western posts, which they did in 1796. For the Amerindians, this meant the loss of a buffer against the steadily increasing pressures from the east. On the positive side, however, the treaty provided for unhindered passage for Indians over the border between Canada and the United States, and exempted them from taxes on personal goods. These have not been provisions that either side has been careful to honour. The treaty did not apply to the Amerindians of Rupert's Land, the vast expanse to the north controlled by the Hudson's Bay Company.[28]

Long before the uprising, the British recognized that pressures on land as well as 'the shameful manner' in which trade was conducted in Amerindian territory were inciting Native reaction. Following the defeat of France, even before the terms of the **Treaty of Paris** were concluded in 1763, officials moved to correct the situation by means of a series of proclamations.[29]

The first one, in 1761, issued to the governors of Nova Scotia, New Hampshire, New York, North and South Carolina, and Georgia, forbade them to grant lands or make settlements that would interfere with Amerindians bordering on those colonies. Settlers found to be unlawfully established upon Amerindian lands were to be evicted. There would also be no more sales of Amerindian lands without a licence, which would be issued only if the Commissioners for Trade and Plantations in London approved.

In 1762, Britain reasserted an earlier proclamation, that the Mi'kmaq had a right to use the sea coast from Cape Fronsac 'onwards'. Hardly had this proclamation been issued, however, than the French blockade of St John's during the summer of 1762 rendered the reservation of coastal territories for the Mi'kmaq meaningless. The Proclamation of 1763, following hard on the heels of the Peace of Paris of that same year, was slow in coming as a result of such continuing confrontations as the Mi'kmaq War. However, conflict in the Far Northwest speeded up the process.[30]

Box 6.1   Excerpt from the Royal Proclamation of 1763

And whereas it is just and reasonable, and essential to our Interest, and the security of our Colonies, that the several Nations or Tribes of Indians with whom We are connected, and who live under our protection, should not be molested or disturbed in the Possession of such Parts of Our Dominions and Territories as, not having been ceded to or purchased by Us, are reserved to them or any of them, as their Hunting Grounds—We do therefore, with the Advice of our Privy Council, declare it to be our Royal Will and Pleasure, that no Governor or Commander in Chief in any of our Colonies of Quebec, East Florida, or West Florida, do presume, upon any Pretence whatever, to grant Warrants of Survey, or pass any Patents for Lands beyond the Bounds of their respective Governments, as described in their Commissions; as also that no Governor or Commander in Chief in any of our other Colonies or Plantations in America do presume for the present, and until our further Pleasure be Known, to grant Warrants of Survey, or pass Patents for any Lands beyond the Heads or Sources of any of the Rivers which fall into the Atlantic Ocean from the West and North West, or upon any Lands whatever, which, not having been ceded to or purchased by Us as aforesaid, are reserved to the said Indians, or any of them.

And We do further declare it to be Our Royal Will and Pleasure, for the present as aforesaid, to reserve under our Sovereignty, Protection, and Dominion, for the use of the said Indians, all the Lands and Territories not included within the Limits of Our Said Three New Governments, or within the Limits of the Territory granted to the Hudson's Bay Company, as also all the Lands and Territories lying to the Westward of the Sources of the Rivers which fall into the Sea from the West and North West as aforesaid;

And We do hereby strictly forbid, on Pain of our Displeasure, all our loving Subjects from making any Purchases or Settlements whatever, or taking Possession of any of the Lands above reserved, without our especial leave and Licence for the Purpose first obtained.

And, We do further strictly enjoin and require all Persons whatever who have either wilfully or inadvertently seated themselves upon any lands within the Countries above described, or upon any other Lands which, not having been ceded to or purchased by Us, are still reserved to the said Indians as aforesaid, forthwith to remove themselves from such Settlements.

And Whereas Great Frauds and Abuses have been committed in purchasing Lands of the Indians, to the Great Prejudice of our Interests, and to the Great Dissatisfaction of the said Indians; In order, therefore, to prevent such Irregularities for the future, and to the End that the Indians may be convinced of our justice and determined Resolution to remove all reasonable Cause of Discontent, We do, with the Advice of our Privy Council strictly enjoin and require, that no private Person do presume to make any Purchase from the said Indians of any Lands reserved to the said Indians, within those parts of our Colonies where, We have thought proper to allow Settlement; but that, if at any Time any of the said Indians should be inclined to dispose of the said Lands, the same shall be Purchased only for Us, in our Name, at some public Meeting or Assembly of the said Indians, to be held for the Purpose by the Governor or Commander in Chief of our Colony respectively within which they shall lie; and in case they shall lie within the limits of any Proprietary Government, they shall be purchased only for the Use and in the name of such Proprietaries, conformable to such Directions and Instructions as We or they shall think proper to give for the Purpose. . . .

Even though the British originally saw it as a temporary measure, to make it operative they had to work out agreements as to where the boundaries lay between Amerindian territory and the colonies. The process took five years and involved 10 treaties.[31] The Proclamation (see Box 6.1) provided that all lands that had not been ceded to or purchased by Britain and that formed part of British North America were 'reserved lands' for the indigenes. In practice, this meant lands beyond the Appalachian Mountains and the western borders of Quebec, about a third of the North American interior, although the Proclamation did not define its western boundaries. The British seem to have meant it to apply to the Maritime colonies as well, but those governments ignored it.[32] It did not apply to Quebec or British Columbia, but did include lands within established colonies that had not yet been ceded, purchased, or set aside for Amerindians. It also did not apply to Rupert's Land, whatever its boundaries were, which was under the jurisdiction of the HBC. Neither was it operative in the Arctic, which, in any event, had a different land-use pattern. The Crown reserved to itself the right to extinguish **'Indian title'**, resurrecting a policy legislated in Virginia in 1655 but that had fallen into disuse.

In the legal terminology of the day, 'Indian title' meant rights of occupancy and use, not ownership. Britain assumed that she held underlying sovereign title. The areas that interested the Crown specifically were those that had potential for settlement. However, it wanted to prevent 'unjust Settlement and fraudulent Purchase' of Indian lands, thus slowing the pace of colonization to keep the peace on the frontier. This protection did not extend to unceded Mi'kmaq and Wuastukwiuk lands, however, because the British still persisted in their view, dealt with in Chapter 3, that their title had already been extinguished twice over—first by French occupation and then by the Treaty of Utrecht.[33]

A question that arose later is whether the Proclamation recognized a pre-existing title or created it.[34] There was a movement in the courts towards the position that Amerindian title preceded colonization, but recent decisions have seen Amerindian rights as arising out of the Proclamation (see Chapter 16).

The English Approach to Treaties

The English, not trusting oral agreements, insisted on European-style written treaties. In relying on European traditions, they assumed that Amerindian societies had hierarchies and centralized authorities.[35] As this usually did not fit with the political realities of the communities they met, however, they, too, had to adapt. Sometimes, they entered into unwritten agreements, but they preferred not to.

Even with the written treaties, moreover, it is not clear what legal status the English gave them, even at the time. As far as we know, the English put none of these treaties through the procedure in the British Parliament that they usually did for international agreements, nor have Canadian courts acknowledged them as such. The colonizers admitted 'Indian title' but did not agree as to what it included. They did agree, however, that a 'savage' could never exercise valid sovereignty. Only peoples living within organized states could do that. Some Europeans further specified that the states had to be Christian. The legal nature of the treaties has never been fully clarified.[36]

The first British treaties that included Amerindians in what is now Canada was the Treaty of Portsmouth, New Hampshire, signed in 1713 and involving Amerindians of the Saint John River, largely Wuastukwiuk but perhaps also some Mi'kmaq and Abenaki. The treaty was for peace and friendship, similar to previous agreements. It also broke new ground by adding that the British would not interfere within the territories where they lived, and the Amerindians would enjoy 'free liberty for Hunting, Fishing, Fowling, and all other [of] their Lawful Liberties & Privileges'.[37]

The British repeated these provisions in the Treaty of Boston, 1725 (see Chapter 3). This treaty included Mi'kmaq of Cape Sable and other areas, as well as Wuastukwiuk. At the same time, the British took advantage of the disarray of Indians following the defeat at Norridgewock to insist on another agreement, Treaty No. 239 (Mascarene's Treaty).[38] Its purpose was to get Mi'kmaq, Wuastukwiuk, and Abenaki to agree that the Treaty of Utrecht made the British Crown 'the rightful possessor of the Province of Nova Scotia or Acadia according to ancient boundaries'.[39]

That the British took such measures to get the Amerindians to 'acknowledge His said Majesty King George's jurisdiction and dominion over the territories of the said Province of Nova Scotia or Acadia' and submit to him indicates the troubles they were having in this regard. However, the Amerindians did not accept that one could sign for all. At most, a chief could sign for his immediate band, and then only if its members agreed. In the case of the two treaties signed at Boston, this meant arranging ratifications and confirmations. Tracking down the chiefs and their bands was a slow process that at first did not much influence the course of the Mi'kmaq War.

As well, negotiations had to be conducted through interpreters,[40] who, as Recollect missionary Sagard observed, often missed the point either from 'ignorance or contempt, which is a very dangerous thing as it has often led to big accidents'.[41] Compounding the problems were grave difficulties in translating concepts, such as that of exclusive landownership, which had no counterpart in Amerindian languages. This situation was never satisfactorily resolved throughout the treaty-making period. As confusions—and deceptions—proliferated, so did suspicion and distrust on both sides.

Annuities first appeared in the Halifax Treaty of 1752, signed with the Shubenacadie band of Mi'kmaq. It promised regular gift distributions, probably an indication of the importance the British attached to this treaty, which was a major break in the prolonged hostilities with the Mi'kmaq. It also acknowledged the Mi'kmaq's right to 'free liberty of Hunting and Fishing as usual' and 'to trade to the best Advantage'.[42] During negotiations, the Mi'kmaq chief, Major Jean-Baptiste (Joseph) Cope (Coppe, d. 1758/60), said that 'the Indians should be paid for the land the English had settled upon in this country.'[43] The British, however, were not yet ready to agree, at least in Nova Scotia, for reasons already noted. The peace established by the treaty soon ended, however, when Mi'kmaq killed two Englishmen.

The 1763 Treaty of Paris formally ended the presence of the French in continental North America when, as one historian put it, they handed over the largest extent of territory ever covered 'by any treaty dealing with the American hemisphere before or since'.[44]

From 'Peace and Friendship' to Land Transfers

After the 1763 Proclamation, treaties and administration took on a different character. Priorities changed—instead of being primarily concerned with peace and secondarily (if at all) with land issues, treaties now focused primarily on land. This was a direct result of the Proclamation's reservation to the Crown of the right to acquire Indian lands, which from then on would take place only by a treaty negotiated at a public meeting. The British would sign land cession treaties with the Aboriginal peoples of central and western Canada but not with those of the east or west coasts, the Atlantic provinces, Lower Canada (Quebec), or the Arctic. Amerindians have formally ceded about one-half of Canada's lands to the government.[45]

The year following the Proclamation saw two treaties negotiated in Upper Canada that gave the British use of the portage at Niagara Falls in return for a trade agreement. Other provisions were similar to those of earlier treaties in other areas. The Amerindians were to keep the peace with the British, avoid helping the enemy, help in the defence of British posts and supply routes, and return prisoners of war.

The first was with the Huron/Wyandot of the Detroit/Windsor region, the other with the Seneca.[46] In 1781, the British renegotiated the second treaty with the Mississauga, whom the British now recognized as the rightful owners of the land in question, a strip six kilometres wide along the west bank of the Niagara River. The price agreed on by Wabakinine (Wabacoming, d. 1796) and other chiefs was 'three hundred suits of clothing'.[47] Further surrenders quickly followed. Between 1815 and 1825, Indians signed nine treaties, giving up almost the entire peninsula between lakes Ontario, Erie, and Huron.[48] At first, these treaties were for parcels of land for specific projects.

Until 1798, the government had no problem in obtaining surrenders for about three pence an acre in either cash or goods, although the value of 'wild' land was estimated at from six to 15 pence an acre.[49] At that time, Upper Canada was the western frontier. The British did not record some of the transactions properly, and many were imprecise in their terms or in regard to boundaries, giving rise to later disputes. They soon formed the vast majority of the 483 treaties listed for Canada in 1912, although little more than 20 of the 30 or so major ones account for most of Ontario's geographical area.

A harbinger of the huge land cession treaties that would begin with the Robinson agreements of 1850 was the accord Wabakinine and other chiefs reached with Frederick Haldimand, governor of Quebec, 1778–86, for the Niagara Peninsula in 1784. By it, the Amerindians 'sold' three million acres of land (1.2 million hectares) to the Crown for £1,180 in goods. The purpose was to provide land for the Iroquois loyalists who had sided with the British during the American War of Independence and so had lost their land. Haunted by the fear of an Amerindian war, the British had moved quickly to reassure Iroquois loyalists that Britain had not abandoned them.[50]

By far the largest portion of the territory acquired from the Mississauga went to **Joseph Brant** and his followers. The Iroquois received a tract six miles deep on either side of the Grand River beginning at its mouth—a total of 2,842,480 acres (1,150,311 hectares), 'which them and their posterity are to enjoy forever' (for further details, see Chapter 18). Known as the **Haldimand Grant**, it provided the land base for the Six Nations Reserve.[51] A 1785 reserve census enumerated a population of 1,843. Mohawk were in the majority, with 448 persons counted. Onondaga accounted for 245, Oneida for 162, Tuscarora, 129, and Seneca, 78. Various tribes, such as Delaware and Creek, among others, made up the rest.[52]

There followed a long struggle between the government and Brant as to land policies. Brant held that the Iroquois had a **fee simple title**, which included the right to sell and lease to private individuals. He argued that the hunting way of life was no longer sustainable in that region and that the only source of income available to the Iroquois was from the sale of parts of their grant. He also wanted to establish non-Amerindian farmers amid his people to teach them the settlers' agricultural techniques.

Brant eventually won his argument, but the result was a severe erosion of the original grant. Eventually, 381,480 acres (154,379 hectares) were sold for three to six shillings an acre.[53] Brant lost considerably on all counts, as many of his transactions were never formalized legally. Besides, it was one thing to sell to private purchasers at high prices but quite another to collect from them.[54]

One effect of his dealings was to increase substantially the price of land.[55] The government, alarmed, went back to its former policy of curtailing Amerindian rights to sell their lands. On top of all that, documents related to the original grant went missing, and a government survey of the reserve in 1791 ruled that it was much smaller than that described by the Haldimand Grant, stopping far short of the river's source.[56] The Simcoe Deed of 1793 confirmed what remained. Other Iroquois leaders, with fewer followers, received smaller grants, such as that of Tyendinaga Reserve at the Bay of Quinte to Mohawk Captain John Deserontyon (Desoronto, Odeserundiye, c. 1740s–1811) and his band of 200. Thus, the Iroquois returned to the lands that other branches of their people had once occupied.

Large-scale land cessions also became the order of the day for the Ojibwa and the closely related Odawa between Lake Erie and the Thames River in Upper Canada. For example, in 1790, they surrendered two million acres (809,371 hectares) for £1,200, and two years later ceded three million acres (1.2 million hectares) for the same amount.[57] In the 1810s, cash payments gave way to annuities, which the administration considered to be more economical.

As already noted, the 1752 treaty with the Mi'kmaq introduced annual payments as a variation of gift distributions. By the early nineteenth century, annuities took the place of cash payments for land. Thomas Douglas, Earl of Selkirk (1771–1820), at Red River in 1817, was the first to

Joseph Brant, Mohawk war chief, as portrayed during a visit to England, 1775–6. This portrait was published in *The London Magazine, July 1776. (Metropolitan Toronto Reference Library, J. Ross Robertson Collection, T–15494)*

use this new system. The following year, the Collingwood Treaty used it to settle for 1,592,000 acres (644,259 hectares) ceded in return for a 'perpetual' annuity of £1,200. Ojibwa chief Musquakie (Mayawassino, William Yellowhead, d. 1864) was one of the main negotiators.[58] His father had previously surrendered 250,000 acres (101,171 hectares) in present-day Simcoe County. Annuities could be in the form of housing, equipment, and/or provisions instead of cash, as in 1822 when the Mississauga surrendered 2,748,000 acres (1,112,096 hectares). In that case, the agreement was that each of the 257 band members would receive payments. Annuities were, indeed, very economical for the administration, as the Crown paid them from funds established with the proceeds of sales of surrendered lands.

Regulation of trade was another main concern of Indian administration at this time. In the past, government had exercised its monopoly through government 'truck' houses, which in Nova Scotia had been established in 1760, but that system did not pay for itself. In 1764, the government adopted a plan to implement a provision in the Proclamation of 1763 for the opening of trade to all. However, it restricted trade to designated locations, which in the North meant military posts.[59] As well, anyone who wanted to trade had to obtain a licence and post bond for good behaviour. These requirements proved to be highly unpopular with traders, who launched a vigorous—and ultimately successful—campaign against them.

The Proclamation also guaranteed that the government would continue to extend its authority further into the Indian Territory. The large-scale cessions of land in Upper Canada to the Crown were the prototype for a policy that would extend beyond the Great Lakes to the Petit Nord and into the Great Plains.

Important Names and Terms

Brant, Joseph
Federation of Seven Fires
fee simple title
Haldimand Grant
'Indian title'
Johnson, Sir William

nativistic movements
Neolin
Pontiac
Proclamation of 1763
Quebec Act of 1774
Treaty of Paris

Study Questions

1) What were the objectives of the pan-Indian and nativistic movements?
2) In what ways did the Amerindian world change in 1763?
3) Why did Pontiac fail to achieve his goals?
4) What choices did the Mohawks make during the Revolutionary Wars?

Recommended Readings

Calloway, Colin G. *Crown and Calumet: British–Indian Relations, 1783–1815*. Norman: University of Oklahoma Press, 1987.

Dowd, Gregory Evans. *War under Heaven: Pontiac, the Indian Nations, and British Empire*. Baltimore: Johns Hopkins University Press, 2004.

Graymont, Barbara. *The Iroquois in the American Revolution*. Syracuse, NY: Syracuse University Press, 1972.

Kelsay, Isabel Thompson. *Joseph Brant, 1743–1807: Man of Two Worlds*. Syracuse, NY: Syracuse University Press, 1984.

Wallace, Anthony F.C. *Death and Rebirth of the Seneca*. New York: Vintage Books, 1969.

Washburn, Wilcomb. *Handbook of North American Indians*, vol. 4: *History of Indian–White Relations*. Washington: Smithsonian Institution, 1988.

7 Westward and Northward

On the Great Plains

Some time in the seventeenth century, word began to spread throughout the western Plains of a strange animal, 'swift as deer', which would become known to the Cree as Misstutim, 'big dog'. The use of horses for hunting bison on the Plains, which today is considered traditional, crystallized in Canada between 1600 and 1750, depending on locality. In southern Alberta, Saskatchewan, and Manitoba, it seems to have developed during the first half of the eighteenth century.[1] There is considerable question as to when Amerindians began to own and ride horses after the Spaniards reintroduced them into the Americas. (The horse actually originated in the Americas but became extinct on the continent around the time of the last ice age.) In 1541, Antonio de Mendoza, first viceroy of New Spain, provided mounts for his Mexican allies during a campaign in central Mexico. About 1567, the Indians of Sonora rode horses and used them for food.[2] The Shoshoni (Snake, Gens du Serpent), seasonal residents of grasslands and Plateau, might have been the first on the northwestern Plains to acquire horses.[3] By the 1730s, they were using horses for raiding.[4]

Saukamapee, a Cree who had been adopted by the Peigan, described to geographical surveyor **David Thompson** (1770–1857) his first encounter with the new arrival. Attacking a lone Shoshoni, the Peigan succeeded in killing his mount, then crowded in wonder about the fallen animal, which, like the dog, was a slave to man and carried his burdens.[5] The Blackfoot called it 'Ponokamita', 'elk dog', in recognition of its size and usefulness.

As for the Atlantic seaboard, horses were present since early in the seventeenth century but did not cross the Alleghenies until later. On the southern Plains, Amerindians owned horses by 1630 and may well have had some as early as 1600. Athapaskan-speaking Apache were raiding on horseback by the mid-seventeenth century.[6] Indeed, they evolved their own techniques for mounted warfare and buffalo hunting. Bison herds seem to have reached their great numbers not long before the arrival of

Europeans.[7] Hernando de Soto (*c.* 1500–42) in 1541 reported 'that cattle were in such plenty' in north-central Arkansas, 'no maize-field could be protected from them, and the inhabitants lived on the meat.'[8] The new character of the buffalo hunt influenced some peoples who were farming in the parklands, such as the Cheyenne and some branches of the Sioux, to abandon agriculture for the excitement of the chase.

Time Line

1600–1870	Development and flourishing of bison-hunting way of life.		Confederacy—now armed and on horseback—forces
1630	Indians on southern Plains own horses, after Spanish introduced horses a century earlier in Mexico.		Shoshoni off northern Plains. Gros Ventre, weakened by epidemic, pushed south and east by Assiniboine and Cree.
1730s	Shoshoni using horses for raiding.	1785	First trading ship—British—arrives on Northwest Coast.
mid-1700s	Cree, who had traded with HBC on the Bay and with French now established on Saskatchewan River, introduce guns to Plains culture.	1788	Pond establishes Fort Chipewyan for North West Company.
		1791	A Haida chief, Koyah, disgraced by British, becomes enemy of fur trade and attacks ships and traders.
1754–63	French–Indian War disrupts trade in the West.	1793	Cree wipe out a Gros Ventre band near South Branch House.
1770	British traders back on Upper Mississippi and Saskatchewan after French–Indian War.		Alexander Mackenzie reaches Pacific coast overland after following Amerindian trade routes.
1774	HBC inland post of Cumberland House (near The Pas, Manitoba).		
1778	Captain James Cook sails into Nootka Sound on British Columbia coast. Amerindian guides take Peter Pond to west via Methye Portage, the third great route for fur resources (after St Lawrence and Hudson Bay).	1793–4	Gros Ventre retaliate against Cree by looting HBC's Manchester House and by destroying South Branch House.
		1799	North West Company post at Rocky Mountain House the first in Blackfoot territory. Dene Dháa (Beaver) seek fur-trading post for their territory.
1779	HBC Hudson House post (west of Prince Albert, Sask.). Cree attack independent traders at Eagle Hills Fort on the Saskatchewan.	*c.* 1800	Fur traders bring Iroquois, Nipissings, Algonquins to the West to trap for them, causing considerable resentment among the Blackfoot and
1781–2	Epidemic takes heavy toll on Shoshoni, and Blackfoot		Peigan.

1800–4	Iroquois trappers famed as rivermen, from Kahnawake, Kanesatake, and Akwesasne, most under contract to North West Company, move west, eventually settle in Athabasca and Peace River regions.		Trade ship *Tonquin* blown up by Amerindians on BC coast, leaving no survivors.
		1818	International border between Canada and the United States is established.
1803	Muquinna, a Nuu'chah'nulth chief, attacks the *Boston*— only two crew survive; Muquinna subsequently has elaborate potlatch.	1821	Hudson's Bay Company and North West Company amalgamate.
		1830s	Thriving buffalo robe and pemmican trade such that tipis are large enough to accommodate 100 people.
1807	Nor'Wester David Thompson establishes post in Kutenai territory.	1834	Fort Simpson moved to Tsimshian Peninsula; nine bands of Tsimshian encamp nearby to control and profit from trade.
1811	David Thompson gains access to Athabasca Pass through negotiation with Tsuu T'ina, which becomes the route to the Plateau and Pacific coast until 1841.	1849	Fort Rupert established on north end of Vancouver Island; four Kwakwaka'wakw bands move to area for trade.

Horse stealing also became a favourite activity and was an accepted way of acquiring animals. Around 1800, some Blackfoot, raiding on the northern Plains, were seen riding horses with Spanish brands.[9] David Thompson described a spectacular raid in which a band of Assiniboine disguised as antelopes made off with 50 horses from Rocky Mountain House.[10] The Amerindians carried out such raids against their enemy, and thus, these were acts of war, not theft.[11]

With horses, running buffalo became universally favoured as a hunting technique. Mounted hunters simply chased the herds and killed animals with guns or bows and arrows. Jumps began to fall into disuse between 1840 and 1850. In this method runners would lead a herd towards a cliff. Once there, other hunters would shout and wave robes and blankets, causing some of the confused animals to run off the cliff. A third group of hunters waited at the bottom and dispatched the wounded bison with spears. The last known use of a buffalo jump was by the Blackfoot in 1873.[12] Pounds continued to be used until the end of the herds. In this method a hunter dressed in buffalo robes would lead the herd into a natural ravine or coulee, as they were known on the prairies, and then into a fenced enclosure built into a natural hollow. A large party of hunters then blocked the only exit and killed the animals with spears.[13]

Horses altered not only the hunt, transportation, and warfare, but also—and perhaps most importantly—trade routes. As a result, they became a symbol of wealth and, as always with the growth of affluence, polarized economic status both between individuals and between tribes. For example, in 1833 a Peigan chief, Sackomaph, owned between 4,000 and 5,000 horses, 150 of which were sacrificed on his death. On a more modest scale, an individual Siksika of Painted Feather's band was reported to have owned 50 horses. Among the Peigan, the number belonging to an individual could reach 300.[14]

Horses, Firearms, and Disease: Shifts in Power Balances

At this time, all of the year-round residents of the northwestern Plains were Algonkian or Siouan speakers except the Tsuu T'ina, who spoke an Athapaskan language and who had broken away from the northern Beaver, apparently not long before the arrival of Europeans. Eventually, the Tsuu T'ina became part of the **Blackfoot Confederacy**, along with the Siksika (Blackfoot proper), Kainah (Blood), and Peigan (Peeagan, Peekanow), the most westerly and southerly of the confederates.[15]

Directly to the east of the Confederacy were the allied Algonkian-speaking Gros Ventre (Atsina, originally a division of the Arapaho; also known as Fall or Rapids Amerindians),[16] who may have been the second to arrive in the region, after the Blackfoot.[17] Later, a fur trader, Matthew Cocking (1743–99), described Gros Ventre customs and manners as similar to those of Europeans.[18]

If we exclude the Plains Ojibwa (Saulteaux, Bungi), who reached Saskatchewan by the late eighteenth century but who did not establish a major presence on the high Plains,[19] the newcomers in this northwestern region were the Plains Cree, who began to arrive early in the eighteenth century, possibly in association with their close allies the Siouan Assiniboine, who preceded them.

But the early historic period saw the southwestern parts of the region being dominated by the raiding, mounted Shoshoni. The Shoshoni wore six-ply quilted armour and carried shields, but as yet did not have firearms. The sinew-backed bow was an efficient weapon, however, particularly when used with metal-tipped arrows—both more accurate and more reliable than guns until about the middle of the nineteenth century. With the exception of the late-arriving Cree, Assiniboine, and Saulteaux, all of whom had earlier associations with the fur trade, the bow and arrow was the preferred weapon of the buffalo hunters.[20]

The appearance of the gun heralded the final phase of shifting Amerindian power balances on the northern Plains before the settlers arrived. The Shoshoni first saw guns in the hands of their enemy, the Cree.[21] The Cree, trading with the English on Hudson Bay and with the French, by mid-eighteenth century were established on the Saskatchewan River and had been armed for some time. The Shoshoni quickly discovered that this new weapon seriously lessened the advantage they had gained with the horse.[22]

There is argument as to the extent of the influence of the early smooth-bore gun on Plains warfare patterns.[23] However, there seems little reason to doubt that it had, at the very least, considerable psychological impact. For one thing, a musket ball was harder to dodge than an arrow or a spear. For another, when it hit, it made traditional armour obsolete. In the hands of a mounted warrior, as happened on the Plains, even the smooth-bore musket, unreliable as it was, could be overpowering.[24]

Box 7.1   Communication in the Fur Trade

French was the operative means of communication in the fur trade, although traders also used English.[25] Possibly, the bilingualism (or, perhaps, multilingualism) of the voyageur made the development of a pidgin or creole jargon unnecessary.[26] What did appear among Métis of Plains and parklands was **Michif**, a fully developed language—not a pidgin—that combines French nouns and noun phrases with the Plains Cree verbal system. It is considered a mixed language, a rare phenomenon.[27]

Once believed to have been restricted to the southeastern parklands in the Turtle Mountain region of Manitoba and North Dakota, it is now known to be much more widespread, reaching into northwestern Alberta, where it is called 'Métis Cree'. In parts of its more easterly range, it incorporates Ojibwa as well. The Manitoba Métis Federation was surprised to discover some of this while conducting a project of recording elders' recollections. Serious study of this phenomenon has only just begun.[28]

Before the Shoshoni could get regular access to firearms, the French and Indian War (1754–63)—the New World aspect of the Seven Years' War in Europe—was seriously interrupting trade in the West. By 1770, however, British traders were back on the Upper Mississippi and the Saskatchewan and were beginning to penetrate into the Far Northwest. France as a power had all but disappeared from North America, and her jurisdiction over Louisiana had been transferred to Spain. This dealt a severe blow to whatever hopes the Shoshoni might have had of obtaining enough guns to face their enemies. The Blackfoot confederates, now mounted, already had access to British firearms, and by the end of the eighteenth century they pushed the Shoshoni off the northern Plains.[29]

In achieving this, the Blackfoot had powerful help. Epidemics, especially that of 1781–2, took a heavy toll on the Shoshoni.[30] By the turn of the century, the victorious Peigan, who had been the confederates mainly involved in the struggle, were referring to the once-dreaded Shoshoni as miserable old women, whom they could defeat with sticks and stones.[31] With the Shoshoni threat gone, the fragile alliance of the Confederacy with Assiniboine and Cree lost its main motivation, and the two expanding power groups came into collision.

The Blackfoot and Peigan Resist Efforts To Disrupt Trade Patterns

While they were still allies, the Blackfoot had obtained their first European trade items through the Assiniboine and Cree network rather than directly from Europeans. The French were the first they met,[32] and the French language had a lasting impact on communication in parts of the West (Box 7.1), although the first identifiable meeting was with HBC trader Anthony Henday (*fl.* 1750–62), whom the Cree trading captain

Attikarish (Attickasish) led to them in 1754–5.[33] By then, the Blackfoot likely had horses[34] and were well into a period of expansion.

As the Peigan pushed the Shoshoni south and west, the Tsuu T'ina moved into the North Saskatchewan River basin, and the allied Gros Ventre occupied territories vacated by the Blackfoot around the Eagle Hills. By 1770, the Blackfoot Confederacy and its allies controlled the area along the eastern Rockies north of Yellowstone to the boreal forest.

The Blackfoot never took to trading with Europeans, as had the Cree and Assiniboine. Not only were their needs being served adequately through the Amerindian networks, but they would have faced opposition if they had tried to penetrate Cree and Assiniboine hunting territory that lay on the route to the Bay. There was also the fact that the demands of the fur trade conflicted with those of buffalo hunting. Late fall and early winter was the best season for trapping furs, as pelts were then in their prime. It was also the best time for killing bison and preparing winter provisions.

Trapping was a family affair, whereas buffalo hunting involved the whole community. Of the Blackfoot confederates, the Peigan had the most beaver in their territory and, as a result, became the most active as trappers. The others, as well as the allies, became provisioners for the trade rather than trappers for furs. This independence of the Blackfoot and Gros Ventre spurred the Hudson's Bay Company to establish the inland posts of Cumberland House (near The Pas, Manitoba) in 1774 and Hudson House (west of Prince Albert) in 1779. By the time the **North West Company** (NWC) built Fort Augustus on the North Saskatchewan in 1795 and the HBC countered with Fort Edmonton that same year, trading posts ringed Blackfoot territory.[35] The NWC was a group of floating fur trade partnerships that coalesced into 'companies' based in Montreal, the first in 1779 and the second in 1783. In 1799, Nor'Westers built the first Rocky Mountain House, establishing a post within the Blackfoot sphere of control.

Despite their unwillingness to meet the fur trade on its terms, the Blackfoot and Gros Ventre complained that they were not being treated in trade as well as their enemies, the Cree, particularly in the case of firearms.[36] The traders did not help when they treated Amerindians badly, as happened all too often. The resulting tensions sometimes erupted into violence, as in 1781, when Amerindians burned the prairie around the posts. The traders believed they did it to scare game away.[37] The establishment of the international border between Canada and the United States in 1818 further complicated what was already a complex situation. It did not take long, however, for the Blackfoot to take advantage of the new international boundary. They became adept at raiding posts built in that part of their territory claimed by the United States and then selling the proceeds north of the border.[38]

When the Nor'Westers tried to cross the mountains to make contact with the Kutenai and other Plateau peoples, the Peigan became seriously alarmed, 'for they dreaded the western Indians being furnished with Arms and Amunition'.[39] David Thompson finally succeeded in building a post in Kutenai territory in 1807. At this, the Peigan, already disturbed by the killing of two of their men by members of the Lewis and Clark expedition shortly before, raised a war party. Thompson was able to negotiate a peaceful settlement, but the delay cost the Nor'Westers the right to claim the mouth of the Columbia River for Britain.[40] That same year, a band of Blood and Gros Ventre looted Fort Augustus. When the HBC built Peigan Post (Old Bow Fort) in 1832 in territory controlled by the Kainah, the latter refused to let their allies trade there. This forced the post to close two years later.[41]

The situation became worse when Euro-Americans—the 'Mountain Men' of American western folklore—began trapping in Indian territory, an act the Blackfoot considered trespassing. Canadian **traders** had already, at the end of the eighteenth century, 'brought in a great number of Iroquois, Nepissings, and Algonquins' to act as trappers for them, men who 'with their steel traps had destroyed the Beaver on their own lands in Canada and New Brunswick'.[42]

Since the Blackfoot would not allow them on their lands, the newcomers went north and west, some going to the Upper Columbia, later moving down to the Lower Columbia and the Snake. If they encroached on Peigan lands, they were driven off in attacks that could be bloody. Thompson reported that the Peigan had killed several hundred for that reason, perhaps an exaggeration.[43]

Expansion, Prosperity, and War

In Canada, the opening of the rich fur resources of the Far Northwest—the Athabasca region—and the growing market for buffalo robes shifted the trade's focus and brought about better relations between the Blackfoot and traders. The need for provisions for the Athabasca trade greatly increased the demand for **pemmican**, a product of the buffalo hunt. Pemmican, a highly concentrated food (made from fat, dried bison meat, and occasionally Saskatoon berries) that could be kept indefinitely, had the added advantage of being well suited for transport in small northern canoes.[44]

As this new trade boomed in the North, buffalo robes were finding widening markets in the south. Transportation was the key here also. In this case, the building of railroads made getting the bulky, heavy hides to market possible. Buffalo hunters flourished. The northern Plains, where affluence was traditionally manifested in the size of tipis, by the 1830s saw them becoming large enough to hold 100 persons.[45]

The new commerce placed a premium on the services of women, who prepared the hides and made pemmican and materials for repairing birchbark canoes. Where Plains Indian women had usually married in their late teens, girls as young as 12 years now did so. Polygamy developed, and so did a hierarchy among wives, with the senior wife usually directing the others.[46] Women taken in raids now tended to be kept by their captors rather than sold, a trend that grew stronger after the first third of the nineteenth century.

Commercialism and its emphasis on wealth affected other social institutions as well. Special-interest societies multiplied. The best known were connected with war and maintaining camp and hunt discipline. War as a way of life was a comparatively recent development. For the Blackfoot, it became a means of gaining wealth, making possible the elaborate ceremonies that were the route to prestige.

Alliances shifted and long-standing trade patterns were disrupted as European traders pushed further into the Northwest. Despite the problems, including epidemics, the arrival of the horse and the new fur trade resulted in a flowering of Plains culture. Here, Plains Amerindians negotiate a trade with an HBC factor in the mid-1800s. The travois of both horse and dog are loaded with trade goods. From *Harper's Monthly*, June 1879. *(Glenbow Museum and Archives, NA–1406–40)*

Still, something of the old ways persisted. Although the Blackfoot were a major military power on the northwestern Plains for more than a century, it was still possible in their society to become a chief without combat experience.[47] Even if the path of war was chosen, **counting coups**—literally, hitting one's opponent in battle with a fist or a coup stick—was esteemed a braver act than killing, as touching the enemy and escaping took power. Each coup was rewarded with a notch on the warrior's coup stick or with a feather for a headdress. Bravery and generosity were the requisites, as they were among the Plains Cree and others. Warfare intensified, nonetheless.

The Gros Ventre were weakened by the ravages of the 1781–2 epidemic, and the Assiniboine and Cree pushed them south and east. In 1793, Cree wiped out a Gros Ventre band near South Branch House. Such incidents greatly intensified the resentment shared by the Gros Ventre and the Blackfoot towards the trading success of the Cree and the Assiniboine, which made possible the latter's superiority in arms.[48] In the eyes of the Gros Ventre, HBC traders were, in effect, allies of their enemies. For that reason, they responded to the Cree raid by attacking the Company's Manchester House (on Pine Island in the Saskatchewan River), which they looted that same year. The following year, they destroyed South Branch House. Eventually, like the Shoshoni, they were pushed south of the international border.[49]

In contrast to the Gros Ventre, the Cree and Assiniboine were still expanding since their arrival on the Plains near the end of the seventeenth century. Although they also suffered severely from the epidemics (1776–7 had been particularly hard on them), their numbers were such that they were able to recover and continue their expansion.[50] In the southwest, however, the Blackfoot, their former allies when the Shoshoni were a common enemy, stopped them. Cree and Blackfoot now considered each other their worst foe.

Neither Cree nor Assiniboine had trouble adapting to Plains life. By 1772, Cree were impounding bison, but they preferred the gun to the bow for the hunt, in contrast to peoples longer established on the grasslands. Buffalo hunting lessened dependence on the fur trade. The 'homeguard', so characteristic of the trading posts of the northern forests, was less apparent on the Plains.[51] Instead, buffalo hunters became provisioners for the trade.

Reduced dependence on the fur trade affected relationships with traders. In fact, the Plains Cree took part in one of the most widely remembered confrontations. It occurred in 1779 in reaction to the callous behaviour of a group of independent traders at Fort Montagne d'Aigle (Eagle Hills Fort), on the Saskatchewan between Eagle Hills Creek and Battle River. The Amerindians killed two traders and forced the rest to flee. The post was abandoned and apparently was never again reoccupied permanently. The incident also caused the abandonment that same year of the Nor'Wester Fort du Milieu and the HBC's Hudson House.

Nor was this an isolated occurrence. The Cree, for example, participated in a mêlée in 1781 at Fort des Trembles on the Assiniboine that resulted in the death of three traders and up to 30 Amerindians. Only the outbreak of the 1781–2 smallpox epidemic prevented large-scale retaliations against traders.[52] The much-vaunted peaceful co-operation that was characteristic of the fur trade in the northern forests was not so evident on the Plains.

In spite of this, the influences of the horse and the fur trade fostered a flowering of Plains cultures from 1750 to 1880. The horse made the buffalo hunt and the extension of overland routes easier. The fur trade made available a new range of goods and provided new markets for products of the hunt. This meant that as long as the herds lasted, Plains Amerindians were able to hold their own and, indeed, to reach new heights of cultural expression. They were even able to overcome to a large extent the disasters caused by introduced diseases. They did not have time, however, to adjust to the disappearance of the herds on which all this was based. The dramatic suddenness of that occurrence catapulted events beyond their control.

In the Far Northwest

The invasion of the fur trade into the **Far Northwest**, today's Northwest Territories and British Columbia, received an enormous boost when the British eased restrictions at the interior posts in 1768. The westward movement began in the seventeenth century, when the Cree and Assiniboine headed west, bringing the fur trade with them. It ended in the voyage of Alexander Mackenzie (1764–1820) of the North West Company, who followed Amerindian trading routes from the Peace River down the Parsnip and Liard rivers to the Bella Coola River, reaching the ocean at Bentinck Arm in 1793.

The visit of Captain James Cook (1728–79) to Nootka Sound in 1778 has usually been considered the beginning of coastal movement. However, according to BC geographer Samuel Bawlf, Sir Francis Drake (1541?–1596), while circling the globe in 1578–80, reached the mouth of the Stikine River where it cuts through the Alaska panhandle. He kept the visit secret, however, to hide it from the Spaniards, who were claiming the entire North American west coast.[53]

More than a century and a half later, in 1741, Vitus Bering (1681–1741) claimed Alaska for Russia. Spaniards arrived offshore in 1774, returning in 1789 to build a fort to protect their claims. They stayed until both Britain and Spain agreed to vacate the region in 1794. The British would soon come back, but not the Spanish (see Box 7.2).

Box 7.2   The Lack of Amerindian–European Alliances in the West

The absence of colonial rivalry during the process of settlement was a mixed blessing for the Amerindians of the Pacific coast. For one thing, once trade dropped off, the Indians and Europeans had no common ground, and no alliances developed. Even though agriculture could not take over, as it had in other parts of Canada, the only role for Amerindians in European settlements was as wage labourers in the fisheries and lumber camps.[54] Apart from the treaties that James Douglas negotiated (see Chapter 9), the settlers did not negotiate for the land they took. The idea that Amerindians had neither sovereign nor proprietary rights prevailed. The problems that resulted from such an attitude became acute with the discovery of gold on the Fraser and Thompson rivers in 1857.

Spearheading the Canadian involvement in both land and sea movements was the North West Company.[55] The NWC fought the Hudson's Bay Company at a severe disadvantage, however, as the latter had direct sea access to the fur providers through Hudson Bay, with the much slower land routes left to the NWC. In 1821, with the merger of the rival trading companies into a new Hudson's Bay Company with effective control over a vast territory stretching from Hudson Bay to the Pacific, the HBC became active on the west coast. Its ship, *Beaver*, arrived in Vancouver in 1836, the first steamer to ply those coastal waters. In the meantime, Amerindian coastal trade networks flourished as Amerindian entrepreneurs capitalized on European initiatives.

The head start of the Cree in gaining access to European trade goods was substantial. The Cree bands of Hudson Bay had a century to develop this new connection before the people of the Far Northwest made their first shaky contact. Throughout all this time, however, Amerindian trade networks were operating. Likely, European merchandise worked its way deep into the interior long before traders did. Certainly, this was the case in the Great Lakes region.[56] Samuel Hearne, on his voyage to the Arctic in 1772, found beads of a type not traded by the HBC in an Inuit camp at the mouth of the Coppermine River.[57] Even though contact between Europeans and Amerindians was low-key during this period, however, it affected Amerindian relationships. Integration into an economy based on production for exchange rather than for use, instead of providing for greater security, destabilized Amerindian ways of life. In some aspects, however, this new economy and what it brought to the Amerindians led to an intensification of traditional cultural activities (Box 7.3).

We have seen that the Cree, with their early acquisition of guns, expanded in two arenas—from already established positions in the Northwest and southward to erupt onto the northern Plains. As the tribes readjusted their territories and sought to control a larger share of the fur trade, Athapaskans not only fought Cree, they also came into conflict with other Athapaskans. Thus, the Chipewyan contended with Yellowknives and Dogrib to keep them from direct access to the Hudson Bay posts.[58] Once the HBC posts moved inland, these hostilities lost their reason for being and stopped. The traditional enmity between the woodland Indians and the people of the tundra—the Inuit—had deeper roots, however, and continued far longer.

Another element adding to the complexity of this picture was the arrival of Iroquois trappers, famed as rivermen, at the end of the eighteenth century (already referred to in the previous chapter). Mostly from Caughnawaga (Kahnawake) but also from Oka (Kanesatake) and St Regis (Akwesasne), most came under contract with the NWC, with a few coming on their own.[59] More than 300 arrived between 1800 and 1804. By 1810, they had concentrated along the eastern slopes of the Rockies in the Athabasca and Peace River regions, but by 1821 the movement was tapering off. Most of the newcomers had completed their contracts and were now 'freemen'.

Efficient fur hunters, the Iroquois used the latest technology: metal traps. After the NWC joined with the HBC in 1821, the Lesser Slave Lake post accounted for more

Box 7.3   Amerindian Arts

As on the east coast nearly three centuries earlier, shipboard trade resulted in limited contact with Amerindians and thus at first intensified existing cultural patterns rather than
causing a major reorientation in their way of life.[60] Changes in tool kits and equipment resulted in a flowering of the arts. For example, iron tools meant that totem poles became
taller and more elaborate. More slowly, dress shifted from buckskin to cloth, and capes that
had once been woven of cedar-bark and mountain goat wool (or dog hair) came to be made
of navy blue and red blanket cloth, trimmed with buttons and thimbles. Blankets became the
unit of trade, as **Made Beaver** had been for the rest of Canada.[61] The passion of west coast
Native peoples for carving, sculpting, painting, and weaving and, generally, for decoration
overflowed onto the most utilitarian of objects. Even such items as halibut fishhooks would
be adorned with carvings. If the people were 'art intoxicated', the condition was catching,
as visitors immediately succumbed and collected all they could.

As the coastal fur trade dwindled, enterprising artisans took to producing objects for
this new market. The Haida of the Queen Charlotte Islands (Haida Gwaii) mined the slate
deposits in their territory, carved it into miniature totem poles, pipes, and other objects,
polished the result to a shining black, and a new art form was born for which there was
an instant demand. Leaders in the development of the arts were the Haida chief Charles
Edenshaw (Tahayghen, 'Noise in the housepit'; Nôngkwigetkla_s, 'They gave ten potlatches
for him'; successor to the chiefly title of Eda'nsa, *c.* 1839–1920), a master sculptor who
worked in many media. Later, his great-grandson Robert Davidson followed in his footsteps.
Argillite carving is only one of the new ways in which coastal artists channelled their creative geniuses in response to new challenges.

Amerindian artists and artisans of the Atlantic coast, on the other hand, had not been
so fortunate in the sixteenth and seventeenth centuries. European tastes during those
periods did not acknowledge 'primitive' arts and crafts. What little they collected was as
curiosities, and practically nothing of that has survived. The results of these attitudes are
evident in museums: where Northwest Coast art is probably the most heavily represented
of any of the tribal arts of the world, there is practically nothing to give us a glimpse of the
once-flourishing cultures of the Maritimes.

than a twelfth of the total returns for the Company that year, by far the largest quantity
for a single post.[62] On such evidence, it is hardly surprising that the freemen faced
accusations of overtrapping to the point of stripping the region of its fur resources.
They intermarried locally, which usually meant with Cree or Métis, but later with non-
Aboriginals. Their descendants in Alberta today live at Grand Cache, Lac Ste Anne, and
Lesser Slave Lake, as well as points south.[63]

Into Athabasca Country

In 1778, his Amerindian guides took **Peter Pond** (1739/40–1807) to Methye Portage,[64] opening up the third great route into Canada's fur resources (the others were the St Lawrence and Hudson Bay). Pond established Fort Chipewyan, which became the most important North West Company post in the North. Within four years, the NWC also had established posts near the present sites of Fort McMurray and Peace River, and by 1805 it had important posts at Dunvegan and Fort St John, both on the Peace River, and at Lesser Slave Lake.

Rivalry between the HBC and the NWC intensified. This meant that credit became easy to obtain and liquor flowed. The spread of posts also meant that more tribes gained direct access to white traders, and the Cree lost out as middlemen. When the HBC gained control of the trade with the 1821 merger, it began to curb the use of alcohol and to change the terms of trade, to the disadvantage of the Amerindians. Montreal also lost out to London as the headquarters for the trade. Canoe brigades no longer left Lachine for Fort William each spring. Instead, York Factory on Hudson Bay, at the mouths of the Nelson and Hayes rivers, became the hub. The HBC's position of exclusive dominance lasted for almost half a century. It was during this time that missionaries became a presence in the Northwest.

The Europeans Push Further West, into the Plateau

The breaking of the mountain barrier into central British Columbia by Europeans presented a problem for the local Amerindians.[65] The Blackfoot Confederacy controlled the easier passes to the south, and they feared that their enemies would obtain European firearms. But when the American Lewis and Clark expedition (1804–6) killed some of their tribesmen, distracting the Confederacy, David Thompson was able to push through Howse Pass,[66] only to find the pass under Peigan control. Finally, in 1811, Thompson was able to negotiate with the Tsuu T'ina for the use of the more northerly, longer, and more difficult Athabasca Pass. That would be the route for the European traders until 1841. By mid-century, the decline of the buffalo herds was becoming evident, however, influencing the Blackfoot to reconsider their position in regard to trade.[67]

The Kutenai of the Plateau, anxious to get direct access to trade goods, particularly guns, helped the traders. This was a new expression of an old rivalry with the Blackfoot Confederacy, which long predated the arrival of European trade. In pre-contact days, this rivalry had surfaced over rights to hunt buffalo on the Plains. The Blackfoot network was charging the Kutenai as much as 10 skins for an item that could be obtained for one at a post. Horses were the Kutenai's main stock-in-trade. These were much desired by the Peigan and other Plains peoples, who, as a result, took all the more care to see that the Kutenai did not gain access to the European traders.[68] As the Peigan and their associates watched anxiously, and despite their best efforts to prevent it, however, the Kutenai and other interior tribes slowly acquired arms.

Once Thompson established a post on the border between the Kutenai and the Flathead, other traders quickly followed. Eventually, the Flathead were in a position to face the Peigan, and in 1810 and again in 1812 they defeated them. The Peigan blamed this on the white men and vowed vengeance.[69] As on the Plains, the fur trade in its westward movement was not always peaceful as it encroached on established Amerindian trade networks.

To the north, entrenched interests were less evident, as European traders pushed westward. Quite the contrary, in fact, as far as the Dene Dháa Beaver, an Athapaskan people, were concerned. They sought out a fur-trading post on their own initiative in 1799. Their leader was an unusual chief, Makenunatane (Swan Chief, so-called because his soul could fly high like a swan), who seems to have realized that the new trade meant a shift in lifeways—for one thing, it called for individualized trapping rather than communal hunting for subsistence. This would obviously call for new rituals. Thus, he and his people wanted to learn about Christianity.[70] It is perhaps not surprising that the Dene Dháa still have a living prophet tradition.

Sea Otters and China Clippers

The sea otter motivated the opening of the fur trade of the Pacific coast, repeating—only more quickly—what had happened on the Atlantic coast nearly 300 years earlier with the beaver.[71] But where shipboard trade had continued for more than a century in Acadia and the Gulf of St Lawrence after beginning as an almost incidental spinoff from the more profitable fisheries, on the Northwest Coast it was the main economic activity for a short but intense period, less than half a century. In both regions, the trade depended on Amerindian middlemen, which meant that participants followed Amerindian protocols. Contact on the west coast was comparatively peaceful but still resulted in an 80 per cent drop of the Aboriginal population within a century.[72]

The sea otter trade began as a result of the activities of Captain Cook's crew at Nootka Sound.[73] The ship went on to China (without Cook, who was killed during a stopover in the Hawaiian islands), and there the British discovered the Chinese passion for sea otter fur. This gave rise to the China clipper traffic between Europe (or New England), the Northwest Coast, and China. Sea otter pelts were traded in China for silk, porcelains, and spices, as well as other items commanding high prices in Europe and in eastern North America. A single round trip could take more than three years, but if all went well it could realize a fortune.

The first trading ship arrived on the Northwest Coast in 1785 (Box 7.4). It was British. However, Americans ('Boston men') were soon dominant. During the following 40 years, until 1825, about 330 vessels flying a variety of national flags came into the region to trade. Of these, 60 per cent made only one visit, but 23 per cent made three or more visits. The peak trading years were between 1792 and 1812, but by about 1825 the sea otter was disappearing. The fur seal of the Pribilof Islands off the southwest coast of Alaska suffered a similar fate.

Box 7.4   Early Trading on the West Coast

James Hanna (d. 1787), captain of the first British trading ship on the west coast, obtained 560 otter skins in 1785 on which he realized $20,000, a fortune in those days. John Kendrick (c. 1740–94), commander of the expedition of the *Columbia* and *Lady Washington*, the first vessels from Boston to join the fur rush, made a deal that became legendary when he got 200 sea otter pelts, valued at $8,000, for an equal number of iron chisels, valued at $100.[74] A Russian made a trade matching that in values exchanged, if not in volume, when he obtained 60 pelts for a handful of nails. When an enterprising American trader persuaded his ship's blacksmith to replicate the Amerindians' ceremonial cedar collars in iron, he traded them at the rate of three sea otter skins for one collar. That lasted for about a year, when the region became saturated with iron collars.

Times of Change—and Conflict—on the West Coast

It would be little more than half a century before non-Amerindian settlements would begin, in mid-nineteenth century. British Columbia remained predominantly Amerindian until the 1880s. Even then, however, all was not as before. More wealth meant more power for chiefs (Box 7.5). Those who could quickly claimed monopolies and took over middlemen roles in the brief but highly profitable trade. Some became wealthy. In 1803, the chief **Muquinna** ('Possessor of pebbles', *fl.* 1786–1817)[75] at Nootka Sound held a **potlatch** during which he gave away 200 muskets, 200 yards of cloth, 100 chemises, 100 mirrors, and seven barrels of gunpowder.

This prosperity, however, was short-lived for Muquinna and other chiefs in a similar position for two reasons: the near extermination of the sea otter and the fact that the coastal regions quickly became glutted with trade goods. Even supplies of highly prized copper reached the saturation point around 1800. A third factor was the introduction of the HBC steamer *Beaver*, which made trade easier but also shifted much of its activity to the inside passage.

In the meantime, during those heady early days of the trade, Amerindians soon became skilled in playing off trading ships, and even nations, against each other. For a short period, Yankees and Russians managed to co-operate in the fiercely competitive situation, with the Americans providing the ships and food and the Russians the Aleut hunters whom they had forced into service.[76] This arrangement was for harvesting sea otters off the California coast. It lasted from 1803 until 1813, by which time the animals were so scarce in those southern waters the deal was no longer profitable.

British North Americans did not appear on the scene until 1811, when Nor'Wester David Thompson arrived at the mouth of the Columbia to find Americans (largely former Nor'Westers) already building a post there. The HBC knocked out one competitor after another and eventually dominated the scene. In 1843, it established Fort

Portrait of Muquinna. In 1803, Muquinna held a potlatch at Nootka Sound at which he gave away 200 muskets and seven barrels of gunpowder. Already, however, overhunting of the sea otter on the west coast was taking its toll, and Muquinna's prosperity would be short-lived. *(British Columbia Archives, A–02678)*

Victoria in Songhees territory, on Vancouver Island. By agreeing to supply the Russian posts with food, the HBC undercut the Americans. For the most part, these rivalries did not last long, in contrast to the prolonged confrontation in the *petit nord* and on the Plains.

As elsewhere in British North America, the European arrival on the Northwest Coast soon led to increased tribal warfare. This, however, seems to have been of short duration, and in the maritime trade there were comparatively few incidents. Those that did occur included Amerindian retaliations against outrages committed against them, but the causes of many are now difficult to determine.[77]

One of the best-known incidents involved Koyah (Coya, Kouyer, 'Raven', d. 1795?), a ranking Haida chief, and Captain Kendrick. Kendrick allowed too many Amerindians aboard the *Lady Washington*, and some small items, including some of his personal linen, were pilfered. Kendrick seized Koyah and another chief, bolted each by a leg to a gun carriage, and threatened them with death until amends were made, which included trading all the furs in the village. Not satisfied when his terms were met, Kendrick further disgraced Koyah by whipping him and cutting off his hair, among other indignities.[78] Such a dishonour ruined Koyah's standing as a chief and turned him into an enemy of the fur trade. From then on, he attacked ships and traders whenever he could, including the *Lady Washington* in 1791. He lost his wife and two of his children in one of these episodes.[79]

Muquinna was more successful than Koyah when he overwhelmed the crew of the *Boston* in 1803, allowing only two to survive.[80] In this case, there seems to have been an accumulation of grievances, not the least of which was the fact that the fur trade

---

Box 7.5   Fair Trade?

The Amerindians of the Northwest Coast, so fond of abalone shell that they traded all the way down to California for it, flatly refused to accept artificial shell. While the differences in the scale of values between Amerindians and Europeans had made huge profits possible for the latter, the benefits were not entirely one-sided. In terms of their own priorities and economic value systems, Amerindians also acquired substantial wealth, as we have seen happen in other parts of Canada.

---

was bypassing the Nuu'chah'nulth chief. His lavish potlatch of that year was never repeated.[81] The most successful of all Amerindian attacks on vessels was in 1811, when some Nuu'chah'nulth blew up the *Tonquin*, leaving no survivors.[82]

Amerindian Entrepreneurialism

From about 1806, crews began to winter on the coast. Year-round trade developed, and eventually posts were built. Amerindian bands clustered around forts, but for different reasons than the 'homeguards' of the Northeast. When forts were built in their territory, tribal nations assumed they had the right to control access to these new centres for trade. Thus, when the HBC moved Fort Simpson from the Nass River to the Tsimshian Peninsula in 1834, nine bands of Tsimshian lost no time in setting up camp nearby. Similarly, four bands of Kwakwaka'wakw converged on Fort Rupert soon after its construction on the northern end of Vancouver Island in 1849. This was the reason behind the annoyed reaction of the Nisga'a of the Nass River when Fort Simpson was moved into Tsimshian territory.[83]

On the other hand, if the Amerindians saw little advantage in having a fort in their midst and refused to trade, there was no point in trying to maintain it. An attempt to establish a fort among the Chilcotin in 1829 met with this kind of a reaction and closed after 15 years.[84] Other forts were maintained for even a shorter period. In either case, the HBC had no alternative but to accept the situation.

The Company never did establish the complete control it would have liked in New Caledonia (the central interior region of BC), although it did eventually establish interior posts. The Nor'Westers were the first on the scene, arriving overland across the Continental Divide to establish Fort McLeod on McLeod Lake in 1805, soon to be followed by others. The HBC became active in the area about 1824, following its amalgamation with the Nor'Westers three years earlier.

When coastal traders tried to extend their commerce up the rivers, particularly towards the north, they found themselves facing stiff competition from Amerindian entrepreneurs. The extent of these networks surprised early traders when they found trade goods from the coast as far east as the Sekani of the Finlay and Parsnip rivers.[85]

Nineteenth-century chiefs of the Wolf Crest of Git-lak-damaks, Nass River, surrounded by wealth acquired in trade and warfare. Standing, beginning fourth from the left, Andrew Nash, John Nash, James Percival, Philip Nash, and Charlie Brown (right rear). Seated, second from the right, Mrs Eliza Woods and Matilda Peal, née Brown, aunt of the chiefs. *(Library and Archives Canada, PA 95524)*

In the Far Northwest, the Tsimshian and Tlingit were particularly aggressive in protecting their trade networks, and chiefs such as Legaic (Legex, Legaix) of the Tsimshian, who ran a strict monopoly over the Gitksan on the Upper Skeena, and the Nisga'a Wiiseaks ('Shakes') on the Nass made it clear to whom they thought the trading rights on those rivers belonged.[86]

When the HBC sent combative ex-Nor'Wester Peter Skene Ogden (1790–1854) in 1834 to establish a post on the Stikine River, he backed down in the face of a threatened trade war.[87] Here again, the Company soon learned that in the short run at least it was wiser to co-operate with Amerindian networks than to compete with them. This policy paid off as the maritime trade declined and that between the coast and the interior stepped up. Still, HBC officers were not pleased when they learned of Kwakwaka'wakw traders buying furs at higher prices than the Company was paying and reselling them to Yankee traders. Some groups of Amerindians were obviously more difficult to control than others.

Furs were not the only reason for the activity on the Northwest Coast. The HBC built Fort Rupert, for example, with an eye on the potential of nearby coalfields that the Kwakwaka'wakw had shown the whites in 1835. The intention of the Kwakwaka'wakw had been to work the mines themselves and sell the coal to the HBC.[88]

Amerindian suspension bridge at Hagwilget, BC, built in the 1880s on the Upper Skeena River. *(National Museums of Canada, 60313)*

New Trade Networks Replace the Old, and Societies Are Disrupted

As elsewhere in the Americas, the social consequences of all this change could be drastic. European diseases seem to have been slower in appearing than on the east coast, and the resultant population drops, while severe, seem to have been proportionately somewhat less than what occurred in other regions of the hemisphere, which had drops in some cases of up to 95 per cent. The Northwest Coast population would reach its nadir in 1929, at 22,605,[89] after which it started recovering.

The connection between material wealth and rank, manifested in the potlatch, placed a premium on the control of trading networks. Chiefs who were well placed in this regard, such as Legaic of the Tsimshian or 'Kwah of the Wet'suwet'en (Carrier) (*c.* 1755–1840), both of whom had large interior networks, expanded their spheres of influence and became very powerful.[90] Others who depended mainly on the sea otter, such as Muquinna, did well for a while but then found their position undercut as the trade passed them by. In the boreal forests, on the other hand, material wealth was not a consideration in selecting peace chiefs, nor were these chiefs concerned with trading. Trading chiefs were a response to the European traders' preference for dealing with chiefs, and had little, if any, connection with the general problems of leadership with which the peace chiefs were involved.

Back in New Caledonia, one of the results of the increasing tempo of upriver trade was the spread of coastal cultures into the interior, reaching as far as the Wet'suwet'en on the interior Plateau. Athapaskans around Atlin and Teslin lakes in the North were so affected by these trends they became known as 'interior Tlingit'. Counterbalancing these were influences being brought in by the fur brigades coming from the east. Canoemen were often Iroquois, some of whom reached the coast (and even Hawaii), but most settled in Oregon and northwestern Alberta.

Important Names and Terms

Blackfoot Confederacy	North West Company
counting coups	pemmican
Far Northwest	Pond, Peter
Made Beaver	potlatch
Michif	Thompson, David
Muquinna	traders

Study Questions

1) What changes were brought about by the arrival of horses and guns in the West?
2) Why did the members of the Blackfoot Confederacy resist the arrival of Europeans?
3) How did the arrival of traders affect relations among different Native groups in the West?
4) What made the relations between Natives and newcomers distinctive on the west coast?

Recommended Readings

Abel, Kerry. *Drum Songs*. Montreal and Kingston: McGill-Queen's University Press, 1993.

Carter, Sarah. *Aboriginal People and Colonizers of Western Canada to 1900*. Toronto: University of Toronto Press, 1999.

Dempsey, Hugh A. *Indian Tribes of Alberta*. Calgary: Glenbow-Alberta Institute, 1986.

Fisher, Robin. *Contact and Conflict: Indian–European Relations in British Columbia, 1774–1890*. Vancouver: University of British Columbia Press, 1977.

Hyde, George E. *Indians of the High Plains*. Norman: University of Oklahoma Press, 1959.

Rich, E.E. *The Fur Trade in the Northwest to 1857*. Toronto: McClelland & Stewart, 1967.

Roe, Frank Gilbert. *The Indian and the Horse*. Norman: University of Oklahoma Press, 1951.

8 Turntable of 1812–14

The Peace of Paris of 1783 that ended the American War of Independence stunned Indians in the upper Middle West. The British had ceded the Ohio Valley—their lands—to the United States without any mention of Aboriginal inhabitants, allies or otherwise. The dream of pan-Indian unity that earlier in the century had inspired the Abenaki's Nescambiouit and the Fox's Kiala in their failed attempts to forge chains of alliances from the Great Lakes to the Atlantic was now an urgent political goal.

Thirty-five nations assembled at Sandusky, in Ohio's Wyandot country (scene of one of the last battles in the recent war), in the first of a series of councils to consider the matter. Joseph Brant of the Mohawk lobbied hard for a confederation on the model of the Six Nations. Few delegates were willing to go that far, but realizing all too clearly the need for unity, some of them united in a loose confederacy.

Sir John Johnson (1741–1830), who succeeded his father, Sir William, as superintendent of Indians for the Northern Department,[1] assured the delegates that the Paris peace in no way extinguished their rights to lands northwest of the Ohio River. Spurred by this 'Tomahawk Speech', as it has been called, the council agreed to hold to the line established by treaty in 1768, the Ohio River, as the boundary beyond which European settlement was not to spread. Settlers and even governments, however, showed little inclination to respect Amerindian rights. The new American government assumed that in winning independence it had automatically gained title to all territories east of the Mississippi, whether or not Indians were living on them.[2] In 1783, North Carolina confiscated all Indian lands within the state. Outcries were such that by 1786, the United States acknowledged the right of Amerindians to land and put a policy of purchase in place, but this did little to ease the situation. Not only was it poorly honoured in practice, but the Indians often simply did not want to sell.

In the battles that inevitably erupted, Amerindians twice defeated the Americans. The US then rallied a larger military expedition than ever and destroyed

Time Line

1783	North Carolina confiscates all Indian lands; outcries lead to policy of purchase three years later.
1794	Amerindian alliance is defeated by American military forces in the Battle of Fallen Timbers; British fail to help Amerindians.
1795	Treaty of Greenville demands huge land cessions to Americans, opens Ohio Valley to settlers.
1807	Death of Joseph Brant, Mohawk war chief, and subsequent rise of Tecumseh.
1808	Tecumseh's brother, Tenskwatawa ('the Shawnee Prophet'), founds Prophetown.
1811	William Henry Harrison, Indiana governor, attacks Prophetown while Tecumseh is away on pan-Indian mission.
1812	17 July: Michilimackinac falls to Amerindians and British, following strategy devised by Tecumseh and other Amerindian chiefs. 15 August: Fort Dearborn (Chicago) falls to massacre by Main Poc's Potawatomi.
	16 August: US General William Hull surrenders Fort Detroit after ruse concocted by Tecumseh. 13 October: Battle of Queenston Heights, led by Mohawks John Brant and Major John Norton; British victory tempered by loss of General Isaac Brock, who had taken Fort Detroit with his friend, Tecumseh.
1813	24 June: Battle of Beaver Dams an Iroquoian-led victory for British. 10 September: American naval victory on Lake Erie cuts British supply line to west. 5 October: At Moraviantown in southern Ontario, Tecumseh and his Indian allies save General Henry Proctor, who flees; Tecumseh, severely wounded, fights to death.
1814	5 July: Battle of Chippewa, in which American Iroquois, led by Red Jacket, fight against Canadian Iroquois under Major John Norton. Treaty of Ghent ends hostilities between British and Americans.

the coalition led by the Shawnee Weyapiersenwah (Blue Jacket) in the **Battle of Fallen Timbers**, 1794. At Fallen Timbers, south of Detroit in northern Ohio, the Amerindian coalition was served a double blow: not only did the British not come to the aid of their allies, but they also closed the doors of Fort Miami, their nearest fort to the battle scene.

Fallen Timbers effectively broke Amerindian resistance to the western advance of non-Aboriginal settlement. The land cessions demanded in the **Treaty of Greenville** in 1795 made that only too clear. The continual loss of territory, even with cash compensation, was causing growing worry and resentment.[3]

In a Changing World, the Amerindians Are the 'Only Allies' Who Can Defend the Canadas

The American push for land was not the only reason for worry. By 1808, the fur trade was in a depression.[4] Lacking other economic resources, tribal nations were suffering severe hardships, and they turned to their British allies for help. The British, caught in unresolved antagonisms in the wake of American independence—and by this time more aware of the usefulness of Amerindian allies to preserve their colonies in the event of future hostilities—were only too willing to comply. Between 1784 and 1788, they spent £20,000 a year on Indian gift distributions, an expense with which the fur barons of Montreal willingly helped. As Montreal merchant James McGill (1744–1813) wrote to the governor, 'The Indians are the only Allies who can aught avail in the defence of the Canadas. They have the same interest as us, and alike are objects of American subjugation, if not extermination.'[5]

It was an ironic switch for the British. During the French and Indian War, they had complained bitterly about French maintenance and use of Amerindian allies. When victorious, the British had tried to discontinue the practice with disastrous results (see Chapter 6). Now, 20 years later, they found themselves using the same tactics towards the Americans.[6]

In 1807, convinced that a conflict with the United States was inevitable,[7] London instructed its colony to ensure the loyalty of western Indians. Remembering the support they had received from the Iroquois (particularly the Mohawk) during the recent war with the Americans, the British concluded that Amerindian support was vital to the preservation of Britain's remaining North American colonies.[8] The very people whose pleas for help Britain had ignored at the Battle of Fallen Timbers in 1794, she now tried to win over to her cause.

Amerindians, for their part, needed all the help they could get in their efforts to preserve their territories. In the early post-independence period in the United States, even the wavering British seemed preferable to the aggressively expansionist Americans.

Tecumseh

The death of Joseph Brant in 1807 opened the way for **Tecumseh** ('Shooting Star', 'Panther Crouching in Wait', c. 1768–1813), part Shawnee, part Cree, to move onto centre stage. Having lost his father and a brother to the Americans in the ongoing US frontier wars, he became an advocate of pan-Indianism. He had refused to participate in the Treaty of Greenville, which opened the Ohio Valley for American settlement. Tecumseh sided with the British, not because he liked them particularly but because he saw them as the lesser of two evils.

As with Pontiac, Tecumseh was linked with a prophet, in his case a brother, **Tenskwatawa** ('Open Door', Lalawethika, 1775–1836). More widely known as the

Shawnee Prophet, Tenskwatawa took his name from the saying of Jesus, 'I am the door'.[9] His nativistic religious revival prepared the way for Tecumseh's inter-tribal movement, with its doctrine that land did not belong to particular tribal nations but, rather, to Amerindians as a whole. As a result, he argued, no single tribe had the right to give up land on its own. This should be done only by all the tribal nations of the region in council.[10] His was an Amerindian answer to the Proclamation of 1763, which held that Native lands could be ceded only to the British Crown. It was also a challenge to the policy of divide and rule.

Tecumseh, one of the greatest Indian leaders, came close to uniting Indians against European settlement of their lands. He was killed at Moraviantown, in present-day southwest Ontario, during the War of 1812–14. (*Library and Archives Canada, C3809*)

Although no authentic portrait of Tecumseh exists, there are verbal descriptions of his appearance. Apparently, he cut a striking figure, combining a fine physique with a great sense of style. He dressed in the manner of his people but with a flair that drew the admiration of both Amerindians and non-Amerindians. His personality was equally impressive, combining a passionate concern for his people with a genius for strategy. As his friend **General Isaac Brock** (1769–1812) observed, if he had been British, he would have been a great general.[11] Tecumseh is widely regarded as the greatest of all Amerindian leaders during the period of resistance to European settlement.

Tecumseh challenged the cessions of territory the Americans were obtaining, particularly those that **William Henry Harrison**, governor of Indiana Territory from 1800 to 1812, wrung from Amerindians. He visited as many tribal nations as he could, urging them to unite to prevent further encroachment. His proposal was a radical departure from traditional inter-tribal politics, yet Tecumseh made remarkable headway towards realizing his vision of an Amerindian alliance from Lake Michigan southward.[12] As the influence of Tecumseh and Tenskwatawa spread, the British became interested, and the Americans, apprehensive.

Tecumseh gained the support of the Potawatomi (mainly through Chief Main Poc, until he defected), Ojibwa, Shawnee, Odawa, Winnebago, and Kickapoo. He had less, but some, success with the Delaware, Wyandot, Menominee, Miami, and Piankeshaw, among others. The Creek, who had been strong supporters of the British in the recent war, felt particularly betrayed by the peace (their first reaction to the news had been to call it a 'Virginia lie'[13]), so very few joined. Tecumseh's appeal was to the younger warriors. Older chiefs tended to oppose him, fearing that his proposed inter-tribal council would undermine their authority.

Despite such opposition, however, other factors came to Tecumseh's aid. The loss of markets for furs caused hardship among those who had adapted to the trade, a situation aggravated among Great Lakes Amerindians by crop failures two years in a row and the disappearance of game because of drought.

By this time, the British had developed a cadre of trader/agents who had learned how to negotiate with Amerindians, following the example of the French. Among these was the Irishman Matthew Elliott (c. 1739–1814), who lived with the Shawnee for many years, married among them, and was so assimilated to the Amerindian way that the British did not completely trust him. Once dismissed from Indian Affairs on unproven charges of corruption, he was called back in 1808 as superintendent at Amherstburg, on the Detroit River in extreme southwestern Upper Canada near Detroit, because of his connection with the strategically located Shawnee. One of his first actions was to arrange a council at Amherstburg that attracted 5,000 Amerindians (see Box 8.1).

Another influential figure was the Scot Robert Dickson (c. 1765–1823), whose flaming red hair and beard became part of western folklore. He was a brother-in-law

Box 8.1   Amherstburg

Amherstburg was a major centre for 'gift' distributions. The British concentrated on providing equipment to obtain food, such as nets, traps, and snares, and, of course, guns and ammunition. The Americans were convinced the Amerindians were being armed for war. In the matter of gift diplomacy, the British had made a complete about-face since 1763. With chiefs they saw as influential, such as Tecumseh, they were generous. The problem was now rather the reverse of the earlier policy, as various administrators and officers vied with each other, especially in the distribution of rum.[14] This, in turn, contributed to problems for both sides.[15]

of Yanktonai Dakota chief Red Thunder. A long-time trader, Dickson was British agent for the tribes west of Lake Huron. His was a hard-headed approach that earned him the reputation of being tough but fair, tempered by a strong streak of generosity, although he tended to favour the various Siouan peoples. Nevertheless, he played a major role rallying the western Indians to the British cause, to which they remained loyal during the war.[16]

But the British were more interested in fostering trade than in provoking war. For one thing, the deadly struggle with Napoleon in Europe had left them with neither the troops nor the resources for more military campaigns. Tensions were mounting, however, particularly between Harrison and Tecumseh. Tecumseh was especially annoyed when the governor ordered land surveys, and he moved to prevent them. Harrison bided his time but then seized the moment in 1811 when the Shawnee chief was away rallying southern tribes to his cause. Harrison attacked Prophetown, which Tenskwatawa had established in 1808 at the confluence of the Wabash and Tippecanoe rivers in Indiana. The ensuing battle was less a victory for the Americans than it was a personal defeat for Tenskwatawa. His influence had been slipping, and this bloodshed speeded up the trend.

For Tecumseh, the attack ended his plan to delay military action until Amerindians and British could gather enough forces to deal a decisive blow to the Americans. For the British, it confirmed their suspicions that the Canadian border was not safe from American aggression.

Gains and Losses

The last of the colonial wars in North America, the **War of 1812–14** has been classed as a continuation of the American War of Independence.[17] For Britain and the US, it was an inconclusive contest that left important matters, such as those relating to Amerindians, as unresolved as they had been before the fighting. For the Amerindians, it was a turning point. The Iroquois who fought for the British fought on their own terms, for their own objectives. Unfortunately, the factionalism that had seen some of the Six Nations Confederacy move to the Grand River and others remain in New York continued to plague the Iroquois and at times they found themselves confronting one another on the field of battle. The Iroquoian military contribution to the British war effort in 1812–14 was tremendous. They had retained their old skill at guerrilla warfare, which the French had called *la petite guerre* and which the Americans feared. In fact, American fear of the Iroquois warriors played an important and sometimes crucial role in the war. Similarly, in the West, the Odawa and Ojibwa allies fought for their own objectives and with similar results. They, too, had preserved guerrilla war tactics and weapons, and they, too, inspired fear in the American armies.

The War of 1812 was the last conflict in northeastern North America in which Amerindian participation was important and even decisive. The Indian allies were the key factor in Great Britain's successful defence of Upper Canada.[18] In the West, it was largely an Amerindian war. For instance, the fall of **Michilimackinac** on 17 July 1812 to British and Amerindian forces was an Amerindian victory. Its strategy, worked out by Tecumseh and other chiefs, had been that of surprise.

The psychological effect of the Michilimackinac victory was enormous, well beyond its broader military significance. Tribes now flocked unreservedly to the British flag. Elliott and Dickson had no trouble raising 4,000 warriors. The Michilimackinac victory also had an impact on General William Hull (1753–1825), US commander at Detroit, whose fear of Amerindians was well known. He proclaimed that 'no white man found fighting by the side of an Indian will be taken prisoner.'[19] A ruse led him to believe that British forces on his flank included 5,000 Amerindians, and Tecumseh reinforced it by using the old trick of marching his warriors again and again past a vantage point in full view of the Americans.

Tecumseh then cut American communication lines, and Hull, convinced that the situation was hopeless, surrendered on 16 August without firing a shot. Tecumseh and General Brock rode together into the fallen fort.[20] When Hull learned what had happened the day before at Fort Dearborn (Chicago), when Main Poc's Potawatomi killed most of the garrison, he probably felt justified. American officials disagreed, however, and court-martialled the hapless Hull.

These successes, especially the fall of Detroit, encouraged the Six Nations, previously set on neutrality, to join British forces. They were a major factor in the British success at **Queenston Heights**, on the Niagara Peninsula, on 13 October 1812, when they arrived at a critical moment on the field of battle led by the Mohawk **Major John Norton**

Major John Norton (Teyoninhokarawen), who played an important role in leading Six Nations forces into battle on the British side during the War of 1812–14. (© *Canadian War Museum (CWM), 19950096–001*)

John Brant, son of Joseph Brant, with Major John Norton led the Iroquois forces to victory during the Battle of Queenston Heights, 1812. Brant was elected to the Upper Canadian House of Assembly in 1830 but lost his seat on the charge of irregular voter practices. *(Metropolitan Toronto Reference Library, J. Ross Robertson Collection, T–15499)*

(Teyoninhokerawen, *fl.* 1784–1825) and John Brant ('Tekarihogen', Ahyonwaeghs, 1794–1832), Joseph Brant's youngest son.[21] Again, the American fear of Amerindians had its effect, and the invasion was repelled. The Americans fled across the river. But the cost was high for the British, as they lost Brock.[22]

Tecumseh cut an American force to pieces near Fort Meigs, Indiana, on 5 May 1813.[23] On the Niagara Peninsula, the **Battle of Beaver Dams**, on 24 June 1813, was an Amerindian victory, Iroquoian, to be exact. According to Norton, 'The Cognauguaga [Caughnawaga] Indians fought the battle, the Mohawk got the plunder and [Lieutenant James] Fitzgibbon [1780–1863] got the credit.'[24] But as the months wore on, Tecumseh began to lose the initiative. He was able to get some Creek to open war in the south, but their confederacy was split to the point of civil war. In 1814, the Americans destroyed what was left of their league.[25] In the meantime, the American naval victory on Lake Erie, 10 September 1813, cut the British supply line to Fort Malden (Amherstburg), the main British centre for gift distribution, endangering Amerindian alliances in the West. To complicate matters, a rift was growing between the Amerindians and their allies.

The British general who succeeded Brock, Henry Proctor (1763–1822), did not attract the admiration of Tecumseh, who compared him to a dog running off with its tail between its legs. His frustration with the British general was understandable, in that the Shawnee chief had by this time assembled one of the largest Indian 'armies' the Great Lakes had ever seen, estimated at 2,000–3,000 warriors, or even more. The contrast with the British force was glaring—it counted only about 800 men. When Proctor finally made a stand at **Moraviantown** (Box 8.2) in southern Ontario on 5 October 1813, Tecumseh and his Indians did the fighting, saving the general's life. Tecumseh, severely wounded, fought until his death. Proctor fled.

Box 8.2   Moraviantown

In 1792, the Moravian Brothers established a village for refugee Delaware on the Thames River near the future international border. Although they called it Fairfield, it became popularly known as Moraviantown. Not only was it successful (for one reason, Delaware were traditionally agriculturalists), it was even more prosperous than surrounding colonial settlements. Looted and burned by the Americans in the War of 1812, the town was rebuilt as New Fairfield in 1815 but never fully recovered. Beset by the usual problems of settler encroachments, which became steadily more serious, many of the Amerindians left for the American Middle West. The colonial authorities also refused to grant the Delaware clear title to the land. In 1903, the government turned New Fairfield over to the Canadian Methodist Episcopal Church, a move the Delaware resented.

We do not know what happened to the Amerindian leader's body, any more than who killed him. Some say he was buried near the scene of battle, others say that souvenir hunters soon rendered the Amerindian leader's body unrecognizable.[26] Among the many stories about Tecumseh's fate is an Ojibwa account recorded a century later, which claims that the Shawnee leader was wounded but did not die because he carried medicine.[27]

Status Quo Ante Bellum

Warriors of more than 30 Amerindian nations had fought under Tecumseh. Now he was dead, and his loss would be hard to overestimate. No leader could fill his role as a catalyst for pan-Indian action. With his passing also went the tattered remains of Tenskwatawa's nativistic movement. Effective Amerindian participation in the war, however, did not end with the defeat at Moraviantown.[28] Warriors continued fighting until the end of the war, sometimes in large numbers. But the underlying unity of purpose that Tecumseh had evoked was fatally weakened and eventually died.

The British tried to fill the void by enshrining Tecumseh's memory as an icon. They gave Tecumseh's son, Paukeesaa, a commission in the British army. His brother, the Shawnee Prophet, received a sword and pistols as gifts of the Prince Regent and was named principal chief of the Western Nations, and the British heaped his sister, Tecumpease, with gifts of condolence. But ceremonial protocol could not transform a memory into a new Tecumseh. The British also could not disguise the fact that they were not fully committed to the war, locked as they were in the struggle in Europe with Napoleon. Britain's wooing of the Amerindians in this particular case sprang not so much from humanist or ideological conviction as it did from the need to use all means possible to maintain and preserve her positions in two different parts of the world at once, a circumstance not lost on her North American opponents.

The Americans moved to take advantage of the situation and to turn the Amerindians to their side of the fighting, and they persuaded some. On 5 July 1814, a contingent of American Iroquois, largely Seneca under Red Jacket, fought on the American side at the Battle of Chippewa, north of Fort Erie on the Niagara Peninsula, against British forces that included 200 men of the Six Nations and 100 western Amerindians under Major Norton. The battle saw Iroquois once more pitted against Iroquois, as had happened in the American War of Independence. This time, the Canadian Amerindians sustained their heaviest losses of the war—87 killed and five taken prisoners, against nine American Amerindians killed, four wounded, and 10 missing—although their role was not decisive.

These casualties, incurred in fighting what was now a white man's quarrel, shocked the Amerindians.[29] The American Iroquois sent a deputation to discuss with the Canadian Six Nations a new, and more inclusive, policy of neutrality. As a result, only a few warriors remained to fight the Battle of Lundy's Lane, north of Chippewa, on 25 July, although other Amerindians continued to fight in other theatres.

The British had learned their lesson from the Treaty of Paris of 1783. During the negotiations for the **Treaty of Ghent**, 1814, which formally ended the war, they tried to bargain for the establishment of an Indian territory, the boundaries of which would follow those fixed at the Treaty of Greenville (1795). This, the Americans absolutely refused to agree to. The most they would accept was to recognize Amerindian lands as they had been before hostilities—in legal terms, the status quo ante bellum.

To suggest that this was a disappointment for Amerindians in the US is to put it mildly. All their battles, very often successful in individual cases, did not give them back any lost territories. Despite the assurances of the Treaty of Ghent—'the Treaty of Omissions', as a French diplomat called it[30]—Amerindians continued to lose land. Métis communities in the Great Lakes area were overwhelmed and even occupied militarily.[31] Three years after the death of Tecumseh and five years after Tippecanoe, Indiana became a state. By 1817, forced removal of Amerindians from their traditional lands began in the Ohio Valley, a policy that would reach a peak with the Trail of Tears for the Cherokee in the 1830s.

In some instances, Amerindians themselves decided to migrate. The Potawatami did in the years 1835–40, when they left their Great Lakes homelands to settle in central and southern Ontario, where they are today.[32] Some Oneida of the Six Nations settled around Muncey, Ontario, around 1840. Even though the Oneida had sided with the Americans during the War of Independence, afterwards they had been deprived of most of their lands in New York.

Amerindians were not the only people on the move. Settler expansion was dramatic—the population tripled from approximately 750,000 in 1821 to 2.3 million by 1851. In Upper Canada alone, it rose by a factor of 10, to reach 952,000. By this time, Amerindians east of the Great Lakes were already a minority in their own lands. By 1812, they formed about 10 per cent of the population of Upper Canada.[33]

In the midst of this agricultural expansion, the fur trade continued for most of the nineteenth century as a major economic activity, ensuring a common ground for peaceful interaction between Amerindians and Europeans. But even there, the end was in sight. The time of the ancient way of life had passed.

For Canadian Amerindians, the War of 1812–14 was the end of an era.[34] As long as the colonial wars lasted, they had been able to maintain their positions in return for war service. The loss of that bargaining tool put them at a serious disadvantage. Post-war governmental reorganization reflected this change: in 1830, Indian administration was shifted to the civilian arm. New conditions, however, demanded new adaptations.[35] Adaptation, of course, had always been the key to Amerindian survival. The circumstances might have changed, but the requirement to work out satisfactory life patterns under prevailing conditions remained the same. Traditional values, instead of disappearing, would find new life and new forms in rising to these challenges.

Important Names and Terms

Battle of Beaver Dams
Battle of Fallen Timbers
Brock, General Isaac
Harrison, William Henry
Michilimackinac
Moraviantown
Norton, Major John

Queenston Heights
Tecumseh
Tenskwatawa
Treaty of Ghent
Treaty of Greenville
War of 1812–14

Study Questions

1) What role did Tecumseh play in the conflicts between the British and the Americans?
2) What advantages did the British gain from their Amerindian allies?
3) Why did the Iroquois and the Odawa and Ojibwa allies fight against the Americans?
4) Where did the various peoples move after the War of 1812–14?

Recommended Readings

Allen, R.S. *His Majesty's Indian Allies*. Toronto: Dundurn Press, 1993.
Benn, Carl. *The Iroquois in the War of 1812*. Toronto: University of Toronto Press, 1998.
Edmunds, R. David. *The Shawnee Prophet*. Lincoln: University of Nebraska Press, 1983.
———. *Tecumseh and the Quest for Indian Leadership*. Boston: Little, Brown, 1984.
Stanley, G.F.G. *The War of 1812: Land Operations*. Toronto: Macmillan, 1983.
Sugden, John. *Tecumseh's Last Stand*. Norman: University of Oklahoma Press, 1985.
Tanner, Helen Hornbeck, ed. *Atlas of Great Lakes Indian History*. Norman: University of Oklahoma Press, 1987.

9 The 'Indian Problem': Isolation, Assimilation, and Experimentation

Two ideas concerning Amerindians dominated British civil administration for North America in 1830. First, it was believed that they were disappearing as a people. After all, at the start of the nineteenth century, there had been about 18,000 indigenous people in Upper and Lower Canada (later Ontario and Quebec), not including 'wild' Amerindians of the boreal forest. Twenty years later, the number had dropped to 12,000, lending support for the popular belief of the 'vanishing Indian'. In contrast, between 1818 and 1828, the non-Native population doubled.

The second notion was that Amerindians who did not disappear should either move to communities isolated from whites or else assimilate. Agriculture[1] and education, entrusted to missionaries, would achieve 'civilization'. In the words of a colonial secretary, the aim was 'to protect and cherish this helpless Race. . . [and] raise them in the Scale of Humanity'.[2] Sir John Colborne, lieutenant-governor for Upper Canada, suggested in 1829 that the best way of financing the 'civilizing' of Amerindians would be through the leasing and sale of their lands. Sir James Kempt, governor of Lower Canada, 1828–30, agreed. Amerindians must become self-supporting citizens within the cultural framework of colonial life. The old hunting ways were doomed. In other words, Amerindians would pay their own way into civilization. It was expected that colonial governors would mainly, but not entirely, work out details. Meanwhile, Indian administration in the Canadas changed radically between 1828 and 1845.

The government hived off the administration of Indian affairs in Lower Canada from that of Upper Canada to form a separate unit in 1829, leaving most of the experienced personnel in Upper Canada. (At this time, each colony—Nova Scotia, Prince Edward Island, New Brunswick, Lower Canada, and Upper Canada—had separate administrations. The Hudson's Bay Company administered Rupert's Land and the west coast.) Administrators recruited some Amerindians as interpreters and clerks, but none at the policy-making level. With the Act of Union, passed by the British Parliament in 1840 and proclaimed in 1841, Upper Canada became Canada West and Lower Canada became Canada East. Earlier, Major-General

H.C. Darling, Indian Affairs' chief superintendent, 1828–30, in his 1828 report on Amerindian conditions—the first such for the Canadas—advocated model farms and villages as the best means of 'civilizing' Amerindians, and this policy had enough support to go forward.[3]

Time Line

1637	First Amerindian 'reserve', at Sillery, near Quebec City.		founded by American Methodist missionary William Case.
1765	Moravian missionary Jens Haven intercedes to ease conflict between Labrador Inuit and Europeans, which had forced Inuit up the Labrador coast.	1830s–40s	Upper Canada administration, over Iroquois protests, gives Grand River Navigation Company Six Nations' funds and land, and the company floods more Six Nations territory before going bankrupt. (Iroquois ultimately lose a 1948 court decision over the matter.)
1769	Moravians receive land grant on northern Labrador coast.		
1771	Haven founds first mission at Nain, which includes trading post.		
1784	New Brunswick separated from Nova Scotia; refuses to recognize the only land grant to Amerindians previously made in the colony.	1835	Indian Affairs agent T.G. Anderson begins Ojibwa settlement project at Manitowaning on Manitoulin Island; project eventually deemed a failure, but Ojibwa remain, founding village of Little Current.
1812	Selkirk colony for white settlers established at Red River, site of the largest Métis settlement in the West.		
1820	Whalers operating on east side of Baffin Island.	1836	Grape Island project relocated to Rice Lake at Alderville, Ont. Anglican Herbert Beaver the first permanent west coast missionary, at Fort Vancouver. Sir Francis Bond Head, lieutenant-governor of Upper Canada, arranges large land surrenders by Ojibwa in Manitoulin chain and on Bruce Peninsula (the Saugeen Tract).
1825	Miramichi fire in northern New Brunswick destroys 6,000 square miles of prime forest, the resource base of subsistence for countless Amerindians. Britain grants land along Credit River to Métis Methodist minister Peter Jones and his Mississauga converts.		
1827	Grape Island settlement of Ojibwa in Bay of Quinte	1838	Only 1,425 Mi'kmaq, in wretched condition, listed as living in Nova Scotia.
		1840s	HBC establishes posts in Far Northwest.

(*continued*)

1841	First book printed using Cree syllabics.	1856	Ojibwa band settles on Christian Island in Georgian Bay.
1842	Nova Scotia Act to provide for the Instruction and Permanent Settlement of the Indians.	1859	An Act Concerning Indian Reserves passed in Nova Scotia.
1844	New Brunswick Act for the Management and Disposal of the Indian Reserves.	1862	Utopian experiment of lay Anglican William Duncan begins at Tsimshian village of Metlakatla with support of Tsimshian chief Paul Legaic.
1847	Mississauga join Six Nations to establish New Credit, near Hagersville, Ont.		
1850	Gunboat diplomacy begins on Pacific coast.	1887	Duncan and 600 followers establish New Metlakatla in Alaska; Legaic and others stay behind.
1850–4	Governor James Douglas, recognizing Aboriginal title, signs 14 treaties with Coast Salish on Vancouver Island.	1888	Warship sails up Skeena River to quell Gitksan uprising.

Model Villages Would Immerse Amerindians in Euro-Canadian Culture

The nineteenth century was the era of Utopian experiments—attempts to create communities that would reflect Victorian ideals of the good life. For Amerindians, these **model villages**—which were closely associated with schools (see Chapters 13, 14)—would become an instrument for the inculcation of Euro-Canadian values—or so it was hoped. These experiments all were in Canada West, but they drew much of their inspiration from the long-established Amerindian villages of Canada East. The inhabitants of these earlier villages were officially Christian and living sedentary lives, an 'achievement' the British hoped to copy in Canada West.[4] In fact, they already had the examples in Canada West of two successful Christian Amerindian villages, Credit River and Grape Island.

A Mississauga-Welsh Métis and Methodist minister, **Peter Jones** (Kahkewaquonaby, 'Sacred Feathers', 1802–56), was very successful converting his people to Methodism.[5] Officials would have preferred it if Jones had been an Anglican—Anglicanism, after all, was the established church of Great Britain and had that same status in the Canadas, whereas Methodism had American ties. Nevertheless, in 1825, they offered to build a village of 20 houses for the converts on the west bank of the Credit River and to help them get started as farmers. The Mississauga were under heavy pressure to make the change to agriculture and looked to Jones and his brother to help them find their way into this strange new world. They selected Jones chief at the age of 27, an unusual honour. Officialdom wanted Jones's people to switch to Anglicanism, but they did not relate to that denomination's structured institutionalism, and they resisted. Suspicious of the American ties to Methodism, the government refused the band's application for a deed.[6] They even tried to move the settlement to Manitoulin Island, farther from American influence, a move the people were able to prevent. Eventually, at the invitation of the Six Nations, the Mississauga established New Credit near Hagersville, Ontario, in 1847.

In another instance, an American-born Methodist missionary, William Case (1780–1855), using American funds, established a village in 1827 on Grape Island in the Bay of Quinte, 10 kilometres east of Belleville. Case ran the project like an army camp. Even so, for a while it worked. In 1836, the project moved to a more suitable location at Alderville, on Rice Lake. Two other settlements launched by Indian Affairs, at Coldwater and the Narrows (near Orillia) in 1829, had shorter lives. They both were under the direction of Thomas G. Anderson (1779–1875), Indian Affairs agent. By 1837, financial problems had become acute, and both settlements were abandoned. Ojibwa Chief John Aisance (Ascance, Essens, *c.* 1790–1847) cited fraud. In 1856, his band moved to Christian Island in Georgian Bay.[7]

In 1835, the department tried again, this time at Manitowaning on Manitoulin Island. They improved funding, but friction developed between missionary sects, compounded by the paternalism of Anderson's administration. As an official project, it was dead by 1862, but as a settlement, Manitowaning continued. A group of Ojibwa, acting on their own, established a village at Little Current. A mission launched by the Jesuits, Wikwemikong, was still on the island in the twenty-first century.

The Amerindians who participated in the model villages were perhaps the most committed to their success and to education in particular. Both Amerindians and officialdom saw schooling as the key to the future, but where Amerindians viewed education as a tool for adaptation, administrators saw it as a means of assimilation— and official goals were not always realistic. Combined with a deep pessimism about Amerindian capabilities 'to rise to civilization', it was easy to see failure when difficulties arose. The fact that the survival rate of these projects was as good as it was speaks volumes for the determined efforts of the Amerindians to make the best of a very difficult situation. In *Sacred Feathers*, historian Donald B. Smith showed how Peter Jones personified this struggle:

> [He] lived in a period of oppression for Canada's native peoples. . . . For three decades Peter Jones fought back: to obtain a secure title to the reserves, a viable economic land base for each band, a first-class system of education, and Indian self-government. The white politicians largely ignored him . . . others today fight the political battles that Peter Jones began.[8]

Jones represents one response of the Ojibwa to the new pressures. Another, more deeply rooted in pre-contact traditions, was the rise of Midewiwin, or the Grand Medicine Society. Its ceremonies became central to Ojibwa life. As with other nativistic spiritual movements, it was a cultural reaffirmation in the face of strange new forces.[9]

'The Greatest Kindness We Can Perform' (Attacking a Sinful History)

At least one high official saw attempts at **assimilation** as a waste of time. **Sir Francis Bond Head**, lieutenant-governor of Upper Canada from 1836 to 1838, reasoned this way: hunters showed little if any inclination to become farmers. Model villages implanted more vices than they eradicated. Therefore, the 'greatest kindness we can perform towards these Intelligent, simple-minded people is to remove and fortify them as much as possible from all Communication with the Whites.' He thought Manitoulin, the world's largest freshwater island, and its surrounding region would make a satisfactory refuge, as it was 'totally separated' from non-Amerindians.[10] Bond Head took advantage of a gift distribution (see Box 9.1) at Manitoulin Island in 1836 to arrange two major land cessions. He then convinced a number of Ojibwa leaders to sign over 'the twenty-three thousand islands' of the Manitoulin chain on the promise that the Crown would protect the region as Amerindian territory.

The second agreement (1854) was with the Saugeen Ojibwa of the Bruce Peninsula.[11] After warning them that the government could not control squatters moving into their territory, Bond Head promised that if they would move either to the Manitoulin Island region or the northern end of Bruce Peninsula above Owen Sound, the government would provide them with housing and equipment. Under pressure, the Ojibwa signed over 1.5 million acres (607,028 hectares), the **Saugeen Tract**, leaving them with 'the granite rocks and bog land' of the remainder. Few took advantage of the Manitoulin Island offer. Bond Head wanted the whole of the Bruce Peninsula but settled for what he thought he could get without argument. Using similar tactics, he proceeded to obtain other surrenders to the south.

These huge, peaceful surrenders greatly impressed the imperial government. The Aborigines' Protection Society, however, saw the deals as an exchange of 3 million acres (1,214,057 hectares) of rich lands for '23,000 barren islands, rocks of granite, dignified

Box 9.1   Gift Distributions

Throughout the nineteenth century, the perceived need for Amerindians to march to the white man's drum would dominate administration. In the meantime, the **gift distributions** continued—the lesson of 1763 had not been forgotten, even though there was no more need for Amerindian military services, at least not until 1837–8, which saw armed rebellions by whites in Upper and Lower Canada. Those episodes prolonged the life of the distributions, even as the cost became steadily more unacceptable. The turning point was 1827, when the Ojibwa of Chenail Ecarte and Lower St Clair surrendered large tracts in the London and western districts for annuities and four reserves. In 1858, the British brought the gift distributions to an end.

by the name of Manitoulin Islands'. The Amerindians' attitude was ultimately one of helplessness in the face of the settler juggernaut. Their 'Great Father was determined to have their land.' In fact, at issue was more than land; despite a Royal Declaration in 1847 acknowledging the Saugeen Ojibwa title to their aquatic territory and traditional fishing grounds around the Saugeen Peninsula, it was not long before the colonial government came to regard the Ojibwa's aquatic territory as public waters and to favour non-Aboriginal interests over those of the Indians.[12] Saugeen discontent reached the point of passing the wampum belt to take up the hatchet. Warned that they could not prevail against the whites, they replied:

> We know that very well; but don't you see that we are all doomed to die; all our land is taken from us, and we think that if we kill a few of the white people they will come and kill us off, and then there will be an end of us.[13]

More Than Land Lost to Colonial Interests

During this period, the Six Nations became embroiled in a different sort of problem. Faced in the 1820s with a scheme to develop the Grand River for navigation, they did their best to oppose it on the grounds that parts of their lands would be flooded and their fisheries ruined.[14] In spite of protests, the government agreed to help the Grand River Navigation Company by using Six Nations funds to buy its stock. Between 1834 and 1847, the Upper Canadian administration (and, after 1840, that of the Union of the Canadas) helped the company to the tune of $160,000 from band funds without the consent of the Iroquois. Not only that, it granted 369 acres (149 hectares) of Iroquois land to the company, in addition to the flooded areas, again without band consent.

In the 1830s and 1840s, the company built five dams, five locks, and a towpath on the lower Grand River despite growing protest from the Iroquois. Then, the company, unable to compete with the railways, went bankrupt, leaving the Iroquois holding worthless stock they had never wanted in the first place. Their attempts at restitution got nowhere. The impasse continued after Confederation, when the Canadian government refused to accept responsibility, a position the courts upheld.[15] An attempt to settle out of court proved fruitless.

The Mississauga of the Credit River also had financial claims against the government arising out of the management of monies the Province of Canada received from the sale of surrendered lands. They finally won their case in 1905, in large part because of the work of a young lawyer, Andrew G. Chisholm. Chisholm spent close to 50 years working on Amerindian claims, mostly in southern Ontario, until his death in 1943.[16]

Overall, demand for land drove the colonies' relations with their Amerindian hosts and led to the creation of reserves—lands reserved for the use of Amerindians (see Box 9.2). In

Box 9.2   Early Reserves in Canada

Reserves for Aboriginal people were not a nineteenth-century invention. In Canada East, the Amerindian villages of Odanak (St Francis), Bécancour, Caughnawaga (Sault St Louis, today's Kahnawake), St Regis (Akwesasne), Oka (Lake of Two Mountains, Kanesatake), and Lorette had existed long before the Conquest. In fact, the French had set up the first 'reserve' in Canada, that of Sillery, near Quebec City two centuries earlier, in 1637, on the site of a Montagnais summer fishing station.[17]

In creating Sillery, the French were not trying to compensate Amerindians for lost territories. Quite the contrary, the French King was setting aside land he considered to be French for Amerindian use under certain conditions.[18] Its title rested with the Jesuits until 1651, when the French transferred it temporarily to the Amerindians (most of whom were Huron) but still under the direction of the Jesuits to ensure Amerindian loyalty in the colonial wars.[19]

In the 1640s, Sillery counted about 40 Christian families and many more traditionalists. Only the 'principal' Amerindians lived in government-built, European-style houses.[20] It was, in effect, a residential mission to introduce agriculture to people whose lands had been overhunted and overtrapped. However, restrictive regulations (for one thing, Amerindians were allowed to hunt or fish only if either the Jesuits or a Christian captain gave them permission),[21] compounded by problems associated with war, disease, and alcohol, dampened early enthusiasm.

The final blows were an Iroquois raid in 1655 and, later, a fire that destroyed most of the buildings. The government returned title to the Jesuits.[22] This ethically questionable transfer allowed the missionaries to open the reserve to European settlers during the latter part of the 1660s.[23] By 1688, Sillery was all but 'free' of Amerindians.[24]

the North, where European and Yankee wanted only to pass through, administrations responded mainly to requests from missionaries to be allowed to preach the Gospel. Further south, European immigrants were fleeing overcrowding and famines in Europe, pro-British refugees were arriving on promise of a reward for their loyalty to the Crown, and colonial governments were gazing ever more intently at what 'vacant' reserve land was left.

Indian Administrations

Arctic and Subarctic People Contend with Missionaries, Whalers, and Fur Traders

The Inuit had two main arenas for association with whites—the comparatively mild Labrador coast since the sixteenth century and the central and western Arctic since early in the nineteenth.[25] The hostilities between the Labrador coast Inuit and Europeans, carried over from the French regime, had driven the Inuit northward. In 1765 the conflict was eased, although not ended, through the efforts of Moravian missionary Jens Haven (1724–96), known to the Inuit as Ingoak ('Inuit friend').[26]

In 1769, the Moravians received a land grant of 100,000 acres (40,469 hectares). Haven launched his first mission at Nain two years later. An influential Inuk woman, Mikak (Micoc, c. 1740–95), helped him win local support. Mikak was one of the Aboriginal people who had been sent to London in the hope that she would be impressed with English might and would influence her people to stop harassing English fishing operations.[27]

Three other land grants followed, as the Moravians expanded their operations. When they combined trading with their missionary work, however, they found themselves in competition with the Hudson's Bay Company, a situation that peaked in the second half of the nineteenth century. The Moravians eventually abandoned trade to the HBC in 1926.[28]

In the central and western Arctic, whaling was the attraction, at first mainly for British and Scottish. By 1820, whalers were operating on the east side of Baffin Island and moving westward. By shortly after mid-century, Americans dominated whaling off the west coast of Hudson Bay as well as in the western Arctic. Their main target was the bowhead whale, sought for its oil but especially for its baleen ('whalebone'), much in demand to create the tightly corseted feminine silhouette then so fashionable.[29]

Individual enterprise was the order of the day, particularly in the western Arctic. There was no systematic organization of whaling operations and no government supervision.[30] For the Inuit, the association could be profitable in the short run, as they hired out to the whalers. They also benefited from the debris (such as wood and metal) the outsiders left behind. In the long run, however, the adoption of the gun and trade goods (including foods such as flour, sugar, and tea)[31] led to a decline in ancient hunting skills and a consequent lessening of self-sufficiency. Introduced diseases made the situation worse. The combined effects of these factors would become severe later in the nineteenth century.

The massive attack on whale populations, started in the Strait of Belle Isle in the sixteenth century and fanning northward, had begun to affect the availability of the sea mammals. Although whale meat was only one item of diet (walrus, for example, was used much more),[32] obtaining it was the ultimate challenge for the hunter—very important to self-esteem. More significant, the commercial slaughter of whales and walrus, at its peak from 1868 to 1883, resulted in widespread starvation.[33] By 1900, the original Inuvialuit of the western Arctic had disappeared, to be replaced by Alaskan Inuit who came with the American whalers.[34] This was only one indication of the dislocations resulting from contact that would eventually be more widespread.[35]

Since no one except Inuit was interested in settling permanently in the Arctic, the British did not raise the question of land, leaving the Inuit to pursue their own lives in their own ways. Non-Native intrusions were few and scattered. The HBC, in fact, did not establish a permanent post in the High Arctic until early in the twentieth century. During the 1840s, however, the Hudson's Bay Company began establishing posts in

A Moravian missionary who may be Jens Haven (1724–96) is shown speaking to Inuit at Nain, Labrador. After Maria Spilsbury (1777–1820). *(Library and Archives Canada, C–124432)*

the Far Northwest despite serious doubts as to the legality. The first was Peel River Post, which would later become Fort McPherson in the Northwest Territories.

The Company then pushed westward into the Yukon,[36] where the Amerindians were already trading with Northwest Coast groups and with Russians on the Pacific coast. Locals were pleased to have access to the new trade goods, but coastal traders such as the Tlingit did not take kindly to this double invasion of their trading domains.[37] When the HBC established Fort Selkirk where the Pelly and Yukon rivers meet, in the homelands of the northern Tutchone, the Tlingit defended their commercial interests by wrecking the post and defying both British and Russians. In the midst of that three-cornered fight, the missionaries arrived—the Anglicans in 1861, with the Roman Catholics hard on their heels a year later.[38] To the south and east, of course, the missionaries had arrived several decades earlier, but one, **William Duncan**, sought the isolation of the northern coast for his missionary experiment (Box 9.3).

The Mi'kmaq Continue the Fight for Their Land in the Atlantic Provinces

In 1829, the last known Beothuk died of tuberculosis, leaving no officially recognized Aboriginal peoples in Newfoundland. In Nova Scotia, the 1838 census cited

1,425 Mi'kmaq, in wretched condition and declining so rapidly they were expected to disappear in about 40 years. The government recognized no Aboriginal territorial rights, apart from the right to hunt and fish 'at the pleasure of the sovereign' (see Chapters 3 and 6). If individual Mi'kmaq wanted land, they had to apply for grants like anyone else. What they received, however, were licences of occupation 'during pleasure'. An Order-in-Council set aside 20,050 unsurveyed acres (8,114 hectares) for this purpose,[39] but neither lands nor locations were good, and none were near Halifax, once a favoured hunting ground.[40]

These lands were not reserved for specific bands, which would most often be the case in other parts of

Mikak, an Inuk woman, was sent to England in 1769 in the hope that she would influence her people to stop harassing English fishing operations off the coast of Labrador. She would be instrumental in helping the Moravian missionaries establish a foothold in the Arctic. John Russell (1744–1806) painted this portrait during her stay in London. *(Photo courtesy Institut und Sammlung für Völkerkunde der Universität Göttingen)*

what would become Canada (see Box 9.4). All Amerindians in the province were equally entitled to all reserves, a system that stayed in effect until 1960.[41] Even so, non-Native squatters, whom the government was unable (or unwilling) to control, continually invaded them. Even worse, homesteaders' tickets of location sometimes overlapped reserves.[42] Some chiefs, such as Andrew Meuse (*fl.* 1821–50, chief near Annapolis Royal), lobbied hard for their people with some results. Meuse, for example, won the right for his people to pursue their traditional hunt of the porpoise.[43]

In 1842, Nova Scotia created the post of Indian commissioner to supervise the reserves. The commissioner saw to it that chiefs were acknowledged publicly by making them militia captains. He also provided them with surveys of their reserves to help them organize distribution of lands among their people. The first holder of the new post was Joseph Howe (1804–73), who later opposed Confederation. Frustrated by lack of public and administrative support—he received no pay—and by anti-Amerindian sentiment, he lasted in the position only

Box 9.3   The Saga of Duncan and Legaic

In 1857, William Duncan (1832–1918), an Anglican schoolmaster, arrived at Fort Simpson.[44] He was not the first missionary on the scene. In 1836, an HBC Anglican chaplain had set up a permanent mission,[45] and Roman Catholic missionaries arrived two years later. But the Fraser River gold rush inspired Duncan in 1862 to establish his mission far away from outside influences.

Impressed by the Tsimshian, wealthy traders who were challenging the HBC monopoly, Duncan learned their language and cultivated the friendship of the influential Legaic (d. 1894), third Tsimshian Eagle clan chief to hold that title.[46] Legaic led 200 of his people who had settled near the fort back to Metlakatla. He was baptized and adopted the name Paul, converting the title 'Legaic' into a surname.

Legaic and Duncan transformed Metlakatla into a mission village, blending the traditional with the new.[47] Government was by a council of chiefs (including Duncan) and 10 elected councillors. Amerindian constables maintained order. Initially supported by the HBC, the community established a store as well as other enterprises, including a fish cannery. Within four years, it was self-sufficient.[48] At its peak, it counted up to 2,000 residents and became known worldwide.

The mission lasted from 1862 until 1887. Duncan's authoritarian ways did not sit well with Legaic, and his unorthodox approach to religion led to a parting of the ways with his sponsor, the Church Missionary Society. On the political front, confrontations with government over land led to a commission of inquiry in 1884 recommending an immediate survey, which was completed under protection of a gunboat. The following year, Duncan re-established his village on Annette Island, Alaska, with 600 followers. Legaic stayed behind in the original Metlakatla. Both Metlakatlas survived into the twenty-first century. The last known holder of the Legaic title died in 1938.[49]

In the late 1880s, the Tsimshian were wealthy and powerful enough to rival the Hudson's Bay Company—and to hold their own in a power struggle with missionary William Duncan. In this drawing by Tsimshian artist Fredee Alexcee, Legaic is presiding over a pole-raising ceremony while standing on the stairway leading to the entrance of his residence. The elevated doorway signals that it was a 'skyhouse', indicating Legaic's lofty position. The stairway symbolizes the World Tree, the channel between the underworld, earth, and sky. Two attendants hold coppers, thus displaying Legaic's wealth. *(National Museums of Canada photo)*

Box 9.4   The Iroquois of Kahnawake

Reserves in the modern sense (lands set aside for Amerindians' continued use upon sur-render of most of their territory)[50] did not appear until after the Proclamation of 1763. Under the French regime, which did not recognize Aboriginal title, lands for Amerindian commun-ities had been granted to missionaries 'for the benefit of the Amerindians'. This meant that Aboriginals, such as the Cree and Ojibwa in the North, were powerless to act when their lands were invaded by loggers and settlers without a by-your-leave, as were the Mi'kmaq of Restigouche with respect to their fishing grounds.

Although their problems were not a priority with the new English government, involved as it was in confronting the French, the Natives won their point in one case. In 1761, when the Jesuits took the stand that as the seigneurs of Caughnawaga (Kahnawake) they had the right to sell portions of its lands, the Iroquois complained to General Thomas Gage, military governor of Montreal from 1760 to 1763. Remembering that the Iroquois had been allies of the British in the recent war, the soldier governor saw to it that the Jesuits were deprived of all interest in the reserve, which was turned over to the Amerindians.[51] This was ratified in 1764 by James Murray, governor of Quebec, 1763–6. Gage's action would stand Kahnawake in good stead in the future.

about a year. Failure of the potato crop in 1846–8 added to both the colony's and the Amerindians' woes.

It was not until 1859 that the government enacted legislation under which estab-lished squatters could buy the lands they had already taken, with the proceeds placed in a fund for Amerindian relief. Henceforth, too, the government would eject squat-ters, regularize surveys, and give plots to individual Amerindians. However, very few of the squatters paid anything for their lands, and none paid in full.[52]

Soon, the government announced that the boundaries of the reserves had been es-tablished beyond dispute. By 1866, reserves totalled 20,730 acres (8,389 hectares) for 637 Amerindian families. At that time, not many Mi'kmaq were farmers. Furthermore, they objected to the division of reserves into individual leaseholds, preferring to con-tinue their tribal custom of holding lands in common.

In 1830, New Brunswick counted fewer than a thousand Mi'kmaq, Wuastukawiuk, and Abenaki. Those of the white pine stands of the Miramichi had been devastated by a disastrous fire in 1825, which destroyed 6,000 square miles (15,540 square km) of prime forest along with their subsistence base. When New Brunswick was separated from Nova Scotia and became a colony in 1784, it had refused to recognize the only land grant of the previous administration, 20,000 acres (8,094 hectares) along the Miramichi River to John Julian and his band. By the time the administration confirmed the grant in 1808, it was half its original size.[53]

As in Nova Scotia, the uncontrolled influx of Loyalists aroused resentment. In this case, troops had to be called in. Indian administration was as haphazard as in Nova Scotia. When lands set aside for Amerindians finally were listed, in 1838, 61,293 acres (24,804 hectares) were counted and divided among 15 reserves. Here, also, there was difficulty with squatters who refused to budge from Amerindian lands.[54] The lieutenant-governor of New Brunswick urged that Amerindians be treated as children—an idea widely accepted at the time—thereby limiting their legal rights and capacity for dealing with their own affairs.

Moses H. Perley, Special Commissioner for Indian Affairs, 1841–8, sounded the alarm that Amerindian lands were shrinking fast.[55] Perley played a major role in drafting the 1844 Act for the Management and Disposal of the Indian Reserves in the Province. By the time it was passed, however, it was so altered that his efforts to protect Amerindian wishes and interests were aborted. The colony would reallocate reserves on the basis of 50 acres (20 hectares) per family. The 'surplus' would be sold 'for the benefit of the Indians'. By 1867, Amerindian holdings had been boosted—theoretically—to 66,096 acres (26,748 hectares). In fact, 16 per cent of that acreage had been sold, usually at ridiculously low prices, and squatters still occupied 10,000 acres (4,047 hectares). The only thing that saved Amerindians from losing all their land was the fact that much of New Brunswick was unsuitable for agriculture.[56]

The situation was even worse in Prince Edward Island. In 1767, it had been divided among 66 absentee British proprietors, with nothing left for its Aboriginal inhabitants. Numerous petitions gave rise to much debate, during which the Mi'kmaq raised the point that although they had once 'raised the tomahawk' against the British, they had put it down on being promised fair treatment. 'They promised to leave us some of our land—but they did not—they drove us from place to place like wild beasts—that was not just.'[57]

An 1856 law provided for a commissioner appointed to look after Amerindian affairs. In 1859, the colony set aside 204 acres (83 hectares) on the Morell River for Amerindians, the only such successful transaction on the island.[58] Eventually, interested persons in the colony, along with the Aborigines' Protection Society, bought Lennox Island, 1,400 acres (567 hectares) offshore, for the Amerindians. The group raised funds for the project in Britain and completed the sale in 1870. They provided money to settle seven Amerindian families. Four years later, almost 90 acres (36 hectares) were under cultivation.

Ominous Signs on the Prairies

On the prairies, the buffalo-hunting way of life was in full swing during the first half of the nineteenth century, but indications of things to come were becoming increasingly evident. The fur trade was in decline, and no one doubted the ultimate fate of the buffalo.[59] Herds could still impede travellers on occasion,[60] but already in the 1830s shortages had begun in certain areas. For two years in a row (1848–9), they were increasingly serious.[61] As early as the beginning of the nineteenth century, the Saulteaux and others, on their own initiative, began to take up agriculture.[62] The traditional way of life, however, was still essentially intact.

Soon after the settlers arrived, another agent for change appeared in the form of missionaries, whose direct attack on Amerindian and fur trade practices increased old social divisions and created new ones. Chiefs such as Peguis (Begouais, Pegouisse, 'Destroyer', 'Little Chip', baptized William King, 1774–1864) of the Saulteaux at Red River became actively disenchanted with the treaty they had signed with Selkirk in 1817 (see Chapter 6).[63] The Métis also were becoming uneasy about their land rights.

Confusion in the laws matched this mixture of cultures. Three systems were in effect: Canadian,[64] British, and Amerindian. The 1821 Act for Regulating the Fur Trade had given the HBC, which by now had swallowed up the North West Company, a 21-year monopoly for 'trading with the Indians in all such parts of North America, not being part of the lands or territories hitherto granted to the said Governor and Company of Adventurers of England trading to Hudson's Bay, and not being part of any of His Majesty's Provinces in North America'.[65] The lack of clarity in this wording gave rise to uncertainty and disputes.[66]

Some years later, the mixing of cultures was instrumental in the rise of a religious movement among the Hudson Bay Cree between the Churchill and Albany rivers, in 1842–3. A newly developed system of written language for the Cree (Box 9.5) probably played a special role in the movement, which combined Christian and traditional Native elements and was led by **Abishabis** ('Small Eyes', d. 1843) and his associate Wasiteck ('The Light'). They claimed they could provide their people with the knowledge to find the road to heaven, since they had been there themselves; they even provided a sketch map.

In the end Abishabis was killed by his own people as a windigo (a being with an overweening appetite who preys on humans) because of his increasingly unacceptable

---

Box 9.5   Cree Literacy

In the nineteenth century, a major cultural change occurred among the northern Cree. They adopted a form of writing devised by Methodist missionary James Evans (1801–46) at Norway House, on Lake Winnipeg. This syllabic system drew on shorthand as well as on symbols already in use among the Cree. The use of the syllabary quickly spread throughout the Cree-speaking North. By the turn of the century, the Cree had one of the highest literacy rates in the world.[67] The system is adaptable to other Algonkian languages, such as Ojibwa and Montagnais, both closely related to Cree, but also to such an unrelated language as Inuktitut. When it came to signing treaties, officials expected Amerindians to sign an X, even though some signees could write in syllabics. Cree chiefs prepared their acceptance speeches for Treaty Nine using syllabics.[68]

behaviour, which had included murder. His movement was a reaction to the presence and teachings of non-Natives but it also vividly illustrated the creative response of Native religions in synthesizing the new teachings with their own beliefs. As we have seen, the rise of Native prophets in response to outside pressures was widespread among Amerindians— the prophet Neolin was associated with Pontiac; Tenskwatawa added a mystic element to Tecumseh's campaign; towards the end of the nineteenth century the Ghost Dance movement, originating in a vision of the Paiute prophet Wovoka, rose on the American Great Plains and found its way to the prairies of Canada; and a recent example of the prophet movement has been among the Dene Dháa (Beaver) of the Northwest.

Gunboat Diplomacy on the West Coast

By 1852, there were 500 settlers on Vancouver Island. Although the Proclamation of 1763 did not apply beyond the mountains, Governor **James Douglas** at first tried to deal with the land question based on an 'unequivocal recognition of Aboriginal title'.[69] Between 1850 and 1854, he signed 14 agreements with Coast Salish bands on Vancouver Island, paying in blankets and other goods rather than in cash for surrenders. On Amerindian insistence, he also stopped settlers from enclosing unpaid-for lands. The land area involved in the agreements was limited (about 3 per cent of the island's area), as settlement was slow. By 1855, there were only 774 non-Amerindians living on Vancouver Island, clustered around Fort Victoria and Nanaimo.[70]

When Douglas ran out of funds, however, neither the colony nor Britain would send more. Both paid lip service to Amerindian title, but neither would pay for it. Douglas then did the next best thing. He had reserves surveyed for Amerindians that included their village sites and burial grounds, as well as their cultivated fields and 'favorite places of resort', such as fishing stations. These reserves, although small by central Canadian standards (west coast Amerindians, being non-agricultural and largely dependent on the sea, did not need as much land, according to officials), took Amerindian wishes into account to some extent. When allotments proved to be too small, Douglas had them increased. Once, when Amerindians at Langley wanted to relocate their village, he had a new reserve surveyed for them.[71]

In addition, partly in compensation for the small size of the reserves, Douglas let Amerindians buy Crown lands on the same conditions that applied to settlers.[72] He managed this despite Colonial Office instructions that white settlement should have priority. In other words, Douglas tried to balance Amerindian and settler rights.[73] The weakness of Douglas's policy, according to one historian, lay in its dependence 'on his own personal qualities and that it was never codified in any legislative enactment'.[74] Therefore, when Douglas retired in 1864, the Colonial Office could make sure that his successors gave settlers' interests priority. A new Commissioner of Crown Lands, Joseph W. Trutch (1826–1904), also appointed in 1864, thought Amerindians had no more rights to land 'than a panther or a bear' (to use a journalistic expression of the period). His reductions of reserve sizes for the benefit of settlers have left a continuing legacy of litigation.[75]

Even during Douglas's day, relations between settlers and Amerindians were uneasy, and violence erupted early. In 1844, Cowichan, Songhees, and Klallum killed livestock belonging to Fort Victoria, then attacked the fort when trade was suspended. It took a show of force to restore peace. In 1850, the period of coastal **'gunboat diplomacy'** was launched in Canada. (It was already being practised in other parts of the British Empire.)[76] After the Newitty, a branch of the Kwakwaka'wakw, killed three runaway sailors, a government warship destroyed a village and 20 canoes. The following year, another warship destroyed another village. There were no arguments about how the government would pay for these expeditions, as there were when it came time to pay Amerindians for land.[77]

Then, in 1852, Amerindians killed an HBC shepherd. Douglas persuaded Cowichan and Nanaimo chiefs to give up the persons involved. The murderer and his accomplice were tried and hanged in 1853, the first such criminal trial in the West. Tensions mounted, and settlers, alarmed at the continuing frontier wars in the United States, feared an Amerindian uprising. The sudden appearance of a group of peaceful Amerindians was enough to send settlers fleeing. When a white settler was murdered in 1856, 400 sailors and marines set out to capture the guilty Cowichan. The discovery of placer gold on the Fraser and Thompson rivers in 1857 added to the Amerindians' difficulties, as will be seen in the next chapter.

Meanwhile, discontent had been bubbling in the region of the Skeena for a number of years. At issue were land and social issues. Trutch expressed official sentiment when he told a Kitkatla delegation in 1872, 'the days are past when your heathenish ideas can be tolerated in this land.'[78] In 1888, however, reports of an uprising were reaching Victoria. A Gitksan chief known as Kitwancool Jim (Kamalmuk) had followed Amerindian custom by killing a medicine man believed to have caused the death of several people, including the chief's child. The chief's brother married the medicine man's widow and, as far as the Amerindians were concerned, the matter was settled.

Not so in the eyes of the authorities, however. They tried to arrest Jim but killed him instead. Amerindian outrage aroused fears of an attack. The government sent a gunboat and additional police to the scene. A 'war correspondent' from the *Victoria Daily Colonist* went along as well.[79] The presence of the warship so far upriver impressed the people, who had never seen anything like it. A series of meetings with the chiefs of the area emphasized the point that British law was to prevail. The chiefs agreed, and after 1890 the government no longer used gunboats for this purpose.

During the first half of the nineteenth century, the situation of Canada's Amerindians varied from coast to coast, as this survey makes evident. With the ending of the colonial wars and the decline of the fur trade, however, the era of partnership between Amerindians and Europeans came to an end. If adaptation had been the key to Native survival in the past, it now became the password that would give Amerindians entry into the future.

Important Names and Terms

Abishabis
assimilation
Douglas, James
Duncan, William
gift distributions
'gunboat diplomacy'

Head, Sir Francis Bond
Jones, Peter
Legaic
Metlakatla
model villages
Saugeen Tract

Study Questions

1) What challenges were faced by Peter Jones (Kahkewaquonaby) and others who called on Christianity to help First Nations peoples adapt to a changing world?
2) Why did Sir Francis Bond Head see assimilation as a waste of time?
3) What difficulties confronted Governor James Douglas as he tried to accommodate the peoples of the west coast?
4) What were the troubling signs, both for Amerindians and for settlers, in the West?

Recommended Readings

Bockstoce, John R. *Whales, Ice, and Men: The History of Whaling in the Western Arctic*. Seattle: University of Washington Press, 1986.

Gough, Barry M. *Gunboat Frontier: British Maritime Authority and Northwest Coast Indians, 1846–1890*. Vancouver: University of British Columbia Press, 1984.

Harring, Sidney L. *White Man's Law: Native People in Nineteenth-Century Canadian Jurisprudence*. Toronto: University of Toronto Press, 1998.

Smith, Donald B. *Sacred Feathers: The Reverend Peter Jones (Kahkewaquonaby) and the Mississauga Indians*. Toronto: University of Toronto Press, 1987.

Upton, Leslie F.S. *Micmacs and Colonists: Indian–White Relations in the Maritimes, 1713–1867*. Vancouver: University of British Columbia Press, 1979.

10 Towards Confederation for Canada, Towards Wardship for Amerindians

During the 1830s, Britain held a parliamentary inquiry into the conditions of Aboriginal peoples throughout the empire. The British widely recognized that they had deprived Amerindians, as well as other tribal peoples, of their lands. They did not, however, generally agree on what they should do about it—or even admit that they should do anything at all.

The committee report was clear: unregulated frontier expansion was disastrous for Aboriginal peoples, who almost without exception lost their lands.[1] And trespass was only part of the problem. Another concern was that Amerindians were losing their land, particularly through devious leasing practices, sometimes by Amerindians themselves.[2] Curbing settlers was tough politically, particularly in areas where they were needed for defence. In an attempt to correct this situation, in 1839, Britain legally declared Amerindian lands to be Crown lands, a decision that had consequences beyond landownership, as significant as that was.

At that time, most political rights where land was concerned extended only to property holders. Amerindians, on the other hand, held their land in common (apart from some individuals who had accepted the European way). Making the Crown the guardian of their lands, in effect, excluded most Amerindians from political rights,[3] which supported the belief that Amerindians were like children, in need of paternal protection.[4] Popular imagination during the nineteenth century romanticized this into the '**white man's burden**'.[5]

Not that the British had not tried to lighten their burden. By 1830, British Indian administration was 75 years old and desperately underfunded. Easily, its main interest was acquiring land. In fact, the government paid so little attention to Indian affairs that the Act of Union (1840) forgot to make provision for it—or for the payment of annuities for earlier land cessions, an oversight that was not corrected until 1844.

Although transferred to the civil arm in 1830, the Indian policy of the two Canadas continued to be administered from London until 1860, through the lieutenant-governor of

Time Line

1816	Cuthbert Grant leads Métis in Battle of Seven Oaks after Métis unrest and hardship following export embargo.
1839	Crown Lands Protection Act declares Indian lands to be Crown lands.
1840	Act of Union of Upper and Lower Canada.
1842–4	Bagot Commission examines Indian administration.
1845	Métis sign petition asking for definition of their status.
1847	Métis petition London for recognition of rights, declaration of colony free of HBC control.
1850	Commissioner of Lands position created in United Canadas. Robinson Superior and Robinson Huron treaties: lands surrendered are twice the area of all previous land-cession treaties in Canada West.
1850–1	Legislation passed to protect lands of Indians in the Canadas.
1851	Métis again petition for colony, just as Vancouver Island had become colony in 1849.
1857	An Act to encourage the Gradual Civilization of the Indian Tribes of the Canadas is introduced by John A. Macdonald. Palliser scientific expedition to report on conditions for living, settlement in Plains region. Fraser River gold strike.
1858	'Fraser River War' as Salish outraged by invasion of their territory by 25,000 gold-seekers.
1859	Act for Civilizing and Enfranchising Indians passed in United Canadas.
1860	Amerindian administration passed from British Colonial Office to the colonies.

1862	Manitoulin Island cession. Sioux uprising in Minnesota followed by hangings at Fort Snelling, largest mass execution in US history.
1864	Chilcotin War: after raids and killings, five Amerindians sentenced and hanged.
1867	Confederation of Canada: Amerindians declared a federal responsibility by British North America Act.
1868	Drought and crop failures on prairies; buffalo hunt in precipitous decline.
1869	An Act for the gradual enfranchisement of Indians. . . defines 'Indian' as at least one-quarter Indian blood and introduces three-year elective system for band leadership.
1869–70	First Riel Rebellion, led by Louis Riel, takes control of Red River and establishes provisional Métis-led government.
1870	Canada acquires Rupert's Land and North-Western Territory from Britain. Manitoba Act rushed through federal Parliament to create new province; Riel flees to US. Blackfoot defeat Cree at Battle of Belly River, the last purely Amerindian battle in Canada.
1871	British Columbia joins Confederation, retains control of its Crown lands.
1874	Ottawa disallows BC's Crown Lands Act because it made no provision for Amerindian reserves or rights. (The special problems of Aboriginal land claims in BC continue into the twenty-first century.)

Upper Canada, who was also superintendent-general of Indian Affairs. The superintendent-general, therefore, had to act both for the Crown and for the Amerindians. Inevitably, the two roles came into conflict.[6] As well, funding for Amerindian administration came from five different sources. It was also uncertain, to say the least, reflecting the lack of importance now given to Indian affairs. This attitude would deepen until well into the twentieth century. Although Britain transferred control of Indian affairs to Canada in 1860, it was two years before a single administration was set up. Even then, unification was not complete.[7]

Making matters even more confusing, in the mid-1800s Britain developed the concept of regional approaches.[8] This meant almost as many policies as there were colonies. In the Maritimes, it was one of 'insulation' of the Amerindians; in the Canadas, 'amalgamation'; in Rupert's Land and on the Northwest Coast, support of HBC administration. In other words, centralized imperial administration was not coping very well with the many local problems of colonial government, and the voices of the Amerindians either were not being heard or were being ignored. This policy failure would have repercussions into the twenty-first century, and Native peoples were often the last to know of changes in policy and in effective authority over their affairs (Box 10.1).

Box 10.1 From Marginalization to a New Vision

As with Confederation, no one thought to consult—or even inform—the Inuit before Privy Council issued a proclamation in 1880 transferring Britain's Arctic territories to the Dominion. Similarly, when Newfoundland joined in 1949, no mention was made of either the Inuit of Labrador or Amerindians of St George's Bay and other regions. The government did not extend the right to self-government, which the colonies had so vigorously and successfully claimed for themselves, to its indigenous peoples. The government did not give Indian status to the Mi'kmaq, who had been accustomed to fishing and sealing in Placentia and St George's Bay from time immemorial, and who had migrated to the St George's Bay area since the fall of New France, until 1984, when the province also established its first reserves.

As of 2009, only one Mi'kmaq community (Conne River, Samaijij Miawpukek Reserve) had official recognition as a band. The Federation of Newfoundland Indians was still pressing for recognition of nine other communities.[9] The Mi'kmaq have claimed that they were sharing Newfoundland with the Beothuk and were intermarrying with them before Europeans arrived. In June 2005, however, Bill C-56, the Labrador Inuit Land Claims Agreement, cleared the Senate, setting the stage for Nunatsiavut, a self-governing territory in northern Labrador.[10]

Who Is an 'Indian'?

In the meantime, reports were pouring in from other investigations into Aboriginal affairs (there were three between 1839 and 1857). The most important from Canada was that of the **Bagot Commission** of 1842–4, named after chief commissioner Sir Charles Bagot (1781–1843).[11] It described a lack of direction in Indian administration and urged centralized control for the British North American colonies—the opposite of what the Colonial Office was practising. It also reaffirmed the Proclamation's position that Amerindians had rights of possession in regard to land, including the right to compensation for surrenders. These points were not always being honoured. The Commission recommended, among other things, that:

- reserves be surveyed and boundaries publicly announced;
- a system of timber licensing be instituted for reserves;
- all title deeds be registered and considered binding; and
- Amerindians be taught European techniques of land management and provided with livestock, agricultural implements, furniture, and the like in lieu of presents.

The commissioners thought that bands should be allowed to buy and sell land, at least between themselves. This, they believed, would encourage Amerindians to adopt individual freehold ownership in place of their traditional communal ownership, which the commissioners considered 'uncivilized'.[12] Finally, they urged that banks be established on reserves and that more schools for Amerindians be established, with the co-operation of various religious denominations. The report described Amerindians as 'an untaught, unwary race among a population ready and able to take every advantage of them'.[13]

Identifying goals was one thing; however, doing something about them proved to be something else again. Easiest to achieve were the department's reorganization and centralization under the civil secretary as superintendent-general for Indian Affairs and the measures to improve the protection of Amerindian lands. More controversial was the gradual stop to gift distributions,[14] which Amerindians resisted. Budgetary considerations prevailed, however, and the gifts ended in 1858. Amerindian opposition to individual landownership was not surprising, not only because of their entrenched customs but also because, invariably, they lost a lot of land following its imposition.[15]

In 1850 and 1851, the Canadian legislature approved two land acts incorporating some of Bagot's recommendations. Passed hurriedly because loggers were invading reserved lands, these measures made it an offence for private individuals to deal with Amerindians concerning their lands. However, it was still unclear what 'Indian title' actually meant. In 1850, the government also created the post of Commissioner of Indian Lands.

The next year, Canada East (Quebec) set aside 93,079 hectares (230,000 acres) for the creation of Amerindian reserves and the distribution of up to £1,000 a year. However, only 68,801 hectares (170,012 acres) were actually granted.[16] Furthermore, the Commissioner, not the Amerindians, had control over leasing and rentals.[17] In the meantime, largely because of the amount of property involved, the government decided that it needed to define who, exactly, was an 'Indian'. The 1851 Act for Canada East, accordingly, undertook the task—without consulting Amerindians—and came up with these criteria:

- all persons of Indian blood reputed to belong to the particular body or tribe of Indians interested in Indian lands or their descendants;
- all persons intermarried with any such Indians and living among them, and their descendants;
- all persons residing among such Indians, whose parents on either side were or are Indians of such body or tribe, or entitled to be considered as such; and
- all persons adopted in infancy by any such Indians, and residing in the village or upon the lands of such tribes or bodies of Indians and their descendants.

The administration quickly decided that this definition was too inclusive, however, and revised it, once more without Amerindian input. This time, it excluded non-Indians living among Amerindians and non-Indians married to Amerindian women. It also distinguished between **status Indians**—those who were officially registered—and **non-status Indians**.[18] Amerindian women married to non-Indians kept their status, but their children did not have the right to claim it. The provision allowing non-Indian women married to registered Indians to gain status and to pass it on to their children stayed in: in other words, the male line determined ancestry. After Confederation, Canada would add a 'blood quantum' proviso (see below).

Inquiry followed inquiry. Concerned about charges that its 'civilizing' program was not working, the Canadian government named a commission to investigate. It resulted, in 1857, in An Act to Encourage the Gradual Civilization of the Indian Tribes of the Canadas, which introduced the idea of giving Amerindians the vote in exchange for Indian status. The commissioners also set out a plan to achieve this, most of which would be in effect until 1960. Eligible were males 21 years of age and over, able to read English or French, minimally educated, and 'of good moral character and free from debt', who had passed a three-year probation. By those standards, many in the white community would not have been eligible.[19] The successful candidate would receive 20 hectares of taxable reserve land.

Amerindians rallied in rejecting the Act. They correctly saw the measure as an attempt to destroy Amerindian communities and their way of life. At the same time, it would break up their reserves, allotment by allotment. By 1876, only one candidate had been enfranchised.[20] Two years after the 1857 Act, an Act for Civilizing and Enfranchising Indians still encouraged enfranchisement and consolidated earlier legislation pertaining to Aboriginals but dodged the issue of reserves. Even as it sought to bring Amerindians into white society, however, it extended Canada West's ban on the sale of liquor to Amerindians to Canada East. Later, the government extended this ban to the whole Dominion. It would stay on the books until 1951.

In 1860, the United Canadas took over Amerindian administration from Britain's Colonial Office. The Commissioner of Crown Lands became chief superintendent of Indian Affairs, but the deputy superintendent actually did the job. Although Indian Affairs would not become a full department until 1880, it received its first full-time head in 1862: William Prosperous Spragge, who that same year had assisted William McDougall (1822–1905, Commissioner of Crown Lands, 1862–4) in negotiating the Manitoulin Island surrender. Spragge held his post until his death in 1874. Obviously, Amerindians had not been consulted.

More Land Surrenders

Throughout the Canadas, tensions were increasing, while the resources to maintain the Amerindian way of life shrank. As overexploitation of land progressed, the concept of family hunting territories took on a new importance. What had started among Amerindians as a custom of asking permission to hunt on another's territory became an enforced requirement. In northern Ontario, Pic River band members killed 14 Amerindian trespassers. The colonial government, however, did not see this requirement as extending to its own administrative officials.

The discovery of mineral deposits north of Lake Superior led the government to permit mining without considering Amerindian interests. Chief Shingwaukonse (Little Pine, 1773–1854) of Garden River, near Sault Ste Marie, and other Ojibwa leaders went to Toronto and demanded that the revenues from the mining leases be paid to them as the owners of the region. They got nowhere.[21] Three years later, in 1849, another request, this time for a land settlement, again drew no response. The Ojibwa took matters into their own hands and moved to close the Quebec and Lake Superior Mining Company operation at Mica Bay by force. Within three weeks, troops were on the scene to quell the 'rebellion', sometimes called the Michipicoten War.[22]

One of the two commissioners sent to investigate the situation was Thomas Anderson, of the Upper Canadian model village experiments, by now chief superintendent for Indian Affairs. The commissioners found the Ojibwa eager to sign a treaty with the government, and even willing to let the government decide the amount of compensation. Despite their confidence in the 'wisdom and justice of their Great Father', however, the Ojibwa were clear-sighted about their objectives. The negotiations were not simple, but out of them arose the practice of including provisions for Amerindian reserves in the treaties, setting the pattern for the future. Amerindians had long had this idea, but up to now, the various colonial assemblies had not set aside lands for Amerindians on a regular basis. In the Amerindian view, reserves were not

Box 10.2   Finding a Place in the White Man's World?

Francis Assikinack ('Blackbird', 1824–63) was the son of Jean-Baptiste Assiginack (*c.* 1768–1865), an influential Odawa chief who fought for the British in the War of 1812, made large land cessions, and was an esteemed public servant. Francis was educated at Upper Canada College. He wanted to become a doctor but was twice refused support.[23] Francis ended up being an interpreter and frustrated schoolmaster. In other words, after having been given the benefits of a superior education, he could not define his own role in life. Not only did the dominant society demand assimilation, it reserved to itself the right to dictate the terms by which it could proceed.

something the government granted them. They were simply lands that Amerindians had not shared with the newcomers.[24]

Reserves were 'the cradle of the Indian civilizing effort—and the means of securing the White man's freedom to exploit the vast riches of a young dominion'.[25] For that reason, establishing large reserves in isolated areas came to be seen as counterproductive. Instead, they should be small and close to white settlements to help Amerindians to learn white ways.[26] Chief negotiator for the treaties was ex-fur trader William Benjamin Robinson (1797–1873), who had negotiated land settlements with Musquakie. His mandate: to obtain rights to as much land as possible for as little as possible from Penetanguishine along the north shore of Lake Huron and across to Batchawana Bay on the eastern shore of Lake Superior and down to Pigeon River. Payment was to be by annuities, and each band would be permitted to choose a site for its own reserve. Hunting and fishing rights would continue over the entire surrendered area. Furthermore, there were to be no gift distributions. (Amerindian etiquette required an exchange of gifts on such occasions, however, so Robinson had to compromise on this.) Jean-Baptiste Assiginack (see Box 10.2), at that point an interpreter in the service of Indian Affairs, ably assisted Robinson in the negotiations.

Chief Peau de Chat ('Cat Pelt', L'Avocat, *fl.* 1814–50) and the Lake Superior chiefs signed on 7 September 1850. Two days later, Chief Shingwaukonse and leaders from Lake Huron also signed—after holding out for better terms. Some chiefs would claim later they were pressured into signing and threatened to appeal to London. The land surrendered was twice the area of the land given up in all previous treaties combined in Canada West,[27] extending north to the height of land separating Rupert's Land from Canada. By now, virtually all of Canada West was clear of Amerindian title. The two **Robinson treaties** confirmed the pattern that had been developing since the Proclamation:

- Negotiations were at open and public meetings.
- Lands were 'surrendered' only to the Crown.

- A schedule of reserves to be held in common was annexed to each treaty.
- Each member of the signing band received annuities.
- Finally, Amerindians retained 'full and free privilege to hunt over the territory now ceded by them and to fish in the waters thereof as they have heretofore been in the habit of doing', except for those portions sold to private individuals or set aside by the government for specific uses.

One of the points that bothered the dissident chiefs was the small size of their annuities—£500 to £600—compared to those being handed out in southern Ontario. Robinson replied that southern Ontario lands were good for agriculture, which had destroyed the hunting for the Amerindians of the region. In northern Ontario, on the other hand, the lands were of little or no use for farming. Robinson did not refer to the ecological effects of mining in the mineral-rich region.

Another point that quickly drew attention was the nature of the 'surrender'. Amerindians did not claim absolute ownership of the lands, only the right to their use. How could they surrender them to the Crown, or to anyone else for that matter? Yet another complication lay in the fact that since the Crown already claimed underlying title, what was it accepting from the Amerindians? Questions like these would lead to a series of court cases (Chapter 16).

The influence of the Robinson treaties would soon be evident in the next major cession, that of Manitoulin Island. The region had been set aside as a reserve by the 1836 treaty with the Ojibwa, in the expectation that those living to the south would move there. But by 1860, only 1,000 people had moved in, with 3,000 acres (1,214 hectares) being farmed. Under pressure to open more land for settlement, the government ended the project.

In 1862, William McDougall successfully negotiated for 600,000 acres (242,811 hectares) of the reserve's land. His tactics involved the use of liquor despite a governmental ban, and he concluded the deal for $700 in cash plus the proceeds from sales of the surrendered lands to homesteaders. In return, each Amerindian head of family was allowed 100 acres (40 hectares), compared to the 25 acres (10 hectares) originally proposed. Single persons over the age of 21 received 50 acres (20 hectares), to be selected in such a way as to keep Amerindian communities intact. Also, they were granted fishing rights. (Earlier, there had been a move to exclude them from this activity.) These small concessions were the result of the efforts of Assiginack, who had been one of the signatories to the 1836 treaty that had created the Manitoulin Island Reserve. Now, with all except two of the chiefs of the Catholic mission village of Wikwemikong, he tried to prevent its being torn apart.

The treaties notwithstanding, the question of protection for Amerindian lands remained essentially unsolved as settler encroachments continued in agriculturally attractive areas. Legislation enacted a year before Confederation gave the government the sole right to sell reserved lands that the Amerindians were not using—and to do so without consulting them. Neither were Amerindians included in the Confederation of British North America agreement of 1867. No one even raised the question of their partnership.

Wards of the State

With the creation of the Dominion of Canada in 1867, the three participating provinces that became four (Nova Scotia, New Brunswick, Quebec, Ontario) kept control of Crown lands within their borders. So did Prince Edward Island and British Columbia when they joined a few years later. Saskatchewan and Alberta, after they were created in 1905, did not gain that control until 1930. Amerindians became a federal responsibility in the section of the British North America (BNA) Act on 'Indians and lands reserved for Indians', the only reference in the Act to Canada's Aboriginal peoples. This separated their administration from that of Crown lands. Amerindians continued in a distinct legal category, that of **wardship**. Amerindians could, if they chose, step out of this category to attain the rights and responsibilities of other Canadians, but the price was high.

According to one white historian, reserves were the main institution that the Dominion inherited from colonial administrations.[28] In the Amerindian view, the main inheritance was the tradition of the treaties to regulate relations between Amerindians and settlers, mainly in connection with land. Whites confidently expected that Amerindians would eventually be assimilated. As Sir John A. Macdonald (Prime Minister of Canada, 1867–73, 1878–91) observed in 1887, 'the great aim of our legislation has been to do away with the tribal system and assimilate the Amerindian people in all respects with the other inhabitants of the Dominion as speedily as they are fit to change.'[29]

Canada acquired Rupert's Land[30] and the North-Western Territory (present-day Yukon, portions of today's western and northern Northwest Territories, and parts of northern Saskatchewan, Alberta, and BC) in 1870. This vast expanse was designated the North-West Territories. Manitoba became the fifth province that same year. British Columbia joined Confederation in 1871, and Prince Edward Island became the seventh province in 1873. These expansions meant that in four years, Canada's Amerindian population increased from 23,000 to more than 100,000 (estimates that may be low), from 0.7 per cent of the population to 2.5 per cent.[31] Each area had a separate history made up of a distinctive set of experiences. All of these governments, however, shared a habit of passing laws in the interests of the dominant society without consulting Amerindians.

This pattern was in place in 1868, when the new Dominion formed the Department of Secretary of State and gave it responsibility for Amerindians. In 1869, Joseph Howe became secretary of state for the provinces and also superintendent-general of Indian Affairs. He held this position until 1873, when the Department of the Interior took over Indian administration. 'Indian affairs' involved control of Amerindian lands and property (including resources) as well as Amerindian funds. High on the department's priority list was the consolidation of the various laws inherited from previous administrations, a comparatively simple task in the East, where the Amerindian population was too small to be an important political consideration.

On the prairies and in British Columbia, however, Amerindians still were in the majority, and so could mount an effective resistance. The situation became even more diverse when Britain handed over her Arctic territories to the Dominion in 1880. The year following Confederation, Indian Affairs reaffirmed its 'guardianship policy'. It also introduced a three-year elective system for bands and extended somewhat the powers of chiefs and band councils, but Indian Affairs could still override them. Cabinet could also depose chiefs or band councillors. The cabinet decided, on the recommendation of the superintendent-general, which bands were ready for the three-year elective system, a step that it could take without the band's consent.[32] Once more, it used individual landholdings carved out of reserves to reward enfranchisement, this time by means of 'location tickets' that carried with them rights of inheritance.[33] Those who became enfranchised lost the right to be classed as Indians under the Act, but they maintained their treaty rights (other than treaty payments) and their right to live on a reserve. This meant, among other things, that they could hold a business licence, buy liquor, and send their children to public schools.

The government confidently expected that these new provisions would undermine resistance to **enfranchisement**. However, by 1920, only about 250 Amerindians had chosen to enfranchise.[34] Later, more Amerindians accepted the vote as the government eased the Act's requirements.

Marrying Out

The 1869 Act for the Gradual Enfranchisement of Indians expanded features of the 1851 legislation that treated men and women differently. If a registered Indian man married a non-Indian woman, she gained Indian status, which she passed on to their children. In contrast, the Indian wife of a non-Amerindian lost her Indian status. Another provision added a 'blood quantum' requirement to the definition of an Indian. To qualify, a person born after the passing of the Act must now have at least one-quarter Amerindian blood.[35] In that case, the one-quarter Amerindian wife of a non-Amerindian could claim Indian status, but her children could not.

These measures aroused strong opposition. The General Council of Ontario and Quebec Indians lobbied hard for the rights of indigenous women, but nothing came of their efforts.[36] The Indian Act of 1876, essentially a consolidation of the legislation considered in this and the previous chapter, would keep this feature (see Chapter 11).

The Acts of 1868 and, in particular, 1869 were designed to break down tribal forms of government on the grounds they were 'irresponsible'. The elected band council would be the instrument to achieve this.[37] It was hardly surprising that, with the exception of the Mohawk of the Bay of Quinte, the bands (including the Six Nations) resisted by refusing to exercise even the limited powers given to them. Meanwhile, on the other side of the continent Amerindians were facing a threat of a different sort.

The West Coast and the 'Chilcotin War'

If white settlement was impinging on Amerindian power on the west coast, the discovery of gold overwhelmed it. A precursor was the mini-gold rush in 1850–3 on the Queen Charlottes, followed by another of similar proportions on the Stikine in 1862. Fortunately for the Amerindians involved (Haida and Tsimshian, respectively), both proved to be short. Even so, confrontations led Governor Douglas to assert British authority with shows of force. Soon, news spread of the gold deposits of the Fraser River in 1857 and the Cariboo in 1862. This time, the strike was huge.

The Salish of the Fraser had been quietly mining the placer gold for years and trading it instead of furs at HBC posts, but they were overwhelmed in 1858, when 25,000 gold seekers flooded into Victoria. In short order, 10,000 men were panning for gold along the Fraser. Outraged at this invasion of their territory, Salish chief Spintlum confronted the miners. A hysterical press in Victoria reported the 'Fraser River War' as a massacre of miners. The actual tally was 30 Amerindians and two whites killed. Again, Douglas asserted British power, announcing that British law applied to all, Amerindians as well as miners. He tried to win Amerindian co-operation by appointing some of their leaders as magistrates, but this did nothing to alleviate the havoc being wreaked on their way of life.

The mining operations needed to extract the hard-rock gold of the Cariboo strike, deep in the interior, meant the building of roads for the transport of equipment and supplies. Proceeding with all possible haste and no consideration for the damage to the Amerindian hunting-and-gathering economy, the invaders interfered with Native salmon weirs, raided villages, and even looted graves. As the Amerindians saw it, the non-Natives were destroying their subsistence base, so it was up to them to replace it, but the road gangs turned away Amerindians who asked for food. On top of all this, 1862 also saw smallpox among the Chilcotin.

Matters quickly came to a head. In 1864, the Chilcotin, the main victims of these developments, sent out war parties to attack road gangs. After several bloody encounters in which 13 non-Natives died, government forces tricked eight insurgents, including chiefs Tellot, Alexis, and Klatsassin, into surrendering. Five received death sentences and were quickly hanged en masse. One was sentenced to life imprisonment.[38] The judge acknowledged, however, that the treatment they had received from the usurpers had provoked them. The following year, the looting of Amerindian graves became illegal. Despite the fears of the whites, no generalized Amerindian war developed.

Governor Douglas's touch was sorely missed after he retired in 1864. Where he had accepted Amerindian requests for as much as 200 acres (81 hectares) per Amerindian householder, his successor, Joseph Trutch, set the ceiling at 10 (4 hectares).[39] (On the prairies, Amerindians were being allowed 160 acres—65 hectares. Non-Natives could pre-empt 160 acres and purchase an additional 480 acres.) Beginning in 1865, Trutch, in a program of 'adjustments', took away much of the reserve land set aside for Amerindians. The following year, he issued an ordinance preventing them from pre-empting land without written permission from the governor.[40] In 1870, Amerindians lost altogether the right to pre-empt. What was left was the right of individuals to purchase lands from non-Amerindians. Since the Amerindians saw the land as theirs already, this was not a 'right' they appreciated. Predictably, resentment rose.

When British Columbia entered Confederation in 1871, it kept control of its Crown lands, the only western province granted this privilege up to that time. This did not bode well for the Amerindians, even though the agreement gave Ottawa the responsibility for Amerindian administration and provided for the necessary transfer of lands to the federal authority. Again, no one consulted the Amerindians, although they still outnumbered the newcomers at the time and would continue to do so until the mid-1880s.[41]

One of the first acts of the new member of Confederation was to deprive Amerindians of the provincial franchise, which they did not regain until 1949. With the exception of the adhesion to Treaty Eight in its northeastern corner, no post-Confederation treaties were signed in the province. British Columbia did not even create a ministry of Native Affairs until 1988.

Almost immediately, Ottawa and British Columbia were locked in a battle over the size of allocations for reserves. The federal government thought that a family of five would need 32 hectares (80 acres), but BC thought that four were enough. In 1873, the administrations worked out a compromise of eight hectares (20 acres) per family, regardless of size, but it pleased no one. In 1874, the federal government disallowed BC's Crown Lands Act because it did not make provision for Amerindian reserves, but British Columbia continued doling out lands to Amerindians in minimal lots. By the last decades of the century, the 90 reserves established for the Kwakwaka'wakw totalled 16,500 acres (6,680 hectares), an average of 183 acres (74 hectares) per reserve.[42]

The Métis Challenge

Hardly had Confederation been accomplished than the federal government came face to face with a situation that had been brewing for a long time in the Northwest: the demands of the Métis for recognition. The Métis of Red River saw themselves as a 'New Nation', neither Amerindian nor white but a distinctive blend of both that incorporated farming, buffalo hunting, and the fur trade. They even had their own national bard. Pierre Falcon (1793–1876) was born and lived within the fur trade, and his ballads became favourites with voyageurs.

The Métis way of life developed under the economic umbrella of the trade and in the isolation of the Northwest. They built their log cabins where they fancied, usually along riverbanks without formal arrangements with the HBC—in fact, often without the Company's knowledge. At Red River, in the District of Assiniboia, a Métis sense of identity had crystallized with the troubles that developed after the coming of the Selkirk settlers in 1812—in the clash of cultures but, above all, in the rivalries of opposing fur-trading interests. The amalgamation of the North West Company and Hudson's Bay Company made the Métis the largest element in Red River's population,[43] empowering them to act decisively when things took a turn for the worse—which they soon did.

First, the War of 1812 interrupted Red River's supply lines. Two years later, food shortages led to a ban on the export of provisions without a special licence—the Pemmican Proclamation of 1814. This greatly disturbed the Métis, for whom the pemmican trade was an important economic activity. They reacted by conducting a series of raids against the colony.

In the spring of 1816, after a winter of starvation during which people died, the Métis Nor'Wester captain **Cuthbert Grant** (c. 1793–1854) assembled 60 buffalo hunters and attacked an HBC brigade bringing down pemmican. They then captured and ransacked Brandon House, an HBC post, and took the pemmican to Red River. At Seven Oaks, Robert Semple (1777–1816, governor-in-chief of Rupert's Land since 1815) and 21 settlers challenged them. By the time the smoke cleared, Semple and all his men were dead. Only one Métis had been killed, and Grant's prestige among his people soared. A gathering of Métis leaders at Qu'Appelle Valley that same year named him 'Captain General of all the Half-Breeds'.[44]

As the buffalo herds dwindled, and farming loomed closer as an alternative to the fur trade, both the hunt and traditional communal values began to give way to those of the individual. More Métis became wage labourers, and their relative position within the fur trade hierarchy declined. Now, most were at the level of menial labour rather than at that of the officer class, where some had been earlier. The Métis saw the HBC monopoly as leading to the 'utter impoverishment, if not the ruin, of the Aboriginal people'. They were also upset at the appointment of the anti-French Adam Thom (1802–90) as recorder (a judgeship) for Assiniboia.

The prospect of the government encouraging white settlement spurred the Métis (particularly those who were French-speaking) to become more militant. In 1845, 977 of them signed a petition to Alexander Christie, governor of Red River and Assiniboia, 1833–9, and of Assiniboia, 1844–9, claiming special rights by virtue of their Amerindian blood. The governor told them that they had no more rights than those enjoyed by all British subjects.

Two years later, in 1847, Alexander Kennedy Isbister (1822–83) took their petition to England. Isbister, who was one-quarter Amerindian, had been born at Cumberland House, the grandson of chief factor Alexander Kennedy and Aggathas, a Cree.[45] This time, the Métis asked that the HBC charter be declared invalid and that Red River (reorganized into the District of Assiniboia in 1836) be declared a colony. This petition gave rise to spirited exchanges in the British Parliament. Powerful forces opposed monopolies in principle, but the colonial secretary could not imagine Amerindian self-government. Only those regions that had enough white settlers to ensure they would have control should have colonial status. The Métis could have appealed to the Privy Council but only at their own expense. Their meagre resources strained, they formally dropped the issue in 1850. Other petitions on other issues would follow.

In 1849, the year Vancouver Island became a colony, the Company in effect lost the power to enforce its monopoly. The Métis kept up their campaign against Thom, and in 1851 HBC Governor Sir George Simpson withdrew him from office. Simpson also gave in to demands that the Métis have a wider representation on the Assiniboia Council but managed to fudge its execution. As HBC control eroded, a Canada West group that would later call itself **Canada First** began a campaign to annex Red River to Canada. With Confederation, the Canada Firsters became strident, adding yet another challenge to the fundamentals of the old order of the 'custom of the country', with its elements of Amerindian law. The Métis were divided on the issue.

As the Métis were waging their war of words with the HBC and London for recognition, they continued actual hostilities in the field against their traditional enemies, the Sioux.[46] An 1851 confrontation, the Battle of Grand Coteau, from which they emerged victorious, proved to be even more important than Seven Oaks in encouraging their sense of identity. More problematic, however, was the international border. At first, US officials let them cross over in pursuit of buffalo by virtue of their Amerindian blood. Now, however, the American attitude was stiffening, and the Métis were finding themselves excluded from hunting south of the border.

The clamour became such that the British Parliament established a select committee in 1857 to examine British policy in the Northwest and to determine if the region (particularly the prairies) had potential for anything other than the fur trade. The British Royal Geographical Society also sent out a scientific expedition under Captain John Palliser (1817–87) to report on the region. Canada West, not to be outdone, organized its own expedition. Toronto professor Henry Youle Hind (1823–1908) and engineer S.J. Dawson (1820–1902) went out to determine the best route for transportation and communication to facilitate annexation.

The upshot was that mainland British Columbia was separated from HBC administration and became a Crown colony in 1858. On the other hand, the government did not deem Red River, with its predominantly mixed-blood population, ready for such a status.[47] The disappointment in Red River was profound. As for the Amerindians, their fears for the future had not been calmed. Already, they wanted a treaty.

Increasing immigration did nothing to relieve tensions at Red River. Even Peguis, the local Ojibwa chief who had tried so hard to come to terms with the whites as long as they were not too numerous, became worried. Engulfment was now a real prospect. Peguis claimed that the Selkirk Treaty of 1817 had not properly extinguished Amerindian title, as the four chiefs who had signed it did not have the required powers. The land involved had been a strip a little over three kilometres long on each side of the Red and Assiniboine rivers. The ensuing controversy engendered more heat than light and would culminate with the Peguis band's loss of St Peter's Reserve in 1916 (see Chapter 13).

Confederation Brings Centralization—and Western Isolation

When Confederation became a reality, four western Cree and Saulteaux chiefs agreed among themselves about the extent and limits of their land claims in preparation for the negotiations they foresaw in the not-too-distant future.[48] A Saulteaux band in Assiniboia allowed settlers onto their lands only on the condition that a permanent agreement be negotiated within three years.[49]

In Red River, changing social customs added to the tensions of the political scene. Victorian standards influenced those of the frontier, leading to a series of sex scandals. These, in turn, erupted into open defiance of HBC authority.[50] As the whites were at each other's throats, the balance of power fell to the Métis, the settlement's largest armed force.[51] The 1862 Sioux uprising in Minnesota also had repercussions in Red River, as ragged and starving refugees (largely Dakota) drifted in from the fighting. In the spring of 1863, 600 of them appeared, bringing the medals they had received from the British for their active alliance in the War of 1812.[52] Sioux had been fleeing in small numbers into Canada since the 1820s. Now, however, the problem became acute, as the people of Red River had to provide for their former enemies. When the HBC, as a representative of the British, pledged friendship with the Sioux, Peguis (who died in 1864 at age 90) and his people felt betrayed. That same year, 1864, a group of Ojibwa attacked a refugee Sioux encampment.

Whites also responded with violence. Frightened at the prospect of vengeful Americans invading their territory, a group of settlers drugged two Sioux chiefs, Shak'pay ('Little Six') and Wakanozhan, also known as Medicine Bottle, and handed them over to American agents.[53] The two were among a group executed at Fort Snelling for murder. Eventually, most of the refugees were persuaded to settle at White Horse Plain, west of Fort Garry in Red River. In 1869, about 500 were wintering there.

Amid these swirling tides of change, Red River's isolation from Canada became more evident than ever. This was the era of railroad building, but there were no immediate plans for the Northwest, and communication was slow. It was faster and easier to communicate via the United States. Obviously, the HBC could no longer control the reins of power, but the Colonial Office steadily refused to set up a Crown colony. Prime Minister Macdonald reluctantly agreed to negotiate for the purchase of Rupert's Land and to extinguish Amerindian land rights once the region was under Canadian control but hoped the HBC would do this before the transfer.

These were rough years for many reasons, not just political ones. Drought and grasshopper plagues brought crop failures. The buffalo hunt was also declining and becoming more distant. The fisheries were at low ebb. In 1868, even the rabbits were at the bottom of their cycle. That was also the year Ontario decided to build a road from the northwest angle of Lake of the Woods to Fort Garry. The project proceeded with more haste than foresight: the government did not always clear Amerindian title, nor did it heed Amerindian claims to fees for rights of passage and for timber used. In some cases, Amerindians sold land that the Métis claimed.

Protests soon developed over wages. Métis claimed the government was paying them less than whites. In addition, wages were paid in scrip (temporary paper currency), which they could redeem only at a store owned by the leader of the Canada Firsters. All this, plus the fact that the road had no legal mandate in the first place, as Red River was outside of Ontario's jurisdiction, brought the project temporarily to a halt. The Dawson Road, as it came to be called, eventually connected Red River to Fort William.

In spite of all these difficulties, a land rush was obviously developing—and settlers were staking claims to land without regard for Amerindian rights. The poet and author Charles Mair (1838–1927), who had been paymaster for the Dawson Road, told the Amerindians of Rat Creek that the influx of settlers was 'like the march of the sun, it could not be stopped.' The rush for land threatened the settlement pattern that had developed spontaneously among the fur trade families of Red River: river frontage farms with long, thin ribbons of land stretching back into woodlots. The pattern mirrored that of the old Quebec regime. This system assured each holder of access to the river, the main transportation route. Throughout all this, there was no official effort to consider the needs of the people of Red River.

The slowness of the Canadian government to act in the North West, however, was not lost on an interested spectator to the south. Minnesota offered $10 million for HBC lands but was refused. In 1868, the state protested the impending transfer of HBC lands to Canada without a vote of the settlers (with no mention of Amerindians, who were in the vast majority) and passed a resolution favouring annexation to the United States. That same year, Britain set up a provisional government for Rupert's Land. William McDougall, who had negotiated the Manitoulin Island surrender of 1862 and who was now actively working for the annexation of the North West to Canada, became the first lieutenant-governor in 1869. His job was to 'report upon the state of the Indian tribes now in the Territories' and to make suggestions as to how the tribes could best be protected and 'improved'.[54]

Meanwhile, Ottawa continued oblivious to the situation in Red River. The new North West Council it appointed was English and Protestant in composition, without representation of the region's French-language element. Even the English-speaking settlers protested this. In the meantime, another figure was making his voice heard: **Louis Riel** (1844–85), one-eighth Amerindian,[55] who had attended the Collège de Montréal for several years. A natural leader, with a strong sense that the Métis of Red River were, indeed, a 'New Nation', he represented the opposing force to Canada First. When in 1869 the English-speaking Métis William Dease (fl. 1855–70) organized a meeting demanding that the payment for Rupert's Land be made to Amerindians and Métis as rightful owners of the land, not to the HBC, Riel attended as an observer. He was already a member of the **Comité National des Métis**, which

Concerned about the land transfer from the HBC to Canada, and the power vacuum that would result, the Métis organized a government that could respond effectively to the needs of both Aboriginal and white residents. Seen here are Louis Riel (seated, centre) and his councillors, 1869–70. In front, left to right are Bob O'Lone and Paul Prue. Seated are Pierre Poitras, John Bruce, Riel, W.B. O'Donoghue, François Dauphinais. Standing in the rear are Le Roc, Pierre de Lorme, Thomas Bunn, Xavier Page, André Beauchemin, Baptiste Tereaux, and Thomas Spence. *(William John Topley; Library and Archives Canada, PA 12854)*

had been organized to defend Métis rights with the active support of Abbé Joseph-Noël Ritchot (1825–1905) of St Norbert.

The transfer of lands and authority from the HBC to Canada was scheduled for 1 December 1869, still without official consultation with the people of the North West. When word reached Red River that McDougall and his entourage were coming to the North West before the scheduled date of transfer, Riel and the Comité acted to defend their interests. They blocked the border on the Pembina Trail, by which the official party must travel, and on 31 October refused to let them enter Assiniboia. McDougall had been warned but had not believed that matters would come to that. The new Dominion had finally come face to face with the new nation whose existence it had steadfastly refused to acknowledge.

Red River Takes a Stand

The Métis were not the only ones who viewed the transfer with mistrust. Resident HBC officers, like the Métis, had not been consulted on the terms of the transfer, and the government had made no provision for any claims they might have had. They resented

English indifference to their fate and wondered about Canada's ability to hold the union together, especially in view of the US purchase of Alaska in 1867. Trade was flourishing between Red River and points south of the border.[56] In the American view, it was only natural that the North West should become part of the United States, joining it with Alaska. The English-speaking settlers were also unhappy at what was happening but were not prepared to go as far as the Comité National.

The day after Riel and the Comité turned McDougall back, a roll call revealed 402 men, all bearing arms and prepared to support Riel. Later that day, 100 more were reported to have arrived. Discipline was strict: no alcohol. Two days later, 2 November, Louis Riel informed the HBC officer at Fort Garry that the fort was under the protection of his men, a move that forestalled a Canada First plan to take over. It also ensured the Comité's control over Red River, at least until federal troops arrived, which could not be before spring. McDougall, cooling his heels in Pembina, compounded his errors. In a snowstorm on 1 December, the day originally scheduled for the formal transfer of Rupert's Land to Canada, he crossed the border into Canada and read the proclamation of the transfer. Thus, HBC authority formally ended without any effective official authority to take its place. McDougall tried to correct this by commissioning John S. Dennis (1820–85), surveyor and militia officer, as 'lieutenant and conservator of the peace', authorizing him in the Queen's name to put down the Métis by force. The Canada Firsters greeted this with enthusiasm, but the English-speaking settlers refused to co-operate. A group of Saulteaux at Lower Fort Garry under Chief Henry Prince (Miskoukeenew, 'Red Eagle', 1819–1907, son of Peguis) felt otherwise. They announced they were ready to fight for the Queen. Some Sioux also joined the Canada Firsters.

A week later, on 8 December, Riel issued the 'Declaration of the People of Rupert's Land and the North-West', stating that 'a people, when it has no government, is free to adopt one form of Government in preference to another, to give or to refuse allegiance to that which is proposed.'[57] On 10 December, residents hoisted the Métis flag. On the 27th, they established the first provisional government, with Riel elected president. Riel and his Métis were in control of Red River without having shed a drop of blood.

Back in Ottawa, Prime Minister Macdonald learned on 25 November of the Métis blockade. His immediate reaction was to advise his representative in London not to complete the transaction with the HBC until Canada could be assured peaceful possession of the Northwest. He then sent a message to McDougall, warning him that he was, in effect, approaching a foreign country under HBC control and that he could not force his way in. When McDougall chose to follow the line of the Canada Firsters and to go ahead anyway, he created a political vacuum in Red River. Macdonald had seen the consequences, both nationally and internationally, all too clearly: the United States might acknowledge this provisional government.[58]

What followed is etched in Canadian historical lore. McDougall never did gain entry to Assiniboia and had to return to Ottawa. Riel formed a second provisional

---

Box 10.3   The New Province of Manitoba

Riel suggested the name of the new province: 'Spirit Strait' of the Crees, 'Lake of the Prairies' of the Assiniboine, 'Manitoba' stood for self-government and was already in use for the region. Macdonald made the 'postage stamp' province as small as possible, 28,490 square kilometres (11,000 square miles). He guaranteed the province official equality of French and English and a separate school system. Crown lands were to be under Dominion control, with 1.4 million acres (566,560 hectares) being reserved for the unmarried children of the Métis, an area close to the size of Prince Edward Island. The Dominion would respect all existing occupancies and titles, including those of Amerindians, a principle more easily stated than honoured, as events would prove.

---

government on 8 February 1870, which was more broadly representative of Assiniboia's community than the first had been. In the meantime, the rowdy behaviour of some Canada Firsters led to the execution by court martial of Orangeman Thomas Scott on 4 March.[59] This inflamed racial passions between English-language Protestants and French-language Catholics. Quebec, which had remained aloof, as it had seen the Métis as 'savages', now came to their defence. Macdonald moved quickly to meet with a Red River delegation. The two parties agreed on terms, and Macdonald's government rushed the Manitoba Act, which created the province of Manitoba (see Box 10.3), through Parliament. It obtained royal assent on 12 May.

McDougall fought hard to have the bill rejected, and he was on solid legal ground. The Act had to be amended hastily to make the new province constitutional. Apart from the Selkirk Treaty, neither had Amerindian title to lands been extinguished. This pushed the federal government into negotiating the first of the numbered treaties of the West in 1871 and 1872. In a move to forestall a raid from Ontario, Macdonald sent a military expedition to Red River in 1870 under Colonel G.J. Wolseley (1833–1913). The newly appointed A.G. Archibald, lieutenant-governor, 1870–3, was supposed to arrive ahead of the troops. The Métis were counting on this. Unfortunately, it happened the other way around.

Despite the unfinished state of both the Dawson Road and the transcontinental railway, and the need to negotiate rights of passage with the Ojibwa, through whose territory the expedition had to pass,[60] the military expedition arrived first. Riel, forewarned, went into hiding.[61] The behaviour of the troops in the settlement did more damage than all the previous months of uncertainty. During the 10 months of the resistance, the Métis had served when needed to keep the peace as volunteers, even providing their own arms and ammunition. Their conduct had been exemplary. Now, they had to endure verbal and physical abuse, in two instances to the point of being killed. Wolseley's expedition was Britain's last official military action in present-day

Canada. Oddly enough, 1870 was also the year of the last purely Amerindian battle fought in Canada when the Blackfoot defeated the Cree, inflicting heavy losses, in the Battle of Belly (Oldman) River.

Canada was divided on Riel. Ontario demanded that he be brought to justice. Quebec answered in his defence. Macdonald was able to announce in all truth that he had no idea as to the Métis leader's whereabouts, which he hoped would calm the situation. The Fenians, who were conducting sporadic raids from across the border, hoped for Métis help, particularly as one of them, William B. O'Donoghue (d. 1878), had been one of Riel's top aides. The Métis leader refused, however. In 1871, Archibald publicly shook his hand in thanks, a gesture that cost the lieutenant-governor his office.

Riel was twice elected to Parliament for the constituency of Provencher, at first by acclamation in a by-election in 1873 and then the following year by defeating his Liberal opponent. Although he was never able to take his seat, he did slip into Ottawa long enough to sign the parliamentary oaths book, a gesture that led to his formal expulsion from the House.

The Red River crisis of 1869–70 and the question of amnesty that arose out of it were the first serious racial controversies the Dominion faced. Although the English–French confrontation took centre stage, the underlying Amerindian–Métis–non-Native division had been the major factor. Great Britain might have lobbied for the creation of an Amerindian buffer state in the US during the negotiations for the Treaty of Ghent in 1814, but when it came to creating a Métis domain within her own colonies, she had not been up to the challenge.[62]

Neither the Amerindian people of the North-West Territories nor the government had any reason to believe the racial issue was settled. Settlers of European descent were arriving every day in the Northwest, and the trickle was turning into a flood. Both sides could look to the south, to the violence of the American West, for a glimpse at what the future might be. Canada's vision of a nation from sea to sea did not include disputes over who owned the land when the next wave of settlers arrived. Amerindians wanted to safeguard their rights while they still were in the majority. The answer for both lay in treaties.

Important Names and Terms

Bagot Commission	reserves
Canada First	Riel, Louis
Comité National des Métis	Robinson treaties
enfranchisement	status Indians
Grant, Cuthbert	wardship
non-status Indians	'white man's burden'

Study Questions

1) What were the findings of the Bagot Commission?
2) What were the specific aims of the 1857 Civilizing Act?
3) Account for the disturbances at Pic River and Mica Bay in the middle of the nineteenth century.
4) What led to the crisis in the Red River settlement?

Recommended Readings

Chute, Janet. *The Legacy of Shingwakonse*. Toronto: University of Toronto Press, 1998.

Getty, Ian L., and Antoine S. Lussier, eds. *As Long As the Sun Shines and Water Flows*. Vancouver: University of British Columbia Press, 1983.

Howard, James H. *The Canadian Sioux*. Lincoln: University of Nebraska Press, 1984.

MacLeod, Margaret, and W.L. Morton. *Cuthbert Grant of Grantown*. Toronto: McClelland & Stewart, 1974.

Pannekoek, Frits. *A Snug Little Flock: The Social Origins of the Riel Resistance of 1869–70*. Winnipeg: Watson & Dwyer, 1991.

11

The First Numbered Treaties, Police, and the Indian Act

Treaties characterized relations between Europeans and Amerindians from the very beginning. By the 1870s, however, the government saw them as the final, once-and-for-all means of opening up Amerindian lands for settlement and development by extinguishing Amerindian land title. The Amerindians missed this at first, because by their custom, agreements were not necessarily permanent. Instead, they were subject to changing conditions that could call for renegotiation and renewal. Even pacts of peace and friendship undertaken to last forever had to be renewed from time to time with appropriate ceremonies to keep them 'alive'.

Government representatives soon mastered Amerindian figures of speech for negotiations, borrowing such phrases (among others) as 'as long as the sun shines and the water flows'. When negotiators used these terms in treaty language, Amerindians expected whites to live up to their word.[1] In the Amerindian view, the treaties they were now negotiating with the Canadian government would help them to adapt to the demands of the modern world within the framework of their own traditions. In return, they agreed to be loyal subjects of the Crown, respecting its laws and customs. Missionaries were prominent in a number of these negotiations, sometimes as agents of the government, at other times as mediators.

In the context of Amerindian–Euro-Canadian relations, a treaty has been defined as a compact or set of fundamental principles that formed the basis for future negotiations between Amerindians and non-Amerindians.[2] In the government view, the treaties granted privileges. In the indigenous view, they protected rights.[3] In some areas, settlement had preceded treaties, and this influenced the government's decisions. As can be imagined, in such cases settler reaction to Amerindian land rights was usually openly hostile. Box 11.1 provides a brief synopsis of the history of treaties in Canada.

Again, negotiations were far from being either simple or easy. As S.J. Dawson, the engineer for the Canadian expedition to the West led by Henry Youle Hind, described it:

Time Line

1871	Treaty One (Stone Fort Treaty) with Saulteaux (Ojibwa), Swampy Cree, and others in southern Manitoba. Treaty Two (Manitoba Post Treaty) with Saulteaux, Cree, and other bands in central Manitoba.
1873	Treaty Three (Northwest Angle Treaty) with Ojibwa of northwestern Ontario and southeastern Manitoba. North West Mounted Police force created. Cypress Hills Massacre: American wolfers cross border after some horses were stolen and slay 20–30 Assiniboine encamped at sacred Amerindian meeting place.
1874	Treaty Four with bands in southern Saskatchewan.
1875	Treaty Five with bands in northern Manitoba.
1876	Treaty Six with Plains Indians of central Saskatchewan and Alberta includes provision of a 'medicine chest' that becomes the legal basis for free health care for all Amerindians.

	Indian Act passed, a consolidation and revamping of pre-Confederation legislation from the Canadas.
1877	Treaty Seven, signed at Blackfoot Crossing, covers southern Alberta and opens lands for completion of transcontinental railway.
1880	Amerindian administration becomes a separate department within Department of the Interior.
1884	Potlatch feasts of Northwest Coast groups banned.
1885	Franchise Bill introduced by Macdonald with aim of Amerindian assimilation.
1890s	Ghost Dance spiritual movement of American Sioux, which anticipates disappearance of white man, appears on Siouan reserves in Saskatchewan and Manitoba.
1895	Thirst dances (sun dances) of Plains Amerindians banned. Like the potlatches, these continue secretively.

• Any one who, in negotiating with these Indians, should suppose he had mere children to deal with, would find himself mistaken. In their manner of expressing themselves they make use of a great deal of allegory, and their illustration may at time appear childish enough, but in their actual dealings they are shrewd and sufficiently awake to their own interests, and, if the matter should be one of importance, affecting the general interests of the tribe, they neither reply to a proposition, nor make one themselves, until it is fully discussed and deliberated upon in Council by all the Chiefs.

What was more, added Dawson, negotiators had to be very careful about what they said, as 'there are always those present who are charged with keeping every word in mind.'[4] Once, a Fort Frances chief repeated to him, word for word, what Dawson had said two years earlier. As well, the language difficulties that plagued negotiations from the start continued to be an unsolved problem. If anything, things were worse, because now interpreters were usually government representatives.

Box 11.1   Treaties in Canada

By the time of Confederation, various governments had already negotiated 123 treaties and land surrenders in British North America with Amerindians. Between 1860 and 1923, 66 treaties were signed, covering a little more than half of Canada's Amerindians. The Proclamation of 1763 gave Canada the right to negotiate for land title in the West. This led directly to the **numbered treaties**, which began with Treaty One in 1871 and ended with Treaty Eleven in 1921. (Later treaties had proper names.) Between 1923 and 1973, the government negotiated no new treaties because of legislation banning the use of band funds for land claim actions. By the time of the James Bay and Northern Quebec Agreement in 1975, the number of such actions had approached 500.[5]

In acquiring Rupert's Land, to which the terms of the Proclamation of 1763 did not extend, the Canadian government promised, on behalf of the King, to negotiate with its Amerindians for the extinguishment of their title and the setting aside of reserves for their exclusive use.[6] It considered Amerindians to have the right to use the land for such purposes as hunting and fishing. Title did not include either sovereignty or ownership in fee simple.

Even such limited rights were not universally acknowledged, however. The idea—developed in the sixteenth century—that Amerindians had no land rights at all was still alive, as officials made clear during negotiations. In this view, treaties were a moral, not a legal, obligation.[7] In practical terms, they were a means of avoiding conflict. In any event, Canada's promise to Britain to honour the provisions of the Proclamation of 1763 led directly to the 11 numbered treaties negotiated between 1871 and 1921.

The government moved to clear an area of Amerindian title when the land had significant value or when there were political considerations. Thus, when Manitoba became a province and settlers were already moving in, it moved quickly to extinguish Amerindian title. Canada could not afford to repeat the costly frontier wars of the United States.

Mounting demands from Amerindians led to the Robinson Huron and Robinson Superior treaties negotiated in 1850. Similar agitations were now developing in the West. A.G. Archibald, as lieutenant-governor of Manitoba and the North-West Territories, responded in 1870 by sending out a representative to investigate the Amerindian position.[8] However, the first attempt to reach an accord in Manitoba that year ended in failure.

Treaties One, Two, and Three: Ontario and Manitoba Land Surrendered

Treaty One is called the Stone Fort Treaty because negotiations took place at Lower Fort Garry, which was built of stone. The Saulteaux (Ojibwa), Swampy Cree, and others in southern Manitoba around Portage la Prairie and Winnipeg petitioned Lieutenant-Governor Archibald for a treaty in the fall of 1870. Signed on 3 August 1871, it

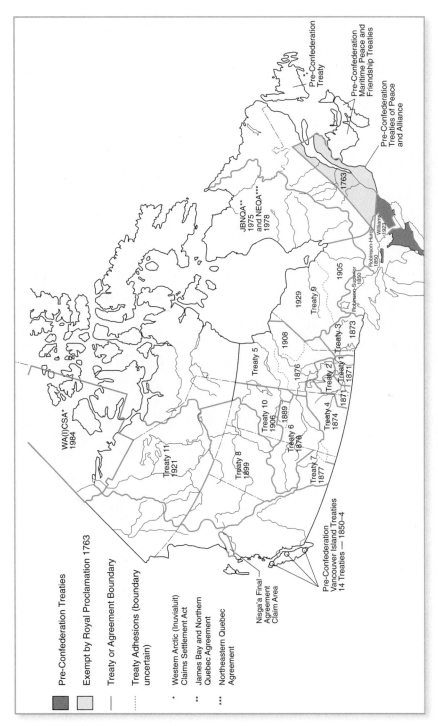

11.1   Areas covered by treaties and agreements

Sources: Alan D. Macmillan, *Native Peoples and Cultures of Canada*; Wilcomb E. Washburn, *History of Indian-White Relations* (Washington: Smithsonian Institution, 1988); *Report of the Royal Commission on Aboriginal Peoples*, II, part 2, 483.

The transfer of Rupert's Land to Canada from the Hudson's Bay Company meant that the government was going to have to embark on a series of treaty negotiations with western Amerindians. Negotiations for Treaty One, in southern Manitoba, as depicted by the *Canadian Illustrated News*, 1871. *(Glenbow Museum and Archives, NA–1406–72)*

included 16,700 square miles (43,253 square kilometres). On 21 August 1871, the Saulteaux, Cree, and other bands in central Manitoba signed Treaty Two, also called the Manitoba Post Treaty. Through the treaties, the government was justifying its creation of Manitoba but also preparing the way for white settlement.

The question of delegates became a concern during the negotiations for Treaty One when a chief complained he could 'scarcely hear the Queen's words'. As it turned out, the HBC's imprisonment of four Amerindians for breach of a service contract was the

Nations whose economies were based on the buffalo hunt went from prosperity to destitution within little more than a generation. A nineteenth-century textbook illustration shows Amerindians begging for food while settlers clear the land. From *Lovell's Advanced Geography*, Montreal, 1880. *(Glenbow Museum and Archives, NA–1374–2)*

cause of his hearing loss. The government released the prisoners, who attended the meeting, and the chief's hearing improved.[9]

The Amerindians opened negotiations by claiming reserves amounting to about two-thirds of Manitoba. Archibald and Wemyss Simpson, then Indian Commissioner, termed this 'preposterous'. They countered with 160 acres (65 hectares) per family of five, and an annuity of $12, and they threatened the Amerindians with being swamped by settlers without any compensation if they did not agree.

The chiefs were disturbed. They could not see that the government's offer would benefit their children. What would happen, one chief asked, if Amerindians had more children after they settled down? Archibald replied that the government would provide for them from lands further west, forgetting that Aboriginals already occupied those lands. Was it really fair, another Amerindian asked, to allow the same amount of land for Amerindians as for non-Amerindians, considering the differences in their circumstances and ways of life? And what about help in getting started in this new life? The government promised schools and schoolmasters, ploughs and harrows. The Amerindians thought there should be more: clothing, housing, and agricultural equipment. They got the impression that the government negotiators agreed.

The terms for Treaties One and Two were similar: $3 for each Amerindian and an annuity of $15 per family of five, prorated for families of different size, payable in goods or cash. The government stood firm on its offer of 160 acres per family of five, which the Amerindians reluctantly accepted. It agreed to maintain a school on each reserve and said it would ban liquor sales on reserves. Archibald promised hunting and fishing rights in his opening speech, but these did not appear in the treaty's final draft. Neither was there any provision for the farm implements, livestock, and clothing that had been a part of the verbal agreement, even though the government expected the Amerindians to take up farming. Even so, the terms that Ottawa accepted had exceeded original instructions.

The Amerindians later complained that the government was not honouring verbal promises made during negotiations. Eventually, in 1875, the government revised the two treaties, but it still did not give all that the government had promised. After that, officials were much more careful about what they said during negotiations.

During the first treaty negotiations, the government gave surprisingly little thought to the terms of the expected surrenders. They paid more attention to the ceremony that would surround the negotiations, expecting to overawe the Amerindians and thus reduce their demands. On the contrary, Amerindians forced major changes in the government's offerings.[10] During these discussions, they raised most of the issues that appeared in later treaties. Their success is a measure of their skill in negotiating, given that the government could, and did, impose a 'take-it-or-leave-it' approach.[11] In two instances, those of Treaty Nine signed in 1905–6 and the Williams treaties of 1923, the Ontario and Canadian governments had worked out the terms before opening negotiations with the Amerindians.[12] There were holdouts among the Amerindians, in some cases until mid-twentieth century.

The Saulteaux of the Lake of the Woods district signed Treaty Three, the North-West Angle Treaty, on 3 October 1873. Most of the 55,000 square miles (142,450 square kilometres) it dealt with were in Ontario, except for a small part in southeastern Manitoba. It cleared title to the Dawson Road and also provided for the railroad right-of-way.

The Ojibwa knew that theirs was 'a rich country'. As Chief **Mawedopenais** of Fort Frances put it, 'the rustling of the gold is under my feet where I stand.'[13] Making the point that it was 'the Great Spirit who gave us this; where we stand upon is the Indians' property, and belongs to them', he observed that non-Amerindians had already robbed them of their lands, 'and we don't wish to give them up again without getting something in their place.'[14]

After prolonged and difficult negotiations, and several refusals by the Amerindians to sign, its final terms were more generous than those of the previous two treaties. The negotiators also made provision for the continuation of hunting and fishing rights and included agricultural equipment and supplies. Schools would be established, and the sale of liquor on reserves would be banned. A request by the Amerindians that they be granted free passes on the Canadian Pacific Railway was rejected out of hand.[15]

The Métis were influential in the negotiations of Treaty Three. This was the first of the numbered treaties specifically to include them, which took place at the request of Mawedopenais after some official hesitation.[16] Similarly, during the bargaining for Treaties Four and Six, the Amerindians requested that their 'cousins' be included. At first, the government accepted this and set aside land for the Métis of Rainy River. However, after the Red River rebellion, Ottawa amended the Indian Act, excluding 'halfbreeds' from both the Act and treaties.[17] In spite of this, the Métis continued to be influential in the negotiations. According to Lord Dufferin, governor-general of Canada (1870–8), they were 'the ambassadors between East and West'.[18]

The better terms of Treaty Three reflected the greater familiarity of the Amerindians of the area with the governmental negotiating process and their greater political assertiveness. Alexander Morris (1826–89), who had succeeded Archibald as lieutenant-governor of Manitoba in 1873, made four attempts over three years before they agreed to sign. At the end of the Treaty Three negotiations, Mawedopenais borrowed from white rhetoric:

> I take off my glove and in giving you my hand I deliver my birthright and lands.
> And in taking your hand, I hold fast all the promises you have made, and I hope
> they will last as long as the sun goes round and the water flows.[19]

Many times, the Euro-Canadians would later reflect on the implications of the rhetoric they used so freely during negotiations.

In the meantime, Treaty Three set precedents for later treaties, particularly where agricultural equipment and livestock were concerned. As well, it contained provisions for hunting and fishing rights in unsettled areas, although the terms improved somewhat in later treaties. Eventually, in 1881, the government extended the boundaries of Manitoba to include those areas ceded by Treaties One, Two, and Three. In the case of Treaty Three, this would lead to a confrontation with Ontario and to Canada's first court case involving Aboriginal rights (a phrase that came into popular usage in the 1960s), *St Catherine's Milling v. The Queen* (Chapter 16). Others would soon follow.

The Liquor Trade Draws the Police into the West

The transcontinental railroad was inching its way from sea to sea. The bison were receding, and settlers were exerting more and more pressure on Amerindian and Métis lands. Ottawa was only too aware of the growing instability in the West. The possibility

Sitting Bull, chief of the Hunkpapa Sioux, who came to Canada in 1877 with 4,000 followers after the Battle of Little Big Horn, 1876. Sitting Bull and his people were denied a reserve, and famine forced his return to the US and surrender in 1881. He was killed while being arrested in 1890 as part of the American government attempt to quell the nativistic Ghost Dance uprising. *(Library and Archives Canada, C 20038)*

of the American frontier wars extending into Canada filled Ottawa with alarm. Under the BNA Act, law enforcement was a provincial responsibility, however, and so a federal force would be able to operate only in those areas not yet organized into provinces. Alternatively, it could come to an agreement with those provinces that did not have their own police.

Macdonald's original plan was to use Métis for at least half of the rank and file of a federal police force for the West, under British officers, following the British colonial model. The revolt of 1869–70, in particular Ontario's violent reaction to the Métis initiative, led him to drop the idea, and the **North West Mounted Police**, created in 1873, was all white.[20]

Almost immediately, an incident brought the new force into action. The Cypress Hills, near the international border where the Alberta/Saskatchewan border would eventually be drawn, was a sacred area for Amerindians (see Box 11.2), where hostile tribes could camp in peace. It was also a favourite resort for American traders, men whose stock-in-trade was liquor, as well as for hunters/trappers called 'wolfers' because of the skins they usually obtained.

A group of these wolfers at Fort Benton, Montana, had some horses stolen. Their search for those they considered guilty brought them to the **Cypress Hills**. There, they attacked an Assiniboine camp, killing 20 or 30 people. In the charges and countercharges that followed, it was never established that the Assiniboine were, indeed, the culprits. In fact, the weight of evidence was to the contrary. Later, it would be established that the horse thieves had been Crees.[21] What was clear at the time was the need for a law enforcement agency in the region. That year, 1873, nearly 100 Amerindians died in drunken brawls.[22]

Canada promptly sent out 150 North West Mounted Police to confront traders and wolfers, whose forts were bristling with cannons, according to rumour. The trip was hard. Many of the animals that formed part of the equipment train died, and at one point the expedition got lost. Among the local guides who came to its rescue was Jerry Potts (Ky-yo-kosi, 'Bear Child', 1840–96), a Métis.[23] The Mounties finally

Box 11.2   After Little Big Horn: The Sioux in Canada

After the Battle of Little Big Horn in the United States in 1876, Ta-tanka-I-yotank (Sitting Bull, *c*. 1836–90), chief of the Hunkpapa Sioux, and 4,000 of his followers streamed north into the Cypress Hills area. At the same time, northern buffalo hunters were heading south into the same region in pursuit of the remaining herds. Not only was there not enough food for so many people, but once more there was fear of an American invasion when the United States demanded that the refugees be forced to return. Most were persuaded by one means or another to do so. Even Ta-tanka-I-yotank gave up after the Canadian government refused his last request for a reserve. Ottawa passed an Order-in-Council setting aside 12,000 acres (4,856 hectares) for the Sioux at two sites in Saskatchewan, based on 80 acres (32 hectares) per family of five. These Sioux refugees had crossed the border from the US over the previous decades in pursuit of bison and to escape the bloodshed on the American frontier. Eventually, the government created other reserves for the Sioux, the last in 1913, at Wood Mountain in Manitoba.[24]

Sioux did not sign any of Canada's treaties, as they did not cede lands in this country. They are registered, however, and so are entitled to the benefits given to status Amerindians except for annuities in payment for land. Once they accepted the fact that buffalo hunting could no longer provide for their needs, they settled down to their ancient way of life, farming, but readjustments were not always smooth, and life could be very hard. Until the end of the nineteenth century, the death rate exceeded the birth rate, so that by 1899 only 897 Sioux were listed for Canada. One of the few who took part in the 1885 rebellion was Wapahaska ('White Cap', 'White Warbonnet'), who was briefly a member of Riel's council— 'Exovidate'—in 1885. He was tried for participating in the rebellion but claimed that he had been forced to join and was acquitted.[25]

arrived at Fort Whoop-Up, a trading post, to find only one trader, who invited the police in to dinner.

Until 1885, the main tasks of the Mounties were to keep the liquor trade in check and establish good relations with the Amerindians. They were successful on both counts. Canada at that point was on good terms with the Cree, an inheritance from the HBC. The attitude of the Blackfoot Confederacy, however, was uncertain. Superintendent James F. Macleod (1836–94) set about cultivating a relationship with one of its chiefs, **Crowfoot** (Isapo-Muxika, 'Crow Indian's Big Foot', *c*. 1830–90), and soon became a personal friend.[26]

The arrival of the police proved to be a boon for the Confederacy, which was suffering from the whisky trade. In 1872–3 alone, at least 70 Blood died in drunken quarrels between themselves, this among a people who in pre-contact days had a very low incidence of violence within their own communities.

Box 11.3   Treaties Four and Six

Paskwaw (Pasquah, d. 1889), a Cree who headed a band of Plains Saulteaux, observed that if a sale of land had really happened under Treaty Six, the Plains people should receive the money. Earlier, he had opposed the entry of surveyors onto the Plains. He was also a lead negotiator for Treaty Four, the Qu'Appelle Treaty, which took two years to be hammered out and resulted in more concessions (in the form of implements and seed to start farming) than the federal government had wished to make. (Paskwaw eventually took a reserve five miles west of Fort Qu'Appelle.) A year later, Piapot (Payipwat, *c.* 1816–1908), who had a larger following than Paskwaw, also signed the treaty, apparently in the mistaken belief that the government had revised it. Treaty Four was the first to recognize trapping as a feature of Amerindian life.

Clearing the Way for White Settlement—Treaties Six and Seven

Treaty Six, signed in two ceremonies at Forts Carlton and Pitt in 1876, included a provision to maintain a **'medicine chest'** for the benefit of the Amerindians. This became the basis for free health care for all Amerindians.[27] It also provided for rations in case of famine, important now that buffalo had become scarce.

Abraham Wikaskokiseyin ('Sweetgrass', d. 1877),[28] chief of the Fort Pitt Crees and leading Amerindian spokesman during the Treaty Six negotiations, told officials, 'We hear our lands were sold and we do not like it. We don't want to sell our lands. It is our property, and no one has the right to sell them.'[29] Other chiefs believed that the Europeans had borrowed the land, as it could not be bought (see Box 11.3). In any event, Sweetgrass signed the 1876 treaty. His people, however, felt that he had signed their lands away without consulting them properly, and they killed him.[30]

Treaty Seven, signed the following year at Blackfoot Crossing, near Gleichen, Alberta, attracted Canada's last great gathering of independent Plains Amerindians. It cleared the way for the construction of the railroad, among other items. Crowfoot agreed to sign on the advice of a shaman, who told him the treaty would change his life and that of his people: 'What you will eat from this money will have your people buried all over these hills. You will be tied down, you will not wander the Plains. The whites will take your land and fill it.'[31] But in spite of these consequences, there was no alternative. With the signing of this treaty, the Canadian government had secured its western settlement frontier.

At least, that's what it thought. But not all Amerindians were enamoured of the treaties. When administrators had sent gifts to smooth the way for Treaty Six negotiations, the most famous and influential of the Plains chiefs, Mistahimaskwa ('Big Bear', *c.* 1825–88), had retorted, 'We want none of the Queen's presents. When we set a trap for a fox we scatter meat all around but when the fox gets into the trap we knock him on the head. We want no baits. Let your Chiefs come to us like men and talk to us.'[32] Pitikwahanapiwiyin ('Poundmaker', *c.* 1842–86), nephew of Mistawasis and adopted son of Crowfoot, told Treaty Six negotiators, 'This is our land. It isn't a piece of pemmican to be cut up and given back to us in little pieces. It is ours and we will take what we want.'[33]

Assimilation Through Legislation: The 1876 Indian Act

In 1873, the government set up separate boards to deal with Amerindian affairs in Manitoba, the North-West Territories, and British Columbia. But Confederation called for centralization, so two years later it replaced the boards with the old superintendency system. This, in turn, called for more legislation. Amerindians, already the most regulated of peoples in Canada, would become even more so. The government would now interfere with their lives at every turn, down to, and including, the personal level.

The **Indian Act** of 1876 consolidated and revamped earlier legislation into a nationwide framework that was still fundamentally in place at the start of the twenty-first century. Its original goal of encouraging assimilation without forcing the issue would be lost

Piapot, in 1885. One of the major leaders of the Plains Cree at the time of the treaty signings on the prairies, he remained loyal to the Crown during the 1885 troubles. This contrasted with his long record of fighting for better treaty terms, the right to choose the location of his reserve, and the right to practise traditional religious rituals. Twice arrested and imprisoned for his persistent efforts, he was finally deposed by Ottawa in 1902. His followers remained loyal, however, and refused to select a successor until after his death in 1908. *(Glenbow Museum and Archives, NA–532–1)*

Box 11.4   Defining Bands, Band Members, and Reserves

According to the Indian Act of 1876, a **band** is a body of Amerindians for whom the government has set aside lands for their common use and benefit; for whom the government is holding monies for their common use and benefit; or whom the Governor-in-Council has declared a band. A member of a band is a person whose name appears on a band list or who is entitled to have his/her name appear on such a list. A reserve, within the meaning of the Act, is a tract of land that the Crown has set aside for the use and benefit of a band.

---

sight of in the repression that followed the 1885 revolt (see next chapter) but was recovered in 1951. But the Act's fundamental purpose—to assimilate Amerindians—has stayed a constant. Furthermore, 'the right of Indians to control the actions of the Department' would not be recognized 'under any circumstances'.[34]

Measures for protection of reserve lands and resources were taken directly from the 1850–1 Acts, although somewhat strengthened, and the enfranchisement provisions of 1857 were kept and expanded. Now, any Amerindian who got a university degree qualifying him as a minister, lawyer, teacher, or doctor could become enfranchised and get a location ticket without going through the otherwise mandatory three-year probation. The regulation depriving Amerindian women married to non-Amerindians of their Indian status also stayed on the books.

One measure that came in for revision was the definition of an Indian. According to the new definition, he or she was 'a person who pursuant of this Act is registered as an Indian, or is entitled to be registered as an Indian' or a person of Amerindian blood reputed to belong to a band and entitled to use its lands.[35] Incidentally, a person could be registered without having signed a treaty. It also defined other terms for the first time, such as 'band', 'member of a band', and 'reserve' (Box 11.4).

In 1869, the government instituted an elective system for the selection of chiefs and band councils in local Amerindian government.[36] The new system, however, was not traditional among Amerindians and met with considerable resistance. The government's goal was administrative uniformity, but it also wanted to speed up assimilation by eliminating tribal systems. According to the Act of 1876, the chief's period of office was three years, but Indian Affairs could remove him at any time for 'dishonesty, intemperance, or immorality'. The Indian Affairs agent also paid the bills, and so he was obviously in a position of power. The Six Nations opposed the new system because of its obvious interference with autonomous choice for forms of government.

Lands held in trust by the Crown for the benefit of indigenous peoples could not be taxed, mortgaged, or seized for debt by any person other than an Amerindian or a band. This severely reduced access to development capital.[37] An Amerindian who held property under lease or outside of the reserve could be taxed. In Manitoba, the North-West Territories, and Keewatin District (today, the mainland central Arctic, which is part of Nunavut, plus portions of northern Ontario and Manitoba bordering on Hudson Bay), Amerindians who signed treaty could not acquire lands by homestead or pre-emption. This was to prevent them from claiming both a share of a reserve and a homestead. The Superintendent-General retained the right to grant allotments on reserve lands in fee simple as a reward for enfranchisement. Most bands resisted the measure and refused to approve location tickets or to sell or lease their lands, even for a limited period.[38]

An Upward Spiral of Regulation

Amerindian administration did not become a separate department until 1880. Even then, however, it continued to be with the Department of the Interior, where it stayed until 1936. The Minister of Interior was also Superintendent-General of Indian Affairs, but effective power lay with the Deputy Superintendent-General. To the superintendent's power to impose the elective system whenever he thought a band was ready for it was added the power to designate only elected officials as band spokesmen. The government would not recognize or deal with traditional leaders.

In 1884, the government banned the elaborate feasts of the Northwest Coast Amerindians, known under the general label 'potlatch',[39] along with dances associated with religious, supernatural **Tamanawas rituals**. In the case of the potlatches, the argument was that their 'give-away' aspect went against the concept of private property.[40] In the case of religious rituals, dancing was against the religious beliefs of some missionaries. The irony, of course, was that Amerindians, in common with many other peoples, considered music and dance to be a gift from the gods—or perhaps stolen from them. Towards the end of the nineteenth century and into the twentieth, missionaries also started a campaign to remove totem poles, seeing them as symbols of an undesirable belief system.

In 1895, the government, in effect, prohibited the **thirst dances** ('sun dances') of prairie Amerindians.[41] The result was to drive the dances underground, as the government could not effectively enforce the prohibition. At this time, Siouan reserves such as the Wahpeton at Round Plain, Saskatchewan, and Wood Mountain, Manitoba, were also holding the **Ghost Dance**, which had originated in 1889 from the prophecy of Wovoka (Jack Wilson), a Paiute spiritual leader in Nevada who foretold a peaceful end to white expansionism. This expectation, and the Ghost Dance, quickly spread among Amerindian nations throughout much of the American West. **Millenarianism** was another type of mystical movement that also appeared from time to time.[42] These movements worried officials, because they strengthened the peoples' inner resources to withstand the intensifying attacks on their culture, and such beliefs found fertile soil in the difficult circumstances the First Nations were facing: loss of land and a way of life; the virtual disappearance of the bison; increasing starvation and poverty.

In the meantime, some Amerindians, with the help of their lawyers, became skilled in fighting these bans.[43] On 21 February 1896, *The Daily Colonist*, Victoria, published a petition signed by three elders of the Na'as band asking for the restitution of their customs:

> If we wish to perform an act moral in its nature, with no injury or damage, and pay for it, no law in equity can divest us of such right. We see the Salvation Army parade through the streets of your town with music and drum, enchanting the town. . . . We are puzzled to know whether in the estimation of civilization we are human or fish on the tributaries of the Na'as River, that the felicities of our ancestors should be denied us.[44]

The traditional way was far from disappearing. In fact, the ceremonies, traditional cultural practices, and values were thriving, and still being disparaged by officials some 40 years after these bans. As late as the 1930s, government reports continued to blame the apparent resistance to the agricultural model for economic self-support on the continuation of traditional ceremonies.[45]

The Indian 'Advancement' Act

An Act for Conferring Certain Privileges on the More Advanced Bands of Indians of Canada, with the View of Training Them for the Exercise of Municipal Affairs—this was the official name of the Indian Advancement Act. Its purpose was to transform tribal regulations into municipal laws. Passed in 1884, it gave tribal councils limited powers of taxation, subject to the approval of the department; responsibility for public health; and the power to enforce bylaws. It also reduced the number of band councillors to six, even though traditional Amerindian councils were large.[46] The Act replaced the three-year election system, in effect since 1869, with annual elections, considered necessary for the municipal type of government the Act was preparing the bands for.

Taking as few chances as it could, the Act stated that chiefs deposed by the Governor-in-Council (i.e., the Governor-General affirming a decision of the federal cabinet) on grounds of dishonesty, intemperance, or immorality could not be re-elected immediately. The decision as to which bands qualified rested with the Governor-in-Council. Bands considered not 'advanced' enough for this system were mostly in the West. In effect, the powers of the Superintendent-General, or his designated agent, to direct the band's affairs had been greatly increased. He could call for and supervise elections, and he could summon and preside over band meetings.[47]

Amerindians across Canada considered these new measures just another attempt 'to force white ideas on the red men'.[48] In all, only nine bands adopted the new system, some of them under pressure. By 1906, the government incorporated what was left of the Indian Advancement Act into the Indian Act (see Chapters 13 and 14 for a discussion of later changes to the Indian Act), but it remained the case that Amerindian and Euro-Canadian views of the Act differed considerably (Box 11.5).

Box 11.5   Two Views of the Indian Act

The Indian Act is something of a 'total institution'.[49] With the treaties, it touches on almost all aspects of the lives of status Indians. Both the treaties and the Indian Act place Canada's First Nations in a separate category from other Canadians, but in different ways. As Amerindians see it, the purpose of the Indian Act is to restrict and control, whereas the treaties aim to accommodate through mutual agreement. To Amerindians, the Act's goal—to remake them, through education and social programs, into contributing members of what has become an industrialized and technological society—is a violation of their treaties.

For non-Aboriginals, the basic purpose of the Act has been to protect Amerindians while setting the stage for their 'advancement'. They see it as paving the way in the long term for Amerindians to become fully participating members of a society based on the liberal democratic traditions of individual initiative supported by equal rights for all.[50] In theory, this should end with the Act's legislating itself out of existence.

In the meantime, on the prairies, Amerindian unrest was growing, as buffalo became fewer and fewer. The Métis were also unhappy about their land situation. The government responded by amending the Indian Act once again, this time to make incitement of Amerindians to riot an offence and to ban the sale or gift of ammunition to Amerindians in Manitoba and the North-West Territories.[51] Obviously, the government had clear warnings of what was to come.

The Franchise Bill

Still pursuing the integration of Amerindians, Macdonald introduced the Franchise Bill into Parliament in March of 1885, four days before the outbreak of the North-West Rebellion. With Amerindians east of the Great Lakes in mind, Macdonald proposed the franchise for all males who were British subjects and who met certain minimum property qualifications, whether or not they held land individually. Amerindians of Ontario and Quebec, he said, might not be contributing to the general assessment of the country:

> but they have their own assessment and their own system of taxation in their own bridges and roads, they build their own school houses. They carry on the whole system in their own way, but it is in the Indian way, and it is an efficient way. They carry out all the obligations of civilized men . . . in every respect they have a right to be considered as equal with the whites.[52]

He added, however, that the Amerindians of the North-West Territories and Keewatin, Manitoba, and 'perhaps' British Columbia were not yet ready for the measure. They should be excluded unless as individuals they were occupying separate tracts of land.

The bill aroused strong opposition on the grounds that Amerindians in general were not paying taxes. The cry went up that it would allow the 'wild hordes' led by the likes of Big Bear and Poundmaker to go 'from a scalping party to the polls'.[53] Macdonald was able to get the bill passed, but the Liberals revoked it in 1898, claiming that it was 'an insult to free white people in the country to place them on a level with pagan and barbarian Indians'.[54]

Clearly, the country was not prepared to accept Amerindians on an equal footing. When it came to choosing between Amerindians and whites, the interest of the latter usually would be provided for. In the situation brewing in the West, the conflict of interests was moving steadily towards violence. It would be amazing how little there was, and of what short duration. Canada has much to be thankful for in the forbearance of her Aboriginal peoples.

Important Names and Terms

band	millenarianism
Crowfoot	'medicine chest'
Cypress Hills	North West Mounted Police
Ghost Dance	numbered treaties
Indian Act	Tamanawas rituals
Mawedopenais	thirst dances

Study Questions

1) What mistakes did the Canadian government make in the treaty process?
2) What led to the troubles at Cypress Hills?
3) Why did the Sioux come to Canada?
4) What were the main provisions of the 1876 Indian Act?

Recommended Readings

Cardinal, Harold. *The Unjust Society: The Tragedy of Canada's Indians*. Edmonton: Hurtig, 1969.
Dempsey, Hugh A. *Crowfoot: Chief of the Blackfeet*. Edmonton: Hurtig, 1972.
Kehoe, Alice B. *The Ghost Dance*. Toronto: Holt, Rinehart and Winston, 1989.
Peterson, Jacqueline, and Jennifer S.H. Brown, eds. *The New Peoples: Being and Becoming Métis in North America*. Winnipeg: University of Manitoba Press, 1985.

12

Time of Troubles as the Old Way Fades

The bounty of nature had its limits. The bison, once 'countless' because they were so many, were rapidly becoming 'countless' because there were none left. It became harder for Amerindians and Métis to pursue their accustomed ways of life.[1] The problem was particularly acute for Amerindians, not so much because they were not willing to change (after all, adaptability had been the key to their survival in the Americas for thousands of years) but because of the suddenness with which it was occurring.[2]

The Cree were among the first to be affected by the decline of the herds. Alarmed, they held a series of councils in the Qu'Appelle region in 1859 in which they maintained that the pursuit of bison should be restricted to Amerindians. They saw the HBC expansion onto the prairies as part of the problem. They wanted trade but did not like to see their lands invaded by strangers—whites or Métis—who also hunted there. If the newcomers wanted meat, pemmican, or hides, they should buy them from the Amerindians.[3]

An outstanding figure of this period was Maskepetoon ('Broken Arm', c. 1807–69), a Cree chief. He was one of the first on the Plains to learn the syllabic script, which may have aided his activities as a roving diplomat. In his efforts to calm growing tensions, in 1869 he entered a Blackfoot camp, traditional enemies of the Cree, with his son and a small party. The Blackfoot killed them all, signalling the eruption of warfare from the Missouri to Fort Edmonton.

This was the setting for the last major battle between Cree and Blackfoot the following year, 1870, at Belly (later, Oldman) River. As many as 300 Cree and perhaps 40 Blackfoot died, according to traders who visited the scene shortly afterwards.[4] This may have been mute testimony to uneven distribution of firearms between the two sides. In 1871, the two peoples signed a treaty allowing the Cree to hunt in Blackfoot territory, where the herds were still comparatively plentiful.[5]

Time Line

1859	Cree hold series of councils in Qu'Appelle region over dwindling bison herds and massive Métis involvement in hunt.
1870s	Groups of Métis leave Red River to form new settlements to north and west.
1871	Cree conclude treaty with Blackfoot to allow them to hunt in Blackfoot territory.
1872	St Laurent founded along South Saskatchewan River by Gabriel Dumont and other Métis. Batoche, another Métis settlement, founded near St Laurent.
1878	John Norquay elected as Manitoba's first and only Métis premier, though he identified with his Orkney heritage.
1880	Louis Riel is instrumental in getting Montana Amerindians to allow Canadian Plains Indians to hunt on their reservations; Canadian Natives raid horses of their traditional southern enemies, which breaks brief alliance.
1881–8	Edgar Dewdney, lieutenant-governor of North-West Territories, seeks to divide Indians just as Cree chief Big Bear seeks to unite them.
1882	Big Bear, leader of largest band of Plains Cree, forced finally to sign Treaty Six in order to get rations for his starving people after he has tried to form Amerindian alliances against white intrusion. He is made to take an isolated reserve.

US military sent to confiscate horses and equipment of Canadian Aboriginals hunting south of the border; border crossings restricted.

1884	Ottawa amends Indian Act to cut off sale or gift of ammunition to Indians in Manitoba and North-West Territories. Big Bear calls a thirst dance on Poundmaker's reserve—more than 2,000 participate. Dumont and other Métis ride south to Montana on 4 June to ask their spiritual leader, Riel, to return and help them in gaining rights that have been often promised but never given. Big Bear losing influence to Cree war chiefs, who advocate violence to regain independence. 16 December: Riel petitions Ottawa for all people of West—white, Amerindian, Métis—to be treated with full dignity as British subjects.
1884–5	Hard winter due to two straight years of poor crops for Amerindians and Métis on western Plains.
1885	Ottawa acknowledges Riel petition but is prepared only to set up a commission. 8 February: Riel replies: 'In 40 days they will have my answer.' 8 March: Riel announces intention to set up provisional government. 18 March: Métis seize Indian agent and other officials and occupy church at Batoche, cut

telegraph lines from Regina to Prince Albert.

19 March: Riel proclaims provisional government.

26 March: Métis attack NWMP sortie at Duck Lake, killing 12. Riel, armed with crucifix, stops pursuit of routed police.

end of March: Poundmaker's and Little Pine's people leave reserves, head towards Battleford.

2 April: Big Bear's war chiefs pillage HBC stores at Frog Lake, killing nine. Big Bear stops onslaught in time to save HBC representative as well as other settlers who had sought refuge at fort.

15 April: Big Bear takes NWMP's Fort Pitt in peaceful surrender.

24 April: Métis ambush Canadian militia, led by F.D. Middleton, at Fish Creek.

2 May: Poundmaker's sleeping camp attacked, and Poundmaker halts pursuit of fleeing militia.

9–12 May: Middleton and militia defeat entrenched Métis, who run out of ammunition, at Batoche.

15 May: Riel surrenders.

26 May: Poundmaker surrenders.

2 July: Big Bear walks into Fort Carlton to surrender.

16 November: Riel, convicted of treason, is hanged at Regina.

17 November: Eight Amerindians hanged at Battleford. Poundmaker, Big Bear, One Arrow sent to prison; all die soon after release.

Pass system introduced to restrict Amerindians to their own reserves.

The Trials of the Métis Continue

Many **Métis** had already accepted agricultural or wage-earning options into their life-style as the bison herd vanished (see Box 12.1). Other problems arose, however, so that the transition for them, too, became painful, if not quite as drastic as it would be for Amerindians. The fur trade, dominant for 200 years, had in many aspects reinforced the cultural and economic positions of Amerindians and Métis, particularly in the West. This, along with the disregard of incoming settlers for Métis or Amerindian land claims, quickly stirred a Native reaction.

In 1872, the Métis asked Lieutenant-Governor Archibald to protect them against settlers occupying their land. Archibald had previously rejected their proposal that a block of land be reserved for their use, as was being done for Amerindians who signed treaty. The federal government also opposed the idea, claiming that the Métis should apply for land on an individual basis, as white settlers did. In Manitoba, after all, speculators had acquired most of the land set aside for 'children of the half-breed heads of families' for only a fraction of its value. Did they want the same thing to happen here, where not more than a quarter of the grants was actually occupied and improved by Métis?[6]

The buffalo had provided food, shelter, and clothing to those who hunted it, and no part of the animal was wasted. Now it was gone, and the Amerindians and Métis who had depended on it were left without skins to make tents. This photograph illustrates the depths to which the once-affluent hunters were reduced. *(Courtesy of Alberta Provincial Archives, B–772)*

Box 12.1   Shifting Populations

Amerindians in the Canadian West are estimated to have numbered about 35,000 in 1870 (a figure considered by some to be too high), the Métis, about 10,000–12,000, and non-Aboriginals, fewer than 2,000. Epidemics and swelling waves of immigration quickly changed these proportions, however. By 1883, whites heavily outnumbered Amerindians.[7]

   Amerindian population on the Plains was highest during the summer, when buffalo herds were at their largest. Bison did not have definite migratory movements, congregating instead where the feeding was most attractive.[8] The shrinking of the herds had the effect of increasing the ceremonial aspect of the hunt, and shamans able to call the animals gained in importance and prestige. Bison were central to the ceremonial life of Plains Amerindians. The disappearance of the herds was a major factor in the rise of the Ghost Dance.

It is not clear whether Ottawa told the Métis about its position concerning treating them as individuals rather than as communities. In any event, groups scattered from Red River to establish independent settlements, a pattern that had been in effect for some time (see Chapter 10). The difference was that now farming was replacing buffalo hunting. The best known of these groups was one led by the buffalo-hunt captain, **Gabriel Dumont** (1838–1906), reputed to speak six Aboriginal languages, besides French and English. In 1872, he led his group north to colonize an area about 45 to 50 kilometres long and some 10 kilometres wide, including a stretch of the South Saskatchewan River and Duck Lake. Its southern boundary was Fish Creek.[9] One of the reasons for choosing this site was that it already had a mission, **St Laurent**, founded in 1871 by Oblate Alexis André (1833–93). Each family had a 'ribbon' lot with river frontage of about 200 metres, following the Red River pattern. Nearby were another two missions, St Louis and St Antoine de Padoue. The settlement connected with the latter dated to 1872 and was called after its founder, trader François-Xavier Letendre *dit* Batoche (*c.* 1841–1901). **Batoche** was the commercial centre for the cluster of Métis settlements, referred to collectively as South Branch, straddling the Carlton Trail (the main route to Edmonton) as well as the South Saskatchewan.

Ottawa, in the meantime, had already decided on the square survey as the settlement pattern for the West. However, anyone who had settled in the region before 1870 could keep the original boundaries. In the case of the Métis, who used ribbon lots, this was important. After 1870, settlers had no legal right to special consideration,

Gabriel Dumont, a buffalo-hunt captain who was fluent in French, English, and many Amerindian languages, was instrumental in the settlement of and in creating a viable government for the St Laurent Métis settlement in Saskatchewan—an administration that the Canadian government would not accept. Later, he was Riel's military leader and strategist during the Northwest Rebellion of 1885. *(Glenbow Museum and Archives, NA-1063-1)*

although the government instructed surveyors to accommodate special claims as best they could. Usually, this took place to the satisfaction of both parties, but at South Branch this did not happen, some say in error. The Métis could not gain recognition of their land claims based on Aboriginal right, as the government had already denied them that, nor could they accomplish this based on prior settlers' rights, as the law considered them to be squatters. On the other side of the picture, the Métis were negligent about filing claims for patent.[10]

On 10 December 1873, Dumont called together the St Laurent Métis, who numbered more than 300, to discuss setting up a governing body. (Later, its population would swell to 1,500.) They unanimously elected Dumont president and chose eight councillors. The new body enacted 28 basic laws modelled on those that governed the buffalo hunt, with the added right to raise taxes. The regulations covered issues such as labour and employment conditions and the settlement of disputes but did not mention theft (apart from horses) or violent crimes such as assault, manslaughter, or murder, all of which were extremely rare among the Métis at that time.

St Laurent was off to a promising start. Dumont, encouraged, visited other South Branch communities suggesting that they do the same. He seems to have hoped that they could eventually work out a self-governing plan, at least for South Branch and perhaps for the whole Northwest, until the time when the North-West Council established by Canada would actually be ready to govern. When that happened, the St Laurent council assured federal officials, it would resign in favour of Ottawa's authority. However, the other communities were not well enough organized to rise to the challenge. In the meantime, the decrease of buffalo caused the St Laurent council to tighten its regulations. It asked the North-West Council to adopt its measures for the whole region. And then, other events intervened.

That summer, 1874, a party of 'free hunters' after buffalo arrived in the area the St Laurent settlers considered to be theirs. Dumont and his men, including some Cree, confronted the intruders and told them they were trespassing and breaking local laws. When the hunters refused to accept this, the Métis issued fines and confiscated their equipment and supplies to the required amount. The hunting party proceeded to the nearest HBC post, Fort Carlton. There, they complained to the chief factor, who then reported the incident to Lieutenant-Governor Morris as an unwarranted attack, maybe even an open revolt against Canada.[11]

The HBC, for its part, had been uneasy about St Laurent from the beginning, particularly as Dumont had offered his services to Riel during a visit in 1870.[12] The press did not improve matters: 'Another Stand Against Canadian Government Authority in the Northwest', headlines screamed. Ten thousand Cree were reported to be on the warpath. Fort Carlton was said to have fallen, and six members of the North West Mounted Police killed. A detachment of the NWMP under Superintendent Leif Crozier (1847–1901) went out to thrash the matter out with the St Laurent council on 20 August 1875.

Crozier examined the council's laws and pronounced them sensible for local conditions. Neither did Edward Blake, federal Minister of Justice, 1875–7, see anything

Box 12.2   Buffalo Robes

In spite of everything, the Métis on the prairies generally were prospering because of the buffalo robe trade with the US, which on the northern Plains peaked during the 1870s.[13] Manufacture of pemmican was no longer the only, or even the main, reason for the buffalo hunt. However, the robe trade prized the winter hides of cows. This encouraged selective killing, which increased pressure on the herds. Short-term profits overwhelmed long-term considerations. Amerindian and Métis alike shared in this quick prosperity, and during the late 1860s and early 1870s the slaughter of the herds reached its greatest intensity.[14]

wrong with them. He observed that the very fact they had been necessary pointed to the need for establishing a properly constituted government on the prairies. The council agreed to disband as a formal body, and the police said they would have no objections to the buffalo hunt being regulated along the suggested lines. But it was 1877 before the North-West Council enacted hunting laws, too little and too late to save the herds (see Box 12.2).

Deprived of their council and thus of the ability to act on their own, the Métis asked the government for schools, or at least for help in getting them established. Ottawa, as usual, was slow but eventually agreed to help. The Métis also wanted two representatives on the North-West Territories Council. In response, the government appointed Pascal Breland (d. 1896), a long-time member of the Assiniboia council but a man whom the Métis did not admire.

In 1878, Manitoba elected its only Métis premier, the English-speaking John Norquay (1841–89). By that time, the flood of immigration was changing Manitoba into an Ontario community. This transition was capped by the language legislation of 1890, which transformed Manitoba from the bilingual province established in 1870 in accordance with Riel's dream into a unilingual English one. Premier Norquay, who identified with his Orkney rather than his Cree background, started the process.

Land title continued to be a problem, and there was no agreement among the Métis as to how to solve it. Some petitioned on the basis of Aboriginal right. Others wanted land grants like those awarded under the Manitoba Act and asked the government to help them in changing over to farming, as it was helping Amerindians. St Laurent wanted the surveyors to recognize its river lot system. Officials said this was not necessary, as the Métis could easily divide the square survey into the desired river lots, but the Métis were seeking government recognition of their system, not just an adaptation. To add to the confusion, survey maps were slow in appearing, so the Métis could not make legal claims. In 1884, a government inspector came out, but he arrived at no solution the Métis could accept. When they had been ignored before, during the political vacuum created by the ending of the Hudson's Bay Company's government, they had got results by taking matters into their own hands. Now, in the midst of a world economic crisis (1883), they met once more to consider their course of action.

At St Laurent, on 30 March 1884, 30 Métis met at Abraham Montour's house. They recalled that Lord Lorne (John Douglas Sutherland Campbell, Governor-General, 1878–83), during his 1881 tour of the West, had promised to bring the Métis situation to the attention of the government. But nothing had happened. The Métis cry was similar to that of the Amerindians: 'the government stole our land, and now is laughing at us.' A few weeks later, at another meeting, the group decided to invite Riel back from his Montana refuge, where he was teaching school. On 4 June 1884 Dumont and some companions rode south to get their leader.

This Is Our Life, This Is Our Land

In 1870, the HBC lands were transferred to Canada. When Amerindians responded with increasing militancy, Ottawa cut their rations, its main weapon for bringing the people into line. The year of the Cypress Hills Massacre, 1873, Big Bear clashed with Gabriel Dumont when the Métis leader tried to direct the hunt on the High Plains. Half Ojibwa, half Cree, **Big Bear** led the largest band of Cree on the Plains at that time, about 2,000 souls. As a young man, he had been noted for his ability to shoot accurately under the neck of his horse while riding at full tilt. Of impressive presence, with a full, rich voice, he did not like dealing with non-Aboriginals.

Like Tecumseh and Nescambiouit before him, he worked for pan-Indianism. He saw that unless the people united in the face of non-Native settlement, they were lost. Refusing official gifts being distributed prior to Treaty Six negotiations, he said he did not want to be baited so that the government could put a rope around his neck (Chapter 11). He was referring not to death but to loss of freedom.[15]

Big Bear did not like the terms being offered for Treaty Six. In particular, he disliked the provision that Canadian law would become the law of the land. As he saw it, the people would lose their autonomy under this treaty. Accordingly, he refused to sign in 1876 but eventually was forced to do so in 1882, at Fort Walsh, to get rations for his people. By then, it was too late for him to have any impact on the treaty's terms. Big Bear was reduced to 247 followers and was in no position to argue when offered a remote reserve at Fort Pitt, well to the north.

Big Bear's campaign to unite Amerindians and to get better treaty terms had seriously alarmed Ottawa, causing officials to increase their efforts to find chiefs, such as Mistawasis ('Big Child', d. 1903) and Ahchacoosacootacoopits ('Star Blanket', c. 1845–1917), willing to negotiate. Of those who did, only Sweetgrass and Minahikosis ('Little Pine', c. 1830–85) had reputations that came close to that of Big Bear. Little Pine, the half Blackfoot, half Cree brother-in-law of Piapot, held out for three years, but finally, his starving people persuaded him. He signed in 1879.

Another holdout was Kamiyistowesit ('Beardy', *c.* 1828–89) of the Parklands People. Like other dissenting chiefs, he maintained that since the Europeans had caused the buffalo to disappear, it was now their responsibility to provide for Amerindians. Beardy carried his objections to the point of threatening to seize the trading post at Duck Lake, in his band's hunting territory, if the government did not meet his demands for support. Authorities responded by sending an NWMP detachment to reinforce the threatened post. The NWMP fed 7,000 from its own rations, an act Ottawa considered to be encouraging the holdouts.

A Plains Cree chief who got along reasonably well with whites was **Poundmaker**, the leading Blackfoot chief.[16] He

Big Bear (Mistahimaskwa) in his prime. *Royal Ontario Museum, 913.13.60)*

inherited his name from his father, a shaman renowned for building pounds. Poundmaker could still argue for his people, however. Faced with government reluctance to go beyond the short term (in fact, it considered the Amerindian concern for their children and grandchildren to be little more than a smokescreen), he observed, 'From what I can hear and see now, I cannot understand that I shall be able to clothe my children as long as the sun shines and water runs.'

In the end, he was one of those who signed in 1876, although he continued to hunt and did not accept a reserve until 1879, about 64 kilometres west of Battleford. By then, all in the Treaty Six area except Big Bear had bowed to the inevitable, but all had not accepted reserves. In the final accounting, the signers of Treaty Six did better than those of Treaty Four, winning such concessions as the 'medicine chest' clause (although it would be 1930 before there was an on-reserve nursing station, at Fisher River, Manitoba) and also the promise of relief in the event of famine or pestilence. But the price was an enormous area of land, 315,000 square miles (815,850 square kilometres).

There were also chiefs who got along so well with whites that their people mistrusted them. One such was Mimiy ('Pigeon', Gabriel Coté, d. 1884), who headed a band of Saulteaux in the Swan River area. His relationship with the HBC was such that his people remembered him as a 'Company chief'. He was one of the signers of Treaty Four.[17]

Looming Preventable Disaster

By 1876, the only place in Canada where there were enough bison left to pursue the old way of life was the Cypress Hills. There were larger herds in Montana, but local Amerindians kept them from moving north by setting fire to the grass along the border. As a result, Canadian Plains tribes converged on the Cypress Hills, a movement that peaked in 1877–9.

Although most of the bands had selected reserves, and some were getting started in their new way of life with government assistance, there were delays in surveying sites and in providing needed supplies and equipment. It was a standoff. As long as there were buffalo around, and the Amerindians wanted to hunt them, why move faster with the new program? The warnings of the NWMP, missionaries, and settlers of a looming but preventable disaster produced no results. As early as 1877, there were complaints that needed equipment was not arriving. Those Amerindians who wanted to get started in their new way of life, and there were many, were, more often than not, frustrated by misguided bureaucratic paternalism compounded by ineptitude. As one anthropologist noted, it is easy, with hindsight, to criticize the government's handling of the situation, for which it had no precedent,[18] but the fact remains that when Amerindians objected, as in the case of Big Bear, the government blamed them for the problems.[19]

Amerindians set old hostilities aside, as Blackfoot, Plains Cree, and Sioux consulted on measures to regulate the hunt. In 1880, Big Bear and Little Pine headed south to the remaining buffalo range on the Milk and Missouri rivers. There, they met with Riel. The Métis leader persuaded the Montana Amerindians—southern Assiniboine, Blackfeet, Crow, and Gros Ventre—to let the northerners hunt on their reservations. The alliance fell apart, however, when the Canadian Amerindians gave in to the temptation to raid the horses of their hosts, who, after all, were still traditional enemies. In 1882, the US army confiscated the horses and equipment of the Canadian Amerindians and sent them back north of the border. From then on, the authorities restricted border crossings.

Meanwhile, Big Bear and other Plains Cree chiefs were discussing a plan to select reserves next to each other, which would have resulted in an Amerindian territory. The reserves they chose took in much of what is now southern Alberta and southern Saskatchewan. They almost succeeded, but Ottawa woke up to what was going on and prevented it, although it meant violating treaty provisions for freedom to select reserve locations. It also meant up-rooting already established Amerindian farmers.[20] Even though Big Bear was finally forced to take a reserve in an isolated location in 1882, he did not give up. With other chiefs, he continued to try to get reserves as close together as possible around Battleford.

Since 1880, Ottawa had enforced a policy of work for rations, except for the or-phaned, sick, or aged. Furthermore, it interpreted the famine clause of Treaty Six to mean that only a 'general' famine warranted free rations. The daily allowance for individuals was 13 ounces (383 grams) of flour, three ounces (99 grams) of bacon, and six ounces (170 grams) of beef. Later, Lawrence Vankoughnet, deputy superintendent-general of Indian Affairs, 1874–93, and such agents as Hayter Reed (1849–1936), who succeeded Vankoughnet, 1893–7, ordered this reduced. Reed did not mention in his reports that Amerindians were starving, perhaps because he saw it as a result of laziness and immorality. To the Cree, Reed was 'Iron Heart'.

Mounting food shortages led to desperate actions, and Amerindians began to kill the cattle that were supposed to get them started as farmers and ranchers.[21] Even government agents realized that stopping rations of offenders would not solve the problem, and so they used fines instead. In 1883, three Cree chiefs, Sehkosowayanew ('Ermineskin'), his brother Keskayiwew ('Bobtail'), and Samson (inheritor of the mantle of Maskepetoon), wrote to Prime Minister Macdonald, who also held the Interior portfolio and thus was Superintendent-General:

> If no attention is paid to our case now we shall conclude that the treaty made with us six years ago was a meaningless matter of form and that the white man has doomed us to annihilation little by little. But the motto of the Indian is, 'If we must die by violence, let us do it quickly.'[22]

Even Poundmaker, who had co-operated at first, became disgruntled. He consulted with Big Bear, who thought it would be a good idea to go to Ottawa to see if someone was really in charge of Indian Affairs, and if so, to deal with him directly. Despite his reputation among whites as a troublemaker, the record indicates that Big Bear opposed violence and even prevented it on occasion. He recognized that negotiation was the way to work out constructive measures. First, though, the Amerindians had to get together and agree among themselves.

In 1884, Big Bear called a thirst dance to be held on Poundmaker's reserve. More than 2,000 participated, the largest united effort managed by the Cree. Authorities were unable to stop it despite frantic efforts (they had been able to prevent others in the recent past). Big Bear's aim was to get Amerindians to select a single representative for a term of four years who would speak for all. He also wanted the Cree to join in obtaining a single large reserve on the North Saskatchewan. He argued that Ottawa had unilaterally changed Treaty Six from what it had agreed to during negotiations: 'half the sweet things taken out and lots of sour things left in'. They needed a new treaty, as well as a new concept for establishing reserves.

As Big Bear laboured to unite Amerindians, Edgar Dewdney, lieutenant-governor of the North-West Territories, 1881–8, worked to divide them, using food as an instrument to keep the people quiet. In 1884, he invited Crowfoot to visit Regina and Winnipeg, where the Blackfoot chief received a royal reception. On seeing the size of the settlements, Crowfoot became all the more convinced that violence was useless. Dewdney also provided for the arrest of any Amerindian found on a reserve not his own without official approval. He was determined that never again would Big Bear or any other chief convoke a large assembly. That this violated the law—not to mention

Crowfoot with his family, 1884. *(Glenbow Museum and Archives, NA–1480–31)*

basic human rights—was overlooked in the fear of an Amerindian war. The police view simplified the situation: 'the government would not permit armed bodies of men, whether Amerindians or Whites, to roam the country at large.'[23]

Although confrontations were increasing, up to this point, there was remarkably little violence. As some observers noted, starving Amerindians were acting with far more restraint than whites would have done under the same circumstances. Only rarely did starving Amerindians kill settlers' cattle.[24] At the time, however, whites did not appreciate this. Ottawa persisted in the view that the situation in the West was really not its responsibility. In contrast, Amerindians held the view that non-Amerindians should pay for having provoked disaster.

Confrontation

The first Métis resistance, in 1869–70, occurred with the passing of the HBC as governing power in the Northwest and the transfer of its lands to Canada. The second, in 1885—this time an uprising—occurred with the passing of the buffalo. It also coincided with the completion of the Canadian Pacific Railway, which would bring in settlers in greater numbers than ever.

In 1869–70:	In 1885:
The HBC had no effective police or military to enforce its decisions.	The NWMP was very much a presence on the northwestern Plains.
Government troops did not arrive until after the passing of the Manitoba Act, 1870.	Troops arrived at Qu'Appelle a week after Riel set up his provisional government.
Riel and the Catholic Church worked closely together.	Riel and the Catholic Church were estranged.
Métis held the balance of power in Red River and were the settlement's effective armed force; white settlers were a small minority.	White settlers heavily outnumbered the Métis.

Two years of poor crops (1883–4) meant that the winter of 1884–5 was hard. At the same time, Ottawa seemed to lose its sense of direction, and it disarmed the North-West Territories militia. In 1884, Hector-Louis Langevin, then Minister of Public Works, cancelled a scheduled visit to Prince Albert on a tour of the West without telling the people. Meanwhile, Big Bear was having his own problems, as his war chiefs gained influence at his expense. His son Ayimisis (Imases, Little Bad Man, 1851–1921) and Kapapamahchakwew (Wandering Spirit, c. 1845–85) advocated violence as the only way of regaining independence.[25] Big Bear recognized that violence was useless but was so involved trying to develop pan-Indianism that he had lost touch with his people. Conditions were so obviously unsettled that in 1884, Ottawa banned the sale or gift of 'fixed ammunition' or 'ball cartridges' to Amerindians of Manitoba and the North-West Territories.[26] That this went against the treaties was either overlooked or brushed aside.

In spite of all this uncertainty and unrest, Riel's return in 1884 did not trigger a call for violence. Riel repeatedly stressed his peaceful intentions, even as he maintained that the North-West Territories should be a self-governing province and that Amerindians should be treated better. He also said that white settlers were being charged too much for land.

The Métis wanted Riel to replace Pascal Breland on the North-West Council. The settlers, however, were not so sure. They were worried about Riel's relations with Amerindians. Although Big Bear did not join up with him, he told Riel he was confident the Métis leader would not forget Amerindians in his fight for Métis rights. Vankoughnet, deeply suspicious of Big Bear, cut his band's rations. The people were becoming hungrier and hungrier. Even co-operative chiefs such as Mistawasis and Ahchacoosacootacoopits were complaining,[27] and rations were not the only issue.

Although there were exceptions, in general the agents and farm instructors Ottawa sent out had little or no knowledge of Amerindians and little, if any, sympathy for them. They usually tried to enforce regulations 'by the book', without consideration for particular situations.[28] Ottawa wanted to transform Amerindians into small-scale farmers, but even that goal was so mired in regulations that there was little prospect of success.

As Riel pointed out in his petition to Ottawa on 16 December 1884, the people of the West had every right to be treated with the full dignity of British subjects, which was not happening. In his list of complaints, he included those of Métis, Amerindians, and whites. This time, Ottawa acknowledged receipt of the petition. The Métis were so jubilant that on New Year's Day 1885, they honoured Riel at a banquet and presented him with a house, some money, and an illuminated address thanking him for his efforts on their behalf. Their optimism was premature.

As it turned out, the most that Ottawa was prepared to do was to establish a commission to list Métis living in the Northwest in 1870 and their claims. At first, it was not empowered to do anything about them. Dewdney realized this was too little too late. He modified the message before relaying it to the Métis, but the ploy did not work. On 8 February, Riel replied, 'in 40 days they will have my answer.' The religious implications of that response were obvious, as the seasonal Lenten fast, which occurred at this time of year, lasted 40 days. Riel's relations with Father Alexis André were already strained, and he was beginning to see himself as a prophet. Aware of the anomaly of his position as an American citizen, he offered to return to the US and leave the Métis to work out their own problems. They refused to let him go and, at a secret meeting, agreed to take up arms if necessary 'to save our country'.

On 8 March, Riel announced his intention to set up a provisional government and presented a 10-point Bill of Rights.[29] Two days later, the Métis began a novena.[30] By this time, Riel had broken with Father André. Both the novena and Riel's '40 days' ended on 18 March. The Métis seized the Indian agent and other officials, and occupied the church of St Antoine de Padoue at Batoche. They cut the telegraph lines from Regina to Prince Albert but left those to Battleford intact. (Battleford had been the capital of the North-West Territories from 1877 to 1883, when Regina had taken over.)

The next day was St Joseph's Day, St Joseph being the patron saint of the Métis. Riel proclaimed his provisional government, and the people armed themselves. Kapeyakwaskonam ('One Arrow', c. 1815–86), chief of the Willow Crees whose reserve was the closest to South Branch, butchered all the cattle on his reserve and joined the Métis. (Later, he claimed that he had been threatened by Dumont and forced into his action.) Riel, emulating events of 1869–70, sent a summons to Fort Carlton on 21 March, calling on it to surrender.

Five days later, on 26 March, Crozier attempted a sortie from the fort with 100 Mounties and volunteers to seize a strategic supply point. The Métis met him at **Duck Lake**, a place they had chosen. Within 15 minutes, 12 of Crozier's men were dead and 11 wounded. Five Métis and one Amerindian were killed. Riel, armed with a crucifix, stopped the pursuit of the routed police, preventing an even worse bloodbath. As the

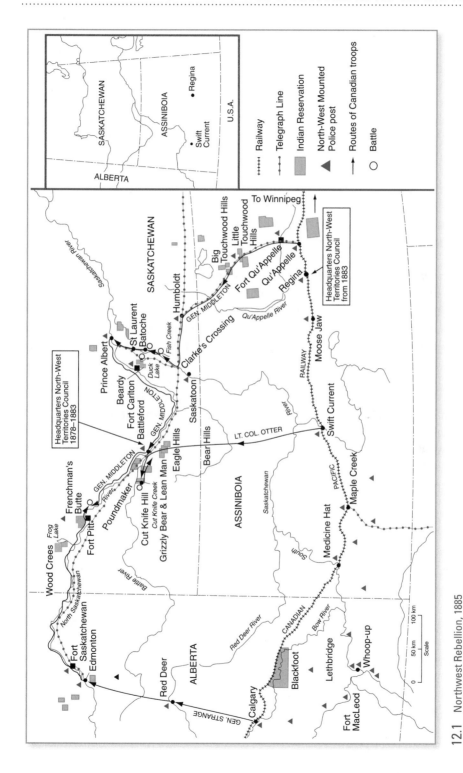

12.1 Northwest Rebellion, 1885

Source: D.G.G. Kerr, *Historical Atlas of Canada*, 3rd rev. ed. (Toronto: Nelson, 1975).

defeated column returned to the fort, reinforcements of 100 men arrived. With this protection, the fort was evacuated to Prince Albert. Thanks to Riel's restraint, there was no further action at this point.

Hard on the heels of these events, Poundmaker's and Little Pine's people left their reserves and headed for Battleford, headquarters for distributing supplies. Settlers took fright and fled into the fort. The Cree looted the abandoned houses and stores during the last two days of March. Little Pine, who had been in poor health for several years, died just afterward.[31] In a separate incident just to the south, Stoneys (Assiniboine) shot and killed a farm instructor and a settler.[32]

Big Bear's war chiefs took matters into their own hands and looted HBC stores at Frog Lake on 2 April. Nine people died in the incident, including the agent, two priests, and settlers. Big Bear stopped the bloodshed in time to save the HBC representative and the women and children.[33] Most of the settlers in the area were able to take refuge in Fort Pitt, an NWMP garrison, which then surrendered to Big Bear. The chief allowed the soldiers to leave, then took over the fort on 15 April.

The call to arms that these events raised brought a quick response across Canada. Since the railway was not completed, transporting troops and supplies meant loading and unloading 16 times before reaching Regina. Even so, by 6 April, **Frederick Dobson Middleton** (1825–98), commander of the Canadian militia, and his troops were marching north to Batoche from Qu'Appelle. From Swift Current, Colonel William Dillon Otter (1843–1929) headed for Battleford on 13 April, and from Calgary, Major-General Thomas Bland Strange (1831–1925) set off for Edmonton, where he arrived on 1 May. The sternwheeler *Northcote*, with armed men aboard, proceeded up the Saskatchewan River to act as support for the ground troops, but it ran into a ferry cable the Métis had strung across the river and lost its stacks and masts. Its crew did not like being targets for Métis sharpshooters, so its brief career as a warship was ended.

On 24 April, Middleton ran into Dumont's ambush at **Fish Creek**, South Branch's southern boundary, but the Métis fired prematurely and Middleton was saved. To the west, on 2 May, Otter attacked Poundmaker's sleeping camp at Cutknife Hill. Poundmaker repelled the attack but refused to let his warriors go off in pursuit, saving Otter and his men from rout. The following week, 9–12 May, Middleton and 850 men confronted entrenched Métis, about 350 strong, at Batoche. After three days, the Métis ran out of ammunition. It was the only clear defeat of the Métis during the uprising, but it was decisive. When the Canadian forces burned and looted after the battle, even Riel's opponent Father André made an indignant protest.[34]

Riel surrendered on 15 May, Poundmaker on 26 May. On 2 July, Big Bear and his youngest son, Horse Child, walked into Fort Carlton to surrender to a startled sentry. The rebellion's toll: 53 non-Natives killed and 118 wounded, and about 35 Amerindians and Métis killed. Less than 5 per cent of the Amerindian population of the Northwest had been involved.[35]

Immediate Consequences

During the revolt, the residents of Wolseley, Manitoba, passed a motion to send to Ottawa:

> It is now time for the Government to take decisive action, and that their first shall be that orders be issued to hang Riel to the first tree when he is caught; but, if there must be delay, that it shall only be long enough to capture Dewdney and hang the two together.[36]

The government, however, turned its anger not against its own representatives but against those who had protested the treatment they had received. The government charged or considered charging more than 200 individuals, most for treason-felony against an empire that had conscripted Amerindians and Métis into its orbit without consulting them and, in the case of Amerindians, without granting them citizenship. In the end, 84 trials were held, 71 of which were for treason-felony, 12 for murder, and one (Riel's) for high treason. Of the 129 individuals who were jailed, there were:

- 46 Métis, of whom 19 were convicted, one hanged, and seven conditionally discharged; the rest were either unconditionally discharged or not brought to trial;
- 81 Amerindians, of whom 44 were convicted and eight hanged for murder; and
- two whites, both charged with treason-felony,[37] who were acquitted, one on the grounds of insanity.[38]

Of the 19 Métis convicted, Riel was charged with treason; he was hanged on 16 November 1885.[39] Most of the other Métis prisoners were convicted on the lesser charge of treason-felony. Eleven were sentenced to seven years, three to three years, and four to one year each. Most of the Amerindians (all Cree except for two Stoney) were charged with treason-felony, but some were tried for murder as well as other of-fences. Eleven were sentenced to hang. Three later had their sentences commuted to life imprisonment. The other eight were hanged together at Battleford on 17 November, one of the two largest mass hangings in Canada's history.[40] Prison sentences ranged up to 20 years for manslaughter and 14 for arson.

Prison terms were virtual death sentences. Big Bear, Poundmaker, and One Arrow all had to be released before their three-year terms were up and died within the year. Big Bear pleaded for amnesty for his band. Many were hiding in the woods, and winter was setting in. (Some of Big Bear's followers went to Onion Lake, where they were fed at government expense until relocated on a new reserve in 1887.) Big Bear served a year and a half of his sentence before his health broke. He died within months of his release, abandoned even by most of his own family, who had fled south. Eventually, all of the Amerindians convicted of treason-felony were pardoned before their sentences were up. Poundmaker had protested in court:

> The bad things they have said against me here are not true. I have worked only at trying to keep the peace. This spring, when my Indians, the halfbreeds and the white men fought, I prevented further killing. As soon as I heard what had happened at Batoche I led my people and went to the white man and gave myself up. If I had not done so, there would have been plenty of bloodshed. For this reason I am here . . . I will not excuse myself for saving the lives of so many people even if I must suffer for it now.[41]

He was at least spared one indignity as a prisoner. Through the intercession of his adoptive father, Crowfoot, his hair was not cut.

As already noted, One Arrow's band had joined Riel the day hostilities broke out. However, as One Arrow was at least 70 years old at the time, it is unlikely that he took part in the fighting. As with the other two chiefs, his trial was a near travesty: One Arrow spoke no English, the language of most of the proceedings, and very little was interpreted for him. He was sentenced to three years. Released after seven months, he was not even able to walk and soon died.[42]

Big Bear and Poundmaker in detention. Big Bear's hair has been cut; at the request of his adoptive father, Crowfoot, Poundmaker was spared this indignity. *(Glenbow Museum and Archives, NA–1315–18)*

After the Conflict

The South Branch Métis, particularly those of St Laurent, had fought to be recognized as a colony, but with special status that would acknowledge their Aboriginal rights and distinctive lifestyle. Although they shared grievances with both Amerindians and whites, the Métis considered themselves to be separate. Each group was fighting for itself, although they had a common enemy: a distant and uncomprehending bureaucracy. One of the ironies of the conflict was that it undid the decade during which Big Bear and other chiefs had worked for the autonomy and self-government of their people.

As for Ottawa, its hostility towards those they saw as inferior—because they were 'others', strangers—has been a historical constant. In 1885, Amerindians might have been appreciated on their own merits in philosophical or artistic circles, but in the political arena they were expected to conform to the dominant power. For the Métis, such attitudes reduced and even ignored the role in which they could have excelled, as mediators between Amerindians and whites. Dufferin was one of the few who appreciated this. He attributed Canada's comparative rarity of frontier wars to the influence of the Métis.[43]

Controversy over the personality of Riel and, above all, over the roles of the government and the Métis in the confrontation is still very much alive. Riel's declaration of rights, labelled revolutionary at the time, seems mild today: he was asking for more liberal treatment for Amerindians and non-Native settlers as well as for the Métis. More heated is the argument over whether the government provoked the uprising to solve its problems in constructing the transcontinental railway. Political scientist Thomas Flanagan asserted that 'Métis grievances were at least partly of their own making' and that 'the government was on the verge of resolving them when the Rebellion broke out.'[44] On the other hand, historian Doug Sprague stated that the uprising 'was not the result of some tragic misunderstanding, but of the government's manipulation of the Manitoba Métis since 1869' for political reasons.[45] The jury is still out. What there is no doubt about is that the defeat at Batoche ended for half a century the Métis struggle for recognition as a people.[46] And it would be a century before that struggle regained a momentum close to that of the days of Riel.

In practical terms, land transfers were made more flexible, and registration of deeds simplified. The North-West Territories gained representation in the House of Commons, with Assiniboia getting two members and the regions that would become Saskatchewan and Alberta one each. In 1887, the Territories got two members in the Senate. This was no mere recognition of the rights of the people living there to representation. The government of Canada had, in fact, set as its goal the destruction of tribal forms of government and the division of Amerindian communities. And the machinery needed to accomplish this was already in place.

Important Names and Terms

Batoche	Métis
Big Bear	Middleton, Frederick Dobson
Duck Lake	Poundmaker
Dumont, Gabriel	St Laurent
Fish Creek	

Study Questions

1) What were the immediate effects of the disappearance of the bison?
2) What did the transfer of land from the HBC to Canada mean for the people of the Northwest?
3) What were Louis Riel's hopes for the region?
4) What were the consequences of the Battle of Batoche?

Recommended Readings

Beal, Bob, and Rod Macleod. *Prairie Fire: The 1885 North-West Rebellion*. Edmonton: Hurtig, 1984.

Carter, Sarah A. *Lost Harvests: Prairie Indian Reserve Farmers and Government Policy*. Montreal and Kingston: McGill-Queen's University Press, 1990.

Dempsey, Hugh A. *Big Bear: The End of Freedom*. Vancouver: Douglas & McIntyre, 1984.

Flanagan, Thomas. *Riel and the Rebellion*. Saskatoon: Western Producer Prairie Books, 1983.

Payment, Diane. *Batoche (1870–1970)*. St Boniface, Man.: Editions du Blé, 1983.

Siggins, Maggie. *Riel: A Life of Revolution*. Toronto: HarperCollins, 1994.

Sluman, Norma. *Poundmaker*. Toronto: Ryerson Press, 1967.

Woodcock, George. *Gabriel Dumont*. Edmonton: Hurtig, 1975.

13 | Repression and Resistance

More Consequences for the Cree. . .

Big Bear and Poundmaker were in prison, and Little Pine was dead. Deprived of their leadership, the Cree now found even their remaining chiefs under attack. Ottawa wanted all those who had not given unwavering support to the government to be deposed. Others could stay in office until their deaths, but they would not be replaced. The goal was the destruction of tribal forms of government and the splitting of Amerindian communities. The government increased the numbers of Indian agents and strengthened the NWMP. It impounded Cree horses, guns, and carts, and discontinued the annuities for five years of those who were implicated in the uprising.[1] It also introduced a **pass system** to keep western Amerindians on their reserves. The argument was that the rebels had violated their treaty rights and thus had lost them.[2]

Ten years later, the NWMP was reporting that Amerindians 'found wandering aimlessly about the prairie have been induced to return to their respective reserves.'[3] What amounted to hysteria among cattlemen and settlers contributed to the repression. In 1906, the ban on certain sun dance practices, previously noted, was extended to include all types of Amerindian dancing. The dances continued anyway, but in hiding. Restrictions on the movements and customs of Natives remained until well into the twentieth century, and not just on the prairies. In Dawson, Yukon, Amerindians were also subjected to a curfew. By 1923, those who wished to move to a city needed a permit. Although the measures were illegal, the government justified them as necessary to protect the Amerindians from evil non-Aboriginal influences.[4]

For the decade following 1885, Amerindians and Métis accepted these growing repressions without violence. When it did erupt, it was on the part of individuals. Between 1895 and 1897, for example, Charcoal, a Blood (Si'k-okskitsis, literally 'Black Wood Ashes', 1856–97), and Almighty Voice, a Cree (Kah-kee-say-mane-too-wayo, 'Voice of the Great Spirit', grandson of One Arrow, 1874–97), between them killed five policemen. The death toll was the result of the police trying to track them down, in separate pursuits.[5]

Time Line

1879, 1884, 1894	Superintendent-General of Indian Affairs empowered to lease undeveloped reserve lands without surrender or band consent.	1908	BC refuses to lay out any more reserves.
		1911	Amendment to Indian Act allows appropriation of reserve lands for public purposes; almost half of Blackfoot Reserve is sold.
1880s–90s	Rapid expansion of church-run residential schools for Native children.		
1885	Many Métis change their names and move to the United States in the aftermath of the Northwest Rebellion.	1916	Royal Commission in BC recommends 'cutting off' parts of reserves and replacing them with lands of lesser value: some reserves thus eliminated, and 36,000 acres of reserve lands are lost. Allied Tribes of British Columbia is formed to fight government action, but united group has little success.
1890	Manitoba and North-West Territories game laws declared applicable to Amerindians.		
1896	The discovery of gold in the Yukon starts a rush that disrupts the way of life of northern residents.		
1901	File Hills Colony, a 'model village', established on Peepeekisis Reserve in Qu'Appelle agency.	1938	BC fulfills obligation taken on when it joined Canada by conveying reserve lands to federal authority.
1906	Ban on sun dances is extended to all Amerindian dances.	1958	James Gladstone first Amerindian appointed to Canadian Senate.

In 1896, a group of Tsuu T'ina defied police attempts to get them to leave Calgary, and the police were becoming steadily more uncomfortable with the task of restricting Amerindian movements. As early as 1893, a police commissioner issued a circular warning about sending Amerindians back to their reserves without legal justification. However, some Indian agents continued to enforce the pass system—described as selectively applied tyranny—until the mid-1940s.[6]

. . . and for the Métis

After the 1885 Rebellion, many Métis, fearing identification as such, changed their names. Others fled to the US, particularly Montana, where they became known as 'Canadian Cree'. Some joined the Cree under Big Bear's son Ayimisis, who had also fled south, and were admitted to reserves. Still others fled north, particularly to the Mackenzie River area.

For those who remained in Canada, land title continued to be a tortured question. The government dealt with Métis land claims—without consultation—by Orders-in-Council. Where Amerindians gained special status through the treaties that extinguished their Aboriginal rights, the Métis did not see long-term benefits with the settlement of their claims. Of the 566,560 hectares set aside in Manitoba for the Métis, only 242,811 had been distributed to them by 1882.[7]

The Manitoba Act of 1870 had acknowledged Métis entitlement to land but provided for the extinguishment of that title through grants of reserved land. In 1874, Ottawa introduced **scrip**, which provided for either a specified amount of land or its equivalent in cash (land scrip or money scrip). The great majority of the Métis agreed to scrip, as many lived in regions that were marginal for agriculture.[8] For them, it seemed better to sell their scrip, often for very little. There are records of scrip sold to speculators for as little as half its face value. Fortunes were made by land speculators at the expense of the Métis, called 'half-breed scrip millionaires' at the time.[9] In some cases, accepting scrip left Métis poorer than before, after a brief orgy of spending. Official attempts to make scrip non-transferable caused such an uproar (mainly on the part of land speculators, according to some) that the government backed down.[10]

The Métis also faced a dilemma. If they took treaty—and those who lived near Amerindian communities sometimes had the option of being included in a treaty—they became legally Amerindian, and many felt that they were a separate people.[11] If they took scrip, they moved into the non-Amerindian camp. Culturally, the line between the two classifications was far from clear-cut, but the legal distinction was enormous. For one obvious point, responsibility for status Indians was (and is) solely that of the federal authority. The Métis, on the other hand, even recognized as an Aboriginal people today in the Constitution Act, 1982, are classed as ordinary citizens and so come under provincial jurisdiction in matters of property and civil rights. Non-status Indians are in the same legal category as the Métis.

The troubles of 1885 galvanized Ottawa into action on Métis land claims. Four days after the encounter at Duck Lake, on 30 March, the government empowered the first of a series of commissions to extinguish Métis land claims. A few weeks later, Métis operating river lots of 40 acres (16 hectares) were allowed to buy that land at a dollar an acre, then select 160 acres (65 hectares) for a homestead. In 1885, the government considered 1,815 claims and allowed 1,678 of them, valued at $279,000 in money scrip and 55,260 acres (22,263 hectares) in land scrip. By 1889, Métis living outside of areas ceded by treaty could apply for scrip.

Treaty Nine (1905–6) did not include Métis, but Treaties Ten (1906) and Eleven (1921) did. In the case of Treaty Eleven, the Métis of the Mackenzie River District each received $240 in cash because of the lack of suitable farmland.[12] The government instructed the land claims commissions to encourage Métis who had taken treaty and who were living on reserves to withdraw and take scrip. Many did, at least partly because of difficult conditions on reserves, where people were living on meagre government handouts. Those who left, however, faced a backlash, as settlers became alarmed at the influx of Métis into their communities. That made the government more cautious about encouraging Métis who were 'living like Indians' to withdraw from treaty.

The Klondike gold strike of 1896 catapulted northern Amerindians and Métis to centre stage. The confrontations of the Fraser gold rush repeated themselves, as fortune hunters flooded into the Yukon, intent on their personal quests and without regard for the rights of the local people. As the government hurriedly prepared to negotiate Treaty Eight, a question arose: should the Métis be included with Amerindians? Most Métis were against the suggestion, so the government established two commissions, one to negotiate treaty with the Amerindians, the other to work out scrip for the Métis.[13] Still intent on encouraging as many as possible to enter treaty—some of those who identified as Amerindian had more non-Amerindian ancestors than some who identified as Métis—the government first negotiated the treaty. It took two years to hammer out terms with Beaver, Cree, Chipewyan, Sekani, and others.[14] For the Métis, the offer was for $240 in cash or 240 acres (97 hectares) of land.

When it came to issuing scrip, officials once again tried not to make it payable to the bearer, but speculators who had come expecting to make a killing refused to accept such scrip. The Métis then also refused to accept it and threatened to influence Amerindians against taking treaty. Officials knuckled under and offered scrip payable on demand. Similarly, when officials tried to postdate scrip issued to children until their age of maturity, parents insisted that it be payable immediately. The first $240 scrip was sold for $75, and soon the price dropped even lower.

During the summer of 1899, the commission issued 1,195 money scrips worth $286,000 and 48 land scrips for 11,500 acres (6,070 hectares), about half of them at Lesser Slave Lake and others at Fort Vermilion, Fort Chipewyan, and Peace River Crossing.[15] Only a fraction of the benefits went to the Métis. In 1900, two new commissions dealt with the Métis of Saskatchewan and those parts of Manitoba that had not been included in its original boundaries.

In its final report on this project in 1929, the year before Crown lands reverted to the provinces, Ottawa issued a statement that 24,000 claims had been recognized in the Northwest Territories, involving 2.6 million acres (1,052,183 hectares) in land scrip and 2.8 million acres (1,133,120 hectares) in money scrip. Later, the situation reversed itself, and during the 1920s and 1930s there were so many applications for reclassification into treaty status that in 1942 the department investigated its band lists and discharged 663 individuals. Of these, 129 were later reinstated.[16]

After the 1885 confrontations, the Department of Indian Affairs assumed more and more control over the lives of Amerindians. Soon, they would not have a free hand even in such personal matters as writing a will or, in the West, selling their own grain or root crops.[17] At the same time, agents' power grew and became more arbitrary. Eventually, they directed farming operations, administered relief in times of need, inspected schools and health conditions on reserves, enforced department rules and provisions, and presided over band council meetings. In effect, they directed the political life of the band. Agents did not vote at those meetings, but they could, and did, influence proceedings.

The main problems facing Aboriginal people were a continuation of old ones: liquor, trespass, poaching, and unauthorized use of reserve resources such as timber. In 1890, furthermore, Manitoba and the North-West Territories declared their game laws applicable to Amerindians. By doing this, they were ignoring the treaties that guaranteed hunting and fishing rights on Crown lands, which led to a series of court cases. While Aboriginal people fought the erosion of their land and sovereignty, however, the government policy continued steadfast in its push towards assimilation, which found its focus in the West, as it had further east, in education.

Assimilation through Education

Amerindians had asked for schools—meaning day schools on their reserves—during treaty negotiations. Many saw them as a means of preparing their children for the new way of life that lay ahead. The final draft of Treaty One had contained a promise that the government would 'maintain a school on each reserve hereby made, whenever the Indians of the reserve should desire it.'[18] Treaty Six negotiators Mistawasis and Ahchacoosacootacoopits tied the need for education to the disappearance of the buffalo. In 1881, Adelard Standing Buffalo (Tatanka-Najin, ?–1922) of Qu'Appelle reminded a visiting dignitary that his band was waiting for the day school they had been promised.[19] What they foresaw was a partnership with the newcomers as they worked out their own adaptations.[20] Officials and their supporters, however, saw another purpose for schools: assimilation. When the government in 1879 commissioned Nicholas Flood Davin, a lawyer and journalist who would later become the first MP for Assiniboia West, to recommend a course of action for western Amerindian education, administrators advised him not to use the schools in the East as a yardstick.[21]

Eastern Schools—'Little or No Good'

The government had already started schooling in the Canadas—day and boarding schools—within a couple of decades of the War of 1812. As with their western counterparts later on, the Amerindian people also took initiative towards education. Chief Shawahnahness (fl. 1833) of the St Clair River Ojibwa wanted his children to learn to read and write so that White traders would not be able to cheat them. Chief Shingwaukonse (Little Pine) was so convinced of the importance of a school, or 'teaching wigwam' as he called it, at Garden River that he postponed harvesting to go fundraising in southern Ontario. Prominent converts like George Copway (Kahgegagahbowh, 1818–69) and the Reverends John Sunday (Shahwundais, 1795–1875), Henry Bird Steinhauer (Sowengisik, 1818–69), and Peter Jones also were active in promoting education within their communities.[22]

But when Jones toured England in the 1830s and 1840s to raise money, he had in mind schools run by Aboriginal people and producing 'men and women able to compete with the White people, able to defend their rights in English, under English law'.[23] In 1846, Ojibwa Chief John Aisance from Beausoleil Island, who had fought with the British during the War of 1812, asked Captain Thomas G. Anderson, a former fur trader and veteran of the same war, for a local school during treaty negotiations, but noted that his band had moved 'four times, and I am too old to remove again.'[24] At this meeting, Anderson expressed the expectation that Amerindians would be running their schools within 25 years, and the chiefs pledged a fourth of their annuities to cover the cost of education during that time period. Within a decade, many would believe that the Amerindians were not getting their money's worth. In setting up schools, the government turned to those who had experience and independent sources of income, and could muster people willing to work in remote areas for low pay: the churches.

Kahkewaquonaby (the Rev. Peter Jones) travelled to Britain in 1845 to raise funds for Ojibwa schools. He had hoped for schools run by Amerindian people that would help them defend their rights. That's not what he got. This photograph, possibly the earliest studio camera study of a Canadian Aboriginal, was taken in Edinburgh. *(Hill & Adamson. Rev. Peter Jones (b). PGP HA 420. Courtesy of the National Galleries of Scotland)*

Like the government, mission-minded churches had not been idle in the eighteenth century and even earlier. New France, after all, had made abortive attempts at boarding schools as part of its assimilation policy. In 1787, the **New England Company**, a non-sectarian Protestant organization, founded several schools, including an 'Indian college' at Sussex Vale, New Brunswick. Its original aim was to teach useful trades to Amerindian children through apprenticeship, but instead, the children ended up as a cheap source of labour for local farms and businesses. By 1826, the Rev. John West (d. 1845), who worked for both the Anglican Christian Missionary Society and Hudson's Bay Company, was able to say, 'little or no good has accrued to the Natives from the Establishment at Sussex Vale.'[25]

Undaunted, the New England Company blamed the Amerindians, claiming that a more 'advanced' group would do better. To prove its point, it moved its operation to the Six Nations reserve at Grand River and several other nearby communities, such as the Bay of Quinte (Grape Island, later Alderville) and Garden River, where the Company financed existing Anglican and Methodist stations (see Chapter 9).[26]

A network of schools was already in place, then, when colonial governments were ready to address the education issue.[27] The advantages of a partnership with the missionaries, who could raise funds independently and provided the labour, were obvious. The administration favoured **residential schools** over **day schools**, as it believed they speeded the process of assimilation.[28] There were two types of residential schools. Boarding schools were usually located on reserves and catered to students between the ages of eight and 14 years. Industrial schools, off reserves, had more elaborate programs and took in students until the age of 18. Curricula combined basic subjects with a half-day of 'practical' training. For boys, this involved agriculture, crafts, and some trades, and for girls, the domestic arts. Both aimed at preparing students for life in the lower fringes of the dominant society.

A school for Amerindian children had existed for some time near Brantford, not far from the Grand River Reserve, amid opposition mainly from among the 20 per cent of reserve residents who followed the **Longhouse religion** of Seneca chief Ganiodaio (Shanyadariyoh, 'Handsome Lake', d. 1815), which combined elements of the Christian religion and the traditional Iroquois belief system.[29] By 1829, it had become a 'mechanic's institution', known as the Mohawk Institute. More successful in attracting children than many of the other schools, by 1867 the Mohawk Institute had 90 students. In 1869, it would hire its first Aboriginal teacher, Isaac Barefoot, and send five of its students to Helmuth College in Brantford for further education.[30] But this success would not last.

From the beginning, many reserve parents refused to send their children away to school, and most of the students who enrolled were either orphans or from destitute families, whose needs were great. To counter parental resistance, the New England Company put three Amerindian people on the school's board of directors, but conditions did not improve. As time went on, funding dropped, and in 1898 the New England Company withdrew all support. As conditions deteriorated, parental resistance increased, prompting Hayter Reed, Superintendent-General of Indian Affairs, to blame the problems on the fact that the children were spending too much time on academic work and were being allowed to go home for vacations. A later school administrator overworked the children in an attempt to save money. **Frederick Ogilvie Loft**, founder of the League of Indians of Canada, said of his time at the Institute, 'I recall the times when working in the fields, I was actually too hungry to be able to walk, let alone work.'[31]

Rebellion against the schools took many forms. On 19 April 1903, Institute residents set fire to the main building. Later, they burned barns and the playhouse. The government rebuilt the school, and Amerindians responded by creating the Indians' Rights Association, which succeeded in getting public curriculum taught in reserve day schools.[32] In 1913, a father sued the Mohawk Institute over the treatment his daughter had received at the hands of the principal. He won only a partial victory in court, but the principal was later fired. Other New England Company schools fared even worse.[33]

Any improvements to physical and sanitary conditions at the schools, however, would go only partway towards helping them gain acceptance in Aboriginal communities. Separation from family was a major issue; 'outing'—the practice of hiring students out as servants or manual labourers, with the schools collecting pay—was another; curriculum, yet another. Although students in industrial schools were supposed to spend a half-day at schooling and a half-day learning a useful trade, lack of funding meant that residents spent most of their time at manual labour. As well, to keep numbers—and grants—up, schools often admitted children who were too young to learn a trade.[34]

All of this, Davin dutifully ignored, and he consulted with no Aboriginal people before completing his report. The administration had seen potential for industrial schools in Ontario because, in their view, the Aboriginal population was 'advanced' enough to benefit from them. Now, in 1879, Davin recommended the same structure as beneficial to the 'warlike' Indians in the West.[35]

Industrial Schools in Western Canada

Despite the lack of success already seen in the East, Ottawa quickly decided it would be more economical to develop the already existing schools run by the churches than it would be to create its own system, an arrangement that would last until 1969. Although education was a provincial responsibility under the BNA Act, Amerindians came under federal authority. The treaties, furthermore, committed the federal government to providing and maintaining schools and teachers on reserves. In practice, this meant that most Amerindian children were to be educated in schools run by the department.

An 1883 Order-in-Council marked the beginning of the first three industrial schools to open on the prairies: at Battleford and Qu'Appelle in the North-West, and at High River in the southern portion of what would become Alberta. The money came from the existing Indian budget, which reduced the amount available for relief—at a time when hunger was widespread on the prairies. Before the turn of the century, seven more schools would open, repeating the same story that had been told in the East.

Almost from the start, the school at Battleford was plagued by lack of funding, truancy, and low staff morale. As local parents refused to send their children, the Department of Indian Affairs recommended that the school start with 'orphans and children who have no natural protectors'.[36] When the Northwest Rebellion broke out, the students were scattered. By the late 1880s, opposition to the school had grown to the point where its viability was being questioned. Dunbow School at High River, which Oblate Father Albert Lacombe (1827–1916) left in 1885 after a brief and unsuccessful tenure, did not fare much better.[37]

Qu'Appelle was the most successful of the initial three, in part because of its distance from the Rebellion and in part because of the tireless efforts of its first principal, Father Joseph Hugonnard (1848–1917), to wrest funding from the government.[38] Even so, throughout the lifespan of the industrial schools, Amerindian parents criticized them and resisted sending their children. At a meeting on the Muskowpetung reserve in northern Saskatchewan early in the twentieth century, parents protested the secrecy surrounding sickness at the Regina school, its use of pupils as labourers, and the breakup of home circles.[39] The children resisted by running away, stealing—often food—and, finally, committing arson. Parents refused to send their children to the point where the government started using the pass system to prevent parents from using their time off the reserves to interfere with their children's schooling. One mother attacked Father Hugonnard with a knife to give her children time to escape into the woods.[40]

In 1910, parents from the Beardy and Okemasis reserves filed a complaint against St Michael's Industrial School at Duck Lake. In particular, they protested the school's practice of 'outing' students to the community. The parents argued that the school should send graduates back to their families. The Indian agent agreed, calling the practice 'slavery'. That same year, he reported that half the children

Oblate Father Albert Lacombe (standing, left) opened an industrial school near Calgary in 1884, but he failed to convince most Blackfoot parents to send their children, in part because he hired the controversial Jean L'Heureux (standing, right) as a recruiter. Also active in western treaty negotiations, Lacombe took a group of western chiefs to Ottawa hoping to impress them. In front, left to right: North Axe, Peigan chief, and One Spot, a Blood subchief. Middle row: Three Bulls, half-brother of Crowfoot; Crowfoot, Blackfoot chief; and Red Cloud, Blood chief. *(Library and Archives Canada, PA 45666)*

who attended St Michael's died, usually from tuberculosis, before reaching the age of 18.[41] But the Oblates who ran the school fought the parents' petition for a day school, and St Michael's remained open.

Further west, Amerindians had been in the majority in British Columbia through much of the nineteenth century, and Governor James Douglas had more or less left them alone. By the 1870s, however, the white population was growing, and the government started encouraging missionaries to found schools. Eventually, the size of the Aboriginal population, combined with furious competition among the Christian denominations, would see the creation of more industrial schools in BC than anywhere else in Canada, most run by the Roman Catholic Oblates, who already had a strong presence in the West.

Like industrial schools elsewhere, BC institutions were plagued by overcrowding and underfunding, which often led them to abandon their stated purpose: to teach young Amerindians a trade. Methodist-run Coqualeetza (St Paul) School near Chilliwack took children out of classes to do drudge work when it was short-staffed. Most of the graduates of the Anglican-run school at Lytton ended up as unskilled farm labourers.[42]

Even so, there were success stories, often the work of exceptional individuals. James Gladstone of the Blood (Akaynamuka, 'Many Guns', 1887–1971, Canada's first Amerindian senator, named in 1958) remarked:

> Over the years I have been grateful for the education I received, and I have always been impressed about St Paul's mission and Calgary Industrial School. In those days, we had dedicated teachers . . . even today you can tell the Indians who went to those schools before 1905. They have been the backbone of our reserves.[43]

Mike Mountain Horse, who attended Calgary Industrial School at the same time as Gladstone and later became prominent in the Indian League of Canada, agreed. However, most disagreed with this assessment. According to author Eleanor Brass (1905–92), who grew up in the **File Hills Colony** (see Box 13.1), a boy who was in an industrial school for 10 years spent only four in the classroom,[44] and parents who kept their children away from these schools understood that the schools were teaching more than a trade.

Box 13.1   The File Hills Colony

The idea of model villages did not die in the nineteenth century. The File Hills Colony was established in 1901 on the Peepeekisis Reserve (named after the chief, 'Little Hawk') at Indian Head in what would soon become the province of Saskatchewan. It was the special project of W.M. Graham, the resident agent. His idea was to extend the training young Amerindians received at government schools,[45] ensuring that they would not 'regress' to their Amerindian ways by returning to their own families and communities. He assigned individual lots, with a portion of the colony being left for hunting and community pasture. Some colonists were able to handle as many as six or seven lots. Others found that the farming life was not for them, and picked up and left.

Graham controlled those who stayed to the point of even having their marriage partners chosen for them. He strictly limited visits between households and banned such gatherings as powwows or dancing of any kind. (This did not mean that there were no such occasions, only that they were held secretly.) In the 1930s, however, it began to lose its younger population. Although many admired the project, the government never repeated the experiment. For one thing, it was very costly. File Hills boarding school is one of those named in connection with charges of student abuse, in this case leading to death.[46]

In 1888, the Indian agent at Alert Bay, BC, noted that parents disliked the local school because it meant 'the downfall of all their most cherished customs', and the principal at Alert Bay cited the elders as the reason for low school attendance. As one historian has noted, 'Respect for other cultures was not included in the training of the nineteenth-century missionary.'[47] The practice of changing students' names served to strip them of their identity, and some schools referred to students by number. A boy who attended Qu'Appelle Industrial School later recalled having his braids cut off without explanation, leaving him wondering if his mother had died because, in the Assiniboine tradition, haircutting is associated with mourning.[48]

The decades of the 1880s and 1890s witnessed the rapid expansion of industrial schools. Increasing costs, however, soon gave rise to second thoughts. Industrial schools cost money that the government was unwilling to pay. Clifford Sifton, who became Minister of the Interior and Superintendent-General in 1896, did not see that Amerindians had 'the physical, mental or moral get-up' to compete with non-Indians on equal terms.[49] Accordingly, he considered industrial schooling for Amerindians a waste of time and effort. He did not mention that it was often hard for Amerindians to find jobs, as many whites refused to work beside them.

By the turn of the twentieth century, enthusiasm for industrial schools had waned. Rising costs and poor administration, including charges of abuse to students, led to a gradual phasing out of the program. As early as 1897, the government had admitted that there was little practical difference between boarding and industrial schools, except that the latter received more government money per capita. Over the next few decades, it would accept that the industrial schools were not bringing about the hoped-for quick assimilation, and one by one they were closed or converted to boarding schools. By 1923, there was one type of boarding facility acknowledged under the general name 'residential school'.

The Right To Choose a Chief

As the nineteenth century drew to a close, confrontations continued over the imposition of the elective form of government,[50] but strong Amerindian resistance made it impractical to insist on annual elections. The Cowessess band (named after the Plains Cree and Saulteaux chief, Kiwisance, 'Little Child', d. 1886, who signed Treaty Four at Fort Qu'Appelle) illustrates the struggles that arose. At its own request, the band went on the three-year elective system in 1887. However, Hayter Reed, the agent from 1881 to 1893, did not approve of the chief elected a few years later, who was an advocate of traditional ways.[51] In 1894, Reed, now deputy superintendent-general of Indian Affairs, denied the band the right to hold another election. In the end, the Amerindians' persistence won out, and the Cowessess band finally held its elections.

As time went on, resistance against government by imposition grew. Bands refused to exercise their police and public health powers, or to spend band funds for those purposes. In response, the department gave the Superintendent-General the power to carry out these functions using band funds. The government let some bands, mainly in the Prairie provinces, continue choosing their chiefs by their traditional methods. The department, in approving the chiefs so selected, saw them as appointees. By 1900, there were four systems of band government: three-year elective (Indian Act), one-year elective (Advancement Act), hereditary (Yukon, NWT, and in varying numbers in the provinces), and appointed.[52]

The Battle over Reserved Lands

As the government reserved lands for Amerindians, it also made provisions for the surrender of these lands by lease or sale. In theory, reserve lands could be surrendered only by a majority of male reserve residents over the age of 21 at a meeting specially called for the purpose. When band councils resisted the leasing of lands even for a limited period, the government handed the power to allot reserve lands without band consent to the Superintendent-General (1879, 1884, 1894).[53]

Band councils continued to fight the imposed regulations. The administration responded in 1898 by granting the Superintendent-General overriding powers. Soon, the government gave itself the power to remove Amerindians from any reserves next to or partly within a town of 8,000 inhabitants or more. In effect, this abolished the St Clair Ojibwa reserve at Sarnia, Ontario, and the Songhees reserve at Victoria, BC.

So died the policy of speeding up assimilation by establishing reserves as close as possible to white settlements. Land was now so valuable that the policy took second place. Instead, more comments were being heard about removing Amerindians to remote areas as settlers flooded in. Their increasing demands, along with those of developers and railway companies, influenced Indian Affairs to decide that many of the reserves were too large for the number of Amerindians living on them—and their populations were declining. Reserve lands beyond immediate requirements came to be regarded as 'surplus' and thus open to negotiations for surrender to the Crown. Those in favour of this claimed the sales were providing Amerindians with cash to get started in their new lives as farmers or ranchers. An amendment to the Indian Act in 1911 empowered municipalities or companies to expropriate Amerindian land for roads, railways, or other public purposes, with up to half of the proceeds to be paid directly to band members.[54]

In Ontario, such deals had taken off after the War of 1812, when the Crown gained some 2.8 million hectares of Amerindian lands.[55] As the tide of immigration moved westward, the Prairie provinces became the major scene for such activity. The period between 1896 and 1911 saw 21 per cent—more than one-fifth—of reserve lands on the prairies thus surrendered.[56] In 1910–11, almost half of the Blackfoot reserve in Alberta was sold for more than a million dollars. In spite of the cash inducement, however, Amerindians were seldom either eager or unanimous about surrendering.

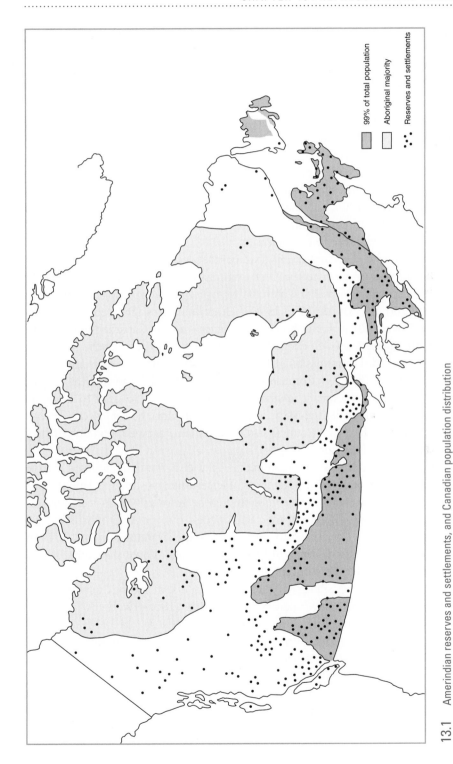

13.1   Amerindian reserves and settlements, and Canadian population distribution

Sources: Report of the Royal Commission on Aboriginal Peoples, II, part 2, 450; adapted from Russel Lawrence Barsh, 'Canada's Aboriginal Peoples: Social Integration or Disintegration?', Canadian Journal of Native Studies 14, 1 (1994), and used with the permission of Brandon University, Brandon, Manitoba.

Far more often, they accepted deals only reluctantly and after persuasion. And matters did not stop there.

Commissions and Expropriations

In 1911, a further amendment to the Indian Act gave municipalities and companies the power to expropriate portions of reserves, with the consent of the Governor-in-Council, for roads, railways, or other public purposes. The surrender initiative did not yield the expected benefits for the Amerindians, however, and resistance grew. The St Peter's band in Manitoba (see Box 13.2) and the Peigan band in Alberta publicly called for the overturn of surrenders but were unsuccessful. Clifford Sifton, Superintendent-General of Indian Affairs, 1896–1905, said that the consent of the Amerindians concerned was necessary but did little to ensure that this happened.[57] The result was that surrenders were eventually phased out in favour of leases.

In British Columbia, the continuing deadlock between the province and Ottawa over Amerindian land gave rise to the Joint Commission for the Settlement of Indian Reserves in the Province of British Columbia to investigate and act on the problem. This it did, off and on, from 1876 to 1910.[58] Other initiatives included a Squamish delegation to Edward VII in London (1906), a petition to the Canadian government (1909),[59] another petition, which elicited Prime Minister Sir Wilfrid Laurier's promise of help (1910),[60] a Royal Commission (1913–16),[61] and a petition by the Nisga'a to the Judicial Committee of the Privy Council in London (1913). The action of the Nisga'a had been spurred by BC's adamant refusal to discuss Aboriginal rights or to allow the Royal Commission to consider the issue. In 1908, the province had refused to lay out any more reserves.[62] The Privy Council said it could consider petitions only if they came from the courts of Canada.

The Royal Commission of 1916 recommended the 'cutting off' of specified reserve lands[63] and their substitution with larger areas of lesser value, costing the Amerindians 36,000 acres (14,569 hectares) and eliminating entire reserves.[64] This led to an increase in the sizes of reserves—if not their land value—but the Amerindians bitterly opposed the cut-offs.[65] They refused to appear before the Commission, and in 1916 they organized into the **Allied Tribes of British Columbia** to fight the Commission's recommendations and to assert Aboriginal right.

In spite of the spirited resistance of Allied Tribes leaders, including Squamish chief Andrew Paull (1892–1959) and Haida Rev. Peter Kelly (1885–1966), BC approved the Commission's report in 1923. Ottawa followed a year later.[66] In 1926, the Allied Tribes carried their petition to the Privy Council in London but were intercepted by the Canadian High Commissioner, who promised to deliver the documents on their behalf. There is no evidence that he did so. The following year, the Canadian government issued a 'final settlement' in which it held that BC's Amerindians had 'not established any claim to the lands of British Columbia based on Aboriginal or other title'.[67] The government recommended that the Amerindians be granted $100,000 a year as compensation for the lack of treaty rights but opposed letting BC Amerindians

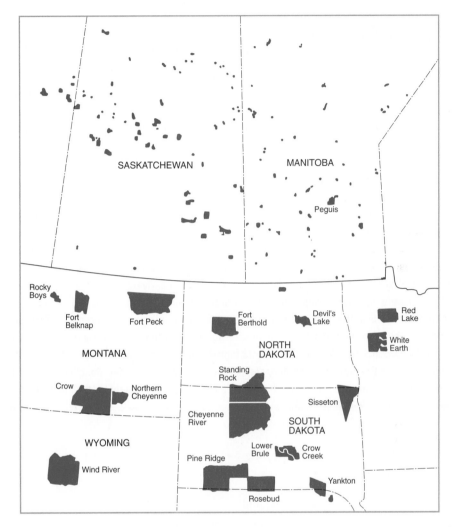

13.2 Plains reserves, Canada and the United States

Sources: *Report of the Royal Commission on Aboriginal Peoples*, II, part 2, 423; adapted, with permission, from Robert White-Harvey, 'Reservation Geography and Restoration of Native Self-Government', *Dalhousie Law Journal* 17, 2 (Fall 1994): 588.

use the courts to settle claims. Three days before the hearings began, the government strengthened the existing prohibitions against using band funds for land claim actions without departmental approval; now, outside fundraising was also banned, a measure that remained in law until 1951.[68]

Soon after, the Allied Tribes collapsed, but by 1931 Paull had organized the Native Brotherhood of British Columbia, which later became the North American Indian Brotherhood (NAIB). Finally, in 1938—67 years late—British Columbia fulfilled the

---

Box 13.2   The Surrender of Reserves

A long and bitter controversy between non-Indians and the Peguis band of Saulteaux over the St Peter's Reserve land, near Selkirk, Manitoba, had resulted in a proposal that the Saulteaux surrender their reserve. The federal government resolved the case by passing St Peter's Reserve Act in 1916. It confirmed individual patents to reserve lands held by Amerindians, as well as those held by non-Indians who were prepared to pay an additional dollar an acre. Monies so raised were to be credited to the band. This 'solution', of course, involved the breakup of the reserve and relocation of the band about 105 kilometres to the north on the shores of Lake Winnipeg. Band members who did not hold patents and who refused to leave the old reserve were evicted. The only thing left to them on the old site was a 53-hectare fishing station. The principle of prior rights had not protected the Saulteaux.

An earlier surrender of a reserve—in fact, the first in the West—was that of the Pahpahstayo (Passpasschase) band, established under Treaty Six. It involved what is today the southeast portion of the city of Edmonton. This was an early example of settlers—some of whom were squatters—objecting not only to the proximity of a reserve to a city but also to rich farmlands in the hands of a people popularly believed to be uninterested in farming. Under intense pressure, most band members agreed to withdraw from treaty and accept scrip. By 1886, the reserve counted only 13 families remaining, who later agreed to join the Enoch band to the west of Edmonton, completing the surrender. Today, descendants of the disbanded group are seeking reinstatement as a band and a settlement for their lost lands.[69]

---

terms of its Act of Union by transferring 592,297 acres (239,694 hectares) to the federal authority (see Box 13.3).

World War I and New Pressures on Land

World War I (1914–18) had seen a renewed wave of pressures on Amerindian lands. Once more, the government had amended the Indian Act so that it could take or lease reserve lands for agricultural production without band permission—financing the projects out of band funds. To add even more insult to injury, the Amerindians in question were at the bottom of the priority list for using the equipment bought for the projects. The Blood of southern Alberta led the protests, but without result.[70]

Amerindians across the land contributed in many ways to the war effort. The Blood raised substantial amounts for the Red Cross despite poverty on the reserves.[71] About 4,000 Amerindians served in the armed forces. As veterans, however, Amerindians soon discovered that they were not getting the same benefits as non-Amerindians. In the words of one official: 'These returned Indian soldiers are subject to the provisions of the Indian Act and are in the same position as they were before enlisting.'[72] Despite some improvements, the equal treatment they received in the armed forces (including the right to vote) would not extend into civilian life.[73]

Box 13.3   The Slow Pace of Settling Land Claims

Other provinces did not move much faster than British Columbia in fulfilling their Confederation obligation to transfer Amerindian reserve land to the federal authority. For instance, it took Ontario 54 years to settle Ojibwa and Mississauga claims, first filed in 1869, even though the claims had long been recognized as valid. The last component of the Manitoulin Island Treaty of 1862 took a final step towards settlement with the agreement in principle involving 90,000 acres (36,422 hectares) that was signed in 1990. In other provinces and territories, claims dating well back into the eighteenth century have still not been settled.[74] In almost all cases, the resolution of such claims owed more to Amerindian persistence than to government acknowledgement of responsibility.

Overseas, however, there was no pass system to prevent Amerindians from different nations from meeting one another, comparing experiences, and discussing shared problems. Fred Loft, a Mohawk from Ontario and by then an officer in the Forestry Corps, was so moved by what he heard from fellow soldiers that, on his own initiative, he met with the Privy Council in London to find out what it could do. They told him that they could not respond to the petition of an individual but advised him to go back home and build an organization that could speak on behalf of Amerindian people.[75] As noted earlier, this is precisely what he did by founding the **League of Indians**, which held its first congress in 1919 at Sault Ste Marie, Ontario.[76] His proposals included giving Indians the vote without losing their special status, allowing them greater control over band funds and properties, and improving the standards of education for Amerindian children. His efforts led to police surveillance and his being branded by Indian Affairs officials as an agitator.

By the 1920s, its leadership was predominantly western. Mike Mountain Horse and Ed Ahenakew were moderates, but later leaders were more radical. The League lobbied against the pass system, petitioned for additional programs, and asserted Amerindians' right to hold thirst dances. By the 1930s, better schooling and assistance for Aboriginal farmers had been added to its list of demands. Aid to farmers was a long-standing issue. Hayter Reed had been a proponent of the 'peasant farmer' policy, whereby Aboriginal people who took up farming would have to sow and harvest by hand. As early as 1893, headmen of the Pasquah and Muscowpetung bands had petitioned the House of Commons to correct this inequity.[77]

Eventually, the League succumbed to pressure from without and within, and inside the organization the diverse and sometimes divergent agendas of status versus non-status Indians and Métis, and of radicals versus moderates, strained relations. By the 1940s, Loft, in his seventies and in failing health, was unable to hold the League together, and it faded from the political scene. But the need for a pan-Indian organization was recognized.

Important Names and Terms

Allied Tribes of British Columbia

day schools

File Hills Colony

League of Indians

Loft, Frederick Ogilvie

Longhouse religion

New England Company

pass system

residential schools

scrip

Study Questions

1) Why did Amerindian leaders George Copway, Shingwaukonse, and Peter Jones request education?
2) What did those who supported the Longhouse religion hope to achieve?
3) By whom were residential schools favoured over day schools? Why?
4) What were the findings of the 1916 Royal Commission?

Recommended Readings

Brass, Eleanor. *I Walk in Two Worlds*. Calgary: Glenbow Museum, 1987.

Carter, Sarah A. *Aboriginal People and Colonizers of Western Canada to 1900*. Toronto: University of Toronto Press, 1999.

Dempsey, Hugh A. *Charcoal's World*. Saskatoon: Western Producer, 1978.

Miller, Christine, and Patricia Chuchryk, eds. *Women of the First Nations: Power, Wisdom, and Strength*. Winnipeg: University of Manitoba Press, 1996.

Miller, J.R. *Shingwauk's Vision*. Toronto: University of Toronto Press, 1996.

Milloy, John S. *A National Crime: The Canadian Government and the Residential School System, 1879–1986*. Winnipeg: University of Manitoba Press, 1999.

14 Tightening the Reins: Resistance Grows and Organizes

As the police pulled back from having to enforce the pass system (see Chapter 13) that restricted the movements of western Amerindians—a measure that violated basic human rights—the department moved to strengthen the other means it had already called into play to achieve the purpose. In 1890, it had empowered Indian agents to enforce the Criminal Code's anti-vagrancy provisions. Then, in 1914, it strengthened the bans on 'giveaway' ceremonies central to the potlatch (1884) and the endurance rituals of the thirst dance (1895). Now, Amerindians could not even appear in Aboriginal clothing or perform their traditional dances at fairs and stampedes. Finally, the government prohibited such dances in any type of dress unless the department gave written approval.[1] This was a direct blow to Amerindian sense of community. Administrators saw any encouragement of Aboriginal culture as undermining its assimilation policy. Encouraged by missionaries, during the 1920s the RCMP conducted raids and confiscated ritual paraphernalia, some of which was sidetracked and sold for private gain by unscrupulous agents. Later, the government would help Aboriginal groups set up museums to house returned objects.[2]

Another aspect of this drive towards assimilation was **compulsory enfranchisement**—the power given to the Superintendent-General to enfranchise Amerindians he considered qualified, whether they or not they wanted to become voters. As well, these individuals would receive title to the reserve lands they occupied and their share of band money. In effect, to the government, enfranchisement meant an end to an individual's status under the Indian Act. The government also eased the way for Métis who had taken treaty to get the vote and paved the way for Amerindian women married to non-Amerindians to give up entirely their Amerindian status.

Although the government designed these measures with Amerindians east of the Great Lakes in mind, the alarm and hostility they aroused spread from coast to coast. The Six Nations found wide support when they petitioned the Governor-General against these arbitrary moves towards enfranchisement. The department's purpose was

Time Line

1890	Indian agents empowered to enforce anti-vagrancy laws.
1896	Land set aside in Alberta for exclusive use of Métis at Saint-Paul-des-Métis.
1914	Amerindians forbidden to perform traditional dances in Native garb at fairs and stampedes.
1920	Indian Act amendment leads to enfranchisement (and loss of Indian status) of nearly 500 Amerindians in less than two years.
1922	Armed confrontation between Iroquois and RCMP.
1923–4	Iroquois take their claim to sovereignty to League of Nations; case is dropped after British intervention at League of Nations.
1924	Ludger Bastien first Aboriginal elected to Quebec legislature.
1930	L'Association des Métis d'Alberta et des Territoires du Nord Ouest organized.
1936	Department of Mines and Resources absorbs Indian administration.
1938	Alberta's Métis Population Betterment Act leads to creation of 10 Métis colonies, of which eight still exist.
1951	Major changes to Indian Act, granting women the vote in band council elections, allowing secret ballot, limited but greater Native control of band affairs, less sweeping ministerial powers.
1958	Tyendinaga Reserve on Lake Ontario first to gain complete control of band funds.
1966	Hawthorn Report criticizes centuries-old policy of assimilation and presents view of Amerindians as 'citizens plus' because of their original inhabitancy.
1967	Amerindian pavilion at Expo 67 brings plight of Canadian Aboriginals to public consciousness.
1969	Federal government White Paper proposes end of Indian Act, termination of treaties, and that Aboriginals be treated equally with all other Canadians.
1970	Supreme Court rules in *Drybones* that Aboriginals have right to drink alcohol in public.
1971	Concerted Amerindian protest results in retraction by Ottawa of White Paper proposals.
1979	Métis legal action for $500 million in oil and gas revenues leads to Alberta government raids on settlement offices.
1985	Indian Act amendments and Bill C-31 grant Indian women rights and status equal to those of men.

clear enough: 'to continue until there is not a single Indian in Canada that has not been absorbed into the body politic and there is no Indian question, and no Indian Department.'[3] In other words, the government's goal was the extinction of Amerindians as Amerindians.[4]

The 1920 amendment lasted only two years. It was revived, however, in a modified form in 1933, with the proviso that the government could not impose the vote in violation of treaty promises. This stayed on the books until the 1951 revision of the Indian Act. Old attitudes died hard, however. Walter E. Harris, who as Minister of Citizenship and Immigration was responsible for Indian Affairs from 1950 to 1954, expressed the hope that the Act, even when revised, would be only temporary, as the 'ultimate goal of our Indian policy is the integration of the Indian into the general life and economy of the country.'[5]

The frustration on all sides was only too clear. The government's approach of treating the Amerindians as minors to be assimilated led to resistance and defiance, both covert and open. The Department of Indian Affairs (DIA) became more arbitrary, and Amerindians refused to co-operate. Time and again, they demonstrated they were prepared to suffer rather than be treated like children. The government paid lip service to consultation, but in practice it could not bring itself to listen and actually take into account what Amerindians were saying.[6] The old idea that Amerindians were human in form only and could not reason may have gone underground, and perhaps even taken on new forms, but its essence was alive and well.

On an individual level, decorated war veteran Francis Pegahmagabow (1891–1952), an Ojibwa from the Parry Island Reserve, and others challenged government authority to such an extent that in 1933 Indian Affairs set as

Corporal Francis Pegahmagabow was Canada's most highly decorated Indian in World War I. An Ojibwa of the Parry Island band in Ontario, he served as a scout and sniper during the war and was reputed to be the greatest sniper on the Western Front. His exploits won him a Military Medal and two bars. Later, as chief of the Parry Island Reserve, he fought against the Indian agent system, for Native control of resources, and for ownership of Georgian Bay islands that the Indians claimed had not been ceded in the Robinson Huron treaty. *(Photo courtesy Fred Gaffen,* Forgotten Soldiers *[Penticton, BC: Theytus Books, 1985])*

official policy that Amerindians could not contact the department directly. All correspondence had to go through the Indian agent, who often wrote off complaints to their superiors as having come from either chronic complainers or outside agitators.[7]

The process of more and stiffer regulations continued until the onset of the Great Depression in 1929. Meanwhile, prices for fur and fish plummeted, putting Amerindians on welfare rolls,[8] and Indian Affairs drifted. In 1936, Amerindian administration was shunted off to the Department of Mines and Resources, which was far more concerned with industrial development than with the social problems of Amerindians. The administration now encouraged northern Amerindians in their traditional hunting and trapping activities,[9] as these enabled them to be self-sufficient.[10] Even if Amerindians could afford the new and larger farm machinery, which rarely was the case, their farms usually were too small to make effective use of it. This situation became acute after World War II, with the result that many Amerindians gave up farming.

More Social Engineering: Residential Schools and Beyond

By the turn of the twentieth century, enthusiasm for industrial schools had waned. Rising costs and poor administration, including charges of abuse to students, led to a gradual phasing out of the program. Even in boarding and day schools, however, problems developed. Investigations in 1907–9 revealed that 28 per cent of the students who had attended Sarcee Boarding School between 1894 and 1908 had died, mostly from tuberculosis.[11] The government shelved a comprehensive plan to deal with the situation because of the cost, but also because it would have undermined the authority of the churches running the schools.

New regulations and financing arrangements led to some improvement.[12] Still, charges of student abuse continued to surface. After the Oka standoff in 1990, these became widespread and received previously unaccustomed media coverage. Until comparatively recently, the system had the backing of society in general,[13] but these administrative problems brought day schools back into favour.

The year of compulsory enfranchisement, 1920, also was the year for strengthening compulsory school attendance to ensure that all Amerindian children between the ages of seven and 15 attended. Ten years later, the government stiffened regulations still more. By this time, Amerindian children could be committed to boarding schools and kept there until the age of 18 on the authority of the Indian agent, a measure far in excess of any applied to non-Amerindians. These regulations might have been responsible for statistics reported by Duncan Campbell Scott (1862–1947), the deputy superintendent-general from 1913 to 1932, indicating that attendance rose from 64 per cent in 1920 to 75 per cent in 1930. This was mostly due to residential schools—by the 1930s, there were more than 80.[14] To Scott, these figures were proof that Amerindians were on their way to becoming 'civilized'.[15]

Other statistics, however, tell a different story. In 1930, three-quarters of Amerindian pupils across Canada were in grades one to three. Only three in 100 went past grade six. By mid-century, the proportion of Amerindian students beyond grade six had risen to 10 per cent, an improvement but only one-third of the comparable level of Euro-Canadian children. As late as 1951, 40 per cent of Amerindians over the age of five were reported to be without formal schooling, in spite of regulations for enforced attendance.[16]

Throughout all this, Amerindians were not allowed to contribute to the content of studies or to exercise any control over schools, although some petitioned to have more emphasis on classwork and less on 'practical' training such as farming. The schools banned the use of Amerindian languages and the practice of traditional religions. Despite their efforts to transform Amerindians, however, educators became aware that Amerindians were using the system to obtain 'the best that the White man had to teach' and were trying to 'work out their own plans and their own self-determination'.[17] The vast majority stayed distinctly Amerindian.

When Amerindians proved they were as adept as Euro-Canadians at their own game, the result could be hostility and rejection instead of acceptance. Diamond Jenness observed in 1920:

In many parts of Canada the Indians had no schools at all, in others only elementary mission schools in which the standard of teaching was exceedingly low. A few mission boarding-schools, subsidized by the government, accepted Indian children when very young, raised them to the age of sixteen, then sent them back to their people, well indoctrinated in the Christian faith, but totally unfitted for life in an Indian community and, of course, not acceptable in any white one.[18]

Amerindians, of course, had another view of the influence of school. In the words of John Tootoosis, who headed the Federation of Saskatchewan Indians in the late 1950s and 1960s:

When an Indian comes out of these places it is like being put between two walls in a room and left hanging in the middle. On one side are all the things he learned from his people and their way of life that was being wiped out, and on the other are the white man's way which he could never fully understand since he never had the right amount of education and could not be part of it. There he is, hanging in the middle of the two cultures and he is not a white man and he is not an Indian. They washed away practically everything an Indian needed to help himself, to think the way a human person should in order to survive.[19]

In the Far North, at least one residential school struck a positive note. The Anglican school at Shingle Point, Yukon, had two Inuit hunters on staff to teach the boys hunting and fishing techniques. The girls received lessons in the domestic arts within the framework of Arctic conditions. Such concessions were rare, however. Gwich'in John Nerysoo of Tuktoyaktuk, when asked in 1981 what he had learned at school, replied, 'mostly about God and being good'.[20]

The parliamentary investigations that preceded the 1951 revision of the Indian Act rejected Indian Affairs' education policy as it then was and proposed instead that Amerindian children be integrated into public schools. Ten years later, of the 38,000 young Amerindians in school, almost one-fourth were attending provincially controlled institutions and the total proportion of Amerindian pupils beyond grade six had doubled.[21] By this time, however, some were advocating autonomous Amerindian schools, separate from those of the dominant society. It was at this time, too, that many Aboriginal children were taken from their homes and communities and placed in foster care or adoptive homes (Box 14.1).

Most of the residential schools that still were operating had closed during the 1970s. The sense of hurt they left in their wake eventually ended in lawsuits by former students seeking damages for their compulsory school attendance and the treatment some had received, and by 2003 thousands of lawsuits had been filed against the churches and individuals involved. The Anglican Church, through Archbishop Michael Peers, initially had issued an apology in 1993 for the personal harm caused by the residential schools. As Archbishop Peers stated, 'I am sorry, more than I can say, that we were part of a system which took you and your children from home and family.' The Anglican Church led the way when it finalized a negotiated settlement with the federal government in late 2002 committing $25 million to reparations. The Presbyterian Church, which had been responsible for fewer schools, offered a formal apology in 1994. The United Church,

Box 14.1   The 'Sixties Scoop'

A phenomenon closely related to the residential schools that temporarily gained strength as residential schools fell into disfavour was the practice of placing 'neglected' or disadvantaged Aboriginal children with white families, either as adoptees or in foster care. The **'Sixties Scoop'**, as it was popularly known, took off in Canada in the 1950s and reached its peak during the 1960s and early 1970s. In all, 15,000 Aboriginal children were adopted into non-Native families, 3,000 from Manitoba alone. By the end of the 1960s, 30–40 per cent of all legal wards were Aboriginal, even though they made up less than 4 per cent of the national population.[22] These children were scattered far and wide after being removed from their families, many of them ending up in the United States and some even farther afield. Their isolation was far greater than if they had been sent to residential school, which was usually located not far from their homes so that contact was not entirely cut off.

The movement began to taper off in the 1980s, as it became apparent that instead of creating a homogeneous society, the practice was producing individuals who were neither white nor Amerindian and whose loss of cultural identity led to social dysfunction. This dysfunction was becoming a tradition in itself, as it was passed on to the next generation.

having previously made a general apology in 1986, issued a formal apology in 1998. Finally, in April 2009, following a private meeting in Rome with a small delegation of residential school survivors, including AFN National Chief Phil Fontaine, the Pope expressed his 'sorrow' on behalf of the Roman Catholic Church, which had been responsible for about 75 per cent of the residential schools in Canada. Although the apologies from the churches in the 1990s met with a cool reception,[23] they preceded any formal apology or announcement of reparations from the federal government (see Chapters 17 and 18).

In December 2003, a unanimous ruling by the British Columbia Court of Appeal that the federal government held 100 per cent liability in the case of the school at Port Alberni[24] moved this issue forward on the government's agenda. In May 2005, the federal government signed an agreement with the Assembly of First Nations outlining the basis on which the government and the AFN would work together to resolve claims and appointed retired Supreme Court Justice Frank Iacobucci to oversee the process.[25] The first results of that process are discussed in Chapter 18.

On the other hand, a study of the Walpole Island First Nation's experience revealed that most of its former students judged their education favourably. More local studies need to be done to balance out the picture as a whole.[26]

Blue Quills, near St Paul, Alberta, in 1970 became the first school in Canada to be controlled by an Amerindian band.[27] Its success encouraged others to follow its example; in 1973 the Métis community at Ile à la Crosse in northern Saskatchewan took over the local school.[28] The following year the Ojibwa of Sabaskong Bay in northern Ontario on its own began the process of taking over their elementary school; three years later, in 1977, they were running the secondary school also.[29] Today, Indian Affairs encourages bands to take over full or partial administration of reserve schools, although its funding policy is not always consistent with this goal. By 2005, Canada counted almost 500 schools being operated on reserves by First Nations.[30]

As to be expected, the influence of the old regime carries over, even as the new regime copes with such problems as the reluctance of Indian Affairs to allow a level of funding for band-operated schools comparable to that of provincially operated schools. Another problem is the transfer of full authority for the schools to the bands. In other words, old attitudes have not disappeared. However, 'aggressive assimilation' is no longer the order of the day, and Amerindian-run schools are chalking up good records.[31] The intensity and duration of the campaign to capture Amerindian minds and hearts reflect the importance accorded to this aspect of nation-building. Control of education goes to the heart of the movement for self-government.

Organized Action and a Revised Indian Act

Early attempts at pan-Indian political unity had been led by such figures as the Abenaki's Nescambiouit, the Fox's Kiala, Joseph Brant of the Mohawks, and, more recently, the returned World War I veteran Fred Loft, the Mohawk founder of the

James Gladstone, of the Blood Reserve, Alberta, was the first treaty Indian appointed to the Canadian Senate. His daughter, Pauline Dempsey, adjusts his headdress while his wife, Janie, looks on. The occasion was his retirement, at age 83, in 1971. *(CP, Canapress Photo Service, Doug Ball)*

League of Indians. Yet, the effective beginning of Amerindian activism in Canadian politics can be dated to a trip to Ottawa in 1943 by Andrew Paull and Dan Assu of the Native Brotherhood of BC to protest taxation of BC's Amerindian fishermen and price ceilings on sockeye salmon.[32] At this time, and even though they were not citizens, Amerindians were serving in the armed forces during World War II in proportionately higher numbers—up to 6,000—than did any other segment of the general population, repeating a pattern that had been evident during World War I. An unexpected area in which they had a unique advantage in World War II was that of language. Amerindian languages were particularly useful for transmitting sensitive information—codes can be broken, but languages have to be learned. Canadian **'code talkers'** used Cree; Americans used Navajo and Comanche.

World War II brought social upheaval and with it a change of attitude. When Amerindians returned to civilian life, the restrictions and inequities of their lot on reserves became glaringly evident. In response, veterans' organizations and church groups mounted a campaign that resulted in the establishment of a Joint Senate and House of Commons Committee on the Indian Act, which held hearings from 1946 to 1948.[33] Amerindians were highly critical of the first draft of the proposed revisions. Led by James Gladstone of the Blood, they claimed that the draft, instead of entrenching their rights, actually would erode them.

Faced with such protests, the government set about revising the revisions. This time, it heard Amerindian witnesses, the first time for such consultations at that level.[34] Treaties and treaty rights concerned the Amerindians most. They wanted these left in place, but with the freedom to govern themselves. Land claims were not far behind. For the government, the goal continued to be assimilation.

The revised Act of 1951 can hardly be called revolutionary, still it heralded the dawn of a new era. Not since the first Indian Act was the minister's power limited as it so became in 1951—but he still had veto power. The new Act did not allow bands to establish their own forms of government but did increase their measure of self-control.[35] In fact, with few exceptions the band could now spend its monies as it wished, unless the Governor-in-Council expressed reservations. This meant, for example, that it could now fund lawsuits to advance claims. It would be 1958, however, before any bands had complete control over their funds.

The government also repealed anti-potlatch and anti-dance measures.[36] It dropped compulsory enfranchisement and restrictions on political organizations, both of which were not working out, in any event. Political organizations, such as the Allied Tribes of British Columbia, had been functioning since early in the twentieth century.[37] A case was fought all the way to the Supreme Court in 1970 for Amerindians to win the right to drink in public.

Although the 1951 Act moved towards self-government, it did not go nearly far enough to satisfy such groups as the Six Nations, who were claiming sovereignty as actively as ever. Even moderates were critical of the revised Act. How could the Act make full citizens of Amerindians, they asked, if they were not going to be allowed the responsibilities that go with citizenship?

A second joint committee for the review of Indian Affairs policy sat from 1959 to 1961. This time, land claims surged to the forefront, and the committee responded by repeating a recommendation of the first joint committee in 1951, that a claims commission be established. That would not happen until 1969 (see Chapter 16). Meanwhile, Andrew Paull and Dan Assu's 1943 petition on fishing rights had triggered a chain of events that eventually led to the formation in 1968 of the **National Indian Brotherhood**. Originally only for treaty Indians, soon it was acting on behalf of Native groups across Canada. It lasted until 1982, when the **Assembly of First Nations** emerged as the national Amerindian voice.[38] In 1966, the Federation of Saskatchewan Indians under Walter Dieter (1916–88) became the first Native organization to receive a federal grant to organize community programs.

Home and Abroad

The centennial of Canada's Confederation in 1967 presented too good an opportunity to miss. At Expo in Montreal, Amerindians, with the support of Indian Affairs, erected a pavilion in which they publicly expressed, for the first time on a national scale, dissatisfaction with their lot.[39] For Amerindians, it was an unheard-of opportunity to present grievances that dated back 300 years or more.

The general public reacted with stunned disbelief that people in Canada were being treated this way. Surely, people thought, Amerindians were exaggerating. Weren't they just being ungrateful for the many good things that Canada had done for them? Most Canadians had no way of knowing what was happening on the reserves and in the North. Canada, in celebrating the centennial of its Confederation, had simply not thought to include First Nations as founding members.

The obviously marginalized position of Amerindians, in the North as elsewhere, spurred the federal government in 1963 to appoint anthropologist Harry B. Hawthorn to investigate their social, educational, and economic conditions. His report, which appeared in 1966, listed 151 recommendations. It stated that an Amerindian should not be forced to 'acquire those values of the majority society he does not hold, or wish to acquire', and that the department should assume a more active role as advocate for Amerindian interests.[40] The report supported the Indian Act but recommended changes. It also revealed that their average per capita annual income was less than half that of other Canadians. Amerindians' schooling also was far below the national average. Hawthorn urged that Amerindians have the opportunity to study in their own languages. He observed that school texts were often not only inaccurate on the subject of Amerindians, they were usually insulting.[41]

Concerning self-government, Hawthorn noted that, between 1951 and 1964, only about a quarter of the bands that Canada counted at that time had passed any bylaws. This reflected the fact that the Governor-in-Council could veto any band decision. When it came to money bylaws, fewer than 50 bands were deemed 'advanced' enough to exercise this power. In other words, outsiders were running the reserves.

According to Hawthorn, Amerindians reacted by orienting themselves primarily to kinship and other groupings. Band councils persisted only because the government insisted on dealing through them. By complying with the system, bands assured themselves of more generous welfare grants, but the price was that they could not make decisions affecting their lives. This pattern of dependency took such root that, in some cases, even urban bands actually voted against local autonomy. Acceptance of welfare also weakened communal activities.[42]

The Amerindian community received the **Hawthorn Report** well. As the report explained, 'in addition to the normal rights and duties of citizenship, Indians possess certain additional rights as charter members of the Canadian community.'[43]

The 1969 White Paper and Some Consequences

In 1969, Ottawa came up with what was described—although not by most Amerindians—as a 'breathtaking governmental recipe for equality'. This was the **White Paper**, a proposal designed to break 'the pattern of 200 years' and to abolish the existing framework of Amerindian administration, widely criticized for setting Amerindians apart and hindering their development.[44]

In fact, rising administrative costs were at the heart of this government initiative, although it was, in part, a response to the American Indian Movement (AIM, or 'Red Power'), which had arisen in Minnesota in 1968 and was spreading into Canada, challenging the administration to allow Amerindians a greater say in running their own affairs. The government, therefore, announced it was going 'to enable the Indian people to be free—free to develop Indian cultures in an environment of legal, social and economic equality with other Canadians'.[45] In other words, instead of Hawthorn's 'citizens plus', Amerindians were to become like all other Canadians. Their special status would end. The White Paper did not recognize Aboriginal rights and, in effect, treaties would be cancelled. When the government announced the new policy, it hit a solid wall of opposition. The National Indian Brotherhood (NIB) said flatly that the proposals were not acceptable:

> We view this as a policy designed to divest us of our aboriginal, residual, and statutory rights. If we accept this policy, and in the process lose our rights and our lands, we become willing partners in culture genocide. This we cannot do.[46]

In the words of Sagkeeng Ojibwa Dave Courchene (Neeghani Binehse, 'Leading Thunderbird'), president of the Manitoba Indian Brotherhood from 1967 to 1974:

> Once again . . . we have not been consulted, we have been advised of decisions already taken. I feel like a man who has been told he must die and am now to be consulted on the methods of implementing that decision.[47]

Later in 1969, the government named Dr Lloyd Barber, vice-president of the University of Saskatchewan, as commissioner for Amerindian land claims but did not initially authorize him to deal with Aboriginal rights (see Chapter 16). This reflected Prime Minister Pierre Elliott Trudeau's personal rejection of the concept of Aboriginal right at that time (see Box 14.2). The NIB rejected Barber's office as an outgrowth of the White Paper. The government's 1970 hiring of a Cree lawyer from Calgary, William I.C. Wuttunee, a former chief of the National Indian Council of Canada and now a supporter of the White Paper, inflamed the opposition. Wuttunee was banned from several reserves, including his own, Red Pheasant.[48]

Box 14.2   Aboriginal Rights

A side effect of the White Paper was to popularize the term **'Aboriginal rights'**, just coming into general use at that time. As originally used, 'Aboriginal rights' referred only to land. Later, it came to include rights to self-determination and self-government. The term 'Aboriginal', which derives from 'Aborigine',[49] was being used in Canada by the early nineteenth century.[50] 'Aboriginal' takes in Amerindians, Métis, and Inuit, and has been adopted by all three. An alternative is 'indigene'.

The official Amerindian response was *Citizens Plus* (known as the 'Red Paper'), written by the Alberta Indian Association. Rejecting wardship, it still advocated special status, but as defined by the treaties.[51] Eventually Trudeau conceded that the government had been 'very naive . . . not pragmatic enough or understanding enough'. His government formally retracted the White Paper on 17 March 1971.

Six Nations, the League of Nations, and the Move towards Autonomy

The Six Nations have a long record of arguing for autonomy, so it is not surprising that they deeply resented the restrictions imposed by the Indian Act of 1876, and particularly by its later amendments, without any Amerindian input. They rejected the authority of the department and the Act it administered. The main advocates of self-government were the hereditary chiefs, who in 1890 petitioned Ottawa for recognition of their autonomy and exemption from the Indian Act. They were rebuffed, as they had been in 1839 when they sought to be governed according to their own laws.

An 1890 amendment to the Indian Act empowered the department to set up an elective system without the approval of the Amerindians involved. In the department's view, the hereditary form of government did not fit the needs of the modern world. Among the Iroquois, supporters of the new system, called 'Dehorners',[52] tended to be younger and Christian. Traditionalists were mainly older followers of the Longhouse religion. In the ensuing power struggle, the traditionalists, led by Levi General (1873–1925), who held the Cayuga title **Deskaheh**, won the day.[53]

— Kahonhes

Deskaheh (Levi General), who travelled on an Iroquois passport, gained support in Europe for Six Nations sovereignty, but London intervened to make his appeal to the League of Nations futile. Upon his return in early 1925, after more than a year in Geneva and London, he was denied entry to Canada and spent the few months before his death later that year at the Tuscarora Reservation near Niagara Falls, New York. *(John Kahionhes Fadden drawing)*

With the close of World War I, the Six Nations established a committee to campaign for sovereignty. The government countered with an amendment to the Indian Act that abolished tribal governments. A Six Nations' petition to the Supreme Court of Canada and to the Privy Council in London got nowhere and aroused little public concern. However, there was much more public sympathy for the Six Nations' cause in Europe than in Canada.

An armed confrontation between Iroquois and the RCMP in 1922, in which shots were fired, led the Iroquois to take their case to the newly formed League of Nations. Canada, on the other hand, argued that it was a domestic matter and thus beyond the League's jurisdiction. At about this time, Deskaheh, waging an effective campaign in London, issued a pamphlet entitled 'The Redman's Appeal for Justice'. In it, he stated that all the Iroquois were asking for was home rule, much as the colonies had done a century earlier. Estonia, Ireland, Panama, and Persia (Iran) rallied to the Six Nations' cause. Norway, the Netherlands, and Albania joined them, but then London intervened, charging that 'minor powers' were interfering in the British Empire's 'internal affairs'. The League of Nations dropped the case in 1924. A direct appeal by Deskaheh to George V brought no result.

In the meantime, Canada appointed an investigator to examine the question of government on reserves as well as charges of mismanagement of Six Nations trust funds. The investigator recommended an elective system. The government implemented the decision without delay and without a referendum, imposing an elective council on the Six Nations and abolishing the hereditary one. The Mohawk rebelled. The next few years saw a traditionalist revival that included an attempt to re-establish links with the Iroquois Confederacy that had been severed 250 years earlier. Providing the spark was Paul Diabo's 1926 arrest in Philadelphia as an illegal alien. Seeing their historical right to free passage between the US and Canada threatened, the Grand Councils at Onondaga and Six Nations argued successfully before the US courts that their existence as nations had been challenged. The following year, the Grand Council met at Kahnawake.[54] Under the hereditary system, women had an important voice in the selection of chiefs, but the elective system did not give women the vote. Ironically, at about this time (1924), a chief of the Loretteville Huron, Ludger Bastien (1879–1948), became the first Amerindian to be elected to a provincial legislature, that of Quebec.[55]

Deskaheh's death in 1925, shortly after his return from Europe, dealt a heavy blow to the Iroquois independence movement, but the movement did not die. In 1942, the Kahnawake council asked that their tribal laws replace the Indian Act. Iroquois from various reserves mounted a campaign against the 1951 changes to the Act, claiming that they were dictatorial and would slow their progress as a nation. During that same decade, Kahnawake took the Canadian government to court over lands seized for the St Lawrence Seaway. Despite their resistance, the Iroquois lost 526 hectares (1,300 acres), including river frontage.[56] This was a cultural and economic blow for a people famed for their river expertise. (Indeed, in the late nineteenth century, when the British needed canoemen for their expeditionary force up the Nile River to relieve Khartoum, they recruited mainly at Kahnawake.[57]) The Mohawk finally won a $1.5 million settlement in 1963 after 17 years of bitter negotiations.[58] Later, after losing an island to Expo 67, the Iroquois moved against the whites living on the reserve and evicted about a thousand of them in 1973 on the grounds of overcrowding.[59]

The result of all this was the deterioration of the band's relationship with the Quebec provincial police, to the point that in 1969 it established its own independent police force. Called **Peacekeepers**, this force eventually became the official law enforcement agency on the reserve.[60] Later, the Warrior movement would gain support among those who felt that the Peacekeepers did not take a strong enough stand.[61]

When the RCMP raided Kahnawake's cigarette stores[62] in 1988, the Warriors rallied the Iroquois to block the south entrance to Mercier Bridge, located on reserve land and connecting the Island of Montreal with the south shore. The standoff lasted 27 hours, with armed Warriors patrolling the bridge, 'the first instance of armed native resistance in Canada's recent history'.[63] The RCMP responded by describing the Mohawk as 'violent'.[64] The government charged 16 persons with smuggling.

Thus was the stage set for the 'Indian summer' of 1990, when Kahnawake again blocked the bridge in support of Kanesatake in its confrontation at Oka. Although the blockade was brief, the standoff lasted 78 days, a member of the Quebec provincial police was shot and killed, and the two besieged communities were virtually cut off from the outside world. The Canadian Police Association called the Mohawk 'terrorists'.[65] The behaviour of the Canadian government once more drew the censure of the international community.

Alberta Métis

As has already been noted, Métis considered that their Amerindian heritage gave them a right to land (Chapters 11, 13). Furthermore, most did not accept that this right could be extinguished by treaty. As non-Aboriginals settled the West, the Métis became more and more scattered in small, impoverished bands. In 1895, Father Albert Lacombe approached Ottawa with a proposal to establish a reserve for Métis where they could learn how to farm. The government approved, seeing this as an alternative to scrip while also avoiding special status, but contributed only $2,000 to the project.

Saint-Paul-des-Métis was established the following year, 1896. It was the first tract of land set aside for the exclusive use of the Métis. The first year, 30 families from across Alberta and Saskatchewan moved to St Paul. By 1897, there were 50 families. Two years later, the Grey Nuns were operating a boarding school like those for Amerindians. Farmsteads were allotted quickly, but far away from each other so that the colony was dispersed. This worked against community cohesiveness. On top of that, the promised livestock and equipment did not appear. This, plus the general underfunding, discouraged the Métis, and they drifted away. In 1908, the

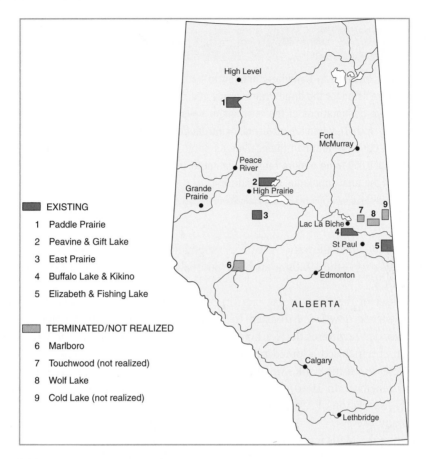

14.1   Métis settlements in Alberta

Source: Adapted from *Metisism, A Canadian Identity* (Edmonton: Alberta Federation of Metis Settlement Associations, 1982).

government ended the Métis leases and, two years later, threw the reserve open for French-Canadian settlement.

The government blamed the Métis for the project's failure. The Métis claimed that even though the government had not fulfilled its obligations, many of their number had succeeded. The real issue, they said, was the prospect of a Canadian Pacific Railway route through the region, which raised the value of the land. That was why white settlers were clamouring to have it opened for general settlement. As the Métis saw it, church, government, and French Canadians had combined to ensure the settlement's failure.

Although some became successful farmers, most of the Métis moved north, squatting on unsurveyed Crown lands where they could hunt, trap, and fish. The Métis settlements that sprang up tended to be on the fringes of Euro-Canadian settlements.

Box 14.3   Métis Population

The number of Métis in Canada is difficult to estimate. In the 1941 census, 27,790 'half-breeds' were listed for the three Prairie provinces, a figure that is almost certainly too low. The negative connotations of the term might have made people reluctant to identify as 'halfbreeds'. In 1981, when the government introduced 'Métis' as a census category, 98,300 across the country identified themselves as such. However, the Métis National Council considers 350,000 to be a more realistic estimate, and others would push the figure to 16 per cent of the total population of Canada.[66]

These were the 'road allowance people', living hand-to-mouth.[67] Alberta's Métis population at this time—the 1920s—has been variously estimated at from 12,000 to 75,000 (see Box 14.3).

The onset of the Great Depression meant that Métis who had been barely eking out an existence now faced disaster. In 1930, they organized l'Association des Métis d'Alberta et des Territoires du Nord Ouest. The first president was Joseph Dion (1888–1960), an enfranchised adopted nephew of Big Bear who was teaching on Keehewin Indian Reserve. In his book, *My Tribe the Crees*, he presented an Amerindian view of the 1885 rebellion. In 1940, the Association was reorganized and its title changed to the Métis Association of Alberta through the efforts of Malcolm Norris (1900–67) and James Brady (1908–67).[68] Taking up the cause of land settlement projects for Métis, l'Association des Métis reported that by the end of October 1933, 348 families had been resettled in northern Alberta. Still, misery was widespread. The Association's efforts caught the attention of the provincial government, which agreed to a public inquiry.

One of the first arguments Alberta Supreme Court Judge Albert Freeman Ewing (1871–1946) heard was that the Métis were nomads by nature and not prepared to change into farmers. Therefore, there was no point in setting aside land for them. Northern Métis were confirmed hunters, trappers, and fishermen, able to support themselves as long as their ecological base stayed sound. Some were even well off, although they lacked education and health services. It soon came out, however, that the situation was totally different in central and southern Alberta, where farming and ranching were widespread and oil exploration was expanding rapidly. All of these activities were threats to game animals. There, the Métis were destitute, malnourished, and had severe health problems. Up to 80 per cent were illiterate.

As the Commission saw it, the only way out of the situation was for the Métis to change their way of life to conform to the dominant society. It did not see that the government had a legal obligation to help them—that had ended with the issuance of scrip—but there were humanitarian considerations. Ewing opposed special status, as had been granted Amerindians.

Box 14.4 Defining Métis

The Ewing Commission accepted the definition of Métis given by the Métis Association of Alberta: 'anyone with any degree of Indian ancestry who lives the life ordinarily associated with the Métis'. The Association would later extend its definition to include anyone who considered himself/herself a Métis and whom the community accepted as such, a position supported by the Royal Commission on Aboriginal Peoples (RCAP).[69]

Eventually, when Alberta amended its Métis Population Betterment Act in 1940, it defined a Métis as 'a person of mixed white and Indian ancestry having not less than one-quarter Indian blood' who was not 'either an Indian or non-Treaty Indian as defined in the Indian Act'. It designed this definition to restrict the numbers of people eligible for provincial benefits. In 1996, the RCAP came out in support of the view that Métis are in the same category as Indians under the Constitution Act (BNA Act) of 1867, and stated that their national culture was 'conceived in Quebec, gestated in Ontario, and born on the western Plains'.[70]

Already, the Métis Association of Alberta had presented the provincial government with a list of 11 possible sites for Métis colonies. Taking its cue from this, the Commission proposed the establishment of farm colonies on good agricultural land, near lakes with plentiful stocks of fish and with access to timber for building. There was no provision for self-government. Later, administrative responsibility was transferred to the Métis Rehabilitation Branch of the provincial Department of Welfare. (A measure of self-government was agreed on in 1989 and confirmed the following year.)

The Commission was recommending colonies as a privilege, not as flowing from Aboriginal right. It recognized the Métis as a distinct socio-economic group that needed help but stopped short of recognizing them as a unique cultural group with a right to preserve their distinctive character (Box 14.4). Those in the colonies would not have special status, but they also would not be ordinary citizens. The commissioners hoped that as the Métis became self-supporting farmers, the colonies would naturally dissolve into individual farms, a process that might take up to 50 years to work itself out.

The report of the **Ewing Commission** also recommended that northern hunting and trapping Métis each be granted 320 acres (130 hectares) of land to be held on the same basis as if they were in the colonies. They should also be allowed free hunting and fishing permits, as well as preference in acquiring them in areas where there was danger of game depletion.

The Métis Population Betterment Act of 1938 implemented the Ewing Commission's recommendations. At that time, it was the most advanced legislation in Canada relating to the Métis. The Act was also unusual in that the government had written it in collaboration with Métis representatives. However, amendments were one-sided on the government's part, and these were not long in coming. In 1940, the definition of Métis was restricted. In 1941, another amendment gave the provincial cabinet the power to create game preserves on the settlements. By the next year, the minister could raise an annual tax. In 1943, the government established a Métis population betterment trust account. It became a fund in 1979.[71]

Initially, the province selected 12 locations in central Alberta and opened 10 of these for Métis settlement. Eventually, two of the colonies were closed so that by the end of the century, there were eight, comprising 539,446 hectares. The two closings, particularly that of Wolf Lake in 1960 over the protests of a dozen resident families, illustrated a weakness of the settlements: the Métis held their lands on leases. They did not have underlying title.

Originally, each of the settlements dealt individually with the provincial government. As this proved unsatisfactory, the Alberta Federation of Métis Settlement Associations was formed in 1975 to co-ordinate administration and also to prevent more closures.[72] Problems continued, however. A legal action started by the Métis against the government for an estimated $500 million in oil and gas revenues from settlement lands culminated in 1979 with raids organized by the provincial Department of Social Services on six of the eight settlement offices, confiscating files pertaining to the suit. The provincial ombudsman handled the dispute, deciding that some of the files were provincial property but that others should be returned to the settlements. The matter had been handled badly, and the Métis were owed an apology. The ombudsman urged that the Métis be given more control in running their own affairs and that more be hired in government service.[73]

At this time, the Alberta government moved responsibility for the Métis from Social Services to Municipal Affairs and created a committee under Grant MacEwan to review the Métis Betterment Act. MacEwan had been lieutenant-governor of the province from 1965 to 1974. His report in 1984 strongly supported self-government and urged that title to Métis lands be transferred to the settlements.[74] The province partially implemented these recommendations. In 1989, it granted title to 512,000 hectares of land, limited self-government, and a cash settlement of $310 million over 17 years.[75] In the 1990s, the provincial government passed legislation establishing a Métis land base, local government, and funding to the Métis Nation of Alberta, formerly the Métis Association of Alberta, for the development of social services and other programs.[76] Ken Noskey, Métis Settlements president, 1991–2000, observed that the accord was a major step for the Métis: 'When it comes to the justice system, we're moving from one place to another; from where justice made decisions about Métis to where justice is made by Métis.' Mineral rights, including royalties on oil and gas wells, still went to Ottawa.

The Feminine Factor

As in the larger Canadian society, women's rights among Aboriginal peoples were slow in being dealt with, although people like Mary Two-Axe Earley (1911–96) of Kahnawake and Nellie Carlson of Saddle Lake had been raising their voices since the

1950s in protest against discriminatory provisions of the Indian Act. It was particularly galling that the Act linked a woman's status to that of her husband. This meant that a white woman acquired Indian status on marrying a status Indian, but a status Indian woman lost hers when she married a non-Indian.

In 1981, as a result of a complaint by Sandra Lovelace of Tobique Reserve in New Brunswick, the United Nations Human Rights Committee found the Indian Act in breach of human rights. The Canadian government granted bands the power to de-cide whether a woman would lose status on marrying a non-Amerindian.[77] Not until the 1985 amendment to the Indian Act (Bill C-31), how-ever, did women obtain the right to keep their status on marrying non-Amerindians and to pass that status on to their children. Also reinstated were persons who had lost their status through such ac-tions as enfranchisement or having obtained a university degree.[78] In effect, Bill C-31 sounded the death knell of the official policy of assimilation.

It was estimated that about 50,000 persons would be eli-gible for reinstatement under the new legislation but that fewer than 20 per cent would apply. A year later, 42,000 had applied, far exceeding ex-pectations. By 1997, the num-ber had reached 100,000.[79] Most have not moved to re-serves. Crowded conditions have been a limiting factor, but the prevailing sentiment among Amerindians is that the legislation was imposed on them. The original injus-tice was not of their making, any more than the law aimed

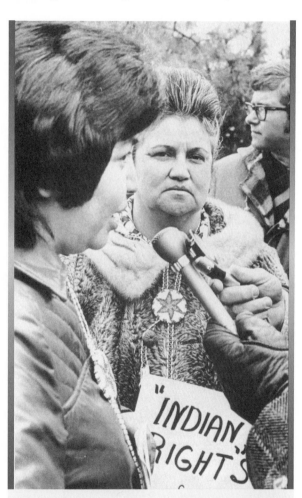

Jenny Margetts (1936–91), left, of Edmonton, and Monica Turner of Geraldton, Ontario, both of Indian Rights for Indian Women, speak to reporters during a demonstration in front of the Parliament buildings, 1973. Jenny fought a lifelong battle against sex discrimination in Indian band membership and also promoted Amerindian language and cultural courses in public schools. (CP, Canapress Photo Service, Bill Brennan)

at its correction. In view of this position, the department redefined Amerindians into two categories, those who are registered federally and those whose bands have accepted them as members. This made it possible to be a band member without being registered, or vice versa.[80]

Important Names and Terms

'Aboriginal rights'   Hawthorn Report
Assembly of First Nations   National Indian Brotherhood
Blue Quills school   Peacekeepers
'code talkers'   Saint-Paul-des Métis
compulsory enfranchisement   'Sixties Scoop'
Deskaheh   White Paper (1969)
Ewing Commission

Study Questions

1) Who is most culpable for the harms caused by the residential schools—governments, churches, individuals, or all Canadians?
2) What accounts for the Sixties Scoop?
3) What were the main recommendations of the Hawthorn Report?
4) What accounts for the political activism of the Six Nations?

Recommended Readings

Alfred, Gerald R. *Heeding the Voices of Our Ancestors: Kahnawake Mohawk Politics and the Rise of Native Nationalism*. Toronto: Oxford University Press, 1995.

Brownlie, Robin Jarvis. *A Fatherly Eye: Indian Agents, Government Power, and Aboriginal Resistance in Ontario, 1918–1939*. Toronto: Oxford University Press, 2003.

Campbell, Maria. *Halfbreed*. Toronto: McClelland & Stewart, 1973.

Coates, Kenneth S., and William R. Morrison, eds. *Land of the Midnight Sun: A History of the Yukon*. Edmonton: Hurtig, 1988.

Fournier, Suzanne, and Ernie Crey. *Stolen From Our Embrace*. Vancouver: Douglas & McIntyre, 1997.

Titley, E. Brian. *A Narrow Vision: Duncan Campbell Scott and the Administration of Indian Affairs in Canada*. Vancouver: University of British Columbia Press, 1986.

York, Geoffrey, and Loreen Pindera. *People of the Pines: The Warriors and the Legacy of Oka*. Toronto: Little, Brown and Company, 1991.

15 Development Heads North

As it happened in the southwestern regions of Canada, so it happened in the Northwest. Canadian jurisdiction expanded through the fur trade, followed by missionaries and, later, the police. After it joined with the North West Company, the Hudson's Bay Company founded posts all over the Subarctic northwest of British North America. This expansion continued after the Company's surrender of Rupert's Land to Britain in 1869 and its transfer to Canada in 1870. However, by 1893, the Company had closed its last post in the Yukon, in the face of competition from Americans (following their purchase of Alaska) and also from whalers.[1]

At first, the appearance of whites, mainly fur traders and missionaries, did not radically alter subsistence patterns, although changes did occur with the emphasis on fur hunting in the boreal forest and whaling in the Arctic, and the availability of trade goods. Metal goods, such as knives, kettles, and axes, soon proved useful, as did nets, twine, and, of course, guns. Even as they traded for these items, however, Amerindians retained a large degree of self-sufficiency. But with time, industrialization slowly invaded the North, and the way of life changed.

Southerners Come to the North to Stay

In the second half of the nineteenth century, transportation was being revolutionized as missionaries and gold-seekers opened new routes to the North. Earlier attempts at discovering passage by sea across the North had largely failed (Box 15.1). In the south, the railway reached Calgary in early 1883 and Edmonton in 1891. Trips that had once taken weeks and months or even years, now took days. Trappers and prospectors were quick to take advantage of the new situation. By 1894, non-Amerindian trappers were established at Fort Resolution, north of the sixtieth parallel. According to a Fort Chipewyan elder, there were:

Time Line

1880	Jurisdiction of High Arctic transferred to Canada by Britain.	1920	Dogribs refuse Treaty Eight payments because of attempts in recent legislation to restrict their hunting and fishing rights.
1883	Railway reaches Calgary.		
1891	Railway reaches Edmonton.		
1892	Sir Wilfred Grenfell begins medical missionary work on Labrador coast.	1921	Treaty Eleven, covering much of Northwest Territories.
1893	HBC closes last Yukon post.	1924	Two Inuit found guilty and hanged on Herschel Island for 1921 murder of police officer, five others.
1895	NWMP establish first permanent post in Far North, in Yukon.		
1898	Yukon becomes separate territory—just in time for Klondike gold rush.		Indian Act amended to include Inuit (later to be excluded by 1951 revisions).
1899	Treaty Eight, covering northern Alberta, northwest Saskatchewan, northeast BC, and parts of Yukon and NWT, is signed as a result of the Klondike gold rush.	1930s	Reindeer herd introduced in western Arctic.
		1934	Relocations of Inuit to more suitable communities and hunting and fishing grounds begun in Arctic; they would fail.
1900s	Collapse of Arctic whaling industry.	1939	Supreme Court rules that all Inuit are a federal responsibility.
1902	Entire band of Sadlermiut, perhaps the last remnant of earlier Dorset culture, perishes on Southampton Island.	1945	Alaska Highway is completed, further opening Northwest to white settlement.
		1953	Forced relocation of Inuit from Arctic Quebec and northern Baffin Island to Ellesmere Island in High Arctic.
1905–6	Treaty Nine (James Bay Treaty), covering northern Ontario, and Treaty Ten in northern Saskatchewan, which clears the way for settlement with creation of province of Saskatchewan.	1974	First NWT reserve, at Hay River.
		1999	Nunavut, a new territory hived off from NWT in eastern Arctic, is officially founded on 1 April.

white trappers all over the place, and we were on very friendly terms with them. I went trapping with them many times. . . . I would guide them and show them how to trap. They were very thankful for that as they took their pelts home.[2]

Some non-Amerindian trappers, however, started using poison. This was anathema to Amerindians.[3] Their reaction was such that the government banned the practice, but enforcement was difficult, to say the least. Amerindian resentment mounted as northern resources soon showed the effects of increased exploitation.[4] In addition, trade added the uncertainties of the marketplace, and subsistence in the North, never easy, began to become problematic. The winters of 1887–8 and 1888–9 saw so many people die of starvation that Ottawa sent relief through the HBC and the missions. This situation would be repeated with increasing frequency. It was 1938 before the Northwest Territories Council restricted trapping licences to territory residents.

At another level, the government had been supporting mission schools—at least in principle—since 1873, although few schools qualified under their regulations, and even then it was years before federal money actually arrived.[5] This association between government and missionaries would last until the 1940s. The government also provided some medical care. Ottawa's official position, however, was that it had no responsibility towards people who had not signed treaty, and it saw no reason for one in those distant regions.

When the North-West Mounted Police arrived in the Yukon in 1895 to establish their first permanent post in the Far North (but south of the Arctic Circle), their instructions were 'not to give encouragement to the idea they [the Amerindians] will be received into treaty, and taken under the care of the government'.[6] Official belief that Amerindians were waiting for the chance to live off government handouts did not take into account the deep satisfaction of living off the land, despite its difficulties.[7] The police would enforce the law of the dominant society but also perform such governmental tasks as recording vital statistics, distributing mail, and collecting customs duties.

Box 15.1   The Northwest Passage

For centuries the British searched for a passage across the top of North America that would provide a shortcut to the riches of the Far East. In fact, these failed explorations, dating back to Martin Frobisher in 1576 (who did return to England with an Inuk captive), led to the European naming and mapping of Canada's Far North. The most famous attempt was the final expedition of Sir John Franklin (1786–1847) of 1845–8, which likely became ice-bound, with all of the men starving or freezing to death or dying of scurvy. In turn, the disappearance of Franklin and his men led to many expeditions in the following years that, though failing to discover either Franklin or the **Northwest Passage**, did continue to add to the British mapping of the Arctic. The first explorer to navigate the Northwest Passage successfully was the Norwegian Roald Amundsen in 1903–6 in a tiny ship, the *Gjoa*. An RCMP icebreaker, *St Roch,* completed a west-to-east passage in 1940–2 and in 1944 completed an east-to-west passage in a single summer. But the commercial attraction of finding the Northwest Passage had died with Franklin.

Two Views of Inuit/White Contacts

The police came to the North in response to pleas from missionaries, who were deeply disturbed by the free flow of liquor. They agreed that liquor was a problem. Otherwise, they thought the missionaries were more concerned about the welfare of Aboriginal peoples than of non-Aboriginals.[8] Charles Constantine of the NWMP (in the Yukon as inspector, 1894–7; as superintendent, 1897–1902) could not see that Inuit society was disintegrating, as the missionaries claimed.[9]

In the western Arctic, more than 1,000 whalers were wintering at Herschel Island, occupying their off-season in living and trading with the 500 Inuvialuit, as the Inuit of the region were called. When gathered for trading, some camped near the whalers, others on islands scattered along the coast. At first, this was highly profitable for both sides, each within the terms of its own culture. For example, 100 primers (a device to detonate the main charge of a gun) that cost 10 cents in New York traded in the Arctic for one muskox skin that sold in the south for $50. When accused of overpricing their goods, traders pointed to their heavy costs.[10] Even so, the trade built fortunes never before seen in the North. The Inuit obtained otherwise unavailable (or very rare) items that made their lives easier. They eagerly sought the new goods, not foreseeing, any

An Inuit settlement, Prince Albert Sound, Victoria Island, NWT. It consists of a large snowhouse with four domes and two entrances. *(Archdeacon Webster, HBC Library, Winnipeg, A–33–4)*

An Inuk seal hunter demonstrates the use of a harpoon. *(Department of Northern Affairs and Natural Resources, 59676)*

more than did the non-Aboriginals, that the use of these goods would eventually help to disrupt both the ecological equilibrium and their social organization.[11]

The growing likelihood of violence and open disregard for authority finally persuaded Canada to act. It organized the Yukon, stretching from the Subarctic into the Arctic, into a district in 1895; three years later, it became a separate territory, under a commissioner named by the federal Minister of Mines and Resources and an appointed council of up to six members.[12] In the western Arctic, the white population numbered about 500, drawn there by furs and minerals. Aboriginal people numbered about 2,600. Already, there had been a severe decline in the Amerindian population, estimated to have been about 8,000 at the beginning of the nineteenth century.

Police protests to the contrary, the missionaries' fears for the Natives were realized. Disease and the disruption of lifestyle took their toll, and by 1920 there were no more of the original Inuvialuit in the Yukon.[13] Some survived around Tuktoyaktuk in the NWT, but most modern Inuvialuit moved in from Alaska. Local disappearances occurred in other areas as well, particularly where white whalers were active. For example, in 1902 an entire band of 68 Sadlermiut (believed by some to be the last of the Dorset people)[14] died of starvation and disease on Southampton Island.[15] To make matters worse, the whaling industry collapsed early in the twentieth century, triggered by a change in women's fashions and the increased use of petroleum products instead

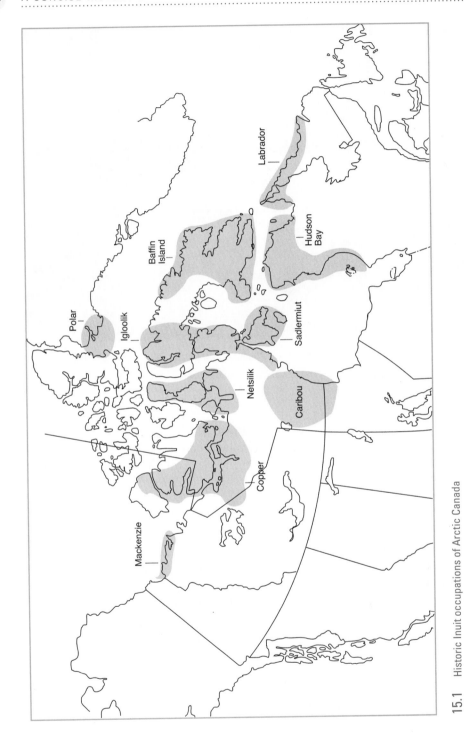

15.1   Historic Inuit occupations of Arctic Canada

Source: Adapted, with the permission of the Canadian Museum of Civilization, from Robert McGhee, *Canadian Arctic Prehistory* (Ottawa: Canadian Museum of Civilization, 1990).

of whale oil. What saved the Inuit from total economic disaster was a new fashion, white fox skins.

Northerners Seek Treaty

Amerindians in the North had been agitating for a treaty since the 1870s despite their fear of the restrictions it could impose and their distrust of non-Amerindians. As the Cree headman Moostoos (c. 1850–1918, 'The Buffalo') put it during Treaty Eight negotiations at Lesser Slave Lake, 'Our country is getting broken up. I see the White man coming in, and I want to be friends. I see what he does, but it is best that we should be friends.'[16] Ottawa, however, held fast to its view that a treaty was unnecessary. It saw little prospect of either industrial development or significant white settlement north of the sixtieth parallel.[17]

As had happened at other times and places, Aboriginal people were not taking kindly to having their trading networks invaded. The Tlingit, for example, controlled the main routes between the coast and the interior, the Chilkoot, Chilkat, and Taku passes. They had long operated a trading monopoly in the region.[18] That was not a position they could maintain, however, when the 1896 strike at Rabbit Creek, later known as Bonanza Creek, set off the **Klondike gold rush**. Ironically, of the three persons who made the strike, two were Tagish—Skookum Jim and Dawson (Tagish) Charlie—as was Kate, the wife of the third, George Carmack.[19] Whether they wanted it or not, the old way was gone forever as one of the most rapid migrations and economic expansions in history began.[20]

The first thing Canada did was reassert its sovereignty. In the Yukon, it reinforced the police force to nearly 300 men. The Amerindians, for their part, were becoming increasingly uneasy. They felt it was unjust 'that people who are not owners of the country are allowed to rob them of their living.'[21] Miners rafted logs down the river, destroying Amerindian fishing weirs and crowding Amerindian villages out.[22] The influx of miners who were only too willing to take the law into their own hands added to the resentment already felt against non-Amerindian trappers. The situation threatened to go out of control, and in 1897 the police set up patrols.[23]

On the whole, Amerindians saw the police presence as positive, except when the NWMP began in 1896 to enforce blanket legislation against hunting wood buffalo. Amerindians depended on wood bison for food. Apparently, this was the only such regulation applied to Amerindians at that time, but this turnabout on the part of the government reinforced Amerindian doubts as to its good faith. Such regulation without regard for local conditions could result in severe economic hardship, especially when game depletion reduced options.[24]

Treaty Eight (1899)

'The Trail of '98' saw the influx of gold-seekers reach serious proportions. By the end of 1898, almost 800 prospectors, most of them Americans, were wintering on the banks of the Mackenzie River.[25] Contemptuous of Amerindians, they shot their horses and dogs, interfered with traplines, and exploited fish and game resources at will. The police were too few and the area too large for them to cope with the situation.[26] In June 1898, several hundred alarmed Amerindians gathered at Fort St John in northeastern British Columbia and announced they would no longer let anyone, even police, pass through their territory until a treaty was signed. This time, Ottawa agreed.

It was not enough, however, for Amerindians to ask for treaty to be included, even if they were suffering hardship.[27] The initial lack of militancy on the part of most of the Yukon Amerindians in defence of their rights seemed to encourage the government to exclude most of their territory from the negotiations. The Oblate missionary turned historian, René Fumoleau, thought it likely that 'Ottawa was afraid that the Amerindians would put too high a price on their rich land.'[28]

The treaty commissioners, headed by David Laird, were soon impressed with the 'keenness of intellect' and 'the practical sense' of the northerners in pressing their claims. 'They all wanted as liberal, if not more liberal terms, than were granted to the Indians on the Plains.'[29] When commissioners tried to impose southern norms, however, the northerners reacted sharply. Moostoos observed that 'a Plains Indian turned loose in the bush would get lost and starve to death.'[30] The northerners, worried about the increasing frequency of famine, were united in wanting help during such periods. They urged that the government care for the aged and needy. They also asked for schools but wanted no interference in their religious beliefs. By this time, most of the Aboriginal people concerned were Roman Catholics.

By far the most important point the commissioners had to deal with was the Amerindians' fear that hunting and fishing rights—the commissioners called them 'privileges'—would be curtailed, as was already happening in the case of the wood buffalo. This was vital for a people living in a land where agriculture, or even ranching, was not generally viable. Provision of ammunition and twine for making nets relieved Amerindian worries to some extent. The matter of selecting reserved land was left for the future.[31] As with earlier negotiations, the Amerindians, not the government, introduced most of the forward-looking parts of the treaty terms.

After two days of negotiations at Lesser Slave Lake, the treaty was signed. Father Lacombe, repeating his earlier success with the Blackfoot, was a major influence in convincing the Amerindians of the government's good intentions and commitment to justice.[32] The government considered that the treaty not only extinguished Amerindian title, it also provided that Amerindian **usufructuary right** would be 'subject to such regulation as may from time to time be made by the Government, and excepting such tracts as may be required for settlement, mining, lumbering, trading, or other purposes'.

The Aboriginal peoples had quite another view. They all held that the negotiators had guaranteed their rights to hunt, fish, and trap without restriction.[33] An elder later recalled:

Moose is our main source of livelihood on this earth. Not like the white man, the King; he lived mainly on bread, he said. But the Indian lived on fish, ducks, anything. The King asked the Indian what he wanted for a livelihood. The Indian chose hunting and fishing not to be limited. As long as he lived.[34]

The Amerindians did not agree, however, as to what they had given up in return for the recognition of this right. In fact, the topic of landownership does not seem to have been clearly brought up during negotiations. In the eyes of one Amerindian, 'the white man never bought the land. If he had bought it, there would have been very large sums of money involved.'[35]

There were other points of disagreement as well. The Amerindians believe they had been assured of health care and social services, but these items do not appear in the written document. Furthermore, provisions that were included, such as aid to start farming where feasible, were not always honoured, at least not in the ways the Amerindians thought they should be. To the Amerindians, Treaty Eight was essentially a peace and friendship treaty. In 1913–15, when the government moved to survey the Treaty Eight area, and particularly the individual allotments, the Amerindians reacted with mistrust and fear, seeing this as a threat to their liberty of movement. At Fort Resolution in 1920, the Dogrib refused to accept their treaty payments as they had become unhappy about attempts to restrict hunting and fishing. They won recognition of their special position in a signed agreement and accepted the treaty payments. Then, the document disappeared.[36]

Similar problems arose at Fort Rae (the largest Amerindian settlement in the Northwest Territories) in 1928 and again at Fort Resolution in 1937. The courts later ruled that federal law prevails over treaty rights, but that of the provinces or territories does not.

In the Northwest Territories, the first reserve was created at Hay River in 1974. In British Columbia, one was established under Treaty Eight at Fort Nelson in 1961, although the province had been laying them out since the 1850s. In 1979, Ottawa set aside 18,000 acres (7,284 hectares) in Wood Buffalo National Park for the Fort Chipewyan Cree, following a breakdown of negotiations with Alberta. The Cree had requested 90,000 acres (36,422 hectares). The same band signed in 1986, when it received 12,280 acres (4,970 hectares) of reserve land with full mineral rights as well as hunting, fishing, and trapping rights, and $26.6 million in cash. The Métis of the region could either enter treaty at the time of signing or take scrip. In the latter case, they received either 240 acres (97 hectares) of land or $240 in cash.

Treaties Nine, Ten (1905–6), and Eleven (1921)

The prospect of mining development and the need to clear railway right-of-way in northern Ontario finally influenced Ottawa to agree to Amerindian demands for a treaty, which had begun as far back as 1884.[37] Treaty Nine (James Bay Treaty) involved 130,000 square miles (336,300 square kilometres). Adhesions in 1929–30 covered territories included in Ontario when the province's final boundary was established in 1912. Treaty Ten, in northern Saskatchewan, was negotiated to clear land title for the province, created the year before, in 1905.

In the Northwest Territories, the years following the signing of Treaty Eight saw conditions go from bad to worse, particularly in the region north of Great Slave Lake and along the Mackenzie River. Even though it was outside the Treaty Eight area, Indian Affairs opened an agency at Fort Simpson in 1911 'to distribute relief and to carry out experiments in farming'. The agent arrived that summer with two horses, four oxen, and 10 tons of equipment and supplies. Local Amerindians, unforewarned, refused to shake hands with him; 'they thought he had come to take their country away from them.' Despite being so far north, the experiment went reasonably well, and the suspicions of the Amerindians were allayed. Their lifestyle remained unchanged, adapted as it was to northern conditions.[38]

In 1908, the HBC established its first permanent post north of the Arctic Circle. Between 1910 and 1920, spurred by the growing presence of independent traders, it opened 14 more.[39] The years 1915–20, a period of international tension, war, and revolution, saw the fur market peaking in value at the same time as the use of currency replaced the old barter system. Amerindians and Inuit, having no experience with this new form of buying and selling, were easily cheated. As well, the post–World War I influenza epidemic hit the North hard, particularly the Inuit. In 1920, the fur market crashed. It was during this period that air travel reached the North.[40]

An Indian encampment on the occasion of Treaty Nine payments in northern Ontario, 1929. Meat is placed high up on scaffolding to protect it from dogs. *(DIAND collection, Library and Archives Canada, C 68950)*

Chief Samson Beardy (standing) and Commissioners Walter C. Cain and Herbert N. Awrey (seated at table) during negotiation of Treaty Nine payments, northern Ontario, 1929. *(Library and Archives Canada, PA 94969)*

As with Treaty Eight, Amerindians agreed to sign Treaty Eleven only after the government and Bishop Gabriel Breynat (1867–1954) assured them of complete freedom to hunt, trap, and fish. For the Dene, the treaty was one of peace and friendship. The negotiators assured them this was their land. 'You can do whatever you want', they told the Amerindians; 'we are not going to stop you.' When the government failed to live up to its word, a disenchanted Breynat publicly campaigned against the way the northern Amerindians were being treated, a campaign that Father Fumoleau later carried on.[41] In 1973 the Dene filed a caveat in Alberta claiming Treaties Eight and Eleven were fraudulent. With the aid of retroactive legislation, the government later denied that they had had the right to file the caveat.

By now, the isolation that had protected the North for so long was broken. The final blow came during World War II with the construction of the Alaska Highway, completed in 1945. Yukon Amerindians helped to lay out its route. In so doing, they opened up their territories to non-Amerindian settlement.[42] By the 1950s, Amerindians were no longer free to hunt and fish as they pleased. In some regions, they had to register their traplines.[43]

Changing Views on Jurisdiction

Although whites had been present in the eastern Arctic, off and on, since the eleventh century, and with increasing frequency since the seventeenth, the first permanent official presence occurred in the western Arctic when Canada sent the NWMP in 1903 to establish posts at Herschel Island and Fort McPherson. The Eastern Arctic Patrol was not instituted on a regular basis until 1922, although there had been occasional government voyages since the late nineteenth century. For most Inuit, first experiences with the new order were through the police, who represented the government until the mid-1950s, when the Department of Northern Affairs and Natural Resources took over.

In the Arctic, problems of first contact were worked out in terms of the Criminal Code rather than of land, as had occurred to the south. The Canadian officers were under orders not to meddle with Native customs as long as they were 'consistent with the general law'. Canada also tempered its justice with cultural considerations when two Oblate missionaries were killed in 1913 near Bloody Falls on the Coppermine River. The two Inuit involved, Uluksuk and Sinnisiak, believed they were acting in self-defence when the priests made threatening gestures during an altercation. After being found innocent in the first trial, a judge sentenced both to be hanged, but this was commuted to life imprisonment. The two men were released after two years and became guides and special helpers to the police.[44]

However, when a police officer fell victim in 1921, along with another non-Native and four Inuit, the government felt that it had to set an example. A trial was held at Herschel Island, and the two Inuit found guilty, one of them about 16 years old, were hanged in 1924. This was the first hanging in the Arctic.[45] It dramatically illustrated the whites' emphasis on the offence and punishing the offender. In the Inuit way, the focus was to preserve the equilibrium of the community.[46] Insisting that the Inuit abide by Canadian law led to what was widely recognized as social injustice; by 1945, some people believed that the Criminal Code should not apply to the Inuit.

With respect to administration, official reaction was to lump Inuit with Amerindians. The first mention of Inuit in Canadian legislation occurred in 1924, when the Indian Act was amended to include them. This drew the comment from Arthur Meighen, who was in between his two terms as Prime Minister (1920–1 and 1926):

> I should not like to see the same policy precisely applied to the Eskimos as we have applied to the Indian. . . . After seventy-five years of tutelage and nursing . . . [the Amerindians] are still helpless on our hands.[47]

Perhaps it was due to such sentiments that the government did not apply the Act to Inuit when the Arctic came under Canada's flag. The Inuit came under Canadian jurisdiction as ordinary citizens, because the government had signed no treaties with them. However, regarding liquor, the police treated the Inuit the same way they did the Amerindians, arguing that they were 'morally', if not legally, the wards of Indian Affairs.[48] In 1927, Inuit affairs were transferred to the Northwest Territories, but the people still starved as game diminished. Quebec took Ottawa to court to get it to accept responsibility for the Inuit within its provincial borders. Historically and politically, Inuit had been habitually classed as Amerindian, as Quebec proved in court. Its *coup de grâce* was to produce official correspondence, dated in 1879, in which

Inuit were referred to as 'Indians'.[49] In 1939, the Supreme Court of Canada ruled that, for administrative purposes, the Inuit were Amerindians and therefore a federal responsibility.

In 1950, the year the Inuit got the vote, an Order-in-Council vested authority for the Inuit in the Minister of Resources and Development. Administration for the Inuit was kept separate from that for Amerindians. For example, there is no national registry for Inuit as there is for Amerindians, and the Inuit were specifically excluded from the Indian Act when it was revised in 1951. In other words, the status of Inuit as ordinary citizens has never changed.

Ironically, Quebec experienced a change of attitude in 1960 and began actively claiming jurisdiction over the Inuit within its borders, a process that it formalized with the establishment of a provincial ministry, Direction générale du Nouveau Québec, in 1962.[50] At one point, federal and provincial authorities were building rival schools.[51] In the meantime, officials remained convinced that Aboriginal people must be encouraged to maintain their traditional way of life, as otherwise they would degenerate.[52] In 1923, two huge game preserves were established for exclusive Aboriginal use, one in the Back and Thelon river basins, the other on Victoria and Banks islands. The latter became the Arctic Islands Game Preserve in 1926, when it was extended it to cover all Arctic islands.[53] At about this time, too, reindeer were introduced to the Canadian Arctic (Box 15.2).

New Strategic Significance

A turning point in official evaluation of the Arctic took place during and after World War II, when its strategic importance in world geopolitics became glaringly evident. The crucial roles of its weather stations and the Distant Early Warning radar line—the **DEW line**—to military operations caused authorities to take another look at the land and its people. Not that there was an immediate change in attitude, however. When

Box 15.2   Reindeer to the Delta

A 1922 Royal Commission recommended that reindeer herds be established in the Canadian Arctic. Following a feasibility study, the federal government bought an Alaskan herd of about 3,000 animals in 1929.[54] The drive was entrusted to Lapp herders under the direction of Andrew Bahr. The press eagerly followed the epic story of their progress over 3,200 kilometres (2,000 miles) across 'the roof of the world'. Finally, in 1935, 2,370 animals (fewer than 700 of which were among those that had left Nome, Alaska, five years earlier) arrived at Kittigazuit in the eastern Mackenzie Delta. There, the government managed the herd for 40 years until it was sold to private interests in 1974. The herd flourished, and two other herds of about 800 animals each were later started further east.[55]

the government introduced family allowances and old age pensions, for instance, it hesitated to include northern Natives. In the end, it did not send them cheques. Instead, it arranged credit at HBC posts for designated food supplies.[56] The requirement that the children attend school led the government to construct the necessary buildings in the 1940s, ending the old reliance on missions.

The destruction of the natural subsistence base in the Far North in the twentieth century proceeded faster than replacements, although there were successes, such as the programs to rehabilitate beaver and muskrat in trapped-out areas.[57] The collapse of the white fox market, 1948–50, when the rest of Canada was experiencing an economic boom, highlighted once again the widespread and complex changes sweeping the Far North. The difficulties of the trapping industry increased even more with the campaign of the anti-fur lobby. At the beginning of the twenty-first century, it was again in a severe depression.

Throughout this period, the policy of 'encouraging' Inuit to relocate to areas selected by the government was in full force.[58] At first the relocations were co-ordinated with the fur trade. Indian Affairs informed the HBC in 1934 that if it wished to continue its operation in the North, it must assume responsibility for Native welfare without expense to the department.[59] That failures resulted is hardly surprising.

The considerations that guided the selections for **relocation** did not always match the conditions the Inuit needed for survival. This was illustrated by a series of attempts that began in 1934, when the government transported 22 Inuit from Cape Dorset, 18 from Pond Inlet, and 12 from Pangnirtung to Dundas Harbour. What appeared to officials to be a suitable location, however, turned out to have ice conditions in winter that impeded both hunting and dog-team travel needed to maintain traplines. After two years, the Inuit had to be evacuated. Some went back to their home bases, but others tried life in still another location. In the succeeding years, the government transported Inuit to one site after another (Croker Bay, Arctic Bay, Fort Ross, Spence Bay), each one of which proved to be unsuitable for the hunting and trapping way of life that officials were convinced must be preserved.[60]

This shifting of the Inuit population reached its peak from 1958 to 1962 but continued at least to the end of the 1970s.[61] Game continued to diminish, and Inuit continued to die of starvation and disease as they were shuttled back and forth. Harassed officials, on receiving reports that there were plenty of fish in the lakes, issued gill nets to a group near Baker Lake, either ignorant of or disregarding a taboo of the Inuit of the region against eating fish harvested by drowning. The Inuit had no objections to fish caught by methods that did not involve drowning, however.

By the mid-1950s and early 1960s, the Inuit had the highest rate of tuberculosis in the world, an ironic situation at a time when the government was establishing an elaborate health-care system in the Arctic.[62] Those sent 'outside' for treatment often vanished without a trace as far as their families and relatives were concerned.

Box 15.3   An Official's View of Northern Resettlement

Gordon Robertson, deputy minister of resources and development and commissioner for the Northwest Territories, reported an impression of the resettlement programs strikingly different from that expressed by the Inuit when he visited Resolute Bay in 1960. On a second visit, in 1976, he was secretary to the cabinet for federal-provincial relations. In his published *Memoirs of a Very Civil Servant*, he said he never heard a word of complaint. 'Nor did I ever, from 1953 to 1963, receive any request by any Inuit or family to move back to their former home. I did receive requests from some of the people of Resolute and Grise Fiord to have friends from Inukjuak come to join them because the hunting at the new settlements was so much better than on the "hungry coast".'[63]

Sometimes, in the case of children, southern families adopted them without informing their parents.[64]

Still convinced of the need to relocate, the government considered, and rejected, a plan to move the Inuit to the south. The North needed its people for a new reason: to support Canada's claims to sovereignty. Spurred by this imperative of international politics, the government began in 1953 to move Inuit from Inukjuak (Port Harrison) in Arctic Quebec to Ellesmere Island in the High Arctic, where game resources were untouched. As well, it brought Inuit in from Pond Inlet, northern Baffin Island. In all, nearly 90 Inuit were relocated to Grise Fiord and Resolute Bay in a forced move to which they did not become reconciled (see Box 15.3). Not only that, but the game resources available were not what the new arrivals were used to. In one historian's view, concern about its sovereignty in the Arctic had been Canada's main motivation for the resettlement policy, which she termed a 'misadventure'. The Inuit put it more strongly. As they see it, they have been the subjects of a social and political experiment.[65]

Nunavut ('Our Land') Is Born

The creation of the territory of Nunavut out of the Northwest Territories on 1 April 1999 was a dramatic moment for the country. Comprising more than 2.2 million square kilometres, better than a fifth of Canada's entire surface, Nunavut is the largest land-claim settlement in the country's history. The agreement involved the surrender of Aboriginal title on the part of the Inuit (who comprise about 85 per cent of a total Nunavut population of 29,357, as of October 2003) but gave them ownership in fee simple of 350,000 square kilometres, an area half the size of Saskatchewan,[66]

15.2   Nunavut, Canada's new territory

Source: Adapted from *The Globe and Mail*, Toronto, 4 May 1996.

the largest private landholding in North America. Nunavut's official languages are English, French, and Inuktitut, and its flag depicts on a white ground a red inukshuk with a blue North Star. The agreement also included a cash settlement of $1.17 billion over 14 years.

The idea for the creation of a northern jurisdiction administered in co-operation with the Inuit developed after World War II and came under active consideration beginning in 1978 as a result of a proposal by Inuit Tapirisat, a national organization representing the four regions of Nunatsiavut (Labrador), Nunavik (northern Quebec), Nunavut, and Inuvialuit (NWT).[67] The concept received a major boost in 1985 when the Royal Commission on the Economic Union and Development Prospects for Canada (the Macdonald Commission) supported it on the grounds that regional governments

Inuit elder Ekalool Juralak lights a traditional 'qulluliq' at the dedication of the Nunavut Legislature in Iqaluit on the day before Nunavut officially became a territory. *(CP PHOTO/ Kevin Frayer)*

adapted to particular circumstances, cultural and otherwise, would better meet the needs of the Canadian North.

That same year, 1985, the project received unexpected outside support when the United States sent the *Polar Sea* through the Northwest Passage without permission from Canada. This was the second such infringement on the part of the Americans (the first occurred in 1971), who wanted those waters to be declared international. Since the Inuit have been in the region for more than 1,000 years, the creation of a self-governing territory was seen as the best possible way of strengthening Canada's claim to Arctic sovereignty. The Northwest Territories endorsed the idea by a margin of 54 to 46 per cent in a plebiscite held in 1992, which led to an accord being signed that same year for the creation of the new territory.[68]

The project took final shape in 1993 with the **Nunavut Land Claim Settlement** and, finally, with the federal Nunavut Act. The territory was given a new style of 'public government', more or less on the elective provincial model but with greater decentralization.[69] In one major aspect, it differs from the party-oriented governments to the south in that in some areas it follows the Inuit practice of reaching decisions by consensus. Native traditions have also influenced the justice system, worked out in co-operation with the Royal Canadian Mounted Police.[70]

Challenges include the training of lawyers and administrators, and housing shortages compounded by rising costs, particularly of fuel and transportation.[71] At the turn of the century, widespread poverty and high unemployment showed no signs of easing, resulting in labour unrest, and the youth suicide rate was the highest in the world. Still, for Inuit elder Nancy Karetak-Lindell, the first elected MP for Nunavut, the creation of the territory has given her people back their lives.[72]

Important Names and Terms

Alaska Highway
DEW line
Klondike gold rush
Northwest Passage

Nunavut Land Claim Settlement
relocation
usufructuary right

Study Questions

1) How did life change in the Arctic after the Klondike gold rush?
2) How did the northern economy adapt to the collapse of the whaling industry?
3) Why did the government become so interested in relocating people across the Arctic?
4) Why was Nunavut created?

Recommended Readings

Fumoleau, René. *As Long As This Land Shall Last*. Toronto: McClelland & Stewart, 1973.

North, Dick. *The Lost Patrol*. Vancouver: Raincoast Books, 1995 [1978].

Pitseolak, Peter, and Dorothy Harley Eber. *People from Our Side*, trans. Ann Hanson. Montreal and Kingston: McGill-Queen's University Press, 1993.

Tester, Frank James, and Peter Kulchyski. *Tammarniit (Mistakes)*. Vancouver: University of British Columbia Press, 1994.

Zaslow, Morris. *The Northward Expansion of Canada, 1914–1967*. Toronto: McClelland & Stewart, 1988.

16 Canadian Courts and Aboriginal Rights

Canada's first Aboriginal rights court case gave rise to two statements that set legal precedents in Canada. One concerned Aboriginal rights, the other, provincial rights. At the time, provincial rights aroused the greater passion. Indeed, Aboriginal rights were considered almost incidental, although they were at the very heart of the dispute.

The case, *St Catherine's Milling v. The Queen,* arose from the long-standing dispute between Ontario and the federal government over the location of the province's northwestern boundary.[1] The Amerindians whose lands were concerned were neither consulted nor brought to the witness stand in the ensuing court action. In 1884, the Privy Council in London decided in favour of Ontario. The government was not so easily defeated, however. It delayed enacting the enabling legislation to put the decision into effect. Ontario responded by filing a legal suit in the High Court of Ontario against the federally licensed St Catherine's Milling and Lumber Company for illegal logging on provincial lands.

The argument boiled down to this: exactly what had the Dominion obtained from the Amerindians in Treaty Three? The lumber company, and hence Ottawa, argued that before the Crown acquired land title—through purchase rather than conquest—Amerindians had been owners of the land but subject to the restriction that they could sell only to the Canadian government. Neither provinces nor individuals had the right to buy lands from Amerindians. The Proclamation of 1763 specifically referred to 'lands reserved for Indians'. Because of the wording of the Proclamation, treaties were an essential prerequisite for the expansion of colonial settlement in British North America, and only the federal authority could engage in that activity.

Oliver Mowat (1820–1903), Premier of Ontario, appeared for the province. He was blunt: 'We say there is no Indian title in law or in equity. The claim of the Indians is simply moral and no more.' Property, so the argument went, was just something created by law. Since Amerindians had no rules or regulations that could be considered laws, they had no title to their ancestral territories that the Crown could recognize. There could be no such thing as Indian title independent of the Crown's law. During

Time Line

1717	Louis XV grants seigneury at Oka (Kanesatake) to Seminary of St Sulpice as Amerindian mission.
1721	Nearly 900 Indians move to area of Sulpician mission.
1781	Mohawk at Kanesatake go to court to prove proprietorship of land held by Sulpicians but lose their case.
1841	British confirm seminary's title at Oka.
1868	Iroquois and Algonquins, citing Oka seminary's tyranny and oppression, unsuccessfully petition Ottawa for clear title to the land and their village.
1875	Sulpicians obtain court order to dismantle Methodist church at Oka.
1877	Iroquois burn the Catholic church at Oka.
1885–9	*St Catherine's Milling v. The Queen*: Judicial Committee of the Privy Council, in complex jurisdictional case between Ontario and Ottawa, upholds validity of Proclamation of 1763 but claims that British, by setting foot in North America, gained title to all Indian lands.
1912	Privy Council upholds Oka seminary title in ongoing land dispute.
1936	Sulpicians sell most of Oka land to Belgian real estate company, which begins to sell parcels of land.
1961	Kanesatake Mohawks' request that land be formally declared a reserve gets no response.
1969–77	Indian Claims Commission headed by Dr Lloyd Barber.
1970	Federal Fisheries Act restricts Aboriginal right.
1973	Supreme Court split decision on Nisga'a land-claim case (*Calder*) opens way for greater recognition of Aboriginal rights, although Nisga'a technically lose in court.
1974	Gull Bay band of Ojibwa organizes reserve police force.
1975	Comprehensive claim by Kanesatake residents for Aboriginal title rejected by Ottawa.
1983	Mi'kmaq Donald Marshall Jr exonerated after spending 11 years in jail for murder he did not commit.
1985	Supreme Court rules in *Simon v. the Queen* that only federal legislation can restrict Aboriginal hunting and fishing rights.
1986	Specific claim to land title at Kanesatake rejected.
1990	A plan by the town of Oka to sell some of the disputed land at Kanesatake leads to a 78-day standoff. A Quebec police officer is killed, and, eventually, more than 40 Mohawk are arrested. Two Warriors received jail terms; all others were acquitted or had charges dropped.
1991	Indian Claims Commission reinstituted.
1999	Supreme Court rules in favour of Mi'kmaq Donald Marshall Jr (the same man who had been wrongfully convicted of murder many years earlier) in case involving Aboriginal right to fish out of season.
2000	Nisga'a Final Agreement Act ratified by federal Parliament. Mi'kmaq lobster fishermen at Burnt Church, NB, emboldened by *Marshall* decision, set their own regulations for lobster fishery and become embroiled in violent confrontations with white lobstermen and Department of Fisheries and Oceans officials. Land governance deal signed by Mohawk of Kanesatake and federal government on 21 December. Chippewa claim for 1,030 hectares of land in Sarnia, Ont., rejected by Ontario Court of Appeal.

Box 16.1   Amerindian 'Ownership' of Land

The pressure of non-Native claims to their territories has led Amerindians to develop trad-itional concepts in terms understandable to Euro-Canadians. Amerindian cyclical and hol-istic ways of viewing the world translate into land being held as common property by the tribal nation as a whole. Tribal members have an undivided interest in the land. Everyone, as a member of the group, has a right to the whole. Furthermore, rights to the use of land belong not only to the living but also to those who have gone before as well as to those who will come. Neither do they belong exclusively to humans, but to other living things as well—animals, plants, and sometimes (under special circumstances) even rocks.

When Amerindians signed treaties, they could not give up absolute ownership of the land, because they never claimed it for themselves. The Crown, to claim absolute title, would have to obtain surrenders from past generations as well as those of the future. As far as Amerindians are concerned, when they signed treaties, they were not alienating their lands but sharing them.[2] They were astonished at the idea that their hunting and fish-ing rights originated with the Proclamation of 1763. In their view, those rights had always existed. The treaties confirmed an already existing situation, subject to limitation only in areas where settlement had occurred.

the course of the province's arguments, Amerindians were described as an 'inferior race . . . in an inferior state of civilization' who had 'no government and no organization, and cannot be regarded as a nation capable of holding lands'.[3] Amerindians' understanding of 'owning' or 'holding' land has always been rather different. Ironically, in an essential respect this view is not unlike the 'trustee' position the government took towards its holding of lands for the Native peoples (Box 16.1).

Three weeks after the first hearing, on 10 June 1885, the Chancellor of Ontario, John Alexander Boyd (1837–1916), presented his decision. His statement on Amerindian rights set a precedent for Canadian courts in its thoroughness. By that date, the Northwest Rebellion was effectively over. Poundmaker had surrendered, and only Big Bear was still at large. Two of Boyd's sons had volunteered against Riel. Boyd described Amerindians as having no fixed residence, moving around as they needed. 'As heathens and barbarians it was not thought that they had any proprietary title to the soil, nor any claim thereto as to interfere with the plantations, and the general prosecution of colonization.'[4] As legal ownership of the land had never been attributed to them, Treaty Three Amerindians had not conveyed any such rights to the federal government. Therefore, the licence the Dominion had granted to St Catherine's Milling Company was invalid.

According to Boyd, in legal terms Treaty Three also was meaningless. If they so chose, Amerindians could treat with the Crown for the extinction of their primitive right of occupancy. But if they refused to do so, the government could go ahead with settlement and development of the country, displacing the Aboriginal peoples if necessary. Boyd's decision was maintained through three appeals, the final one to the **Judicial Committee of the Privy Council** (1888). The *St Catherine's Milling* decision was still in effect in 2005 despite some monumental legal battles since.

As for the Amerindians of Treaty Three, they did not fare well. Ottawa and Ontario could not agree on the promised selection, location, and extent of reserves. For some, it would be a generation, or even several generations, before their reserves were confirmed. For others, the process was still going on into the twenty-first century. Neither has the exact nature of Amerindian interest in reserve lands been fully defined.

During Treaty Three negotiations, Mawedopenais, Fort Frances chief, had repeated a sentiment that Amerindians had been expressing in various terms ever since the first arrival of Europeans in North America: 'This is what we think, that the Great Spirit has planted us on this ground where we are, as you were where you came from. We think where we are is our property.' He added that the Great Spirit had provided the Amerindians with the rules 'that we should follow to govern us rightly'.[5] Mississauga George Copway was even more categorical: 'The hunting grounds of the Indians were secured by right, a law and custom among themselves. No one was allowed to hunt on another's land, without invitation or permission.' Repeated offences could result in banishment from the tribe.[6]

Nearly Three Centuries of Confrontation at Oka

An even older but still only partially resolved case was that of the Amerindians of **Oka** against the Seminary of St Sulpice.[7] It dated from Louis XV's 1717 grant of a seigneury to the Sulpicians on the Ottawa River where it meets the St Lawrence, about 30 kilometres west of Montreal, on the condition that it be used as an Amerindian mission.[8] France thought it wiser to make the grant to the seminary rather than to the Amerindians, as the latter were considered to be incapable of conserving the property for themselves. The grant left unresolved, however, the question of whether the Sulpicians were the sole proprietors or trustees.[9] In 1721, nearly 900 Amerindians moved to the new location at Lake of Two Mountains, with funds provided by a private benefactor.[10]

As far as the Amerindians were concerned (particularly the Iroquois, who eventually predominated), this was their territory. France, however, never recognized Aboriginal title and so never considered it necessary to negotiate with the Amerindians before granting lands to French subjects. The British later recognized the grant as clear title for the seminary and even enlarged it, without the protection of a special treaty. The Amerindians went to court in 1781 to prove their proprietorship. Their evidence was the 'Two-Dog Wampum' belt (the dogs, at each end of the belt, were the protectors of their land, represented by 27 beads). The court rejected their claim.[11] That the Iroquois position at Oka aroused concern was evident in the fact that the British felt it necessary to issue a special ordinance in 1841 confirming the seminary's title. Encouraged by this support and now much less enthusiastic about its missionary role, especially as the Iroquois were deserting Catholicism in favour of Methodism, the seminary pressured the Amerindians to leave. The Sulpicians brought in French-Canadian settlers to replace them.[12]

In 1853 and 1854, the department set aside lands for the Algonquin at Maniwaki, Quebec, and for the Iroquois at Doncaster, Ontario. Some moved to the new locations, but most rejected the compromise.[13] They continued to assert their claims to the land at Kanesatake by selling wood and staking out lots. Some went to jail, as the seminary claimed right to the trees.[14] The situation again boiled over in 1868, when both the Algonquin and Iroquois, led by new Iroquois chief Joseph Onasakenarat (Sosé, Joseph Akirwirente, 1845–81), petitioned Ottawa for clear title to the land and to their village, Kanesatake.[15] The result was the arrest and jailing of three chiefs, including Joseph (who would end up in jail eight times on land-related charges), and an Order-in-Council in 1869 reaffirming the seminary's title.

The violence escalated. The Sulpicians dismantled the Methodist church with the authority of a court order in 1875. Two years later, provincial police raided in the dead of night. The Catholic church burned down, and 14 Amerindians were charged with arson. One trial after another produced only hung juries. Finally, in the sixth, an English-speaking jury acquitted them.[16]

Another inquiry, this one in 1878, found that the seigneury was the property of the seminary.[17] Faced with the Amerindians' refusal to accept this decision, the department arranged for the seminary to buy land in the Township of Gibson, Ontario, as compensation for the Amerindians and as a 'final solution' to the problem. Although the seminary built houses on the newly acquired lands and offered lots for each family, few finally agreed to the move. For one thing, no one had consulted them as to the location of the new reserve. For another, they considered the compensation too little.[18]

This rejection led to still another report, in 1883. It spoke of a deep-seated public conviction that 'although the Indians may not have a legal claim to the lands, as owners thereof, they are nevertheless entitled to compensation for the loss of lands which they had been led to suppose were set apart for their benefit.'[19] In the meantime, not all was confrontation. Between 1886 and 1910, Mohawk and whites collaborated on a reforestation project to stabilize the region's sandy soil. It became a model for other such efforts in the province.[20]

Since neither side would budge on the land issue, the case was eventually fought out in the courts, with Ottawa paying the expenses of both sides. In 1912, the Privy Council decided in favour of the seminary but suggested that a charitable trust that could be enforced be set up for the Amerindians.[21] The implication was that Amerindian rights in the case could be dealt with outside the judicial system. No immediate action resulted, either in or out of the courts.

Then in 1936, the seminary, faced with a financial crisis, sold most of its seigneury, including the forest at Oka, to a Belgian real estate company.[22] The company set up a sawmill operation and, after World War II, began to sell off the land for agricultural development. This upset the Amerindians so much that, in 1945, the alarmed department bought the seminary's unsold lands, except those used for religious purposes, plus an additional 500 acres (202 hectares) of woodland for fuel, and assumed responsibility for the Amerindians.[23] The department administered the newly acquired land as if it were a reserve but without granting it that status.

All this took place without input from the residents of Kanesatake, who continued to press their claims. Their request in 1961 that the land in question be formally declared a reserve brought no response. They followed up in 1975 with a comprehensive claim asserting Aboriginal title, which the department rejected. The Amerindians came back two years later with a specific claim, but it, too, was eventually rejected in 1986. The Iroquois, for their part, continued to reject proposals that they settle on nearby federal lands. In the meantime the **Warrior movement**—described as the defence arm of the Longhouse religion but not universally accepted as such—was steadily gaining ground.

That the problem was not only unresolved but had intensified became dramatically evident in the summer of 1990, when the town of Oka announced that it was going to expand a golf course, built in the 1950s, into the disputed area. Oka took this stand after months of fruitless negotiations. The Iroquois responded by barricading the location. Quebec police

A Mohawk Warrior sits in golf cart and uses binoculars to view approaching Canadian army armoured vehicles on highway 344 on the Kanesatake Reserve at Oka, Quebec *(CP Photo/Tom Hanson)*

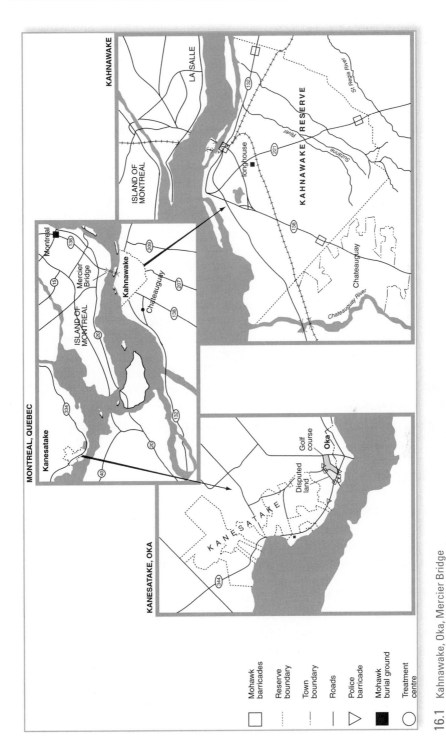

16.1   Kahnawake, Oka, Mercier Bridge

Sources: Associated Press Graphic, 1990; Rick Horning, *One Nation Under the Gun* (Toronto: Stoddart, 1991).

tried to storm the barricade, failed, and one police officer was killed.[24] Kahnawake residents, about 30 kilometres away, came to the support of their kin by blocking highways crossing their reserve, as well as the Mercier Bridge between Montreal and the mainland. The standoff at Kanesatake lasted for 78 days. Quebec tried to cut off food supplies to the holdouts, a move the Amerindians thwarted with the aid of the Red Cross.

In the end, the province asked Ottawa to send in the army. In the trials that followed, two Mohawks were found guilty of 29 of 56 charges: Ronald Cross (known as 'Lasagna', 1957–99) was sentenced to four years and four months and Gordon ('Noriega') Lazore to 23 months. A third, Roger Lazore, was acquitted. Of 39 Mohawks brought to trial a few months later, five were freed for lack of evidence. The rest were acquitted.[25]

More than a decade later there was still no agreement on what had been learned from Oka.[26] The old arguments that Amerindians have no rights to the land they have lived on for thousands of years, unless they have been asserted by special arrangements, are still alive. In some cases, they are more entrenched than ever. Unsolved problems, unlike old soldiers, have a habit of staying and growing instead of fading away.[27] On the positive side, the crisis heightened public interest in the situation of Aboriginal peoples in general.

Another positive development has been Ottawa's increase in funding for land claim settlements, somewhat speeding up a still all-too-slow process.[28] More specifically, the federal government has continued an already launched policy of buying land in the disputed area to prevent another confrontation. Finally, 10 years after the crisis, it signed a land governance deal with the Mohawks on 21 December 2000, which some people have hailed as a step towards self-government. Still, for most Mohawks, it was a bittersweet victory. As far as they were concerned, the land has always been theirs.[29]

Some Other Arenas

In other cases before the courts, there has been more accommodation with regard to hunting and fishing rights than in the matter of land rights. Even so, the record is inconsistent. In Nova Scotia, for instance, a series of cases beginning in the 1920s found against hunting and fishing rights,[30] based on the understanding that Amerindian sovereignty had never been recognized. That decision was upheld in appeals.[31] On another level, in 1970, the federal Fisheries Act did away with the treaties of 1725, 1752, and 1779. That situation remained until 1985, when the Supreme Court ruled that the 1752 agreement was still valid. In the eyes of the Mi'kmaq, the new decision meant that their rights were neither outdated nor set aside.[32] Although the courts have upheld the validity of the 1752 treaty, they have not upheld its status as an international treaty.[33]

Similarly, other provincial courts have in general upheld usufructuary rights—but based on treaty, not on Aboriginal, rights. A major exception has been Quebec. Since it had no treaties to override its legislation, it has claimed the right to regulate hunting and fishing. In New Brunswick, on the other hand, Amerindian resistance in 1981 led to 400 heavily armed provincial police, backed by bulldozers and helicopters, raiding the Restigouche Reserve community and confiscating 250 kilograms of salmon and more than 75 nets. A second raid followed two days later, in which tear gas was used and the bridge linking the reserve to Campbellton, New Brunswick, was blocked. The Amerindians in their turn blockaded the four roads leading into their reserve. After the police left the reserve, the two sides reached an agreement on fishing rights.[34] Federal game laws, on the other hand, have prevailed over treaties.

In other aspects of Aboriginal rights, the courts have been less tolerant of Amerindian claims. For example, in British Columbia in 1969, Frank Calder, founder and president (1955–74) of the Nisga'a Tribal Council (later the Nisga'a Nation),[35] maintained that his people's Aboriginal title had never been extinguished and that they had not ceded their territory to Britain. In **Calder v. Attorney General,** he repeated what another spokesman had told a Royal Commission in 1888:

> What we don't like about the government is their saying this: 'We will give you this much land.' How can they give it when it is our own? We cannot understand it. They have never bought it from us or our forefathers. They have never fought or conquered our people and taken the land in that way, and yet they say now that they will give us so much land—our own land. . . . It has been ours for a thousand years.[36]

As a result, Calder argued, provincial land legislation was invalid.

The BC Supreme Court ruled, however, that any rights Amerindians had at time of contact were overruled by the mere enactment of white man's law, in spite of the fact that none of the legislation stated that fact. In 1973, the Supreme Court of Canada upheld the ruling on a technicality.[37] Pierre Trudeau, Prime Minister, 1968–79 and 1980–4, assessing this judgement, conceded that Amerindians might have more rights than he had recognized in the White Paper of 1969 (see Chapter 14).[38] He entrenched Aboriginal rights without definition in the Constitution of 1982 despite a determined assault by the provincial premiers to prevent it. This partial constitutional victory for Aboriginal rights did not mean acceptance by the courts, however, as the *Bear Island* case illustrates.

At issue in *Attorney General of Ontario v. Bear Island Foundation*, 1984, was the legal nature of the continuing interest of the Teme-agama Anishnabay (Bear Island people) in their ancestral lands, about 10,360 square kilometres (4,000 square miles) in and around Lake Temagami (100 kilometres north of North Bay, Ontario), against a provincial government that wished to open up the area for resource and tourist development. When the Teme-agama claim finally came before the court, Justice Donald Steele ruled that the British Crown had acquired its rights in Canada by conquest, first against the French (he did not explain how that related to Amerindian title) and then against Pontiac in 1763. He made no mention of the Amerindian allies who had fought for the British on those occasions. The primitive level of Amerindian social organization, the judge wrote, meant that 'the Indian occupation could not be considered true and legal, and that the Europeans were lawfully entitled to take possession of the land and settle it with colonies.'[39] Judge Steele's decision was upheld in 1989 on the basis of new evidence to the effect that during the Robinson negotiations the Teme-agama had sold their land for $25.

The British North America Act gave Ottawa responsibility for 'Indians and lands reserved for Indians', a responsibility that time and again has not been fulfilled (see Box 16.2). However, 'all lands, mines, minerals and royalties' from the land were to be the proprietary interest of the four provinces that first made up Confederation. (The Prairie provinces gained control of their natural resources in 1930.) This separation of powers has meant that the provinces have a vested interest in opposing Aboriginal land claims.[40] Thus, there were (and are) serious concerns as to the adequacy of existing systems—whether by direct negotiation with the government or through the courts—to deal with Amerindian claims, dating back to the nineteenth century.

Box 16.2   *Guerin v. The Queen:* First Nations as Leasers

The pre-existence of Aboriginal right before colonization and its survival afterward was acknowledged in *Guerin v. The Queen* (1984, the Musqueam case), when it was found to be a 'burden on the radical or final title of the Sovereign'.[41] The *Guerin* case also recognized the federal government's fiduciary responsibility towards Amerindians, a direct consequence of the Crown reserving to itself the right to acquire Amerindian lands in the Proclamation of 1763. In assuming that role, the government had also implicitly assumed the responsibility of always acting in the best interest of the Indians.

In *Guerin* the government had leased 65 hectares of the band's lands to a Vancouver golf club at a rental far below prevailing rates and then had misrepresented the situation to the band. When the Musqueam finally got their hands on a copy of the lease 12 years later, they lost no time in going to court, which found that Indian Affairs had failed in its duties as a trustee.[42]

On the other side of the picture, a consequence has been the Musqueam band's move to raise its rents to bring them into line with prevailing Vancouver real estate values. As a result, 73 non-Aboriginal leaseholders who had built homes in the area found their rents skyrocketing from around $375 a year to $20,000 and even higher. When they complained, the federal government ruled in the band's favour. The Supreme Court of Canada later overturned the decision when it assessed the Musqueam's land as being worth only half the market value because of 'the political uncertainty and potential unrest' it saw as being typical of Indian reserves. Consequently, it ruled, the band could not charge more than $10,000 for a leaseholder's annual rent. For Musqueam Chief Ernie Campbell it was 'a sad day for this country' that saw land value being determined by the race of the owner. In the view of the leaseholders, the value of reserve land is governed by the fact that they cannot buy it outright rather than on the racial factor.[43] In the meantime, the move to raise rents had caused a split in the band.[44] Incidentally, another BC nation, the Katzie of Pitt Lake, announced that it would not renew current leases or renegotiate rents on its lands when they became due in 2004.[45]

In 1890 formal arbitration was attempted with the establishment of a board to deal with disputes between Canada and the provinces of Ontario and Quebec. Amerindians were allowed little opportunity to participate, and in only one case were they permitted even to select their own lawyers. During its decade of existence, the board heard about 20 cases dealing with disputes over financial matters and lands. It succeeded in settling only three of these cases; the courts later reversed two other decisions.

In the wake of the 1969 White Paper, the first hint of a change in Prime Minister Trudeau's position came during the second year of the Indian Claims Commission, in 1970, when its terms of reference were broadened to include comprehensive claims (claims arising in non-treaty areas). This opened the door for the Indian Claims Commissioner, Lloyd Barber, to consider Aboriginal rights. Although government policy did not officially change until after the Nisga'a (*Calder*) decision in 1973, and the Commission's life was short (it lasted until 1977), Barber won praise because of his even-handed approach and willingness to listen to all sides.[46]

In his final report, Barber observed that it was up to the Amerindians to establish their claims, rather than waiting for others to do the right thing by them. He did not, however, resolve the basic principles for evaluating claims or determine the kind of mechanism that would be best for their resolution. A joint National Indian Brotherhood/cabinet committee, established in 1975, lasted for only three years before the Amerindians withdrew. A Canadian Indian Rights Commission did not last much longer. Reconciling national and regional priorities was a major difficulty. It would be 1991 before the present Indian Claims Commission was established.

The department has consistently considered the courts to be a last resort for dealing with claims. As far as the Amerindians are concerned, litigation presents hazards, not the least of which is cost. While restrictions against Amerindians raising funds for such a purpose were removed in 1951, departmental funds available to them for research cannot be used for litigation without departmental consent.[47] Other aspects of the problem are considered in Chapter 17.

Turning Points and Setbacks

Three court cases have been widely viewed as representing a turning point in the Canadian legal approach to Aboriginal right.[48] In the first, *Sparrow v. The Queen* (1987), the Court found that Aboriginal fishing, land, and hunting rights for food, social, and ceremonial purposes had priority over later legislation.[49] This interpretation of Aboriginal right was supported in *The Queen v. Adams* (1996), when the Supreme Court of Canada ruled that George Weldon Adams, a Mohawk, had a right to fish for food in Lake St Francis,[50] contrary to Quebec fishery regulations. In the *Sioui* case (1990), the Court ruled that a 230-year-old safe-conduct was in effect a treaty and so took precedence over later laws.[51] The rights in question relate to self-government, a result of what has been called 'the Indians' historic occupation and possession of their tribal lands'.[52]

Donald Marshall Jr (centre) during a protest march. Marshall, a Mi'kmaq, was acquitted in 1999 by the Supreme Court of charges concerning the taking and sale of fish as a treaty right outside of the regulated season. *(CP, Andrew Vaughan, Canapress)*

This trend received a sharp check in March 1991, however, when Justice Allan McEachern, in ***Delgamuukw v. British Columbia,*** rejected the claim of the Gitksan and Wet'suwet'en to Aboriginal right over traditional lands in northern British Columbia, a resource-rich area about the size of Nova Scotia that had never been ceded by treaty and whose people had never been conquered. In 1997, the Supreme Court of Canada overturned the judgement with the argument that the lower courts had not given enough weight to oral tradition. In the Court's opinion, the laws of evidence must be adapted to place oral history on an equal footing

A Gitksan dance group performs outside the Supreme Court of Canada at the opening of the Gitksan-Wet'suwet'en appeal (*Delgamuukw*) in 1997. *(CP, Fred Chartrand, Canapress Photo Service)*

Box 16.3   The Nisga'a Treaty

The **Nisga'a Final Agreement Act** (Nisga'a treaty) was ratified by Parliament in 2000 after 22 years at the bargaining table and nearly 200 years of lobbying on the part of the Nisga'a (see Chapter 17). The decision to accept oral history as evidence in court helped to bring it to a conclusion. The agreement gave them self-governing rights to 1,900 square kilometres of land (8 per cent of the area they originally claimed) in exchange for giving up their tax-free status under the Indian Act. Hailed as a breakthrough marking 'a new understanding between cultures',[53] its basic land claim had been enormously strengthened by the Supreme Court's decision regarding oral evidence. In the meantime, however, it has met strong opposition from both Aboriginal and non-Aboriginal sources. The Aboriginal challenges come from both within and without the Nisga'a Nation. From without, they concern competing claims for the land assigned to the Nisga'a: a neighbouring nation, the Gitanyow, has already resorted to the courts to press its counterclaim. Another neighbour, the Gitksan, is still negotiating. From within, the challenge concerns the authority of the Nisga'a Tribal Council, which tribal dissenters see as not acting in accord with Aboriginal law.[54] The non-Aboriginal challenge, by the provincial Liberal Party, claims that the treaty is in violation of the Constitution Act of 1982 on the grounds that the self-government powers granted by the treaty to the Nisga'a will effectively make the band a state within a state. This claim was defeated by the BC Supreme Court when it ruled that the self-government powers in question are limited, and that the treaty expressly provides that in the case of conflict between Nisga'a laws and federal or provincial laws, the latter will prevail.[55]

---

with other types of evidence accepted in law, instead of being classed as hearsay, as was the prevailing practice[56] (see also Box 16.3).

The Supreme Court of Canada reached an explosive decision in 1999 when it acquitted **Donald Marshall Jr** (1953–2009), a Mi'kmaq from Nova Scotia, of charges concerning the taking and sale of fish as a treaty right outside of the regulated season. (Marshall had previously been jailed for 11 years for murder but was found innocent in 1983.) This decision led to out-of-season fishing by other Native fishers in the region. Non-Native fishermen reacted against the differential restrictions by destroying lobster traps belonging to the Burnt Church band in New Brunswick's Miramichi Bay. The confrontation escalated in spite of a clarification from the Supreme Court that 'the treaty right . . . can be contained by regulation', a qualification the band did not accept.[57]

The government finally brokered an agreement by which the Burnt Church band agreed to stop fishing on 7 October 2000, more than three weeks earlier than they had planned. By then, however, the lobsters had already started their seasonal migration to colder waters, making them harder to catch. Also by then, Amerindian fishing gear had been seized, a Department of Fisheries and Oceans boat had rammed an Amerindian boat broadside, demolishing it and hurling its Mi'kmaq occupants into the water, and several Amerindians had been arrested.[58]

Another landmark decision, this one applying to hunting, was that of the Ontario Court of Appeal, when it ruled early in 2001 that the Métis, as a distinct Aboriginal people, have the constitutional right to hunt for food out of season and without a licence. The jubilant reaction of the Métis had less to do with hunting than with the fact that this was the first time a Canadian court of appeal has recognized the legal existence of the Métis nation, even though it stopped short of defining the Métis as a people. Justice Robert C. Sharpe stated, 'While I do not doubt there has been considerable uncertainty about the nature and scope of Métis rights, this is hardly a reason to deny their existence.' He added that in spite of their 1982 constitutional recognition, there has been no serious effort anywhere in Canada to deal with Métis rights.[59]

First Nations within the Canadian Criminal Justice System

Public awareness that the justice system has not served Aboriginals well has also grown. At the beginning of the twenty-first century, Aboriginal people were three times more likely to go to jail than non-Aboriginals. This was dramatically illustrated by the

Two Mi'kmaq in a dory check out one of their boats that was rammed and sunk by a Department of Fisheries and Oceans boat, 29 August 2000. The clash occurred when Fisheries personnel sought to retrieve lobster traps set by Mi'kmaq off the coast of Burnt Church Reserve in northern New Brunswick. (Jacques Boissinot, CP photo)

Donald Marshall case in Nova Scotia. Marshall, a Mi'kmaq, was convicted in 1971 for a murder he did not commit and was jailed for 11 years before being exonerated in 1983. A subsequent investigation pilloried the justice system for failing Marshall at every turn.[60] Similarly, in Alberta a Royal Commission found that 'Systemic discrimination exists in the criminal justice system. There is no doubt that aboriginal people are over-represented in this system and that, at best, the equal application of the law has unequal results.'[61] Former Indian Affairs Minister Tom Siddon (in office, 1990–3) agreed that Canadian justice in general has displayed 'inadequate sensitivity' to the particular needs of the First Nations[62] (see Box 16.4).

On the other side of the picture, on 6 October 2000, Canada's first Aboriginal court opened on the Tsuu T'ina reserve just west of Calgary. With Aboriginal judges, prosecutors, and peacemakers, it is geared to recognize Amerindian traditions, values, languages, and customs. Chief Roy Whitney saw it as 'providing the opportunity to create our own system of justice'.[63] In 1990, the death of Neil Stonechild, last seen in police custody, and the deaths of other Aboriginal men in Saskatoon led to criminal convictions for local police officers and the most extensive investigation of Aboriginal people and the justice system to date.

Instituted on 15 November 2001, armed with a $2.5 million budget, and chaired by Alberta lawyer and former MP Wilton Littlechild, the Commission on First Nations and Métis Peoples and Justice Reform undertook a thorough examination of the criminal justice system. In its final report, released in June 2004, the Commission cited racism as central to Aboriginal peoples' mistrust of police services and recommended better screening of police candidates; more First Nations and Métis officers, legal aides, and judges; and better training for existing police forces. Other recommendations included an independent complaints investigation agency, a 'therapeutic court' that would deal with such issues as fetal alcohol syndrome and family violence, and allowing individual communities to deal with some cases that under the current system would appear before the courts. The Commission also recommended that alternatives to prison sentences be sought, with input from First Nations and Métis elders.[64] Another promising development was pioneered earlier by Ontario's Gull Bay band (Ojibwa) when it organized its own reserve police force in 1974, a first for Canada. Others have followed suit, with encouraging results: a drop in the crime rate on reserves serviced by their own police.[65]

Still, the legal position of Amerindians in Canada is determined not only by the Indian Act but also by the Constitution and the treaties. Despite the Canadian Charter of Rights and Freedoms, which in theory overrides all other statutes, the Indian Act continues to define Amerindian rights even as 'it reflects so little faith in the Indians.'[66] Far from viewing Amerindians as equals, however, its goals of protection and assimilation have led to an emphasis on control rather than development.[67] Initiative and enterprise have been stifled, ensuring poverty and underachievement. Even with enfranchisement, Amerindians, whether veterans or otherwise, did not have access to equality of opportunity and social benefits. In the words of Amerindian spokesman Harold Cardinal, the Indian Act has 'subjugated to colonial rule the very people whose rights it was supposed to protect.'[68]

Box 16.4   Two Justice Systems

The calls for a separate Aboriginal justice system have arisen from the recognition that traditional Aboriginal culture and values are in some ways at odds with the European-derived system in place in Canada. Below are examples of some general differences.

	Western Justice	Traditional Aboriginal Justice
Justice system	Adversarial	Non-confrontational
Function of justice	Ensure conformity, punish deviant behaviour, and protect society	Heal the offender, restore peace and harmony to the community, reconciliation between offender and victim/family
Guilt	European concept of guilty/ not guilty	No concept of guilty/not guilty
Pleading guilty	The accused has the right against self-incrimination; thus, it is not seen as dishonest to plead not guilty when one has actually committed the offence	It is dishonest to plead not guilty when one has committed the offence (values of honesty and non-interference)
Testifying	Witnesses testify in front of the accused as part of the process	Reluctance to testify, as it is confrontational to testify in front of the accused
Truth	Expectation to tell the 'whole truth'	It is impossible to know the 'whole truth' in any situation
Witnesses	Only certain people are called to testify in relation to specific subjects	Everyone is free to have their say; witnesses do not want to appear adversarial and often try to give answers that will please counsel, often changing their testimony
Eye contact	Maintaining eye contact sends the message that the individual is telling the truth	In some Aboriginal cultures, maintaining eye contact with a person in authority is a sign of disrespect
Verdict	The accused is expected to show signs of remorse during proceedings and on receiving a guilty verdict	The accused must accept what happens without any signs of emotion
Incarceration/ probation	Means of punishing and rehabilitating the offender	Absolves the Aboriginal offender of the responsibility to make restitution to the victim

Source: 'Aboriginal Peoples and the Criminal Justice System', special issue of the *Bulletin of the Canadian Criminal Justice Association*, Ottawa, 15 May 2000, from Corrine Mount Pleasant-Jette, 'Creating a climate of confidence: Providing services within Aboriginal communities', in *National Round Table on Economic Issues and Resources* (Ottawa: Royal Commission on Aboriginal Peoples, 27–9 April 1993). Reproduced by permission of the Canadian Criminal Justice Association.

Important Names and Terms

Calder v. Attorney General

Delgamuukw v. British Columbia

Judicial Committee of the Privy Council

Marshall, Donald, Jr

Nisga'a Final Agreement Act

Oka

St Catherine's Milling v. The Queen

Warrior movement

Study Questions

1) What caused the Oka crisis?
2) Why is *St Catherine's Milling* a landmark case?
3) What is the long-term significance of the *Delgamuukw* case?
4) What finally brought about the resolution of the Nisga'a land claim?

Recommended Readings

Clark, Bruce A. *Native Liberty, Crown Sovereignty*. Montreal and Kingston: McGill-Queen's University Press, 1990.

Maclane, Craig, and Michael Baxendale. *This Land Is Our Land: The Mohawk Revolt at Oka*. Montreal and Toronto: Optimum Publishing, 1990.

McNab, David T. *Circles of Time: Aboriginal Land Rights and Resistance in Ontario*. Waterloo, Ont.: Wilfrid Laurier University Press, 1999.

Miller, J.R. *Skyscrapers Hide the Heavens*. Toronto: University of Toronto Press, 1989.

Purich, Donald. *Our Land: Native Rights in Canada*. Toronto: James Lorimer, 1986.

Wiebe, Rudy, and Yvonne Johnson. *Stolen Life: The Journey of a Cree Woman*. Toronto: Alfred A. Knopf, 1998.

17 The Road to Self-Government

The White Paper had been withdrawn. This meant that in the 1970s the Indian Act still was in effect. Thirty years later, at the turn of the century, the government still had the legal right to make unilateral decisions, even to the point of terminating treaties. As early as 1971, however, it was funding Native political organizations to act as forums for policy discussions.[1] This, of course, was a complete turnabout from its move in the 1920s to curb such organizations by cutting their funding.

In other areas, such as social assistance programs, the government abandoned its expectation that Amerindians would assimilate to white ways. Where it once saw reserves as temporary expedients for easing Amerindians into mainstream society, now it sees them as homelands that Amerindians have a right to control. It will take a long time to rectify the poor social conditions that have developed on many of them,[2] and settling land claims has been seen as key to economic development.

At the close of 1990, 500–600 **specific claims**[3] were outstanding, some of them not having been resolved for 15 years or more. The struggle of the Lubicon of northern Alberta (Box 17.1), for example, began during the 1930s, when the Great Depression drove many non-Amerindians into their land. About 100 of the outstanding claims had been settled by the end of the century. The Indian Specific Claims Commission, with increased funding to speed up the process, was established in 1991 in response to the Oka crisis. Despite some success, it has also met with frustrations, often complicated by the **division of powers** between Ottawa and the provinces.[4] Long negotiations, sometimes lasting for years, are the result. There is no end in sight for settling land claims that have already been brought forward, let alone those that have yet to be made.

In 1973, the Canadian government, responding to various Aboriginal land claims, reaffirmed its continuing responsibility for Amerindians and Inuit under the BNA Act. It also referred to the Proclamation of 1763 as 'a basic declaration of the Amerindian people's interests in land in this country'. It recognized the loss of traditional use and

Box 17.1   The Lubicon Cree

One of the best-known and longest-standing claims, which remained unresolved in 2009, is that of the Lubicon Cree band of the Treaty Eight area in oil-rich northern Alberta.[5] Missed at the treaty signing, the band did not apply for a land settlement until 1933. Ottawa, responding in 1939, promised a reserve. In 1940 both federal and provincial governments approved a site at the western end of Lubicon Lake, but the site was never surveyed, and disputes arose about band lists. A judicial inquiry in 1944 did not lead to a settlement acceptable to the band. There matters lay until 1952, when mining and oil explorations expanded into the Lubicon's area. In 1979, the band's attempt to prevent the construction of a road into the area failed. By 1982 there were 400 oil wells within a 24-kilometre radius of the Lubicon band community,[6] whose main settlement was called 'Little Buffalo'. Alberta's approval for a pulp mill in the general region, while not directly affecting lands claimed by the Lubicon, did not simplify the situation.[7] In 1978, a new young chief, Bernard Ominayak, who held office into the twenty-first century, took over the band's leadership.

Federal objections to names on the band list have been one sticking point through numerous court hearings, judicial inquiries, and a vigorous public relations campaign by the Lubicon Cree. Another sticking point has been the band's insistence on compensation for what it claims is irreparable damage to its way of life, a point that neither the courts nor Ottawa has been willing to grant. The band, once a self-sustaining hunting community, now depends on wage work and transfer payments to supplement hunting, which has been reduced because of the erosion of the wildlife base. This situation, of course, has become prevalent throughout the North. In spite of a changing lifestyle, cultural identity remains strong; for one thing, the Lubicon still retain Cree as their first language.

In 1989, 350 band members broke away and won Ottawa's recognition as a separate band, 'Woodland Cree'. Within a year the Woodland Cree reached an agreement-in-principle with federal and provincial governments.[8] Another group, the Loon River people, won federal recognition as an independent band under Treaty Eight in 1991, but it took eight years of negotiation with Alberta for them to win a land and cash settlement. With the Woodland Cree, the Loon River people represent about 30 per cent of the Lubicon's claimed membership. In the meantime, Ominayak announced an agreement between the Lubicon band and Petro-Canada allowing for oil exploration under certain conditions on lands claimed by the band.[9]

occupancy of lands in BC, northern Quebec, Yukon, and the Northwest Territories in areas where 'Indian title was never extinguished by treaty or superseded by law.' For those areas, the government offered to negotiate a settlement involving compensation or benefits in return for relinquishment of the Native interest.

Time Line

1933	Lubicon Cree band in northern Alberta, missed in Treaty Eight signing, applies for land settlement.
1940–79	Reserve site established for Lubicon Cree, but resource explorations and provincial road on Lubicon land create problems still unresolved.
1966	Indian administration and northern resources management combined in Department of Indian Affairs and Northern Development (later called Department of Indian and Northern Affairs).
1968	Smallboy's Camp, a traditionalist encampment on Crown land in southern Alberta, is established by hereditary Cree chief Johnny Bob Smallboy.
1970	Mercury pollution of English-Wabigoon River system in northwestern Ontario, which devastated Grassy Narrows and Whitedog reserves since 1950s, is traced to Reed Paper Company mill at Dryden, Ontario.
1971	Inuit Tapirisat of Canada formed in response to announcement of Quebec's proposed James Bay hydroelectric project.
1972	Cree and Inuit of northern Quebec get injunction to stop James Bay project, but it is suspended on appeal.
1974–7	Mackenzie Valley Pipeline Inquiry (Berger Inquiry) sets new standard for listening to and accounting for Aboriginal concerns about development projects.
1975	James Bay and Northern Quebec Agreement reached between governments and Inuit and Cree of northern Quebec falls short of entrenching Native rights.
1976–7	Len Marchand first Amerindian federal cabinet minister.
1982	Patriation of Canadian Constitution; Constitution Act, 1982 recognizes and affirms 'existing aboriginal and treaty rights'.
1983	Report of the Special Parliamentary Committee on Indian Self-Government (Penner Report) urges distinct form of Aboriginal self-government.
1983–7	Three First Ministers' Conferences on Aboriginal rights, mandated in Constitution Act, 1982, accomplish little.
1984	Cree-Naskapi Act of Quebec, hailed as the first self-government legislation for Amerindians, replaces Indian Act for regions it covers. Western Arctic Claim Agreement extinguishes Inuvialuit Aboriginal title in exchange for $55 million and ownership of 96,000 square kilometres.
1989–90	Woodland Cree break from Lubicon band, gain band status, and cut lucrative deal

	with federal and provincial governments.	1995	Standoff over disputed land on shore of Lake Huron between Kettle and Stoney Point First Nation (Chippewa) and Ontario Provincial Police results in shooting death of Native activist Dudley George.
1990	Manitoba MLA Elijah Harper withholds vote on ratification of Meech Lake Accord, effectively killing agreement that would have given Quebec special status while ignoring Amerindians.		
		1997	First Nations Bank of Canada begins operations in Saskatoon.
1991	Loon River people break from Lubicon band, gain band status.		
1991–6	Royal Commission on Aboriginal Peoples concludes with five-volume, 3,537-page report including 440 specific recommendations.	1998	Formal government regret expressed for residential school abuses and $350 million healing fund established.
		1999	Loon River band signs land settlement agreement.

By now, however, Aboriginal people were more interested in entrenchment of their rights than in extinguishment. In 1975, the Joint Council of Chiefs and Elders adopted the Declaration of the First Nations:

We, the original peoples of this land know the Creator put us here.

The Creator gave us laws that govern all our relationships to live in harmony with nature and mankind.

The laws of the Creator defined our rights and responsibilities.

The Creator gave us our spiritual beliefs, our languages, our culture, and a place on Mother Earth which provided us with all our needs.

We have maintained our freedom, our languages, and our traditions from time immemorial.

We continue to exercise the rights and fulfill the responsibilities and obligations given to us by the Creator for the land upon which we were placed.

The Creator has given us the right to govern ourselves and the right to self-determination.

The rights and responsibilities given to us by the Creator cannot be altered or taken away by any other Nation.

By the end of the twentieth century, the Canadian public, in general, was supportive of—or at least did not strongly oppose—the Amerindian position, particularly in regard to land claims.[10]

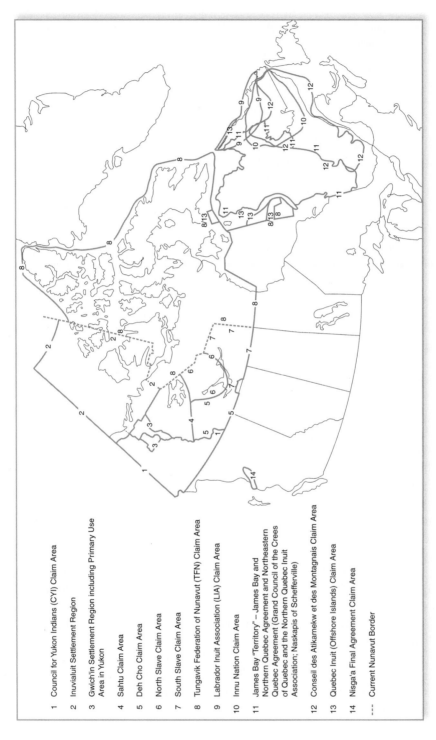

1 Council for Yukon Indians (CYI) Claim Area

2 Inuvialuit Settlement Region

3 Gwich'in Settlement Region including Primary Use Area in Yukon

4 Sahtu Claim Area

5 Deh Cho Claim Area

6 North Slave Claim Area

7 South Slave Claim Area

8 Tungavik Federation of Nunavut (TFN) Claim Area

9 Labrador Inuit Association (LIA) Claim Area

10 Innu Nation Claim Area

11 James Bay "Territory" – James Bay and Northern Quebec Agreement and Northeastern Quebec Agreement (Grand Council of the Crees of Quebec and the Northern Quebec Inuit Association; Naskapis of Schefferville)

12 Conseil des Atikamekw et des Montagnais Claim Area

13 Quebec Inuit (Offshore Islands) Claim Area

14 Nisga'a Final Agreement Claim Area

--- Current Nunavut Border

17.1 Major comprehensive claim areas

Source: Adapted from Indian and Northern Affairs, Comprehensive Land Claims in Canada, Revised map June 1992, Comprehensive Claims Branch, DIAND, Ottawa.

The Push for Technology Underscores the Need for Self-Government

Developing technology has meant greater industrial attention to northern resources. In 1957, John George Diefenbaker (1895–1979) led the Conservatives to an overwhelming victory with his vision of the 'New North'. His model was a colonial one: improve transportation to the North, so that people and industrial know-how could come in to exploit northern resources and ship the benefits south. Changes in federal procedure also reflected this attitude. In 1966, Indian administration and northern resources management were combined in the Department of Indian Affairs and Northern Development, which is how matters stood at the end of the twentieth century, except that the name had been shortened to Indian and Northern Affairs. Industrialization continued in the earlier pattern with little consideration for the needs of northern peoples.

In the 1950s, for example, the water supplies of the Grassy Narrows and Whitedog reserves in Ontario's Treaty Three area showed signs of mercury pollution, but it was 1970 before the cause was discovered. The Reed Paper Company was dumping methylmercury into the English-Wabigoon river system. The contamination forced reserves to close their commercial fisheries. Still, government reaction was slow. Eventually, the Ojibwa called in specialists from Minamata, Japan, where a similar situation had occurred, to assess what was happening. They confirmed mercury poisoning.

The Ojibwa then found out that treaty assurances provided little protection. When Reed announced plans for a new mill in 1974, the people had to prepare their own case on land use and forest management. In the midst of the public scandal, an agreement for the new mill, containing some provision for environmental protection, was signed in 1976. Meanwhile, the people had to restrict their intake of fish.[11] An out-of-court settlement for $8.7 million, reached in 1985, paved the way for the reserves to develop a program encouraging environmentally friendly industries.

The discovery of oil at Prudhoe Bay, Alaska, in 1968, seven years after oil exploration had begun in the Canadian High Arctic, led to a proposal for a pipeline running south down the Mackenzie Valley for 3,800 kilometres (2,400 miles) to connect into existing pipeline systems, crossing regions covered by Treaties Eight and Eleven. Three years later, in 1971, Quebec announced its plan to develop the James Bay watershed in that province as a gigantic hydroelectric project in a region where no treaties had been signed. In neither case was thought given to consulting the peoples of the regions involved.[12] After all, in the past, railways had been built, dams constructed, and whole villages relocated without any such consultations, but times had changed. Now, even the churches, traditional instruments for assimilation and upholders of government policy, were questioning the high social price of economic development undertaken without regard to local situations.

Quebec launched the James Bay project without consultation with the Amerindians and Inuit who would be affected. The Inuit reacted by forming a number of associations,[13] which Tagak Curley (grandson of a whaler) and Meeka Wilson co-ordinated in 1971 under a new organization, Inuit Tapirisat of Canada. It became a major voice for Inuit across the Arctic as they worked towards political and economic control while preserving their culture, identity, and way of life.

Quebec already had a record of refusing to delay development projects pending the resolution of Native claims. In 1972, Judge Albert Malouf granted the Grand Council of the Crees (Quebec) and the Northern Quebec Inuit Association an injunction to halt the James Bay hydroelectric project, only to see it suspended on appeal a week later. The Quebec Court of Appeals eventually ruled that Aboriginal rights in the territory had been extinguished by the HBC charter of 1670. The uproar stirred by the Inuit and Cree was unprecedented. Besides speeches, meetings, and public demonstrations, the First Nations held theatrical evenings in which they put on performances that ranged from the traditional to the contemporary. The James Bay Cree publicly burned a Quebec government communiqué written in the wrong Cree dialect for the region to which it was sent. After they reached an agreement, Billy Diamond, chief of the Waskaganish band of James Bay Cree, observed: 'It has been a tough fight, and our people are still very much opposed to the project, but they realize that they must share their resources.'[14]

The James Bay and Northern Quebec Agreement of 1975[15]—the term 'treaty' was temporarily out of fashion—left the Inuit and Cree communities of Quebec with substantial control of their own political, economic, and social affairs, although the final say still rested with the government.[16] More generous than the numbered treaties, the accord still fell far short of entrenching First Nations rights. As far as the Aboriginal peoples involved are concerned, the expectations to which it gave rise have not been met.[17] Critics have pointed to the price: the flooding of 10,500 square kilometres of once productive hunting land without consideration of wildlife factors. Their point was dramatically reinforced in 1984, when Hydro-Québec inadvertently drowned 10,000 caribou by releasing a large volume of water during their migration. On top of everything else, expected contracts for hydroelectric power did not materialize. Of the project's three phases originally planned for, only the first (La Grande) had approached completion by the turn of the century.[18]

Mackenzie Valley Pipeline Inquiry

In 1974, Prime Minister Trudeau appointed Justice Thomas Berger to chair a **Mackenzie Valley Pipeline Inquiry**. In carrying out his mandate, Berger not only decided to consult the people directly, he broke with tradition by seeing to it that the media covered the hearings. The resulting publicity outdid even that of James Bay. Public interest was intense, as southern Canadians learned about life in the North, many of them for the first time. A witness to the hearings reminded them that northerners, too, had a way of life to protect:

> I wonder how people in Toronto would react if the people of Old Crow went down to Toronto and said, 'Well, look, we are going to knock down all those skyscrapers and high rises . . . blast a few holes to make lakes for muskrat trapping, and you people are just going to have to move out and stop driving cars and move into cabins.'[19]

Oil Spill Threats
Recent Oil & Gas Discoveries
Oil Spill Threats
Oil Spills
Oil Spills
INTERPROVINCIAL PIPELINE (NW)
RADIO-ACTIVE CESIUM POLLUTION
Arsenic Pollution
W.A.C. Bennett Dam
PEACE ATHABASCA DELTA AREA
CHURCHILL RIVER DIVERSION PROJECT AREA
JAMES BAY PROJECT AREA
Oil Spills
Proposed Moran Dam Site
Big Horn Dam
Upper Howe Sound
Oil Spills
Manicouagan Outardes Hydroelectric Developments
Oil Spills
Sewage Pollution
Oil Spills
Oil Spills
1 Canada Tungsten Mining Co. Ltd, W*
2 Giant Yellowknife Mines Ltd, Au, Ag, Nerco Ltd, (Con Mine) Au, Ag
3 Cominco Ltd, (Polaris Mine) Zn, Pb
4 Nanisivik Mines Ltd, Pb, Zn, Ag
5 Echo Bay Mines Ltd,* Ag, Pb, Cd, Zn
6 United Keno Hill Mines Ltd,* Ag, Pb, Cd, Zn
7 Curragh Resources Corp., Pb, Zn, Ag
8 Nadahini Mining Corp., Coal
9 Canamax, (Ketza River) Au
10 BHP Diamonds Ltd
11 Voisey's Bay Nickel Co., Ni, Zn
*Temporary Closure
△ Principal mining industries
▼ Industrial chemical plants discharging mercury contaminants
○ Dams and/or hydroelectric developments as indicated
Mercury polluted waters

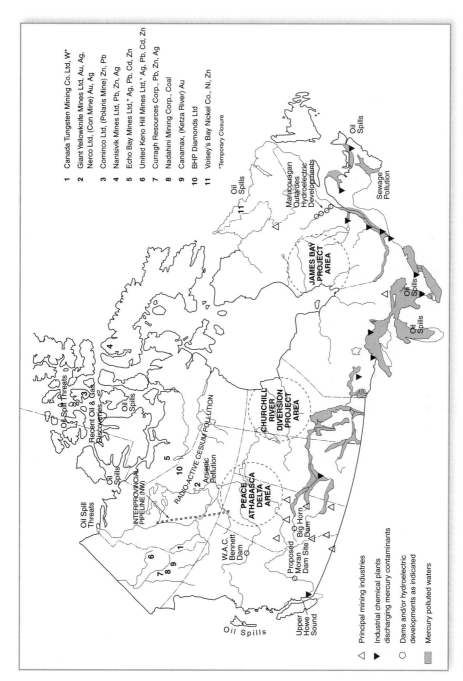

17.2 Principal industrial development areas and effects on Aboriginal peoples

Sources: Canada, *Aboriginal People of Canada and their Environment* (Ottawa: NIB, 1973); Canada, *Looking North: Canada's Arctic Commitment* (Ottawa: DIAND, 1989).

Another was more blunt:

> Your nation is destroying our nation. . . . We are a nation. We have our own
> land, our own ways, and our own civilization. We do not want to destroy you
> and your land. . . . your Prime Minister is willing to say that Louis Riel was not
> all wrong. He is willing to say that, a hundred years later, but is he willing to
> change the approach that destroyed Louis Riel?[20]

When Berger's report appeared in 1977, it became a best-seller.[21]

Berger's recommendation that the pipeline be put on hold for 10 years to allow time for Aboriginal concerns to be considered was a shocker to many Canadians, accustomed as they were to development being given top priority. Eventually, large quantities of natural gas were discovered in Alberta and British Columbia, providing more easily available sources of fuel.[22] In 1985, an oil pipeline running about half the length of the Mackenzie Valley, from Norman Wells to northern Alberta, was completed, two years before Thomas Berger's recommended moratorium would have ended.

The lapsing of the moratorium revived interest in the original proposal, but with a difference. This time, the First Nations, instead of opposing it, have indicated support, provided that the Natives are major participants. This turnabout was influenced by dramatic price increases for oil and gas. The Inuvialuit of the western Arctic, whose land claim was settled in 1984, lost no time in taking advantage of this favourable turn of the market and negotiated four oil and gas concessions that netted them $75.5 million.[23]

On the Political Front

The period between the rejection of the 1969 White Paper and the patriation of the British North America Act in 1982 was marked by protest and confrontation, bureaucratic dissension, and policy confusion.[24] This came to a head in a 1974 clash between west coast Amerindians and an RCMP riot squad in Ottawa that disrupted the opening of Parliament. About 200 Amerindians had come from Vancouver—'Native Peoples' Caravan'—in what was supposed to have been a peaceful protest against poor living conditions. Nervous authorities called out the riot squad and then brought out the military, the first time the government used such measures against Native demonstrators.[25]

The negotiations that preceded the adoption of the Canadian Constitution saw considerable Native political activity. As a Dene leader observed, 'While others are trying to negotiate their way out of Confederation, we are trying to negotiate our way in.'[26] Amerindians, Inuit, and Métis, concerned that Aboriginal rights be enshrined in the new constitution and convinced they were not being given a fair hearing in Canada, sent delegation after delegation to Britain and continental Europe to press their cause on the international scene. At one point, 300 Amerindians went to Britain to present their case to the Queen, but at the request of the short-lived Tory government of Joe Clark (1979–80) they were denied an audience.

Eventually, when the **constitutional patriation** was accomplished in 1982, First Nations peoples won recognition of 'existing' Aboriginal rights but without a definition of the term. However, there was provision that such rights could not be harmed by anything in the Charter of Rights and Freedoms.[27] Its recognition of Métis as Aboriginals was a consequence of their earlier recognition by the Manitoba Act of 1870. As a sop for First Nations having been excluded from the constitutional negotiations, the government made provision for three conferences between Aboriginal leaders and Canada's first ministers.

What these conferences, held in the mid-1980s, made clear was that, constitutionally, the Aboriginal role is at best advisory. Whatever the justification for Aboriginal self-government, it rests at the local level. When it comes to constitutional matters that concern the country as a whole, the final say rests essentially with the federal Parliament and provincial legislatures. The term 'constitution' as used here is a European political concept. It provides 'a set of rationally conceived and formalized rules for the exercise of political powers and, equally important, for the restraint of political power'.[28] For Amerindians, the Constitution not only embodies the internal sovereignty of the tribe but also symbolizes the aspiration for self-determination for the people.

Amerindians are not seeking to be granted self-government so much as to win recognition that viable Amerindian governments existed long before the arrival of Europeans. Cree lawyer Delia Opekokew elaborated: 'Aboriginal right', she wrote, 'recognizes our ownership over lands we have traditionally occupied and used and our control and ownership over the resources of the land—water, minerals, timber, wildlife and fisheries.' What was more, she added, such a right 'recognizes our Indian government's sovereignty over our people, lands and resources.'[29] In 1983, this position received a powerful boost from the Report of the Special Parliamentary Committee on Indian Self-Government, known as the **Penner Report** after the committee's chairman, Keith Penner, Liberal MP for Kenora, 1968–88. The report urged that Amerindians be allowed to establish their own level of government, distinct from those of the municipality and the Indian Act. A major result would be the reinforcement of Aboriginal rights.

Hopes were high at the launching of the first of the three constitutionally mandated First Ministers' Conferences on Aboriginal affairs in 1983. As Inuit delegate Zebedee Nungak cheerfully put it, 'We're here to do constructive damage to the status quo.'[30] That was just what some of the provincial premiers feared, however. Brian Mulroney, Conservative Prime Minister, 1984–93, at first apparently enthusiastic about resolving the question of Aboriginal rights, pulled back, so that the third and last of the conferences, in 1987, was even more frustrating than the first two.

Not many weeks later, Mulroney and the provincial premiers signed the Meech Lake Accord, recognizing Quebec as a distinct society and granting that province special status, to be ratified within three years. The disillusionment among the Amerindians

Elijah Harper, then an NDP member of the Manitoba legislature, holds an eagle feather for spiritual strength as he uses delaying tactics to prevent the 1990 Meech Lake Accord from being ratified. *(CP, Canapress Photo Service, Wayne Glowacki)*

and Inuit was profound. What the government had denied to them was now being given to Quebec!

Amerindians and Inuit rallied. When the opportunity presented itself to kill the Accord by legislative means, they took it. All of the provincial legislatures had to ratify the agreement. **Elijah Harper**, an Oji-Cree chief from Red Sucker Lake and the only Amerindian member of the Manitoba legislature (NDP, Rupertsland),[31] withheld his vote on the grounds that procedural rules were not being followed. The Speaker of the House agreed, observing that the Accord was too important 'to open the door for some future legal challenge because all the rules weren't obeyed'. The matter had been introduced to the legislature at the last minute. Harper's delaying tactics meant that the 23 June 1990 deadline could not be met, and so the Accord died.[32] Harper, incidentally, was one of the chiefs who had gone to London in 1980 to lobby the Queen for fair treatment of Aboriginals in the patriation of the Canadian Constitution. He had refused an invitation to attend the royal signing of the Constitution in Ottawa in 1982.[33]

The stalling of Aboriginal rights at the constitutional level has to some extent been counterbalanced by an inching towards recognition at local levels.[34] Between 1913 and 1954, the deputy minister of the Department of the Interior and a council consisting of missionaries, an HBC trade commissioner, and an RCMP commissioner governed the three districts of Keewatin, Mackenzie, and Franklin in the Northwest Territories. Following epidemics that swept through the Dene and Inuit, the government transferred political control to the Department of Indian Affairs and Northern Development. The NWT government has seen a dramatic increase in Native participation since it became fully elective in 1975. Aboriginal participation has influenced the character of the Legislative

Council, which has abandoned the party system in favour of indigenous consensus politics. In other words, the move is towards decentralization. Yukon, on the other hand, has had an elective council since 1908, but its government is more centralized than that of the NWT.[35]

Northern Self-Government

The Cree-Naskapi Act of Quebec, 1984, was a result of the Penner Report, as well as being a consequence of the James Bay and Northern Quebec Agreement (JBNQA) and its related accords of 1975–8. Hailed as the first **self-government** legislation for Aboriginals in Canada, the Cree-Naskapi Act replaced the Indian Act for the regions it serves and establishes the communities as corporate entities, over and above their members' legal existence as individual persons.[36] However, disagreement soon arose as to the extent to which Ottawa had implemented the agreed-upon funding formula. The government maintained in 1988 that it had effected 80 per cent of its commitments. Chief Henry Mianscum of the Mistassini band took an opposite view: 'probably 70 per cent of that Agreement hasn't been implemented.'[37]

The Western Arctic Claim Agreement (Inuvialuit Final Agreement) was also reached in 1984.[38] It extinguished Inuvialuit Aboriginal title to the western Arctic in return for ownership of 96,000 square kilometres stretching up to Banks Island, along with payments of $45 million in benefits and $10 million for economic development. The administration of all this came under the umbrella Inuvialuit Regional Corporation (IRC), organized the following year. Its concerns include wildlife conservation and management, as is generally the case in these northern agreements. Its business arm, the Inuvialuit Development Corporation, bought a transportation firm for $27 million with a virtual monopoly on barge transportation in the Canadian Arctic. Among their many enterprises, the Inuvialuit are exclusive owners of the government-set muskox quotas for their region.[39] Similarly, Aboriginal business activities and entrepreneurialism, both on a band level and individually, have increased significantly in recent years (Box 17.2).

In Yukon, after nearly two decades of negotiation, an Umbrella Final Agreement was signed in 1993 whereby the territory's 14 Amerindian bands retain ownership of 44,000 square kilometres and receive compensation of $260 million while avoiding complete extinguishment of Aboriginal title. Besides protection for wildlife, the agreement also creates a constitutional obligation to negotiate self-government.[40]

The federal government, however, is far from conceding that entrenchment of Aboriginal rights is a feature of land-claim settlements. This was dramatically illustrated by the cancellation of the Dene/Métis Western Arctic Land Claim agreement late in 1990,[41] after the Dene/Métis demanded to renegotiate a clause in the preliminary agreement that required the surrender of Aboriginal and treaty rights in return for the

Box 17.2   First Nations Enterprise

First Nations increasingly are participating in the world of business. Branching out from such traditional sectors as fishing, farming, and arts and crafts, First Nations have turned to resource development—oil and gas, forestry, and mining, for three obvious examples. At the start of the twenty-first century, there were 1,600 active oil wells on Aboriginal lands and at least 12 band-owned oil and gas companies, not to mention a myriad of service contractors. In forestry, a half-dozen mills are owned by Native bands. Aboriginal Business Canada, an arm of Industry Canada, estimates more than 20,000 Aboriginal-owned businesses across the land. Although they account for only 1 per cent of Canada's businesses, their growth rate between 1981 and 1996 was 170 per cent.[42]

Such activity is not without its problems. For example, in the mid-1990s the Stoney Nation of Morley, Alberta, taking advantage of stricter forestry regulations introduced in British Columbia that meant BC mills were undersupplied with cut timber, engaged in extensive clear-cutting on their reserve with the permission of the Department of Indian Affairs. Some band members protested, and the Rocky Mountain Ecosystem Coalition, a non-Native environmental group, pressured Indian Affairs to stop the activity. Following a CTV report on the clear-cutting and its environmental impact, the work finally was halted in February 1995, but only after a wide swath had been cut in the foothills between Calgary and Banff.[43]

settlement. As the Dene put it, 'Our laws from the Creator do not allow us to cede, release, surrender or extinguish our inherent rights.'[44]

Extending Self-Government

Ottawa, meanwhile, has been extending self-government at the municipal level to some Amerindian bands, in line with the long-held legal opinion that if Amerindians have the national vote they should be allowed to run their own affairs at the local level. In 1986, for example, the 650-member Sechelt band assumed legal and political control in fee simple of a reserve of 10 square miles (26 square kilometres), 50 kilometres north of Vancouver, after a decade of effort on their part. Alberta's tiny but wealthy Sawridge band also has negotiated a self-government agreement, and others have followed suit.

In 1990, Dene Georges Erasmus, the Assembly of First Nations' National Chief, 1985–91, described the Amerindian vision of the new order of things as one of 'sharing, recognition, and affirmation'.[45] In contrast, at the same time, Chief Ben Michel of the Innu argued that 'an attack on the economic base of Canada' would not be an insurrection. Rather, he said, it would be an exercise in sovereignty, at least for the Innu, who have never surrendered it.[46]

Coercion, Standoffs, an Agreement, and a Royal Commission

A consequence of the Oka crisis was Prime Minister Mulroney's announcement in 1991 of the **Royal Commission on Aboriginal Peoples** (RCAP) to investigate and report on the situation of Aboriginal peoples across the country. Mulroney appointed seven commissioners, but none of the four Aboriginal members represented the western numbered treaties. Of the two co-chairs, Georges Erasmus was formerly president of the Dene Nation, Northwest Territories, and more recently National Chief of the Assembly of First Nations. René Dussault was a judge of the Quebec Appeals Court. It was 'the first time in modern history that the non-Aboriginal people have sat down with Aboriginal people and together . . . reviewed where they've been together and tried to chart a course on where they want to go.'[47] It would be the most thorough official investigation ever undertaken of Aboriginal life in Canada.[48]

In the newly built Innu community of Natuashish, the technologies of two very different worlds adorn the outside of a house. *(Photo by Dominick Tyler)*

In the meantime, the ending of the Oka standoff did not mean the end of tensions and demonstrations, as Aboriginal leaders continued their arguments for a larger constitutional role for their people.[49] Protests in various forms, such as occupations of land or offices, or the erection of barricades at strategic places, erupted sporadically across the land. In January 1993, six children on the Innu reserve at Davis Inlet, Labrador, whose history of forced relocations had started in 1948, tried to commit suicide after sniffing gas fumes. The incident quickly blew up into an international scandal: 'Tragedy at Davis Inlet. The near-suicides of six teens display the hollowness of government promises to improve the community', according to a headline in *The Gazette*,

Montreal.[50] The Innu of Davis Inlet finally were relocated in 2003 to a new community, Natuashish, built at a cost of more than $150 million on the Labrador mainland near their former island community. In 1995, a land occupation at Ipperwash, Ontario, saw Canada's first Amerindian casualty in a land-claim standoff, Dudley George.[51] An Ontario provincial court found Police Sergeant Kenneth Deane guilty of criminal negligence causing death,[52] but Deane spent no time in jail.

BC's First Land Claims Agreement: The Nisga'a Treaty

British Columbia's position in relation to its First Nations peoples was for a long time unique in Canada. For one thing, apart from the 14 small treaties on Vancouver Island negotiated by Governor James Douglas, 1850–4, and the overlap of Treaty Eight into its northeastern corner in 1899, the province had not negotiated treaties with its First Nations. Not recognizing Aboriginal rights, it denied having any outstanding obligations that could be settled by way of land claims. It maintained this position until 1990 when—following court rulings, federal pressure, and a change in public attitude—it agreed to open talks. Two years later, the newly formed New Democratic government promised to resolve the 47 open claims, which covered most of the province. This raised the hopes of Amerindian leaders, whose sometimes overlapping demands soared to encompass more than 110 per cent of the province's land. The government responded by announcing that only 5 per cent would be available for settling claims.[53]

The Nisga'a were the first of BC's claimants to have their case heard. A nation of 5,500 in the Nass Valley and spreading to the northwest, they had filed their claim 70 years earlier.[54] Originally, it involved 24,000 square kilometres of the northern part of the province. Finally, after intensive negotiations (behind closed doors for the final two years), the Nisga'a agreed to accept 1,930 square kilometres.[55] The land turned over to the Nisga'a, to be communally owned in fee simple, is valued at $100 million and remains exempt from provincial property and resource taxes. Still, it is a fraction of what was once theirs.

The persistence of the Nisga'a had paid off. Parliament ratified their treaty in 2000. The *Calder* case of 1973 (Chapter 16) set the scene. Although that decision had gone against the Nisga'a on a technicality, the judges had agreed that the First Nation did indeed have Aboriginal title to its ancestral lands. From there, the Nisga'a never stopped pressing, first the federal government, then, after 1990, the provincial government as well. The discussions were neither simple nor easy. At one point, they broke off entirely.

It took a tragedy to break the deadlock: the shooting of Dudley George at Ipperwash. The prospect of spreading violence very quickly brought the negotiators back to the table, and the terms of British Columbia's first land-claims preliminary agreement soon were settled.[56] Not surprisingly, in view of its past policies, BC faces the largest roster of unsettled **comprehensive claims**[57] of any of the provinces. As of 2000, the number had climbed to 51. Across the country at the same time, there were more than 1,000 claims in process in various categories.

B.C. Premier Glen Clark and Nisga'a Tribal Council President Joe Gosnell shake hands before signing the Nisga'a Final Agreement in Terrace, BC, 27 April 1999. The historic ratification of the Nisga'a Treaty and Nisga'a Constitution won a majority vote by the Nisga'a Nation on 6 November 1998 after 113 years of negotiations. *(CP PHOTO/Nick Procaylo-str)*

The RCAP Report

The commissioners' five-volume, 3,537-page report, when it finally appeared, was stunning in its size and the scope of its proposals for Canada and Canadians. It involved a fundamental reorganization of the country's social and political institutions in relation to Aboriginal peoples. In the commissioners' words:

> We advocate recognition of Aboriginal nations within Canada as political entities through which Aboriginal people can express their distinctive identity within the context of Canadian citizenship. . . . At the heart of our recommendations is the recognition that Aboriginal peoples are peoples, that they form collectives of unique character, and that they have a right to governmental autonomy.[58]

In other words, the relationship between Aboriginal and non-Aboriginal people is central to Canada's heritage. With this in mind, the commissioners identified four key issues: the need for a new relationship between Aboriginal and non-Aboriginal peoples, self-determination through self-government, economic self-sufficiency, and healing for Aboriginal peoples and communities. They made 440 recommendations detailing specific measures to achieve these goals, including:

- An Aboriginal parliament—the House of First Peoples—elected as a third order of government to advise the federal and provincial legislatures on matters relating to Aboriginal peoples.
- The merging of 1,000 or more separate bands, Inuit villages, and Métis settlements into 60 to 80 Aboriginal nations entitled to self-government. Aboriginal peoples should be recognized as possessing a unique form of dual citizenship, as citizens both of an Aboriginal nation and of Canada.
- The enactment of an Aboriginal Nations Recognition and Government Act to establish criteria for the recognition of Aboriginal nations and to complete a citizenship that is consistent with international norms of human rights and with the Canadian Charter of Rights and Freedoms.

In addition to self-government, the recommendations dealt with such matters as co-management of wildlife resources, keeping Aboriginal customary usage in mind when establishing national parks, ownership and management of cultural historic sites, and even a proposal for the establishment of an electronic worldwide information clearing office. In the view of the RCAP, there are four dimensions to social change in reference to Natives: (1) healing; (2) improving economic opportunity; (3) developing human resources and Aboriginal institutions; and (4) adapting mainstream institutions to both Aboriginal and non-Aboriginal needs.[59]

On the subject of self-government, the commissioners proposed for urban Aboriginal people a 'Community of Interest Government'. Such a government would operate based on voluntary membership within municipal boundaries with powers delegated from Aboriginal national and/or provincial governments.[60] The Commission commended Quebec for its hunter income support programs, which were developed as part of its northern land-claim agreements.[61]

Self-Government in Any Context

Even as the commissioners were hammering out their recommendations, some of them had already been realized, at least in part. Others were in the process. A notable example is the northern Quebec community of Oujé-Bougoumou.

Oujé-Bougoumou, counting between 500–600 persons at the turn of the twenty-first century, was one of the nine northern Quebec bands listed under the James Bay and Northern Quebec Agreement of 1975. The United Nations has recognized the village as one of 50 world-class models for integrating as it does traditional concepts with modern engineering techniques and architectural designs.

It was not always like this. The Oujé-Bougoumou's troubles had started in the 1920s, when their territory became the focus of mining development. There followed a period during which the government displaced the Cree time and again as they got in

Chief Morris Scennacappo of the Rolling River, First Nations reserve in Manitoba, holds up an eagle feather below the Peace Tower on Parliament Hill, 14 June 2002, during a demonstration by First Nations over the government's tabling of the First Nations Governance Act. *(CP PHOTO/Tom Hanson)*

the way of mining interests. It would take years of persistent effort on the part of such individuals as Chief Jimmy Mianscum. Eventually, in the 1980s, they won recognition as a band and renamed themselves the Oujé-Bougoumou Cree Nation. After still more administrative battles, and with a new chief, Abel Bosum, they chose a site at Lake Opémisca, hired one of Canada's leading architects, Douglas Cardinal, a Blackfoot from Alberta, and set about building yet another village. When negotiations with the federal and provincial governments collapsed, they declared jurisdiction over their territory of 10,000 square kilometres. As Aboriginal leaders across the country rallied to their cause, Quebec (1989) and Ottawa (1991) finally signed deals. In the words of Bosum, from 'the very beginning, our objective has been to build a place and an environment that produces healthy, secure, confident and optimistic people.'[62]

In an urban context, the Tsuu T'ina Nation administers and is developing land adjacent to Calgary, Alberta, as is the Nippissing First Nation at North Bay, Ontario. The Squamish Nation Capilano Indian Reserve, including its business park, is situated entirely within the city of Vancouver, BC. In Saskatchewan, on the other hand, bands have targeted nearby cities for the creation of satellite reserves within the city limits but affiliated with the parent reserve. Their purpose is to provide centres of business activity and social service distribution for areas of the cities, such as Prince Albert, with large Aboriginal populations.[63] While many Aboriginal bands and individuals

Box 17.3   Smallboy's Camp

In 1968, Johnny Bob (Robert) Smallboy (Apitchitchiw, 1898–1984), a hereditary chief of the Ermineskin band at Hobbema, Alberta, left the reserve and with 143 followers set up camp on an old Amerindian hunting ground on the shores of Lake Muskiki, 65 kilometres north-west of Nordegg. For some time, the chief had been worried about overcrowding on the reserve. But even more, he was concerned about the loss of traditional values under the stresses of today's technology-dominated ethos. His camp remained on Kootenay Flats at the start of the twenty-first century and had developed a wilderness program for the re-habilitation of problem youths, 'the best of the worst from streets and reserves, society's rejects', in the words of Wayne Roan, president of the Nihtuskinan Society, which is in charge of the project.[64]

have embraced and taken advantage of the opportunities provided in modern society, others have sought and found strength in a retreat from that society and a return to more traditional practices (Box 17.3).

Directly related to the RCAP—in fact, launched within three weeks of its report—was Canada's first Aboriginal bank. The First Nations Bank of Canada began operations in Saskatoon in 1997 as a co-operative enterprise involving the Saskatchewan Federation of Indian Nations, the Saskatchewan Indian Equity Foundation, and the Toronto-Dominion Bank. Matthew Coon Come, National Chief of the Assembly of First Nations, 2000–3, an original board member, saw the benefits as including a greater degree of Native economic control and greater sensitivity to needs of First Nation communities and businesses, as well as an opportunity to share in the profits.[65]

On the political front, an initiative of Ronald Irwin (Indian Affairs Minister, 1993–7) to amend the Indian Act to give Aboriginal nations more control over their own affairs met with an angry reception on the part of Amerindian leaders, who felt that the proposed measures did not go far enough and that the Act should be abolished. National Chief Ovide Mercredi moved quickly to warn Ottawa that implementing the RCAP recommendations was its 'last best chance' to improve the lot of marginalized Aboriginal peoples, thus avoiding rising remedial expenditures for social and economic ills, not to mention the possibility of violence. The bill died unpassed on the order paper when a federal election was called for 2 June 1997.

The idea behind the bill was not dead, however. In January 2001, Robert Nault, Irwin's successor as Minister of Indian Affairs, proposed supplementing the Indian Act with a First Nations Governance Act (FNGA). The proposed Act would give bands increased powers to levy taxes on reserves, as well as the right to garnishee wages and seize assets. Nault saw the proposed measure as a step towards self-government. The reaction of the Amerindians was predictable: unless they would be involved in working out the new format, it would not get the support it needed to succeed.[66]

Concerns, Hopes, and Fears

It surprised no one that Aboriginal leaders hailed the RCAP report as an 'inspiring road map to the future', all the more because it so clearly expressed the Aboriginal position. Erasmus denied an early criticism that it 'listens only to Indians',[67] saying that the Commission was neither an Aboriginal organization nor an advocacy group.[68] Towards the end of the twentieth century, Indian Affairs was involved in self-government and jurisdictional negotiations at 81 tables across the country, involving about half of all First Nations.

In general, Indian Affairs acknowledged the need to build a new partnership with Aboriginal peoples, as well as to strengthen their communities to enable them to govern themselves. It also acknowledged that 'the inherent right of self-government is an existing Aboriginal and treaty right.'[69] Early in 1998, Jane Stewart, Minister of Indian Affairs and Northern Development, 1997–9, officially expressed the government's regret for the residential school abuses and announced a $350 million healing fund to help those who had suffered. At the same time, Stewart announced an action plan called 'Gathering Strength' to develop a partnership with the First Nations to carry out needed reforms in general administration.

The reaction of Native leaders was mixed, to say the least, particularly as the Minister of Indian Affairs, not the Prime Minister, had made the statement of regret.[70] Still, the department was able to report a year later that it had developed with the Assembly of First Nations an agenda to correct the situation and that, in fact, it was already in operation at national, regional, and community levels. AFN National Chief Matthew Coon Come, however, said the apology was not good enough. Instead, he asked for a national Truth and Reconciliation Commission to be established by Order-in-Council to act as a national forum for venting feelings and working out problems that have resulted from the residential school experience.[71]

On the matter of self-government, everyone agrees that arrangements have to take into account the differing circumstances of each case.[72] Fiscal restraint means that federal funding must be achieved through reallocation of existing resources, which involves taking the interests of other Canadians into account. Where their jurisdictions or interests are affected, provincial or territorial governments must be included in negotiations. In general, three-way (federal, provincial, Aboriginal) processes seem to be the most effective. Whatever the approach, no one expects easy answers, nor are any in sight. On the positive side, the country now has its first thoroughly thought-out blueprint for incorporating its First Nations as full partners in the Canadian confederation. However, Amerindian leadership must also accept its share of responsibility in mapping out the future, Coon Come said at an Aboriginal health conference held in Ottawa. In a speech entitled 'Our Voice, Our Decisions, Our Responsibility', he made the point that solutions to the social ills that plague the Amerindian community cannot all come from outside. 'We are the ones who have to do something. We must act.' High on his list of priorities was leadership accountability. In his words, 'we need to clean up our own act.'[73]

More recently, in another realm involving Amerindians' control of their future, the AFN National Chief, Phil Fontaine, at the end of June 2005, on the twentieth anniversary of Bill C-31 becoming law, called for a joint First Nations–government process to establish Aboriginal citizenship. Fontaine stated that Bill C-31 'has not resolved any of the problems it was intended to fix and has . . . created new problems.' Gender discrimination continues, for example, and the status Indian population 'is declining as a direct result of Bill C-31.' The National Chief emphasized:

> It is morally, politically and legally wrong for one government to tell another government who its citizens are, and we are calling for a process to move citizenship to the jurisdiction where it properly belongs . . . with First Nations governments. . . . Canada is in a clear conflict of interest . . . because the number of registered Indians creates financial implications for the government.[74]

Reactions to these calls for action will profoundly affect Canada's future as a nation.

Important Names and Terms

comprehensive claims
constitutional patriation
division of powers
Harper, Elijah
James Bay and Northern Quebec Agreement

Mackenzie Valley Pipeline Inquiry
Penner Report
Royal Commission on Aboriginal Peoples
self-government
specific claims

Study Questions

1) What makes the situation of the Lubicon Cree unique?
2) Explain the connections between the Penner Report and the Cree-Naskapi Act.
3) What were the key recommendations of the Royal Commission on Aboriginal Peoples?
4) What steps towards self-government were made at the end of the twentieth century?

Recommended Readings

Asch, Michael. *Home and Native Land: Aboriginal Rights and the Canadian Constitution*. Toronto: Methuen, 1984.
Goddard, John. *Last Stand of the Lubicon Cree*. Vancouver: Douglas & McIntyre, 1991.
Hornig, James F., ed. *Social and Environmental Impacts of the James Bay Hydroelectric Project*. Montreal and Kingston: McGill-Queen's University Press, 1999.
Samson, Colin. *A Way of Life That Does Not Exist: Canada and the Extinguishment of the Innu*. St John's and London: ISER Books and Verso, 2003.
Shkilnyk, Anastasia M. *A Poison Stronger Than Love: The Destruction of an Ojibwa Community*. New Haven: Yale University Press, 1985.

18 We Are Sorry

On 11 June 2008, the Prime Minister of Canada rose in the House of Commons and made history with three words: 'We are sorry.' His statement, and those made that day by the leaders of the other parties in Parliament, and responses by the leaders of five national Aboriginal organizations, mark a watershed in Canada's Aboriginal history. The apology was made for the many harms wrought on stolen children by the residential schools since the middle of the nineteenth century. The apology marks a new beginning, but it is only a beginning, and the real work of healing the relationship between the government of Canada and Canada's First Nations is yet to be done.

An April 2008 *Globe and Mail* article, headlined 'Natives threaten Olympic disruptions', quoted the then Assembly of First Nations National Chief, Phil Fontaine, as stating that the 'The situation here is compelling enough to convince Canadians that while it is okay to express outrage with the Chinese government's position against Tibet and the Tibetans, they should be just as outraged, if not more so, about our situation here.'[1] Many Canadians reading that headline would be shocked that Canada's treatment of First Nations peoples could be compared to China's treatment of the people of Tibet, but the fact remains that the legacy of abuse still must to be addressed and that the apology of 11 June 2008 is merely a beginning rather than an end to the healing process.

In addition to the residential schools apology, other important signs suggest that the healing process is gaining momentum. This chapter will examine some of these signs. Across Canada one of the most important and cherished First Nations traditions is oral history, the passing of a people's storehouse of knowledge from one generation to the next. The historic 1997 decision by the Supreme Court of Canada in *Delgamuukw v. British Columbia* overturned a decision of the British Columbia Court of Appeal and ruled that oral history must be considered 'as a repository of historical knowledge for a culture'.[2] Other Aboriginal and treaty rights cases continue to push the legal and administrative agenda towards fairness and healing. The priority of resource allocation that came from the landmark ***Sparrow v. R.*** case of 1987 is a good example of a step forward. This case involved a BC Native who had used a fishing net larger than allowed by law. The Supreme Court

Time Line

1982	Patriation of Canadian Constitution; Constitution Act, 1982 recognizes and affirms 'existing aboriginal and treaty rights'.
1987	Supreme Court rules in *Sparrow v. R.* The *Sparrow* case was the first in which the Supreme Court of Canada dealt with section 35 of the Constitution Act of 1982, which recognizes and affirms 'the existing aboriginal and treaty rights of the aboriginal peoples of Canada.'
1990	Supreme Court rules in *R. v. Sioui.* In this case, a document signed by General James Murray, Military Governor of Quebec in 1760 in which the Hurons were guaranteed the free exercise of their customs and religion, was held to be a treaty.
1996	Supreme Court rules in *R. v. Adams.* The Adams case was another Aboriginal rights case that supported the right to resource use as found in *Sparrow.*
1997	Supreme Court overturns British Columbia Court of Appeals decision in *Delgamuukw v. British Columbia.* The most important element in this case was the Court's allowance of oral history on an equal footing with other types of evidence.
2000	The Canadian government ratifies the Nisga'a Final Agreement Act, granting 1,900 square kilometres to the Nisga'a.
2003	In September, with the decision in *Powley*, the Supreme Court of Canada affirms that Métis have rights that are recognized and protected by Canada's Constitution.
2005	In October Henco Industries decides to develop the Douglas Creek Estates, adjacent to the Six Nations Reserve, which later causes clashes between residents of Caledonia, near Hamilton and Brantford in southern Ontario, and the Six Nations.
2007	On 19 September, the federal government announces a $1.9 billion compensation deal for an estimated 80,000 former residential school students.
2008	On 11 June, the Prime Minister of Canada makes a statement of apology to former residential school students in the House of Commons.
2009	On 23 July, Shawn A-in-chut Atleo sworn in as new National Chief of the Assembly of First Nations following an election spanning 23 hours and eight ballots, which ended only with the concession of his nearest rival.

found that Aboriginal fishing, land, and hunting rights for food, social, and ceremonial purposes had priority over later restrictive legislation, and Sparrow was acquitted.

On the other hand, there is still work to be done. The ongoing (as of 2010) Douglas Creek land claim in Caledonia, Ontario, is an example of the challenges that need to be confronted. Although the Ontario Provincial Police seem determined not to repeat the tragic events of Ipperwash, the Douglas Estates land claim remains a volatile and difficult situation and has excited a great deal of media and public attention. Similarly, the Samson Cree Nation lawsuit (see Box 18.2) against the federal government reveals that high-stakes claims create special problems that need to be addressed with fairness and resolve.

Delgamuukw and Oral History

As we have seen in Chapter 16, Justice Allan McEachern ruled to reject the Aboriginal rights claim of the Gitskan and Wet'suwet'en to 58,000 square kilometres of their traditional lands in northern British Columbia. The case relied heavily on oral history and on the testimony of more than 100 witnesses. McEachern, Chief Justice of the Appeal Court of British Columbia, denied the existence of Aboriginal rights of ownership, but then, in 1997 the Supreme Court of Canada overturned the judgement and found that oral history evidence had not been given sufficient weight in the original trial. Justice Brian Dickson stated: 'Claims to aboriginal title are woven with history, legend, politics, and moral obligation.'[3] In addition to the obvious importance of a land claim of such a vast size, the *Delgamuukw* case is of special significance in terms of the importance placed by the Court on oral history. With a few exceptions—including pictographs and wampum belts—most First Nations history lives in the memories of the people. Stories are told and passed on from one generation to another, and from time immemorial these stories have constituted the storehouse of people's knowledge.

From the very first contacts between Europeans and Amerindians oral history has played an important role. When Samuel de Champlain travelled up the Ottawa River in the summer of 1613 in his first attempt to visit the Hurons in their villages he kept a careful record of his travels and noted several elements of oral history. When he landed at Allumette Island the Algonquin chief Tessouat invited him and his party to a feast. Later, Champlain complained bitterly about the Algonquin habit of repetition and he marvelled at how long his hosts discussed matters of import.[4] What Champlain saw and heard that night was the careful repetition of facts that would enable his hosts to remember events long after Europeans—and others trained in the written tradition—had forgotten them.

Oral histories take many forms and can be repeated as stories. Some of them were recorded. Two famous examples of oral histories that were written down in the nineteenth century are those of Francis Assikinack and Andrew Blackbird.[5] Francis Assikinack was an Odawa from Manitoulin Island who wrote down his histories at the urging of the chief clerk for the Indian Department, Daniel Wilson. Assikinack had been educated at Upper Canada College in Toronto and came to understand the importance of the written word in the changing world around him. His histories are clearly written and, as far as they can be checked against other sources, factual. Blackbird, another Odawa, who had been sent away to get a European education, is often used as an example of the validity of oral history. In one section of his history Blackbird refers to a group of people as Stockbridges, a term that referred to a New England town where they had been sent after being forced off their ancestral land. By the time Blackbird wrote his history this term had gone out of use completely and the only way Blackbird could have known it was from the oral tradition he had learned from his parents and from his extended family.[6] This kind of validation is not possible in most cases because of the paucity of written sources.

Box 18.1 Discovery Doctrine

Some critics have pointed to Chief Justice McEachern's original ruling as an example of the old concept of **discovery doctrine**. The origins of this policy may be found in the middle of the fifteenth century. In 1452, Pope Nicholas V issued to King Alfonso V of Portugal the papal bull *Romanus Pontifex*, a virtual declaration of war against all non-Christians and an official sanction of the conquest, colonization, and the eventual exploitation of non-Christian peoples and their territories.[7] The importance of this doctrine was put into high relief with the arrival of Columbus in the Americas in 1492. The policy was further strengthened when Columbus returned to Europe and Pope Alexander VI issued the papal bull *Inter Caetera* in 1493, which granted to Spain (Pope Alexander was from Valencia) the right of conquest over those lands that Columbus had already explored, as well as any non-Christian territories that Columbus or other Spanish explorers might find in the future. By this means, Pope Alexander hoped to please King Ferdinand and Queen Isabella, expand the influence of Spain and Christianity, and through the doctrine of *propaganda fide* or propagation of the faith he hoped to bring the conquered people to Christianity.[8]

The main principle of the discovery doctrine was accepted by European colonizers and remained an unspoken assumption until the famous US Supreme Court case of *Johnson v. McIntosh* in 1823.[9] Writing for a unanimous court, Chief Justice John Marshall noted that the European colonizers had assumed dominion over North and South America during the Age of Discovery, and that the indigenous peoples had lost their rights to absolute sovereignty, but they did retain a right of occupancy in their own lands. In addition, Marshall claimed that the United States of America, upon winning its independence from Great Britain, simply assumed this right of discovery and the authority of dominion from the British. Succinctly put, the colonizing powers assumed the right to claim possession of the Americas by virtue of their belief in the superiority of Christianity and its adherents. In turn, the US Supreme Court ruled that they had inherited their right of possession, by way of the British, from the doctrine of a fifteenth-century pope who was attempting to curry favour with the King and Queen of Spain.[10]

The Supreme Court ruling to allow appropriate weight to oral history testimony reveals that the Court has come to accept what historians have known for some time: oral history provides the best way to overcome the evidentiary shortcomings of the written record and the best way to find the Aboriginal perspective. Cases that have benefited from this acceptance include that of the Nisga'a, where the Court allowed a great deal of oral history testimony to help clarify the issues around the Nisga'a land claim in British Columbia. Oral history greatly helped a case that was extremely complex.[11]

Caledonia Land Claims

One complex case still awaiting a resolution is the **Douglas Creek** dispute in Caledonia. Like many First Nations issues, the problems at Douglas Creek in Caledonia have deep roots. Before we can hope to understand what seems to be an ill-conceived fiasco on the part of the Henco property developers, we first must examine the history of the Six Nations people in the Grand River region. In many ways the story of the settlement of the Six Nations in the so-called **Haldimand Tract** along the Grand River resonates with some of the critical themes of Canadian history: settlement; the clash of cultures between the Europeans and the Aboriginal people; the clashes between French and English; and worries over American expansionism. At the heart of the story is one of Canada's most famous Amerindians, Joseph Brant, or, to give his Mohawk name, Thayendanegea.[12] The territory in question, the Haldimand Tract in what is now southern Ontario, lies west of the Niagara Peninsula, north of Lake Erie, south of Lake Ontario, and east of Lake Huron. This area had been a kind of no man's land for much of the seventeenth century. The warriors of the Iroquois Confederacy who lived to the east of the Niagara River had made the area too dangerous to occupy.

By the dawn of the eighteenth century, however, this was to change. After being decimated by the so-called Mourning War, delegates of the Five Nations went to Montreal to forge the 'Great Peace' with the Hurons, the Odawa, and the Ojibwa and their allies, the French. After the treaty, the Five Nations returned to their ancestral homeland in the region to the south of Lake Ontario and to the east of the Niagara River. In 1722 the five (Mohawk, Onandaga, Oneida, Seneca, and Cayuga) were joined by the Tuscaroras, the sixth nation in the confederacy, who had migrated north to escape settler encroachment in the Carolinas.[13]

When the Revolutionary War broke out in 1776 the Six Nations Iroquois first chose to pursue a policy of neutrality. They made a treaty with the newly formed Second Continental Congress to formalize this arrangement. The colonists pledged to protect the Six Nations from encroachment on their lands in exchange for this neutrality. Events soon made it evident that the Six Nations had misjudged the Americans. With its energies devoted to the epic struggle with the British, the Continental Congress had no time to spare to see that the niceties of the treaty were respected. Thousands of Anglo-Americans soon began to occupy Iroquoia—what we now call the Finger Lakes region of New York. After being let down by the Continental Congress the Six Nations turned to the British for help against the land-hungry colonists.

The leading figure in this drama was Joseph Brant. A long-time ally of the British, Brant had been made 'Interpreter for the Six Nations Language' by the British agent to the Iroquois, Sir William Johnson, whose common-law spouse and mother of nine children was the highly influential Mary Brant, Joseph's sister. After Sir William's death in 1774, Joseph Brant continued to work for the British and in particular for Sir William's successor, Colonel Guy Johnson. In the autumn of 1775 Johnson and Brant travelled to London on a mission of goodwill to the British government.

Brant used this extraordinary opportunity to express his concerns about the intentions of the American settlers and land speculators to the Secretary of State for the American Colonies, Lord George Germain. Brant warned that the settlers wanted to cheat the Iroquois out of the small territory that remained to them. Lord George listened sympathetically and promised Brant, 'every support England could render' as soon as the disputes with the Americans were resolved.[14]

This meeting convinced Brant that the interests of the Six Nations were best served by allying with the British. Even while they were talking in London the problem in Iroquoia was growing much worse and by the time of Brant's return the situation was desperate. When Brant arrived back in North America he went to see Six Nations leaders. They were skeptical of an alliance with the British, and Brant had little influence with his own people. In Iroquois culture, age and tradition carried a huge amount of authority and Brant was relatively young and too closely associated with the British for some of his compatriots. His claims that a British alliance was in the Six Nations' interest were met with suspicion. Eventually, however, the actions of the Americans became increasingly hostile and the entire Six Nations force sided with the British.

The struggles of 1777 and 1778 were hard fought. Gradually the Americans' superior numbers wore down the British and their allies. Brant and his men fought with Major-General John Butler and won a number of battles, but the tide of the war turned against the British and allied forces. By 1779 Butler and Brant had been forced as far west as the Genesee River by the American forces under Major-General John Sullivan. Sullivan's forces destroyed every Iroquois village they took. They burned the longhouses to the ground and set fire to the cornfields. Iroquoia was destroyed forever. Brant and his small force had little choice but to continue the fight along the Niagara frontier for the remainder of the war. By 1782, however, the British commanders instructed their Iroquois allies to abandon the hostilities as peace negotiations were announced.[15]

For the loyalty of the Iroquois allies to the British Crown, and for their courage on the battlefield, the British government informed Brant that the Six Nations people would be accommodated as soon as possible with a new home. Such a home had a number of very specific requirements. First, the climate and soil had to be right for growing corn, beans, and squash, the 'three sisters' that formed the staple of the Iroquois diet. Second, Iroquois hunters would need good access to deer, their main prey. Third, second-growth forests—forests that were not yet fully mature—were necessary to provide the people with the raw materials they would need to build longhouses and other structures and equipment. Finally, the Six Nations required an uninhabited area that would not bring them into conflict with an established group.[16]

The Grand River region, from its source to its mouth, fit the bill perfectly. The soil and climate of the region were nearly identical to old Iroquoia. The crops would thrive just as they had further east. Deer and other game were abundant, all the more so because the region had not had many human visitors since the end of the seventeenth century. Second-growth forests were plentiful and there was a lot of choice for village sites close to these forests. Most importantly, the area was available for settlement. The

Iroquois had long driven off the ancestral inhabitants, the Eries and the oddly named Neutrals, and the Mississaugas who had recently moved into the region did not want to settle. The land was purchased by the British from the Mississaugas, whose economic orientation to the resources of the lakes was ill-suited to it.[17] In fact, the only problem with the Grand River was its proximity to the frontier and to the American colonists.

Accordingly, on 25 October 1784, the Governor of Quebec, Sir Frederick Haldimand, made the so-called Haldimand Proclamation. Acting for the Crown, Haldimand conveyed to the Mohawks 'and such others of the Six Nations Indians as wish to settle in that quarter' the Grand River tract of land as restitution for their losses in the Revolutionary War. Haldimand's grant was quite specific and the Six Nations were authorized to settle along the banks, from its head to its mouth 'six miles deep from each side' of the Grand River.[18] In the early spring of 1785 Brant led a group of 1,843 Six Nations people from Lewiston, New York, across the Niagara to their new home. The Cayugas (and a few of their Delaware compatriots) built a village on the northeast side of the river just upstream from Lake Erie. The Onandagas and Senecas built villages a little further upstream and still on the northeast side of the river. Just along from them the Tuscaroras built a village. Closer to the present city of Brantford, the Mohawks, Oneidas, and another group of Cayugas (called Upper Cayugas to distinguish them from the group near Lake Erie) built their villages.[19]

What appears to be a clear and unequivocal document, however, soon gave rise to a set of controversies that still rage today. There were two problems with the Haldimand Proclamation from the outset. First, the region was largely unknown at the time of the proclamation and not properly surveyed. The Six Nations never went beyond the vicinity of present-day Brantford and the region beyond was never clearly delineated. Much more serious, however, was the divergence in the interpretation of the meaning of the grant. The agents of the British Crown, from Haldimand forward, asserted that the land granted was not transferable and that the Haldimand Proclamation did not recognize the political sovereignty of the Six Nations Confederacy. Understandably, Joseph Brant interpreted matters differently. He argued that the Proclamation was a de facto recognition of Iroquois sovereignty and that the title to the land was, therefore, held in what British law called 'an estate in fee simple'. To prove this, he quickly sold and leased huge sections of the Grand River to British settlers.[20]

These actions alarmed the Crown. In 1793 the lieutenant-governor of the new province of Upper Canada, John Graves Simcoe, drafted the 'Simcoe Patent', a document stipulating that all land transactions in the Haldimand Tract had to be approved by the Crown. Brant simply ignored Simcoe and his 'Patent' and continued to invite British settlers into the Haldimand Tract. Somewhere between Haldimand's grant and Simcoe's action, Brant and other Iroquois leaders began to change their minds about the presence of British settlers. In the early days they had been invited in as a means of demonstrating Iroquois sovereignty, but as time went by Brant realized the extent of the huge changes sweeping across the region. Simcoe was inclined to allow Brant to have his own way as he feared losing the Six Nations as military allies.[21]

Brant seems to have recognized that the days of the longhouse and the traditional economy of the Iroquois were numbered. He felt the presence of British farmers would serve as a good example for the Iroquois people and that the Iroquois would learn to farm like the British. The Crown continued to oppose Brant's actions and interpretations, but Brant by this time was a wise and skilled politician and the newly formed Indian administration was not equipped to handle him.

In 1834 the first inquiry into the situation in the Haldimand Tract was held. The Crown determined that Brant had acted illegally, but by then it was deemed too costly and difficult to move all of the British settlers from their farms. The only option open to the Crown at this juncture was to confirm the legality of Brant's leases. At the same time the inquiry raised a number of concerns about the rapid growth of Brantford and the other communities within the Haldimand Tract.

In response to the ongoing problems, the Superintendent of Indian Affairs, Samuel Peters Jarvis, went to the Onandaga Council House in January 1841 and suggested the Iroquois voluntarily surrender their lands (save some reserve lands and the areas of the villages, a total of about 20,000 acres) back to the Crown so that the Crown could administer the Haldimand Tract 'for their exclusive benefit and interest'. Jarvis argued that one contiguous reserve would allow for more economical construction of schools, churches, and other public buildings. The chiefs agreed, but the agreement did little to alleviate the confusion that resulted from Brant's earlier interpretation of the Haldimand Proclamation.[22] After Jarvis got the Six Nations to surrender their lands the ownership question of most of the land that had been sold and leased was resolved, at least in the eyes of the Crown. Various interests in the Six Nations continued to maintain a different point of view.[23]

Following the Order-in-Council of 1843 that affirmed the surrender, a delegation of Iroquois chiefs appealed to the government to grant an additional 35,000 acres. This was

The landscape of present-day Caledonia. *(Bill Newbigging)*

Box 18.2   Samson Cree Nation

In 1989 legal proceedings were instituted in the Federal Court of Canada by the **Samson Cree Nation** and its members against the federal government with regard to the royalties from oil and gas revenues that the federal government holds in trust for the band. The Samson Cree Nation, part of Treaty Six in central Alberta, seeks to have the federal government, in particular the Department of Indian Affairs, declared in breach of its treaty, trust, fiduciary, and other obligations and duties with respect to the management of the oil and gas revenues relating to the Pigeon Lake Reserve. This case has crept along for years and the Samson Cree are now pursuing costs for the delays as well. The sums of money involved are huge—a reflection of the demand for oil and gas—and the case points to the critical need for Aboriginal development corporations that will have the real interest of Aboriginal people at heart.

---

affirmed, and in 1847 the reserve was formally established at approximately 55,000 acres, although subsequent surrenders reduced its size to 44,900 acres. The government also forced squatters off the reserve land, but many of them simply returned. The particular land in question at Caledonia falls into this grey area. It was never legally surrendered, but as long as the descendants of the original British settlers were on the property, nothing was done. When the land was sold to Henco Industries for development, the trouble started. The history of this piece of land was faithfully recorded by Canadian historian Charles Johnston in *The Valley of the Six Nations* and his painstaking work does help us to understand the issues now confronting the people of Caledonia and the members of the Six Nations who are protesting the development at Douglas Creek. Understanding is one thing, however, and resolution is another.

In 2006 the Ontario government negotiated the purchase of the Douglas Creeks Estates property from Henco Industries, for $21.1 million, and a year later the federal government contributed $15.8 million towards the Ontario purchase. Nonetheless, bitterness between some residents of Caledonia and the Six Nations people has not entirely subsided, and a final resolution of this land issue that dates back more than two centuries must await the resolution of many other specific land claims relating to the Haldimand Tract that have been filed over the past several decades.

The Residential Schools Settlement Agreement, 2007

An agreement to compensate the estimated 80,000 recognized survivors of designated Indian residential schools was ratified by the federal government on 19 September 2007. This agreement was not only for those who attended and survived but also for those who did not survive or who have since died. The issues surrounding the profound damage to individuals, communities, and cultures are the focus of the **Indian Residential Schools Truth and Reconciliation Commission**, but this symbolically important body got off to a less than encouraging start. Ontario Court of Appeal Justice Harry S. LaForme of the Mississauga of New Credit First Nation was appointed to head the Commission in May 2008 and began his work in June 2008, but in October of that year he resigned, citing the insubordination of the other two commissioners, who, among other things, were less interested than Justice LaForme in the reconciliation aspect of the Commission's mandate. These two commissioners held onto their positions, without a chair, until January 2009, when they finally stepped down.[24] A reconstituted Commission was established in June 2009, headed by Justice Murray Sinclair, the first Aboriginal judge in the Manitoba court system.

The September 2007 agreement with the federal government was to provide at least $1.9 billion to residential school survivors. The last federally run residential school had been closed in 1996 in Saskatchewan.[25] There have been many painful stories and memories from indigenous persons of a legacy of mental, physical, and even sexual abuse. The path to a settlement agreement with the federal government and the Canadian churches who also ran these schools took over 10 years from the time, in January 1998, when the federal government announced an **Aboriginal Action Plan**, which called for a renewed partnership with many Aboriginal people and Aboriginal organizations to recognize the past mistakes and injustices.[26]

Students at Shingwauk residential school, 1956.

Residential school survivors return to Shingwauk, 2002.

With many lawsuits related to the residential schools still pending, the federal government proposed payments for all former residential school students who were alive as of 30 May 2005. The proposal included an initial payout of $10,000 plus $3,000 for each year the student attended the school. However, this proposal included a provision that such an offer would release the government and the involved churches from all further liability relating to the Indian residential school experience, except in serious cases of sexual abuse or any physical abuse. For this purpose the **Independent Assessment Process** (IAP) was set up to address these serious cases of abuse.[27] As with other Aboriginal issues, lawyers and civil servants have managed to turn this process into a cottage industry and a tremendous amount of resources that could benefit the abused students are wasted on legal wrangling and bureaucratic inefficiencies.

In the current deal, each eligible person who attended a designated residential school is expected to receive about $28,000. Not everyone, however, was happy with the agreement or its payment, and legal actions remain outstanding. The former students who decided to take the settlement money will not be able to sue the government, the churches, or any other defendant in a class action lawsuit, the government stated. While the Indian residential schools settlement brought some closure for the federal government and the churches accused in the lawsuits, financial compensation can never equal the suffering and anguish. The long-term damages to Aboriginal individuals, families, and communities are incalculable.[28]

The Proposed Governance Act and Aboriginal and Treaty Rights

Early in the twenty-first century the federal government attempted, but failed, to do away with the Indian Act. As we have seen in the previous chapter, the **First Nations Governance Act** (FNGA), first proposed in January 2002 by the Department of Indian Affairs, was designed to amend the original Indian Act (1876). Introduced by former Liberal Indian Affairs Minister Robert Nault as Bill C-7, it created much discussion on the issue of Aboriginal governance. The proposed legislation, which died when then Prime Minister Paul Martin ended the parliamentary session in 2004, set forth a wave of debate between the federal government and many Aboriginal groups across Canada. Many First Nations leaders opposed the legislation, first, because it did not recognize the inherent right of self-government, and second, because it was seen as an attack on existing Aboriginal and treaty rights. For its part the federal government claimed that the proposed Act would increase the accountability of both First Nations and their governments. However, discussions about how the proposed Act would improve education, health care, and housing and eradicate poverty revealed obvious disagreements regarding the achievement of these important goals.

The main principles of the Act included the development of a system by First Nations to choose their leaders and to establish clear rules on financial spending and accountability. First Nations wished to have their form of governance based on their customs, laws, and cultures as well as their Aboriginal and treaty rights. The major opposition to this Act concerned the process under which it would come into existence, and great concern was expressed over the lack of prior consultation. Opposition demonstrated that a considerable amount of mistrust and discontent continued to plague the relations between the First Nations and the federal government. First Nations leaders could not help but notice that the FNGA was put on the back burner while members of the ruling Liberal Party fought an internecine war that ended in their electoral defeat.

Still, it remains clear that the Indian Act is badly in need of replacement. It can no longer accommodate the existing governance structures in that it fails to address major issues such as the financial regulations of First Nations band councils, economic development, economic sustainability, and the ability to delegate authority.[29] These issues have been dealt with in Canada's Far North, where the Inuit have established development corporations to handle the funds from claims settlements. These corporations are kept separate from democratic governance structures. Some treaty bands, too, have been successful in establishing development agencies. The Lac La Ronge band of Treaty Six in northern Saskatchewan, for example, has established successful developmental agencies.[30]

The federal government's stated goals for the FNGA were to give First Nations communities the 'tools they need to operate effective, responsible, and accountable governance structures' and to 'improve the lives of Aboriginal people by

---

Box 18.3   Treaty Land Entitlement

One area where progress is being made concerns the question of treaty land entitlement in western Canada. Land claims in the West had long been hampered by the shifting nature of responsibility. The boundaries of the province of Saskatchewan were different when the treaties were signed than they are at present. When the Hudson's Bay Company sold the huge tract of the Northwest known as Rupert's Land to Britain in 1869 and it was transferred to the new Confederation of Canada in 1870, these transactions occurred without consideration of the land rights of the region's people. Naturally, the First Nations involved complained of this violation of a policy established as far back as the Royal Proclamation of 1763. The federal government recognized that a number of First Nations did not receive the reserve lands they were entitled to under the original surveys for the numbered treaties. The federal government did little about this situation until 1930 when it signed the Natural Resources Transfer Agreement.

By this agreement, responsibility for outstanding treaty land obligations shifted from Canada to Saskatchewan at the time the province finally gained control over its Crown lands, minerals, and resources. In 1992, by the Saskatchewan Treaty Land Entitlement Framework Agreement, 25 Saskatchewan First Nations, the federal government, and the provincial government moved to ensure that all of the First Nations receive the amount of reserve land to which they are entitled. Saskatchewan provides the Crown land for sale; the federal government provides the funds to purchase the land; and the First Nations select and purchase the land for the reserves. The Manitoba Treaty Land Entitlement Framework Agreement, following the exact pattern as the Saskatchewan agreement, and for the exact same reasons, was signed in 1997.

---

providing tools for greater self-sufficiency and economic development.'[31] This latter ideal eventually became part of the **Kelowna Accord** of November 2005. This attempt, brokered by Prime Minister Paul Martin and First Nations leaders, was to provide some equity for First Nations people after the failure of the FNGA. Unfortunately, the Kelowna Accord, which had promised $5 billion over its initial five-year phase for economic development, education, and various other services, fell by the wayside after the election of a minority Conservative government in February 2006.

Throughout the spring, summer, and fall of 2003, First Nations across Canada participated in community meetings, information sessions, and discussion groups; they also provided written proposals in their submissions to the minister. Over 10,000 First Nations people participated in the process and discussed their views on the matter of how Bill C-7 could be implemented to improve the lives of Aboriginal people across Canada. The minister also appointed a joint ministerial advisory committee, made up of First Nations representatives and federal government officials, to provide expert advice and guidance on the various legislative options. The committee presented its report to Nault in March 2004.

The federal government's initiative sought to bring together what it regarded as all of the indigenous leaders from across Canada in an effort to consult them on the proposed legislation. Although this was an admirable and inclusive goal, it proved difficult to implement. The different governance structures across Canada meant that a clear definition of 'indigenous leaders' was problematic and the federal government's attempt to be inclusive led to division and opposition. In addition to this practical problem, the old problems of mistrust asserted themselves. For some, the consultation effort was a reminder of the White Paper of 1969 and the politicization of First Nations people, which that initiative had helped to galvanize. People opposed the White Paper because its authors argued for the abolition of the treaties and an end to Aboriginal rights. To some extent the FNGA seemed to be advocating the same things.[32]

The opposition to the proposed FNGA rose steadily, and included many non-Aboriginal groups. Amnesty International and the Anglican, Catholic, and United churches of Canada joined the Assembly of First Nations in condemning the proposed legislation. As Grand Chief Matthew Coon Come noted, the proposed legislation would 'leave a

---

Box 18.4   Indian Activism in the 1960s and 1970s

In many ways the steps forward, such as the entrenchment of Aboriginal rights in the Constitution Act of 1982, the Charter of Rights and Freedoms, and the federal government's interest in consultation in the First Nations Governance Act, were the result of the Indian activism of the 1960s and 1970s. The National Indian Brotherhood—later the Assembly of First Nations—led the opposition to the 1969 White Paper on the grounds that indigenous people enjoyed certain rights *because* of their indigenous status. This resistance to government heavy-handedness struck a chord across Canada, and indeed across the continent, as people began to question authority more vociferously than ever before. The American Indian Movement, with its slogan of 'Red Power', rose in Minnesota in 1968, and was one of several other significant grassroots social movements of the period—civil rights, anti-war, the women's movement. The beginnings of the self-government movement in Canada can also be traced to the activism of the 1960s and 1970s as the federal government was forced to respond to the political activism of the National Indian Brotherhood and other Aboriginal groups. Treaty rights and Aboriginal rights were not simply gifts of the government, they were the birthright of Aboriginal people across the country, and the grassroots move to defend them resonated with people who were more ready than ever to challenge entrenched political power.

legacy of shame, a legacy of despair, and a legacy of colonialism when we were looking for a legacy of hope for our future generations.'[33] Opposition focused on the federal government's failure to address self-government and on the vagueness that appeared to threaten treaty rights and Aboriginal rights. Under Bill C-7 there was no explicit reference to the right of self-government. In the final analysis the FNGA related more to federal legislation and policy issues—to a desire to streamline an administrative quagmire—than to important constitutional rights. Its aim was federal housekeeping, not a new deal for Canada's Amerindians.[34]

In some sense the failure of the FNGA was the failure of a caretaker federal government that had come to power as a result of a palace coup rather than on a platform of good new ideas for the country. With the failure of the Paul Martin Liberals the initiative to replace the Indian Act shifted away from the federal government and to First Nations communities across Canada. By 2009 various self-governance models had taken form. Recently established self-governance agreements with the Kwanlin Dün First Nation in the Yukon, various First Nations in Manitoba, and with the Anishinabek Nation in Ontario provide models for new government-to-government relationships based on partnership and mutual respect. Another model exists in Nunavut, where the democratically elected territorial government is responsible for all citizens regardless of ethnicity but the reality is a government of Inuit people. An agreement-in-principle has been signed for a similar public (but mainly Inuit) government, the Nunavik Regional Government, in northern Quebec. This Nunavik government may serve as a model for others.[35] These steps are indeed in the direction of self-government, and they all have been accomplished without compromising treaty and Aboriginal rights.

In the end, as self-government becomes a reality for First Nations and other Aboriginal communities in Canada, we must remember that this will not be easy and there will be setbacks. For example, the Lheidli T'enneh near and within Prince George, BC, in 2007 rejected an agreement that their leaders had achieved. A bottom-up approach that comes from within First Nations will be needed, rather than solutions imposed by governments or simply by Aboriginal elites. We also must remember that Aboriginal people sometimes will fail the expectations of their own people—for example, a payroll administrator for a northern Manitoba First Nation was charged in December 2009 with embezzling over $1 million of band funds; and in the same month, some members of the Peguis First Nation, also in Manitoba, made public their objection that their chief and councillors received salaries and other payments comparable to or exceeding those of the province's premier and the mayor of Winnipeg.[36] Self-government, as it evolves, will require economic reform and economic development, something that, as we have seen, a number of communities have achieved. But others have not, and continue to live in conditions of poverty unimagined by most Canadians.

Shawn A-in-chut Atleo of the Ahousaht First Nation on the west coast of Vancouver Island was elected as the new National Chief of the Assembly of First Nations in

Shawn Atleo, a hereditary Nuu'chah'nulth chief from Vancouver Island, was elected National Chief of the Assembly of First Nations in July 2009. *(The Canadian Press/Jeff McIntosh)*

July 2009, following a potentially divisive and extended (eight ballots over 23 hours) election process. After campaigning on the importance of education, economic reform, and First Nations unity, Atleo explained: 'We know economic independence is political independence; economic power is political power.'[37] Achieving such independence and power will be the challenge in the years to come.

Important Names and Terms

Aboriginal Action Plan
discovery doctrine
Douglas Creek
First Nations Governance Act
Haldimand Tract
Independent Assessment Process

Indian Residential Schools Truth and
    Reconciliation Commission
Kelowna Accord
Samson Cree Nation
Sparrow v. R.

Study Questions

1) Why is oral history so vital in First Nations claims cases?
2) In what ways is Douglas Creek a unique land claim?
3) What is the task of the Indian Residential Schools Truth and Reconciliation Commission?
4) Outline the failings of the proposed First Nations Governance Act.

Recommended Reading

Bone, Robert M. *The Canadian North: Issues and Challenges*, 3rd edn. Toronto: Oxford University Press, 2009.

Graymont, Barbara. *The Iroquois in the American Revolution*. Syracuse: Syracuse University Press, 1972.

————. 'Thayendanegea', *Dictionary of Canadian Biography Online*.

Havard, Gilles. *The Great Peace of Montreal*. Montreal and Kingston: McGill-Queen's University Press, 2001.

Johnston, Charles M. *The Valley of the Six Nations*. Toronto: University of Toronto Press, 1964.

Kelsay, Isabel Thompson. *Joseph Brant: Man of Two Worlds*. Syracuse: Syracuse University Press, 1984.

Miller, J.R. *Shingwauk's Vision: A History of Native Residential Schools*. Toronto: University of Toronto Press, 1996.

Epilogue

If any one theme can be traced throughout the history of Canada's Amerindians, it is the persistence of their identity. The confident expectation of Europeans that Indians were a vanishing people, the remnants of whom would finally be absorbed by the dominant society, has not happened.[1] If anything, Indians are more prominent in the collective conscience of the nation than they have ever been, and if anyone is doing the absorbing it is the Indians. Adaptability has always been the key to their survival; it is the strongest of Amerindian traditions. Just as the dominant society has learned from the Indians, so the Indians have absorbed much from the dominant society, but they have done it in their own way. In other words, Indians have survived as Indians, and have preferred to remain as such even at the cost of social and economic inequality.[2]

In the Canadian multicultural mosaic, the Aboriginal peoples are reported to be the least happy with their lot.[3] In part, this is a reaction to cultural loss, particularly evident in the realm of language. Of the 50 or so Aboriginal tongues spoken in Canada at the time of contact, several are now extinct (Beothuk, Huron, Neutral) and most of the others are endangered, some seriously. Cree, Ojibwa, and Inuktitut appear to have the best chances of survival.[4] On the other hand, Aboriginal spiritual beliefs have displayed a remarkable vitality and indeed have been enjoying a renaissance. An expression of this has been the introduction of Aboriginal elements into Roman Catholic ritual, a movement that began in the prairie West, particularly in Edmonton. Recently there has been a convergence of Aboriginal and science-based knowledge that holds exciting promise for both the Aboriginal and non-Aboriginal communities.

All this has gone hand in hand with the rise of political activism and the campaign for self-determination and self-government. This is the opposite of a separatist movement. What Indians are asking for is full and equal participation in the Canada of today and of the future, and this was the clear message of the *Report of the Royal Commission on Aboriginal Peoples*. This movement is not without its problems, as the old ways are widely held by First Nations to be the best expression of their identity, and there is resistance to the party politics of representative democracy, which is regarded by some as an imposition. 'Self-government' is interpreted by many First Nations to mean participation on their own terms.[5] On the other side of the coin, change is the very essence of Aboriginal tradition. It recognizes that the cycle of life is one of constant motion. While basic patterns can be detected, there is no guarantee that they will be repeated in exactly the same way. No society today is the same as it was a century ago, even though there is continuity in many of its elements. Living traditions, like living societies, also change; what worked in one set of circumstances may not work in another. Identity is not an issue, but survival is, and adaptation continues to be the key. This is true not only for the First Nations, but for everyone.

The reaffirmation of Aboriginal identity has not been a sudden development—Amerindians have always had a clear idea of who they are. What is new is the demand for recognition of this by the dominant society. Several factors have contributed to this development, some of them of comparatively long standing and others very recent.

First of all, there has been the growing international recognition of Aboriginal art, especially since World War II. West coast art has long been appreciated—dating back to the days of first meetings in the eighteenth century, in fact—but that of other regions has been slower in gaining acknowledgement. In the 1940s, largely through the efforts of Toronto artist James A. Houston, Inuit learned printmaking. Carving in soapstone and ivory and the creation of tapestries also were encouraged; with the support of the Canadian government, the Hudson's Bay Company, and the Canadian Handicrafts Guild and the development of co-operatives to handle production and marketing, Inuit art became known worldwide. Another success story that developed somewhat later, that of Eastern Woodlands art, favours painting over printmaking, although both forms are practised.[6] Crafts such as porcupine quill work, beading, embroidery, and leather work have also come into their own and are much in demand. This flowering of Native arts and crafts illustrates very well the Aboriginal capacity to use new techniques to bring traditional arts, whose antiquity approaches those of Europe, Africa, and Australia,[7] into the contemporary world. In the literary, musical, and theatrical arts also, Native expression is winning respectful attention. The message is clear: Canada's first peoples, far from being interesting relics of the past, are a vital part of Canada's persona, both present and future.

It was only a matter of time for this growing cultural self-confidence to express itself, and to be listened to, in other arenas as well. A key area is education, and the First Nations have demonstrated their effectiveness in taking control of the schooling of their children. The justice system has been slower to respond, but there, too, the Native input is becoming more evident as it becomes more confident. If one were to pinpoint the moment of truth for this cultural momentum, it would be when Elijah Harper said 'No' to the Meech Lake Accord. The occasion could not have been more appropriate: not only was the whole nation watching and listening, but a good part of the world as well. Harper rose to the occasion, withstood the pressures mounted to bring him into line, and spoke for himself and his people. He even took himself by surprise: 'I never realized that I would have such an impact on this country.'[8]

Canada's Natives had finally caught the attention not only of their fellow Canadians but of the international community as well. And they had fundamentally altered the nation's course of events. The standoff at Oka quickly followed, as Amerindians took a determined position against an ancient wrong. The point was emphasized when 300 indigenous leaders held a summit of their own concurrently with the Summit of the Americas, at Quebec City in April 2001. AFN National Chief Coon Come was invited to attend the general summit, but without provision for him to meet with the top leaders from the Americas.[9] Still, this set a precedent that indicated that the message is being heard: no longer will Aboriginal people stand meekly by as others run things to suit themselves, without taking into serious account the people who were on the scene first. As the case of Canada so well illustrates, its confederation may be young, but it has components that are ancient.

The early twenty-first century included new challenges for Aboriginal people across Canada, as well as unresolved problems from the past. The federal Conservative government elected in early 2006 wasted no time undoing the efforts of its predecessors by immediately scrapping the Kelowna Accord and by its refusal in 2007 to accept the United Nations Declaration on the Rights of Indigenous Peoples. Only three other countries—Australia, New Zealand, and the United States—rejected the Declaration, and more recently the Australian government has affirmed its support. On 8 April 2008, the opposition parties in Canada sought to repudiate the government's stance by passing a resolution in the House of Commons endorsing the Declaration. The Tories opposed it.

The new century also brought some closure to other issues, such as the release of the final report of the Ipperwash Inquiry into the death of Dudley George, along with the Ontario government's pledge in December 2007 to return the provincial park to the Chippewas of Kettle and Stony Point First Nation. But such issues, as we have seen, are often complicated, especially in a federal state such as Canada. In May 2009, the First Nation and the provincial government reached agreement on the transfer of the park land to the federal government so this land then can be added to the reserve lands of the Chippewas of Kettle and Stony Point. Similarly, the residential schools settlement provided some of the Aboriginal survivors of designated residential schools at least some compensation for their tragic experiences of assimilation over the course of the twentieth century. However, the pain of all of these experiences can never be taken back, and many Aboriginal people, individually and collectively, will never recover what they lost.

While there remains hope that the twenty-first century will bring positive change for all Aboriginal people across Canada, many of the issues now confronting them are dramatically evident. There is still a significant gap in the standard of living compared to the rest of Canada, in terms of economic development, housing, education, and health care. Unresolved land rights issues, which have always posed a tremendous strain on the relationship with the federal and provincial governments, continue to be a central issue. The Specific Claims Tribunal Act, which came into effect in October

2008, is intended to speed up the specific claims process through the establishment of a Specific Claims Tribunal, made up of sitting provincial superior court judges. The Tribunal, consisting of three members, from British Columbia, Ontario, and Quebec, was appointed in November 2009, and the following month one of these three, Justice Harry Slade of the BC Supreme Court, was named as the chair. Yet, despite this important change, the slow pace of negotiations in the past has created a deep mistrust on the part of First Nations people towards government commitments to resolve long-standing disputes.

The foreign policy stance on indigenous rights by the federal government was a startling reminder that Canada's policy on Aboriginal rights—as human rights—always has been one of denial, and thus a failure. Nevertheless, to many Aboriginal people in Canada, the federal government stance at the UN has become all too familiar. In the early twenty-first century one of many unanswered questions relating to the future of Aboriginal peoples in Canada is whether they can become partners in building a more equitable nation of nations, or if they will be forced, by governments and by the indifference of public opinion, to focus exclusively, in piecemeal fashion, on their own often desperate needs. Many questions still remain in spite of the words: 'We are sorry.'

National Historic Sites of Canada Commemorating Aboriginal History

ALBERTA

64. **Blackfoot Crossing**
Traditional meeting place on Blackfoot reserves

63. **British Block, Cairn & Suffield Tipi Rings**
Aboriginal site on CFB Suffield

65. **Earthlodge Village**
Remains of Aboriginal village

62. **Frog Lake Massacre** (Parks Canada Administered)
Site of Cree uprising, 1885

68. **Head-Smashed-In Buffalo Jump**
World Heritage Site—Aboriginal bison drive

67. **Old Women's Buffalo Jump**
Aboriginal bison drive in use for 1500 years

66. **Treaty No. 7 Signing Site**
Treaty signed in 1877 with Blackfoot Nation

BRITISH COLUMBIA

72. **Kiix?in Village and Fortress**
Archaeological sites of First Nations village and fortress with significant architectural remains

82. **Kitselas Canyon Area**
Remains of 2 Aboriginal villages and petroglyphs

84. **Kitwanga Fort** (Parks Canada Administered)
Tsimshian village

83. **Kitwanga Totem Poles**
Totem poles record families of Kitwanga Fort

85. **Kitwankul**
Gitksan village

79. **Kiusta Village**
Former Haïda village

70. **Marpole Midden**
Site of midden, excavated in 1892

81. **Metlakatla Pass Area Indian Site**
Site of winter villages of Tsimshian Peoples

75. **Nan Sdins** (Parks Canada Administered)
Remains of Haïda longhouses and totem poles

78. **New Gold Harbour Area**
Site of Haïda village

77. **Skedans**
Former Haïda village

76. **Tanu**
Former Haïda village

71. **Weir's (Taylor's) Beach Earthworks Site**
Pre-contact site on Vancouver Island

74. **Whaler's Shrine Site**
Aboriginal ritual site

69. **Xa:ytem/Hatzic Rock**
Habitation site of Stó:lo peoples

80. **Yan Village Indian Site**
Former Haïda village

73. **Yuquot**
Spanish settlement site, 1789–95

MANITOBA

48. **Battle of Seven Oaks**
Conflict between Métis and Red River settlers, 1814

50. **Brockinton Indian Sites**
Late prehistoric site, Blackduck phase

51. **Linear Mounds** (Parks Canada Administered)
Aboriginal burial mounds from 1000–1200 AD

49. **Riel House** (Parks Canada Administered)
Family home of Métis leader Louis Riel

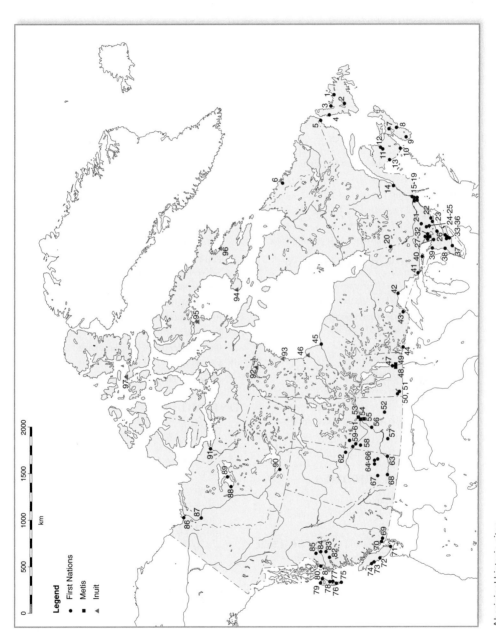

Aboriginal historic sites

46. **Sea Horse Gully Remains**
Large Dorset and Pre-Dorset site

47. **The Forks** (Parks Canada Administered)
Historic meeting place, junction of the Red and Assinboine rivers

45. **York Factory**
(Parks Canada Administered)
Hudson's Bay Company's principal fur trade depot from 1684–1870s

NEW BRUNSWICK

11 **Augustine Mound Site**
Pre-contact burial mound

13. **Meductic Indian Village/Fort Meductic**
Principal Maliseet settlement

10. **Minister's Island Pre-contact Sites**
Pre-contact shell midden, 500 BC–1500 AD

12. **Oxbow Sites**
Well-preserved, 3000-year archaeological record

NEWFOUNDLAND & LABRADOR

1. **Beothuk Site**
Major archaeological site for Beothuk history

3. **Fleur de Lys Soapstone Quarries**
Resource extraction by Dorset culture

2. **Indian Point**
Well-documented Beothuk site

5. **L'Anse Amour Burial**
Burial site, Maritime Archaic culture

6. **Okak**
Archaeological site, several cultures occupied

4. **Port au Choix** (Parks Canada Administered)
Pre-contact burial and habitation sites

NORTHWEST TERRITORIES

88. **Déline Fishery/Franklin's Fort**
Wintering quarters of Sir John Franklin and his second expedition

89. **Grizzly Bear Mountain and Scented Grass Hills**
Expression of cultural values through the interrelationship between landscape, oral histories, graves, and cultural resources

90. **Hay River Mission Sites**
Mission buildings, significant to Dene community

86. **Kittigazuit Archaeological Sites**
Beluga Hunting, Kittegaryumiut and Mackenzie Delta

87. **Nagwichoonjik (Mackenzie River)**
Flows through Gwichya Gwich'in traditional home-land and continues to be culturally, socially, and spiritually significant

NOVA SCOTIA

8. **Bedford Petroglyphs**
Spiritually significant petroglyph site

7. **Debert Palaeo-Indian Site**
Archaeological remains of Aboriginal caribou hunting

9. **Kejimkujik** (Parks Canada Administered)
Important Mi'kmaq cultural landscape

NUNAVUT

93. **Arvia'juaq and Qikiqtaarjuk**
Inuit summer occupation sites with rich history and surviving in situ resources

96. **Blacklead Island Whaling Station**
Aboriginal and European bowhead whaling

91. **Bloody Falls**
Pre-contact hunting and fishing sites

92. **Fall Caribou Crossing**
Site of critical importance to the historical survival of Inuit community

95. **Igloolik Island Archaeological Sites**
Archaeological sequence, 2000 BC–1000 AD

94. **Inuksuk**
Inuit complex of 100 stone landmarks

97. **Port Refuge**
Pre-contact occupations, trade with Norse colonies

ONTARIO

26. **Bead Hill**
Remains of 17th-century Seneca village

23. **Carrying Place of the Bay of Quinte**
Site of 1787 treaty between British and Mississauga

36. **Chiefswood**
Italianate style birthplace of poet Pauline Johnson

22. **Christ Church Royal Chapel**
Historic royal chapel linked with establishment of Mohawk Peoples in Ontario

43. **Cummins Pre-contact Site**
Extensive late Palaeo-Indian stone quarry

39. **Donaldson Site**
Aboriginal site, 500 BC–300 AD

31. **Etharita Site**
Main village of Wolf Tribe of Petun, 1647–9

30. **Fort Sainte Marie II**
Jesuit mission to Hurons, 1649–50

33. **Her Majesty's/St Paul's Chapel of the Mohawks**
First Protestant church in Upper Canada, 1785

44. **Manitou Mounds**
Religious and ceremonial site for 2,000 years; Rainy River Mounds

21. **Mazinaw Pictograph Site**
Largest Algonkian pictograph site in Canada

34. **Middleport Site**
Archaeological site, Middle Ontario Iroquois

29. **Mnjikaning Fish Weirs (Parks Canada Administered)**
Aboriginal fishing site

28. **Ossossane Sites**
Principal village of Bear Clan of Hurons

38. **Parkhill Site**
Palaeo-Indian habitation site, c. 8000 BC

24. **Peterborough Petroglyphs**
Algonkian petroglyph site

42. **Pic River Site**
Complex of pre-contact Woodland culture sites

27. **Saint-Louis Mission (Parks Canada Administered)**
Site of Huron village destroyed by Iroquois in 1649

32. **Sainte-Marie Among the Hurons Mission**
Headquarters of Jesuit mission to Hurons from 1639–49

25. **Serpent Mounds Complex**
Aboriginal peninsula site, 60 BC–300 AD

40. **Sheguiandah**
Site of pre-contact stone quarry

37. **Southwold Earthworks (Parks Canada Administered)**
Site of Attiwandaronk Indian village, c. 1500 AD

35. **Walker Site**
Large Iroquoian site, historical Attiwandaronk tribe

41. **Whitefish Island**
Ojibwa historic site

QUEBEC

19. **Battle of the Lake of Two Mountains**
Site of defeat of Iroquois by French, 1689

15. **Caughnawaga Mission/Mission of St Francis Xavier**
Jesuit mission to Mohawks established 1647

16. **Caughnawaga Presbytery**
Oldest surviving building at mission, eighteenth century

17. **Fort St-Louis**
Built in 1725 for protection of Christian Iroquois

18. **Hochelaga**
Iroquois village visited in 1535 by Jacques Cartier

14. **Notre-Dame-de-Lorette Church**
Mission church to the Hurons with seventeenth-century art objects, 1865

20. **Pointe Abitibi**
Traditional summering area and sacred place for the Algonquin

SASKATCHEWAN

54. **Batoche** (Parks Canada Administered)
Métis village; site of 1885 Battle Batoche

58. **Battle of Cut Knife Hill**
Cree repulse Canadian attack, 1885

53. **Battle of Duck Lake**
First battle of 1885 North West Rebellion

55. **Battle of Fish Creek** (Parks Canada Administered)
Site of battle between Métis and Canadian forces, 1885

60. **Fort Pitt**
Site of Hudson's Bay Company Post, signing of Treaty No. 6

52. **Fort Qu'Appelle**
Hudson's Bay Company post, Negotiation of Treaty No. 4

59. **Frenchman Butte** (Parks Canada Administered)
Site of 1885 battle, Cree and Canadian Troops

57. **Gray Burial Site**
One of the oldest burial sites in Plains, c. 3000 BC

61. **Steele Narrows**
Last engagement of North West Rebellion, 1885

56. **Wanuskewin**
Complex of Plains Indian cultural sites

Glossary

Abishabis ('Small Eyes', d. 1843) Cree prophet of a millenarian religious movement that swept through northern Manitoba and Ontario during the 1840s; murdered a First Nations family near York Factory, was arrested, and was murdered during his imprisonment.

Aboriginal Action Plan A renewed partnership with Aboriginal people and Aboriginal organizations to recognize past mistakes and injustices, especially in regard to residential schools, announced by the federal government in January 1998. This Plan led to an agreement on reparations in 2007 and a formal apology from the Prime Minister in June 2008.

'Aboriginal rights' A term originally signifying the rights that Canada's Aboriginal peoples hold as a result of their ancestors' long-standing use and occupancy of land, including the right to hunt, trap, and fish, but later encompassing the right to traditional self-government.

Alaska Highway A 1,520-mile (2446-km) road built in 1942 from Dawson Creek, Yukon, to Fairbanks, Alaska, as a supply route for World War II.

Allied Tribes of British Columbia The first province-wide coalition of BC First Nations formed in 1916 to pursue land claims; declared illegal following 1927 amendments to the Indian Act.

Assembly of First Nations The national representative organization of the First Nations in Canada. It grew out of the National Indian Brotherhood (NIB), which changed not only its name in 1982 but also its structure to become an 'Organization of First Nations Government Leaders'.

assimilation The process of being absorbed into the culture or customs of another group.

Bagot Commission (1842–4) Commission headed by Sir Charles Bagot (1781–1843) that examined Indian administration and affirmed the government's assimilation policy.

band The definition in the Indian Register, 1997, is a 'group of First Nation people for whom lands have been set apart and money is held by the Crown. Each band has its own governing band council, usually consisting of one or more chiefs and several councillors. Community members choose the chief and councillors by election, or sometimes through traditional custom. The members of a band generally share common values, traditions, and practices rooted in their ancestral heritage.'

Batoche The headquarters of Louis Riel's provisional government and the site of the last battle of the Northwest Rebellion, 1885, in present-day central Saskatchewan; named after François-Xavier Letendre *dit* Batoche (*c.* 1841–1901), the founder of the community.

Battle of Beaver Dams Battle of the War of 1812–14 near Thorold, Ontario, 24 June 1813, in which Kahnawake and other Mohawk warriors ambushed almost 500 American troops.

Battle of Fallen Timbers Defeat of Amerindians by Americans under the command of Major-General 'Mad' Anthony Wayne on 20 August 1794. The British refused to open the gates of Fort Miami to the retreating Amerindians, including Shawnee leader Tecumseh, which caused a breach in Amerindian–British relations.

Beothuk Aboriginal inhabitants of Newfoundland at the time of the arrival of the Europeans. The last known Beothuk died in 1829.

Beringia The name scientists have given to the land bridge that spanned the Bering Strait between what are now Asia and North America during the Wisconsin glaciation (last Ice Age).

Big Bear (Mistahimaskwa) (*c.* 1825–88) Cree-Ojibwa chief who refused to sign Treaty Six, working instead to unite the Cree and create an Indian territory. His band participated in the 1885 Northwest Rebellion, and Big Bear was convicted of treason-felony.

Blackfoot Confederacy Plains Indian coalition composed of the Siksika (the Blackfoot, the Blood, and the Peigan), the Sarcee, and the Gros Ventre. At its peak, it extended from the North Saskatchewan River, south to the Missouri, and from the present Alberta–Saskatchewan border to the Rocky Mountains.

Blue Quills School Opened in 1970, the first school in Canada run by Aboriginal people, near St Paul, Alberta, approximately 200 km northeast of Edmonton.

Brant, Joseph (Thayendanegea) (1742–1807) Mohawk chief, spokesman for his people, Anglican missionary, and British military officer during the US War of Independence. Brantford, Ontario, is named after him.

Brébeuf, Jean de (1593–1649) Jesuit missionary to the Huron who was captured and killed by the Iroquois during Huron–Iroquois hostilities.

Brock, Major-General Isaac (1769–1812) British officer who fought alongside Tecumseh at Fort Detroit. He was killed in the Battle of Queenston Heights. Brockville, Ontario, and Brock University, St Catharines, Ontario, are named after him.

Cabot, John (Giovanni Caboto) (*c.* 1451–1498?) Italian explorer financed by England who reached the shore of North America in 1497. He set out for the New World again in 1498, but his ship disappeared.

Cahokia Only pre-contact Amerindian city north of Mexico. Covering about 4,000 acres that included massive earthworks, the Cahokia site was occupied between about AD 700 and 1400.

Calder v. Attorney General (1973) Court case in which the Nisga'a of British Columbia claimed continued Aboriginal rights in their traditional territory. The Nisga'a lost on a technicality, but the case led the federal government to negotiate land claims based on outstanding Aboriginal title.

Canada First Activist group that campaigned to annex Red River to Canada in the mid-1850s.

Cartier, Jacques (1491–1557) French explorer who reached what is now eastern Canada. France used his three voyages, between 1534 and 1542, as a basis for its claim to sovereignty of North America.

Champlain, Samuel de (*c.* 1570–1635) French geographer, explorer, and founder of Quebec (1608). His writing and maps provide the only extant written information on the first 15 years of French occupation.

chiefdoms Amerindian communities characterized by hierarchy and led by chiefs.

'code talkers' Amerindians who served as radio operators during World Wars I (US, Chocktaw) and II (Canada, Cree; US, Navajo) receiving and transmitting coded messages in their native language.

Comité National des Métis (Métis National Committee) Association formed in 1869 with John Bruce as president and Louis Riel as secretary, and actively supported by Abbé Joseph-Noël Ritchot (1825–1905) of St Norbert, for the purpose of negotiating with the federal government concerning the rights of the residents of Red River.

Compagnie des Cent Associés One of the societies that received a charter (1627) from France authorizing it to explore, develop, and exploit New France.

comprehensive claims Claims arising in areas where rights of traditional use and occupancy have not been extinguished by treaty or superseded by law.

compulsory enfranchisement Department of Indian Affairs policy, dating from early twentieth century to mid-century, whereby the Superintendent-General had the power to enfranchise Amerindians he considered qualified, whether they wanted it or not. This meant that the individuals concerned had the rights of other Canadian citizens, including the right to vote, but no longer had status under the Indian Act.

constitutional patriation Process of transfer of the authority to amend a country's constitution to that country, signifying independence from a colonial power. In the case of Canada, it refers to the 1981 amendment of Canada's Constitution from being a British statute to being held in Canada.

Council of Three Fires Confederacy aimed at a joint defence against the Five Nations. It was made up of the Potawatomi (Fire Keepers), the Odawa (Trader Nation), and the Ojibwa (Faith Keepers).

counting coups Acts of skill and bravery that involved touching, but not killing, an enemy with a weapon. A person's status was determined by the number of touches made.

coureurs de bois Europeans who assimilated to First Nations culture and who were particularly active in the fur trade.

Crowfoot (Isapo-Muxika) (*c.* 1830–90) Blackfoot chief in what is now southern Alberta, a chief negotiator for Treaty Seven, and adoptive father of Poundmaker.

'custom of the country' Marriage not formalized by churches but accepted by local communities, usually between European men and Aboriginal women.

Cypress Hills Amerindian sacred place, and gathering place, in southern Saskatchewan and Alberta; the site of the murders of 20–30 Assiniboine (Nakoda) at the hands of American 'wolfers' in 1873.

day schools Schools on reserves that students attended while living with their families.

Delgamuukw v. British Columbia A 1991 court case in which the Gitksan and Wet'suwet'en claimed Aboriginal right over traditional lands in northern British Columbia. The BC Court of Appeal rejected their claim, but in 1997, the Supreme Court of Canada overturned the earlier judgement, arguing that the lower courts had not given enough weight to oral tradition.

Deskaheh Cayuga title held by Six Nations traditionalist leader Levi General (1873–1925) who sought sovereignty for his people at the League of Nations.

DEW (Distant Early Warning) line Line of radar installations built across northern Canada and Alaska that began operation in 1954 meant to serve as a warning system for over-the-pole attacks on North America.

discovery doctrine Principle first enunciated in 1452 by Pope Nicholas V that officially sanctioned the conquest, colonization, and the eventual exploitation of non-Christian peoples and their territories by those European powers that first 'discovered' new lands and peoples in the Americas.

division of powers Situation in which different levels of government in a federal system have authority over different aspects of public policy.

Donnacona (d. 1539) Chief of Stadacona before 1536, when he and his sons Domagaya and Taignoagny were kidnapped by Samuel de Champlain and taken to France, where he died.

Dorset Name given by scientists to a culture that thrived for more than 3,000 years in what is now northern Canada and Alaska but disappeared around AD 1000, replaced by the Thule. Their name derives from Cape Dorset, on Baffin Island.

Douglas, Sir James (1807–73) Governor of Vancouver Island (1851–63) and of British Columbia (1858–64), a man of mixed West Indian black and Scottish heritage who earlier was Chief Trader (1835–9) and then Chief Factor at Fort Vancouver, and who was responsible for 14 treaties (1850–4) granting Aboriginal title to Coast Salish bands on southern Vancouver Island.

Douglas Creek A real estate development on lands claimed by Six Nations Iroquois on the edge of Caledonia, Ontario, near Brantford and Hamilton,

that led to Native occupation of the disputed land and bitter confrontations between Six Nations activists, local residents, and outside agitators. The Ontario government purchased the land from the developer, Henco Industries, in June 2006, but a final agreement between governments and the Six Nations has not been reached.

Duck Lake Town in Saskatchewan, 88 km north of Saskatoon, and site of a battle on 26 March 1885 wherein Métis provisional government forces led by Gabriel Dumont routed government forces.

Dumont, Gabriel (1837–1906) Buffalo hunter, Métis chief, and military strategist. Dumont was Louis Riel's military commander during the Northwest Rebellion, 1885.

Duncan, William (1832–1918) Protestant lay missionary who, along with Tsimshian Chief Paul Legaic, founded the 'model' Aboriginal community of Metlakatla (1862–87). The community became increasingly totalitarian, and eventually, following a violent confrontation, Duncan led a breakaway group to form New Metlakatla on Annette Island, Alaska.

egalitarian societies Communities characterized by a lack of distinction of social ranks, in which leadership is often assumed temporarily and for a specific purpose.

enfranchisement Acquisition of the right to vote.

Ewing Commission Commission appointed in 1935 by the Alberta government to investigate social and economic conditions of the province's Métis population and chaired by Justice Albert Freeman Ewing. It resulted in the Métis Population Betterment Act (1938) and the creation of Métis settlements (colonies) in Alberta.

Far Northwest Term used by Euro-Canadians to describe present-day Northwest Territories, Yukon, and northern British Columbia, Alberta, and Saskatchewan.

Federation of Seven Fires A mid-eighteenth-century alliance network linking French mission Indians, led by Pontiac with an intent to resist European settlement, that did not survive the dislocations caused by US War of Independence or colonial distrust of pan-Indianism. It consisted of the Iroquois mission villages on the St Lawrence (Kahnawake, Kanesatake, Oswegatchie, and St Regis), the Abenaki at St Francois and Bécancour, and the Huron at Lorette.

fee simple title The most complete form of ownership. A fee simple buyer acquires ownership of both land and buildings and has the right to possess, use, and dispose of the land as he or she wishes.

File Hills Colony Model village established on the Peepeekisis Reserve near Indian Head, Saskatchewan, and the last of such government experiments.

'first meetings' First communication between peoples who have no prior knowledge of each other. One historian has listed three basic types: collisions, relationships, and contacts.

First Nations Governance Act Legislation proposed in January 2002 by the Department of Indian Affairs that was designed to amend, and effectively do away with, the original Indian Act. Known as Bill C-7, it created much discussion on the issue of Aboriginal governance but was never enacted and died when the parliamentary session ended in 2004.

Fish Creek Southern boundary of the South Branch Métis settlement, which had Batoche as its commercial centre. It was the site of an ambush, 26 April 1885, of government soldiers by Métis led by Gabriel Dumont.

Five Nations Iroquoian confederacy founded in the sixteenth century or before in the present-day Finger Lakes region of northern New York. They were, from east to west, the Mohawk, Oneida, Onondaga, Cayuga, and Seneca. The league later became the Six Nations around 1720 when the Tuscaroras migrated north to join the Iroquois.

fluted points Stone points with flutes (round grooves) around the edge used as spear or arrow heads.

Fox War (1710–38) Name given by historians to the resistance by the Fox and other Amerindian nations to French forays inland to the Upper Midwest. The war chief Kiala rose to prominence during this time as a proponent of pan-Amerindian solidarity.

Ghost Dance (Spirit Dance) Religious circle dance of numerous western US Amerindian groups, derived from the 1889 prophecy and subsequent teaching of the Paiute pacifist prophet Wovoka (Jack Wilson) foretelling a peaceful end to white expansion. White fears of Indian activism related to the Ghost Dance contributed to the 1890 massacre of Lakota Sioux by the US Army at Wounded Knee in South Dakota and in the 1890s the dance appeared on Sioux reserves in Canada.

gift distributions Custom begun by the Amerindians and continued by the British colonial administration of giving goods to Amerindian nations periodically as a way of maintaining agreements and alliances.

gift exchanges Diplomatic ritual involved in the sealing of agreements between Amerindian nations and, later, between New France and Amerindians through the trade of goods or hostages, which resulted in blood ties.

Grant, Cuthbert (c. 1793–1854) Métis fur trader, North-West Company employee, and political leader who advanced the concept of the Métis nation; killed Robert Semple, governor of the HBC-administered territories, near Seven Oaks (present-day Winnipeg) in a Métis route of HBC personnel.

Great Peace of Montreal Agreement reached in 1701 between the Five Nations and the French to end the nearly century of conflict known as the Iroquois (Mourning) War.

guerrilla warfare Warfare characterized by irregular forces using 'hit-and-run' tactics in small-scale, limited actions against European-style military forces.

'gunboat diplomacy' Diplomacy backed by the use or threat of military force, specifically gunboats.

Haldimand Grant Land on the Grand River in Upper Canada (Ontario) granted in 1784 to loyalist Iroquois by Frederick Haldimand, governor of Quebec. The Iroquois had ceded 3 million acres (1,214,100 hectares) on the Niagara Peninsula to the colonial government.

Haldimand Tract The extent of the Haldimand Grant, from the source of the Grand River north of Grand Valley in southwestern Ontario to its mouth, where it discharges into Lake Erie at Port Maitland, and including six miles (10 km) deep on each side of the river—a total of 2,842,480 acres (1,150,311 hectares).

Harper, Elijah Oji-Cree chief from Red Sucker Lake and member of the Manitoba legislature (NDP, Rupertsland) who was instrumental in the failure of the Meech Lake Accord by withholding his vote for ratification.

Harrison, William Henry (1773–1841) Governor of Indiana Territory from 1800 to 1812, later ninth president of the United States. Harrison participated in the Battle of Fallen Timbers (1794), and during his governorship promoted white settlement at the expense of Amerindians.

Hawthorn Report (1966) Report by anthropologist Harry B. Hawthorn on Aboriginal social, educational, and economic conditions. Hawthorn criticized the existing assimilation policy and presented a view of Amerindians as 'citizens plus'.

Head, Sir Francis Bond (1783–1875) Soldier and colonial administrator who was lieutenant-governor of Upper Canada during the 1837 rebellion and arranged the surrender by the Ojibwa of the Saugeen ('mouth of the river') tract on the Bruce Peninsula in 1836.

Head-Smashed-In Bison jump site in present-day southern Alberta in use for more than 5,000 years.

It was also a trade centre for the nations that used the site. It was declared a UNESCO World Heritage Site in 1981.

Hearne, Samuel (1745–92) HBC fur trader and explorer who, with his Amerindian guide Matonabbee, reached the Coppermine River (present-day NWT) in 1772 and later rebuilt Fort Churchill. Hearne's adoption of Amerindian methods of travel allowed him to become the first white man to reach the Arctic Ocean overland.

Heyerdahl, Thor (1914–2002) Norwegian anthropologist who developed a theory that people from South America, not Asia, had populated Polynesia. To prove his thesis, that sailors on rafts could travel the distances required for this, Heyerdahl sailed from Peru to Polynesia in the *Kon Tiki*, a replica of the balsa rafts made by South American Aboriginal people. He later sailed from Morocco to the Caribbean in a replica of an ancient Egyptian papyrus boat.

Hochelaga Iroquoian settlement at the site of present-day Montreal.

homeguards Bands of Amerindians that settled near French or English trading posts.

Hudson, Henry (*fl.* 1607–11) English explorer who searched for a northwest passage to China on behalf of first the English Muscovy Company and then the Dutch East India Company, for whom he also explored the Hudson River.

Hudson's Bay Company (HBC) Company that received its charter from Great Britain in 1670 to trade for furs, explore, and settle Rupert's Land, which consisted of the Hudson Bay drainage system, all of Manitoba, most of Saskatchewan, southern Alberta, and extended north to the Arctic.

Huronia Territory in present-day south-central Ontario extending eastward from Georgian Bay that was controlled at the time of early European contact by a confederacy of Iroquoian communities whom the French called Huron but who called themselves Wendat.

Independent Assessment Process Process set up to deal with serious cases of physical and sexual abuse as part of the residential schools reparations policy.

Indian Act Canadian legislation enacted in 1876 that continues with amendments to the present day and that defines the relationship between Amerindians and the federal government.

Indian Residential Schools Truth and Reconciliation Commission Government commission of inquiry established in May 2008 as part of the resolution of damages and harm caused by residential schools in Canada; after a troubled start, the Commission is now chaired by Justice Murray Sinclair, the first Aboriginal judge in the Manitoba court system.

'Indian title' Seventeenth-century concept involving rights of occupancy and use, but not ownership. *See* **usufructuary right**.

Iroquois War (1609–1701) Conflict between Iroquois and French that lasted almost a century and was interspersed with attempts at peace.

James Bay and Northern Quebec Agreement (JBNQA) Land claim agreement of 1975 between Inuit and Cree of northern Quebec and federal and provincial governments that involves a transfer of money in exchange for cession of land but fails to entrench Aboriginal rights. The JBNQA resulted from Aboriginal objections to the province's James Bay hydroelectric project, begun in 1971.

Jesuits Members of the Society of Jesus, a Roman Catholic order of priests. They were principal actors in the missionary activity in New France.

Johnson, Sir William (1715–74) Military commander who was colonial Superintendent of Indian Affairs from 1755 until his death. He was married 'after the custom of the country' to Mary Brant.

Jones, Rev. Peter (1802–56) Mississauga-Welsh Métis and Methodist minister who advocated Amerindian control of their education system.

Judicial Committee of the Privy Council A board of the British Privy Council that had jurisdiction over the courts of Great Britain's colonies, including, until 1949, Canada.

Kelowna Accord A 'national treaty' achieved by Liberal Prime Minister Paul Martin and Aboriginal leaders in meetings in Kelowna, BC, that would provide $5 billion over a five-year period to improve the daily lives of Aboriginal Canadians in terms of housing, health care, education, and economic development. The Accord, reached in late November 2005, was never ratified by the House of Commons after the Conservatives, under Stephen Harper, gained a minority government in February 2006.

Kiala (Quiala) (*fl.* 1733–4) Fox chief who sought to unify the First Nations of the eastern seaboard to oppose the French. The Fox were based in the Great Lakes area.

King Philip's War (1675–6) Last Amerindian attempt to oust Europeans from New England, led by Wampanoag chief Metacom, called King Philip by the English. It resulted in the exodus of Western Abenaki to Canada.

Klondike gold rush Massive influx of southerners into the Klondike area, Yukon, following news of the discovery of gold that led to the negotiation of Treaty Eight.

League of Indians One of the first attempts at national organization by Aboriginal people founded in 1919 by F.O. Loft, a Mohawk from Brantford, Ontario, to fight treaty violations. Following Loft's death in 1934, the League split into regional organizations.

Legaic Title for a Tsimshian chief meaning 'chief of the mountain'.

Legaic (Legaik, Legex), Paul (d. 1894) Tsimshian chief who took Paul as his baptismal name. In 1862, he and 200 followers settled in the model village created by missionary William Duncan at Metlakatla, a Tsimshian ancestral village.

Little Ice Age Period between 1450 and 1850 when global temperatures fell, causing the northern sea ice to stay all year. This affected wildlife, which caused hardship for hunters. In Europe, it resulted in increased demand for furs, which spurred New World exploration.

Loft, Frederick Ogilvie (1861–1934) Mohawk from Brantford, Ontario, and officer in the Forestry Corps who served in World War I; founder of the League of Indians in 1919.

longhouse Communal dwelling of some First Nations, such as the Iroquois (Hodenosaunee, 'People of the Longhouse').

Longhouse religion Synthesis of traditional beliefs and ceremonies combined with the teachings of nineteenth-century Seneca prophet Handsome Lake (Shanyadariyoh, d. 1815) that combined elements of the Christian religion and the traditional Iroquois belief system.

Mackenzie Valley Pipeline Inquiry (1974–7) Investigation commissioned by the Canadian federal government and headed by Justice Thomas Berger to study the social, economic, and environmental impact of a proposed gas pipeline and energy corridor from the western Arctic to Alberta and further south.

Made Beaver Prime beaver skin in good condition, used as unit of trade by HBC in negotiations with Amerindians.

Marshall, Donald, Jr (1953–2009) Mi'kmaq man released from prison in 1983 after spending 11 years in jail for a murder he did not commit; was acquitted in 1999 in a landmark court case involving Aboriginal right to fish out of season.

Mascarene's Treaty (1725) Treaty No. 239, signed between English and Abenaki after Amerindian military defeat at Norridgewock and later ratified by other Amerindian nations, which stated that Amerindians must behave as British subjects; named after chief negotiator, Paul Mascarene, administrator of Nova Scotia at the time of the treaty.

Matonabbee (c. 1737–92) Chipewyan leader who worked for HBC and guided Samuel Hearne on his third excursion in search of the Coppermine River (1772). Matonabbee ensured the success of this expedition by using the Amerindian manner of travel.

Mawedopenais Ojibwa chief and leading participant in Treaty Three negotiations at Fort Francis in 1873.

'medicine chest' Phrase included in Treaty Six, negotiated between Amerindians of central Saskatchewan and Alberta and the federal government in 1876, that became the legal basis for free health care for all Amerindians.

Megumaage Mi'kmaq name for their land, in the present-day Maritime provinces.

Métis A constitutionally recognized Aboriginal people created by intermarriage between Europeans and Amerindians whose culture reflects both influences.

Metlakatla Traditional Tsimshian settlement on the coast of what is now British Columbia, and site of an Anglican mission and model village, which lasted from 1862 to 1887.

Michif Mixed language that developed in what is now western Canada during the years of the active fur trade that features French nouns and noun phrases and the Plains Cree verbal system.

Michilimackinac An early eighteenth-century British fort located at the Straits of Mackinac connecting Lakes Huron and Michigan.

Middleton, Frederick Dobson (1825–98) Army and militia officer who led Canadian forces in the Northwest Rebellion, 1885, and accepted the surrenders of Louis Riel and Poundmaker.

Mi'kmaq War (1749–53) Mi'kmaq resistance to English settlement of Acadia (Megumaage).

millenarianism Religious belief in and anticipation of a sudden, imminent change in the social order, anticipating prosperity and happiness; related to the prophecy in the Book of Revelation of the return of Christ and a peaceful reign of 1,000 years on earth.

model villages Amerindian settlements organized and administered by government officials or missionaries for the purpose of promoting assimilation of Aboriginal people.

Mohawk Warrior Movement Iroquois association based in traditional beliefs and social structures that has as its goal to preserve the Mohawk Nation. It has been described as the defence arm of the Longhouse religion but is not universally accepted as such.

Moraviantown Village established in 1792 by the Moravian Brothers, a Protestant missionary group founded in 1727, for refugee Delaware on the Canadian side of the future international border and originally called Fairfield. It was the site of a battle on 5 October 1813, part of the War of 1812–14, in which Tecumseh died.

Mourning War (1609–1701) Iroquois term for the Iroquois War, an almost century-long conflict between the Five Nations and the French.

Muquinna Chiefly title of the Mochat band (Nootka). One particular Muquinna (*fl.* 1786–1817) quarrelled in 1803 with the captain of a fur-trading ship over a defective gun, which led to the destruction of the *Boston* by a group of Nootka. Muquinna was renowned for the magnificence of a potlatch he gave that same year.

National Indian Brotherhood (NIB) (1968–82) National association resulting from the split of the National Indian Council into a body representing status and treaty Aboriginal groups (NIB), and non-status and Métis (Native Council of Canada).

nativistic movements Organized and conscious efforts by members of a community to build a more satisfying culture, often by revitalizing traditional beliefs and customs.

Neolin Mid-seventeenth-century Delaware prophet who urged Amerindians to avoid contact with whites and to return to their traditional values. His teachings influenced Pontiac. Neolin was one of two men known as the 'Delaware Prophet'.

Nescambiouit ('He who is so important and so highly placed because of his merit that his greatness cannot be attained, even in thought', *c.* 1660–1722) Pigwacket (Abenaki) chief who was taken to France but returned in 1716 and attempted to form a pan-Amerindian alliance.

New England Company Non-sectarian Protestant missionary organization that founded a school for Amerindians at Sussex Vale, New Brunswick, in 1787.

Nisga'a Final Agreement Act Legislation ratified by Parliament in 2000 in which the Nisga'a gained self-governing rights to 1,900 km² of land but gave up the tax-free status they had under the Indian Act.

non-status Indians Amerindians who have not or whose ancestors have not signed treaties and so are not covered by the provisions of the Indian Act.

North West Company (NWC) Consortium of fur-trading firms and individuals formed in the late eighteenth century to compete with Hudson's Bay Company in the western fur trade. The HBC absorbed the NWC in 1821.

North West Mounted Police (NWMP) Police force created by 1873 legislation and sent to what is now western Canada in 1874 to maintain order, primarily by curtailing the whisky trade, and to encourage white settlement. In 1904, the force was given the prefix 'Royal', and in 1920 it was merged with the Dominion Police to form the Royal Canadian Mounted Police.

Northwest Passage Hoped-for and sought-after shortcut from northern Europe to China, which was the reason for the voyages of John Cabot and other early European explorers.

Northwest Rebellion Armed uprising in present-day Saskatchewan in 1885 of Métis, Amerindians, and some whites, who were concerned about encroachment of white settlers and for their own future with the demise of the vast buffalo herds of the western Plains. The Rebellion, led by Louis Riel, was quelled by troops sent from eastern Canada.

Norton, Major John (Snipe, Teyoninhokarawen) (*fl.* 1784–1825) Mohawk chief and army officer who worked as an interpreter and emissary for Captain Joseph Brant (Thayendanegea) in dealing with Six Nations land claims and led Amerindian forces in several important battles of the War of 1812–14.

numbered treaties Series of 11 treaties signed between First Nations and the Canadian government following the cession of Hudson's Bay Company land to the Canadian government. These treaties, signed between 1871 and 1921, resulted in the cession of much of present-day Ontario, Manitoba, Saskatchewan, Alberta, and the Mackenzie District of the Northwest Territories to the government.

Nunavut Land Claim Settlement (1993) Legislation that paved the way for the creation of the self-governing territory of Nunavut and the largest land claim settlement in Canadian history.

Odanak Present-day Saint-François-de-Sales, near Sorel, Quebec. In the 1700s, it was the largest Abenaki settlement in New France.

Oka (Kanesatake, Lake of Two Mountains) Land near Montreal granted by France in 1717 to the Seminary of St Sulpice as an Amerindian mission. A long-standing dispute over ownership of the land culminated in a standoff in 1990 in which Canadian Armed Forces intervened.

pass system Regulation introduced after the Northwest Rebellion that required Amerindians in the West to obtain permission from the Indian agent to leave their reserves. Although not based in any legislation, the policy was later extended to Amerindians throughout Canada and was enforced until the mid-1940s.

pays d'en haut ('Upper Country') Great Lakes region west of Michilimackinac.

Peacekeepers Self-governed police force formed in Kahnawake, near Montreal, following a breakdown in relations with the Quebec Provincial Police. It eventually became the reserve's official law enforcement body.

pemmican Concentrated food used by Plains Métis and Amerindians consisting of dried meat, pounded fine and mixed with melted fat and sometimes berries. It became a staple food of the fur trade. One kilogram of pemmican had the food value of four to eight kilograms of fresh meat or fish.

Penner Report (1983) Report of the Special Parliamentary Committee on Indian Self-Government, headed by Liberal MP Keith Penner, that recommended a distinct form of Aboriginal self-government.

Pond, Peter (1739/40–1807) Fur trader and explorer who recorded descriptions of the Fox and Sauk and later explored the North-West with the assistance of Amerindian guides, producing in 1784–5 a map of the Great Lakes and Hudson Bay and the area westward to the Rocky Mountains and northward to the Arctic.

Pontiac (1712/1725–69) Odawa war chief who attempted to unite First Nations to resist European settlement in the Great Lakes area. Some later turned against him, and he was assassinated by an Illinois at Cahokia.

potlatch Ceremonial feast of Northwest Coast First Nations involving the host's lavish distribution of gifts. A means of redistributing wealth within communities, it was banned by the Canadian government in 1884 as being contrary to European values.

Poundmaker (Pitikwahanapiwiyin) (c. 1842–85) Adopted son of Isapo-Muxika (Crowfoot) and a leader in Treaty Six negotiations. He was convicted of treason-felony following the 1885 Northwest Rebellion though he sought to be a peacemaker during the hostilities.

Proclamation of 1763 Proclamation by England declaring a British system of government for North American land surrendered by France but also declaring land not under European settlement as land reserved for Indians, which set the stage for later land surrenders by treaty.

Quebec Act of 1774 British legislation that defined the boundaries of Quebec as extending south to the Ohio Valley, recognized the Roman Catholic Church, and established French civil law as the basis for business and other day-to-day transactions.

Queenston Heights Site near Niagara Falls, Ontario, of a battle in October 1812 that saw invading American forces defeated by English and Amerindian forces led by Mohawk Major John Norton and British General Isaac Brock, who died in the battle.

relocation As a policy of the Canadian federal government, it meant moving Amerindian or Inuit communities to new locations.

reserves Tracts of land, the legal title to which is vested in the Crown, set apart for the use and benefit of a band.

residential schools Boarding schools for First Nations children usually run as joint government–church enterprises with the purpose of assimilating these children into white society.

Riel, Louis (1844–85) Métis leader, founder of the province of Manitoba, and spiritual leader of the 1869–70 Riel Rebellion and the 1885 Northwest Rebellion; hanged for treason on 16 November 1885. His father, Louis Riel Sr, had been a leader in the Métis community.

Robinson treaties Two treaties negotiated by William Benjamin Robinson. Lake Superior chiefs signed the Robinson-Superior Treaty, 7 September 1850; chiefs from the Lake Huron region signed the Robinson-Huron Treaty, 9 September 1850.

Royal Commission on Aboriginal Peoples (RCAP) (1991–6) Commission set up in the wake of the Kanesatake standoff and chaired by Georges Erasmus, a former National Chief of the Assembly of First Nations, and René Dussault, a judge of the Quebec Appeals Court. Its final report included 440 specific recommendations.

sagamore (sagamo, saqmaw, saqmawaq) Chief (Mi'kmaq, Abenaki).

St Catherine's Milling v. The Queen (1885–9) Ontario court case in which the question of federal and provincial jurisdiction was central and which led to a ruling of the Judicial Committee of the Privy Council that the Proclamation of 1763, which recognized Amerindian land, was valid, but also that the British had gained title to all Amerindian lands simply by setting foot in North America.

St Laurent Oblate mission founded in 1871, and the site of a settlement on the South Saskatchewan River founded by Gabriel Dumont and other Métis in 1872; one of the cluster of Métis settlements known collectively as the South Branch.

Saint-Paul-des-Métis First tract of land set aside for Métis settlement, in 1896 in Alberta.

Samson Cree Nation Central Alberta First Nation that has sought payments for oil and gas royalties through the courts since 1989.

Saugeen Tract Triangular area of 1.5 million acres on the western edge of Lake Huron adjacent to the Bruce Peninsula ceded to the federal government by the Saugeen Ojibwa nation in August 1836 in exchange for assistance to those who moved to the Bruce Peninsula.

scrip Document used as evidence that the holder or bearer is entitled to receive something, such as cash or an allotment of land.

self-government Government controlled and directed by the inhabitants of a region rather than by an outside authority.

Six Nations, League of Expansion of the Iroquoian confederacy by the addition of the Tuscarora, who fled north from the Carolinas and sought refuge among the Five Nations around 1720.

'Sixties Scoop' Expression referring to the practice during the 1960s of removing Aboriginal children from their communities and encouraging them to be adopted into non-Aboriginal families.

Sparrow v. R. Supreme Court case in 1987 in which the court ruled in favour of a BC Amerindian who had used a fishing net larger than allowed by law. The Court found that Aboriginal fishing, land, and hunting rights for food, social, and ceremonial purposes had priority over later restrictive legislation.

specific claims Claims concerning outstanding legal obligations on the part of the government, such as non-fulfillment of a treaty, breach of an obligation under the Indian Act, or improper actions in connection with the acquisition or disposition of land by government employees or agents.

Stadacona Major Iroquois settlement on the St Lawrence River at the time of first contact near present-day Quebec City.

status Indians Amerindians who have, or their ancestors have, signed a treaty with the government and are covered by the Indian Act.

Tadoussac Innu settlement at the mouth of the Saguenay River and an important fur-trading centre in the mid-1600s.

taiga Subarctic coniferous (evergreen) forest.

Tamanawas rituals Religious ceremonies of western Amerindians involving dancing. These and other rituals were banned from 1884 to 1951.

Tecumseh (*c.* 1768–1813) Shawnee chief who fought American settlement in the Ohio area in the 1790s and later transformed a prophetic movement led by his brother, Tenskwatawa, into a movement aimed at retaining Amerindian land. Tecumseh sided, reluctantly, with the British in the War of 1812–14 and died at the Battle of Moraviantown in 1813.

Tenskwatawa ('Open Door') (1775?–1836) Brother of Tecumseh who, following a series of prophetic visions in 1803, promoted a revival of traditional customs and values.

Tessouat, Paul (d. 1654) Algonkin orator chief of Allumette Island, also known as Le Borgne de l'Isle as he was blind in one eye, initially resisted the missionary efforts of the Jesuits but was later baptized; one of at least three chiefs named Tessouat, he extracted tolls (i.e., forced gift exchanges) from traders along the Ottawa River. An earlier Tessouat (Besouat; *fl.* 1603–13) met Champlain. A third Tessouat, also known as Le Borgne de l'Isle, died in 1636.

Thanadelthur (d. 1717) A Chipewyan referred to as the Slave Woman in the HBC records who was enslaved by Cree in 1713 but escaped and travelled overland to Fort York. She was instrumental in negotiating peace between the Chipewyan and Cree.

thirst dances (sun dances) Amerindian rituals practised primarily in the Plains area involving privation and self-torture. The Canadian government banned them in the 1895 because they fuelled Amerindian resistance of assimilation. The ban was lifted in 1951.

Thompson, David (1770–1857) HBC and, later, NWC fur trader and explorer who surveyed a route to the Churchill River and the area west of Lake of the Woods along the 49th parallel, and was the first European to travel the Athabasca Pass through the Rockies to the west coast.

'three sisters' Corn, squash, and beans, the three crops central to Aboriginal agriculture. They complement each other nutritionally and agriculturally, with the beans adding nitrogen to the soil, corn providing support for the beans, and squash providing ground cover to prevent weed growth and preserve soil moisture.

Thule Name given by scientists to the northern people who preceded the Inuit and whose culture spread from Alaska across what is now northern Canada to Labrador, Newfoundland, and Greenland about AD 1000.

traders Individuals working for large companies who accepted furs and other goods from Amerindians and Inuit in exchange for agreed-upon items such as knives, pots, beads, and guns.

Treaty of Boston (1725) Treaty signed at the end of the English-Indian War between the English and Abenaki, Wuastukwiuk, and Mi'kmaq.

Treaty of Ghent (1814) Treaty that concluded the War of 1812–14, in which the British tried to negotiate for the establishment of an Indian territory but failed.

Treaty of Greenville (1795) Treaty of peace between the US government and the Wyandot, Delaware, Shawnee, Odawa, Chippewa, Potawatomi, Miami, Eel River, Wea, Kickapoo, Piankeshaw, and Kaskaskia involving huge land cessions on the part of the Amerindians and opening the Ohio Valley to European settlement.

Treaty of Paris (1763) Peace treaty between Britain and France following the latter's military defeat that effectively ended the French colonial presence in North America.

Treaty of Utrecht (1713) Treaty in which France ceded Acadia to the British that ended French–British hostilities in Acadia that had begun in 1701.

usufructuary right The legal right to use something, such as land, without ownership.

War of 1812–14 British interference in US trade during Napoleonic Wars led to conflict in North America, on both land and sea, between US and Britain, with the US seeking to annex British North America. It was the last colonial war in which First Nations people held the balance of power.

wardship The state of being under the care of another person or group of people. In the case of First Nations people, the term refers to the relationship between First Nations and the colonial or Canadian government.

'white man's burden' A phrase first used by British poet Rudyard Kipling to describe what Britain saw as her role with respect to the indigenous people of the countries she colonized.

White Paper (1969) A white paper, or parliamentary paper, is a document in which the government presents its policy or proposed policy on a specific topic. In the Statement of the Government of Canada on Indian Policy, 1969, the Liberal government put forward its proposal to end Aboriginal treaty rights and special status.

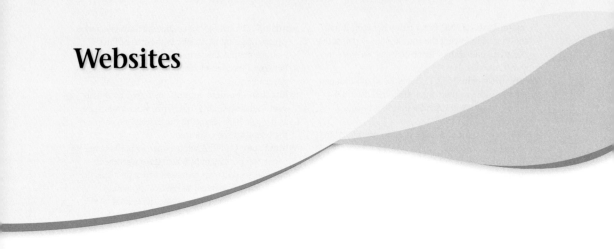

Websites

Note: This is not meant to be a comprehensive list, as the Internet is always changing.

General Sites

http://atlas.gc.ca/site/english/index.html—
Atlas of Canada.

http://collections.ic.gc.ca—Canada's Digital
Collections. Links to web pages and
on-line publications, with a section on
First Nations.

http://library.usask.ca/native/directory/english/
index.html—Directory of First Nations, Métis,
and Inuit Library Collections in Canada
(University of Saskatchewan).

www.aboriginalcanada.gc.ca/—Aboriginal Canada
Portal. Federal government site that provides
links to sites relating to a variety of topics, e.g.,
cultural, legal, and economic.

www.ainc-inac.gc.ca—*Report of the Royal Commission
on Aboriginal Peoples.* This series of documents includes an overview of primarily post-Confederation
history, including post-1885 repressive measures
and residential schools.

www.ammsa.com/windspeaker/index.htm—
Windspeaker is a First Nations news
publication.

www.biographi.ca/—*Dictionary of Canadian Biography*
on-line.

www.canadiana.org—*Early Canadiana Online.* This site
contains downloadable early historical documents,
books, and journals. Many of the texts are available without subscription. The website contains a
list of the universities and libraries that have full
access to the site.

www.civilization.ca/cmc/home/cmc-homel—Wright,
J.V. *History of the Native People of Canada*, vols 1

and 2 (Ottawa, 1995). This on-line publication
of the Museum of Civilization concerns
pre-contact history.

www.johnco.com/nativel/—First Nations
Information Project. This site provides links
to First Nations communities, businesses,
organizations, cultural websites, and
publications.

www.thecanadianencyclopedia.com/,
http://tceplus.com—*Canadian Encyclopedia*
on-line.

www.turtleisland.org/—Turtle Island. The site
features news and links to subjects of current
interest.

www.ucalgary.ca/applied_history/tutor/firstnations/
home.html—University of Calgary–Red
Deer College Applied History Research
Group. Pages include an overview of pre-contact
history.

www.virtualmuseum.ca/—Virtual Museum.
This site contains more than 100 virtual
exhibits, some of which relate to Aboriginal
history and culture, from Canadian museums.

Glossaries and Dictionaries

www.abheritage.ca/alberta—Alberta Heritage, First
Nations and Métis Glossary.

www.ainc-inac.gc.ca—Indian and Northern Affairs
Canada (INAC) Terminology.

www.civilization.ca/cmc/home/cmc-home—Glossary
of the Fur Trade. This list includes definitions
and biographies of Europeans involved in the
fur trade.

www.usask.ca/nursing/aboriginalglossary/—
Aboriginal Health Glossary (University of
Saskatchewan).

www.wisconsinhistory.org/dictionary/—*Dictionary of
Wisconsin History.*

Libraries, Museums, and Archives

Note: In addition to the larger sites, a few examples
of community-run museums and archives,
most of which are specific to a nation, are
provided here.

http://pwnhc.learnnet.nt.ca/—Prince of Wales
Northern Heritage Centre. The site includes ref-
erences and photographs related to Northwest
Territories

www.archivescanada.ca—Canadian Archival
Information Network. This site contains links to
provincial and territorial archives. Some, such as
the BC Archives, have scanned photo collections
in addition to textual material.

www.civilization.ca—The Canadian Museum of
Civilization site contains illustrations of artifacts,
maps, and so on.

www.collectionscanada.ca/archivianet/—Library and
Archives Canada.

www.glenbow.org/collections/archives/—The
Glenbow Archives site contains a large search-
able database of scanned photographs, including
many of First Nations, in addition to textual
information.

www.iroquoismuseum.org—The Iroquois Indian
Museum, New York, includes information and
links to other Iroquois-related sites.

www.nmai.si.edu/—National Museum of the
American Indian, Smithsonian Institution.
This site includes on-line exhibitions relating
to indigenous people, primarily of the
present-day United States but including the
rest of North and Central America. At one
time the Smithsonian sponsored a great deal
of fieldwork among First Nations and the
collection of Aboriginal material culture;
the site also contains information on the
repatriation of artifacts.

Associations and Organizations

Note: These sites contain a variety of information on
history and current issues, plus links to other
sites. It is not possible to provide a complete list
of First Nations organizations.

www.abegweitfirstnations.com/—Abegweit First
Nation, Prince Edward Island

www.abheritage.ca/abpolitics/people/influ_indian
.html —Indian Association of Alberta history

www.abo-peoples.org/—Congress of Aboriginal
Peoples, provides links related to legal Métis
and non-status Indians

www.afn.ca/—Assembly of First Nations

www.anishinabek.ca/—Anishinabek, Union of
Ontario Indians

www.chiefs-of-ontario.org/—Chiefs of Ontario

www.cyfn.ca/—Council of Yukon First Nations

www.fni.nf.ca/—Federation of Newfoundland
Indians

www.fsin.com/—Federation of Saskatchewan
Indian Nations

www.gcc.ca/—Eeyou Istchee, Grand Council of
the Crees; includes a link to the James Bay and
Northern Quebec Agreement.

www.itk.ca/—Inuit Tapiriit Kanatami

www.metisnation.ca/—Métis National Council

www.nwac-hq.org/—Native Women's Association of
Canada

www.nwt2000.com/aborig.html—Northwest
Territories Aboriginal Organizations and Services.
Few websites are provided, so the names would
have to be searched separately.

www.ubcic.bc.ca/—Union of British Columbia
Indian Chiefs

www.unbi.org/—Union of New Brunswick Indians

www.unsi.ns.ca/—Union of Nova Scotia Indians

www.aiai.on.ca—Association of Iroquois and Allied
Nations

Specific Topics

Agreements, treaties, and negotiated settlements:
www.canadiana.org/citm/themes/aboriginals_e
.html; www.bctreaty.net relates to British
Columbia; www.atns.net.au/ contains a database
produced by the University of Melbourne,
Australia, of events, treaties, etc., that includes
Canada.

Canada's Constitution:
www.pco-bcp.gc.ca/premier.asp Language=E&Page=c
onsfile&Sub=ThehistoryofConstitution

Inuit history:
www.civilization.ca/cmc/home/cmc-home—
David Morrison, *Canadian Inuit History*, including
reference list.

Mackenzie Valley Pipeline Inquiry: www.allwestbc
.com/MVP/MVP_AllTranscripts.html

Métis, Michif:
www.gdins.org/home.html—Gabriel Dumont
Institute of Native Studies and Applied Research

Mi'kmaq College Institute Resource Centre:
http://mrc.uccb.ns.ca/default.htm

North-West Mounted Police:
www.nwmpmuseum.com/

Northwest Resistance:
  http://library.usask.ca/
Nunavut:
  www.gov.nu.ca/—government site includes links
  to photographs; see also Nunavut Tunngavik:
  www.tunngavik.com/
Quebec history:
  http://faculty.marianopolis.edu/c.belanger/
  QuebecHistory/index.htm—on-line entries
  from W.S. Wallace, ed., *Encyclopedia of Canada*
  (Toronto, 1948); updating is ongoing; site also
  contains transcripts of major legislation.

Residential schools:
  www.collectionscanada.ca/native-residential/
  index-e.html; see also an abridgement of
  Shingwauk's Vision (J.R. Miller): http://collections
  .ic.gc.ca/shingwauk/
Technology:
  www.nativetech.org/
Yukon:
  www.gov.yk.ca/—brief overview of history on
  government website.

Notes

Introduction

1. On 18 June 1936, William Lyon Mackenzie King, Liberal Prime Minister of Canada (1921–6, 1926–30, 1935–48), observed in the House of Commons 'that if some countries have too much history, we have too much geography.' John Robert Colombo, ed., *Colombo's Canadian Quotations* (Edmonton, 1974), 306.

2. As political economist Harold Innis (1894–1952) expressed it, 'the Indian and his culture were fundamental to the growth of Canadian institutions.' Innis, *The Fur Trade in Canada* (Toronto, 1962), 392.

3. Izumi Shimada and John F. Merkel, 'Copper Alloy Metallurgy in Ancient Peru', *Scientific American* 265, 1 (July 1991): 80–6.

4. Ian Hodder, *Reading the Past* (Cambridge, 1986), 102, 147–70.

5. 'Professor warns of native rift', *Edmonton Journal*, 19 Oct. 1990; 'Oka standoff sparked fears of IRA-type crisis, Ciaccia says', *Globe and Mail*, 15 Jan. 1991; Sarah Schmidt, 'New-Age Warriors', *Saturday Night*, 14 Oct. 2000, 22–9.

6. See Ives Goddard's discussion of the subject in David Damas, ed., *Handbook of North American Indians*, 5: *Arctic* (Washington, 1984), 5–7.

7. Denys Delâge, 'Les Iroquois chrétiens des "réductions", 1667–1770: I—Migration et rapports avec les Français', *Recherches amérindiennes au Québec* 20, 1–2 (1991): 64.

8. Where the original manuscript has survived, this can be checked, but that is rare with early imprints. See I.S. MacLaren, 'Samuel Hearne's Accounts of the Massacre at Bloody Falls, 17 July 1771', *Ariel: A Review of English Literature* 22, 1 (1991): 25–51; MacLaren, '"I came to rite thare

portraits": Paul Kane's Journal of His Western Travels, 1846–1848', *American Art Journal* 21, 2 (1989): 6–88.

Chapter 1

1. Brian M. Fagan, *The Great Journey* (London, 1987), 26; see also, for example, Jeffrey Goodman, *American Genesis* (New York, 1981). Some of the various approaches to the study of early humanity in the Americas are found in William S. Laughlin and Albert B. Harper, eds, *The First Americans: Origins, Affinities and Adaptation* (New York, 1979).

2. Knut R. Fladmark demonstrates the complementarity of myth and scientific discourse by using legends to amplify his text in *British Columbia Prehistory* (Ottawa, 1986).

3. Norval Morrisseau, *Legends of My People the Great Ojibway* (Toronto, 1965), 15; Mircea Eliade, *Gods, Goddesses, and Myths of Creation* (New York, 1974), 135–6.

4. A variation of this myth is found among the Athapaskan Wet'suwet'en of the Cordilleran plateau. See A.G. Morice, *Au pays de l'ours noir* (Paris, 1897), 76–8.

5. A survey of types of creation myths and their distribution in North America is that of Anna Birgitta Rooth, 'The Creation Myths of the North American Indians', *Anthropos* 52 (1957): 497–508. See also, for example, George Blondin, *When the World Was New: Stories of the Sahtú Dene* (Yellowknife, 1990).

6. Knut R. Fladmark, 'Times and Places: Environmental Correlates of Mid-to-Late Wisconsinan Human Population Expansion in North America', in Richard Shutler Jr, ed., *Early Man in the New World* (Beverly Hills, Calif., 1983), 27. See also William N. Irving, 'The First Americans: New Dates

for Old Bones', *Natural History* 96, 2 (1987): 8–13. Irving and paleobiologist Richard Harrington claim that a campsite at Old Crow River dates back 150,000 years. The oldest skeleton found so far (in Texas) has been dated to 11,600 years ago; 'Hemisphere's oldest remains identified, geologist says', *Toronto Star*, 1 Nov. 1992. Joseph H. Greenberg, *Language in the Americas* (Stanford, Calif., 1987), 331–7; Greenberg, 'Linguistic Origins of Native Americans', *Scientific American* (Nov. 1992): 94–9. See also Jared M. Diamond 'The Talk of the Americas', *Nature* 344 (1990): 589–90.

7. For one, 'The Origin of Gitxawn Group at Kitsumkalem', in Marius Barbeau and William Beynon, coll., *Tsimshian Narratives 2* (Ottawa, 1987), 1–4. Others are in Marius Barbeau, *Tsimshian Myths* (Ottawa, 1961).

8. For an argument supporting Aboriginal traditional beliefs, see Vine Deloria Jr, *Red Earth, White Lies: Native Americans and the Myth of Scientific Fact* (Golden, Colo., 1997).

9. Joseph de Acosta, *The Natural and Morall History of the East and West Indies*, tr. E.G., 2 vols (London, 1880; reprint of 1604 edition), I, 57–61; first published in Latin in 1590. A joke among Indians illustrative of their attitude towards the Bering Strait migration route has it that the reason why their people wound up in the Americas instead of staying in Asia was that 'they couldn't get their bearings straight.' See also Steven B. Young, 'Beringia: An Ice-Age View', in William W. Fitzhugh and Aron Crowell, eds, *Crossroads of Continents: Cultures of Siberia and Alaska* (Washington, 1988), 106–10. On the debate about pre-Clovis sites, see Eliot Marshall, 'Clovis Counterrevolution', *Science* 249 (1990): 738–41.

10. 'What the Stone Tools Tell Us', *Archaeology* 49, 6 (1996): 61.

11. D. Wayne Moodie, Kerry Abel, and Alan Catchpole, 'Northern Athapaskan Oral Traditions and the White River Volcanic Eruption', paper presented at 'Aboriginal Resource Use in Canada: Historical and Legal Aspects' conference, University of Manitoba, 1988. See also Catherine McClellan, *Part of the Land, Part of the Water: A History of the Yukon Indians* (Vancouver, 1987), 54–5; Peter Schledermann, *Crossroads to Greenland: 3000 Years of Prehistory in the Eastern High Arctic* (Calgary, 1990), 314–15. Four possible ways by which the Arctic could have been peopled are presented in schematized form by Robert McGhee in *Canadian Arctic Prehistory* (Scarborough, Ont., 1978), 18–21. See also 'Relics suggest that humans came to New World 36,000 years ago', *Edmonton Journal*, 2 May 1991.

12. Knut R. Fladmark, 'The Feasibility of the Northwest Coast as a Migration Route for Early Man', in Alan Lyle Bryan, ed., *Early Man in America from a Circum-Pacific Perspective* (Edmonton, 1978), 119–28; Fladmark, 'The First Americans: Getting One's Berings', *Natural History* (Nov. 1986): 8–19; Margaret Munro, 'Underwater world of B.C. could be missing link in early man's travels', *Edmonton Journal*, 9 Aug. 1993; Richard Shutler Jr, 'The Australian Parallel to the Peopling of the New World', in Shutler, ed., *Early Man in the New World*, 43–5. See also E.F. Greenman, 'Upper Paleolithic in the New World', *Current Anthropology* 3 (1962): 61; Edwin Tappen Adney and Howard I. Chapelle, *The Bark Canoes and Skin Boats of North America* (Washington, 1964), 94–8; Alice B. Kehoe, 'Small Boats Upon the North Atlantic', in Carrol Riley et al., eds, *Man Across the Sea: Problems of Pre-Columbian Contacts* (Austin, Texas, 1971), 275–92; Ruth Gruhn, 'Linguistic Evidence in Support of the Coastal Route of Earliest Entry into the New World', *Man*, new series 23, 2 (1988): 77–100. For the view that the western corridor could have been used for migrations, see N.W. Rutter, 'Late Pleistocene History of the Western Canadian Ice-Free Corridor', *Canadian Journal of Anthropology* 1, 1 (1980): 1–8. This entire issue of *CJA* is devoted to studies of the corridor.

13. William H. Hodge, *The First Americans Then and Now* (New York, 1981), 15–16; Paul S. Martin, 'Prehistoric Overkill', in Martin and H.E. Wright Jr, eds, *Pleistocene Extinctions: The Search for a Cause* (New Haven, 1967), 75–105. Also Martin, 'The Pattern and Meaning of Holarctic Mammoth Extinctions', in David M. Hopkins et al., eds, *Paleoecology of Beringia* (New York, 1982), 399–408.

14. Although the Inca were skilled metallurgists, they used their craft largely, although not entirely, for ceremonial purposes. However, copper alloy metallurgy was more important than previously thought and was used for mundane purposes. See Izumi Shimada and John F. Merkel, 'Copper Alloy Metallurgy in Ancient Peru', *Scientific American* 265, 1 (1991): 80–6. Inca architecture, roads, and engineering projects were based on Stone Age technology. This technology, of course, was no more confined to stone than that of the Bronze Age was to bronze, or the Iron Age to iron. It may well be that bone and wood were just as important as stone, or even more so; their perishability, however, particularly that of wood, has made it highly unlikely that this can ever be determined with any precision. As stone and bone technology

gave way to that of metals, some tribal peoples came to regard stone tools as thunderbolts. See C.J.M.R. Gullick, *Myths of a Minority* (Assen, 1985), 25; Miguel León-Portilla, *Aztec Thought and Culture* (Norman, Okla., 1963).

15. The Siberian find, at a site near Magadan Oblast, has been radiocarbon dated to 8,300 years ago. 'Discovery raises questions over settling of New World', *Globe and Mail*, 2 Aug. 1996. On fluted points in Canada, see R. Cole Harris, ed., *Historical Atlas of Canada*, I (Toronto, 1987), plate 2. The view that Siberia was not peopled before 20,000 years ago is maintained by Nikolai N. Dikov, 'On the Road to America', *Natural History* 97, 1 (1988): 14.

16. Harris, ed., *Historical Atlas*, I, plates 5 and 6.

17. Carl Ortwin Sauer, *Land and Life*, ed. John Leighly (Berkeley, Calif., 1969), 237–40.

18. Alan L. Bryan, 'An Overview of Paleo-American Prehistory from a Circum-Pacific Perspective', in Bryan, ed., *Early Man in America*, 306–27. The oldest stone tools known so far, crafted more than 2.5 million years ago, have been found in Ethiopia. 'Oldest known stone tools found, but makers remain anonymous', *Ottawa Citizen*, 23 Jan. 1997. See also Robin Ridington, 'Technology, world view, and adaptive strategy in a northern hunting society', *Canadian Review of Sociology and Anthropology* 19, 4 (1982): 469–81.

19. Archery was practised at least 10,000 years ago in Japan. See Fumiko Ikawa-Smith, 'Late Pleistocene and Early Holocene Technologies', in Richard Pearson, ed., *Windows on the Japanese: Studies in Archaeology and Prehistory* (Ann Arbor, Mich., 1986), 212.

20. *Lost Visions, Forgotten Dreams*, exhibit guide, Canadian Museum of the American Indian (n.p., 1996).

21. Brian O.K. Reeves, 'Communal bison hunters of the Northern Plains', in L.B. Davis and Reeves, eds, *Hunters of the Recent Past* (London, 1990), 170–1.

22. Sauer, *Land and Life*, 284. The recent discovery of a 6,000-year-old wooden walkway buried in a peat bog in England has pointed to the existence of very early stable communities. See John M. Coles, 'The World's Oldest Road', *Scientific American* 201, 5 (1989): 100–6. On the difficulties of interpreting archaeological data, see Hodder, *Reading the Past*.

23. Canada's ecology, subsistence bases, and population distribution for 1500 are mapped in Harris, ed., *Historical Atlas*, I, plates 17, 17A, 18. Seasonal Algonkian and Iroquoian cycles are schematized in plate 34.

24. 'Increase in carbon dioxide spurred farming, article says', *Globe and Mail*, 9 Oct. 1995; 'Earliest Agriculture in the New World', *Archaeology* 50, 4 (July–Aug. 1997): 11.

25. The section on agriculture is partly adapted from my '"For Every Plant There Is a Use": The Botanical World of Mexica and Iroquoians', in Kerry Abel and Jean Friesen, *Aboriginal Resource Use in Canada: Legal and Historical Aspects* (Winnipeg, 1991), 11–34. My thanks to Dr Walter Moser, University of Alberta, for providing the Latin names.

26. Chili peppers, first domesticated on the Gulf coast, made their way to India, where they now form part of the traditional cuisine. India is also the leading grower of peanuts, another New World crop.

27. Virginia Morell, 'Confusion in Earliest America', *Science* 248 (1990): 439–41.

28. Barry Kaye and D.W. Moodie, 'The Psoralea Food Resource of the Northern Plains', *Plains Anthropologist* 23, 82, pt. 1 (1978): 329–36. Use of the wild turnip as a food resource intensified with the growth of population that followed the advent of the horse. Prairie turnip flour is a good source of vitamin C.

29. Peter McFarlane and Wayne Haimila, *Ancient Land, Ancient Sky: Following Canada's Native Canoe Routes* (Toronto, 1999), 120.

30. Stephen Lewandowski, 'Three Sisters—An Iroquoian Cultural Complex', *Northeast Indian Quarterly* 6, 1–2 (1989): 45. The story of O-na-tah, spirit of corn, tells how corn became separated from her sister plants in modern agriculture. ('O-na-tah Spirit of Corn', ibid., 40.) Archaeologist Norman Clermont has observed that in the St Lawrence Valley, early agricultural communities developed in conjunction with fishing sites. He theorizes that a series of hard winters about AD 1000 encouraged farming as a means of obtaining enough food to store for the cold months. See Clermont, 'Why Did the St. Lawrence Iroquois Become Agriculturalists?', *Man in the Northeast* 40 (1990): 75–9.

31. Patricia S. Bridges, 'Changes in Activities with the Shift to Agriculture in the Southeastern United States', *Current Anthropology* 30, 3 (1989): 385–94. Skeletal studies also indicate changes in the division of labour between men and women as a result of the shift to maize agriculture. An increase in the variety of chores is indicated for women; men show fewer changes.

32. Chrestien Le Clercq, *New Relation of Gaspesia*, ed. William F. Ganong (Toronto, 1910), 296. See also Reuben Gold Thwaites, ed., *Jesuit Relations and*

Allied Documents, 73 vols (Cleveland, 1896–1901), XXII, 293.

33. Virgil J. Vogel, *American Indian Medicine* (Norman, Okla., 1970), 9; Daniel E. Moermon, *Medicinal Plants of Native America*, 2 vols (Ann Arbor, Mich., 1986); Charles H. Talbot, 'America and the European Drug Trade', *First Images* 2: 813–32. Early settlers soon learned to appreciate Amerindian medical lore and incorporated it into their own practice. See Alfred Goldsworthy Bailey, *The Conflict of European and Eastern Algonkian Cultures 1504–1700* (Toronto, 1969 [1937]), 120–1.

34. For an overview of subsistence patterns, see Harold E. Driver, *Indians of North America* (Chicago, 1970), 53–83.

35. Despite their usefulness, dogs were regarded by some northern peoples as fundamentally hostile to humans and were associated with evil and witchcraft. See Catharine McClellan, *My Old People Say: An Ethnographic Survey of Southern Yukon Territory*, 2 vols (Ottawa, 1975), I, 161–7. Others had a much different view, not only demonstrating considerable respect, but in the case of some groups, such as the Dogrib, believing they were descended from a dog. Kerry Abel, *Drum Songs* (Montreal and Kingston, 1993), 131. See also Carl Ortwin Sauer, *Sixteenth-Century North America: The Land and People as Seen by Europeans* (Berkeley, Calif., 1971), 239, 293. The use of dogs as packers predates their use for traction. In southern Yukon, for example, dog teams pulling toboggans did not appear until the nineteenth century. (McClellan, *My Old People Say*, I, 162.)

36. Henry T. Lewis and Theresa A. Ferguson, 'Yards, Corridors, and Mosaics: How to Burn a Boreal Forest', *Human Ecology* 16, 1 (1988): 57–77. Fire, of course, had many more uses than those pertaining to agriculture and game management. See 'Our Grandfather Fire: Fire and the American Indian', in Stephen J. Pyne, *Fire in America* (Princeton, NJ, 1982), 71–83.

37. Brian Swarbrick, 'A 9,000-year-old housing project', *Alberta Report* 18, 34 (1991): 50–1.

38. See Ron Brunton, 'The Cultural Instability of Egalitarian Societies', *Man* 24, 4 (1989): 673–4.

39. See Thwaites, ed., *Jesuit Relations*, VI, 243; V, 195.

40. Concerning the Plains Amerindians in this regard, see Chapters 4 and 13.

41. Torture as practised in Europe was part of the judicial system rather than that of warfare. At a time when nation-states were consolidating their positions, it was used as a means of control of certain elements within their own societies that for various reasons were considered undesirable.

The majority of Amerindians who followed the practice (most prevalent in the East) belonged to non-state societies and used torture of outside enemies to demonstrate their community solidarity and superiority over hostile alien forces. They did not torture those within their own communities. See Olive Patricia Dickason, *The Myth of the Savage and the Beginnings of French Colonialism in the Americas* (Edmonton, 1984), xi; Dickason, 'Louisbourg and the Indians: A Study in Imperial Race Relations, 1713–1760', *History and Archaeology* 6 (1976): 91–2; Nathaniel Knowles, 'The Torture of Captives by the Indians of Eastern North America', *Proceedings of the American Philosophical Society* 82, 2 (Mar. 1940), reprinted in Georg Friederici, *Scalping and Torture: Warfare Practices Among North American Indians* (Oshweken, Ont., 1985).

42. The Cree word for leader, of which 'okima' is one form, contains the root 'to give away'. See Colin Scott, 'Hunting Territories, Hunting Bosses and Communal Production among Coastal James Bay Cree', *Anthropologica* 28, 1–2 (1986): 171 n2. On what was expected of Montagnais chiefs, see Thwaites, ed., *Jesuit Relations*, XXVI, 155–63.

43. Le Clercq, *Nouvelle relation*, I, 379–81.

44. Thwaites, ed., *Jesuit Relations*, IX, 235; Chrestien Le Clercq, *Nouvelle relation de la Gaspésie*, 2 vols (Paris, 1691), I, 381–6.

45. Thwaites, ed., *Jesuit Relations*, VI, 243.

46. One study goes so far as to say the chief's authority was 'absolute' within certain spheres but in practice was constrained by the well-being of the community. See Arthur E. Hippler and Stephen Conn, *Traditional Athabascan Law Ways and Their Relationship to Contemporary Problems of 'Bush Justice'* (Fairbanks, Alaska, 1972). This would accord, at least in part, with the observation of HBC Captain Zachariah Gillam (1636 o.s.–1682) that Amerindians had 'some chief persons that are above the rest, yet working with them'. Cited by Toby Morantz, 'Old Texts, Old Questions—Another Look at the Issue of Continuity and the Early Fur Trade Period', paper presented to the American Society for Ethnohistory, Chicago, 1989.

47. Thomas Jefferys, *The Natural and Civil History of the French Dominions in North and South America*, I: *A Description of Canada and Louisiana* (London, 1760), 67.

48. Kenneth M. Ames, 'The Evolution of Social Ranking on the Northwest Coast of North America', *American Antiquity* 46, 4 (1981): 797.

49. 'Moiety': half. This division of a community into two halves was for ceremonial purposes.

50. Thomas E. Emerson and R. Barry Lewis, eds, *Cahokia and the Hinterlands* (Urbana, Ill., 1990); Melvin Fowler, *The Cahokia Atlas* (Springfield, Ill., 1989).

51. The processes by which this can occur are examined by Ames, 'Evolution of Social Ranking', 789–805.

52. Harris, ed., *Historical Atlas*, I, plate 8.

53. Kuang-chih Chang, 'Radiocarbon dates from China: some initial interpretations', *Current Anthropology* 14, 5 (1973): 525–8.

54. On the white-bone, white-meat variety, see George F. Carter, 'Pre-Columbian Chickens in America', in Riley et al., eds, *Man Across the Sea*, 178–218; Carter, 'Chinese Contacts with America: Fu Sang Again', *Anthropological Journal of Canada* 14, 1 (1976): 10–24. On the black-boned, dark-meated 'melanotic' chicken, found in Mexico, Mesoamerica, and Guatemala, see Carl L. Johannessen, 'Folk Medicine Uses of Melanotic Asiatic Chickens as Evidence of Early Diffusion to the New World', *Social Science and Medicine* 15D (1981): 427–34; Johannessen, 'Melanotic Chicken Use and Chinese Traits in Guatemala', *Revista de Historia de América* 93 (1982): 73–89. Melanotic chickens were not eaten but used in magical and curing rituals by both Mayans and Chinese.

55. Peter Caley, 'Canada's Chinese Columbus', *The Beaver* Outfit 313, 4 (1983): 8–9. Although living in China, Hwui Shan was an Afghan and apparently spoke Chinese imperfectly, which did not help his credibility upon his return. Still, his story was officially recorded, although in condensed form. It has been inferred, from his description of people keeping herds of deer and drinking the milk, that he first arrived at the Aleutian Islands before heading south to Fu-Sang, held by some to be Mexico.

56. Japanese pottery dates from before 12,000 BP: Fumiko Iwaka-Smith, 'Late Pleistocene and Early Holocene Technologies', in Pearson, ed., *Windows on the Japanese*, 199–216. Childe called pottery 'the earliest conscious utilization by man of a chemical change'. V.G. Childe, *Man Makes Himself* (New York, 1951), 76. Earliest pottery is associated with cooking.

57. Kehoe, 'Small Boats Upon the North Atlantic', 288–9; Stuart J. Fiedel, *Prehistory of the Americas* (Cambridge, 1987), 109.

58. Terry Grieder, *Art and Archaeology in Pashash* (Austin, Texas, 1979), maintains there is evidence of the potter's wheel having been used to produce Recuay ceramics, AD 290–360.

59. *Sweat of the Sun: Gold of Peru* (Edinburgh, 1990). This is the catalogue for the exhibition of the same name.

60. See Gordon F. Ekholm, 'A Possible Focus of Asiatic Influence in the Late Classic Cultures of Mesoamerica', in Jesse D. Jennings, ed., *Memoirs of the Society for American Archaeology*, 9, supplement to *American Antiquity* 18, 3, part 2 (1953): 72–97.

61. S.G. Stephens, 'Some Problems of Interpreting Transoceanic Dispersal of the New World Cottons', in Riley et al., eds, *Man Across the Sea*, 401–5.

62. For the argument that the two New World species were developed in the Americas with plants that came from Africa, see Fiedel, *Prehistory of the Americas*, 161. For the case that cotton was domesticated from naturally hybridized plants growing wild in the Americas, see Joseph Needham and Lu Gwei-Djen, *Trans-Pacific Echoes and Resonances: Listening Once Again* (Philadelphia, 1985), 62. The case for the Indian origin of New World cotton, both as a crop and its manufacture into textiles, is presented by J.B. Hutchinson, R.A. Silow, and S.G. Stephens, *The Evolution of Gossypium and Differentiation of the Cultivated Cottons* (London, 1947), 79–80, 136–9.

63. Stephen Jett, 'Trans-oceanic Contacts', 636, in Jesse D. Jennings, ed., *Ancient Native Americans* (San Francisco, [1978]); John Barber, 'Oriental Enigma', *Equinox* 49 (1990): 86.

64. It is not known how long amaranth has been cultivated in such Chinese provinces as Yunan and Kwaichow. In western China, amaranth seeds are popped, dipped in syrup, and eaten as candy. Needham and Lu, *Trans-Pacific Echoes*, 62–3.

65. A detailed description of these correlations is in Barber, 'Oriental Enigma', 82–95. See also B.J. Meggers, 'The Trans-Pacific Origin of Meso-American Civilization: A Preliminary Review of the Evidence and its Theoretical Implications', *American Anthropologist* 77 (1975): 1–27.

66. Only 20 per cent of Andean crops reproduce readily above 2,700 metres. On the distribution of maize as a crop, see Victor A. Shnirelman, 'Origin and Early History of Maize', *European Review of Native American Studies* 3, 2 (1989): 23–8, particularly the map on page 25. On the contributions of Amerindian farmers to world agriculture, see Earl J. Hamilton, 'What the New World Gave to the Economy of the Old', in Fredi Chiapelli, ed., *First Images of America: The Impact of the New World on the Old*, 2 vols (Berkeley, Calif., 1976), II, 853–84; Barrie Kavash, *Native Harvests* (New York, 1979); Jack Weatherford, *Indian Givers: How the Indians*

of the Americas Transformed the World (New York, 1988). Maize is also used as raw material for a wide variety of industrial products. It has been estimated that maize as a crop is worth more each year than all the gold and silver taken out of the Americas by the conquistadors. See Arturo Warman, 'Corn as Organizing Principle', *Northeast Indian Quarterly* 6, 1 and 2 (1989): 22. Maize, incidentally, was the staple for the transatlantic slave trade, as it prevented scurvy.

67. Corn requires 60 to 70 days to produce a crop; rice requires 120–40 days. Pierre Chaunu, *L'Amérique et les Amériques* (Paris, 1964), 19. In Europe at the time of contact, the standard yield of Old World cereals was six units of seed collected for each unit of seed planted, a rate that under favourable circumstances could increase to 10:1. The standard for corn was 150:1; in bad years, the yield could drop to 70:1. Warman, 'Corn as Organizing Principle', 21.

68. There has been spirited debate about the origin of corn as a cultigen and, consequently, an extensive list of publications. Among the articles (being shorter and perhaps more readable) are: Steve Connor, 'Stone Age People Modified Crops', *The Independent*, 18 Mar. 1999, 12; Paul C. Mangelsdorf, 'Mystery of Corn', *Scientific American* 183, 1 (1950): 20–4; Mangelsdorf, 'Mystery of Corn: New Perspectives', *Proceedings of the American Philosophical Society* 127, 4 (1983): 215–47; Mangelsdorf, 'The Origin of Corn', *Scientific American* 255, 2 (1986): 80–6; George W. Beadle, 'The Ancestry of Corn', *Scientific American* 242, 2 (1980): 112–19; Walton C. Galinat, 'The Origin of Maize', *Annual Review of Genetics* 5 (1971): 447–78; J.M.J. de Wet and J.R. Harlan, 'Origin of Maize: The Tripartite Hypothesis', *Euphytica* 21 (1972); James H. Kempton, 'Maize as a Measure of Indian Skill', *Symposium on Prehistoric Agriculture*, University of New Mexico (Millwood, NY, 1977); Louis Werner, 'Caught in a maize of genes', *Américas* 52, 3 (May–June 2000): 6–17.

69. Thor Heyerdahl, *Early Man and the Ocean: A Search for the Beginnings of Navigation and Seaborne Civilizations* (New York, 1980), 376–7. Zoologist and amateur linguist Barry Fell has been one proponent of North African and European connections with the New World. A reasoned assessment of the strengths and failings of his arguments is David H. Kelley's 'Proto-Tifinagh and Proto-Ogham in the Americas', *Review of Archaeology* 11, 1 (1990): 1–10. Kelley concludes: 'We need to ask not only what Fell has done wrong in his epigraphy, but also where we have gone wrong as archaeologists.'

70. Jared Diamond, *Guns, Germs, and Steel* (New York, 1999), 217–38. Diamond observes that the task of developing writing was so difficult that it occurred comparatively late in human cultural development. According to Diamond, one of the reasons that hunting and gathering societies neither developed nor adopted writing was their lack of institutional needs for its use. When Spaniards arrived in the sixteenth century, they found 18 different writing systems in Mesoamerica. See Alice B. Kehoe, *North American Indians, A Comprehensive Account* (Englewood Cliffs, NJ, 1981), 41.

71. Michael H. Brown, *The Search for Eve: Have Scientists Found the Mother of Us All?* (New York, 1990), 315. Polynesians, in their turn, are genetically similar to Chinese and Indonesians.

72. Julian H. Steward advocates multilinear evolution in *Theory of Culture Change* (Urbana, Ill., 1976). Cultures have been described as symbolic structures that provide the means for human satisfaction once survival has been assured. See David Rindos, 'The Evolution of the Capacity for Culture: Sociobiology, Structuralism, and Cultural Evolution', *Current Anthropology* 27, 4 (1986): 326.

73. Bob Connolly and Robin Anderson, *New Guinea Highlanders Encounter the Outside World* (London, 1988).

74. Nigel Davies, *Voyagers to the New World* (Albuquerque, NM, 1979).

75. Needham and Lu, *Trans-Pacific Echoes*, 64.

Chapter 2

1. This section was developed from my 'Three Worlds, One Focus: Europeans Meet Inuit and Amerindians in the Far North', in Richard C. Davis, ed., *Rupert's Land: A Cultural Tapestry* (Calgary, 1988), 51–78.

2. William R. Morrison, *Under the Flag: Canadian Sovereignty and the Native People in Northern Canada* (Ottawa, 1984), 97. The term 'Inuit', meaning 'human beings' ('Inuk' in the singular), widely used among the people for themselves, was adopted by the Inuit Circumpolar Conference in 1977 for all the people formerly referred to as 'Eskimo'. People of the western Arctic are called Inuvialuit; other regional terms include 'Inuinait' and 'Inumagit'. (Bishop John R. Sperry, Yellowknife, in a letter published in *Arctic* 40, 4 [1987]: 364.) 'Inuit' has been officially adopted in Canada. See José Mailhot, 'L'Etymologie de "Esquimau": Revue et Corrigée', *Études/Inuit/Studies* 2, 2 (1978): 59–69; Yvon Csonka,

Collections arctiques (Neuchâtel, Switzerland, 1988), 11, 18. On the question of first contacts with Europeans, see Robert McGhee, *Canada Rediscovered* (Hull, Que., 1991).

3. Morrison, *Under the Flag*, 100.

4. Urs Bitterli, *Cultures in Conflict: Encounters Between European and Non-European Cultures, 1492–1800*, tr. Ritchie Robertson (London, 1989).

5. This is the thesis of Tryggvi J. Oleson, *Early Voyages and Northern Approaches* (Toronto, 1963), 9.

6. Kaj Birket-Smith, *Eskimos* (Copenhagen, 1971), 13. An account of the first meeting of Greenland Skraelings with Norsemen is reproduced, ibid., 28–9. See also L.H. Neatby, 'Exploration and History of the Canadian Arctic', in Damas, ed., *Handbook of North American Indians*, 5: *Arctic*, 337–90.

7. Wendell H. Oswalt, *Eskimos and Explorers* (Novato, Calif., 1979), 11.

8. By way of comparison, French cosmographer André Thevet (*c.* 1517–92) reported that Amerindians at first honoured Spaniards as prophets and even as gods. Thevet, *Les singularitez de la France Antarctique*, ed. Paul Gaffarel (Paris, 1878), 139–40. See also Bruce G. Trigger, 'Early Native North American Response to European Contact', *Journal of American History* 77, 4 (1991): 1195–1215; Nathaniel Wachtel, *The Vision of the Vanquished: The Spanish Conquest of Peru through Indian Eyes, 1530–1570* (London, 1977).

9. Harris, ed., *Historical Atlas*, I, plate 16; Joel Berglund, 'The Decline of the Norse Settlements in Greenland', *Arctic Anthropology* 23, 142 (1986): 109–35.

10. See temperature graph in Harris, ed., *Historical Atlas*, plate 16.

11. The argument that the Norse communities did not adapt either culturally or technologically to changing conditions is presented by Thomas H. McGovern, 'The economics of extinction in Norse Greenland', in T.M. Wigley, M.J. Ingram, and G. Farmer, eds, *Climate and History* (Cambridge, 1981), 404–33. For example, they never adopted Inuit sea-mammal hunting technology (the most advanced in the world at that time) or skin boats, despite the unavailability of timber. Culturally, they concentrated on bigger and more elaborate churches and the latest in European fashion and dress.

12. Alan D. McMillan, *Native Peoples and Cultures of Canada: An Anthropological Overview* (Vancouver, 1988), 246.

13. Samuel Hearne, *A Journey from Prince of Wales's Fort in Hudson's Bay to the Northern Ocean in the years 1769 ·· 1770 ··1771 ··1772*, ed. J.B. Tyrrell (Toronto, 1911), 163.

14. W.A. Kenyon, *Tokens of Possession* (Toronto, 1975), 41, 121.

15. The term 'Qallunaat' or 'Kabloona' is thought to have originated from the Inuktitut term meaning 'people who pamper their eyebrows', perhaps a variation of 'qallunaaraaluit', which refers to materialism, interference with nature, and greed. See Minnie Aodla Freeman, *Life among the Qalunaat* (Edmonton, 1978), after Foreword. Another translation that has been proposed is 'people with bushy eyebrows'.

16. Charles Francis Hall, *Arctic Researches and Life among the Esquimaux* (New York, 1865), 251, 290, 385.

17. William C. Sturtevant and David Beers Quinn, 'This New Prey: Eskimos in Europe in 1567, 1576, and 1577', in Christian F. Feest, ed., *Indians and Europe* (Aachen, 1987), 80.

18. Miller Christy, *The Voyages of Captain Luke Foxe of Hull, and Captain Thomas James of Bristol, in search of a North-West Passage, in 1631–32*, 2 vols (London, 1894), I, 50ff.; Nicholas Jérémie, *Twenty Years at York Factory, 1694–1714* (Ottawa, 1926), 16.

19. This technology was used by the Thule of the eastern Arctic as well as the Punuk of the west, and had been adopted by the whalers of the west coast, such as the Nuu'chah'nulth (Nootka) of Vancouver Island. See Jean-Loup Rousselot, William W. Fitzhugh, and Aron Crowell, 'Maritime Economics of the North Pacific Rim', in Fitzhugh and Crowell, eds, *Crossroads of Continents*, 163–72. A toggling harpoon found at L'Anse Amour Mound in Labrador, dating back to 7500 BP, may be the oldest such weapon in the world. See James A. Tuck and Robert McGhee, 'Archaic Cultures in the Strait of Belle Isle Region, Labrador', *Arctic Anthropology* 12, 2 (1975): 76–91. For a general description of Inuit whaling technology, see J. Garth Taylor, 'Inuit Whaling Technology in Eastern Canada and Greenland', in Allen P. McCartney, ed., *Thule Eskimo Culture: An Anthropological Perspective* (Ottawa, 1979), 292–300.

20. Ethnologist June Helm, University of Iowa, divides the Subarctic into the shield with associated Hudson Bay lowlands and Mackenzie borderlands, the cordillera, the Alaska plateau, and the region south of the Alaska range. The first division, that of the Subarctic shield and borderlands, covers approximately three-quarters of the land mass of the Arctic. June Helm, ed., *Handbook of North American Indians*, 6: *Subarctic* (Washington, 1981), 1.

21. On the importance of reciprocity, see Le Clercq, *Nouvelle relation*, I, 324. Europeans, not

appreciating the principle of 'I give to you that you might give to me', quickly denigrated it as 'Indian giving', particularly when Amerindians, perceiving that the Europeans did not reciprocate, asked for their gifts back.

22. Chrestien Le Clercq, *First Establishment of the Faith in New France*, 2 vols, tr. John Gilmary Shea (New York, 1881), I, 124.

23. Fladmark, *British Columbia Prehistory*, 50. Trade in the region is at least 10,000 years old.

24. Recent research by historian Laurier Turgeon has revealed that copper, particularly in the form of kettles, was important in early Indian–Basque trade. See Turgeon, 'Basque–Amerindian Trade in the Saint-Lawrence during the Sixteenth Century: New Documents, New Perspectives', *Man in the Northeast* 40 (1990): 81–7.

25. Harris, ed., *Historical Atlas*, plate 14.

26. A.I. Hallowell, 'Some Psychological Characteristics of the Northeastern Indians', in Frederick Johnson, ed., *Man in Northeastern North America* (Andover, Mass., 1940), 25. Amerindians much admired emotional control, giving rise to the European stereotype of the 'haughty Indian'.

27. Caley, 'Canada's Chinese Columbus', 4.

28. Thwaites, ed., *Jesuit Relations*, VI, 233. Later, Le Jeune referred to the Montagnais as 'real buffoons' (ibid., 243).

29. Le Clercq made the remark in reference to the Mi'kmaq (*Nouvelle Relation*, 388); however, hospitality is characteristic of tribal societies generally. It was also practised in pre-Renaissance Europe. Unfortunately, Europeans forgot their own traditions and did not generally reciprocate Amerindian hospitality. As a result, Amerindians continued the custom among themselves, but with Europeans they soon began to demand payment, much to the latter's disgust. Le Clercq, *New Relation*, 246.

30. *An Account of the Customs and Manners of the Micmakis and Maricheets, Savage Nations, Now Dependent on the Government of Cape Breton* (London, 1758), 4. An early description of them is that of Jesuit Pierre Biard (1567?–1622) in Thwaites, ed., *Jesuit Relations*, II, 73–81. At Quebec, Jesuit Paul Le Jeune was vividly impressed with the facial painting of Amerindians, as well as by their general appearance when he saw a group of 600 warriors, 'tall, powerful', wearing, among other skins, those of elk, bear, and beaver. Thwaites, ed., *Jesuit Relations*, V, 23; VI, 25. See also Daniel N. Paul, *We Were Not the Savages: A Micmac Perspective on the Collision of European and Aboriginal Civilization* (Halifax, 1993).

31. Jay Miller, 'People, Berdaches, and Left-handed Bears', *Journal of Anthropological Research* 38, 3 (1982): 274–87. See also Colin Scott, 'Knowledge Construction among Cree Hunters: Metaphors and Literal Understanding', *Journal de la Société des Américanistes* 75 (1989): 193–208, particularly 194–5. Stephen A. McNeary discusses these beliefs as expressed by the Tsimshian in 'Image and Illusion in Tsimshian Mythology', in Jay Miller and Carol M. Eastman, eds, *Tsimshian and Their Neighbors of the North Pacific Coast* (Seattle, 1984). The Amerindian estimation of the reasoning capacity of beavers is found in *Nouveaux Voyages de Mr. le Baron de Lahontan dans l'Amérique septentrionale*, 2 vols (The Hague, 1703), 155–9. The Jesuits observed that Amerindians considered all souls—minds—to be immortal, whether human or otherwise. (Thwaites, ed., *Jesuit Relations*, VI, 175–7.)

32. A. Irving Hallowell, 'Ojibway Ontology, Behavior and World View', in Hallowell, *Contributions to Anthropology* (Chicago, 1976). See also McClellan, *My Old People Say*, 86–8; Brian Swarbrick, 'A 9,000-year-old housing project', *Alberta Report* 18, 34 (1991): 50–1, concerning the belief of the Sto:lo of British Columbia (a subgroup of the Coast Salish) that certain 'transformer' rocks were actually 'men of stone'. The Indians believed that being turned into stone was the fate of chiefs who did not share their wealth with their people.

33. Claude Lévi-Strauss has explored the general nature of these myths in *The Jealous Potter*, tr. Bénédict Chorier (Chicago, 1988). Nicolas Denys describes Indian love for storytelling in *The Description and Natural History of the Coasts of North America (Acadia)*, ed. William F. Ganong (Toronto, 1908), 418–19.

34. For a general study of the phenomenon, see Diana Claire Tkaczuk and Brian C. Vivian, eds, *Cultures in Conflict: Current Archaeological Perspectives* (Calagary, 1989).

35. Ernest S. Burch Jr, 'War and Trade', in Fitzhugh and Crowell, eds, *Crossroads of Continents*, 231–2.

36. By the end of the seventeenth century, a French officer would observe that northeastern Indians were 'never rash in declaring war; they hold frequent Councils before they resolve upon it.' Louis Armand de Lom d'Arce de Lahontan, *New Voyages to North America by Baron de Lahontan*, ed. R.G. Thwaites, 2 vols (Chicago, 1905), II, 507. Le Clercq agreed: war, he wrote, was never declared except as a last resort on the advice of Old Men. (Le Clercq, *New Relation*, 269.) By mid-eighteenth century Thomas Jefferys expressed a different view. Indians,

he wrote, rarely 'refuse to engage in a war to which they have been invited by their allies: on the contrary, they seldom wait till they are called to take up arms, the least motif being sufficient to determine them to it' (Jefferys, *Natural and Civil History*, I, 53, 68). See also Daniel K. Richter, 'War and Culture: The Iroquois Experience', *William and Mary Quarterly* 40, 4 (1982): 528–59.

37. Le Clercq, *Nouvelle Relation*, 89.

38. John Webster Grant, *Moon of Wintertime: Missionaries and the Indians of Canada in Encounter since 1534* (Toronto, 1984), 24.

39. For example, in the *Jesuit Relations* there is a chapter devoted to the differences between Europeans and Amerindians (XLIV, 277–309), but little, if any, mention is made of resemblances.

40. Le Clercq, *Nouvelle Relation*, 379–81.

41. Thwaites, ed., *Jesuit Relations*, III, 91. Although Biard was speaking about the Mi'kmaq, this was reported for other Amerindian societies as well. For example, see George Henry Loskiel, *History of the Missions of the United Brethren Among the Indians in North America*, tr. C.I. LaTrobe (London, 1794), 132; Nicolas Perrot (1644–1718), *Mémoire sur les moeurs, coustumes et relligion des sauvages de l'Amérique Septentrionale* (Leipzig and Paris, 1864; Johnson Reprint, 1968), 78.

42. If an 'e' is substituted for the second 'o', Oupeeshepow becomes Oupeeshepew, which means 'always busy', according to Reg Louttit, chief of the Attawapiskat Cree north of Moose Factory. (Personal communication.)

43. Glyndwr Williams, ed., *Andrew Graham's Observations on Hudson's Bay 1767–91* (London, 1969), 204.

44. Christy, *Voyages*, I, 137.

45. Toby Morantz, 'Oral and Recorded History in James Bay', in William Cowan, ed., *Papers of the Fifteenth Algonquian Conference* (Ottawa, 1984), 181–2.

46. John S. Long, 'Narratives of Early Encounters between Europeans and the Cree of Western James Bay', *Ontario History* 80, 3 (1988): 230. The earliest mention of the 'Kristinaux' is in the *Jesuit Relations* of the 1640s.

47. Harris, ed., *Historical Atlas*, I, plate 23.

48. Colonial Office 194/27, 263, Palliser to the Secretary of the Admiralty, 25 Aug. 1766. Cited by W.H. Whiteley, 'The Establishment of the Moravian Mission in Labrador and British Policy, 1763–83', *Canadian Historical Review* 45, 1 (1964): 31, 39–40.

49. Jean Alfonce (Jean Fonteneau), *Les Voyages aventureux du Capitaine Ian Alfonce, Sainctongeois* (Poitiers, 1559), 27v; Giovanni Battista Ramusio, *Navigations et Voyages (XVI siècle)*, tr. Général Langlois and M.J. Simon (Paris, 1933), 111.

50. J. Callum Thomson, 'Cornered: Cultures in Conflict in Newfoundland and Labrador', in Tkaczuk and Vivian, eds, *Cultures in Conflict*, 199.

51. Sir Richard Whitbourne, *A Discourse and Discovery of New-found-land, with many reasons to prove how worthy and beneficiall a Plantation may there be made, after a far better manner than now is* (London, 1620), 2–4.

52. Leslie Upton, 'The Extermination of the Beothucks of Newfoundland', *Canadian Historical Review* 58 (1977): 144–53; Ingeborg Marshall, *A History and Ethnography of the Beothuk* (Montreal and Kingston, 1996), 158–9.

53. See George W. Brown, David M. Hayne, and Frances G. Halpenny, eds, *Dictionary of Canadian Biography (DCB)* (Toronto, 1966), VI, s.v. 'Demasduwit', 'Shawnadithit'. Harold Horwood, 'The people who were murdered for fun', *Maclean's*, 10 Oct. 1959, 27–43; Ingeborg Constanze Luise Marshall, *The Red Ochre People* (Vancouver, 1982); Marshall, *A History and Ethnography of the Beothuk* (Montreal and Kingston, 1996); Leslie F.S. Upton, 'The Extermination of the Beothuks of Newfoundland', *Canadian Historical Review* 58, 2 (1977): 133–53.

54. Victor P. Lytwyn, 'Waterworld: The Aquatic Territory of the Great Lakes First Nations', in *Gin Das Winan: Documenting Aboriginal History in Ontario* (Toronto, 1996), 14. Gilles Havard, in *La grande paix de Montréal de 1701* (Québec, 1992), 132–5, lists 27 Great Lakes nations.

55. Harris, ed., *Historical Atlas*, plate 12.

56. Iroquoian languages are related to Siouan and Caddoan. The Caddo, of the US Southwest, were organized into hierarchical chiefdoms at the time of European contact; the Sioux had been connected earlier with the Mississippian Mound Builders. There is some evidence that chiefdoms had appeared among some of the Iroquois. See William C. Noble, 'Tsouharissen's Chiefdom: An Early Historic 17th Century Neutral Iroquoian Ranked Society', *Canadian Journal of Archaeology* 9, 2 (1985): 131–46.

57. Succotash, an Amerindian dish adopted by early settlers, was made with corn and beans boiled with fish or meat.

58. A description of Huronia as first seen by Europeans is in Thwaites, ed., *Jesuit Relations*, XVI, 225–37.

59. On the possible Basque origin of the word 'Iroquois', see Peter Bakker, 'A Basque Etymology for the Word Iroquois', *Man in the Northeast* 40 (1990): 89–93.

60. They called themselves Wendat, People of the Peninsula, and their land Wendake. 'Wendat' could also refer to the confederacy. The name 'Huron' was given them by the French because of the coiffures of the warriors, which reminded them of the bristles on the spine of a boar. Diamond Jenness, *Indians of Canada* (Ottawa, 1932), 82. Odawa men affected a similar hairstyle. Apparently the term 'huron' also referred to manner of dress, implying rusticity. See also Georges Sioui, *Les Wendats: Une civilisation méconnue* (Québec, 1994).

61. Gabriel Sagard, *The Long Journey to the Country of the Hurons*, tr. H.H. Langton (Toronto, 1939), 104.

62. Gabriel Sagard, *Histoire du Canada, et voyages que les frères mineurs Recollects y ont faicts pour la conversion des infidelles*, 4 vols (Paris, 1636), III, 728.

63. The 30,000 estimate for the Hurons was made by Champlain, who spent a winter in Huronia. Geographer Conrad Heidenreich believes it is probably about one-third too large; he uses the figure 20,000. Heidenreich, *Huronia: A History and Geography of the Huron Indians 1600–1650* (Toronto, 1971), 96–103.

64. The Arendarhonon, 'the People of the Rock', had the second largest population among the Huron confederates. They may have joined about 1590, long after the two founding tribes confederated, perhaps early in the fifteenth century. Their late date of joining raises the question whether the Arendarhonon came from Stadacona.

65. Bruce G. Trigger, *The Children of Aataentsic: A History of the Huron People to 1660*, 2 vols (Montreal and Kingston, 1976), I, 197.

66. The Five Nations languages were, from east to west, Mohawk, Oneida, Onondaga, Cayuga, and Seneca. According to the Huron historian Margaret Vincent Tehariolina, the Huron were an offshoot of the Seneca and thus essentially the same people. Tehariolina, *La nation huronne, son histoire, sa culture, son esprit* (Québec, 1984), 96–7.

67. A report in the *Jesuit Relations* says that the Onondaga alternated men and women as head sachems (XXI, 201).

68. Daniel K. Richter, 'War, Peace, and Politics in Seventeenth Century Huronia', in Tkaczuk and Vivian, eds, *Cultures in Conflict*, 285–6.

69. 'Oka and its Inhabitants', in *The Life of Rev. Amand Parent, the first French-Canadian ordained by the Methodist Church* (Toronto, 1887), 167.

70. Hiawatha has been identified as an Onondaga by birth and a Mohawk by adoption, and also as a Huron. Some of the versions of the origins of the league are told by Christopher Vecsey, 'The Story of the Iroquois Confederacy', *Journal of the American Academy of Religion* 54, 1 (1986): 79–106. Cree-French historian Bernard Assiniwi gives his version in *Histoire des Indiens du haut et du bas Canada: moeurs et coutumes des Algonkins et des Iroquois*, 3 vols (Québec, 1973), I, 111–24.

71. Alice Beck Kehoe, *The Ghost Dance* (Toronto, 1989), 115. Hiawatha's name, 'One Who Combs', was earned because he combed the snakes out of Thadodaho's hair. There are several versions of the story, one of which is recounted by Paul A.W. Wallace, *The White Roots of Peace* (Port Washington, NY, 1968), 11–17.

72. 'Anishinabe' (plural, Anishinabeg) means 'the people'. 'Ojibwa' translates as 'the talk of the robin'. The subsistence basis of the Odawa was dealt with by William Newbigging, 'The Ottawa Settlement of Detroit', paper presented to the Canadian Historical Association, 1992. In the seventeenth century, the closely related Ojibwa, Odawa, and Algonquin were loosely confederated into the Council of Three Fires. Today they are more or less merged as Ojibwa (Anishinabe), a process that took off during the nineteenth century. Nipissings, Saulteaux, and Mississauga are among others who are included.

73. A detailed study of the exploitation of wild rice and its cultural ramifications is that of Thomas Vennum, *Wild Rice and the Ojibway People* (St Paul, Minn., 1988). See also Kathi Avery and Thomas Pawlick, 'Last Stand in Wild Rice Country', *Harrowsmith* 3, 7 (May 1979): 32–47, 107.

74. Sagard, *Histoire du Canada*, IV, 846.

75. Catharine McClellan, verbal communication.

76. The expression is borrowed from the Navajo's Blessingway ceremony.

77. Anthropologists once argued that the Great Plains could not have been inhabited to any extent before the advent of the horse and the gun. Clark Wissler wrote in 1906, 'the peopling of the plains proper was a recent phenomenon due in part to the introduction of the horse and the displacement of tribes by white settlement.' Wissler, 'Diffusion of Culture in the Plains of North America', International Congress of Americanists, 15th session (Quebec, 1906), 39–52. Although Wissler later modified his position, A.L. Kroeber in 1939 was still arguing that the Plains had developed culturally 'only since the taking over of the horse from Europeans'. Kroeber, *Cultural and Natural Areas of Native North America* (Berkeley, 1939), 76. William Duncan Strong, 'The Plains Culture Area in the Light of Archaeology', *American Anthropologist* 23, 2 (1933): 271–87, held that horse nomadism represented no more than a 'thin and strikingly uniform veneer' on earlier cultural

manifestations. On the lack of specific rites among the Plains Cree for the increase of horses even though they were the symbol of wealth, see David G. Mandelbaum, *The Plains Cree* (Regina, 1979 [1940]), 63. See also John C. Lewis, *The Horse in Blackfoot Indian Culture* (Washington, 1955); Lewis, *The Blackfeet* (Norman, 1958).

78. Head-Smashed-In has been named a World Heritage Site by UNESCO. For a detailed description of the site, see Jack Brink and Bob Dawe, *Final Report of the 1985 and 1986 Field Season at Head-Smashed-In Buffalo Jump* (Edmonton, 1989), 298–303. Also <www. head-smashed-in.com>.

79. Thomas F. Kehoe, 'Corralling Life', in Mary LeCron Foster and Lucy Jane Botscharow, eds, *The Life of Symbols* (Boulder, Colo., 1990), 175–93.

80. Richard G. Forbis, *A Review of Alberta Archaeology to 1964* (Ottawa, 1970), 27.

81. Harris, ed., *Historical Atlas*, I, plate 15. See also Brian O.K. Reeves, *Culture Change in the Northern Plains: 1000 B.C.–A.D. 1000* (Edmonton, 1983); H.M. Wormington and Richard G. Forbis, *An Introduction to the Archaeology of Alberta, Canada* (Denver, 1965), particularly the summary and conclusion, 183–201.

82. Eleanor Verbicky-Todd, *Communal Buffalo Hunting Among the Plains Amerindians: An Ethnographic and Historic Review* (Edmonton, 1984), 25–32. At a later date an offender risked being flogged or even (among the Kiowa) having his horse shot.

Chapter 3

1. H.P. Biggar, ed., *The Voyages of Jacques Cartier* (Ottawa, 1924), 61–2. For an Amerindian view of 'an adventurer called Jacques Cartier' on the St Lawrence, see Assiniwi, *Histoire des Indiens du haut et du bas Canada*, II, 29–81. See also Ramsay Cook, ed., *The Voyages of Jacques Cartier* (Toronto, 1993).

2. The generally accepted version of the origin of the name 'Canada' is that it derived from the Iroquoian 'ka-na-ta', meaning village. A good argument can be made, however, that it comes from the Montagnais 'ka-na-dun', meaning clean land. During the sixteenth century, the term 'Canadian' referred to the people of the North Shore, today's Montagnais, closely related to Cree and speaking a variation of the same language. These people were among the first trading partners of the French, which the Iroquois were not. Amerindian languages, besides being complex, used a wider variety of sounds and ways of making sounds than did European languages. As a result, during the early days of contact, it was simpler for an Amerindian to learn a European language than for a European to learn an Amerindian one.

3. Olive Patricia Dickason, 'Concepts of Sovereignty at the Time of First Contacts', in L.C. Green and Dickason, *The Law of Nations and the New World* (Edmonton, 1989), 223–4.

4. François de Belleforest and Sebastian Münster, *La Cosmographie universelle de tout le monde . . .*, 2 vols (Paris, 1575), II, 2190–2.

5. Christopher Carlile's report in Richard Hakluyt, *The Principal Navigations, Voyages, Traffiques and Discoveries of the English Nation*, 12 vols (Glasgow, 1903–5), VIII, 145–6; Pierre-François-Xavier de Charlevoix, *Histoire et description générale de la Nouvelle France*, 3 vols (Paris, 1744), I, 21.

6. Biggar, ed., *Voyages of Cartier*, 264; H.P. Biggar, ed., *A Collection of Documents Relating to Jacques Cartier and the Sieur de Roberval* (Ottawa, 1930), 463.

7. Marcel Trudel, *Histoire de la Nouvelle-France I: Les vaines tentatives, 1524–1603* (Montréal, 1963), 151–75; Antoine de Montchrestien, *Traicté de l'oeconomie politique . . .* (Paris, 1889 [1615]), S.l., s.d., 214.

8. Biggar, ed., *Voyages of Cartier*, 158. It should be remembered that Cartier spent only a day at Hochelaga.

9. Bruce G. Trigger and James F. Pendergast, 'Saint Lawrence Iroquoians', in Trigger, ed., *Handbook of North American Indians*, 15: *Northeast* (Washington, 1978), 358–9.

10. Belleforest and Münster, *La Cosmographie*, II, 2190–2.

11. Thwaites, ed., *Jesuit Relations*, I, 105.

12. Trigger, *Natives and Newcomers*, 146. In general, I am following Trigger, who discusses the question of the Laurentian Iroquoians in detail, 144–8.

13. John Witthoft, 'Archaeology as a Key to the Colonial Fur Trade', in *Aspects of the Fur Trade* (St Paul, Minn., 1967), 57. John M. Cooper describes early trapping techniques in *Snares, Deadfalls, and Other Traps of the Northern Algonquians and Northern Athapaskans* (Washington, 1938).

14. Bruce G. Trigger, *Natives and Newcomers: Canada's 'Heroic Age' Reconsidered* (Montreal and Kingston, 1985), 96–100, 105–8.

15. Biggar, ed., *Voyages of Cartier*, 177–8. See also Trigger, *Natives and Newcomers*, 137, 147. Although Cartier's is a second-hand account and should therefore be treated with caution, there is archaeological evidence of large-scale warfare, as Trigger points out.

16. Trigger, *Natives and Newcomers*, 106–8. See also J.B. Jamieson, 'Trade and Warfare: Disappearance of

the St. Lawrence Iroquoians', *Man in the Northeast* 39 (1990): 79–86. Jamieson argues that the dynamics of the St Lawrence Iroquois disappearance had nothing to do with European trade.

17. Bailey, *The Conflict of European and Eastern Algonkian Cultures*, xviii.

18. Henry P. Biggar, ed., *The Works of Samuel de Champlain*, 6 vols (Toronto, 1922–36), II, 96.

19. Biggar, ed., *Voyages of Cartier*, 76.

20. Charles A. Martijn, 'Innu (Montagnais) in Newfoundland', in William Cowan, ed., *Papers of the Twenty-first Algonquian Conference* (Ottawa, 1990), 227–64.

21. Thwaites, ed., *Jesuit Relations*, VI, 233.

22. Champlain was entering into an alliance according to Amerindian ritual, by which, in effect, the council was the treaty. The French had developed this practice a century earlier in Brazil. Biggar, ed., *Works of Champlain*, I, 98–102.

23. Bruce G. Trigger, *Indians and the Heroic Age of New France* (Ottawa, 1970), 10–11.

24. Eleanor Burke Leacock and Nancy Oestreich Lurie, eds, *North American Indians in Historical Perspective* (New York, 1971), 351.

25. Jan Kupp, 'Could the Dutch Commercial Empire have influenced the Canadian Economy during the First Half of the Eighteenth Century?', *Canadian Historical Review* 52, 4 (1971): 367–88.

26. Thwaites, ed., *Jesuit Relations*, XXVI, 155–63; XVIII, 205; Pierre d'Avity, Seigneur de Montmartin, *Description générale de l'Amérique, troisième partie du Monde . . .* (Paris, 1660), 42–3. See also Trigger, *Natives and Newcomers*, 204–5.

27. See, for example, Bruce G. Trigger, 'Champlain Judged by His Indian Policy: A Different View of Early Canadian History', *Anthropologica* 13 (1971): 94–100. This was a special issue devoted to essays in honour of anthropologist Diamond Jenness.

28. Thwaites, ed., *Jesuit Relations*, VI, 7–19; Marcel Trudel, *Histoire de la Nouvelle France III: La seigneurie des Cent-Associés, 1627–1663* (Montréal, 1979), 128.

29. Trigger, *Indians and the Heroic Age*, 15; Denys Delâge, *Le pays renversé: Amérindiens et européens en Amérique du nord-est 1600–1664* (Montréal, 1985), 108.

30. Sagard, *Histoire du Canada*, II, 512.

31. Sagard, *Long Journey*, 45–6, 268.

32. Le Clercq, *First Establishment of the Faith in New France*, I, 136. See also Marc Lescarbot, *The History of New France*, ed. W.L. Grant, 3 vols (Toronto, 1907–14), III, 25–6; Denys, *Description and Natural History*, 447–8; Thwaites, ed., *Jesuit Relations*, III, 81.

33. Charlevoix, *Histoire et description*, III, 87–8.

34. J.B. Tyrrell, ed., *David Thompson's Narrative of His Explorations in Western America, 1784–1812* (Toronto, 1916), 206.

35. Claude C. Le Roy dit Bacqueville de la Potherie (1663–1736), *Histoire de l'Amérique septentrionale*, 4 vols (Paris, 1722), III, 176–7; Lahontan, *New Voyages to North America*, I, 82. There are reports of wasteful hunting for food as well. See, for example, Glyndwr Williams, ed., *Andrew Graham's Observations on Hudson's Bay 1767–91* (London, 1969), 154, 280.

36. Charlevoix, *Histoire et description*, I, 126. According to popular rumour, Basque whalers had been operating off the North Atlantic coast for so long that by the time French merchants arrived in the seventeenth century, they found the Amerindians and Inuit using Basque words, and Spaniards reported that Montagnais and Basques were able to converse with each other. Peter Bakker, 'Two Basque Loanwords in Micmac', *International Journal of American Linguistics* 55, 2 (1989): 258–60; Bakker, 'The Mysterious Link Between Basque and Micmac Art', *European Review of Native American Studies* 5, 1 (1991): 21–4. An early eighteenth-century observer reported that Inuktitut resembled Basque. See also Nicolas Jérémie, *Twenty Years at York Factory, 1694–1714* (Ottawa, 1926), 17; Selma Huxley, ed., *Los vascos en el marco Atlantico Norte Siglos XVI y XVII* (San Sebastian, 1988). Basque is an agglomerative language, as are those of Amerindians and Inuit.

37. Johannes de Laet, *L'Histoire du Nouveau Monde, ou Description des Indes occidentales . . .* (Leyden, 1640), 36.

38. Bernard G. Hoffman, *Cabot to Cartier* (Toronto, 1961); David Sanger, 'Culture Change as an Adaptative Process in the Maine-Maritimes Region', *Arctic Anthropology* 12, 2 (1975): 60–75. A Penobscot whale hunt is described in 'A True Relation of the Voyage of Captaine George Waymouth, 1605, by James Rosier', in Henry Sweetser Burrage, ed., *Early English and French Voyages, Chiefly from Hakluyt, 1534–1608* (New York, 1952), 392. Abbé J.A. Maurault (1819–70) makes the point that all the Natives of Acadia and New England shared a similar culture and lived in much the same manner. Maurault, *Histoire des Abenakis depuis 1605 jusqu'à nos jours* (Sorel, Québec, 1866), 9; see also Ruth Holmes Whitehead, *The Old Man Told Us: Excerpts from Micmac History 1500–1950* (Halifax, 1991).

39. Thwaites, ed., *Jesuit Relations*, XLVII, 223; Denys, *Description and Natural History*, 196; D.B. Quinn,

ed., *New American World: A Documentary History of North America to 1612*, 5 vols (New York, 1979), III, 348; Lescarbot, *History of New France*, II, 309.

40. 'Mi'kmaq' is widely accepted as meaning 'allies' (Jenness, *Indians of Canada*, 267), although this is not entirely certain. The term the Mi'kmaq used for themselves was 'El'nu', 'true men'. They were probably the Toudamans of Cartier and were certainly the Souriquois of Lescarbot; they were also called Taranteens, a reference to their trading proclivities. Wuastukwiuk (Maliseets) were known to Champlain and the early Jesuits as Etchemin or Eteminquois. The language of the Mi'kmaq shares certain characteristics with Cree, the most widespread of the Algonkian group, as well as with Arapaho of the central Plains.

41. Lescarbot, *History of New France*, III, 312–13, 358–9.

42. E.B. O'Callaghan and J.R. Brodhead, eds, *Documents Relative to the Colonial History of the State of New York*, 15 vols (Albany, NY, 1853–87), IX, 161.

43. Denys, *Description and Natural History*, 446–9.

44. Charlevoix, *Histoire et description*, I, 128; Denys, *Description and Natural History*, 195–6. See also Virginia Miller, 'Social and Political Complexity on the East Coast: The Micmac Case', in Ronald J. Nash, ed., *The Evolution of Maritime Cultures on the Northeast and Northwest Coasts of America* (Burnaby, BC, 1983), 51. In another article, Nash argues that the Mi'kmaq at the time of contact were on their way to becoming organized into chiefdoms. Ronald J. Nash, 'An Alternative History: Uninterrupted Views of Micmac Society', in Tkaczuk and Vivian, eds, *Cultures in Conflict*, 187–94.

45. Archives de la Marine, Series B3, vol. IX, Sieur de Narp to Minister of the Marine, 23 Sept. 1671, f.374. Cited by Cornelius J. Jaenen, *Friend and Foe: Aspects of French-Amerindian Cultural Contact in the Sixteenth and Seventeenth Centuries* (Toronto, 1976), 123. See also Jaenen, *The French Relationship with the Native People of New France and Acadia* (Ottawa, 1984).

46. Library and Archives Canada (LAC), AC, C11B 10:4–5, lettre de Joseph de Monbeton de Brouillan dit Saint-Ovide (governor of Ile Royale 1718–39), le 13 septembre 1727 en délibération du conseil, le 17 février 1728. Similar episodes occurred in the Caribbean. See Gullick, *Myths of a Minority*, 25.

47. Ellice B. Gonzalez, *Changing Economic Role for Micmac Men and Women: An Ethnohistorical Analysis* (Ottawa, 1981), 63, 87–8.

48. For more detail, see my article, on which this section is based, 'Amerindians between French and

English in Nova Scotia, 1713–1763', *American Indian Culture and Research Journal* 20, 4 (1986): 31–56.

49. 'Les Sauvages qui seront amenés à la foi et en feront profession seront censés et réputés naturels français, quand bon leur semblera, et y acquérir, tester, succéder et accepter donations et legs, tous ainsi que les vrais régnicoles et originaires français, sans être tenus de prendre aucune lettre de déclaration ni de naturalité.' *Edits, ordonnances royaux, déclarations et arrêts du Conseil d'état du roi concernant le Canada*, 3 vols (Québec, 1854–6), I, 10.

50. *Collection de manuscrits contenant lettres, mémoires et autres documents historiques relatifs à la Nouvelle-France*, 4 vols (Québec, 1883–5), I, 175, Instructions pour le Sieur de Courcelle au sujet des indiens. See also Dickason, 'Louisbourg and the Indians', 38, 109–25.

51. This was the opinion of Sir Edward Coke (1552–1634), England's influential Chief Justice of the Common Pleas. See W.S. Holdsworth, *A History of English Law* (London, 1944), IX, 83–4; also, Robert A. Williams, *The American Indian in Western Legal Thought* (New York, 1990), 269–70.

52. *Collection de documents inédits sur le Canada et l'Amérique publiées par le Canada Français*, 3 vols (Québec, 1888–90), I, 196.

53. Similarly, when France was defeated in 1760, southern tribes refused to recognize the British takeover, as they had never given up their lands. See Jack M. Sosin, *Whitehall and the Wilderness* (Lincoln, Neb., 1961), 66.

54. 'Les sauvages sont peu de chose, étant nos alliées, mais pourraient devenir quelque chose de considérable, étant nos ennemis.' (LAC, AC, C11B 4:251–6, 17 nov. 1719.)

55. LAC, AC, C11B 12:37v, Saint-Ovide à Maurepas, 25 nov. 1731. See also *Account of the Customs and Manners*, 85, 'Letter from Mons. de la Varenne'. A major work on French missionary activity in Acadia is Lucien Campeau's compilation of documents, *Monumenta Novae Franciae I: La première mission d'Acadie (1602–1616)* (Québec, 1967). A second volume, *Monumenta Novae Franciae II: Etablissement à Québec (1616–1634)*, appeared in 1979.

56. LAC, Nova Scotia A 32:222, Maillard to Peregrine Hopson (governor of Nova Scotia, 1752–5), 11 Sept. 1748.

57. Thomas Pichon, *Lettres et Mémoires pour servir à l'histoire Naturelle, Civile et Politique du Cap Breton* (La Haye and London, 1760; Johnson Reprint, 1966), 101–2.

58. Thomas B. Akins, ed., *Selections from the Public Documents of the Province of Nova Scotia* (Halifax,

1869), 178–9, Cornwallis to Captain Sylvanus Cobb, 13 Jan. 1749.

59. LAC, AC, C11B, vol. 31:63, Raymond to minister, 19 nov. 1751. On French concern that the Mi'kmaq (as well as their other allies) had no causes for complaint about gift distributions, see LAC, AC, B, vol. 45/2:260–6 [122–9]; ibid., 267–73 [129–34].

60. Dickason, 'Louisbourg and the Indians', 111–14.

61. Thwaites, ed., *Jesuit Relations*, I, 177. There were also reports of them having lived to great ages in past times. Denys told of one Mi'kmaq said to have reached the age of 160 years. He attributed such long life to the Mi'kmaq habit of drinking 'only good soup, very fat'. He also reported that some Mi'kmaq could recite their genealogies back for 20 generations. Denys, *Description and Natural History*, 400, 403, 410.

62. LAC, AC, C11A, vol. 122:13, 30 sept. 1705.

63. Later, they were referred to as 'Canibas', wolves.

64. This section is a revision and extension of Olive P. Dickason, 'The French and the Abenaki: A Study in Frontier Politics', *Vermont History* 58, 2 (1990): 82–98.

65. Dean R. Snow, *The Archaeology of New England* (New York, 1980), 38; Thwaites, ed., *Jesuit Relations*, III, 111.

66. Marc Lescarbot, 'La Deffaite des Sauvages Armouchiquois', *History of New France*, III, 497–508. An English version of the poem, translated by Thomas Goetz, is in William Cowan, ed., *Papers of the Sixth Algonquian Conference, 1974* (Ottawa, 1975), 159–77.

67. Early accounts of the two military expeditions are to be found in Maurault, *Histoire des Abenakis*, 178–84, 186–93. Le Febvre de La Barre (1622–88) was governor-general of New France, 1682–5.

68. Pierre-Victor-Palma Cayet (1525–1610), *Chronologie septenaire de l'Histoire de la Paix entre les Roys de France et d'Espagne*, 2 vols (Paris, 1605), II, 423. This description was repeated by Lescarbot, *History of New France*, II, 169. He at first attributed it to Champlain but later said that Champlain had admitted that it was 'fabulous' and that the Armouchiquois really were 'as good looking men . . . as ourselves, well built and agile'. (Ibid., 172.)

69. Biggar, ed., *Works of Champlain*, I, 356–7. Marc Lescarbot expresses the same sentiments in *History of New France*, II, 327. The suspicion of cannibalism is found in Thomas Corneille, *Dictionnaire universel, géographique et historique . . .*, 3 vols (Paris, 1708), I, s.v. 'Armouchiquois'; and Thwaites, ed., *Jesuit Relations*, II, 73.

70. In 1613, it was reported that there 'has always been war . . . between the Souriquois [Mi'kmaq] and Iroquois'. Thwaites, ed., *Jesuit Relations*, I, 105.

71. Ibid., III, 71.

72. Biggar, ed., *Works of Champlain*, I, 103, 109; V, 313–16; P.-André Sévigny, *Les Abénaquis habitat et migrations (17e et 18e siècles)* (Montréal, 1976), 64–5.

73. Thwaites, ed., *Jesuit Relations*, XII, 187; XXXIV, 57; XXXVIII, 41.

74. Gordon M. Day, 'Western Abenaki', in Trigger, ed., *Handbook of North American Indians*, 15: *Northeast*, 150. See also Thwaites, ed., *Jesuit Relations*, XXIV, 183–5; XXXVI, 103.

75. Native settlement patterns for 1625–1800 are mapped in Harris, ed., *Historical Atlas*, I, plate 47.

76. The phrase is used by Gordon Day, 'English-Indian Contacts in New England', *Ethnohistory* 9 (1962): 28.

77. Colin G. Calloway, *Western Abenaki of Vermont, 1600–1800* (Norman, Okla., 1990), 248–51.

78. Thomas Charland, *Histoire des Abénakis d'Odanak (1675–1937)* (Montréal, 1964), 44, 75–6; Jean Lunn, 'The Illegal Fur Trade Out of New France, 1713–60', *Canadian Historical Association Annual Report* (1939): 61–76.

79. *Account of the Customs and Manners of the Micmakis and Maricheets*, 89, 'Letter from Mons. de la Varenne'.

80. Abbé Joseph A. Maurault held that intermarriage in New France was at its peak during the first three-quarters of the seventeenth century. Maurault, *Histoire des Abenakis*, 75. See also H.R. Casgrain, 'Coup d'oeil sur l'Acadie', *Le Canada Français* 1 (1888): 116–17.

81. O'Callaghan and Brodhead, eds, *Documents*, IX, 871, M. de Vaudreuil to the Duke of Orleans, 1716; LAC, CO 217/1:364–6, 'Answer of Indians of Penobscot to the Commissioners', Apr. 1714; LAC, AC, C11B 1:340v–42, lettre de Bégon, 25 sept. 1715, dans les déliberations de Conseil; 28 mars 1716, ibid., lettre de Costebelle, 7 sept. 1715, 335–6; Pierre-François-Xavier de Charlevoix, 'Mémoire sur les limites de l'Acadie', *Collection de manuscrits*, III, 50–1.

82. *Journal of the Honorable House of Representatives of His Majesty's Province of Massachusetts-Bay in New-England* (Boston, 1744), 57, William Shirley to the General Court, 18 July 1744.

83. O'Callaghan and Brodhead, eds, *Documents*, IX, 940, 'Memoir on the Present Condition of the Abenaquis, 1724'.

84. Dickason, 'Louisbourg and the Indians', 66–9. See also the warning of Jesuit Pierre de La Chasse

(1670–1749) concerning what the Abenaki reaction to such a proposition would be, in *Collection de manuscrits*, III, 51, Memoire sur les limites de l'Acadie.

85. LAC, AC, B, vol. 47:1263–4 [279], 16 juin 1724; ibid., C11B, vol. 7, 191–193v, 10 déc. 1725.

86. Sévigny, *Les Abénaquis*, 160–1.

87. LAC, AC, C11B, vol. 5:187–187v, Saint-Ovide to minister, 5 sept. 1720.

88. O'Callaghan and Brodhead, eds, *Documents*, IX 902, Vaudreuil to Governor William Burnett, 11 July 1721.

89. Dickason, 'Louisbourg and the Indians', 111–14; Victor Morin, *Les médailles décernées aux Indiens: Etude historique et numismatique des colonisations européennes en Amérique* (Ottawa, 1916).

90. O'Callaghan and Brodhead, eds, *Documents*, IX, 948–9, Abstract of M. de Vaudreuil's Despatch; ibid., 939–40, Memoir on the Present Condition of the Abenaquis, 1724.

91. An overview of Amerindian contributions to the establishment of New France is that of John H. Dickinson, 'Les Amérindiens et les débuts de la Nouvelle-France', *6e Convegno Internazionale di studi canadesi* (Selva di Fasano, 1985), Sezione III, 87–108.

92. This follows my 'Louisbourg and the Indians', with additions and some changes.

93. O'Callaghan and Brodhead, eds, *Documents*, IV, 206–11, London Documents 10, 'Mr. Nelson's Memorial about the state of the Northern Colonies in America', 24 Sept. 1696.

94. Ibid. The English quickly followed suit. One of the most famous of these episodes occurred in 1710, when four Iroquois sachems were brought to London and presented to Queen Anne as kings of the League of Five Nations. See John G. Garratt, *The Four Indian Kings* (Ottawa, 1985).

95. LAC, AC, B, vol. 57/1:639 [139], Maurepas à Beauharnois, 8 avr. 1732. See also O'Callaghan and Brodhead, eds, *Documents*, IV, 206–11.

96. In his words, 'heureux celui qui en sçait monter les ressorts pour les faire jouer à Sa Volonté, depuis tout ce tems je n'ai encore pu parvenir à ce point de Science.' NAC, CO, Nova Scotia A, vol. 32:232, Maillard to Hopson, 11 Sept. 1748. See also Nicholas Perrot, *Mémoire sur les moeurs, coustumes et relligion des sauvages de l'Amérique septentrionale*, ed. J. Tailhan (Montréal, 1973), 78.

97. Thomas C. Haliburton, *An Historical and Statistical Account of Nova Scotia*, 2 vols (Halifax, 1829), I, 101.

98. Francis Parkman, *The Jesuits in North America in the Seventeenth Century* (Toronto, 1907), 44.

99. *Collection de manuscrits*, I, 175, 'Instructions pour le Sieur de Courcelle au sujet des indiens', 1665.

100. Thwaites, ed., *Jesuit Relations*, V, 145; VI, 85; VII, 227; IX, 105; XI, 53.

101. Dickason, *Myth of the Savage*, 219–20. On the subject of the program's failure, particularly with the Montagnais Pierre Pastedechouan (*fl.* 1620–36), see Thwaites, ed., *Jesuit Relations*, VI, 85–9.

102. These efforts are summarized by Cornelius J. Jaenen, *The Role of the Church in New France* (Toronto, 1976), ch. 2; Jaenen, 'Education for Francization: The Case of New France in the Seventeenth Century', in Jean Barman, Yvonne Hébert, and Don McCaskill, eds, *Indian Education in Canada*, 2 vols (Vancouver, 1986), I, 45–63; Trigger, *Children of Aataentsic*.

103. Dickason, *Myth of the Savage*, 258–62.

104. *Massachusetts Historical Society Collections*, 2nd ser. 8 (1826): 260, Eastern Indians' letter to the Governor, 27 July 1721.

105. The town had developed as a consequence of a mission founded by Sébastian Rale at Norridgewock (today's Old Point, South Madison, Maine) in 1694. Both he and Mog were killed there in 1724; see Kenneth M. Morrison, *The Embattled Northeast: The Elusive Ideal of Alliance in Abenaki-Euramerican Relations* (Berkeley, 1984), 155–93.

106. R.O. MacFarlane, 'British Policy in Nova Scotia to 1760', *Canadian Historical Review* 19, 2 (1938): 160.

107. Morrison, *Embattled Northeast*, 182–3.

108. For one such episode, see Charland, *Histoire*, 83.

109. *DCB*, III, s.v. 'Atecouando'. This chief is not to be confused with the earlier one of the same name, *fl.* 1701–26. Chiefs were referred to by their titles rather than their personal names.

110. Ibid., III, s.v. 'Nodogawerrimet'.

111. *Collection de manuscrits*, II, 54, Mémoire sur les limites de l'Acadie.

Chapter 4

1. Thwaites, ed., *Jesuit Relations*, XVI, 231; XXXIX, 49. The leader of the French was Samuel de Champlain (*c.* 1570–1635), who is thus the Father of New France although he was never named governor.

2. Thwaites, ed., *Jesuit Relations*, XVI, 229; XXXIX, 49. There is a possibility that Hurons had met French earlier, perhaps in 1600. See Trigger, *Children of Aataentsic*, I, 246.

3. Ibid., I, 30. Thwaites, ed., *Jesuit Relations*, XVI, 227–9.

4. Trigger, *Children of Aataentsic*, I, 244; Thwaites, ed., *Jesuit Relations*, XVI, 227–9. Huron settlement

patterns and missions are mapped in Harris, ed., *Historical Atlas*, I, plate 34. A good, short overview of the Huron is Conrad E. Heidenreich, 'Huron', in Trigger, ed., *Handbook of North American Indians*, 15: *Northeast*, 368–88.

5. Trigger, *Children of Aataentsic*, I, 30.

6. Thwaites, ed., *Jesuit Relations*, XVIII, 103–7. Jesuit historian Lucien Campeau challenges this, on the grounds that the Amerindian tradition of tolerance allowed Christians and non-Christians to live in peace. Campeau, *La Mission des Jésuites chez les Hurons 1634–1650* (Montréal, 1987), 276–8.

7. Barbara Alice Mann, '"Are you delusional?": Kandiaronk on Christianity', in B.A. Mann, *Native American Speakers of the Eastern Woodlands: Selected Speeches and Critical Analyses* (Westport, Conn., 2001).

8. Thwaites, ed., *Jesuit Relations*, LII, 179; Henry Warner Bowden, *American Indians and Christian Missions* (Chicago, 1981), 88; Trigger, *Natives and Newcomers*, 255.

9. Thwaites, ed., *Jesuit Relations*, XVI, 33; Trigger, *Children of Aataentsic*, II, 547, 700; Trigger, *Natives and Newcomers*, 254–5; Bowden, *American Indians and Christian Missions*, 87–8. Converts denied commercial reasons for their actions (Thwaites, ed., *Jesuit Relations*, XX, 288). Some saw Amerindians as being capable of feigning acceptance of Christianity if they thought it was in their interest to do so. Another explanation for such behaviour would be that the Amerindians saw nothing wrong in following the new practices when with whites, and then reverting to their own when in their own encampments. In other cases, evangelization had the effect of giving new life and new strength to Native religions. John S. Long makes this point in connection with the Cree and Montagnais of James Bay, in 'Manitu, Power, Books and Wiihtikow: Some Factors in the Adoption of Christianity by Nineteenth-Century Western James Bay Cree', *Native Studies Review* 3, 1 (1987): 1–30. Even as the missionaries saw elements in Native spiritual beliefs that were similar to their own, so Amerindians identified Christian spiritual beings with those of their own beliefs. For the Montagnais, the Christian God resembled their Atahocan. In their view, there was plenty of room in the cosmos for both sets of spiritual beings, each with its own requirements at the appropriate times and places. Thwaites, ed., *Jesuit Relations*, V, 153–5; Jean-Guy Goulet, 'Religious Dualism among Athapaskan Catholics', *Canadian Journal of Anthropology* 3, 1 (1982): 1–18.

10. Trigger, *Children of Aataentsic*, I, 220–1. For sixteenth-century patterns of trade and warfare in the St Lawrence Valley, see Harris, ed., *Historical Atlas*, plate 33.

11. Sagard, *Histoire du Canada*, I, 170.

12. Thwaites, ed., *Jesuit Relations*, XX, 221; XXII, 179, 307, concerning the number of guns among the Hurons; Elizabeth Tooker, 'The Iroquois Defeat of the Huron: A Review of Causes', *Pennsylvania Archaeologist* 33, 1–2 (1963): 115–23. On the reasons why the Iroquois adopted firearms despite their inefficiency at that period, see Thomas B. Abler, 'European Technology and the Art of War in Iroquoia', in Tkaczuk and Vivian, eds, *Cultures in Conflict*, 173–282.

13. Antonio de Ulloa (1716–95), *A Voyage to South America . . .*, 2 vols, tr. John Adams (London, 1806), II, 376–7.

14. W.J. Eccles, *The Canadian Frontier, 1534–1760* (Toronto, 1969), 78.

15. *Account of the Customs and Manners of the Micmakis and Maricheets*, 88–9.

16. There were three Huron chiefs of that name recorded during the seventeenth century. The other two were both baptized: Jean Baptiste Atironta (d. 1650) and Pierre Atironta (d. 1672). See *DCB*, I.

17. Allumette Island is today's Morrison Island, near Pembroke, Ontario.

18. Of two other known chiefs with the name Tessouat, one met Champlain in 1603; his successor, also known as Le Borgne de l'Isle, died in 1636. See *DCB*, I.

19. Trigger gives a detailed account of Champlain's dealings with Tessouat in *Children of Aataentsic*, I, 281–6.

20. Thwaites, ed., *Jesuit Relations*, V, 263–5.

21. Ibid., X, 77.

22. Trigger, *Children of Aataentsic*, I, 311. Biggar's identification of the village as Onondaga has been discounted by Trigger.

23. Thwaites, ed., *Jesuit Relations*, XXI, 203–5.

24. Ibid., XI, 207–9.

25. Trigger, *Children of Aataentsic*, II, 473–6. Brûlé had apparently retained more of his French connections than previously believed. See Campeau, *Monumenta Novae Franciae II*, 808–9.

26. A description of the beaver, its living habits, how it was hunted, and how its pelts were processed for the fur trade is in Charlevoix, *Histoire et description*, III, 94–107. See also Tyrrell, ed., *David Thompson's Narrative*, 1–4, 10–11, 198–200; Innis, *The Fur Trade in Canada*. The Huron trade is examined in detail in Heidenreich, *Huronia*, 242–99.

27. Philippe Jacquin, *Les indiens blancs* (Paris, 1989).

28. Thwaites, ed., *Jesuit Relations*, I, 103–7.

29. Charlevoix describes the clash in *Histoire et description*, I, 150–2.

30. Ibid., 142. See also Trigger, *Children of Aataentsic*, I, 220.

31. In Acadia there had been confrontations between Jesuits and traders. See Lescarbot, *History of New France*, III, 48, 53.

32. The first missionary in Canada was the secular priest Jessé Fleché (d. ?1611), who spent a few weeks in Acadia in 1610, during which he baptized the paramount Mi'kmaq chief Membertou, his family, and members of his band, for a total of 21 individuals. He was followed by the Jesuits, who arrived the following year, in 1611, and were incensed to find a Mi'kmaq with eight wives who considered himself a Christian. (Thwaites, ed., *Jesuit Relations*, I, 109–13.) The first two Jesuits to work in Canada were Pierre Biard (1567–1622) and Enemond Massé (1575–1646). The latter, trying to live Amerindian-style during the winter of 1611–12, lost so much weight that his host, Louis Membertou (son of the famous chief), feared he would die and that the French would accuse the Mi'kmaq of having killed him. (Lescarbot, *History of New France*, III, 56.)

33. The Recollects were naturally unhappy about this. For their views on the Jesuits, see Pierre Margry, *Découvertes et établissements dans l'ouest et dans le sud de l'Amérique septentrionale (1614–1754)*, 6 vols (Paris, 1976–86), I, 5–15.

34. *Treizième tome du Mercure François* (Paris, 1629), 32; Thwaites, ed., *Jesuit Relations*, VI, 25; Lescarbot, *History of New France*, I, 184. Also, Dickason, *Myth of the Savage*, 251.

35. Sagard's dictionary is reproduced in Sagard, *Histoire du Canada*, IV. On Le Caron, see Le Clercq, *First Establishment of the Faith in New France*, I, 248–50. Brébeuf's translation into Huron of Ledesma's catechism is reproduced by Tehariolina, *La nation huronne*, 436–50.

36. Thwaites, ed., *Jesuit Relations*, XI, 1472.

37. Sagard, *Histoire du Canada*, I, 165. '. . . le sang me gelle quand je r'entre en moymesme, & considere qu'ils faisoient plus d'estat d'un castor que du salut d'un peuple . . .' An article denying the Jesuit involvement in the fur trade is that of Patrick J. Lomasney, 'The Canadian Jesuits and the Fur Trade', *Mid-America* 15 (new ser., vol. 4), 3 (1933): 139–50.

38. Thwaites, ed., *Jesuit Relations*, V, 83; IX, 171–3; VI, 80–2.

39. Jaenen, *Friend and Foe*, 75.

40. Thwaites, ed., *Jesuit Relations*, IX, 53.

41. Ibid., XVI, 53–5; IX, 239.

42. Trigger, *Children of Aataentsic*, I, 429–33; Sagard, *Long Journey*, 118, 183. Floppy-eared dogs would later fascinate Amerindians in British Columbia. On the French reaction to the Hurons' dogs, see Thwaites, ed., *Jesuit Relations*, VII, 43–5.

43. Thwaites, ed., *Jesuit Relations*, VIII, 109–13; Trigger, *Children of Aataentsic*, II, 495. The Jesuits did not make much use of their mill, as they found that sagamité was better when made from corn pounded in a wooden mortar, after the manner of the Hurons.

44. This reached such proportions that the Maliseet were reputed to be descendants of Malouins: Jacquin, *Les Indiens blancs*, 32. This comes from Maurault, *Histoire des Abenakis*, 6 n3. Maurault claimed the Abenaki called the mixed-bloods Maliseets because most of the fathers came from St Malo.

45. Thwaites, ed., *Jesuit Relations*, V, 211; X, 26.

46. Le Clercq, *First Establishment of the Faith in New France*, I, 74–7, 'Brief of Pope Paul V for the Canada mission, 1618'.

47. See, for example, Biard's ruminations on the subject. He concluded that the reasons for Canada's severe climate were the presence of so much water and the fact that the land had not been cleared and cultivated. (Thwaites, ed., *Jesuit Relations*, III, 55–61.)

48. Amerindians who depended on hunting and gathering did not generally use salt, which they claimed shortened life, and some even regarded it as poisonous (agricultural peoples, however, valued it, and used it as an item of trade). See Dickason, *Myth of the Savage*, 325 n50; Thwaites, ed., *Jesuit Relations*, V, 103. 'French snow'—sugar—was also seen in the same light (ibid., XIV, 51). Diets, imposed by different ways of life, influenced salt preferences.

49. Dom Guy Oury, *Marie de l'Incarnation (1599–1672) Correspondance* (Solesmes, 1971), 112, lettre du 4 sept. 1640. Nearly three-quarters of a century later, similar sentiments were expressed by Father Pierre-Gabriel Marest (1662–1714): '. . . the horror of our forests, those vast uninhabited Regions in which I would certainly perish if I were abandoned, presented themselves to my mind and took away nearly all my courage.' Thwaites, ed., *Jesuit Relations*, LXVI, 269. See also Marcel Trudel, *Histoire de la Nouvelle France II: Le comptoir 1604–1627* (Montréal, 1966), 384–6. My thanks to Claire Gourdeau, Laval University, for these references.

50. Dickason, *Myth of the Savage*, 144–7; Biggar, ed., *Works of Champlain*, II, 48. Le Jeune shared this belief: 'Their natural color is like that of those French beggars who are half-roasted in the Sun, and I have no doubt the Savages would be very white if they were well covered.' (Thwaites, ed., *Jesuit Relations*, V, 23.) Some even extended this belief to Africans: 'The children of this country are born white, and change their colour in two days to a perfect black.' E.G. Ravenstein, ed., *The Strange Adventures of Andrew Battell of Leigh in Angola and the Adjoining Regions* (London, 1901; reprint, 1967), 49.

51. Bacqueville de la Potherie, *Histoire de l'Amérique septentrionale*, IV, 180–1.

52. Peter N. Moogk, 'Les Petits Sauvages: The Children of Eighteenth-Century New France', in Joy Parr, ed., *Childhood and Family in Canadian History* (Toronto, 1982), 27.

53. Trigger, *Children of Aataentsic*, I, 325.

54. Thwaites, ed., *Jesuit Relations*, XLVII, 203; lxv, 69, 263. Marriage 'à la gaumine' also appeared in the colony, an import from France. The contracting couple, wishing to avoid the required formalities, would attend Mass and raise their hands together as the officiating priest blessed the worshippers, thus inadvertently sanctifying the union. For a discussion of these issues, see my 'From "One Nation" in the Northeast to "New Nation" in the Northwest: A Look at the Emergence of the Metis', *American Indian Culture and Research Journal* 6, 2 (1982): 1–21. See also Robert-Lionel Séguin, *La vie libertine en Nouvelle-France au XVIIe siècle*, 2 vols (Montréal, 1972), I, 47. Several members of the Chabert de Joncaire and Le Moyne families followed this path. See LAC, AC, C11A 18:82, 147–8; Marcel Giraud, *The Métis in the Canadian West*, tr. George Woodcock, 2 vols (Edmonton, 1986), I, 232–4. Biographies of members of the Chabert de Joncaire family are in *DCB*, II, III, IV; for Le Moyne de Maricourt and his brother Charles Le Moyne de Longueuil, II. See also O'Callaghan and Brodhead, eds, *Documents*, IX, 580. The *Documents* index lists Philippe-Thomas Chabert de Joncaire (1707–*c.* 1766) as a French Indian. Other sources of information include the Michilimackinac table of marriages, 1698–1765, in Jacqueline Peterson, 'A Social Portrait of the Great Lakes Métis', *Ethnohistory* 25, 1 (1978): 50; Marcel Giraud, *Histoire de la Louisiane française*, 2 vols (Paris, 1953–8), I, 315–16; Louise Phelps Kellogg, *The French Régime in Wisconsin and the Northwest* (New York, 1968), 386–405; Natalie Maree Belting, *Kaskaskia under the French Regime* (New Orleans, 1975), 13–16.

55. Gaston du Boscq de Beaumont, comp. and ed., *Les derniers jours de l'Acadie (1748–1758)* (Paris, 1899), 85.

56. Lisa Poirier, 'J'étions un Métis', *L'Actualité* (juillet 2000): 39–40.

57. Belting, *Kaskaskia*, 74–5; Jaenen, *Friend and Foe*, 164–5. For the Métis, with a foot in both European and Amerindian camps (more often the latter), it placed a premium on their services as interpreters and go-betweens. An interesting example of such an envoy was 'Colonel Louis Cook' (Atiatoharongwen, *c.* 1740–1814) of the American army, a half-Abenaki from Caughnawaga, who served as go-between to the Oneida during the American War of Independence. His father was black. See *DCB*, V, s.v. 'Atiatoharongwen'; F.B. Hough, *A History of St. Lawrence and Franklin Counties, New York, from their Earliest Period to the Present Time* (Albany, NY, 1853), 182.

58. Thwaites, ed., *Jesuit Relations*, V 237; VIII, 119; XIII, 171. Biard reported a similar reaction on the part of the Mi'kmaq. Ibid., III, 123.

59. Cornelius J. Jaenen, 'Amerindian Views of French Culture in the Seventeenth Century', *Canadian Historical Review* 55, 3 (1974): 261–91.

60. Thwaites, ed., *Jesuit Relations*, XXVIII, 41.

61. Ibid., VIII, 43; XV, 113. At one point, Hurons rejected French kettles as possible sources of contagion. Ibid., XV, 21.

62. Ibid., XIII, 147.

63. Le Clercq, *Nouvelle relation*, 285–6; Sagard, *Histoire du Canada*, I, 166–7; Thwaites, ed., *Jesuit Relations*, VIII, 5–59.

64. Thwaites, ed., *Jesuit Relations*, XXVIII, 49–65.

65. Ibid.

66. Ibid., xxi, 45.

67. Sagard, *Histoire du Canada*, I, 166. See also Daniel A. Scalberg, 'Seventeenth and Early Eighteenth-Century Perceptions of Coureurs-de-Bois Religious Life', *Proceedings of the Annual Meeting of the Western Society for French History* 17 (1990): 82–95.

68. Sagard, *Histoire du Canada*, II, 457.

69. Charlevoix, *Histoire et description*, III, 322.

70. 'La relation dernière de Marc Lescarbot, Paris, 1612', in Campeau, ed., *Monumenta Novae Franciae I*, 184: 'On ne peut arracher tout d'un coup les coutumes et façons de faire invétérées d'un peuple quel que soit.'

71. Bruce G. Trigger, 'Early Iroquoian Contacts with Europeans', in Trigger, ed., *Handbook of North American Indians*, 15: *Northeast*, 352; Karl H. Schlesier, 'Epidemics and Indian Middlemen: Rethinking the Wars of the Iroquois, 1609–1653', *Ethnohistory* 23, 2 (1976): 129–45.

72. Delâge, *Le pays renversé*, 106.

73. *DCB*, I, s.v. 'Oumasasikweie'.

74. Biggar, ed., *Works of Champlain*, VI, 379.

75. Thwaites, ed., *Jesuit Relations*, XXVII, 89–91; XXVIII, 47.

76. See Chapter 5.

77. Guy Laflèche, *Les saints martyrs canadiens*, 2 vols (Québec, 1988), I, 32. In an attempt to curb Iroquois attacks, which were stepped up during the 1640s, French soldiers sometimes reinforced the warriors accompanying the flotillas. This was done in 1644 and again in 1645, when 60 canoes and 300 Huron came to Trois-Rivières (Jacquin, *Les indiens blancs*, 251 n37). Such commerce brought prosperity to everyone involved; at its height, the Huron were reported to account for 50 per cent of the French fur trade. Despite the Iroquois blockade, furs valued at 200,000 to 300,000 livres were shipped to France. W.J. Eccles, *France in America* (New York, 1972).

78. Thwaites, ed., *Jesuit Relations*, XXXII, 99.

79. José António Brandão, *Your Fyre Shall Burn No More* (Lincoln, Neb., 1998), 98–9. See also Roland Viau, *Enfants du néant et mangeurs d'âmes: guerre, culture et sociétés en Iroquoisie ancienne* (Montréal, 1997), 40–4.

80. The two were Brébeuf and Gabriel Lalement (1610–49). They were canonized in 1930, along with six others, all Jesuits except Jean de la Lande, a donné. See Laflèche, *Les saints martyrs*, I, 33, 299.

81. *DCB*, III, s.v. 'Orontony'.

82. LAC, MG 8: Documents relatifs à la Nouvelle-France et au Québec (XVIIE–XXE siècles), E1, f60, James Murray, Report of the Government of Quebec and dependencies thereof, *c.* 1762. The promise contained in the document was defined by the Supreme Court of Canada as a treaty. See John Thompson, 'The Treaties of 1760', *The Beaver* 76, 2 (1996): 23–8.

83. '230-year-old treaty guaranteeing Hurons' rights is valid: top court', *The Gazette*, Montreal, 25 May 1990, A5. For the historical background, see Georges Sioui, *Pour une autohistoire amérindienne* (Québec, 1989), 111–30. (Published in English as *For an Amerindian Autohistory*, tr. Sheila Fischman [Montreal and Kingston, 1992]). The Hurons had been arrested for cutting saplings in a provincial park north of Quebec City to build a sweat lodge.

84. Delâge, 'Les Iroquois chrétiens', 64.

85. Tehariolina, *La nation huronne*, 306–9; *DCB*, II. Kondiaronk was 'Adario' in Lahontan's dialogues.

86. See Eccles, *Canadian Frontier*, ch. 6.

87. Thwaites, ed., *Jesuit Relations*, XL, 215.

88. For a study of the factors that led to the 1701 peace, see Havard, *La grande paix*.

89. Much of the material for this section has been drawn from my 'Three Worlds, One Focus', 51–78.

90. On the prehistoric trade of the Huron, see Trigger, *Children of Aataentsic*, I, 176–86; on its development after the arrival of the French, ibid., II, 608–12.

91. Thwaites, ed., *Jesuit Relations*, I, 101.

92. Five northern routes, some of them said to be ancient, were described by the Jesuits, with the comment that they were 'more difficult to travel than the high road from Paris to Orleans'. The fifth route was for peoples north and west of Lake Superior. Ibid., XLIV, 239–45; LVI, 203. See also Toby Morantz, 'The Fur Trade and the Cree of James Bay', in Carol M. Judd and A.J. Ray, eds, *Old Trails and New Directions: Papers of the Third North American Fur Trade Conference* (Toronto, 1980), 23–4.

93. Kehoe, *The Ghost Dance*, 115.

94. James W. VanStone, 'Northern Athapaskans: People of the Deer', in Fitzhugh and Crowell, eds, *Crossroads of Continents*, 68. The increase in famine manifested itself very early. In 1635, starving Amerindians of the Gaspé allegedly killed and ate a young boy whom the Basques had left with them to learn their language. (Thwaites, ed., *Jesuit Relations*, VIII, 29.) Pierre-François-Xavier Charlevoix would later observe that although Amerindians knew how to endure hunger, they still died from it. See Charlevoix, *Histoire et description*, III, 338.

95. Denys, *Description and Natural History*, 440–1.

96. Missionaries and traders soon noted how much the northerners prized tobacco. Thwaites, ed., *Jesuit Relations*, LVI, 189.

97. Christopher L. Miller and George R. Hamell, 'A New Perspective on Indian-White Contact: Cultural Symbols and Colonial Trade', *Journal of American History* 73, 3 (1986): 311–28.

98. Arthur Dobbs, *An Account of the Countries adjoining to Hudson's Bay* (London, 1744; reprint New York, 1967), 59.

99. Peter A. Cumming and Neil H. Mickenberg, eds, *Native Rights in Canada* (Toronto, 1972), 142.

100. HBC Official London Correspondence Book Outwards 1679–1741, A.6/1.6, HBC Archives; E.E. Rich, ed., *Letters Outward 1679–1694* (Toronto, 1948), 9; Cumming and Mickenberg, eds, *Native Rights in Canada*, 142 n36; Daniel Francis and Toby Morantz, *Partners in Furs: A History of the Fur Trade in Eastern James Bay*

1600–1870 (Montreal, 1983), 23. These instructions were repeated to Nixon's successor, Henry Sergeant, in 1683. See A.6/1:30v, HBC Archives.

101. These were probably oral agreements along the French/Amerindian model. Francis and Morantz, *Partners in Furs*, 213–24; John Oldmixon, *The History of Hudson's-Bay, Containing an Account of its Discovery and Settlement, the Progress of It, and the Present State; of the Indians, Trade and Everything Else Relating to It*, in J.B. Tyrrell, ed., *Documents Relating to the Early History of Hudson Bay* (Toronto, 1931), 400–1; Edwin Thompson Denig, *Five Indian Tribes of the Upper Missouri*, ed. John C. Ewers (Norman, Okla., 1961), 112. For a discussion of gift-giving in the context of the fur trade, see Mary Black-Rogers, 'Varieties of "Starving": Semantics and Survival in the Subarctic Fur Trade, 1750–1850', *Ethnohistory* 33, 4 (1986): 368; Bruce M. White, '"Give Us a Little Milk": The Social and Cultural Significance of Gift Giving in the Lake Superior Fur Trade', in T.C. Buckley, ed., *Rendezvous: Selected Papers of the Fur Trade Conference 1981* (St Paul, Minn., 1984), 187. See also Arthur J. Ray and Donald Freeman, *'Give Us Good Measure': An Economic Analysis of Relations between the Indians and the Hudson's Bay Company before 1763* (Toronto, 1978), 60–1; E.E. Rich, 'Trade Habits and Economic Motivation among the Indians of North America', *Canadian Journal of Economics and Political Science* 26 (1960): 35–53 (reprinted, with illustrations added, under the title 'The Indian Traders' in *The Beaver* Outfit 301 [1970]: 5–20); A. Rotstein, 'Trade and Politics: An Institutional Approach', *Western Canadian Journal of Anthropology* 3, 1 (1972): 1–28.

102. The French had earlier experienced difficulty in this regard. Galinée reported that even in his day (the second half of the seventeenth century) they had not yet mastered the techniques of fishing in the northern rivers. Margry, *Découvertes et établissements*, I, 163–4.

103. Carol M. Judd, 'Sakie, Esquawenoe, and the Foundation of a Dual-Native Tradition at Moose Factory', in Shepard Krech III, ed., *The Subarctic Fur Trade* (Vancouver, 1984), 87.

104. Hearne, *Journey*, 185n. For a similar reaction on the part of the Inuit at a later period, see Hall, *Arctic Researches*, 297. Jesuits reported in 1646 that when Amerindians killed animals, 'they eat the meat of these without bread, without salt, and without other sauce than the appetite.' (Thwaites, ed., *Jesuit Relations*, XXIX, 75.)

105. HBC Archives, 1742, B.135/a/11:67, Moose Fort

Journal, 1742, cited by Francis and Morantz, *Partners in Furs*, 58–9.

106. Hearne, *Journey*, 306.

107. Ibid., 85–6n.

108. Dobbs, *An Account*, 42.

109. Apparently the Hurons had a more restrained reaction and refused to eat salted foods because they said they smelled bad. See Sagard, *Long Journey*, 118. The belief developed among the Amerindians that the reason Europeans were able to resist their witchcraft was because they ate so much salt.

110. The French had long since learned the truth of this. Gabriel Sagard said the French should never go into the woods without an experienced guide, as even such travel aids as a compass could fail. He told of Étienne Brûlé, an experienced coureur de bois, who had once lost his way and mistakenly wandered into an Iroquois village, where he escaped torture and death only by a lucky happenstance. Sagard, *Histoire du Canada*, I, 466–7; II, 429–30. Champlain had got lost in Huronia. See Trudel, *Histoire de la Nouvelle France II*, 221. A young Amerindian lad, raised by the French and christened Bonaventure, died as a result of being lost in the woods following an accident. (Thwaites, ed., *Jesuit Relations*, IX, 221.) There has never been a study of the economic value of Amerindian contributions to European voyages of discovery in the interior of the Americas, if such would be possible. It must have been considerable.

111. John Tanner, *The Captivity and Adventures of John Tanner During Thirty Years' Residence Among the Indians in the Interior* (New York, 1830). See also Jennifer S.H. Brown, *Strangers in Blood: Fur Trade Company Families in Indian Country* (Vancouver, 1980); Sylvia Van Kirk, *Many Tender Ties: Women in Fur Trade Society, 1670–1870* (Norman, Okla., 1983).

112. Sylvia Van Kirk, 'Thanadelthur', *The Beaver* Outfit 304, 4 (1974): 40–5; Keith Crowe, *A History of the Original Peoples of Northern Canada* (Montreal and Kingston, 1991), 76–8. James Houston, *Running West* (Toronto, 1989), is a historical novel detailing Thanadelthur's life. Oral traditions concerning Thanadelthur are recorded in Julie Cruikshank, *Reading Voices: Dän dhá ts'ledeninthth'é=Oral and Written Interpretations of the Yukon's Past* (Vancouver, 1991).

113. Actually, the French had encountered bison in 'Florida' much earlier, as attested by an engraving of bison-hunting in André Thevet's *La Cosmographie Universelle*, 2 vols (Paris, 1575), II, 1007v.

114. When Hearne returned from his voyage, his guides Matonabbee and Idotlyazee provided a map of the lands they had visited. June Helm's study of the chart revealed how it co-ordinates with modern maps. See Helm, 'Matonabbee's Map', *Arctic Anthropology* 26, 2 (1989): 28–47. For other Amerindian maps, see Harris, ed., *Historical Atlas*, I, plate 59. Arctic explorer Sir John Franklin (1786–1847) availed himself of Amerindian and Inuit sketch maps. See Charles Mair, *Through the Mackenzie Basin* (Toronto, 1908), 96–7. About 100 Inuit maps drawn on paper for explorers have survived. Among themselves, Inuit either gave verbal instructions or drew maps on sand or snow. See David F. Pelly, 'How the Inuit find their way in the trackless Arctic', *Canadian Geographic* 3, 4 (1991): 58–64.

115. Trigger, *Natives and Newcomers*, 184–94. For the varying effects of the trade on northern Native societies and economies, see Krech III, ed., *Subarctic Fur Trade*.

116. For a nineteenth-century observation of this characteristic, see Arthur J. Ray, *The Canadian Fur Trade and the Industrial Age* (Toronto, 1990), 91.

117. HBC Archives, B.135/a/11:69, cited by Francis and Morantz, *Partners in Furs*, 59.

118. HBC Archives, B.135/a/31:27v–29v, Moose Fort Journal 1758–9.

119. HBC Archives, A.6/4:86v, cited by Francis and Morantz, *Partners in Furs*, 91.

120. Eric Ross, *Beyond the River and the Bay* (Toronto, 1970), 29–31.

121. Ibid., 31.

122. Daniel Will Harmon, *Sixteen Years in the Indian Country*, ed. W. Kaye Lamb (Toronto, 1957), 55.

123. Charles Bishop, 'The Henley House Massacres', *The Beaver* Outfit 307 (1976): 36–41; Van Kirk, *Many Tender Ties*, 43–4. Marcel Giraud wrote that the coureurs de bois instigated the massacre: *The Métis in the Canadian West*, I, 141.

124. Perrot, *Mémoire sur les moeurs, coustumes et relligion des sauvages*, ed. J. Tailhan, 126–8, 292–4; Thwaites, ed., *Jesuit Relations*, LV, 105–15; Margry, *Découvertes et établissements*, I, 96–9; William W. Warren, *History of the Ojibway People* (St Paul, 1984; 1st edn 1885).

125. 'Ainsy cette nation peut connoistre qu'on prétend d'en demeurer le maistre.' (Margry, *Découvertes et établissements*, I, 89, second extrait de 'l'addition au mémoire de Jean Talon au Roy', 10 nov. 1670.) Voyages of exploration were usually undertaken for the purpose of territorial expansion; for example, La Vérendrye on his western voyage left a trail of lead plaques indicating that the region was claimed by France (ibid., VI, 609), as did Galinée and Dollier de Casson, whose ostensible mission was the spreading of the faith.

126. Thwaites, ed., *Jesuit Relations*, LXVIII, 283.

127. Donald B. Smith, 'Who are the Mississauga?', *Ontario History* 67, 4 (1975): 211–23; Leroy V. Eid, 'The Ojibway–Iroquois War: The War the Five Nations did not Win', *Ethnohistory* 17, 4 (1979): 297–324.

128. James G.E. Smith, 'The Western Woods Cree: Anthropological Myth and Historical Reality', *American Ethnologist* 14 (1987): 434–48.

129. L.J. Burpee, ed., *Journals and Letters by Pierre Gaulthier de Varennes et de La Vérendrye* (Toronto, 1927), 25.

130. John S. Milloy, *The Plains Cree: Trade, Diplomacy and War, 1790–1870* (Winnipeg, 1988), 41–66, 119–20.

Chapter 5

1. There is an enormous body of literature on the Iroquois wars. Besides George T. Hunt's *The Wars of the Iroquois* (Madison, Wis., 1967), see W.J. Eccles, *Canada Under Louis XIV, 1663–1701* (Toronto, 1964), especially chs 7–10; Eccles, *Frontenac the Courtier Governor* (Toronto, 1959), especially chs 8–10; Francis Jennings, *The Ambiguous Iroquois Empire* (New York, 1984). A detailed account of the war to 1646 is Leo-Paul Desrosier's *Iroquoisie* (Montréal, 1947). Bruce G. Trigger deals with aspects of Iroquoian conflicts in *Natives and Newcomers*. See also Keith F. Otterbein, 'Why the Iroquois Won: An Analysis of Iroquois Military Tactics', *Ethnohistory* 11 (1964): 56–63; Otterbein, 'Huron vs. Iroquois: A Case Study of Intertribal Warfare', *Ethnohistory* 26, 2 (1979): 141–52.

2. *DCB*, I, s.v. 'Pieskaret'; Bacqueville de la Potherie, *Histoire de l'Amérique septentrionale*, I, 297–303.

3. Desrosiers, *Iroquoisie*, 304.

4. Charlevoix, *Histoire et description*, II, 160–1.

5. François Dollier de Casson, *A History of Montreal 1640–1672*, tr. and ed. Ralph Flenley (London, 1928), 131; originally published in Montreal, 1868, from a copy of a Paris manuscript brought to Canada by Louis-Joseph Papineau, leader of the 1837–8 rebellions in Lower Canada. The manuscript does not bear Dollier de Casson's name but has been attributed to him on the strength of internal evidence.

6. Ibid., 117–18, 139.

7. LAC, MG 7, 1a, 10, Collection Moreau, vol. 841:251v, d'Endemare à François de la Vie, Fort Richelieu, 2 sept. 1644.

8. Bibliothèque Nationale, Paris, Fonds Français, vol. 10204, ff. 203–4.

9. Thwaites, ed., *Jesuit Relations*, XXVIII, 57.

10. Cited by William Kip, *The Early Jesuit Missions in North America* (New York, 1846), 54. These observations would be repeated almost exactly by the British in Australia during the nineteenth century as they settled in lands the Aborigines considered theirs. See, for example, Henry Reynolds, *Frontier* (Sydney and London, 1987), 3–57.

11. Thwaites, ed., *Jesuit Relations*, XXXIII, 229–49; Trigger, *Natives and Newcomers*, 265.

12. John A. Dickinson, 'La guerre iroquoise et la mortalité en Nouvelle-France, 1608–1666', *Revue d'histoire de l'Amérique française* 36, 1 (1982): 31–47; Trigger, 'Early Iroquoian Contacts', 352.

13. LAC, AC, C11G, vol. 6:69–70v, Mémoire sur les compagnies sauvages proposées par le Sieur de La Motte envoyé à Monseigneur en 1708; ibid., C11A, vol. 122:10–42, unsigned letter from Quebec, 30 sept. 1705. On chiefs receiving commissions, see LAC, AC, C11B, vol. 23:28v, Du Quesnel to Maurepas, 19 oct. 1741; ibid., vol. 29:63v, Des Herbiers to Rouillé, 27 nov. 1750; ibid., 68, Des Herbiers to Rouillé, 6 déc. 1750.

14. O'Callaghan and Brodhead, eds, *Documents*, IX, 363.

15. Margry, *Découvertes et établissements*, I, 141, Récit de ce qui c'est passé de plus remarquable dans le voyage de MM. Dollier et Galinée, 1669–70.

16. O'Callaghan and Brodhead, eds, *Documents*, IX, 95, Journal of Count de Frontenac's Voyage to Lake Ontario in 1673.

17. For a detailed account of this expedition and the factors leading up to it, see Eccles, *Frontenac the Courtier Governor*, 161–72.

18. Louis Armand de Lom d'Arce de Lahontan was one French officer who saw advantages in the Amerindian style of warfare: Lahontan, *Nouveaux voyages*, I, 238–9.

19. Bacqueville de la Potherie says that 40 Iroquois were taken. *Histoire de l'Amérique septentrionale*, I, 332–3.

20. Richter, 'War and Culture', 548–53.

21. Yves F. Zoltvany, 'New France and the West, 1701–1713', *Canadian Historical Review* 46, 4 (1965): 304.

22. Richter, 'War and Culture', 549.

23. Anthony F.C. Wallace, *Death and Rebirth of the Seneca* (New York, 1969), 111–14; Wallace,

'Origins of Iroquois Neutrality: The Grand Settlement of 1701', *Pennsylvania History* 24 (1957): 223–35.

24. Zoltvany, 'New France and the West', 302–5.

25. The Iroquois claimed they had conquered lands from the Appalachians to the Kentucky River and then by the Ohio River and Mississippi to the Great Lakes and the Ottawa River. This included long-past conquests being disputed rather than only territory actually occupied. Sosin, *Whitehall and the Wilderness*, 74 n58.

26. Ibid., 551.

27. Lahontan, *Nouveaux voyages*, II, 84–9.

28. A detailed description is by Jefferys, *Natural and Civil History*, I, 62–3. The practice of adopting war captives was not unique to the Iroquois.

29. W.A. Kenyon and J.R. Turnbull, *The Battle for the Bay 1686* (Toronto, 1971); Arthur S. Morton, *A History of the Canadian West to 1870–71*, ed. Lewis G. Thomas (Toronto, 1973), 92–103.

30. C.S. Mackinnon, 'The 1958 Government Policy Reversal in Keewatin', in Kenneth S. Coates and William R. Morrison, eds, *For Purposes of Dominion* (Toronto, 1989), 159.

31. Daniel K. Richter, 'Iroquois versus Iroquois: Jesuit Missions and Christianity in Village Politics, 1642–1686', *Ethnohistory* 32, 1 (1985): 1–16; *DCB*, I, s.v. 'Garakontié'.

32. Bacqueville de la Potherie, *Histoire de l'Amérique septentrionale*, I, 346–64. He wrote that their Catholic faith was the only common ground between the newcomers and the French. See also Henri Béchard, *The Original Caughnawaga Indians* (Montreal, 1976).

33. Milo Milton Quaife, ed., *The Western Country in the 17th Century: The Memoirs of Antoine Lamothe Cadillac and Pierre Liette* (New York, 1962), 67–8.

34. He was the eldest son of Nicolas-Antoine de Villiers, who led the winter raid at Grand Pré against the English in 1749.

35. An account of the last phase of the Fox War is by Joseph L. Peyser, 'The Fate of the Fox Survivors: A Dark Chapter in the History of the French in the Upper Country, 1726–1737', *Wisconsin Magazine of History* 73, 2 (1989–90): 93.

36. Louise Phelps Kellogg, *The Fox Indians during the French Regime*, reprinted from *Proceedings of the State Historical Society of Wisconsin 1907* (Madison, Wis., 1908), 178.

37. Akins, ed., *Public Documents of Nova Scotia*, 486, General Edward Whitmore to Lawrence, Louisbourg, 20 June 1760. See also John Stewart

McLellan, *Louisbourg from its Foundation to its Fall, 1713–1758* (London, 1918).

38. The texts of these treaties are in Cumming and Mickenberg, eds, *Native Rights in Canada*, 300–6; William Daugherty, *Maritime Indian Treaties in Perspective* (Ottawa, 1983), 75–8; Canada, *Indian Treaties and Surrenders*, 3 vols (Toronto, 1971), II, 199–204.

39. LAC, AC, B 49/2:705–7, de Maurepas, 28 mai 1726, and B 8:34–8v, 18 sept. 1726. The charge was in a letter from Longueuil and Bégon, 31 oct. 1725 (Collection de manuscrits, III, 126).

40. LAC, AC, C11B 35:125, Chevalier Augustin Boschenry de Drucour (governor of Ile Royale, 1754–8), au ministre, 18 nov. 1755.

41. LAC, MG 18, E29, vol. 2, section 4, Discours fait aux sauvages du Canada par M. de Saint-Ovide, gouverneur de l'Acadie avec les Responses que les sauvages on faites.

42. There are two versions of this declaration. The earlier one is reproduced in *Report Concerning Canadian Archives*, 1905, 3 vols, 1906, 2: App. A, pt. III, in 'Acadian Geneaology and Notes' by Placide Gaudet, 239. The later one is in *Collection de documents inédits sur le Canada et l'Amérique publiées par le Canada français*, 3 vols (Québec, 1888–90), I, 17–19.

43. Akins, ed., *Public Documents of Nova Scotia*, 581, Council aboard the *Beaufort*, 1 Oct. 1749; ibid., 581–2, Proclamation of Governor Cornwallis, Oct. 1749.

44. LAC, Nova Scotia A 17:129–32; Nova Scotia B 1:53–5.

45. Dickason, 'Louisbourg and the Indians', 99–100. 'Humanity cries out against such things', a contemporary observer wrote, 'which should cause a just horror.' LAC, AC, C11C, vol. 8:88v, Couagne to Acaron, directeur de Bureau des Colonies, 4 nov. 1760. The proclamation authorizing the bounty still remains on Nova Scotia's books, although such bounties are prohibited by the Criminal Code. According to newspaper accounts, the government fears that revoking the law and apologizing for it would precipitate a rash of lawsuits. Richard Foot, 'Colonial bounty on Mi'kmaq scalps still on the books', *National Post*, 5 Jan. 2000, A1, A2.

46. J.B. Brebner, 'Subsidized intermarriage with the Indians', *Canadian Historical Review* 6, 1 (1925): 33–6.

47. LAC, AC, C11B, vol. 31:62–3.

48. LAC, AC, C11B, vol. 32:163–6, Prevost à Antoine Louis Rouillé, Comte de Joüy (minister of the marine, 1749–54), 10 sept. 1752; ibid., vol.

33:159v, Prevost à Rouillé, 12 mai 1753; Akins, ed., *Public Documents of Nova Scotia*, 672–4, Council minutes, Halifax, 16 Sept. 1752.

49. LAC, CO, 217/18:277–4, Ceremonials at Concluding a Peace . . ., 25 June 1761.

50. LAC, AC, C12, vol. 1:3v, Mémoire du Roy pour servir d'instruction au Sr. Dangeac nommé au gouvernement des Iles St. Pierre et de Miquelon, 23 fév. 1763.

51. Denis A. Bartels and Olaf Uwe Janzen, 'Micmac Migration to Western Newfoundland', paper presented to the Canadian Historical Association, Victoria, 1990.

Chapter 6

1. Article 40 reads: 'The savages or Indian Allies of His Most Christian Majesty shall be maintained in the lands they inhabit, if they choose to reside there; they shall not be molested on any pretense whatsoever, for having carried arms and served His Most Christian Majesty; they shall have, as well as the French, liberty of religion, and shall keep their missionaries.' See also Maurice Torrelli, 'Les Indiens du Canada et le droit des traités dans la jurisprudence canadienne', *Annuaire Français de Droit International* 20 (1974): 227–49, 236.

2. James Sullivan, Alexander C. Flick, and Milton W. Hamilton, eds, *The Papers of Sir William Johnson*, 14 vols (Albany, NY, 1921–65), VII, 785.

3. English watchdog sloops reported that 'the French . . . are very busy carrying on a trade with the Indians.' MG 12: Great Britain, Admiralty 106, vol. 1123:369, letter from Jacob Hurd.

4. See, for instance, the complaints of the Seneca: Wallace, *Death and Rebirth of the Seneca*, 114–15.

5. Johnson's Journal of Indian Affairs, 9–12 Dec. 1758, in Sullivan et al., eds, *Papers of Sir William Johnson*, X, 69, 73. Amerindian complaints in this regard were of long standing, and they had frequently requested authorities to ban the sale of liquor. See, for example, the plea in 1722 of the Mahican to William Burnett, governor-in-chief of New York and New Jersey, 1720–8. O'Callaghan and Brodhead, eds, *Documents*, V, 663–4.

6. The governor of Virginia reported this to the Board of Trade in 1756. See Sosin, *Whitehall and the Wilderness*, 30.

7. Peter Wraxall, *An Abridgement of Indian Affairs . . . Transacted in the Colony of New York for the Year 1678 to the Year 1751*, ed. Charles H. McIlwain (Cambridge, Mass., 1915), IX, 153 n2.

8. David A. Armour, ed., *Attack at Michilimackinac 1763* (Mackinac Island, Mich., 1988), 25. This is

a reproduction of Alexander Henry's *Travels and Adventures in Canada and the Indian Territories between the years 1760 and 1764* (New York, 1809).

9. Sosin, *Whitehall and the Wilderness*, 31.

10. Gordon M. Day and Bruce G. Trigger, 'Algonquin', in Trigger, ed., *Handbook of North American Indians, 15: Northeast*, 795; Robert J. Surtees, 'The Iroquois in Canada', in Francis Jennings, ed., *The History and Culture of Iroquois Diplomacy* (Syracuse, NY, 1985), 70.

11. Delâge, 'Les Iroquois chrétiens'.

12. Sullivan et al., eds, *Papers of Sir William Johnson*, III, 965.

13. The question of Pontiac's origins is unresolved. Howard H. Peckham discusses the evidence in *Pontiac and the Indian Uprising* (Chicago, 1947), 15–16 n2. Contemporary reports inform us that he was of better than medium height and not handsome. Ibid., 28–9.

14. Ibid., 29.

15. Robert Rogers, *Concise Account of North America . . .* (London, 1765), 240, 243. An extract is reprinted in Peckham, *Pontiac*, 59–62 n8.

16. Ibid.

17. Carl F. Klinck, ed., *Tecumseh, Fact and Fiction in Early Records* (Englewood Cliffs, NJ, 1961), 184–5. See also Colin Calloway, *Crown and Calumet: British–Indian Relations, 1783–1815* (Norman, Okla., 1987), 217.

18. *DCB*, III, s.v., 'Pontiac'. The other 'Delaware Prophet' had a religious message.

19. Helen Hornbeck Tanner, ed., *Atlas of Great Lakes Indian History* (Norman, Okla., 1987), 48. For a detailed account of the uprising, see 48–53.

20. For a contrary view, see Wilbur R. Jacobs, 'The Indian Frontier of 1763', *Western Pennsylvania Historical Magazine* 34, 3 (1951): 185–98.

21. Peckham, *Pontiac*, 316.

22. At the time the fort was built, the Dakota–Ojibwa War had been going on for something like a century. During a temporary peace in 1787 the combatants agreed to recognize the British King. Clayton W. McCall, 'The Peace of Michilimackinack', *Michigan History Magazine* 28, 3 (1944): 367–83.

23. Mary 'Molly' Brant, consort of Sir William Johnson, superintendent of Northern Indian Affairs who had died in 1774, was a more powerful figure among the matrilineal Mohawk than her famous younger brother. On her importance among her people, it was reported that 'one word from her goes farther with them than a thousand from any white Man without

Exception who in general must purchase their Interest at a high rate.' The Iroquois did not regard Joseph as their leading war chief; that honour was accorded the Seneca Kaien?kwaahto'n (Sayenqueraghta, d. 1786), who also fought for the British. See Barbara Graymont, *The Iroquois in the American Revolution* (Syracuse, NY, 1972), 159; Earle Thomas, *The Three Faces of Molly Brant* (Kingston, Ont., 1996).

24. Red Jacket took part in a council that removed Brant from office in 1805, but Brant managed to stay on another two years. Red Jacket, employed as a runner for the British during the American War of Independence, had been rewarded for his services with a richly embroidered red jacket. He later threw in his lot with the Americans, although he would have preferred neutrality. See Mary H. Eastman, *The American Aboriginal Portfolio* (Philadelphia, 1853), 9–13.

25. On the participation of the Six Nations in the American War of Independence, see George F.G. Stanley, 'The Six Nations and the American Revolution', *Ontario History* 56, 4 (1964): 217–32.

26. George F.G. Stanley, *The War of 1812: Land Operations* (Toronto, 1983), 13–14.

27. A.L. Burt, 'A New Approach to the Problem of the Western Posts', *Canadian Historical Association Report* (1931): 61–95.

28. John Leslie discusses the treaty and its background in *The Treaty of Amity, Commerce and Navigation, 1794–1796: The Jay Treaty* (Ottawa, 1979).

29. The texts of the proclamations of 1761 and 1762 and excerpts from that of 1763 are reproduced in Cumming and Mickenberg, eds, *Native Rights in Canada*, 285–92. See also Bradford W. Morse, ed., *Aboriginal Peoples and the Law: Indian, Metis, and Inuit Rights in Canada* (Ottawa, 1985), 52–4, 191–6.

30. For a detailed study of the Proclamation, see Jack Stagg, 'Anglo-Indian Relations in North America to 1763 and an Analysis of the Royal Proclamation of 7 October 1763', Ottawa, 1981.

31. Dorothy V. Jones, 'British Colonial Indian Treaties', in Wilcomb Washburn, ed., *Handbook of North American Indians, 4: History of Indian-White Relations* (Washington, 1988), 189–90.

32. Robert J. Surtees, 'Canadian Indian Treaties', in Washburn, ed., *Handbook of North American Indians, 4: History of Indian–White Relations*, 202.

33. Stagg, 'Anglo-Indian Relations', 386.

34. Torrelli, 'Les Indiens du Canada', 237–9.

35. Jones, 'British Colonial Indian Treaties', 185.

36. Torrelli, 'Les Indiens du Canada', 227–49.

37. The text of the treaty is in Cumming and Mickenberg, eds, *Native Rights in Canada*, 296–8. In the Amerindian view, this guarantee was for pre-existing rights. See *Indian Treaty Rights*, Federation of Saskatchewan Indians, n.d.

38. For a Wuastukwiuk view of the two 1725 treaties, see Andrea Bear Nicholas, 'Maliseet Aboriginal Rights and Mascarene's Treaty, not Dummer's Treaty', in William Cowan, ed., *Actes du dix-septième Congrès des Algonquinistes* (Ottawa, 1986), 215–29.

39. The text is in Cumming and Mickenberg, eds, *Native Rights in Canada*, 302–6.

40. David L. Ghere, 'Mistranslations and Misinformation: Diplomacy on the Maine Frontier, 1725 to 1755', *American Indian Culture and Research Journal* 8, 4 (1984): 3–26.

41. Sagard, *Histoire du Canada*, II, 444: '. . . Truchemens, qui souvent ne rapportent pas fidellement les choses qu'on leur dit, ou par ignorance ou par mespris, qui est une chose fort dangereuse, & de laquelle on a souvent vue arriver de grands accidents.'

42. Akins, ed., *Public Documents of Nova Scotia*, 682–5; Daugherty, *Maritime Indian Treaties*, 75–8; Canada, *Indian Treaties and Surrenders*, 50–1, 84–5; Cumming and Mickenberg, eds, *Native Rights in Canada*, 307–9.

43. Akins, ed., *Public Documents of Nova Scotia*, 671, Council minutes, Halifax, 14 Sept. 1752. Amerindian resistance to land surveys had long been troubling the British. Ibid., Council minutes, Halifax, 4 Sept. 1732.

44. Max Savelle, *The Diplomatic History of the Canadian Boundary 1749–1763* (New Haven, 1940), 147.

45. Surtees, 'Canadian Indian Treaties', 202.

46. Lisa Patterson, 'Errant Peace Treaty', *The Archivist* 16, 6 (1989): 15.

47. Donald B. Smith, 'The Dispossession of the Mississauga Indians: A Missing Chapter in the Early History of Upper Canada', *Ontario History* 73, 2 (1981): 72. Wabakinine was a signatory to several land-cession treaties. See *DCB*, IV.

48. Canada, *Indian Treaties and Surrenders*, 3 vols (Toronto, 1971), I, 42ff.

49. Lillian F. Gates, *Land Policies of Upper Canada* (Toronto, 1968), 49, 51. According to historian Robert J. Surtees, the average price was four pence an acre. Surtees, 'Canadian Indian Treaties', 204.

50. The importance of Amerindians in colonial policy was indicated by the wish of John Graves Simcoe, first lieutenant-governor of Upper Canada, 1791–6, to establish the capital on the site of London, to be near the Amerindian allies.

See R.J. Surtees, 'The Changing Image of the Canadian Indian: An Historical Approach', in D.A. Muise, ed., *Approaches to Native History in Canada: Papers of a conference held at the National Museum of Man* (Ottawa, 1977), 121.

51. The text of the grant is reproduced in Isabel Thompson Kelsay, *Joseph Brant, 1743–1807: Man of Two Worlds* (Syracuse, NY, 1984), 363. See also Gates, *Land Policies*, 14–15.

52. Charles M. Johnston, ed., *The Valley of the Six Nations: A Collection of Documents on the Indian Lands of the Grand River* (Toronto, 1964), 52. See also Kelsay, *Joseph Brant*, 370.

53. Gates, *Land Policies*, 49. On Brant's struggle with the administration, see Charles M. Johnston, 'Joseph Brant, the Grand River Lands and the Northwest Crisis', *Ontario History* 55 (1963): 267–82.

54. A later court case that involved Brant's leasing activities was *Sheldon v. Ramsay*, 1852. The issue was whether or not lands believed to belong to a certain Mallory (not a Native) would be forfeited for treason. It developed that the lands in question had been leased by Brant; the court ruled that the Mohawk chief had had no authority for such an action, as neither he nor the Six Nations had possessed title in fee simple. See Bruce A. Clark, *Native Liberty, Crown Sovereignty* (Montreal and Kingston, 1990), 19 and n15.

55. Surtees, 'The Iroquois in Canada', 76. An outline of Brant's real estate dealings is in Johnston, ed., *Valley of Six Nations*, xlii–liv. For a study of the legal dissensions that ensued, see Sidney L. Harring, *White Man's Law* (Toronto, 1998), ch. 2.

56. Kelsay, *Joseph Brant*, 555–6. Brant had initially maintained that the purchase from the Mississauga had not been necessary, as these had been Iroquois lands from time immemorial. Later he became land agent for the Mississauga, indicating a de facto acknowledgement of their title.

57. Surtees, 'Canadian Indian Treaties', 203; Boyce Richardson, 'Kind Hearts or Forked Tongues?', *The Beaver* Outfit 67, 1 (1987): 16.

58. Canada, *Indian Treaties and Surrenders*, I, 47. Musquakie's band eventually settled in Rama Township in 1839, after several moves.

59. R.A. Humphreys, 'Governor Murray's Views . . .', *Canadian Historical Review* 16 (1935): 166–9.

Chapter 7

1. This section is an adaptation of my paper, 'A Historical Reconstruction for the Northwestern Plains', *Prairie Forum* 5, 1 (1980): 19–37.

2. F.G. Roe, *The Indian and the Horse* (Norman, Okla., 1951), 54.

3. Richard Glover, ed., *David Thompson's Narrative 1784–1812* (Toronto, 1962), 241–2; Frank Raymond Secoy, *Changing Military Patterns on the Great Plains*, Monographs of the American Ethnological Society, 21 (Seattle, 1953), 33; Oscar Lewis, *The Effects of White Contact Upon Blackfoot Culture* (New York, 1942), 11; George E. Hyde, *Indians of the High Plains* (Norman, Okla., 1959), 121, 133–4. See also Harris, ed., *Historical Atlas*, I, plate 57, for a schematic diagram of the diffusion of horses.

4. James Teit, *The Salishan Tribes of the Western Plateau*, 45th Annual Report, US Bureau of Ethnology (1927–8) (Washington, 1930), 109–10; Bernard Mishkin, *Rank and Warfare Among Plains Indians* (Seattle, 1940), 9.

5. Glover, ed., *David Thompson's Narrative*, 240–4.

6. Roe, *Indian and Horse*, 74–5.

7. Dolores A. Gunnerson, 'Man and Bison on the Plains in the Protohistoric Period', *Plains Anthropologist* 17, 55 (1972): 2. It has been theorized that the custom of burning altered the ecology of river valleys so that the subsistence base of the communities was undermined. The average life of a Plains farming village has been estimated at about 30 years.

8. T.H. Lewis, ed., 'The Narrative of the Expedition of Hernando de Soto by the Gentleman of Elvas', in Frederick W. Hodge, ed., *Spanish Explorers in the Southern United States 1528–1543* (New York, 1907), 213.

9. John Price, *Indians of Canada: Cultural Dynamics* (Scarborough, Ont., 1979), 176.

10. Mishkin, *Rank and Warfare*, 10; Glover, ed., *David Thompson's Narrative*, 267–8. For other such raids, see Arthur S. Morton, ed., *The Journal of Duncan M'Gillivray of the Northwest Company at Fort George on the Saskatchewan, 1794–1795* (Toronto, 1979), 27.

11. John McDougall, *Wa-pee Moostooch or White Buffalo* (Calgary, 1908), 132–50.

12. George W. Arthur, *An Introduction to the Ecology of Early Historic Communal Bison Hunting among the Northern Plains Indians* (Ottawa, 1975), 72.

13. Philip Duke, *Points in Time: Structure and Event in a Late Northern Plains Hunting Society* (Niwot, Colo., 1991), 69–74.

14. Elliott Coues, ed., *New Light on the Early History of the Great Northwest 1799–1814*, 3 vols (New York, 1897), II, 526.

15. John C. Ewers, 'Was There a Northwestern Plains Subculture? An Ethnographic Appraisal', in Warren W. Caldwell, ed., *The Northwestern Plains: A Symposium* (Billings, Mont., 1968), 71. See also Hugh A. Dempsey, *Indian Tribes of Alberta* (Calgary, 1986).

16. 'Gros Ventre' translates as 'Big Bellies', an appellation said to have been earned because of their big appetites. They called themselves Willow People. F.W. Hodge, *Handbook of Indians of Canada* (Ottawa, 1913), 51–2.

17. Ewers, 'Was There a Northwestern Plains Subculture?', 73. 'Atsina' was the Blackfoot term for these people and 'Gros Ventre' the French. Another name for them was 'Haaninin', 'chalk men' or 'men of soft white stone'.

18. Regina Flannery, *The Gros Ventres of Montana, Part I: Social Life*, Anthropological Series #15 (Washington, 1953), 5; Alfred L. Kroeber, *Ethnology of the Gros Ventre* (New York, 1908), 145. Another fur trader, however, found them to be lazy and 'good only at stealing horses'. Morton, ed., *M'Gillivray*, 26–7, 73–4.

19. Cf. James H. Howard, *The Plains-Ojibwa or Bungi, Hunters and Warriors of the Northern Prairie* (Vermillion, SD, 1965). Edwin Thompson Denig says that the Ojibwa and Cree were so intermingled as to be difficult to distinguish. See John C. Ewers, ed., *Five Indian Tribes of the Upper Missouri* (Norman, Okla., 1961), 100.

20. Coues, ed., *New Light*, II, 713–14. For a Spanish governor's ingenious argument in favour of providing guns to *indios barbaros* in order to make them less formidable, see Max L. Moorhead, *The Apache Frontier* (Norman, Okla., 1968), 127–8.

21. A Cree tradition from the Churchill River area has it that the first time they met non-Aboriginals they were presented with a gun, but without live ammunition. Once they obtained ammunition, the Cree found the gun to be 'a good hunting weapon'. Long, 'Narratives of Early Encounters', 230, 231.

22. Secoy, *Changing Military Patterns*, 52.

23. Brian J. Smith, 'How Great an Influence Was the Gun in Historic Northern Plains Ethnic Movements?' in Tkaczuk and Vivian, eds, *Cultures in Conflict*, 253–61. Diamond Jenness, for his part, had no doubts that the gun disturbed the equilibrium not only between humans and the animals they hunted, but also between human groups. Jenness, *Eskimo Administration*, II: *Canada* (Montreal, 1972), 7.

24. Delegates to a Peigan-Salish (Flathead) peace council vividly described the effect that guns could have. See Glover, ed., *David Thompson's Narrative*, 390–1.

25. Peter Bakker, 'Canadian Fur Trade and the Absence of Creoles', *The Carrier Pidgin* 16, 3 (1988): 1–3.

26. George Lang, 'Voyageur Discourse and the Absence of Fur Trade Pidgin', paper presented to the American Society for Ethnohistory, Toronto, 1990; in *Canadian Literature* 133 (Winter, 1992): 51–63.

27. Peter Bakker, 'The Genesis of Michif: A First Hypothesis', in William Cowan, ed., *Papers of the Twenty-first Algonquian Conference* (Ottawa, 1990), 12–35; Bakker, 'Relexification: The Case of the Métif (French Cree)', in N. Baretzy, W. Enninger, and T. Stolz, eds, *Sprachkontakt. Beiträge zum s. Essener Kolloquium über Grammatikalisierung: Naturlichkeit un System Okonomie*, 2 vols (Bochum, 1989). See also Sarah Grey Thomason and Terrence Kaufman, *Language Contact, Creolization, and Genetic Linguistics* (Berkeley, Calif., 1988), 228–33. Patline Laverdure and Ida Rose Allard have compiled *The Michif Dictionary: Turtle Mountain Chippewa Cree*, ed. John C. Crawford (Winnipeg, 1983).

28. A study by Peter Bakker of Aarhus University, Denmark, has been acclaimed as 'an analytical breakthrough'. Bakker, *A Language of Our Own* (New York, 1997).

29. See Glover, ed., *David Thompson's Narrative*, 207, 240. The Shoshoni were doubly unfortunate, as they were also confronted by Sioux armed with guns who pushed them westward into the mountains and sagebrush desert.

30. Hyde, *Indians of the High Plains*, 164–5.

31. Coues, ed., *New Light*, II, 726.

32. Peter Fidler's Journal, HBC Archives, E 3/2:19, 31 Dec. 1792. See also F.W. Howay, 'David Thompson's Account of His First Attempt to Cross the Rockies', *Queen's Quarterly* 40 (1933): 337. A touching account of the Blackfoot's first encounter with non-Aboriginals is told by George Bird Grinnell, *The Story of the Indians* (New York, 1911), 224–40.

33. Various voyages into the interior are described by Morton, *History of the Canadian West*, 263–90.

34. Glyndwr Williams, 'The Puzzle of Anthony Henday's Journal, 1754–55', *The Beaver* Outfit 309, 3 (1978): 53.

35. Lewis, *Effects of White Contact*, 17–18.

36. Morton, ed., *M'Gillivray*, 31. That there might have been some grounds for the Blackfoot suspicions is indicated by French practices in the Huron trade, in which preferential treatment was accorded to converts.

37. E.E. Rich, *The Fur Trade in the Northwest to 1857* (Toronto, 1967), 158. It should be noted that Amerindians regularly used fire to control vegetation, which in turn influenced the movements of the herds.

38. Lewis, *Effects of White Contact*, 24.

39. Howay, 'David Thompson's Account', 335; Glover, ed., *David Thompson's Narrative*, 272–9, 389.

40. Lewis, *Effects of White Contact*, 23.

41. Tyrrell, ed., *David Thompson's Narrative*, xc. For a different version, see J.E.A. Macleod, 'Peigan Post and the Blackfoot Trade', *Canadian Historical Review* 24, 3 (1943): 273–9.

42. Glover, ed., *David Thompson's Narrative*, 229. Thompson, of course, was repeating hearsay.

43. Ibid., 392–4. He called the intruders 'French Canadians'.

44. Pemmican was made from dried, pounded buffalo meat mixed with buffalo fat, about five parts meat to four parts fat, to which berries were sometimes added. One kilogram of pemmican had the food value of four to eight kilograms of fresh meat or fish. The development of its manufacture, believed to have occurred about 3000 BC, was a major factor in the emergence of the classic period of the Northern Plains Bison Hunting Culture. Brian O.K. Reeves, 'Communal bison hunters of the Northern Plains', in Davis and Reeves, eds, *Hunters of the Recent Past*, 169–70.

45. Lewis, *Effects of White Contact*, 35–6.

46. Mandelbaum, *The Plains Cree*, 246. Lewis says that among the Blackfoot, the third or fourth wife had such an inferior status that she was referred to as a 'slave'. Lewis, *Effects of White Contact*, 38–40.

47. Mandelbaum, *Plains Cree*, 57.

48. Daniel Williams Harmon, *Sixteen Years in the Indian Country: The Journals of Williams Harmon*, ed. W. Kaye Lamb (Toronto, 1957), 69.

49. Glover, ed., *David Thompson's Narrative*, 177–8.

50. David G. Mandelbaum, *Anthropology and People: The World of the Plains Cree* (Saskatoon, 1967), 6.

51. Ibid.

52. Coues, ed., *New Light*, I, 292–3; II, 498–9; Morton, *History of the Canadian West*, 253; Alexander Mackenzie, *Voyages from Montreal on the River St. Lawrence Through the Continent of America* (London, 1801), xiii–xiv. Mackenzie's work is reported to have been ghost-written. See Franz Montgomery, 'Alexander Mackenzie's Literary Assistant', *Canadian Historical Review* 18, 3 (1937): 301–4.

53. Stephen Hume, 'Was B.C. discovered by Francis Drake?', *Ottawa Citizen*, 6 Aug. 2000, A5.

54. See Rolf Knight, *Indians at Work: An Informal History of Native Indian Labour in British Columbia 1858–1930* (Vancouver, 1978).

55. W.J. Eccles, 'The Fur Trade in the Colonial Northeast', in Washburn, ed., *Handbook of North American Indians, 4: History of Indian–White Relations* (Washington, 1988), 332.

56. Witthoft, 'Archaeology as a Key to the Colonial Fur Trade', 56–7.

57. Hearne, *Journey*, 330n. Archaeologist Clifford Hickey speculates that these beads could have been of Russian origin; Hearne thought they might be Danish from Davis Strait.

58. For a detailed account of these hostilities, see Abel, *Drum Songs*, ch. 5.

59. Trudy Nicks, 'The Iroquois and the Fur Trade in Western Canada', in Judd and Ray, eds, *Old Trails and New Directions*, 86. See also Nicks, 'Origins of the Alberta Métis: Land Claims Research Project 1978–1979', workpaper for the Métis Association of Alberta.

60. Leslie F.S. Upton, 'Contact and Conflict on the Atlantic and Pacific Coasts of Canada', *B.C. Studies* 45 (1980): 103–15.

61. Made Beaver was a beaver pelt cleaned, stretched, and dried for the trade.

62. Trudy Nicks, 'Mary Anne's Dilemma: The Ethnohistory of an Ambivalent Identity', *Canadian Ethnic Studies* 17, 2 (1985): 106.

63. Trudy Nicks and Kenneth Morgan, 'Grand Cache: the historic development of an indigenous Alberta métis population', in Jacqueline Peterson and Jennifer S.H. Brown, eds, *The New Peoples: Being and Becoming Métis in North America* (Winnipeg, 1985), 163–81.

64. Methye Portage was also known as Portage La Loche. 'Methye' is the Cree word for a freshwater fish, the burbot.

65. Rich, 'Trade Habits', 35–53.

66. Glover, ed., *David Thompson's Narrative*, 273–4.

67. W.A. Sloan, 'The Columbia link—native trade, warfare, and European penetration of the Kootenays', paper presented to the Orkney-Rupert's Land Colloquium, Orkney Islands, 1990.

68. Morton, ed., *M'Gillivray*, 56.

69. Glover, ed., *David Thompson's Narrative*, 305–6; Coues, ed., New Light, II, 713.

70. Kehoe, *The Ghost Dance*, 100. See, for example, Pat Moore and Angela Wheelock, eds, *Wolverine Myths and Visions: Dene Traditions from Northern Alberta* (Edmonton, 1990). Compiled by the Dene Wodih Society, this work deals with Dene prophets, particularly Nógha ('Wolverine', *fl.* 1920s) of the Dene Dháa, and recounts wolverine stories as told by the people. On northern shamanism, see McClellan, *My Old People Say*, II, 529–75.

71. Upton, 'Contact and Conflict', 103–15.

72. Robert T. Boyd, 'Demographic History, 1774–1784', in Wayne Suttles, ed., *Handbook of North American Indians*, 7: *Northwest Coast* (Washington, 1990), 135.

73. F.W. Howay, 'An Outline Sketch of the Maritime Fur Trade', *Canadian Historical Association Report* (1932): 5–14.

74. Robin Fisher, *Contact and Conflict* (Vancouver, 1977), 3; F.W. Howay, 'Early Days of the Maritime Trade on the Northwest Coast', *Canadian Historical Review* 4 (1923): 26–44.

75. 'Muquinna' was a chiefly title of the Mochat band and was held by several chiefs. The holder of the title referred to here not only controlled the trade of his own people, but also that of the Kwakwaka'wakw of the Nimkish River.

76. Arrell Morgan Gibson, *The American Indian: Prehistory to the Present* (Lexington, Mass., 1980), 177.

77. Fisher, *Contact and Conflict*, 16. See also F.W. Howay, 'Indian Attacks upon Maritime Traders of the Northwest Coast, 1785–1805', *Canadian Historical Review* 6, 4 (1925): 287–309.

78. *DCB*, IV, s.v. 'Koyah'.

79. Fisher, *Contact and Conflict*, 15. Various versions of the incident are given by F.W. Howay, 'The Ballad of the Bold Northwestman: An Incident in the Life of Captain John Kendrick', *Washington Historical Quarterly* 20 (1929): 114–23.

80. One of the survivors was John Jewitt, who published his experiences in *A Journal Kept at Nootka Sound . . .* (Boston, 1807).

81. Possible motivations are discussed in Fisher, *Contact and Conflict*, 16.

82. Gabriel Franchère, *Journal of a Voyage to the Northwest Coast of North America during the Years 1811, 1812, 1813 and 1814*, ed. W. Kaye Lamb (Toronto, 1969), 124–7.

83. Fisher, *Contact and Conflict*, 30.

84. Ibid., 35.

85. Ibid., 31. 36. Both 'Legaic' and 'Wiiseaks' were chiefly titles by which the incumbents were known. For example, there were five recorded Legaics, a title held by the Eagle clan. The first known holder of the title built a trade empire during the second half of the eighteenth century, which the second Legaic expanded by establishing a trading relationship with the HBC. This relationship was cemented in 1832 by the marriage of his daughter to Dr John Frederick Kennedy, an official with the Company.

86. See Michael P. Robinson, *Sea Otter Chiefs* (Vancouver, [1978]), 61–87; *DCB*, XII, s.v. 'Legaic, Paul'. Tsimshian stories of Legaic and Wiiseaks are in Marius Barbeau and William Beynon, coll., *Tsimshian Narratives 2* (Ottawa, 1987).

87. Fisher, *Contact and Conflict*, 32.

88. E.E. Rich, ed., *The Letters of John McLaughlin from Fort Vancouver to the Governor and Committee, First series, 1825–38* (London, 1941), IV, app. A, Duncan Finlayson to John McLaughlin, 334–5.

89. Some estimates place the pre-contact population much lower, and the nadir at 10,000. See Thomas Berger, *Fragile Freedoms: Human Rights and Dissent in Canada* (Toronto, 1981), 229.

90. On 'Kwah, see Charles A. Bishop, 'Kwah: A Carrier Chief', in Judd and Ray, eds, *Old Trails and New Directions*, 191–204. 'Kwah is remembered mainly for a confrontation with Douglas, in which he spared the latter's life.

Chapter 8

1. For purposes of administration, the English colonies were divided into two departments, the northern and the southern.

2. Reginald Horsman, *Expansion and American Indian Policy, 1783–1812* (East Lansing, Mich., 1967), 171.

3. On the intolerance of American frontiersmen to Amerindian rights, see Robert L. Fisher, 'The Western Prologue to the War of 1812', *Missouri Historical Review* 30, 3 (1936): 272.

4. This was a period of profound changes in the Western world. In Europe, the French Revolution of 1789 led to the Napoleonic Wars (1793–1815), another in the long series of Anglo-French conflicts, which drained human resources from such peacetime activities as the fur trade and cut off markets.

5. LAC, RG 8, series C, vol. 257:31, McGill to Prevost, Montreal, 19 Dec. 1812; George F.G. Stanley, 'The Indians in the War of 1812', *Canadian Historical Review* 31, 2 (1950): 152–3.

6. Stanley, *War of 1812*, 64–5.

7. Britain, in its pursuit of the Napoleonic Wars, had insisted on its right to stop neutral vessels on the high seas in search of contraband and British deserters. In 1807, when the American *Chesapeake* refused to allow the British to take off suspected runaways, the British HMS *Leopard* fired on her, killing three of her men. The Americans retaliated with economic sanctions against Britain, though these were ineffective. See John Sugden, *Tecumseh's Last Stand* (Norman, Okla., 1985), 20.

8. Stanley, 'Indians in the War of 1812'; George F.G. Stanley, 'The Significance of the Six Nations' Participation in the War of 1812', *Ontario History* 55, 4 (1963): 215–31.

9. John 10:9. See R. David Edmunds, *The Shawnee Prophet* (Lincoln, Neb., 1983), 28–41.

10. For a reaction to this policy, see 'Tecumseh's Claims: An American View', in Carl F. Klinck, ed., *Tecumseh: Fact, Fiction and Early Records* (Englewood Cliffs, NJ, 1961), 75.

11. Apparently the admiration was mutual. See 'Brock and Tecumseh', ibid., 138.

12. R. David Edmunds, *Tecumseh and the Quest for Indian Leadership* (Boston, 1984), 148–53.

13. Calloway, *Crown and Calumet*, 11.

14. Haldimand Papers 21763: 225–6, Brigadier General Allen Maclean to Haldimand, 8 Aug. 1783; cited ibid., 62.

15. Ibid., 69.

16. *DCB*, VII, Dickson, James. The Dakota call the War of 1812 Pahinshashawacikiya, 'when the Redhead begged for our help'. Peter Douglas Elias, *The Dakota of the Canadian Northwest: Lessons for Survival* (Winnipeg, 1988), 8.

17. In the account that follows, only some battles of this war are touched on, mainly those that relate in some way to Canada.

18. Robert S. Allen, *His Majesty's Indian Allies: British Indian Policy in the Defence of Canada, 1774–1815* (Toronto, 1992), 120.

19. Stanley, *War of 1812*, 95–6.

20. A description of the battle is in Edmunds, *Tecumseh and the Quest for Indian Leadership*, 180.

21. 'Tekarihogen' was the name of a chieftainship of the Six Nations (alleged by the Mohawks to be the primary one), hereditary in Brant's mother's clan. *DCB*, VI, s.v. 'Tekarihogen'.

22. Stanley, *War of 1812*, 65–6, 122, 128–31.

23. Edmunds, *Tecumseh and the Quest for Indian Leadership*, 192–3.

24. Calloway, *Crown and Calumet*, 202–3; Stanley, *War of 1812*, 196–9.

25. Reginald Horsman, *The Frontier in the Formative Years, 1783–1815* (New York, 1970), 179–83.

26. Matthew Elliott's description of the battle is in Calloway, *Crown and Calumet*, 236–7; another version is in Stanley, *War of 1812*, 211–12. On the reported desecration of Tecumseh's body, see Sugden, *Tecumseh's Last Stand*, 136–81.

27. Edwin Seaborn, *The March of Medicine in Western Ontario* (Toronto, 1944), 9–10. For other versions, see Klinck, ed., *Tecumseh*, 200–19.

28. Sugden is particularly emphatic on this point: *Tecumseh's Last Stand*, 193–5. See also the list of battles in which Amerindians took part, and the percentage of their participation, in Helen Hornbeck Tanner, ed., *Atlas of Great Lakes Indian History* (Norman, Okla., 1987), 108–15. More

than a third of these battles were fought after Moraviantown.

29. Many more Indians than whites fought in the war, with a number of the battles involving only Indians. As a consequence, apart from a few specific battles, there are no statistics available for Indian casualties.

30. Stanley, *War of 1812*, 394.

31. Kerry A. Trask, 'Settlement in a Half-Savage Land: Life and Loss in the Métis Community of La Baye', *Michigan Historical Review* 15 (1989): 1–27.

32. Allen, *His Majesty's Indian Allies*, 197–8; Edward S. Rogers and Donald B. Smith, eds, *Aboriginal Ontario* (Toronto, 1994), 123–4.

33. Robert J. Surtees, 'Canadian Indian Treaties', in Washburn, ed., *Handbook of North American Indians, 4: History of Indian-White Relations*, 204.

34. John F. Leslie, 'Buried Hatchet', *Horizon Canada* 4, 40 (1985): 944–9.

35. Delâge, *Le pays renversé*, 339–47.

Chapter 9

1. As Alexandre Taché (bishop of St Boniface, Man., 1853–71, archbishop, 1871–94) acidly observed, farming, 'although so desirable, is not the sole condition in the state of civilization'. Canada, Sessional Papers 1885, No. 116, 'Papers . . . in connection with the extinguishment of the Indian title preferred by Half-breeds resident in the North-West Territories', 85, Taché to Col. J.S. Dennis, deputy minister of the interior, 29 Jan. 1879. Later, ranching would be advocated, as the 'work suits the Indians better'. Not only that, but ranching could be co-ordinated with hunting. In the view of the NWMP, 'Farming is too steady and monotonous work for them, although some have fine fields.' (Canada, *N.W.M.P. Report*, 1895, 5.)

2. Cited by L.F.S. Upton, 'The Origins of Canadian Indian Policy', *Journal of Canadian Studies* 10, 4 (1973): 59.

3. The Sarnia, Kettle Point, and Stony Point reserves and Moore Township. William Henderson, *Canada's Indian Reserves: Pre-Confederation* (Ottawa, 1980), 10 and n56.

4. Richardson, 'Kind Hearts or Forked Tongues?', 18.

5. Donald B. Smith, *Sacred Feathers: The Reverend Peter Jones (Kahkewaquonaby) and the Mississauga Indians* (Toronto, 1987), chs 6, 7. Other Amerindian clerics, all Methodists, included George Copway (Kahgegagahbowh, 'He Who Stands Forever', 1818–69); Peter Jacobs (Pahtahsaga, 'One Who Makes the World Brighter', c. 1807–94); and War of 1812 veteran John Sunday (Shah-wun-dais, 'Sultry Heat', c. 1795–1875). Two of these, Copway and Jacobs, ran into funding difficulties that resulted in their expulsion from their ministries.

6. John F. Leslie and Ron Maguire, *The Historical Development of the Indian Act* (Ottawa, 1978), 18–19.

7. For more on Aisance, see Smith, *Sacred Feathers*, 212–13; *DCB*, IX, s.v. 'Musquakie'; VIII, s.v. 'Aisance'.

8. Smith, *Sacred Feathers*, 349.

9. On such movements in general, see Anthony F.C. Wallace, 'Revitalization Movements: Some Theoretical Considerations for Their Comparative Study', *American Anthropologist* 58, 2 (1956): 264–81. See also Selwyn Dewdney, *The Sacred Scrolls of the Southern Ojibway* (Toronto, 1975); Ruth Landes, *Ojibwa Religion and Midéwiwin* (Madison, Wis., 1968); A. Irving Hallowell, *Culture and Experience* (Philadelphia, 1955), 308.

10. Francis Bond Head, *A Narrative*, 2nd edn (London, 1839), app. A, 'Memorandum on the Aborigines of North America'. This memorandum is reproduced in part in Adam Shortt and Arthur G. Doughty, eds, *Canada and Its Provinces*, 23 vols (Toronto, 1914–17), V, 337–9. Sir Francis had been knighted in 1831, reportedly because of his demonstration of the military usefulness of the lasso.

11. Peter S. Schmaltz, *The History of the Saugeen Indians* (Ottawa, 1977), 82–4. 'Saugeen' is Ojibwa for 'mouth of the river'.

12. Peggy J. Blair, 'The Supreme Court of Canada's "Historic" Decision in Nikal and Lewis: Why Crown Fishing Policy in Upper Canada Makes Bad Law', Master's thesis (University of Ottawa, 1998), 52–9. See also Victor P. Lytwyn, 'Waterworld: The Aquatic Territory of the Great Lakes First Nations', in Dale Standen and David McNab, eds, *Gin Das Winan: Documenting Aboriginal History in Ontario* (Toronto, 1996), 14–28. A valuable recent study of the experiences of the peoples who moved to reserves around Georgian Bay after signing the Bond Head Treaty of 1836, the Robinson Huron Treaty (1850), and the Manitoulin Island Treaty (1862) is Robin Jarvis Brownlie, *A Fatherly Eye: Indian Agents, Government Power, and Aboriginal Resistance in Ontario, 1918–1939* (Toronto, 2003).

13. Smith, *Sacred Feathers*, 163–4; Schmaltz, *History of the Saugeen Indians*, 56–148.

14. B.E. Hill, 'The Grand River Navigation Company and the Six Nations Indians', *Ontario History* 63, 1 (1971): 31–40; Richard C. Daniel, *A History of Native Claims Processes in Canada 1867–1979* (Ottawa, 1980), 122–30.

15. Sidney L. Harring, *White Man's Law: Native People in Nineteenth-Century Canadian Jurisprudence* (Toronto, 1998), 58, 148.

16. According to Daniel (*History of Native Claims*, 198), Chisholm was the most active of the lawyers who worked on Amerindian cases. Others included R.V. Sinclair of Ottawa and Walter O'Meara in British Columbia.

17. Thwaites, ed., Jesuit Relations, VI, 151; Lucien Campeau, 'Roman Catholic Missions', in Washburn, ed., *Handbook of North American Indians, 4: History of Indian-White Relations*, 465–8.

18. Henderson, *Canada's Indian Reserves*, 2–5.

19. George Stanley, 'The First Indian "Reserves" in Canada', *Revue d'histoire de l'Amérique française* 4 (1950): 178; Thwaites, ed., *Jesuit Relations*, LXVI, 43.

20. Thwaites, ed., *Jesuit Relations*, XXIII, 303; LX, 131.

21. Stanley, 'First Indian "Reserves"', 185.

22. Léon Gérin, 'La Seigneurie de Sillery et les Hurons', *Mémoires de la Société Royale du Canada*, ser. 2, vol. 6 (1900): sec. 1, 75–115. See also Georges E. Sioui, *Pour une autohistoire amérindienne: Essai sur les fondements d'une morale sociale* (Québec, 1989), 124–5.

23. Thwaites, ed., *Jesuit Relations*, XLVII, 263, 299; LXVI, 43–7; Henderson, *Canada's Indian Reserves*, 3. On Sillery's religious and social failure as far as the Montagnais were concerned, see Kenneth M. Morrison, 'Baptism and Alliance: The Symbolic Mediations of Religious Syncretism', *Ethnohistory* 37, 4 (1990): 416–37.

24. Stanley, 'First Indian Reserves', 186–7; Richard H. Bartlett, *Indian Reserves in Quebec* (Saskatoon, 1984), 2 n6.

25. J. Garth Taylor, *Labrador Eskimo Settlements of the Early Contact Period* (Ottawa, 1974); W. Gillies Ross, *Whaling and Eskimos: Hudson Bay 1860–1915* (Ottawa, 1975).

26. *DCB*, IV, s.v. 'Haven, Jens'. See also Jenness, *Eskimo Administration*, 9–10. The Moravian Brethren, also known as Unitas Fratrum, was a pietist Protestant missionary group founded in 1727 by Count Nikolaus Ludwig von Zinzendorf (1700–60). They already had missions in Greenland when they were invited by the British to establish in Labrador.

27. *DCB*, IV, s.v. 'Mikak'.

28. Barnett Richling, 'Without Compromise: Hudson's Bay Company and Moravian Trade Rivalry in Nineteenth Century Labrador', in Bruce G. Trigger, Toby Morantz, and Louise Dechêne, eds, *Le Castor Fait Tout* (Montreal, 1987), 456–84.

29. An adult whale would have as much as 2,000 pounds of baleen in its jaws; in 1883, baleen brought $4.75 a pound.

30. Ross, *Whaling and Eskimos*, 138.

31. On adaptation to Euro-Canadian foods, see Morris Zaslow, *The Northward Expansion of Canada, 1914–1967* (Toronto, 1988), 153.

32. John R. Bockstoce, *Whales, Ice, and Men: The History of Whaling in the Western Arctic* (Seattle, 1986), 130, 136.

33. Ibid., 135–42.

34. Morris Zaslow, *The Opening of the Canadian North, 1870–1914* (Toronto, 1971), 258.

35. On the effects of the change of diet, see Morrison, *Under the Flag*, 74–6.

36. The name 'Yukon' (Youcon, Ou-kun-ah) derives from an Indian word, probably Gwich'in, meaning great river or white water river. If the Bering Strait migration hypothesis is correct, then the Yukon, with Alaska, is North America's oldest inhabited region. Kenneth S. Coates and William R. Morrison, *Land of the Midnight Sun: A History of the Yukon* (Edmonton, 1988), 2, 5.

37. Ibid., 13, 25, 50.

38. McClellan, *Part of the Land*, 67–70, 75–84; Coates and Morrison, *Land of the Midnight Sun*, 23–30.

39. L.F.S. Upton, *Micmacs and Colonists: Indian-White Relations in the Maritimes, 1713–1867* (Vancouver, 1979), 82–7.

40. Ibid., 91.

41. Douglas Sanders, 'Government Indian Agencies in Canada', in Washburn, ed., *Handbook of North American Indians, 4: History of Indian-White Relations*, 279.

42. Upton, *Micmacs and Colonists*, 95.

43. During the nineteenth century the porpoise was particularly valued for its oil, which was used in the manufacture and maintenance of fine watches. A bill before the Nova Scotia House of Assembly to ban the shooting of porpoises in the bay had passed two readings when Meuse made his plea that resulted in the bill's defeat.

44. Fort Simpson has been labelled the 'London of the Northwest Coast' because it was the largest settlement in the region and was the hub for trading activity.

45. Herbert Beaver (1800–58) was highly critical of HBC dealings with Amerindians; after two years, he was transferred out but kept up his campaign

even after his departure. Nellie B. Pipes, 'Indian Conditions in 1836–38', *Oregon Historical Quarterly* 32, 4 (1931): 332–42.

46. Jean Usher, *William Duncan of Metlakatla* (Ottawa, 1974); 'Duncan of Metlakatla: the Victorian origins of a model Indian community', in W.L. Morton, ed., *The Shield of Achilles: Aspects of Canada in the Victorian Age* (Toronto, 1968), 286–310; Fisher, *Contact and Conflict*, 125–36; Grant, *Moon of Wintertime*, 129–32. On Legaic, see *DCB*, XII, s.v. 'Legaic, Paul'; Michael P. Robinson, *Sea Otter Chiefs* (Vancouver, c. 1978).

47. Usher, *William Duncan of Metlakatla*, 135.

48. Frederick Temple Blackwood, 1st Marquess of Dufferin and Ava, governor-general of Canada, 1872–8.

49. Thomas Crosby, *Up and Down the Pacific Coast by Canoe and Mission Ship* (Toronto, 1914), 65–6.

50. More precisely, a reserve is 'a tract of land in which the aboriginal interest is permanently preserved for a particular group of native people'. Jack Woodward, *Native Law* (Toronto, 1989), 222. See also Brian Slattery, 'Understanding Aboriginal Rights', *Canadian Bar Review* 66 (1987): 743–4, 769–71. A Cree term applied to reserves is 'iskonikun', what is left over, scraps. This refers to the fact that many reserves are ill-suited for agriculture and have long since become useless for hunting and trapping. See Eleanor Brass, *I Walk in Two Worlds* (Calgary, 1987), 71.

51. Henderson, *Canada's Indian Reserves*, 4–5. See also Richard H. Bartlett, 'The Establishment of Indian Reserves on the Prairies', *Canadian Native Law Reporter* 3 (1980): 3–56.

52. Upton, *Micmacs and Colonists*, 96.

53. Ibid., 99; Cumming and Mickenberg, eds, *Native Rights in Canada*, 308–9.

54. Upton, *Micmacs and Colonists*, 99–100.

55. Cumming and Mickenberg, eds, *Native Rights in Canada*, 102.

56. Upton, *Micmacs and Colonists*, 112.

57. *Journals of the Legislative Assembly of Prince Edward Island*, 7 Jan. 1812, 11–12; cited by Upton, *Micmacs and Colonists*, 115.

58. Ibid., 118.

59. Maurice F.V. Doll, Robert S. Kidd, and John P. Day, *The Buffalo Lake Métis Site: A Late Nineteenth Century Settlement in the Parkland of Central Alberta* (Edmonton, 1988), 13–14.

60. Paul Kane, *Wanderings of an Artist* (Edmonton, 1968 [1859]), 89.

61. Overhunting had, by this time, become a serious problem; the Nor'Westers alone regularly prepared 30 to 50 tons of pemmican each season for the company's fur brigades. A.S. Morton, *History of Prairie Settlement and Dominion Lands Policy* (Toronto, 1938), 208.

62. The Cree told Palliser that the bison were disappearing and that they hoped to be provided with farming implements. Irene M. Spry, *The Palliser Expedition: An Account of John Palliser's British North American Expedition, 1857–1860* (Toronto, 1963), 60; see also F.G. Roe, 'Early Agriculture in Western Canada in Relation to Climatic Stability', *Agricultural History* 26, 3 (1952): 109. On pre-contact agriculture in the Red River area, see *Prehistory of the Lockport Site* (Winnipeg, 1985), 11.

63. Laura L. Peers, 'Rich Man, Poor Man, Beggarman, Chief: Saulteaux in the Red River Settlement, 1812–1833', in William Cowan, ed., *Papers of the Eighteenth Algonquian Conference* (Ottawa, 1987), 265–9.

64. Both the Jurisdiction Act of 1803 and the Fur Trade Act of 1821 were concerned with extending the Canadian court system into the Northwest. The 1803 Act had been inspired by the Louisiana Purchase of the same year.

65. Morton, *History of the Canadian West*, 628.

66. Hamar Foster, 'Long-Distance Justice: The Criminal Jurisdiction of Canadian Courts West of the Canadas, 1763–1859', *American Journal of Legal History* 34, 1 (1990): 6.

67. J.A.H. Bennett and J.W. Berry, 'The Future of Cree Syllabic Literacy in Northern Canada', paper presented at the Fifteenth Algonquian Conference, Winnipeg, 1986. For a discussion of the religious background, see Jennifer S.H. Brown, 'The Track to Heaven: The Hudson Bay Cree Religious Movement of 1842–1843', in William Cowan, ed., *Papers of the Thirteenth Algonquian Conference* (Ottawa, 1982), 59. See also *DCB*, I, s.v. 'Abishabis'; John S. Long, 'The Cree Prophets: oral and documentary accounts', *Journal of the Canadian Church Historical Society* 31, 1 (1989): 3–13. A page of the letter is reproduced in René Fumoleau, *As Long As This Land Shall Last* (Toronto, 1973), 33.

68. Duncan Campbell Scott, 'The Last of the Indian Treaties', *Scribner's Magazine* 40, 5 (1906): 581–2.

69. Paul Tennant, *Aboriginal Peoples and Politics* (Vancouver, 1990), 20.

70. Knight, *Indians at Work*, 236.

71. Fisher, *Contact and Conflict*, 154–6.

72. Tennant, *Aboriginal Peoples and Politics*, 21–38.

73. For example, according to Robert Cail, 'So long as Douglas was governor, the Indians had only to ask to receive additional land.' Cail, *Land, Man,*

and the Law: The Disposal of Crown Lands in British Columbia, 1871–1913 (Vancouver, 1974), 179.

74. Fisher, Contact and Conflict, 153–6.

75. Dennis Madill, British Columbia Treaties in Historical Perspective (Ottawa, 1981), 31.

76. Barry M. Gough, Gunboat Frontier: British Maritime Authority and Northwest Coast Indians, 1846–1890 (Vancouver, 1984).

77. J.E. Michael Kew, 'History of Coastal British Columbia Since 1849', in Suttles, ed., Handbook of North American Indians, 7: Northwest Coast (Washington, 1990), 159.

78. Fisher, Contact and Conflict, 208.

79. Gough, Gunboat Frontier, 205–8.

Chapter 10

1. John H. Bodley, ed., Tribal Peoples and Development Issues: A Global Overview (Mountain View, Calif., 1988), 63–9.

2. Some of these problems are still continuing. For example, the community of Shannonville, Ontario, occupies lands that were leased by the Iroquois of Tyendinaga early in the nineteenth century to a certain Turton Penn for 999 years. Henderson, Canada's Indian Reserves, 38 n48.

3. Leslie and Maguire, Historical Development of the Indian Act, 11.

4. A clear exposition of this position is that of Herman Merivale, 'Policy of Colonial Governments Towards Native Tribes, as Regards Their Protection and Their Civilization', in Bodley, ed., Tribal Peoples, 95–104.

5. The phrase 'white man's burden' owes its origin to Rudyard Kipling, who used it in reference to colonial powers and their relationship to the Aboriginal people whose territories they took over.

6. Dennis Madill, 'Band Council Powers', in W.E. Daugherty and Madill, Indian Government Under Indian Act Legislation 1868–1951 (Ottawa, 1980).

7. John E. Hodgetts, Pioneer Public Service: An Administrative History of the United Canadas, 1841–1867 (Toronto, 1955), 223.

8. David McNab, 'The Colonial Office and the Prairies in the Mid-Nineteenth Century', Prairie Forum 3, 1 (1978): 21–38.

9. 'Nfld. Mi'kmaq, Ottawa set to bargain', Cape Breton Post, 22 Nov. 2003, A11. The Federation of Newfoundland Indians website is: <www.fni.nf.ca>.

10. Jamie Baker, 'One Done, Two to Go', St. John's Telegram, 26 June 2005, A5.

11. It was published in two parts, in Journals of the Legislative Assembly of the Province of Canada, 1844–5, app. EEE; and ibid., 1847, app. T.

12. Ibid., 1847, app. T.

13. Cited by Richardson, 'Kind Hearts or Forked Tongues?', 23. The commissioners appear to have considered that Amerindian loss of lands was in large part due to alienation by the Amerindians themselves. Such a view would have been re-inforced by the lack of Amerindian action in launching suits against trespass or for the recovery of lost lands. See the Bagot Commission Report, Journals of the Legislative Assembly of the Province of Canada, 1844–5, app. EEE; and 1847, app. T.

14. Thomas Anderson, for example, opposed the discontinuance, arguing that it would result in serious deprivation; see Leslie and Maguire, Historical Development of the Indian Act, 21.

15. Smith, Sacred Feathers, 184.

16. Toby Morantz, 'Aboriginal Land Claims in Quebec', in Ken Coates, ed., Aboriginal Land Claims in Canada (Toronto, 1992), 107.

17. Schedule of Indian Bands, Reserves and Settlements (Ottawa, 1987), 11–17. Amerindian settlements, of which there are about a dozen, are not in-cluded, as they do not have lands specifically set aside for them.

18. Some reserve the term 'Indian' for those who are registered. See, for example, J. Rick Ponting and Roger Gibbins, Out of Irrelevance (Toronto, 1980), xv.

19. John L. Tobias, 'Protection, Civilization, Assimilation: An Outline History of Canada's Indian Policy', Western Canadian Journal of Anthropology 6, 2 (1976): 16. This article was reprinted in A.L. Getty and Antoine S. Lussier, eds, As Long As the Sun Shines and Water Flows (Vancouver, 1983), 39–55.

20. Peter Jones, the Mississauga chief, had warned that Amerindians must feel like full partners in the new order. He pinpointed such measures as security of ownership of reserve lands and civil rights; see Smith, Sacred Feathers, 238–9.

21. For a study of the long Ojibwa struggle with the mining companies, see Janet E. Chute, The Legacy of Shingwaukonse: A Century of Native Leadership (Toronto, 1998).

22. Douglas Leighton, 'The Historical Significance of the Robinson Treaties of 1850', paper pre-sented to the Canadian Historical Association, Ottawa, 1982; Richardson, 'Kind Hearts or Forked Tongues?', 24–7; George Brown and Ron Maguire, eds, Indian Treaties in Historical Perspective (Ottawa, 1979), 26.

23. DCB, IX, s.v. 'Assikinack, Francis'.

24. This view is expressed in a pamphlet issued by the Federation of Saskatchewan Indians, *Indian Treaty Rights*, n.d., n.p.

25. Allen G. Harper, 'Canada's Indian Administration: Basic Concepts and Objectives', *América Indígena* 5, 2 (1945): 132. See also Roger Gibbins and J. Rick Ponting, 'Historical Overview and Background', in Ponting, ed., *Arduous Journey: Canadian Indians and Decolonization* (Toronto, 1986), 25.

26. Hodgetts, *Pioneer Public Service*, 209–10.

27. A rule of thumb for determining their size was to allow 80 acres (32 hectares) per family; however, there was considerable variation in practice.

28. Douglas Sanders, 'Government Indian Agencies', in Washburn, ed., *Handbook of North American Indians, 4: History of Indian–White Relations*, 279.

29. Malcolm Montgomery, 'The Six Nations Indians and the Macdonald Franchise', *Ontario History* 56 (1964): 13.

30. The price was $1.5 million, or about one penny for every three hectares.

31. *Census of Canada*, 1871, I, 332–3; 1881, I, 300–1; 1941, 684–91.

32. Wayne Daugherty, 'The Elective System', in Daugherty and Madill, *Indian Government Under Indian Act Legislation*, 4.

33. Ibid., 3.

34. Tobias, 'Protection, Civilization, Assimilation', 17–18.

35. Ibid., 22–3. On current legal meanings of 'Indian', see Jack Woodward, *Native Law* (Toronto, 1989), 5–12.

36. Kathleen Jamieson, *Indian Women and the Law in Canada: Citizens Minus* (Ottawa, 1978), 69–73.

37. Dennis Madill, 'Band Council Powers', in Daugherty and Madill, *Indian Government Under Indian Act Legislation*, 2.

38. N.L. Barlee, 'The Chilcotin War of 1864', *Canada West Magazine* 6, 4 (1976): 13–23. Another version of Klatsassin's behaviour has it that his people had been decimated by smallpox in 1862, and when a Euro-Canadian threatened him with a return of the disease he went on his rampage. See *DCB*, IX, s.v. 'Klatsassin'.

39. Robin Fisher, 'Joseph Trutch and Indian Land Policy', *B.C. Studies* 12 (1971–2): 17. See also Berger, *Fragile Freedoms*, 222.

40. 'Ordinance further to define the law regulating acquisition of Land in British Columbia'.

41. Kew, 'History of Coastal British Columbia Since 1849', 159.

42. *Report of the Royal Commission on Aboriginal Peoples*, 5 vols (Ottawa, 1996), II, part 2, 784.

43. The 1871 Census counted 9,800 Métis out of a total population of 11,400. Nathalie J. Kermoal, 'Le "Temps de Cayoge": La vie quotidienne des femmes métisses au Manitoba de 1850 à 1900', Ph.D. thesis (University of Ottawa, 1996), xliii n23, 40.

44. For the story of Grant, see Margaret MacLeod and W.L. Morton, *Cuthbert Grant of Grantown* (Toronto, 1974).

45. Barry Cooper, 'Alexander Kennedy Isbister: A Respectable Victorian', *Canadian Ethnic Studies* 17, 2 (1985): 44–63; *DCB*, XI, s.v. 'Isbister, Alexander Kennedy'. He had gone to England at the age of 20.

46. Most of the Métis of Red River were of Cree descent and so had inherited the animosity that existed betweeen Cree and Sioux.

47. For some of the colonial secretary's views, see Herman Merivale, 'Policy of Colonial Governments Towards Native Tribes, as Regards Their Protection and Their Civilization', in Bodley, ed., *Tribal Peoples*, 95–204; David T. McNab, 'Herman Merivale and Colonial Office Indian Policy in the Mid-Nineteenth Century', in Getty and Lussier, eds, *As Long As the Sun Shines and Water Flows*, 85–103.

48. Alexander Morris, *The Treaties of Canada with the Indians* (Toronto, 1880; reprint, 1971), 169.

49. NAC, RG 6, C–1, vol. 316, file 995, William McDougall to Secretary of State for the Provinces, 5 Nov. 1869; 'Copy of the Indian Agreement', *The Globe*, Toronto, 4 Sept. 1869, 3. Both references cited by Richard C. Daniel, *A History of Native Land Claims Processes in Canada, 1867–1979* (Ottawa, 1980), 3.

50. For details of these troubles, see Frits Pannekoek, *A Snug Little Flock: The Social Origins of the Riel Resistance of 1869–70* (Winnipeg, 1991).

51. Although the French language predominated among Red River Métis, in biological fact they were more mixed than that would indicate. Historian Diane Payment has illustrated this with names: MacGillis (Magillice), Bruce (Brousse), Sayer (Serre), McKay (Macaille), and McDougall (McDoub). Payment, *Batoche (1870–1970)* (St Boniface, Man., 1983), 1.

52. Their story is told by Elias, *Dakota of the Canadian Northwest*. See also James H. Howard, *The Canadian Sioux* (Lincoln, Neb., 1984); Roy W. Meyer, 'The Canadian Sioux Refugees from Minnesota', *Minnesota History* 41, 1 (1968): 13–28; George F.G. Stanley, 'Displaced Red Men: The Sioux in Canada', in Ian A.L. Getty and Donald B. Smith, eds, *One Century Later:*

Western Canadian Reserve Indians Since Treaty 7 (Vancouver, 1978), 55–81.

53. According to Elias, the pair were taken by Americans in a raid: *The Dakota of the Canadian Northwest*, 23. See also Howard, *The Canadian Sioux*, 28.

54. Daniel, *History of Native Land Claims*, 4, citing John Leonard Taylor, 'The Development of an Indian Policy for the Canadian North-West, 1869–70', Ph.D. thesis (Queen's University, 1975), 28.

55. Riel was the grandson of Jean-Baptiste Lagimodière (1778–1855) and Marie Anne Gaboury (1780–1875), first non-Aboriginal woman in the West. During the winter of 1816–17, Jean-Baptiste and a companion had travelled by foot from Red River to Montreal (17 Oct. 1816–10 Mar. 1817) to inform Lord Selkirk about the Battle of Seven Oaks. Riel's parents were farmers and did not participate in either the fur trade or the buffalo hunt.

56. On the St Paul trade, see Rhoda R. Gilman, Carolyn Gilman, and Deborah M. Stultz, *The Red River Trails: Oxcart Routes between St. Paul and the Selkirk Settlement 1820–1870* (St Paul, Minn., 1979).

57. Proclamation of the Provisional Government & 'Declaration of the People of Rupert's Land and the North-West', 8 Dec. 1869, in E.H. Oliver, ed., *The Canadian North-West: Its Early Development and Legislative Records* (Ottawa, 1915), 904. The full Declaration is at: <www.mhs.mb.ca/docs/pageant/09/rupertslanddeclaration.shtml>.

58. LAC, Macdonald Papers, vol. 516, Macdonald to McDougall, 27 Nov. 1869; cited by Donald Creighton, *John A. Macdonald*, 2 vols (Toronto, 1966 [1955]), II, 51.

59. Ontario was particularly enraged because the court martial that had condemned Scott had been made up of Métis and Amerindians. See Arthur Silver, 'French Quebec and the Métis Question, 1869–1885', in Carl Berger and Ramsay Cook, eds, *The West and the Nation* (Toronto, 1976), 91–113.

60. George F.G. Stanley, *The Birth of Western Canada: A History of the Riel Rebellion* (Toronto, 1960 [1936]), 129, 135–6.

61. In 1872 Macdonald sent $1,000, via Archbishop Taché, for both Riel and Ambroise-Dydime Lépine (1834–1923) to stay out of the country. Riel took advantage of the offer, but Lépine, who had headed the court martial that had condemned Scott, came back.

62. Ironically, an ultimate result of the confrontations was to split the Métis into two groups: those of Red River and Rupert's Land (the 'New Nation') who had stood up for their rights, and the 'others' in the rest of the country who had not made such a stand. See the *Report of the RCAP*, IV, ch. 5, 'Métis Perspectives', 199–384.

Chapter 11

1. The *Report of the RCAP*, while acknowledging that Aboriginal treaties were kept 'alive' through periodic renegotiations to adapt them to changing circumstances (II, part 1, 11), later observed that 'their central feature makes them irrevocable' (19).

2. The United States stopped making treaties with Amerindians in 1871, the year that Canada signed the first of its 11 numbered treaties.

3. John S. Long, '"No Basis for Argument?" The Signing of Treaty Nine in Northern Ontario, 1905–1906', *Native Studies Review* 5, 2 (1989): 36.

4. Canada, Parliament, *Sessional Papers*, 1867–8, no. 81, 18; 1869, no. 42, 20–1.

5. There are 483 agreements listed in Canada, *Indian Treaties and Surrenders from 1680 to 1902*, 3 vols (Ottawa, 1891–1912; facsimile, 1971). Since then a few have been added.

6. Brown and Maguire, eds, *Indian Treaties in Historical Perspective*, 32.

7. Richard C. Daniel, 'Indian Rights and Hinterland Provinces: The Case of Northern Alberta', MA thesis (University of Alberta, 1977), ch. 2.

8. Taylor, 'Development of an Indian Policy', 45–6.

9. David J. Hall, '"A Serene Atmosphere"? Treaty 1 Revisited', *Canadian Journal of Native Studies* 4, 2 (1984), 325.

10. For an examination of the negotiations for Treaty One, see Hall, 'Treaty 1 Revisited'.

11. Harold Cardinal, *The Unjust Society: The Tragedy of Canada's Indians* (Edmonton, 1969), 36.

12. Daniel, *History of Native Claims Processes*, 12. Canada had agreed, in 1894, that any future treaties within Ontario would require the province's concurrence. Similarly, later adhesions presented little, if any, opportunity for negotiations. The territories involved could be considerable—in Treaty Nine, for instance, most of northern Ontario was involved in the adhesion of 1929.

13. Morris, *Treaties of Canada with the Indians*, 62.

14. Ibid.

15. The idea of train passes was not out of line, of course. The railways handed them out to privileged customers, such as persons in certain professions. In the United States, Amerindians

were allowed free rides on western railroads but were not entitled to free seats; they could ride in boxcars.

16. Morris, *Treaties of Canada with the Indians*, 69.

17. John S. Long, 'Treaty No. 9 and fur trade company families: Northeastern Ontario's halfbreeds, Indians, petitioners and métis', in Peterson and Brown, eds, *The New Peoples*, 145; *Report of the RCAP*, IV, 261.

18. Morris, *Treaties of Canada with the Indians*, 293–5. George F.G. Stanley referred to 'the invaluable assistance of the half-breeds' in maintaining comparative peace on Canada's frontier. Stanley, *Birth of Western Canada*, 214. A contrary view, claiming that the Métis were no more than facilitators, interpreters, reporters, and witnesses, is presented by David T. McNab, 'Hearty Co-operation and Efficient Aid, the Metis and Treaty #3', *Canadian Journal of Native Studies* 3, 1 (1983): 131–49.

19. Taylor, 'Development of an Indian Policy', 29.

20. In 1904 the force was renamed the Royal North-West Mounted Police; in 1920, it became the Royal Canadian Mounted Police, which is still its designation today. On the NWMP, see R.C. Macleod, *The North-West Mounted Police and Law Enforcement, 1873–1905* (Toronto, 1976).

21. Philip Goldring, *Whiskey, Horses and Death: The Cypress Hills Massacre and its Sequel*, Occasional Papers in Archaeology and History No. 21 (Ottawa, 1973).

22. Paul F. Sharp, 'Massacre at Cypress Hills', *Saskatchewan History* 7 (1954): 81–99; Zaslow, *Opening of the Canadian North*, 15–17.

23. B.D. Fardy, *Jerry Potts, Paladin of the Plains* (Langley, BC, 1984).

24. Meyer, 'Canadian Sioux Refugees', 13–28; Alice B. Kehoe, 'The Dakotas in Saskatchewan', in Ethel Nurge, ed., *The Modern Sioux* (Lincoln, Neb., 1970), 148–82.

25. Elias, *Dakota of the Canadian Northwest*, 172. A closer look at White Cap's trial is in Bob Beal and Rod Macleod, *Prairie Fire: The 1885 North-West Rebellion* (Edmonton, 1984), 327–30.

26. Hugh A. Dempsey has written a biography, *Crowfoot: Chief of the Blackfeet* (Edmonton, 1972). Dempsey points out (pp. 93–107) that Crowfoot was not the head chief of the Blackfoot Confederacy, as generally believed by non-Natives, but one of the chiefs of the Blackfoot proper. The other members of the Confederacy, the Blood, Tsuu T'ina, and Peigan, each had their own chiefs, and they all participated in the treaty negotiations. Crowfoot, however, was particularly highly regarded by the Euro-Canadians,

and this increased his influence among his fellow chiefs in treaty matters.

27. Leslie and Maguire, eds, *Historical Development of the Indian Act*, 59.

28. Sweetgrass had become a chief by achieving what Maskepetoon had failed to do: he entered a Blackfoot camp alone, killed a warrior, and captured 40 horses. By 1870 he had become principal chief of the River Cree; in the meantime, in 1865, he had adopted the name Abraham when he had been converted by Father Albert Lacombe. The HBC dubbed him 'Chief of the Country'. See *DCB*, X, s.v. 'Wikaskokiseyin'.

29. Arthur J. Ray, *Indians in the Fur Trade: Their Role as Trappers, Hunters, and Middlemen in the Lands Southwest of Hudson Bay, 1660–1870* (Toronto, 1974), 228.

30. Hugh A. Dempsey, *Big Bear: The End of Freedom* (Vancouver, 1984), 77–8.

31. Dempsey, *Crowfoot*, 102.

32. Cited in Dempsey, *Big Bear*, 63.

33. Ibid., 67.

34. Leslie and Maguire, eds, *Historical Development of the Indian Act*, 100.

35. The 'Indian Register' is a list maintained by the government; it consists of Band Lists and General Lists. Those who are registered and subject to the Indian Act are 'status' Amerindians.

36. Leslie and Maguire, eds, *Historical Development of the Indian Act*, 65.

37. *Report of the RCAP*, II, part 2, 809.

38. Leslie and Maguire, eds, *Historical Development of the Indian Act*, 67.

39. The term 'potlatch' included several different types of feasts, of which the 'giveaway' was one. Jay Miller described feasts as 'knots holding together the . . . social fabric'. Miller, 'Feasting with the Southern Tsimshian', in Margaret Seguin, ed., *The Tsimshian: Images of the Past, Views for the Present* (Vancouver, 1984), 27–39; Tina Loo, 'Don Cranmer's Potlatch: Law as Coercion, Symbol and Rhetoric in British Columbia, 1884–1951', *Canadian Historical Review* 73, 2 (1992): 125–65; Stuart Piddocke, 'The Potlatch System of the Southern Kwakiuktl: A New Perspective', *Southwestern Journal of Anthropology* 21 (1965): 244–64.

40. For a contemporary view of the matter, see Morice, *Au pays de l'ours noir*, 146–61.

41. Edward Ahenakew, *Voices of the Plains Cree* (Toronto, 1973), 182.

42. Kehoe, *The Ghost Dance*, 129–34; F.L. Barron, 'The Indian Pass System in the Canadian West, 1882–1935', *Prairie Forum* 13, 1 (1988): 31.

See also Katherine Pettipas, *Severing the Ties that Bind: Government Repression of Indigenous Religious Ceremonies on the Prairies* (Winnipeg, 1994).

43. George Manuel and Michael Posluns, *The Fourth World: An Indian Reality* (Don Mills, Ont., 1974), 78–9.

44. Cited by Cody Poulton, 'Songs from the Gods: "Hearing the Voice" in the Ascetic Rituals of West Coast Indians and Japanese Liturgic Drama', paper presented to the Thirty-third International Congress of Asian and North African Studies, University of Toronto, 1991.

45. Pettipas, *Severing the Ties that Bind*, 160–6.

46. On the role of the Indian Act, see John F. Leslie, *A Historical Survey of Indian–Government Relations, 1940–1970* (Ottawa, 1993), esp. 12–19.

47. Tobias, 'Protection, Civilization, Assimilation', 19–20.

48. Leslie and Maguire, eds, *Historical Development of the Indian Act*, 77, 85–6.

49. The concept of the total institution is presented by Erving Goffman in *Asylums: Essays on the Social Situation of Mental Patients and Other Inmates* (Chicago, 1962).

50. LAC, RG 10, vol. 2116, file 22:155, letter to Sir John A. Macdonald from Chief Peter Jones, 11 Feb. 1884; cited by Daugherty, 'The Elective System', 14.

51. Ibid., 81.

52. Ibid., 87.

53. This cry was raised by David Mills, who under Prime Minister Alexander Mackenzie had been Minister of the Interior, 1876–8. *House of Commons Debates*, 1885, vol. 2, 1580: The Franchise Bill, 4 May 1885; cited by Leslie and Maguire, eds, *Historical Development of the Indian Act*, 86.

54. Montgomery, 'The Six Nations Indians and the Macdonald Franchise', 20.

Chapter 12

1. At the same time a similar situation was being experienced in the western Arctic with the whale and walrus populations, and for similar economic reasons. See Bockstoce, *Whales, Ice, and Men*, chs 7, 8. There the similarity ends, as the decimation of the sea mammals did not have side benefits, such as the freeing of land for agricultural settlement.

2. John L. Tobias, 'Indian Reserves in Western Canada: Indian Homelands or Devices for Assimilation', in D.A. Muise, ed., *Approaches to Native History in Canada* (Ottawa, 1977), 89–103.

3. Henry Youle Hind, *Narrative of the Canadian Red River Exploring Expedition of 1857 and of the Assiniboine and Saskatchewan Exploring Expedition of 1858*, 2 vols (Edmonton, 1971), I, 360–1; Milloy, *The Plains Cree*, 107–8.

4. Alexander Johnston, comp., *The Battle at Belly River: Stories of the Last Great Indian Battle* (Lethbridge, Alta, 1966). Belly River became the Oldman in 1890.

5. Sarah Carter, *Lost Harvests: Prairie Indian Reserve Farmers and Government Policy* (Montreal and Kingston, 1990), 36.

6. Morton, *History of Prairie Settlement*, 236–8.

7. P.R. Mailhot and D.M. Sprague, 'Persistent Settlers: The Dispersal and Resettlement of the Red River Metis, 1870–1885', *Canadian Journal of Ethnic Studies* 17 (1985): 1–30.

8. D.W. Moodie and Arthur J. Ray make the point that hunters understood the factors that influenced bison behaviour, so they knew where to look for the herds. See Moodie and Ray, 'Buffalo Migrations in the Canadian Plains', *Plains Anthropologist* 21, 71 (1976): 45–51.

9. Beal and Macleod, *Prairie Fire*, 41. Dumont had become buffalo-hunt captain at the age of 25.

10. Thomas Flanagan has analyzed the situation in detail in *Riel and the Rebellion: 1885 Reconsidered* (Saskatoon, 1983).

11. Some hold that Clarke was an agent provocateur for Macdonald, actively fomenting trouble as a way out of solving financial difficulties that were plaguing the construction of the Canadian Pacific Railway. See Don McLean, *Home from the Hill: A History of the Metis in Western Canada* (Regina, 1987).

12. George Woodcock, *Gabriel Dumont* (Edmonton, 1975), 81–4.

13. In the south, where transportation facilities were better, the buffalo robe trade had been active since the second half of the eighteenth century.

14. Frank Gilbert Roe, *The North American Buffalo* (Toronto, 1970), 467ff.

15. Dempsey, *Big Bear*, 77–8; see also R.S. Allen, 'Big Bear', *Saskatchewan History* 25, 1 (1972): 1–17; William B. Fraser, 'Big Bear, Indian Patriot', *Alberta Historical Review* 14, 2 (1966): 1–13; *DCB*, XI, s.v. 'Mistahimaskwa'.

16. Before contact, there were not the clear distinctions between 'tribes' that were later imposed by Europeans. Thus, even though the Blackfoot and Cree considered each other enemies, Crowfoot saw nothing anomalous in adopting Poundmaker because of his striking resemblance to a son he had lost.

17. *DCB*, XI, s.v. 'Mimiy'.

18. T.J. Brasser, *Blackfoot* (Ottawa, n.d.), 3.

19. Carter, *Lost Harvests*, 30. This carefully documented study imputes the failure of the agricultural programs to government policy rather than to the supposed inability of Amerindians to become farmers.

20. Ibid., 112.

21. Long before the demise of the buffalo herds—in the very early days of the fur trade, in fact—some Amerindians had already successfully taken up farming. Within a century of the establishment of the fur trade, the 'three sisters', corn, beans, and squash, were being grown at their northern limit. This was in response to the needs of the posts for provisioning. See D. Wayne Moodie and Barry Kaye, 'Indian Agriculture in the Fur Trade Northwest', *Prairie Forum* 11, 2 (1986): 171–84; Moodie and Kaye, 'The Northern Limit of Indian Agriculture in North America', *Geographical Review* 59, 4 (1969): 513–29.

22. Cited by Beal and Macleod, *Prairie Fire*, 74.

23. *Report of the Commissioner of the North-West Mounted Police Force, 1884*: Commissioner A.G. Irvine, 8.

24. Macleod, *The NWMP and Law Enforcement*, 29.

25. John L. Tobias, 'The Subjugation of the Plains Cree, 1879–1885', *Canadian Historical Review* 64, 4 (1983): 539; *DCB*, XI, s.v. 'Kapapamahchakwew'.

26. Leslie and Maguire, eds, *Historical Development of the Indian Act*, 81.

27. Beal and Macleod, *Prairie Fire*, 63, 115–16, 120; Isabel Andrews, 'Indian Protest against Starvation: The Yellow Calf Incident of 1884', *Saskatchewan History* 28, 2 (1975): 41–51. Mistawasis was Poundmaker's uncle and was renowned as a hunter.

28. Robert Jefferson, *Fifty Years on the Saskatchewan: Being a history of the Cree in Canadian domestic life and the difficulties which led to the serious agitation and conflict of 1885 in the Battleford locality* (Battleford, Sask., 1929).

29. The Métis Declaration of Rights is reproduced in full in Beal and Macleod, *Prairie Fire*, 136.

30. In the Roman Catholic Church, a novena is a series of devotions made on nine successive days for some special purpose.

31. Pihew-kamihkosit ('Red Pheasant'), whose reserve was also in the region, had died just before the sortie began.

32. A. Blair Stonechild, 'The Indian View of the 1885 Uprising', in J.R. Miller, ed., *Sweet Promises: A Reader on Indian–White Relations in Canada* (Toronto, 1991), 273.

33. A Cree Anglican clergyman's view of the event is that of Dr Edward Ahenakew, 'An Opinion of The Frog Lake Massacre', *Alberta Historical Review* 8, 3 (1966): 9–15. Another Cree view, this time by a descendant of Big Bear, is Joseph F. Dion, *My Tribe the Crees* (Calgary, 1979). Contemporary accounts were compiled and edited by Rudy Wiebe and Bob Beal in *War in the West: Voices of the 1885 Rebellion* (Toronto, 1985). The sensationalized press accounts that contributed to public hysteria at the time are described by Sarah Carter, *Aboriginal People and Colonizers of Western Canada to 1900* (Toronto, 1999), 159ff.

34. Payment, *Batoche*, 61–2. Despite the defeat and subsequent difficulties, Batoche expanded and prospered in later years. Ibid., 136.

35. Stonechild, 'The Indian View of the 1885 Uprising', 259–76. Gabriel Dumont's account of the rebellion was translated by George F.G. Stanley and published in the *Canadian Historical Review* 30, 3 (Sept. 1949): 249–69.

36. *Manitoba Free Press*, 7 Apr. 1885, front page.

37. D.H. Brown, 'The Meaning of Treason in 1885', *Saskatchewan History* 28, 2 (1975): 65–73.

38. Will Jackson (1861–1952), one-time secretary to Riel, was acquitted as insane. The two had parted ways over the question of Aboriginal rights. The other was Tom Scott, the non-Native leader of the English-language Métis.

39. This was the same statute under which eight men had been hanged in Burlington Heights, Ontario, in 1814 for high treason during the War of 1812. See William R. Riddell, *The Ancaster 'Bloody Assize' of 1814* (Toronto, 1923; reprinted from Ontario Historical Society Papers and Records 20 [1922]: 107–25). Wandering Spirit was one of those hanged at North Battleford.

40. The other occasion was described in note 38. In neither case do the consequences compare with those of the Sioux uprising of 1862–3 in the United States. Of 303 Sioux who were condemned to death, 38 were executed at Fort Snelling, Minnesota, the largest mass hanging in American history.

41. Norma Sluman, *Poundmaker* (Toronto, 1967), 270. See also Donald C. Barnett, *Poundmaker* (Don Mills, Ont., 1976).

42. Sandra Estlin Bingaman, 'The Trials of Poundmaker and Big Bear, 1885', *Saskatchewan History* 28 (Autumn 1975): 81–94.

43. Morris, *Treaties of Canada with the Indians*, 294.

44. Flanagan, *Riel and the Rebellion*, viii. See also Flanagan's study of Riel's millennialism, *Louis*

'David' Riel, Prophet of the New World (Toronto, 1979).

45. D.N. Sprague, *Canada and the Metis, 1869–1885* (Waterloo, Ont., 1988), 184.

46. John E. Foster, 'The Plains Metis', in R. Bruce Morrison and C. Roderick Wilson, eds, *Native Peoples: The Canadian Experience*, 3rd edn (Toronto, 2004), 310–11.

Chapter 13

1. Tobias, 'Subjugation of the Plains Cree', 547–8. See also F.L. Barron and James B. Waldram, eds, *1885 and After: Native Society in Transition* (Regina, 1986).

2. Barron, 'Indian Pass System', 28; Sarah A. Carter, 'Controlling Indian Movement: The Pass System', *NeWest Review* (May 1985): 8–9. The system lasted until 1941, but some northern reserves reported that it was still being enforced during the 1960s. Although only 28 reserves were officially designated as disloyal during the disturbances, the system was generally applied in the prairie west.

3. *Annual Report of the North-West Mounted Police, 1895*, app. B, Superintendent W.B. Steele, 45.

4. Coates and Morrison, *Land of the Midnight Sun*, 206–7.

5. Hugh A. Dempsey, *Charcoal's World* (Saskatoon, 1978). Dempsey argues that Charcoal's behaviour was culturally appropriate. On Almighty Voice, see Frank W. Anderson, *Almighty Voice* (Aldergrove, BC, 1971); Carter, *Aboriginal People and Colonizers*, 174–5.

6. Barron, 'Indian Pass System', 39. In 1902, a delegation from South Africa came to study the Canadian pass system as a method of social control.

7. See Sprague, *Canada and the Metis*, 104–5, 124.

8. Payment, *Batoche*, 73–4. See also John Leonard Taylor, 'An Historical Introduction to Métis Claims in Canada', *Canadian Journal of Native Studies* 3, 1 (1983): 151–81.

9. Marcel Giraud, 'The Western Metis after the Insurrection', *Saskatchewan History* 9, 1 (1956): 5.

10. A detailed study of the situation is that of Paul L.A.H. Chartrand, *Manitoba's Métis Settlement Scheme of 1870* (Saskatoon, 1991).

11. Joanne Overvold sees the role of women as being central to the struggle of the Métis to maintain a separate identity. She depicts the Métis of the Northwest Territories in *Our Metis Heritage . . . a portrayal* (n.p., 1976). Her comment on the role of women is on p. 103; see also Sarah Carter, 'First Nations Women of Prairie Canada in the Early Reserve Years, the 1870s to the 1920s: A Preliminary Inquiry', in Christine Miller and Patricia Chuchryk, eds., *Women of the First Nations: Power, Wisdom, and Strength* (Winnipeg, 1996). A personal statement on being Métis is by Dorothy Daniels, 'Metis Identity: A Personal Perspective', *Native Studies Review* 3, 2 (1987): 7–15.

12. Fumoleau, *As Long As This Land Shall Last*, 207–8; Daniel, *History of Native Claims*, 24.

13. A readable contemporary account of the two commissions is Charles Mair, *Through the Mackenzie Basin* (Toronto, 1908).

14. On Treaty Eight, see Chapter 15.

15. Zaslow, *Opening of the Canadian North*, 225–6.

16. Daniel, *History of Native Claims*, 25.

17. Government control over the sale of Amerindian crops was officially described as a 'kindly supervision' to ensure that Amerindians were 'getting a fair deal'. See Ahenakew, *Voices of the Plains Cree*, 147. This book is an eloquent depiction of Plains Cree life before and after contact.

18. Morris, *Treaties of Canada with the Indians*, 315.

19. J.R. Miller, *Shingwauk's Vision: A History of Native Residential Schools* (Toronto, 1996), 98–100. Louie Phillip Adelard Standing Buffalo (Tatanka-Najin, ?–1922) was a hereditary chief of the Dakota for over 50 years and the son of Standing Buffalo (Tatanka-Najin, c. 1820–70), the Dakota Sioux chief who brought his people to Canada to avoid further conflict in the United States. See <www.mendel.ca/henderson/standing-buffalo/>.

20. Federation of Saskatchewan Indians, *Indian Treaty Rights*, undated pamphlet. See also Suzanne Fournier and Ernie Crey, *Stolen from Our Embrace: The Abduction of First Nations Children and the Restoration of Aboriginal Communities* (Vancouver, 1997), 54.

21. Jennifer Lorretta Pettit, 'To Christianize and Civilize', Ph.D. thesis (University of Calgary, 1997), 56.

22. Miller, *Shingwauk's Vision*, 76–80.

23. Smith, *Sacred Feathers*, 160.

24. Minutes of the General Council of Indian Chiefs and Principal Men held at Orillia, Lake Simcoe Narrows, on Thursday, the 30th, and Friday, the 31st, July, 1846, on the proposed removal of the smaller gommunities [sic] and the establishment of manual labour schools (Orillia, Ont., 1846), 20–1. At: <www.canadiana.org>.

25. Cited in Pettit, 'To Christianize and Civilize', 26–7.

26. Ibid., 22.

27. In 1820, West used the opportunity given to him as HBC chaplain to attempt evangelizing and schooling on behalf of the Anglican Church Missionary Society. In his journal, he noted that Saulteaux chief Peguis questioned him very closely but, in the end, did not hand over his children. West, *The Substance of a Journal During a Residence at the Red River Colony, British North America* (London, 1824).

28. Federation of Saskatchewan Indians, *Indian Treaty Rights*. See also Fournier and Crey, *Stolen from Our Embrace*, 56.

29. Handsome Lake's story is told in Kehoe, *The Ghost Dance*, 116–23. The standard work on the prophet is Wallace, *Death and Rebirth of the Seneca*.

30. Pettit, 'To Christianize and Civilize', 25–6.

31. Ibid., 51–2.

32. Ibid., 68.

33. Ibid., 36–40.

34. Two of the most recent studies of residential schools are Miller's *Shingwauk's Vision* and John Sheridan Milloy, *A National Crime: The Canadian Government and the Residential School System* (Winnipeg, 1999). There are many published eyewitness accounts of the industrial and residential schools.

35. N.F. Davin, 'Report on Industrial Schools for Indians and Halfbreeds', 10.

36. Department of Indian Affairs (DIA), *Annual Report, 1883*, CSP (No. 4) 1884, xi; cited in Miller, *Shingwauk's Vision*, 106.

37. Father Albert Lacombe complained that his Blackfoot students were too big and too 'well acquainted with the Indian fashion' to accept in-stitutionalization. He also created controversy by hiring Jean L'Heureux, a local man rumoured to be a pedophile, as a recruiter. When he stepped down in 1885, Father Lacombe left behind a school with only three students. His successor resigned after three years as principal, claiming that only two of 25 graduates had enough education and skill to succeed. DIA, *Annual Report, 1884*, 89; cited in Pettit, 'To Christianize and Civilize', 109. For a description of the Dunbow School, see Raymond J.A. Huel, *Proclaiming the Gospel to the Indians and Métis* (Edmonton, 1996), 128–31. The author claims that the Oblates were aware of the allegations concerning L'Heureux.

38. Success was relative; by Father Hugonnard's statistics, about 20 per cent of students died under his care. Milloy, *National Crime*, 92.

39. Miller, *Shingwauk's Vision*, 350.

40. Huel, *Proclaiming the Gospel*, 151.

41. Cited in Arlene Roberta Greyeyes, 'St. Michael's Indian Residential School, 1894–1926', MA thesis (Carleton University, 1995), 129, 138.

42. For a description of the Lytton, BC, school, see Miller, *Shingwauk's Vision*, 318–9.

43. James Gladstone, 'Indian School Days', *Alberta Historical Review* 15, 1: 24; cited in Pettit, 'To Christianize and Civilize', 147–8.

44. Brass, *I Walk in Two Worlds*, 45.

45. Eleanor Brass, 'The File Hills Ex-Pupil Colony', *Saskatchewan History* 6, 2 (1953): 66. Mrs Brass was the daughter of Fred Dieter, one of the colony's outstanding farmers who was awarded a silver shield. Born and raised in the colony, she reminisces about her life in her autobiography, *I Walk in Two Worlds*. See also E. Brian Titley, *A Narrow Vision: Duncan Campbell Scott and the Administration of Indian Affairs in Canada* (Vancouver, 1986), 18–19; Titley, 'W.M. Graham: Indian Agent Extraordinaire', *Prairie Forum* 1 (1983): 25–41; 'Indian students forced into marriage, farm life', *Globe and Mail*, 10 Dec. 1990.

46. 'Assault, death common at schools, natives say', *Globe and Mail*, 11 Dec. 1990. Complaints about mission-run schools had been voiced at least since the 1940s.

47. Historian Robert Choquette, cited in Pettit, 'To Christianize and Civilize', 17.

48. Greyeyes, 'St. Michael's Indian Residential School', 66.

49. D.J. Hall, 'Clifford Sifton and Canadian Indian Administration 1896–1905', in Getty and Lussier, eds, *As Long As the Sun Shines and Water Flows*, 126.

50. Daugherty, 'The Elective System', 6.

51. The Cowessess band's election problems have been dealt with in detail by Daugherty, 'The Elective System', 28–35.

52. Tobias, 'Protection, Civilization, Assimilation', 21, 24.

53. Ibid., 21.

54. Canada, Indian Affairs, *Report, 1910–11*, 196; cited by Zaslow, *Opening of the Canadian North*, 232–3. From 1909 to 1914, Laird was adviser to Indian Affairs in Ottawa.

55. Robert J. Surtees, 'Indian Land Sessions in Upper Canada, 1815–1830', in Getty and Lussier, eds, *As Long As the Sun Shines and Water Flows*, 66; Peggy Martin-McGuire, *First Nation Land Surrenders on the Prairies, 1896–1911* (Ottawa, 1998), xiii. This is a detailed study of 25 surrenders, prepared for the Indian Claims Commission.

56. Richard H. Bartlett, *Indian Reserves and Aboriginal Lands in Canada: A Homeland* (Saskatoon,

1990), 26. See also Stewart Raby, 'Indian Land Surrenders in Southern Saskatchewan', *Canadian Geographer* 17, 1 (Spring 1973), 36–52; Carter, *Lost Harvests*, 244–9.

57. Martin-McGuire, *First Nation Land Surrenders on the Prairies*, 461–2. See also Hall, 'Clifford Sifton', 120–44.

58. Heading the Commission were Gilbert Malcolm Sproat (1876–9, for the first two years in office, as co-commissioner with Alexander C. Anderson and Archibald McKinley), Peter O'Reilly (1880–98), and A.W. Vowell (1899–1910). By 1892, the Commission was granting reserves that ranged in size from seven to 230 acres (three to 93 hectares) per capita, depending on the region. Complaints from non-Native settlers concerning these amounts led the province to refuse to sanction any more, leading to the dissolution of the Commission in 1910.

59. The delegation of 1906 was led by Chief Joe Capilano of the North Vancouver Squamish and other chiefs. They were listened to politely but did not get any action. See Cumming and Mickenberg, eds, *Native Rights in Canada*, 188.

60. Cumming and Mickenberg, eds, *Native Rights in Canada*, 188–9.

61. Usually called the McKenna-McBride Commission, after J.A.J. McKenna, assistant Amerindian commissioner for the Northwest, 1901–9, and Richard McBride, Premier of BC, 1903–15. McBride did not actually serve on the Commission.

62. Berger, *Fragile Freedoms*, 231. During this time also, commercial fishing licences were not being issued to west coast Indians; in 1923 they were allowed to apply for them. See E.E. Laviolette, *The Struggle for Survival* (Toronto, 1973), 138.

63. These were described by Lloyd Barber as 'prime development land'. Barber, 'The Implications of Indian Claims for Canada', address given at the Banff School of Advanced Management, Banff, Alberta, 9 Mar. 1978.

64. Reuben Ware, *The Lands We Lost: A History of Cut-Off Lands and Land Losses from Indian Reserves in British Columbia* (Vancouver, 1974), 1; Kew, 'History of Coastal British Columbia Since 1849', 160. The land issue became a factor in the saga of British Columbia's most famous outlaw, Peter Simon Gunanoot (*c.* 1874–1933), who eluded police for 13 years, from 1906 to 1919. Gunanoot ('Little Bear that Walks up a Tree'), a prosperous Gitksan trapper and storekeeper of Hazelton (Gitenmaks), BC, upon being wanted for murder, took to the woods with his family. Their success in evading capture was at least partly due to the complicity of the Amerindians of the region, who were agitating for an extension of their reserve and for payment for lands occupied by non-Aboriginals. Gunanoot eventually voluntarily surrendered, was tried, and acquitted. David R. Williams, *Simon Peter Gunanoot: Trapper Outlaw* (Victoria, 1982); Thomas P. Kelley, *Run Indian Run* (Markham, Ont., 1972).

65. The text of the Commission's report is reproduced in Ware, *Lands We Lost*, 179–98, along with the texts of the Commission's 98 interim reports proposing land alienations for a variety of reasons, pp. 114–77. A study that takes a sympathetic view of British Columbia's position on the land question is Cail, *Land, Man, and the Law*, chs 11–13.

66. The story of the political adaptation of British Columbia Indians to non-Native pressures and the development of Native organizations in the province is told by Paul Tennant, 'Native Political Organization in British Columbia, 1900–1960: A Response to Internal Colonialism', *B.C. Studies* 55 (1982): 3–49. The Allied Tribes lasted until 1927; its battles would be picked up by the Native Indian Brotherhood in 1931.

67. Daniel, *History of Native Claims*, 50–2. See also Wilson Duff, *The Indian History of British Columbia*, vol. 1, *The Impact of the White Man* (Victoria, 1964), 69–70; Cail, *Land, Man, and the Law*, 243.

68. James S. Frideres, *Native Peoples in Canada: Contemporary Conflicts* (Scarborough, Ont., 1983), 233–66; Leslie and Maguire, eds, *Historical Development of the Indian Act*, 120. Anthropologist Peter Kulchyski thinks that the measure may have contributed to the breakup of the Allied Tribes of BC in 1927. Kulchyski, 'Headwaters: A new history', *The Press Independent* 21, 27 (12 July 1991): 5.

69. 'South Edmonton claimed by Pahpahstayo First Nation', *Windspeaker* 14, 14 (1996): 8; 'Papapschase wants to re-establish land base', ibid. 12, 14 (1994): 5; 'Indians lured into giving up rich lands', *Edmonton Journal*, 2 Apr. 1983.

70. Hugh A. Dempsey, *The Gentle Persuader* (Saskatoon, 1986), 50–2.

71. Ibid., 49. Similarly, the Inuit, even those in remote communities, raised money for famine relief for Ethiopia in 1984. See 'Northern Generosity Snowballs', *Globe and Mail*, 29 Nov. 1984. See also Fred Gaffen, *Forgotten Soldiers* (Penticton, BC, 1985); Terry Lusty, *Metis, Social-Political Movement* (Calgary, 1973); Gaffen, *Native Soldiers, Foreign Battlefields* (Ottawa, 1993), 9–11.

72. Cited by James Dempsey, 'Problems of Western Canadian Indian War Veterans', *Native Studies Review* 5, 2 (1989): 5, 6. See also James St G. Walker, 'Race and Recruitment in World War I: Enlistment of Visible Minorities in the Canadian Expeditionary Force', *Canadian Historical Review* 70, 1 (1989): 5.

73. Peter S. Schmaltz, *The Ojibwa of Southern Ontario* (Toronto, 1991), 233–4; Gaffen, *Forgotten Soldiers*, 70–2.

74. An example is the Walpole Island dispute, in which a framework agreement was finally reached in 1989. David T. McNab, 'Exchanging Time and the Ojibwa: An Exploration of the Notions of Time and Territoriality', paper presented to the American Ethnohistory Society, Toronto, 1990.

75. Peter McFarlane, *Brotherhood to Nationhood: George Manuel and the Making of the Modern Indian Movement* (Toronto, 1993).

76. Peter Kulchyski, '"A Considerable Unrest": F.O. Loft and the League of Indians', *Native Studies Review* 4, 1–2 (1988): 95–113; Stan Cuthand, 'The Native Peoples of the Prairie Provinces in the 1920's and 1930's', in Ian A.L. Getty and Donald B. Smith, eds, *One Century Later: Western Canadian Reserve Indians Since Treaty 7* (Vancouver, 1978), 31–5; Titley, *A Narrow Vision*, 102–9; Zaslow, *Northward Expansion*, 165–6.

77. See Sarah Carter, '"We Must Farm To Enable Us To Live": The Plains Cree and Agriculture to 1900', in R. Bruce Morrison and C. Roderick Wilson, eds, *Native Peoples: The Canadian Experience*, 3rd edn (Toronto, 2004), 320–40; J.R. Miller, *Skyscrapers Hide the Heavens: A History of Indian–White Relations in Canada*, rev. edn (Toronto, 1989), 217; Kulchyski, '"A Considerable Unrest"'.

Chapter 14

1. Michael Asch, *Kinship and the Drum Dance in a Northern Dene Community* (Edmonton, 1988), 89–97.

2. Ira Jacknis, *The Storage Box of Tradition: Kwakiutl Art, Anthropologists, and Museums, 1881–1981* (Washington, 2002).

3. Titley, *A Narrow Vision*, 50.

4. Harper, 'Canada's Indian Administration', 127.

5. Leslie and Maguire, eds, *Historical Development of the Indian Act*, 191.

6. A documentary novel vividly portraying the incomprehension and frustration of Euro-Canadians who very much want to help Amerindians, but who think they can do it by telling them what to do, is Alan Fry, *How a People Die* (Toronto, 1970).

The view that the administration was really concerned with non-Aboriginal goals and not with those of Amerindians is expressed by Shelagh D. Grant in 'Indian Affairs under Duncan Campbell Scott: The Plains Cree of Saskatchewan, 1913–1931', *Journal of Canadian Studies* 18, 3 (1983): 21–39.

7. Brownlie, *A Fatherly Eye*, 57. Pegahmagabow's military career is described in Gaffen, *Forgotten Soldiers*.

8. Canada, *Annual Report of Indian Affairs Branch, 1937*.

9. To combat overtrapping, in the 1920s British Columbia introduced registered traplines. The program initially hurt Amerindians, as it interfered with traditional allocations of territory, but in the long term made it possible to maintain the trapping way of life. Registration was introduced in 1940 in Manitoba, and six years later in Saskatchewan. At the end of the century, it was in general use throughout the North and in the Arctic. Oblate Archives, St Albert, Alberta, Fort Good Hope file #1, vol. 5: 28. See also Martha McCarthy, *From the Great River to the Ends of the Earth: Oblate Missions to the Dene, 1847–1921* (Edmonton, 1995).

10. For an example of this policy, see Kenneth S. Coates, 'Best Left as Indians: The Federal Government and the Indians of the Yukon, 1894–1950', *Canadian Journal of Native Studies* 4, 2 (1984): 179–204.

11. One estimate places the total number of deaths among students in all residential schools in Canada at 50,000. See the letter of Rev. Kevin D. Annett, Ganges, BC, in the *Guardian Weekly*, 6–12 July 2000, 13.

12. Titley, *A Narrow Vision*, 82–7.

13. *The fifth estate*, CBC-TV, 8 Jan. 1991.

14. Fournier and Crey, *Stolen from Our Embrace*, 50, 61. According to *Windspeaker* (May 1998) in a special section entitled 'Classroom Edition', 4, the number of residential schools peaked at 88. Geoffrey York writes about some of these schools in *The Dispossessed: Life and Death in Native Canada* (London, 1990).

15. Titley, *A Narrow Vision*, 91, 93.

16. *Report of the RCAP*, I, 388–9 n15.

17. Jean Barman, Yvonne Hébert, and Don McCaskill, 'The Legacy of the Past: An Overview', in Barman et al., eds, *Indian Education in Canada*, I, 7.

18. Cited ibid., 9.

19. Norma Sluman and Jean Goodwill, *John Tootoosis* (Ottawa, 1982), 109; cited ibid., 11. On residential schools in British Columbia, see Celia

Haig-Brown, *Resistance and Renewal: Surviving the Indian Residential School* (Vancouver, 1988).

20. Coates and Morrison, *Land of the Midnight Sun*, 141–2; Shelagh D. Grant, *Sovereignty or Security? Government Policy in the Canadian North, 1936–1950* (Vancouver, 1988), 33–4 n37.

21. Barman, Hébert, and McCaskill, 'Legacy of the Past', 13. See also Assembly of First Nations, *Breaking the Silence: An Interpretive Study of Residential School Impact and Healing* (Ottawa, 1994).

22. Fournier and Crey, *Stolen from Our Embrace*, 81–114; Jason Clayworth, '"Stolen" native wants family, culture back', *Ottawa Citizen*, 10 Oct. 2000 (reprint from *Des Moines Register*); Brad Evenson, 'Native adoption policy—a Canadian tragedy', *Edmonton Journal*, 19 Apr. 1999; 'Indian boy returned to adoptive kin in U.S.', *The Gazette*, Montreal, 21 Mar. 1999.

23. Catherine Ford, 'Apology does not mean instant forgiveness', *Calgary Herald*, 9 Sept. 2000, O7; CBC News, 'Indian residential schools', 16 May 2008, at: <www.cbc.ca/canada/story/2008/05/16/f-faqs-residential-schools.html>.

24. Richard Foot, 'Feds responsible for native school abuse', *Calgary Herald*, 12 Dec. 2003, A17.

25. Cristin Schmitz, with Richard Foot, 'Billions for Natives: Talks to Compensate Residential School Students Start at $4-billion', *National Post*, 31 May 2005, A1.

26. James Miller and Edmund Danziger, Jr, '"In the Care of Strangers": Walpole Island First Nation's Experiences with Residential Schools after the First World War', *Ontario History* 92, 1 (Spring 2000): 71–88. See also Janet Steffenhagen, 'Minister traces activism to residential school', *Vancouver Sun*, 3 Nov. 2000, A12. Another such graduate, although from a different school, is Matthew Coon Come, National Chief of the Assembly of First Nations, 2000–3. For a profile on Coon Come, see Graham Fraser, 'Chief hunter', *Toronto Star*, 16 Dec. 2000, J1, J4.

27. The story of the Amerindian takeover of the school is told by Diane Persson, 'The Changing Experience of Indian Residential Schooling: Blue Quills, 1931–1970', in Barman et al., eds, *Indian Education in Canada*, I, 150–67.

28. Howard Adams, *Prison of Grass: Canada from the Native Point of View* (Toronto, 1975), 213–14.

29. 'A lesson in misery: Canadian Indians look back in anger at residential school days', *Globe and Mail*, 2 Dec. 1989. This is an excerpt from York's *The Dispossessed*.

30. Information on First Nations schooling is available at the Indian and Northern Affairs Canada website: <www.ainc-inac.gc.ca/>. An early example of indigenous curriculum development was the Cree Way Project of Rupert House during the 1970s. See Richard Preston, 'The Cree Way Project: an experiment in grass-roots curriculum development', in William Cowan, ed., *Papers of the Tenth Algonquian Conference* (Ottawa, 1979), 92–101.

31. See, for example, 'Sweet success for native school', *Edmonton Journal*, 1 Oct. 1990; 'Bias absent in all-native school', ibid., 25 Nov. 1989.

32. Leslie, *Historical Survey of Indian-Government Relations*, 3–4.

33. Years later the lot of Amerindian war veterans was still giving rise to complaints and investigations. See, for example, 'Indian war veterans mistreated: report', *Globe and Mail*, 7 June 1984. The joint committee, during its three years of existence, heard 122 witnesses and studied 411 written briefs. Zaslow, *Northward Expansion*, 298. Particularly irritating was the practice of awarding the traplines of registered Indians to non-Aboriginal veterans.

34. There were exceptions. For one, in 1920, Indian spokespersons had been invited to attend House of Commons hearings on amendments to the Indian Act that proposed compulsory enfranchisement. In spite of their opposition, however, the bill was passed.

35. *Indian Conditions: A Survey* (Ottawa, 1980), 84.

36. Alice B. Kehoe, 'The Giveaway Ceremony of Blackfoot and Plains Cree', *Plains Anthropologist* 25, 87 (1980): 17–26.

37. E. Palmer Patterson II, *The Canadian Indian: A History Since 1500* (Toronto, 1972), 171–2.

38. A detailed history of the National Indian Brotherhood and analysis of its operations is in Ponting and Gibbins, *Out of Irrelevance*, 195–279.

39. Little of this is reflected in the pamphlet, *Indians of Canada Pavilion*, given to visitors, although it presented a spectrum of Amerindian views. Its general approach is expressed in the statement: 'I see an Indian, tall and strong in the pride of his heritage. He stands with your sons, a man among men.' Such romanticism was more effective in literature than in politics.

40. H.B. Hawthorn, *A Survey of the Contemporary Indians of Canada: Economic, Political, Educational Needs and Policies*, 2 vols (Ottawa, 1966–7), I, 6.

41. A seminal article on historians' approach to Amerindians is James W. St G. Walker, 'The Canadian Indian in Historical Writing', Canadian Historical Association, *Historical Papers*

(1971): 21–51. A follow-up report, also by Walker, 'The Indian in Canadian Historical Writing, 1971–1981', appeared in Getty and Lussier, eds, *As Long As the Sun Shines and Water Flows*, 340–57.

42. The social dislocations that have resulted from these shifts in values and circumstances were the subject of a special report, 'A Canadian Tragedy', *Maclean's* 99, 28 (14 July 1986): 12–25.

43. Hawthorn, *A Survey of Contemporary Indians*, I, 13.

44. R.W. Dunning, 'Indian Policy—a proposal for autonomy', *Canadian Forum* 49 (Dec. 1969): 206–7. A detailed analysis of the birth of the White Paper is Sally Weaver, *Making Canadian Indian Policy: The Hidden Agenda 1968–1970* (Toronto, 1981).

45. *Statement of the Government of Canada on Indian Policy, 1969*, 3. See also Bradford W. Morse, 'The Resolution of Land Claims', in Morse, ed., *Aboriginal Peoples and the Law*, 618–21.

46. 'Statement of National Indian Brotherhood', in *Recent Statements by the Indians of Canada*, Anglican Church of Canada General Synod Action 1969, Bulletin 201, 1970, 28.

47. Cited by Weaver, *Making Canadian Indian Policy*, 174. See also Marie Smallface Marule, 'The Canadian Government's Termination Policy: From 1969 to the Present Day', in Getty and Smith, eds, *One Century Later*, 103–16.

48. 'Wuttunee Termed "Traitorous", Barred from his Home Reserve', *Globe and Mail*, 4 May 1970. William I.C. Wuttunee, *Ruffled Feathers* (Calgary, 1971), 136–41.

49. Alpheus Henry Snow, *The Question of Aborigines in the Law and Practice of Nations* (Washington, 1919), 7.

50. A circular published by the Society for Converting and Civilizing the Indians of Upper Canada, 20 Oct. 1830, read, in part: '. . . it must be a matter of deep concern to reflect that there exist in this Province a very great number of Aborigines in this Country, the original possessors of the soil on which we are now living, and enjoying the blessings of civilized life, to whom the glad tidings of Salvation, as published in the gospel of Jesus Christ, are still altogether unknown.' (Metropolitan Toronto Reference Library, History, H-1830.)

51. The text of *Citizens Plus* was reproduced in *The First Citizen* 7 (June 1970). Other Amerindian responses appear ibid. 8 (July 1970). See also Menno Boldt, *Surviving as Indians* (Toronto, 1993), 46, 66.

52. Traditionally, horns (deer antlers, buffalo horns) were considered to be instruments of power

and were worn by shamans and leaders. The 'Dehorners' opposed the traditional power structure.

53. This section owes a special debt to Titley, *A Narrow Vision*, 110–34; Joëlle Rostkowski, 'The Redman's Appeal for Justice: Deskaheh and the League of Nations', in Feest, ed., *Indians and Europe*, 435–53; Ann Charney, 'The Last Indian War', *The Idler* 29 (July–Aug. 1990): 14–22.

54. Gerald R. Alfred, *Heeding the Voices of Our Ancestors: Kahnawake Mohawk Politics and the Rise of Native Nationalism* (Toronto, 1995), 58–60.

55. Tehariolina, *La nation huronne*, 317–18.

56. The original grant to the seigneury of Sault St Louis was for 44,000 acres (17,806 hectares); Kahnawake today comprises 13,000 acres (5,261 hectares).

57. C.P. Stacey, 'Canada and the Nile Expedition of 1884–1885', *Canadian Historical Review* 33 (1952): 319–40; Louis Jackson, *Our Caughnawagas in Egypt* (Montreal, 1885). Jackson, leader of the Caughnawaga (Kahnawake) canoemen, recounts the adventures of the Iroquois as non-combatants in the expeditionary force. A brief excerpt is reproduced in Penny Petrone, ed., *First People, First Voices* (Toronto, 1983), 136–8.

58. Morantz, 'Aboriginal Land Claims in Quebec', 105.

59. Charney, 'The Last Indian War', 14, 17.

60. Ibid., 16. In 1996, the Peacekeepers came fully under the Quebec Police Act.

61. The Iroquoian term that translates into English as 'warrior' is more nearly equivalent to 'young man'. The meaning of the term and the role of the Warriors in Iroquois society are discussed in *Akwesasne Notes* 22, 4 (1990): 6. The Mohawk *Akwesasne Notes*, which began publication in 1969, is published in the New York section of St Regis Reserve. The 'ideological father' of the current Warrior movement was Louis Hall of Kahnawake (1916–93).

62. Because of an Indian Act provision that no taxes be paid on goods owned or used by Amerindians on Amerindian land, cigarettes can be sold more cheaply on reserves than elsewhere. The cigarette trade has become an important source of revenue for some reserves, particularly those near the international border. See Charney, 'The Last Indian War', 17–18.

63. Ibid., 14.

64. '"Armed, violent" poster stuns fugitive Mohawks', *Edmonton Journal*, 20 Oct. 1988.

65. 'Police call Mohawks "terrorists" in national ad', *Edmonton Journal*, 19 Sept. 1990. The

advertisement, headed 'We Oppose Terrorism', ran that same day in newspapers across Canada. The role of the Warriors in the 1990 standoff is discussed in *Akwesasne Notes* 22, 4 (1990): 8.

66. Statistics for First Nations in Canada are available at: <www12.statcan.ca/english/ census01/home/ index.cfm> and <www.firststats.ca/>.

67. See Maria Campbell's classic *Halfbreed* (Toronto, 1973).

68. Their story is told by Murray Dobbin, *The One-and-a-Half Men* (Vancouver, 1981). Both Norris and Brady were veterans of World War II, Norris having served in the RCAF and Brady with the Royal Canadian Artillery. Dr Adam Cuthand, who had seen service with the Canadian army, became the founding president of the Manitoba Metis Federation in 1968.

69. *Report of the RCAP*, IV, 203.

70. Ibid., 209, 258.

71. Donald Purich, *The Metis* (Toronto, 1968), 144. Sources for this section are Judith Hill, 'The Ewing Commission, 1935: A Case Study of Metis Government Relations', MA thesis (University of Alberta, 1977); Metis Association of Alberta et al., *Metis Land Rights in Alberta: A Political History* (Edmonton, 1981); Dan Smith, *The Seventh Fire* (Toronto, 1993).

72. Nicks, 'Mary Anne's Dilemma', 110.

73. Purich, *The Metis*, 148–9.

74. For a discussion of the Métis and Aboriginal right, see *Metisism: A Canadian Identity* (Edmonton, 1982).

75. 'Pact makes history: "It's our land," Metis say as Getty signs', *Edmonton Journal*, 2 July 1989, 1.

76. Marie Burke, 'Métis sign provincial agreement', *Alberta Sweetgrass* 6, 4 (May 1999): 3; 'Deal allows Alberta Metis to create justice programs', *Edmonton Journal*, 9 Nov. 1999.

77. The best known of the cases contesting Amerindian women's loss of status when they married non-Amerindians was that of *Attorney General of Canada v. Lavell* (1974). Jeannette Lavell, an Ojibwa, fought the issue all the way to the Supreme Court of Canada, where the decision finally went against her, as well as against Yvonne Bedard in a companion case that was heard at the same time. See Jamieson, *Indian Women and the Law*, 79–88; Janet Silman, *Enough Is Enough* (Toronto, 1994), 13–14; Pauline Comeau and Aldo Santin, *The First Canadians* (Toronto, 1990), 32–3.

78. For the criticism that Bill C-31 has substituted one form of inequality for another, see the report prepared for the Assembly of First Nations by Stewart Clatworthy and Anthony H. Smith, 'Population Implications of the 1985 Amendment to the Indian Act', 1992. Incidentally, the 1999 court decision in *Corbière v. Canada* allowing off-reserve band members to vote in band elections has particularly affected reinstated Indian women, as many of them live off-reserve. The bands were given until 20 November 2000 to implement the decision; a request by the Assembly of First Nations and treaty chiefs across the nation that they be allowed more time was turned down by the Supreme Court. The first band council election under the new regulations was held by the Ojibwa reserve in Manitoba called 'Ebb and Flow'. Thomas Isaac, *Aboriginal Law Cases, Materials, and Commentary* (Saskatoon, 1995), 429–30; 'Supreme Court dismisses delay in off-reserve voting', *Ottawa Citizen*, 4 Nov. 2000.

79. Bill Tremblay, 'Status or non-status—that is the cultural question', *Wawatay News* 24, 22 (6 Nov. 1997): 4.

80. *Report of the RCAP*, IV, 46–7.

Chapter 15

1. Morrison, *Under the Flag*, 32–4; Coates and Morrison, *Land of the Midnight Sun*, 43–7; Morton, *History of the Canadian West*, 708–9. Concerning whalers as traders, see Bockstoce, *Whales, Ice, and Men*, 192–4.

2. Interview with Felix Gibot recorded by Richard Lightning, Treaty and Aboriginal Rights Research of the Indian Association of Alberta, 5 Feb. 1974, in Richard Price, ed., *The Spirit of the Alberta Indian Treaties* (Edmonton, 1987), 157.

3. *Report of the North-West Mounted Police 1898*, Part II, Patrol Report, Fort Saskatchewan to Fort Simpson, inspector W.H. Routledge, 96.

4. A fine study of the relationship between the northern Cree and the animals upon which they depend is by Robert Brightman, *Grateful Prey* (Berkeley, 1993).

5. Kerry Abel, '"Matters are growing worse": Government and Mackenzie Missions, 1870–1921', in Coates and Morrison, eds, *For Purposes of Dominion*, 75. The Yukon's first Indian residential school was established at Carcross in 1901 by Anglican bishop W.C. Bompas.

6. Department of Indian Affairs, vol. 1115, Deputy Superintendent's Letterbook, Hayter Reed to Charles Constantine, commander of the first Yukon police contingent, 29 May 1894; cited by Coates, 'Best Left as Indians', 181.

7. For example, John Tetso, *Trapping Is My Life* (Toronto, 1970); Maxwell Paupanekis, 'The Trapper', in Malvina Bolus, ed., *People and Pelts* (Winnipeg, 1972), 137–43. See also Hugh Brody, *The People's Land: Eskimos and Whites in the Eastern Arctic* (Harmondsworth, 1975).

8. Coates and Morrison, *Land of the Midnight Sun*, 112–13.

9. Richard Diubaldo, *The Government of Canada and the Inuit, 1900–1967* (Ottawa, 1985), 13–14.

10. Morrison, *Under the Flag*, 45–6.

11. A film, Barry Greenwald's *Between Two Worlds*, tells the story of Joseph Idlout of Pond Inlet and Resolute Bay, a leading hunter who embraced the Euro-Canadian way. He was successful enough that he and his family were the subject of a National Film Board classic, *Land of the Long Day*, directed by Doug Wilkinson in 1951; the family also adorned the back of the Canadian $2 bill. Idlout ended up as a barfly, surviving on handout jobs. On 2 June 1968 he died in an accident. The happier story of another hunter who made the same transition is I, Nuligak, ed. and tr. Maurice Metayer (Toronto, 1966).

12. Gurston Dacks, *A Choice of Futures: Politics in the Canadian North* (Toronto, 1981), 90; David R. Morrison, *The Politics of the Yukon Territory, 1898–1909* (Toronto, 1968), ch. 3.

13. McClellan, *Part of the Land*, 43. Diamond Jenness says that by 1930 not more than a dozen—if that—could claim descent from the western Arctic's original inhabitants. (*Eskimo Administration*, 14.)

14. McMillan, *Native Peoples and Cultures of Canada*, 246.

15. Jenness, *Eskimo Administration*, 11 and n1. According to one report, four children survived. However, even after the arrival of the NWMP, self-help was still the rule in the North. In the eastern Arctic in the 1860s an Inuk shaman, Qitdlarssuaq (d. 1875), led a four-year trek to find isolated Polar Inuit in need of help. Father Guy Mary-Rousseliere, *Qitdlarssuaq: The Story of a Polar Migration* (Winnipeg, 1991).

16. Mair, *Through the Mackenzie Basin*, 60. The speech has also been attributed to Wahpeehayo ('White Partridge'), who was also in attendance.

17. Jenness was strong on this point, and highly critical of Canada's performance. *Eskimo Administration*, 17.

18. Julie Cruikshank and Jim Robb, *Their Own Yukon* (Whitehorse, 1975), 2.

19. Their sudden wealth did not make life better for Skookum Jim Mason or Dawson Charlie, Kate's brothers. The latter fell off a bridge in 1908 and was drowned; Skookum Jim retired to his home grounds at Carcross, where he died in 1916. Kate Carmack was abandoned by her husband, who went to California and remarried; Kate stayed at Carcross, where she became something of a tourist attraction. See Zaslow, *Opening of the Canadian North*, 145. The oral history related to the gold rush and its discoverers has been published in Cruikshank, *Reading Voices*.

20. H.A. Innis, 'Settlement and the Mining Frontier', in W.A. Mackintosh and W.L.G. Joerg, eds, *Canadian Frontiers of Settlement*, IX, Part II (Toronto, 1936), 183.

21. *Report of the Commissioner of the North-West Mounted Police*, Northern Patrol 1897, 170. The observation was made in connection with the custom of non-Native trappers to use poison bait.

22. For some recollections of what happened on the Klondike River, see Cruikshank and Robb, *Their Own Yukon*, 13–15.

23. Fumoleau, *As Long As This Land Shall Last*, 58; Richard C. Daniel, 'Spirit and Terms of Treaty Eight', in Price, ed., *Spirit of the Alberta Indian Treaties*, 63. The story of the 'lost patrol', 1910–11, when four policemen died, is one of the many reminders of the dangers of overconfidence in the North. The patrol, headed by Inspector F.J. Fitzgerald, was to go from Dawson to Fort McPherson; Fitzgerald not only did not take along a Native guide, he had refused help when it had been offered. The story has been the subject of a CBC television drama. See Dick North, *The Lost Patrol* (Vancouver, 1995).

24. The problem as it applied in the North in general is touched upon by Ray, *Canadian Fur Trade and the Industrial Age*, 197–221.

25. Fumoleau, *As Long As This Land Shall Last*, 47. See also J.G. MacGregor, *The Klondike Rush Through Edmonton 1897–1898* (Toronto, 1970).

26. Mair, *Through the Mackenzie Basin*, 23–4.

27. Daniel, 'Spirit and Terms of Treaty Eight', 58.

28. Fumoleau, *As Long As This Land Shall Last*, 51.

29. Official report of Treaty Eight Commission, 1899, in Fumoleau, *As Long As This Land Shall Last*, 84. The account that follows is drawn from this report.

30. Ibid., 74, citing a sworn affidavit by James K. Cornwall ('Peace River Jim'), 1937, on his recollections of the treaty negotiations. Cornwall was involved in transportation projects.

31. Ibid., 86.

32. Mair, *Through the Mackenzie Basin*, 63.

33. Price, ed., *Spirit of Alberta Indian Treaties*, 106.

34. Daniel, 'Spirit and Terms of Treaty Eight', 82.

35. Interview with Felix Gibot in Price, ed., *Spirit of Alberta Indian Treaties*, 159.
36. Fumoleau, *As Long As This Land Shall Last*, 192–6.
37. John S. Long, '"No Basis for Argument"? The Signing of Treaty Nine in Northern Ontario, 1905–1906', *Native Studies Review* 5, 2 (1989): 26.
38. Fumoleau, *As Long As This Land Shall Last*, 142.
39. Jenness, *Eskimo Administration*, 23. See also Ray, *Canadian Fur Trade in the Industrial Age*; Zaslow, *Northward Expansion*.
40. Abel, Drum Songs, 205–6; Zaslow, *Northward Expansion*, 177–81.
41. Abel, '"Matters are growing worse"', 82. A typescript copy, dated 5 June 1938, of Breynat's memorandum denouncing government treatment of Indians is in the Alberta Provincial Archives, 17.220, item 994, box 25. A marginal note says the memorandum was published in the *Toronto Star* towards the end of June and in *Le Soleil* (Quebec), 3 July 1938.
42. McClellan, *Part of the Land*, 90.
43. On some of the problems of the trapping life today, see James W. VanStone, 'Changing Patterns of Indian Trapping in the Canadian Subarctic', in William C. Wonders, ed., *Canada's Changing North* (Toronto, 1976), 170–86.
44. R.G. Moyles, *British Law and Arctic Men* (Saskatoon, 1979); Gaston Carrière, *Dictionnaire biographique* (Ottawa, 1979), VIII, 141.
45. For details of this and other cases about the same time, see Diubaldo, *Government of Canada and the Inuit*, 15–17. A detailed study of the first murder trial in the Arctic, in 1917, in which the two Inuit charged were found guilty but granted clemency, is Moyles, *British Law and Arctic Men*.
46. *The Inuit Way: A Guide to Inuit Culture* (Ottawa, [1990]), 6. A less idealized version, as practised by the Copper Inuit, is described by Diamond Jenness, *Report of the Canadian Arctic Expedition 1913–18*, vol. 12: *The Life of the Copper Eskimos* (Ottawa, 1922), 94–6. Oddly enough, the pregold rush mining communities in the Yukon developed a system of justice that had certain resemblances to that of the Inuit. Not only was the offence itself judged, but also the character of the accused and what he was likely to do in the future. This was called 'forward-looking justice'. Coates and Morrison, *Land of the Midnight Sun*, 60–1; see also Penny Petrone, ed., *Northern Voices: Inuit Writing in English* (Toronto, 1988); Peter Pitseolak and Dorothy Harley Eber, *People from Our Side*, tr. Ann Hanson (Montreal and Kingston, 1993).
47. Leslie and Maguire, eds, *Historical Development of the Indian Act*, 119.
48. Jenness, *Eskimo Adminstration*, ch. 2.
49. The letters are reproduced in Diubaldo, *Government of Canada and the Inuit*, 46–7. The practice of classifying 'Esquimaux' as Amerindian endured until well into the twentieth century. See, for example, the 1934 edition of *Webster's International Dictionary* (cited ibid., 45).
50. Louis-Edmond Hamelin, *Canadian Nordicity: It's Your North Too*, tr. W. Barr (Montreal, 1979), ch. 6.
51. The fuss over the legal status of Inuit is examined by Frank James Tester and Peter Kulchyski in *Tammarniit (Mistakes)* (Vancouver, 1994), 13–42.
52. C.S. Mackinnon, 'The 1958 Government Policy Reversal in Keewatin', in Coates and Morrison, eds, *For Purposes of Dominion*, 161.
53. Diubaldo, *Government of Canada and the Inuit*, 57.
54. Diubaldo, *Government of Canada and the Inuit*, 74. See also R.M. Hill, 'Reindeer Resource in the Mackenzie Delta—1968', in Wonders, ed., *Canada's Changing North*, 225–9.
55. Zaslow, *Northward Expansion*, 145.
56. Mackinnon, 'The 1958 Government Policy Reversal', 162.
57. Ibid., 145–6.
58. Jenness, *Eskimo Administration*, 9.
59. Diubaldo, *Government of Canada and the Inuit*, 118.
60. Jenness, *Eskimo Administration*, 59–64; Zaslow, *Northward Expansion*, 168–73. See also E. Lyall, *An Arctic Man* (Edmonton, 1979).
61. Diubaldo, *Government of Canada and the Inuit*, 118–30; Mackinnon, 'The 1958 Government Policy Reversal', 166–7. One observer likened the northern service officers who were placed in charge of these villages to the agents on Amerindian reserves.
62. Robert G. Williamson, *Eskimo Underground: Socio-Cultural Change in the Canadian Central Arctic* (Uppsala, 1974), 82. See also David E. Young, ed., *Health Care Issues in the Canadian North* (Edmonton, 1988); P.G. Nixon, 'Early Administrative Developments in Fighting Tuberculosis among Canadian Inuit: Bringing State Institutions Back In', *Northern Review* 2 (1988): 67. Widespread adoption of the foods, clothing, and housing of non-Natives has been seen as injurious to Native health. Zaslow, *Northward Expansion*, 153.
63. Gordon Robertson, *Memoirs of a Very Civil Servant* (Toronto, 2000); cited by Andrew Duffy and Paul Gessell, 'Retired Trudeau "chose to destroy"', *Ottawa Citizen*, 8 Oct. 2000, A2.

64. 'Decades later, Inuit far from home', *Toronto Star*, 27 Dec. 1988; 'Lost Inuk's family found, N.W.T. brings him home', *Edmonton Journal*, 5 Jan. 1989; 'Families still search for Inuit sent south in '40s and '50s', ibid., 23 Jan. 1989; 'Inuit unlock mystery of 1950s epidemic', ibid., 23 Jan. 1989.

65. The Inuit relocations of 1939–63 are studied by Tester and Kulchyski, *Tammarniit*. See also *Report of the RCAP*, I, 411ff., and the three-volume interim report issued in 1994 under the general title, *The High Arctic Relocation*. See also, for example, Ila Bussidor and Üstün Bilgen-Reinart, *Night Spirits: The Story of the Relocation of the Sayisi Dene* (Winnipeg, 1997); 'No apology from the federal government to uprooted Inuit', *Edmonton Journal*, 20 Nov. 1990.

66. Keith Watt, 'Uneasy Partners', *The Globe and Mail Report on Business Magazine* (Sept. 1990): 46–7; 'Inuit, gov't strike land deal' and 'Inuit dream carries high price tag', *Edmonton Journal*, 17 Dec. 1991.

67. The pros and cons of the Nunavut proposal are discussed in John Merritt et al., *Nunavut Political Choices and Manifest Destiny* (Ottawa, 1989).

68. 'N.W.T. residents narrowly approve Nunavut', *The Gazette*, Montreal, 5 May 1992; 'Accord signed to create Nunavut by '99', *Edmonton Journal*, 31 Oct. 1992. See also E. Quinn Duffy, *The Road to Nunavut: The Progress of the Eastern Arctic Inuit since the Second World War* (Montreal and Kingston, 1988); John David Hamilton, *Arctic Revolution* (Toronto, 1994).

69. *Report of the RCAP*, II, part 1, 149.

70. Relations between the Inuit and the RCMP had been strained ever since the latter's campaign in the 1950s and 1960s to kill Inuit sled dogs on the grounds that they spread diseases and were a danger to the communities. The Inuit considered the dogs an important part of their lifestyle. The RCMP later changed its tactics and apologized to the Natives. In 1998 the dispute boiled over again when dogs killed a six-year-old girl in Iqaluit. This time a compromise was worked out, with the dogs being banned from certain areas. Janice Tibbetts, 'When Mounties shot down sled dogs', *Ottawa Citizen*, 30 Mar. 1999; Adrian Humphries, 'New compromise may save Iqaluit's dog sled tradition', *National Post*, 25 Jan. 2001, A2.

71. Rob Weber, 'New government, old problem: Shivering in Nunavut', *Toronto Star*, 8 Apr. 2000, K4.

72. Jennifer Pritchett, 'Nunavut MP faces the future', and Nick Forster, 'It will give us back our lives', both in *Ottawa Citizen*, 1 Apr. 1999.

Chapter 16

1. Donald B. Smith, 'Aboriginal Rights a Century Ago', *The Beaver* 67, 1 (1987): 7. See also Anthony J. Hall, 'The St. Catherine's Milling and Lumber Company vs. The Queen: A Study in the Relationship of Indian Land Rights to Federal-Provincial Relations in Nineteenth-Century Canada', unpublished manuscript, 10. A survey of Indians' legal position in Canada is by Paul Williams, 'Canada's Laws about Aboriginal Peoples: A Brief Overview', *Law and Anthropology* 1, (1986): 93–120.

2. The legal argument follows Hall, 'St. Catherine's Milling', 10–15.

3. For the example of the Ojibwa's misunderstanding in this regard, see Smith, *Sacred Feathers*, 24–5.

4. Smith, 'Aboriginal Rights', 12. See also Bruce A. Clark, *Indian Title in Canada* (Toronto, 1987).

5. Morris, *Treaties of Canada with the Indians*, 59. On Treaty Three, 'The North-West Angle Treaty', see 44–76.

6. George Copway, *Life, History and Travels of Kah-ge-ga-gah-bowh* (Philadelphia, 1847), 20.

7. This account follows Richard C. Daniel, *History of Native Claims*, 77–83. Donald Smith compiled the most complete bibliography on pre-1990 Oka in *Le Sauvage: The Native People in Quebec: Historical Writing on the Heroic Period (1534–1663) of New France* (Ottawa, 1974), 129–31. For a post-1990 bibliography, see Geoffrey York and Loreen Pindera, *People of the Pines* (Toronto, 1991).

8. Stanley, 'The First Indian "Reserves"', 206–7. The 1718 deed, in English translation, as well as other documents pertaining to the case are reproduced in Beta (pseud.), *A Contribution to a Proper Understanding of the Oka Question; and a Help to its Equitable and Speedy Settlement* (Montreal, 1879), 77–92. 'Oka and Its Inhabitants', in *The Life of Rev. Amand Parent, the first French Canadian ordained by the Methodist Church* (Toronto, 1887), 186.

9. In the words of Philippe de Vaudreuil, governor-general of New France, 1703–25, the Amerindians 'ne sont point capable de conserver les choses qui leur sont les plus nécessaires.' Stanley, 'First Indian "Reserves"', 206.

10. Jean Lacan, *An Historical Notice on the Difficulties Arisen Between the Seminary of St. Sulpice of Montreal and Certain Indians, at Oka, Lake of Two Mountains: A Mere Case of Right of Property* (Montreal, 1876), 14–17. On François Vachon de Belmont, see *DCB*, II, s.v. 'Vachon'.

11. Jan Grabowski, 'Mohawk Crisis at Kanesatake and Kahnawake', *European Review of Native American Studies* 5, 1 (1991): 12.

12. 'Oka and Its Inhabitants', 190–1, 193; Beta (pseud.), *Contribution*, 14–15. In 1870, Parent reported 110 Amerindian Methodists at Oka.

13. Cited by Rev. William Scott, *Report Relating to the Affairs of the Oka Indians, made to the Superintendent General of Indian Affairs* (Ottawa, [1883]), 53.

14. Ibid., 29; 'Oka and Its Inhabitants', 191, 202, 235.

15. In 1874, Chief Joseph became an assistant to Amand Parent. He translated the four gospels into Iroquois. For more on the chief, see *DCB*, XI; John MacLean, *Vanguards of Canada* (Toronto, 1918), 167–79.

16. Albert R. Hassard, 'When the Oka Seminary Went Up in Flames', *Famous Canadian Trials* (Toronto, 1924), 106–23.

17. 'Oka and Its Inhabitants', 205–18; Beta (pseud.), *Contribution*, 15.

18. Scott, *Report Relating to the Affairs of the Oka Indians*, 53–4.

19. Ibid., 59.

20. Michel F. Girard, 'La crise d'Oka à la lumière de l'ecologie historique', *NHSG Newsletter* (Oct. 1990): 4–8. The Native History Study Group is part of the Canadian Historical Association.

21. Privy Council, Angus Corinthe and Others . . . Plaintiffs, and Ecclesiastics of the Seminary of St. Sulpice of Montreal, Defendants, in Canadian Indian Rights Commission Library, box 85 (1). Also, Daniel, *History of Native Claims*, 79–82.

22. Registration office, district of Two Mountains, Acte de vente entre La Compagnie de Saint-Sulpice et la Compagnie immobilière Belgo, 21 oct. 1936; cited by Michel F. Girard, *Étude historique sur la forêt du village d'Oka* (Québec, 1990).

23. Department of Indian and Northern Affairs, Miscellaneous Correspondence, Oka, 1945–1953, vol. 1, file 0/121–1–5, Order-in-Council of 2 Apr. 1945.

24. The events leading up to the raid, and the raid itself, are described by Loreen Pindera, 'The Making of a Warrior', *Saturday Night* 106, 3 (1990): 30–9. See also Craig Maclane and Michael Baxendale, *This Land Is Our Land: The Mohawk Revolt at Oka* (Montreal and Toronto, 1990); Linda Pertusati, *In Defense of Mohawk Land* (Albany, NY, 1997).

25. Rene Laurent, 'Two Mohawks get prison terms for Oka violence', *The Gazette*, Montreal, 20 Feb. 1992, A1–2; Catherine Buckie, 'Jury-selection process ends in trial of Mohawks', ibid., 30 Apr. 1992; Rene Laurent, '5 Mohawks freed for lack of evidence', ibid., 11 June 1992, A4; Rene Laurent, 'Jury acquits all defendants in Oka trial', ibid., 4 July 1992, A1, A5; 'Quebec says it won't appeal jury's acquittal of Mohawks', ibid., 25 July 1992.

26. *Windspeaker* 18, 3 (July 2000): 2–3; *Calgary Herald*, 11 July 2000, A3; *Ottawa Sun*, 15 July 2000, 8; *Le Droit*, 12 juil. 2000, 28.

27. 'Oka still confounds us', *Edmonton Journal*, 9 May 1991. Quebec's Parti Québécois, at its 1991 convention, resolved that a sovereign Quebec state would recognize autonomous Native nations within its borders. According to the resolution, drafted with the help of Aboriginals, Native laws would take precedence over Quebec laws in specific areas where agreement had been reached by both parties. 'Delegates agreed on allowing native autonomy', *Globe and Mail*, 28 Jan. 1991.

28. British Columbia's Hartley Bay band (near Prince Rupert), frustrated with the slow progress of settlements, has started signing its own deals with industry, environmental groups, and other First Nations. 'Fed up, B.C. Indian band goes it alone in signing deals', *The Gazette*, Montreal, 22 July 2000, A15.

29. 'Mohawks sign historic land deal', *Ottawa Citizen*, 22 June 2000; 'Mohawks to get land near Oka', *Globe and Mail*, 21 June 2000.

30. Cumming and Mickenberg, eds, *Native Rights in Canada*, 98. The case was *Rex v. Syliboy*, [1929] 1 D.L.R. 307, (1928), 50 C.C.C. 389 (NS Cty Ct).

31. Cumming and Mickenberg, eds, *Native Rights in Canada*, 99.

32. *The Mi'kmaq Treaty Handbook* (Sydney and Truro, NS, 1987), 13. Also Donald Marshall Sr, Alexander Denny, and Putus Simon Marshall, 'The Covenant Chain', in Boyce Richardson, ed., *Drum Beat: Anger and Renewal in Indian Country* (Ottawa, 1989), 71–104.

33. *Simon v. The Queen*, [1985] 2 S.C.R. 387 at 404.

34. See National Indian Brotherhood, *Inquiry into the Invasion of Restigouche*, Preliminary Report, 15 July 1981.

35. Calder graduated from the Anglican Theological College of the University of British Columbia and in 1949 was elected to the BC legislature, where he served for 26 years, first for the New Democratic Party, then for Social Credit. He was Minister without Portfolio, 1972–3. In 1996, he received the National Aboriginal Achievement Award.

36. The original statement had been made by David McKay, a Greenville chief, to the Joint Reserves Allotment Commission that had been established in 1876. See David Raunet, *Without Surrender, Without Consent: A History of the Nishga Land Claims* (Vancouver, 1984), 90.

37. The case had been brought to the Supreme Court without provincial authorization.

38. See Cumming and Mickenberg, eds, *Native Rights in Canada*, 331–2; Thomas R. Berger, 'Native History, Native Claims and Self-Determination', *B.C. Studies* 57 (1983): 16; David W. Elliott, 'Aboriginal Title', in Morse, ed., *Aboriginal Peoples and the Law*, 74.

39. 'The Bear Island Decision', *Ontario Reports* (2nd ser.), 49, part 7, 17 May 1985: 353–490. A review of the issues at stake, particularly those of forestry management, is by Bruce W. Hodgins and Jamie Benidickson, *The Temagami Experience* (Toronto, 1989). See also David T. McNab, *Circles of Time: Aboriginal Land Rights and Resistance in Ontario* (Waterloo, Ont., 1999). The Indian view is presented by Gary Potts, 'Last-Ditch Defence of a Priceless Homeland', in Richardson, ed., *Drum Beat*, 203–28.

40. Anthony J. Hall, 'The Ontario Supreme Court on Trial: Justice Donald Steele and Aboriginal Right', unpublished manuscript, 2.

41. Clark, *Native Liberty*, 31. Prior to *Guerin, in Baker Lake v. Minister of Indian Affairs and Northern Development* in 1980, the court listed the conditions that had to be met for it to find an Aboriginal title to be valid: Natives had to establish that they and their ancestors lived within, and were members of, organized societies; these societies occupied the specific territory over which they were claiming Aboriginal title; their occupation was exclusive; and this occupation was in effect when England claimed sovereignty over the region. The people at Baker Lake met these conditions and won their case. Donald Purich, *Our Land: Native Rights in Canada* (Toronto, 1986), 57.

42. The question of the Crown's responsibility to act in the best interests of the Indians is dealt with extensively by Leonard Ian Rotman in *Parallel Paths: Fiduciary Doctrine and the Crown-Native Relationship in Canada* (Toronto, 1996). See also Purich, *Our Land*, 58–9; Miller, *Skyscrapers Hide the Heavens*, 263.

43. Kirk Makin and Robert Matas, 'Reserve land worth half of market value: court', *Globe and Mail*, 10 Nov. 2000, A5.

44. Barbara Yaffe, 'Musqueam factions engage in battle of petitions', *Vancouver Sun*, 27 July 2000, A3.

45. Scott Simpson, 'Leaseholders on Indian Lands at Pitt Lake Upset over Ouster', ibid., 2 Mar. 2000, A1; 'Aboriginal Landlords Act at Cross-Purposes', ibid., 3 Mar. 2000, A14; Byron Churchill, 'Katzie Indians Within Rights to Vote Against Lease Renewals: About 56 Non-Natives Have Cabins on Rented Land', ibid. 8 Mar. 2000, B1.

46. See, for instance, Harold Cardinal's views on the subject in *The Rebirth of Canada's Indians* (Edmonton, 1977), 164–5.

47. Daniel, *History of Native Claims*, 237–8.

48. On the Constitution's adoption, see Chapter 17.

49. Woodward, *Native Law*, 66–7.

50. 'R. v. George Weldon Adams (Appellant) v. Her Majesty the Queen (Respondent) and the Attorney General of Canada (Intervenor)', *Canadian Native Law Reporter* 4 (1996): 1–26. On the question of commercial fishing, however, the courts have ruled that Aboriginal right can be subjected to regulation.

51. For details of the *Sioui* case, see Chapter 4; also 'Confrontation gets natives into land talks', *Edmonton Journal*, 20 Aug. 1990.

52. Clark, *Native Liberty*, 31.

53. 'Nisga'a ceremony seals historic deal', *Globe and Mail*, 5 Aug. 1998. Tom Molloy, chief negotiator, and Donald Ward tell the story of the making of the treaty in *The World Is Our Witness: The Historic Journey of the Nisga'a into Canada* (Calgary, 2000).

54. Concerning Aboriginal challenges from without the Nisga'a nation, see Neil Sterritt, 'The Nisga'a Treaty: Competing Claims Ignored!', *B.C. Studies* 120 (Winter 1998–9): 73–97; Rick Mofina, 'B.C. Band challenges Nisga'a deal', *Ottawa Citizen*, 8 Nov. 1999; 'Nisga'a Treaty leaves issues unresolved for Gitanyow', *Vancouver Sun*, 22 May 2000, A9. Concerning challenges from within the Nisga'a nation, see Neil Seeman, 'Nisga'a land claim challenged by band dissidents', *National Post*, 23 Mar. 2000.

55. Mark Hume, 'Nisga'a treaty survives B.C. Liberals' challenge', *National Post*, 25 July 2000, A2; Rod Mickleburgh, 'Court rejects legal challenge to Nisga'a Treaty', *Globe and Mail*, 25 July 2000, A5.

56. 'Supreme Court: Accept oral history as evidence', *Globe and Mail*, 15 Dec. 1997, A25.

57. Peggy Blair, 'Taken for "Granted": Aboriginal Title and Public Fishing Rights in Upper Canada', *Ontario History* 92, 1 (Spring 2000): 31–55.

58. Kevin Cox, 'Native lobster fishery ends but dispute doesn't', *Globe and Mail*, 7 Oct. 2000, A7; Graeme Hamilton, 'Burnt Church votes to end fall fishery early', *National Post*, 20 Sept. 2000; 'Nova Scotia tribe to fish for lobster despite lack of agreement with Ottawa', Associated Press state and local wire, 20 Nov. 2000. For the Mi'kmaq view of the dispute, see Paul Barnsley, 'Anger mounts', *Windspeaker* (Oct. 2000): 1, 11; for the lobster situation, see Kevin Cox, 'The real lobster problem', *Globe and Mail*, 2 Sept. 2000; 'Ottawa, natives reach compromise on fishing', *Globe and Mail*, 23 Apr. 2001, A4.

59. This was a situation that Aboriginal people across the board were keenly aware of. Rick Mofina, 'Government ignores rights rulings, natives say', *Ottawa Citizen*, 28 Feb. 2001, A3.

60. The findings of the Royal Commission into the Donald Marshall Jr prosecution were reported in *Globe and Mail*, 27 Jan. 1990, A9.

61. 'Justice on trial', *Edmonton Journal*, 30 Mar. 1991, H1, H3. The commission was headed by Justice Allan Cawsey.

62. 'Justice system falls short, Siddon says', *Edmonton Journal*, 27 Mar. 1991. A woman's experience with the criminal justice system is described in Rudy Wiebe and Yvonne Johnson, *Stolen Life: The Journey of a Cree Woman* (Toronto, 1998).

63. Shelley Knapp, 'Country's First Aboriginal Court Opens Today', *Calgary Herald*, 6 Oct. 2000, B7. See also Eric Ross, *Returning to the Teachings: Exploring Aboriginal Justice* (Toronto, 1996).

64. The Stonechild Inquiry has been published in print and electronically. Justice David H. Wright, *Report of the Commission of Inquiry into the Death of Neil Stonechild* (Saskatoon, 2004), at: <www.stonechildinquiry.ca/>.

65. 'A breakthrough in Kanesatake', *The Gazette*, Montreal, 27 Dec. 1996.

66. Harper, 'Canada's Indian Administration', 313.

67. Ponting and Gibbins, *Out of Irrelevance*, 100; Dacks, *A Choice of Futures*, 199.

68. Cardinal, *The Unjust Society*, 44.

Chapter 17

1. Douglas Sanders, 'Government Agencies in Canada', in Washburn, ed., *Handbook of North American Indians*, 4: *History of Indian-White Relations*, 282.

2. See, for example, Heather Robertson, *Reservations Are for Indians* (Toronto, 1970).

3. The term 'specific claim' came into use in 1973 following the Nisga'a decision, when Ottawa issued its policy on Amerindians and Inuit land claims. Specific claims are those that concern obligations arising out of the treaties, the Indian Act, or regulations.

4. 'Land claims office getting no results', *Edmonton Journal*, 26 May 1996, A3. A more positive picture is presented by the *Report of the RCAP*, II, part 2, 547.

5. This account is based on Darlene Abreu Ferreira, 'Need Not Greed: The Lubicon Lake Cree Band Claim in Historical Perspective', MA thesis (University of Alberta, 1990). See also Boyce Richardson, 'Wrestling with the Canadian System:

A Decade of Lubicon Frustration', in Richardson, ed., *Drum Beat*, 231–64.

6. Ferreira, 'Need Not Greed', 93.

7. 'Lubicon Cree Defy Japanese Logging Plans', *Akwesasne Notes* 22, 6 (1991): 10–19.

8. 'Cree sign land-claim agreement', *Edmonton Journal*, 20 Dec. 1990, 1. By this agreement, they received a reserve of 142 square kilometres, $35.1 million for the construction of a new community, plus $13 million for socio-economic development and $512,000 in cash. What the Woodland Cree gave up in return was not announced.

9. In 2003, Amnesty International published a report entitled *Time Is Wasting: Respect for the Land Rights of the Lubicon Cree is Long Overdue*. See also John Goddard, *Last Stand of the Lubicon Cree* (Vancouver, 1991).

10. Ponting and Gibbins, *Out of Irrelevance*, 81.

11. 'Indians eating contaminated fish', *Globe and Mail*, 5 Nov. 1990, A4. See also Anastasia M. Shkilnyk, *A Poison Stronger Than Love: The Destruction of an Ojibway Community* (New Haven, 1985); George Hutchison and Dick Wallace, *Grassy Narrows* (Toronto, 1977).

12. Dacks, *A Choice of Futures*, 148. One-third of the world's fresh water is found in Canada, half of which is in Quebec, and concern was expressed in some quarters. Paul Charest, 'Les barrages hydro-électriques en territoires montagnais et leurs effets sur les communautés amérindiennes', *Recherches amérindiennes au Québec* 9, 4 (1980): 323–37. Churches also spoke out. Charles E. Hendry, *Beyond Traplines: Assessment of the Work of the Anglican Church of Canada with Canada's Native Peoples* (Toronto, 1969). See also Hugh and Karmel McCullum, *This Land Is Not for Sale* (Toronto, 1975).

13. Outstanding among these was the Committee for Original People's Entitlement (COPE), founded in 1969 by Agnes Semmler, a Gwich'in Métis who became its first president, and Nellie Cournoyea. With headquarters in Ottawa, it became the voice of the Inuvialuit.

14. Cited by Colin Scott, 'Ideology of Reciprocity between the James Bay Cree and the Whiteman State', in Peter Skalník, ed., *Outwitting the State* (New Brunswick, NJ, 1989), 103.

15. The agreement was signed by the government of Quebec, three Quebec Crown corporations, the Grand Council of the Crees (of Quebec), the Northern Quebec Inuit Association, and the government of Canada. It involved 6,650 Cree living in eight communities and 4,386 Inuit in 15 communities.

16. Harvey Feit, 'Legitimation and Autonomy in James Bay Cree Responses to HydroElectric Development', in Noel Dyck, ed., *Indigenous Peoples and the Nation-State: 'Fourth World' Politics in Canada, Australia and Norway* (St John's, 1985), 28–9. For an overview of the treaty's impact, see James F. Hornig, ed., *Social and Environmental Impacts of the James Bay Hydroelectric Project* (Montreal and Kingston, 1999).

17. *James Bay and Northern Quebec Agreement Implementation Review February 1982* (Ottawa, 1982). See also Billy Diamond, 'Villages of the Dammed', *Arctic Circle* 1, 3 (1990): 24–30.

18. Stanley Warner and Raymond Coppinger, 'Hydroelectric Power Development at James Bay: Establishing a Frame of Reference', in Hornig, ed., *Social and Environmental Impacts*, 19–38; Philip Authier and Graeme Hamilton, 'Quebec shelves Great Whale', *The Gazette*, Montreal, 19 Nov. 1994, A1, A8.

19. Berger Community Hearings, Rainer Genelli, Whitehorse, vol. 23, 2374–5; cited by Robert Page, *Northern Development: The Canadian Dilemma* (Toronto, 1986), 212.

20. Berger Community Hearings, Philip Blake, Fort McPherson, vol. 12, 1081; cited by Page, *Northern Development*, 213.

21. Thomas R. Berger, *Northern Frontier, Northern Homeland*, 2 vols (Ottawa, 1977). See also Martin O'Malley, *The Past and Future Land* (Toronto, 1976); Hugh and Karmel McCullum and John Olthuis, *Moratorium: Justice, Energy, the North, and the Native People* (Toronto, 1977).

22. Peter Foster, 'Exploring Mackenzie', *National Post*, 4 Mar. 2000, D1, D8.

23. Carol Howes, 'N.W.T. gives conditional support to Mackenzie Valley pipeline', *National Post*, 11 Apr. 2000; Steven Chase, 'NWT natives push for big role in Mackenzie Valley pipeline', *Globe and Mail*, 19 July 2000, B1, B4; Dan Westell, 'Ownership dispute clogs plans for northern pipeline', *Financial Times*, London, 2 Aug. 2000, 34; Two other commissions that have been influential in the development of Aboriginal claims were those of law professor Kenneth Lysyk to study a Yukon pipeline route as an alternative to the proposed Mackenzie Valley route and that of Justice Patrick Hartt to study the environment of northern Ontario. Daniel, *History of Native Claims*, 226.

24. Ponting, ed., *Arduous Journey*, 34–41. Also, David Alan Long, 'Trials of the Spirit: The Native Social Movement in Canada', in Long and Olive Patricia Dickason, eds, *Visions of the Heart* (Toronto, 1996), 377–96.

25. 'Status Indians number half a million', *Globe and Mail*, 30 Aug. 1990, A5.

26. Michael Asch, *Home and Native Land: Aboriginal Rights and the Canadian Constitution* (Toronto, 1984), 105.

27. On possible legal implications of the constitutional provisions, see Brian Slattery, 'The Constitutional Guarantee of Aboriginal and Treaty Rights', *Queen's Law Journal* 8, 1–2 (1982): 232–73.

28. J. Anthony Long, Leroy Little Bear, and Menno Boldt, 'Federal Indian Policy and Indian Self-government in Canada: An Analysis of a Current Proposal', *Canadian Public Policy* 8, 2 (1982): 194.

29. Delia Opekokew, *The First Nations: Indian Government and the Canadian Confederation* (Saskatoon, 1980); see also Opekokew, *The First Nations: Indian Governments in the Community of Man* (Regina, 1982).

30. Ponting, ed., *Arduous Journey*, 321. Nungak later became president of Quebec's Makavik Corporation. With Eugene Arima, he co-authored *Eskimo stories—unikkaatuat* (Ottawa, 1969).

31. Harper, a treaty Amerindian, was the provincial Minister for Northern Affairs, 1986–8. Ovide Mercredi, a Cree of Grand Rapids, Manitoba, at that time Manitoba regional chief of the Assembly of First Nations, and Phil Fontaine, Ojibwa grand chief of the Assembly of Manitoba Chiefs, were Harper's advisers on Meech Lake. First Mercredi and then Fontaine were later elected National Chief of the Assembly of First Nations.

32. 'Foes stall accord again', *Edmonton Journal*, 15 June 1990.

33. 'Elijah Harper: one man, one feather', *The Gazette*, Montreal, 23 June 1990. Amerindians were not opposed to recognizing Quebec as a distinct society, as Phil Fontaine, then head of the Assembly of Manitoba Chiefs, 1989–97, pointed out. Quite the contrary: 'We recognize that and support that. But if Quebec is distinct, we are even more distinct. That's the recognition we want, and will settle for nothing less.' 'Native leaders turn tables on Quebec', ibid., 18 June 1990.

34. A study on Indian self-government has been prepared by the Institute for Research and Public Policy: Frank Cassidy and Robert L. Bish, *Indian Government: Its Meaning in Practice* (Halifax and Lantzville, BC, 1989). See also Frank Cassidy, ed., *Aboriginal Self-Determination: Proceedings of a conference held September 30–October 3, 1990* (Toronto, 1991).

35. Dacks, *A Choice of Futures*, 92–3; Kenneth Coates and Judith Powell, *The Modern North: People, Politics, and the Rejection of Colonialism* (Toronto,

1989); Abel, *Drum Songs*, 258–61. On the need for local control for such matters as health care, see Nancy Gibson, 'Northern Medicine in Transition', in Young, ed., *Health Care Issues*, 110–21. For the early struggles for responsible government, see Lewis H. Thomas, *The Struggle for Responsible Government in the North-West Territories 1870–97* (Toronto, 1978), 234–63. For information on disease, see J.F. Marchand, 'Tribal Epidemics in Yukon', *Journal of the American Medical Association* 123 (1943): 1019–20.

36. *Report of the Cree-Naskapi Commission* (Ottawa, 1988), 10.

37. Ibid.

38. The agreement was signed by the government of Canada with COPE representing the Inuvialuit.

39. 'Gourmets from New York to Tokyo feast on North's Guerin woolly musk-ox', *Edmonton Journal*, 21 May 1991. Muskox meat was recently awarded a gold medal by the Chefs of America; the wool, eight times warmer by weight than sheep's wool, competes with cashmere.

40. *Report of the RCAP*, IV, 420.

41. In this matter, the government has not followed the report of its Task Force to Review Comprehensive Claims Policy (Coolican Report), which urged that extinguishment of all Aboriginal rights be abandoned as a requirement for a claim settlement. See *Living Treaties: Lasting Agreements* (Ottawa, 1985), 43.

42. Carol Howes, 'The new native tycoon', *National Post*, 27 Jan. 2001, D5.

43. Greg Poelzer, 'Aboriginal Peoples and Environmental Policy in Canada: No Longer at the Margins', in Debora L. VanNijnatten and Robert Boardman, eds, *Canadian Environmental Policy: Context and Cases*, 2nd edn (Toronto, 2002), 100–4.

44. Deh Cho First Nation, *Declaration of Rights*, 1993, 1. See also *Report of the RCAP*, IV, 427.

45. Assembly of First Nations, *Self-Determination Symposium Summary Report* (Ottawa, 1990), 60. Erasmus was president of the Dene Nation, Northwest Territories, 1976–83.

46. 'Innu chief warns government', *Globe and Mail*, 2 Oct. 1990. A survey of various Amerindian priorities is in Richardson, ed., *Drum Beat*. See also J. Anthony Long and Menno Boldt, eds, *Governments in Conflict? Provinces and Indian Nations in Canada* (Toronto, 1988); Leroy Little Bear, Menno Boldt, and J. Anthony Long, eds, *Pathways to Self-Determination: Canadian Indians and the Canadian State* (Toronto, 1984).

47. Quoted by Rudy Platiel, 'Vast changes sought to aid natives', *Globe and Mail*, 22 Nov. 1996, 1.

48. Gilles Gauthier, 'Le départ d' "un long débat"', *La Presse*, 22 nov. 1996, B1; Dan Smith, 'New deal urged for First Nations', *Toronto Star*, 22 Nov. 1996; 'Paying the price: How a report plays on two reserves', *Maclean's* 109, 49 (2 Dec. 1996): 16–19; Scott Feschuk, 'Cost of reforms $30-billion, report on Aboriginals says', *Globe and Mail*, 22 Nov. 1996; Marty Logan, 'Last chance for Canada—report', *Windspeaker* 14, 9 (Jan. 1997): 1.

49. *People to People, Nation to Nation: Highlights from the Report of the Royal Commission on Aboriginal Peoples* (Ottawa, 1996), ix. Also issued in French, Cree, and Inuktitut.

50. *The Gazette*, Montreal, 4 Feb. 1993. Also see 'Moved far from their homes, natives seek a deadly escape', *Globe and Mail*, 6 Feb. 1996.

51. A detailed account of the incident, based on official documents, is Peter Edwards, 'Death in the Dark: What happened at Ipperwash', *Toronto Star*, 24 Nov. 1996, F1, F6.

52. Michael Grange, 'Officer guilty in Ipperwash Killing', *Globe and Mail*, 29 Apr. 1997.

53. Ross Howard, 'A terrible territorial tangle', *Globe and Mail*, 29 May 1995. The figure of 110 per cent was the apparent result of different bands laying overlapping claims.

54. For an account of the early phase of the Nisga'a claim, see Kristin Jackson, 'Drawing the Line: B.C. Indians claim a rich chunk of the province', *Pacific* (*Seattle Times/Seattle Post-Intelligencer*), 2 Oct. 1988.

55. *Nisga'a Treaty Negotiations Agreement-in-Principle*, issued jointly by the Government of Canada, the Province of British Columbia, and the Nisga'a Tribal Council, 15 Feb. 1996. The agreement involved the return of almost 200 artifacts held by the Canadian Museum of Civilization. Buzz Bourdon, 'Nisga'a artifacts heading home', *Ottawa Citizen*, 19 Nov. 1999.

56. Ross Howard, 'Native standoffs heat up BC talks', *Globe and Mail*, 13 Sept. 1995; Art Wilson, 'Nisga'a sign historic treaty with B.C., federal governments', *Native Network News* (Feb. 1996): 1. For a negative view of the agreement, see Foster J.K. Griezic, 'The Nisga'a agreement: a great deal or a great steal?', *Globe and Mail*, 5 Mar. 1996.

57. The term 'comprehensive claims' came into use in 1973 (see note 3, above). Comprehensive claims are those arising in areas where rights of traditional use and occupancy have not been extinguished by treaty or superseded by law. Some cases involving Aboriginal right in the English-speaking world are surveyed in Brian Slattery,

Ancestral Lands, Alien Laws: Judicial Perspectives on Aboriginal Title (Saskatoon, 1983). The first comprehensive claim Ottawa accepted for negotiation was that of the Council for Yukon Indians, a claim that was not resolved until 1993. W.R. Morrison, *A Survey of the History and Claims of the Native Peoples of Northern Canada* (Ottawa, 1983), 44–53; 'Siddon says Yukon land claim deal won't mean Indian self-government', *Edmonton Journal*, 22 Oct. 1990. The tentative agreement provides for 44,440 square kilometres (8.6 per cent of Yukon's land mass) to be retained by the Natives, who also receive $257 million in compensation.

58. *Report of the RCAP*, V, 1.

59. *Report of the RCAP*, V, 12. Highlights of the *Report* are available at many websites, including <www.uni.ca/rcap.html>.

60. Ibid., II, part 1, 154–6; *People to People, Nation to Nation*, 29.

61. *Report of the RCAP*, IV, 478.

62. Quoted by John Goddard, 'In from the cold', *Canadian Geographic* 114, 4 (1994): 36–47. This account is based on his article. See also *Report of the RCAP*, III, 396, 419.

63. F. Laurie Barron and Joseph Garcea, eds, *Urban Indian Reserves: Forging New Relationships in Saskatchewan* (Saskatoon, 1999). See also Lynda Shorten, *Without Reserve: Stories of Urban Natives* (Edmonton, 1980).

64. 'Smallboy's Camp seeks support', *Edmonton Journal*, 13 Oct. 1991. The event received wide press coverage; for example, 'Here we are, here we stay, chief says: Smallboy's squatters look to old ways', *Edmonton Journal*, 30 May 1975; 'I'd trade my award for more real estate', ibid., 17 Jan. 1980; 'Cree leader: "I'll hang before moving"', *Akwesasne Notes* 3, 4 (1971): 1.

65. Rudy Platiel, 'First native bank to open next year', *Globe and Mail*, 10 Dec. 1996. See also Marybelle Mitchell, *From Talking Chiefs to Corporate Elite* (Montreal and Kingston, 1996).

66. Brian Laghi, 'New law to reform native voting', *Globe and Mail*, 16 Jan. 2001, A1; Laghi, 'Natives seek role in Nault initiative', ibid., 17 Jan. 2001, A4.

67. Michelle Lalonde, 'Aboriginals panel listens only to Indians' supporters: MP', *The Gazette*, Montreal, 8 May 1993, A4.

68. 'Commission staff divided on advocacy for natives', *Edmonton Journal*, 9 Mar. 1995.

69. The government's position was presented by Allan MacDonald, senior policy adviser, Indian and Northern Affairs Canada, at a conference on archaeological resource management in a land claims context held by Parks Canada, Ottawa, 20–2 Jan. 1997.

70. The mixed reaction was reflected in newspaper reports. Some examples: Erin Anderssen and Edward Greenspon, 'Federal apology fails to mollify native leaders', *Globe and Mail*, 8 Jan. 1998, A4; Jack Aubry, 'Native leaders disappointed, but some see reason for hope', *Edmonton Journal*, 8 Jan. 1998, A3; Laura Eggertson, 'An Apology, at long last', *Toronto Star*, 13 Feb. 1998, A20; Tod Mohamed, 'The politics of saying sorry', *Ottawa Citizen*, 1 Mar. 1998. Even the Inuit, who were not involved, had a comment, in the person of Zebedee Nungak, 'Apology to Indians soothes and jars', *The Gazette*, Montreal, 28 Jan. 1998.

71. Lorna Dueck, 'Sorry isn't good enough', *Globe and Mail*, 31 Oct. 2000. See also James Brooke, 'Facing ruin from lawsuits, Anglicans in Canada slash budgets', *New York Times*, 23 Aug. 2000; Rick Mofina, 'Churches have no easy exit from native lawsuits', *National Post*, 18 Sept. 2000.

72. Something of the complexity of the current Aboriginal scene is caught in Ron F. Laliberte et al., eds, *Expressions in Canadian Native Studies* (Saskatoon, 2000). See also Ovide Mercredi and Mary Ellen Turpel, *In the Rapids: Navigating the Future of First Nations* (Toronto, 1993).

73. 'Coon Come tells native leaders to sober up', *National Post*, 28 February 2001, A7; 'Coon Come's Call', *Ottawa Citizen*, 1 Mar. 2001, A14; 'Mr Coon Come steps into line of fire', *Globe and Mail*, 2 Mar. 2001, A12; Rick Mofina, 'Chiefs aren't all drunkards, natives insist', *Ottawa Citizen*, 1 Mar. 2001, A4.

74. AFN website, 28 June 2005: <www.afn.ca/article.asp?id=1548>.

Chapter 18

1. 'Natives threaten Olympic disruptions', *Globe and Mail*, 18 Apr. 2008, 1.

2. 'Supreme Court: Accept oral history as evidence', *Globe and Mail*, 15 Dec. 1997, A25.

3. Ibid.

4. H.P. Biggar, ed., *The Works of Samuel de Champlain* (Toronto, 1922), 2: 283–4.

5. Francis Assikinack, 'Social and Warlike Customs of the Odawah Indians', *Canadian Journal of Industry, Science, and Art* 3, 16 (1858): 297–309; Francis Assikinack, 'Legends and Traditions of the Odawah Indians', *Canadian Journal of Industry, Science, and Art* 3, 14 (1858), 115–25; Andrew J. Blackbird, *History of the Ottawa and Chippewa Indians of Michigan* (Ypsilanti, Mich., 1887).

6. Blackbird, *History of the Ottawa and Chippewa Indians*, 79–80.

7. Frances Gardiner Davenport, *European Treaties Bearing on the History of the United States and Its Dependencies to 1648*, vol. 1 (Washington, 1917), 20–6.

8. Ibid., 61.

9. Steve Newcomb, 'Five hundred years of injustice', *Shaman's Drum* (Fall 1992): 18–20.

10. Ibid.

11. *Nisga'a Treaty Negotiations Agreement-in-Principle*, issued jointly by the Government of Canada, the Province of British Columbia, and the Nisga'a Tribal Council, 15 Feb. 1996.

12. Barbara Graymont, 'Thayendanegea', *Dictionary of Canadian Biography Online*.

13. Gilles Havard, *The Great Peace of Montreal* (Montreal and Kingston, 2001), 8.

14. Graymont, 'Thayendanegea'.

15. Barbara Graymont, *The Iroquois in the American Revolution* (Syracuse, NY, 1972), 55.

16. Charles M. Johnston, *The Valley of the Six Nations* (Toronto, 1964), 40–3.

17. Ibid., 68–9.

18. Ibid., 50–1.

19. Isabel Thompson Kelsay, *Joseph Brant: Man of Two Worlds* (Syracuse, NY, 1984), 555.

20. Johnston, *Valley of the Six Nations*, 128.

21. S.R. Mealing, 'John Graves Simcoe', *Dictionary of Canadian Biography Online*.

22. Johnston, *Valley of the Six Nations*, 128.

23. Douglas Leighton and Robert J. Burns, 'Samuel Peters Jarvis', *Dictionary of Canadian Biography Online*.

24. Linda Diebel, 'Seeking truth about lost children', *Toronto Star*, 29 May 2008; CBC News, 'Chairman quits troubled residential-school commission', 20 Oct. 2008, at: <www.cbc.ca/canada/story/2008/10/20/truth-resignation.html>.

25. Jane O'Hara with Patricia Treble, 'Residential church school scandal', *Maclean's*, 26 June 2000.

26. Ibid.

27. Jonathon Gatehouse, 'Residential schools cash draws closer', *Maclean's*, 16 Apr. 2007.

28. Miller, *Shingwauk's Vision* , 579–82.

29. Indian and Northern Affairs Canada, Summary of the First Nations Governance Act (Ottawa, 2002), at: <www.fng-gpn.gc.ca>.

30. <www.llrib.ca>.

31. Robert D. Nault, Minister of Indian and Northern Affairs Canada, 'First Nations governance', 9 Oct. 2002.

32. 'Statement of National Indian Brotherhood', in *Recent Statements by the Indians of Canada*, Anglican Church of Canada General Synod Action 1969, Bulletin 201 (1970): 28.

33. Fred R. Fenwick, 'First Nations Governance Act', *Law Now* 27, 3 (Dec. 2003): 3–4.

34. Paco Francoli, 'Showdown on Governance Act', *Hill Times* 685 (5 May 2003): 3–4.

35. Robert M. Bone, *The Canadian North: Issues and Challenges*, 3rd edn (Toronto, 2009), 241–5.

36. Richard Cuthbertson, 'As new First Nations chief, Atleo calls for unity', *National Post*, 22 July 2009, at: <www.nationalpost.com/news/story.html?id=1819970>.

Epilogue

1. Even Diamond Jenness subscribed to the idea of the 'vanishing Indian'. In his words: 'Doubtless all the tribes will disappear. Some will endure only a few years longer, others, like the Eskimo, may last several centuries. Some will merge steadily with the white race, others will bequeath to future generations only an infinitesimal fraction of their blood.' In any event, he added, Indians had already contributed everything they had that was culturally valuable to the dominant civilization. Jenness, *Indians of Canada*, 264.

2. Menno Boldt, 'Social Correlates of Nationalism: A Study of Native Indian Leaders in a Canadian Internal Colony', *Comparative Political Studies* 14, 2 (1981): 205–31.

3. Dave Brown, 'Measuring the happiness of Canada's ethnic groups: Aboriginals report least satisfaction with life, study finds', *Ottawa Citizen*, 18 Nov. 2000, C1.

4. McMillan, *Native Peoples and Cultures of Canada*, 6.

5. *Report of the RCAP*, V, 5.

6. Selwyn Dewdney, 'Birth of a Cree-Ojibway Style of Contemporary Art', in Getty and Smith, eds, *One Century Later*, 117–25.

7. Niède Guidon, 'Cliff Notes', *Natural History* 96, 8 (1987): 10.

8. 'Harper speaks on Native Awareness', *Native Sports, News, and Culture* 2, 4 (1991): 26. See also Pauline Comeau, *Elijah: No Ordinary Hero* (Vancouver, 1993).

9. Rick Mofina, 'Coon Come invited to Quebec summit', *Ottawa Citizen*, 31 Mar. 2001, A6.

Index